VISIT US AT

www.syngress.com

T0227133

Syngress is committed to publishing high-quality books for IT Professionals and delivering those books in media and formats that fit the demands of our customers. We are also committed to extending the utility of the book you purchase via additional materials available from our Web site.

SOLUTIONS WEB SITE

To register your book, visit www.syngress.com/solutions. Once registered, you can access our solutions@syngress.com Web pages. There you may find an assortment of value-added features such as free e-books related to the topic of this book, URLs of related Web sites, FAQs from the book, corrections, and any updates from the author(s).

ULTIMATE CDs

Our Ultimate CD product line offers our readers budget-conscious compilations of some of our best-selling backlist titles in Adobe PDF form. These CDs are the perfect way to extend your reference library on key topics pertaining to your area of expertise, including Cisco Engineering, Microsoft Windows System Administration, CyberCrime Investigation, Open Source Security, and Firewall Configuration, to name a few.

DOWNLOADABLE E-BOOKS

For readers who can't wait for hard copy, we offer most of our titles in downloadable Adobe PDF form. These e-books are often available weeks before hard copies, and are priced affordably.

SYNGRESS OUTLET

Our outlet store at syngress.com features overstocked, out-of-print, or slightly hurt books at significant savings.

SITE LICENSING

Syngress has a well-established program for site licensing our e-books onto servers in corporations, educational institutions, and large organizations. Contact us at sales@syngress.com for more information.

CUSTOM PUBLISHING

Many organizations welcome the ability to combine parts of multiple Syngress books, as well as their own content, into a single volume for their own internal use. Contact us at sales@syngress.com for more information.

SYNGRESS®

MICROSOFT®

Vista for

IT Security

Professionals

Anthony Piltzecker   Technical Editor

Larry Chaffin   **Daniel Sheperd**
Scott Granneman   **Matt Sheperd**
Laura E. Hunter   **Robert J. Shimonski**
Alun Jones   **Henrik Walther**
Jan Kanclirz
Marc Perez

KEY	SERIAL NUMBER
001	HJIRTCV764
002	PO9873D5FG
003	829KM8NJH2
004	8932KLPERN
005	CVPLQ6WQ23
006	VBP965T5T5
007	HJJJ863WD3E
008	2987GVTWMK
009	629MP5SDJT
010	IMWQ295T6T

PUBLISHED BY
Syngress Publishing, Inc.
800 Hingham Street
Rockland, MA 02370

Microsoft Vista for IT Security Professionals

Printed and bound by CPI Group (UK) Ltd, Croydon, CR0 4YY

Transferred to digital print 2012

ISBN-10: 1-59749-139-X
ISBN-13: 978-1-59749-139-6

Publisher: Andrew Williams
Acquisitions Editor: Gary Byrne
Technical Editor: Tony Piltzecker
Cover Designer: Michael Kavish

Page Layout and Art: Patricia Lupien
Copy Editor: Audrey Doyle
Indexer: Richard Carlson

For information on rights, translations, and bulk sales, contact Matt Pedersen, Commercial Sales Director; email m.pedersen@elsevier.com.

Technical Editor

Tony Piltzecker (CISSP, MCSE, CCNA, CCVP, Check Point CCSA, Citrix CCA), author and technical editor of Syngress Publishing's *MCSE Exam 70-296 Study Guide and DVD Training System,* is a Consulting Engineer for Networked Information Systems in Woburn, MA. He also contributed to *How to Cheat at Managing Microsoft Operations Manager 2005* (Syngress, ISBN: 1597492515).

Tony's specialties include network security design, Microsoft operating system and applications architecture, as well as Cisco IP Telephony implementations. Tony's background includes positions as IT Manager for SynQor Inc.; Network Architect for Planning Systems, Inc.; and Senior Networking Consultant with Integrated Information Systems. Along with his various certifications, Tony holds a bachelor's degree in Business Administration. Tony currently resides in Leominster, MA, with his wife, Melanie, and his daughters, Kaitlyn and Noelle.

Contributors

Larry Chaffin is the CEO/Chairman/Founder of Pluto Networks, a virtual worldwide network consulting company spanning 23 countries and specializing in book authoring, VoIP, WLAN, and security. He is an accomplished author. He was a contributor to *Managing Cisco Secure Networks* (Syngress, ISBN: 1931836566), *Skype Me!* (Syngress, ISBN: 1597490326), Practical VoIP Security (Syngress, ISBN: 1597490601), *Configuring Check Point NGX VPN-1/Firewall-1* (ISBN: 1597490318) and author of *Building a VoIP Network with Nortel's Multimedia Communication Server 5100* (Syngress, ISBN: 1597490784). He has also coauthored or ghostwritten 11 other technology books about VoIP, WLAN, security and optical technologies. Larry has over 29 vendor certifications from companies such as Avaya, Cisco HP, IBM, isc2, Juniper, Microsoft, Nortel, PMI, and VMware. Larry has been a Principal Architect designing VoIP, security, WLAN, and optical networks for many Fortune 100 companies in 22 countries. He is viewed by his peers as one of the most well-respected experts in the field of VoIP and Security in the world. Larry has spent countless hours teaching and conducting seminars/workshops around the world in the field of Voice/VoIP, security and wireless networks. Larry is currently working on a follow-up to *Building a VoIP Network with Nortel's Multimedia Communication Server 5100* as well as new books on Cisco VoIP networks, Microsoft Vista, and Practical VoIP case studies.

Larry cowrote Chapter 1.

Scott Granneman is an author, teacher, and consultant. A monthly columnist for both *SecurityFocus* and *Linux Magazine*, Scott has also authored three books on open source technologies, each of which focuses on security issues in a different way: *Don't Click on the Blue E!: Switching to Firefox*; *Hacking Knoppix*; and *Linux Phrasebook*. As an adjunct professor at Washington University in St. Louis and Webster University, Scott teaches a variety of popular courses about security, technology, and the Internet. As a Principal of WebSanity, he manages the firm's UNIX-based server environment and helps develop the company's Content Management System, which is used nationally by educational, business, and nonprofit clients.

Scott wrote Appendix A and Appendix B.

Laura E. Hunter (CISSP, MCSE: Security, MCDBA, Microsoft MVP) is an Active Directory architect with a publicly held engineering and staffing firm, where she provides network planning, implementation, and troubleshooting services for Active Directory and other Microsoft technologies. Her specialties include Windows 2000 and 2003 Active Directory design and implementation, troubleshooting, and security topics. Laura has more than a decade of experience with Windows computers; her previous experience includes a position as an IT Project Leader with the University of Pennsylvania and as the Director of Computer Services for the Salvation Army. She is a contributor to the TechTarget family of Web sites and to *Redmond Magazine* (formerly *Microsoft Certified Professional Magazine*).

Laura has previously contributed to the Syngress Windows Server 2003 MCSE/MCSA DVD Guide & Training System series as a DVD presenter, author, and technical reviewer. Laura is the author of the *Active Directory Consultant's Field Guide* (ISBN: 1-59059-492-4) from APress, and the coauthor of the *Active Directory Cookbook, Second Edition* (ISBN: 059610202X) from O'Reilly Media. Laura is a four-time recipient of the prestigious Microsoft MVP award in the area of Windows Server—Networking. Laura holds a Master's Degree in Computer Science from the University of Pennsylvania and also works as a freelance writer, trainer, speaker and consultant.

Laura wrote Chapter 6.

Alun Jones (MVP, MCP) is the President of Texas Imperial Software. Texas Imperial Software develops secure networking software and provides security engineering consulting services. Texas Imperial Software's flagship product is WFTPD Pro, a secure FTP server for Windows, written entirely by Alun.

Alun entered the security engineering field as more and more of WFTPD's support needs indicated that few companies were trying to meet their needs for security on the Internet. His current day job is as an Information Systems Security Engineer at Premera Blue Cross, a health insurance provider based in the Pacific Northwest of the USA.

Alun has attended, but not completed, University at Corpus Christi College, Cambridge, and Bath University, and now lives in Seattle, Washington, with his wife, Debbie, and son, Colin.

Alun wrote Chapter 5.

Jan Kanclirz Jr. (CCIE #12136-Security, CCSP, CCNP, CCIP, CCNA, CCDA, INFOSEC Professional, Cisco WLAN Support/Design Specialist) is currently a Senior Network Information Security Architect at IBM Global Services. Jan specializes in multivendor designs and post-sale implementations for several technologies such as VPNs, IPS/IDS, LAN/WAN, firewalls, content networking, wireless, and VoIP. Beyond network designs and engineering, Jan's background includes extensive experience with open source applications and Linux. Jan has contributed to several Syngress book titles: *Managing and Securing Cisco SWAN*, *Practical VoIP Security*, and *How to Cheat at Securing a Wireless Network*.

In addition to Jan's full-time position at IBM G.S., Jan runs a security portal, www.MakeSecure.com, where he dedicates his time to security awareness and consulting. Jan lives in Colorado, where he enjoys outdoor adventures. Jan would like to thank his family, slunicko, and friends for all of their support.

Jan wrote Chapter 7.

Marc Perez (MCSE:Security, Security+) is a senior consultant at Networked Information Systems in Boston, MA. Representing Network Information Systems' Microsoft practice, he provides strategic and technical consulting services to midsize and enterprise-level clients located throughout the Northeast. Focusing on securely integrating directory services with messaging and collaboration solutions, he provides the guidance necessary for enterprises to leverage their technology investments toward more effective communication with an emphasis on presence.

Educated at the University of Southern Maine, Marc has consulted privately for several organizations in the Boston area and has held roles throughout New England, including four years as an Information Security Manager for MBNA America Bank. He currently lives on the North Shore with his wife, Sandra, and his two sons, Aidan and Lucas.

Marc wrote Chapter 8.

Daniel Shepherd (MCP, GSEC) is IT Manager for an oil and gas trade association, headquartered in Washington, D.C. Dan provides the association with a full range of IT services, including designing, administering, and troubleshooting the corporate network. The small staff of roughly 30 employees supports more than 40,000 individual association members. The projects Dan has designed and implemented for the organization range from a whole office VoIP implementation, a network infrastructure upgrade, a complete overhaul of aging server hardware and software, and virtualization of the server environment for increased resource utilization and security through role isolation.

Dan's background includes positions as the Network Administrator for the fastest-growing restaurant point-of-sale company in the southeast and as a Consultant for Faith Based Design Inc., where he provided training, technical writing, and field engineering services for the U.S. Military.

Daniel wrote Chapter 9 and cowrote Chapter 1.

Matt Shepherd (CISSP, MCSE, GCFW, GSEC, CEH) is a consultant for Project Performance Corporation of McLean, VA. Project Performance Corporation synthesizes its capabilities in security architecture, engineering, and compliance with best-of-breed tools to provide effective security solutions to customers in the public and private sectors. Matt uses his experience as a network administrator, IT manager, and security architect to deliver high-quality solutions for Project Performance Corporation's clients. Matt holds bachelor's degrees from St. Mary's College of Maryland, and he is currently working on his Master's of Science in Information Assurance.

Matt would like to thank his wife, Leena, for her wonderful support during this project, and throughout their relationship. He thanks his family for a lifetime of love and support and Olive for making every day special. Matt also thanks his brother Daniel for tackling this project with him.

Matt thanks Mike Nigro, Martin Wright, and Jan Hill at PPC for supporting him on this project, and he also sends thanks to Shon

Eizenhoefer at Microsoft for taking the time to provide clear, timely answers when he needed them.

Matt wrote Chapter 4.

Robert J. Shimonski (MCSE) is an Entrepreneur and best-selling author and editor of hundreds of published books and thousands of magazine and industry articles. Rob consults within today's most challenging business and technology environments and brings front-line industry knowledge to the reader in every page he writes. Rob is always on top of the latest trends and reporting the state of the business and technology industry from a real-world perspective. As of the writing of this book, Rob is currently on assignment testing and developing secure Vista images and designing a Longhorn upgrade for a large global firm.

For Syngress, Rob has written many cutting-edge "in demand" titles, including The *(ISC)2 SSCP Study Guide and DVD Training System* (ISBN 1931836809), *The Best Damn Firewall Book Period!* (ISBN 1931836906), *Designing and Building Enterprise DMZs* (ISBN 1597491004), *Nokia Network Security Solutions Handbook* (ISBN 1931836701), *Sniffer Pro Network Optimization and Troubleshooting Handbook* (ISBN 1931836574), *Configuring and Troubleshooting Windows XP Professional with CD-ROM* (ISBN 1928994806), *Configuring Symantec Antivirus Corporate Edition* (ISBN 1931836817), and the *Network+ Study Guide & Practice Exams: Exam N10-003* (ISBN 1931836426). Rob also helped to develop the first DVD video with Syngress for the launch of *The Security + Study Guide and DVD Training System* (ISBN 1931836728), which has become a best seller.

Rob owns and operates Sound Room Studios Inc, a media development company in Long Island, NY. His role there is to produce and engineer audio and video content for TV, radio, and digital distribution.

Rob wrote Chapters 2 and 3.

Henrik Walther (Exchange MVP, MCSE Messaging/Security) is a senior consultant working for Interprise Consulting A/S (a Microsoft Gold Partner) based in Copenhagen, Denmark. Henrik has more than 14 years of experience in the IT business, where he primarily works with Microsoft Exchange, ISA Server, MOM, IIS, clustering, Active Directory, and virtual server technologies.

In addition to his job as an Exchange System specialist, Henrik also runs the Danish Web site Exchange-faq.dk. He also is the primary content creator, forums moderator, and newsletter editor at the leading Microsoft Exchange site, MSExchange.org. Henrik is the author of *CYA: Securing Exchange Server 2003 & Outlook Web Access* (Syngress, 2004), and he has been a reviewer on several other messaging books (including another Exchange 2007 book).

Henrik wrote Chapter 10.

Foreword Contributor

Brien Posey is Relevant Technologies' Vice President of Research and Development (www.relevanttechnologies.com). Brien has previously served as the Director of Information Systems for a large nationwide chain of healthcare facilities and as the Department of Defense's senior network engineer at Fort Knox. He has also served as Editor in Chief of several technical publications and also as a network administrator for one of the country's largest insurance companies.

Brien is an award-winning technology author, a Microsoft Certified Systems Engineer (MCSE), and a Microsoft MVP. He has written or contributed material to 28 books and published more than 3,000 articles for a variety of Web sites and printed publications, including *CNET, Jupiter Media, Microsoft's TechNet Magazine, Windows Magazine, Windows Networking, TechTarget,* and *ZDNet.*

Contents

Foreword

In 2001, the IT community was celebrating the long-awaited release of Microsoft's Windows XP. The release of Windows XP was a major milestone for Microsoft because it was the first time that the company had created an NT kernel-based operating system intended for both businesses and consumers. Windows XP was designed to render DOS-based operating systems such as Windows 9x and Windows ME obsolete forever. Sadly, the celebration was short-lived, though, as it became apparent that Windows XP and Internet Explorer were both plagued with security problems.

At first these security problems were mostly a concern for businesses. It wasn't long, however, before consumers began to feel the consequences of these security holes as well. Nuisances such as Trojans, spyware, pop-ups, and browser hijackers quickly went from existing in relative obscurity to becoming an almost overnight epidemic.

In 2003, Microsoft was hard at work on Service Pack 2 for Windows XP, which was originally intended to consist of a set of critical security patches and hotfixes that had been rolled up into a service pack. But everything changed when the Slammer worm hit.

The development team in Redmond was already hard at work on a new desktop operating system, code-named Longhorn (now known as Windows Vista). Longhorn was slated to include code that would prevent Slammer-type worms from being effective, but the new operating system was still years away from being ready to be released.

Fearing another Slammer-type attack, Microsoft Vice President Jim Allchin made the decision to halt the development of Longhorn and mandated that much of the Longhorn code be adapted to Windows XP and included in Service Pack 2.

Service Pack 2 was released on August 6, 2004. However, the service pack didn't fix all of Windows XP's security problems, although it did help to some extent. In retrospect it was probably good that Microsoft created Service Pack 2 from Longhorn code. This strategy gave the company the chance to see that the code was not completely secure, thus providing Microsoft with a chance to rewrite the code prior to Vista's release.

All this hard work apparently has paid off, though. Windows Vista is the first desktop operating system released under Microsoft's Trustworthy Computing Initiative, and it is without a doubt the most secure OS that Microsoft has released to date.

Even so, Vista isn't completely secure right out of the box. Like every previous Windows operating system, Vista is highly customizable, and the settings that you configure Vista to use play a role in how secure the operating system really is. For example, there will undoubtedly be security updates released for Vista as new security threats are discovered. If Vista isn't configured to receive these updates, though, then it will be less secure than an updated version of Vista.

That's where *Microsoft Vista for IT Security Professionals* is helpful. This book discusses all of the enhanced security mechanisms that are present in Vista. It also shows you how to configure these mechanisms for optimal security.

—*Brien M. Posey*
Vice President of Research and Development,
Relevant Technologies
www.relevanttechnologies.com

About the Companion Material

 The CD icon that appears beside certain sections of the chapters in this book indicates that this material is available on the companion website. Companion material is available at http://booksite.elsevier.com/9781597491396/ and also includes scripts and other adjunct material. We hope this material is helpful to you.

Chapter 1

Microsoft Vista: An Overview

Solutions in this chapter:

- **The User Interface**
- **Internet Explorer 7**

☑ **Summary**

☑ **Solutions Fast Track**

☑ **Frequently Asked Questions**

Introduction

The long-anticipated successor to Windows XP is just now making its debut to the world. Windows Vista has spent the last five years in development and has undergone many feature additions, deletions, and changes. Vista features a heavily altered core, and to many users, it will look and feel entirely different. The fact is that Vista is still built on the now mature and robust Windows NT kernel. Vista is intended to improve reliability, security, and manageability. It also was designed to provide an improved user experience.

The reliability factor has long been an issue to most Windows users, and as sys admins we all have stories of failed systems and frequent BSODs. As sys admins we also understand that a truly effective operating system (OS) doesn't need to be rebooted, or rebuilt on a regular basis; an effective OS provides a great user experience and wide application support, as well as a stable base on which to run those applications. The Windows NT kernel and its iterations, Windows 2000, Windows XP, and Windows 2003, have focused on improving the reliability of the OS with each release and with each service pack. Windows Vista again takes a much-needed step forward in reliability. Microsoft has built the code for Vista on top of Windows Server 2003 Service Pack (SP) 1. This design not only helps with reliability but also brings with it all the security improvements brought about by the Windows 2003 Server line of operating systems.

The recent focus of most electronic systems vendors has been security, security, security, and there is good reason for this push toward effective security controls for everything from electronic voting machines to home computers. The hacker is not a new enemy to computer systems, but the fact that electronic systems are now in use throughout our society makes available a host of new, poorly protected systems. The availability of high-speed Internet access is also a contributing factor. Previously, when people were connected to the Internet only via a slow dial-up connection for a couple hours each night, hackers had a very small window of opportunity to attack home systems. Now with ubiquitous always-on broadband connections, hackers have ample opportunity to attack home systems that rarely have strong security controls in place.

Windows Vista continues the efforts of the developers of Windows XP SP 2 and Windows Server 2003 SP 1. Vista includes an updated host-based firewall, User Account Control (UAC), Internet Explorer 7, and Windows Defender. Vista code also underwent an intensive code security audit process by Microsoft, and independent hackers in the security community were invited by Microsoft to attack Vista and make recommendations on how security could be improved. From these third-party suggestions came features such as, Address Space Layout Randomization

(ASLR), which helps protect systems from buffer overflow attacks by randomizing the memory location where system files are loaded. This isn't a new feature to operating systems in general; it has been used in Linux and BSD for some time now, but it is new to the Windows line of operating systems.

Manageability is another important subject related to administering Windows machines. Applying application and system patches is one of the main areas of concern when it comes to managing any OS. In previous versions of Windows, most application or system updates required a reboot of the entire system. With Vista, however, Microsoft has added the Restart Manager, which is called by the installer to look at a particular application or portion of the system and determine whether the update can be applied without rebooting the entire OS. The Restart Manager also helps in the event of a required reboot by taking a snapshot of the system and applications open on the machine. After the reboot the applications and any file resources that were in use by the system are reopened and presented to the user as if the machine were never shutdown. By separating user-mode and kernel-mode code and improving the isolation between the two, the developers of Vista have also changed the responsibility of third-party vendors.

Much concern has been expressed by the community as a whole about the requirements to run Vista. If you are wondering whether your system meets the requirements, Table 1.1 lists the Microsoft's recommendations. You can also go to www.microsoft.com/windowsvista/getready/upgradeadvisor/default.mspx and the upgrade advisor will analyze your current system specs. Any new software will have a few bugs, and we did experience bugs when upgrading a current system from XP to Vista, but our fresh installation with Vista went very smoothly. We have installed Vista on several different systems and only experienced a few problems during the process. The only issue that we found was on an AMD system with an NVIDIA 7300 graphics card installed. Vista was unable to properly allocate system resources for the graphics card, resulting in a 4-bit default display. A quick search revealed that others were experiencing the same issue with Vista and this particular graphics processor. Unfortunately, no fix was currently available. Minimum supported requirements for running Vista include an 800MHz 32-bit (x86) or 64-bit (x64) processor; 512 MB of system memory; an SVGA (800 x 600) GPU; a 20 GB HDD with 15 GB of free space; and a CD-ROM optical drive. Table 1.1 lists the requirements that Microsoft recommends for new Vista installations and upgrades.

Table 1.1 Microsoft-Recommended Requirements for Running Vista

	Windows Vista-Capable PC	Windows Vista Premium Ready
Processor	At least 800 MHz	1GHz 32-bit (x86) or 64-bit (x64)
System memory	512 MB	1 GB
GPU	DirectX 9-capable	DirectX 9-capable
Graphics memory		128 MB
HDD		40 GB
HDD free space		> 15 GB
Optical drive		DVD-ROM

For more information, visit the Vista Tech Center site at http://technet. microsoft.com/en-us/windowsvista/aa905075.aspx.

NOTE

We were able to successfully run the 32-bit version of Vista on a machine with 10 GB of disk space and 512 MB of memory. The performance wasn't ideal, but it was still usable, and we experienced no issues with installation or operation.

Microsoft offers six different versions of Vista for consumers and business users (see Table 1.2). The Home versions will fit into the same niche that Windows XP Home edition fit into; unfortunately, they both lack some of the higher end features that power users desire. For example, the Home Basic version is intended for people who just want to surf the Web, have e-mail access, and create documents, whereas the Home Premium version includes features for users who are interested in using the system for video, music, and mobile computing. The Vista Business edition is more centered on typical business use. It lacks the media center features of the Home premium edition. Windows Ultimate edition is for power users who require all the features. The unfortunate reality of this highly diverse field of editions is that most users will end up either missing out on features they desire or simply shelling out more money for the Ultimate edition. For example, Home premium doesn't include Remote Desktop, the lowest cost edition to support remote desktop is the Business edition, which doesn't include the media center features. To have both features users will need to get the Ultimate edition. Another example is the lack of

BitLocker drive encryption in the Business edition, a feature that you would expect to see in the purported "business" edition of a product.

Vista also comes in an Enterprise edition, which is available to large enterprise customers through the volume licensing program. The Enterprise edition includes support for things such as BitLocker drive encryption, OS deployment features, and advanced application compatibility. It also includes the right to run four virtual operating system sessions without the need to purchase more licenses from Microsoft. Table 1.3 lists the retail and upgrade prices of the different versions of Vista.

Table 1.2 Vista Features

Features	Vista Home Basic	Vista Home Premium	Vista Business	Vista Ultimate
Windows Defender and Windows Firewall	x	x	x	x
Instant Search and Windows Internet Explorer 7	x	x	x	x
Elegant Windows Aero desktop experience with Windows Flip 3D navigation		x	x	x
Windows Mobility Center and Tablet PC support		x	x	x
Windows Meeting Space		x	x	x
Windows Media Center		x		x
Windows Media Center output on TVs, Xbox 360, and other devices		x		x
Advanced business backup features			x	x
Business networking and Remote Desktop			x	x
Windows BitLocker Drive Encryption				x

TIP

Choosing an edition for your personal needs will be somewhat difficult, but using the information in Table 1.2 and in the comparison chart located at www.microsoft.com/windows/products/windowsvista/editions/choose.mspx will help you in the process. If you are a home user who needs only basic Web, e-mail capability, then the Home basic edition is probably right for you. On the other hand, if you are an amateur film guru you will probably want the Home Premium or Ultimate editions.

Table 1.3 Vista Pricing

Vista Edition	x64 Version	Licensing Available	Retail Price	Upgrade Price
Vista Starter	No	Select countries only, with new PC purchase	N/A	N/A
Vista Home Basic	Yes	Retail	$199	$99.95
Vista Home Premium	Yes	Retail	$239	$159
Vista Business	Yes	Retail	$299	$199
Vista Enterprise	Yes	Volume license only	N/A	N/A
Vista Ultimate	Yes	Retail	$399	$259

Whether to upgrade is a big question that everyone will be asking this year. To answer that question, first you need to make sure your computer has the recommended hardware to run Vista; if it doesn't, you will need to upgrade or purchase a new computer. If your computer runs fine on its current OS, you could find it difficult to justify switching to Vista. It may be a good idea to wait and see how Vista fares in the community before considering an upgrade.

Microsoft is shipping 32- and 64-bit versions of Vista, and consequently, there are a few things to remember. In the long term, the 64-bit version of Vista will help move companies and vendors to the next generation of computer hardware. But if you move to a 64-bit version now, you need to be sure all the applications and hardware you need to run have 64-bit support. There also is no support in the 64-bit version for 16-bit DOS and Windows applications.

The User Interface

The new user interface, Vista Aero, is much different from the current XP interface. The new interface implements the functionality of currently available 3D graphics accelerators, thereby enabling Vista to provide the following features:

- Translucent window frames
- Live previews of documents
- Live previews of windows
- Scalable icons

Figure 1.1 displays the main logon window that appears when Vista starts. Users of current Linux distributions will find this interface familiar. From this screen you can enter your password and press **Enter** or click the right-facing **Arrow** button to log on. This screen also enables you to *shut down, restart,* or put the computer to *sleep* by using the red button at the bottom of the screen.

Figure 1.1 Main Logon Screen

One of the main issues with Vista is the new logon process. Many users and sys admins are not happy with having to relearn or reeducate users on how to log in. Another problem with the logon screen, when the system is a member of a domain, is the extra button presses required to login as a different user. In previous versions of Windows logging in as a different user was as simple as typing in that user name, entering the password, and pressing enter. Now the user must click the **Switch User** button and choose **Other User,** at which point the user will be allowed to enter a new username (Figure 1.2).

The next area of concern is related to the new log-on process. To log in to the local machine instead of the domain, users have to enter their usernames in the machine\username format. Many sys admins have expressed concern over having to remember and correctly type the machine name of each computer under their control.

TIP

Yes a shortcut does exist for the aforementioned problem. To log in as a user on the local machine, simply type .\ and the **username**. The dot is simply a shortcut specifying the local machine. See Figure 1.2 for an example of this step.

The button at the bottom left of the screen takes you to the Ease of Access Center, where you can select various options to make your computer easier to use (see Figure 1.3). These options include the familiar, sticky keys, filter keys, and high-contrast settings. Another option is the Narrator, which will read screen text, user input, and system messages allowed.

Figure 1.2 Log On under Different User by Using the Dot-Slash Trick

Figure 1.3 Ease of Access Center

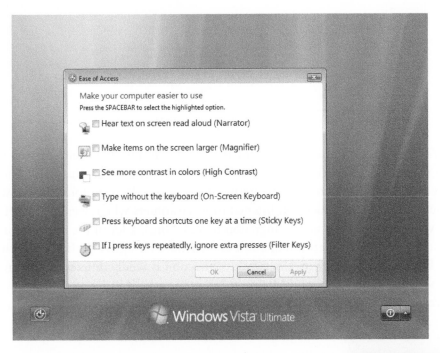

The Welcome Center

After you have successfully logged in, you are taken to the Welcome Center, shown in Figure 1.4. The Welcome Center is new with Vista, and it provides a quick view of the computer's hardware, as well as quick access to many of the initial functions most users will want to perform after installing a new system. At the bottom of the Welcome Screen, you can deselect the option to have the Welcome Center start at startup.

Figure 1.4 The Welcome Center

With this new interface, Microsoft has been able to put useful information into places where users can find it quickly and easily. Everyone knows that sometimes it can be frustrating trying to find the information you are looking for in Windows XP. But it appears that Microsoft listened to its customers when deciding how to build Vista. This also aids in the migration to Vista, since a lot of the standard functions users are used to performing a certain way have changed significantly with Vista. For example, setting up a network connection is wildly different from any previous version of Windows, and Microsoft hopes to make it easier to perform using the Welcome Center. A useful function is the Files and Settings transfer wizard.

Other new functions are available for changing display settings and viewing the hardware installed on the system.

Figure 1.5 shows the basic information concerning our computer. We were able to access this information quickly and easily by clicking on the **Show more details** arrow in the top right of the Welcome Center. The information in Figure 1.5 represents what most users need to know concerning their hardware and software. This information is the same data that one would access in Windows XP by going to **System** in the Control Panel or by right clicking on **My Computer | Properties**. From the System Information window we can change our workgroup\domain membership, computer name, and even our product key. We can also access the remote desktop settings, device manager, system restore, and other advanced system settings.

Figure 1.5 System Information

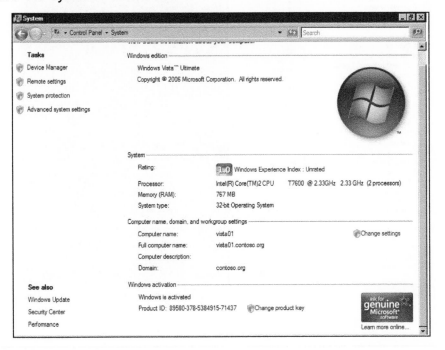

The Start Menu

The Start Menu has undergone another redesign in an effort to provide a better user experience, and we personally think Microsoft hit the target with this change. The menu still utilizes a familiar architecture, but instead of the dropdown menu that would often span the entire width of a user's screen, Vista utilizes a folder-based sub-menu structure.

Clicking **Start | All Programs** shows you the familiar list of programs available in the current start menu but without drawing extra dropdown menus across the user's screen (see Figure 1.6). From this list you can select an available program to run or you can click on a subfolder such as **Accessories**, which brings up the list of programs available under the Accessories folder. Moving the start menu away from submenus and toward a simple and familiar folder-based layout makes it much easier for new users to grasp, but this new feature might cause a bit of confusion for existing users who will need to relearn the structure once again.

Figure 1.6 The Start Menu

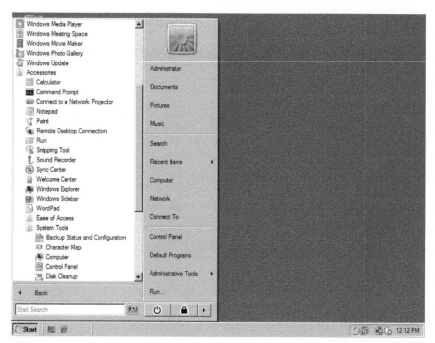

TIP

Remember that after you click on a folder within the Start menu, you can just click the **Back** button at the bottom of the screen to move back one level.

User Accounts

Selecting the user icon at the top right of the Start menu (refer to Figure 1.6) will take you to the User Accounts screen (see Figure 1.7). This screen provides the user with quick access to account management in Vista without having to go into the Control Panel. From this screen the user can add or delete users, change passwords, change user pictures, and manage account permissions. UAC can also be enabled or disabled from this screen.

Figure 1.7 User Accounts Screen

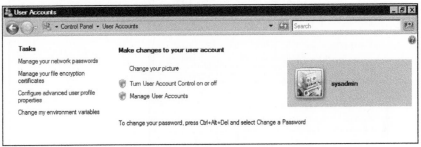

This screen will differ depending on whether your system is a member of a domain or in a simple workgroup. Figure 1.7 shows the User Account screen when the system is a joined to a domain. To change a password the user will need to press **Ctrl+Alt+Del** and select **Change a Password**. To change advanced user settings, click **Manage User Accounts**, which will launch the User Accounts property page (Figure 1.8). From this page we can add and remove local users, change group membership, reset passwords, turn the "press ctrl+atl+del to logon" feature on or off, and launch the Local User Management Console.

The Local User Management Console is the familiar user management interface that most sys admins will want to use to control local accounts (Figure 1.9). From this interface you can quickly alter user settings, create new users, reset passwords, change group membership, and create new groups. This console is a Microsoft Management Console (MMC) 3.0 snap-in. MMC 3.0 is available for download for Windows XP or Windows Server 2003. It also is included in Windows Server 2003 R2, Windows Vista, and Windows Server Longhorn by default.

Figure 1.8 User Accounts Property Page

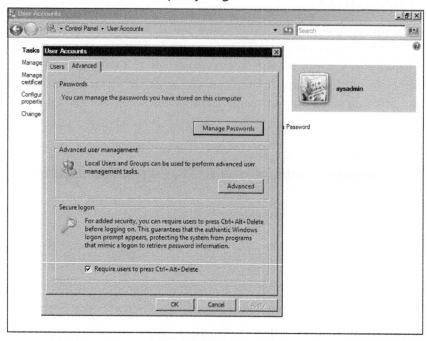

Figure 1.9 Local User Management Console

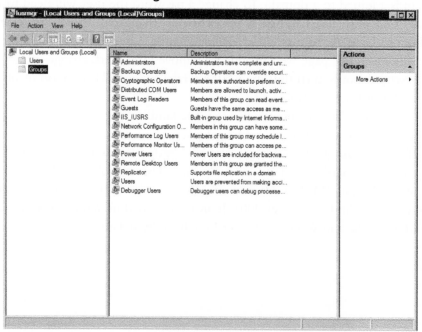

Internet Explorer 7

Microsoft recently released another long-awaited software package, Internet Explorer (IE) 7. IE 7 is available through Windows Update for Windows XP, and Windows Server 2003 and Windows Vista will ship with the new version of Internet Explorer. Microsoft has improved Internet Explorer with new features and options in this latest version.

Internet Explorer 6 was plagued by security issues, and sys admins have been just as focused on the security of IE 7 as they have been on Vista's security. Some of the security features included in IE 7 are an improved pop-up blocker and the anti-phishing filter. There have also been changes in the way IE asks users for input when a suspect digital certificate is encountered or an ActiveX control needs to be installed. These changes all aim to increase the overall security of IE 7 as well as the systems running the browser.

Internet Explorer 7 Features

Internet Explorer 7 also aims to improve the user's experience. Microsoft has been pushing for a change in its basic user interface by eliminating the standard menu system present at the top of program windows. The familiar menus (File, Edit, View, etc.) have been cast aside for context- and task-oriented systems. The first program to make these changes was Windows Media Player 10, but IE 7 and Office 2007 have quickly followed suit. The change is quite a departure from the way users are used to navigating and interacting with programs in Windows, and it will be interesting to see if the community can adapt.

Internet Explorer 7 also introduces tabbed browsing, a feature that will be familiar to users of Firefox and Opera. Tabbed browsing consolidates newly opened pages into a single main window.

TIP

To turn the menu bar on for quick access to the File, Edit, View, Favorites, Tools, and Help menu, simply press the **Alt** key. Press the **Alt** key again to hide the bar. If you wish to turn the menu bar on by default simply click **Tools** and select **Menu Bar**. See Figure 1.10.

Figure 1.10 Internet Explorer 7

RSS Feeds

RSS feeds allow Web sites and users to subscribe to content on the Web that is of interest to them. Many news sites and blogs offer this feature so that users can receive updated stories and content as soon as it is posted to the feed. This technology is also employed by many news aggregators that offer quick views of the top stories from many different news sites. Internet Explorer 7 provides new features to support RSS feeds from your favorite sites. The RSS Feed feature in IE 7 is simply just an addition to the Favorites bookmark feature in IE. Feeds are separated from your standard bookmarks, and as the content in the feed is updated, the link to that feed is also updated. In Figure 1.11 we have navigated to www.digg.com, a popular news site that aggregates news stories from many different sources on its main page. As you can see the RSS Feed icon, the icon sandwiched between the Home Page and Printer icons, is no longer grayed out as in Figure 1.10. This means there is an RSS feed, or multiple RSS feeds, available on this page.

Figure 1.11 RSS Feed Icon

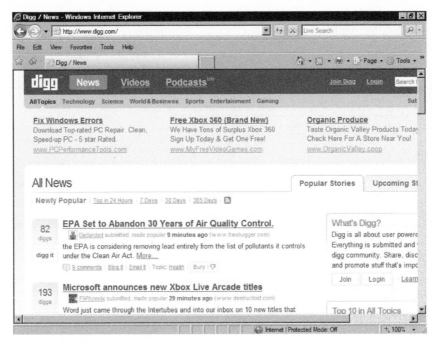

Clicking the **RSS Feed** icon will take you directly to the RSS feed Web page (Figure 1.12). If you aren't subscribed to this feed, you can select **Subscribe to this Feed,** which will bring up the *Subscribe to this Feed* dialog box (Figure 1.13).

From the *Subscribe to this Feed* dialog box, you can assign a descriptive name to the feed and choose where to file the feed under the Feeds section of your Favorites Center. To subscribe to this feed click **Subscribe**, and the feed will be added to your Favorites Center. After you subscribe to feeds, IE 7 will monitor these feeds for changes and provide notification of updated content by showing the feed in bold text in the Favorites Center (Figure 1.14).

Figure 1.12 RSS Feed from a Web Page

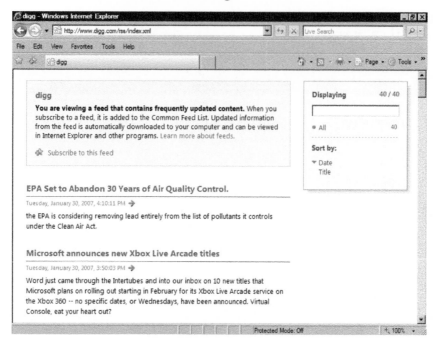

Figure 1.13 Adding an RSS Feed

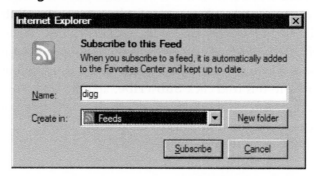

Figure 1.14 Viewing RSS Feeds

If you right-click on the **RSS feed** in your Favorites and select **Properties**, you will see the box shown in Figure 1.15, which lists the RSS feed properties for that Web page. From this page, you can select when and how many times the RSS feed should be updated throughout the day. This feature will help those RSS feed junkies who have hundreds of feeds. You can also select how many items from each feed you want to remain archived on your system.

Figure 1.15 RSS Feed Properties

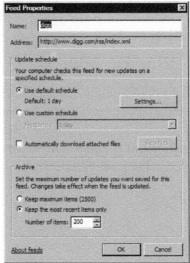

Pop-up Blocker

A Pop-up Blocker comes with Internet Explorer 7 to help you with all of those nasty pop-ups you're prone to getting when you surf the Web. Within Internet Explorer 7, you can control the Pop-up Blocker by going to the **Tools** setting on the far right of Internet Explorer 7 and selecting **Pop-up Blocker Settings**. From here, you can change how the Pop-up Blocker works on certain sites (see Figure 1.16).

Figure 1.16 Pop-up Blocker Settings

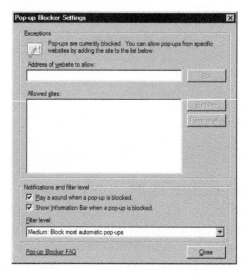

Phishing Filter

Also new with Internet Explorer 7 is a Phishing Filter that helps you understand which Web sites are safe to visit and which are trying to steal information from you. Phishing is an attempt by hackers to obtain sensitive user information such as passwords and credit card information while masquerading as a trustworthy person or business.

The Phishing Filter in Internet Explorer 7 is turned on by default, but you can turn it off from the Tools setting on the far right of the Internet Explorer screen. Figure 1.17 shows the icon you will see at the top of Internet Explore 7 if there is a problem with a Web site you're visiting. Figure 1.18 shows different icons that you might see while surfing with the Phishing Filter turned on.

Figure 1.17 The Phishing Filter Indicating that There Is a Problem with This Web Site

Figure 1.18 Phishing Filter Icons

Summary

Windows Vista represents Microsoft's view of the future of computing. With Vista Microsoft wants to improve the user's experience, as well as change the minds of the public about the insecurity and reliability of Windows operating systems. Microsoft has taken a hard stance on security through an improved code review process and the employment of third-party individuals to scrutinize its software. The implementation of innovative security controls such as ASLR and a layered approach to total system security has also helped Microsoft produce a much more secure OS.

Microsoft is also seeing the benefit of having a code base that is now maturing and becoming more robust with each release and service pack. Vista also includes several mature add-on products such as Internet Explorer 7 and Windows Media Player 11. IE 7 offers users improved security and a much more efficient user interface with features such as tabbed browsing and the phishing filter. Are these new features enough to warrant an upgrade in the home or office, though? This is the battle that Microsoft must now fight. Wide adoption of Vista will be slow at first, and the main source of new Vista machines will not be users upgrading their current systems. Most new Vista machines will be from OEMs such as Dell and Gateway. Another factor will be the fact that DirectX (DX) 10 will not be available for Windows XP. Gamers will need to upgrade their systems with new graphics cards as well as Vista to support DX 10 and the new games coming out that will take advantage of DX 10.

The next year will be interesting for Microsoft and the IT world in general. Most sys admins will choose to wait before fully adopting Vista as their platform of choice. What happens in the first year, how many security flaws and bugs are found, and how Microsoft responds to those issues will greatly affect the choices of many IT departments.

Solutions Fast Track

The User Interface

- ☑ The new Aero user interface in Windows Vista is nice to work with and provides useful system information at your fingertips.

- ☑ The new tree-like menu in the Start menu works well and eliminates the old problem of clicking on the wrong program or file.

☑ The Ease of Access Center is where you can select various options to make your computer easier to use.

Internet Explorer 7

☑ Microsoft has updated Internet Explorer with a Phishing Filter and a Pop-up Blocker to help users secure their surfing on the Internet.

☑ Tabbed browsing allows you to surf the Web with multiple tabs open, but within one Internet Explorer application.

☑ The new RSS Feeder is a great feature for people who are on the go and like to get their news automatically downloaded to their computers.

Frequently Asked Questions

The following Frequently Asked Questions, answered by the authors of this book, are designed to both measure your understanding of the concepts presented in this chapter and to assist you with real-life implementation of these concepts. To have your questions about this chapter answered by the author, browse to **www.syngress.com/solutions** and click on the **"Ask the Author"** form.

Q: How can I determine whether upgrading to Windows Vista is right for me?

A: First, you need to make sure your computer has the recommended hardware to run Vista; if it doesn't, you will need to upgrade your computer or purchase a new computer. If your computer runs fine on its current OS, you could find it difficult to justify switching to Vista. It may be a good idea to wait until some of the bugs are worked out of Vista before considering an upgrade.

Q: Do I need to upgrade my computer to the specifications that Microsoft has published, or will Vista crash on me?

A: You should always go by the hardware requirements put forward by the vendor. This will ensure that the software will operate correctly when installed on the computer.

Q: I really don't like Internet Explorer 7. Will Firefox run on Vista?

A: Yes, it will, and we have been using it on our test box with no problems so far.

Q: Is it better for me to go with a 64-bit or a 32-bit version of Vista?

A: We recommend the 32-bit version for now because there are still many programs and hardware devices that are not supported on 64-bit Windows. If you have researched what programs and hardware devices are supported and feel comfortable going with the 64-bit version, then the 64-bit version may be right for you.

Q: Can I expect any glitches when upgrading from XP to Vista?

A: We experienced only a few when we upgraded to Vista in our lab. When we did a fresh install, we had no problems.

Q: I was told that Vista is a memory hog and that it would crash computers with less than 1 GB of RAM. Is this true?

A: We ran Vista on a machine with only 600 MB of RAM and it ran okay, but remember, when you add more programs, you need more RAM.

Chapter 2

Microsoft Vista: The Battle Against Malware Lives On

Solutions in this chapter:

- Malware Fundamentals

- Improvements in Internet Explorer 7

- Windows Security Center

- Windows Defender

☑ Summary

☑ Solutions Fast Track

☑ Frequently Asked Questions

Introduction

Microsoft's Vista is by far the most secure version of its client-based operating system (OS) to date. Living by its motto of "Trustworthy Computing," Microsoft has taken many steps to ensure new levels of security to the Windows Vista base OS. Along with other tools and programs, Microsoft has released Internet Explorer 7, which is the most secure version of the famous browser released to date. Microsoft has also updated and released a plethora of documentation on the company's main Web site and on TechNet in coordination with the Vista release, to help you harden and prepare your system for use on the Internet or on a corporate network.

With all of these tools, documentation updates, and newly developed forms of technology and security you should be wondering why we still have to deal with so many computer-related issues. The fact is that every time we browse the Internet, we open our doors to danger. It's also a fact that we may never catch up to quell the growing threat. In the world of IT, the playing field is constantly changing, so as programming code becomes more bloated and newer features are added, consequently more exploits are added. Newly made software and software that has been updated will always have issues that will be resolved only through update installations, hotfixes, service packs (SPs), and/or complete OS or program upgrades. As this chapter's title implies, the battle against malware does in fact live on. You do have an option to protect yourself, though.

Security is not only a practice, it's also a mindset. Those of you who leave your front doors open and unlocked invite danger. This doesn't mean you will inevitably be a target; it just means you are making it easier to become a target. It's always better to make sure your assets are secure before inviting danger. You can apply the same way of thinking to your Internet surfing habits. Knowing that you could be a victim every time you venture onto the Web will help you develop a mindset to make sure your doors are locked before you do. By preparing for risk, you will ultimately be more secure. To lessen the risk of attack, you would want to ensure that your OS is secure and hardened and that the Web browser you use will not invite danger. You will also want to make sure you aren't surfing sites where you may be an even bigger target, such as downloadable warez sites, pornographic content sites, and music download sites. These are generally havens for unwanted malware. With Microsoft's new tools and more secure software, you are definitely going to be able to lock your doors at night and feel better about your security posture. If you also apply common-sense browsing skills to your Web surfing, you could very well keep your OS malware-free for a long period of time.

With the release of Microsoft's Vista OS, security has once again been brought to a new level. When Microsoft started to take security extremely seriously (after its federal antitrust case), the biggest area that needed work was its Web browser. From its inception, Internet Explorer has been the target of many exploits. Due to its widespread deployment (it came with the base OS and was one of the first browsers available for use), Internet Explorer became the biggest target of exploit writers. Because of its flawed code and many bugs, exploit writers had no problem creating one exploit after another, with no end in sight. Tie in that the Internet is the main catalyst in an ever-changing world of technology and you can clearly see why Internet Explorer has had so many problems to date. This would also explain why other browsers had not seen as many exploits as Internet Explorer did. They just weren't as big a target and, to some extent, may have been programmed better.

Ever since Microsoft invested considerable time, money, and resources into securing its software, each release had gotten better and less susceptible to attack and exploit. This obviously doesn't stop the ongoing plague of exploits that surface each month; it only helps to "stem the tide." Because malicious software (malware) is an ongoing problem and one that is growing each year, Microsoft has stepped up to the challenge once again with its newest releases of Vista and Internet Explorer Version 7. In this chapter, we will look at how Vista and Internet Explorer make for a safer browsing experience, and how Microsoft is combating problems with malware.

NOTE

When you connect to the Internet, you are connecting to one of the biggest networks in use today, aside from the public telephone system. Millions of people use the Internet each day. Therefore, you need to take securing your computer, your data, and your identity seriously. To remain secure you should constantly stay abreast of threats by keeping your system updated with antivirus definitions and other updates, and exercise due diligence by making sure you do not visit questionable sites. Stay vigilant, because all you need to do is let your guard down once and you could infect your system with so much malware that you may have to completely reinstall your OS.

Malware Fundamentals

Intruders, hackers, or attackers who access networks and systems without authorization and with malicious motives can plant various types of programs to cause damage to the network, your system, and your data. These programs—often lumped together under the general term *viruses*—perform many different functions and are classified under different categories. In this section, we will look at how granular the term *malware* can actually be. It's important to have a general understanding of the different classifications of malware, and it's equally important to understand their general behavior.

Malware is any software product or program that has been created with an intent to cause damage or harm. The word *malice* is a legal term used to define the intention of one party to harm or cause injury to another party. When applied to computer technology, the word holds equal meaning. A malicious party creates software to cause havoc on any host that downloads and installs it, whether knowingly or unknowingly. When discussing malware, it's important to classify it. The term *malware* is generally used to describe a broad spectrum of different types of software, such as computer viruses, Trojans, worms, adware, and spyware. Just about any form of hostile, intrusive, or annoying software or program code can be classified as malware.

NOTE

You should not confuse malware with defective software, which is software that has a legitimate purpose but contains bugs that cause the program not to work as advertised. Malware is intended. A software bug is not intended.

Viruses, Worms, and Trojan Horses

Many of the original MS-DOS-based viruses and other types of malware were written as experiments intended to be either harmless or destructive, and many were created as simple and harmless pranks. As time went on, the level of skill used to create such malware grew by leaps and bounds, and the severity of each payload grew exponentially as well. This inevitably caused many software programmers to stop coding, learn security fundamentals, and start coding again while applying those fundamentals. Because it appeared that the exploit writers were outpacing the software developers, this practice became "mandatory" within Microsoft's own camp.

Notes from the Underground…

Vista Is Still Susceptible to Older Malware

Since its release, Microsoft Windows Vista has already been reported to be affected by old malware. In particular, Vista has been found to be susceptible to three common malware exploits:

- **Stratio-Zip** W32/Stratio-Zip is a family of Zip files containing worms in the Stration family.
- **Netsky-D** W32/Netsky-D is a worm that spreads via e-mail. When e-mailing itself the worm can spoof the sender's e-mail address.
- **MyDoom-O** W32/MyDoom-O is an e-mail worm that creates a file named services.exe in the Windows or Temp folder, and then runs the file. Services.exe is a backdoor component. The worm then searches the hard disk's e-mail addresses.

When deploying Vista, be aware that although malware defense has been fortified, it still has its faults. For more information on this subject, visit www.sophos.com/pressoffice/news/articles/2006/11/toptennov.html and http://news.zdnet.co.uk/security/0,1000000189,39284939,00.htm.

Young, inexperienced software programmers and script kiddies learning about viruses and the techniques used to write them were getting more advanced as the tools they created or had at their disposal expanded in number. Some of these malware attacks proved to hurt a global economy that now thrived on the use of the Internet. As time went on, a chase seemed to ensue, and it appeared as though the exploit writers were outpacing the product's legitimate software development teams. As the use of the Internet exploded, it seemed as though malware grew more and more destructive on a daily basis. Newer exploits were coming out rapidly that were designed to destroy files on a hard disk or to corrupt the file system so that it could not be used. Viruses were created to cause traffic flooding to legitimate Web servers, putting them out of business. The list goes on and on. It wasn't until malware became extremely destructive that action was taken on a grand scale. In 1999, Melissa (a well-known computer virus) really showed us how fast (and far) a virus could spread. It also showed us how vulnerable our systems were to attacks that could hurt a company's bottom line. Melissa was the first virus to be widely disseminated via e-mail. It is a macro virus, written in Visual Basic for Applications (VBA), and it was embedded in a Microsoft Word 97/2000 document. When the infected document was opened, the macro ran (unless Word was set not to run macros), sending itself to the first 50 entries in every Microsoft Outlook MAPI address book it could find. These included mailing list addresses, which resulted in very rapid propagation of the virus. The virus also made changes to the Normal.dot template, which caused newly created Word documents to be infected. Because of the huge volume of mail it produced, the virus caused a denial of service (DoS) attack on infected e-mail servers.

Are You Owned?

Script Kiddies and DoS Attacks

A *script kiddie* is an inexperienced hacker who uses already developed tools and methods to exploit a system or penetrate a system's defenses, instead of creating those tools and methods on his own. Advanced hackers and code programmers are generally considered to be elite. These experienced individuals can create a rootkit, whereas a script kiddie will only obtain and execute it.

A DoS attack is an attack on a network or system that is designed to tie up the system's or network's resources so that legitimate requests for service cannot be answered. For all known DoS attacks, there are software fixes that system administrators can install to limit the damage caused by the attacks, and steps they can take to attempt to prevent the attacks. Since 2003, the majority of widespread viruses and worms have been designed to take control of users' computers for use in DoS attacks to hide the identity of the true attacker. Infected computer system hosts (called *zombies*) are used to send large amounts of data, spam, pornography, and other random data to legitimate hosts. A DoS attack is usually sourced from one or multiple locations to attack a single location. A distributed denial of service (DDOS) attack is the "distributed" form of the same attack, using multiple zombie hosts to perform a larger-scale attack more quickly.

Viruses

A virus is a malicious program that is commonly installed on a target host with the intent to cause harm or damage. A virus (just like the medical version of the term) infects the host, usually by being installed by the end user of the target host. A virus is almost always executed by the end user without him knowing the true intention of the malware. Viruses are made to perform undesirable actions. Viruses are also created to replicate themselves, infecting other systems by writing themselves to any disk that is used in the computer or sending themselves across a network when activated. Viruses are often distributed as attachments to e-mail or as macros in word processing documents easily sent via e-mail and opened by unsuspecting e-mail users. Some viruses activate immediately on installation, and others lay dormant until a specific date or time, or until a particular system event triggers their payload.

Viruses come in literally thousands of varieties. They can do anything from sending a pop-up message on your desktop to scare you (which is considered a prank), to erasing the entire contents of a computer's hard disk (which is considered destructive and harmful). The proliferation of computer viruses has also led to the phenomenon of the virus hoax, which is a warning—generally circulated via e-mail or Web sites—about a virus that does not exist or that does not do what the warning claims it will do. The same malicious effect takes place because through the hoax, the end user can cause the same damage to the target system without creating a software tool using programming languages. In the past, some of these hoaxes have prompted computer users to manually delete needed system files, either because they sounded malicious or because the icon image they used by default looked malicious. Real viruses, on the other hand, present a real threat to your network. Companies such as Symantec and McAfee make antivirus software that is aimed at detecting and removing virus programs, and is updated daily to thwart newly created ones, which seem to also come out on a daily basis.

TIP

Because new viruses are created constantly, it is very important to download new virus definition files regularly. These updates contain information required to detect each virus type, to ensure that your virus protection stays up-to-date, and to take action when certain parameters are tripped.

Although viruses come in many varieties, they can be classified into four general categories: e-mail-based, boot sector-based, application-based, and macro-based. The common thread that holds these types together is that they need to be executed on the target host.

- **E-mail viruses** E-mail viruses are transmitted via e-mail and contain a payload that is activated when the end user is provoked to activate it, or when something in the e-mail client and how it reads e-mail (and scripts) activates the payload upon delivery or viewing, without opening the e-mail (such as with an automatic reading pane found in most e-mail clients).

- **Boot sector viruses** Boot sector viruses are often transmitted via disk. The virus is written to the master boot record on the hard disk, from which it is loaded into the computer's memory every time the system boots.

- **Application or program viruses** Application viruses are executable programs that, when run, infect your system. Viruses can also be attached to other, harmless programs and installed at the same time the desirable program is installed.

- **Macro viruses** Macro viruses are embedded in documents (such as Microsoft Word documents) that can use macros, which are small applications or "applets" that automate the performance of some task or sequence. Although Microsoft Office documents are not executable files, they can contain macros. Thus, Office documents should be treated as though they are executables, unless the ability to run macros is disabled in the Office program.

WARNING

A virus can be programmed to mutate into something else, and can be written with defense mechanisms to protect itself from detection and/or deletion. One type of virus that can avoid detection is called a *polymorphic virus*. Polymorphic viruses are written to use encryption routines that constantly change to avoid detection.

Worms

Worms are ugly, regardless of whether they are dangling from a fish hook or taking down your public Internet connection. Worms can also be very destructive. History has shown us that since its inception, the worm has consistently transferred itself over networks to infect target hosts, whereas common viruses typically infect a single target host only. The worm is then transferred via e-mail or floppy disk to other hosts in hopes that they become infected as well. A worm is written to propagate quickly, and to infect as many target hosts via propagation as possible, thereby causing as much turmoil as possible. Although the line between malware terms such as *worm* and *virus* is sometimes blurred, this is the major distinction between the two.

A worm is programmed to "scan" the network from the infected host to find other hosts with open and vulnerable services and ports. As an example, a worm may infect a target host via a network port and then find 30 hosts on the connected subnet with the same open port. Once this criterion is met, the worm then propagates to those 30 hosts, and so on. Examples of this come in the form of the Sasser and Slammer worms. The Sasser worm exploited Transmission Control Protocol (TCP) port 5554. The Slammer worm exploited a known SQL Server vulnerability by sending a single packet to User Datagram Protocol (UDP) port 1434.

TIP

Although most ports are programmable, many well-known services operate on designated ports such as domain name system (DNS), which operates on TCP and UDP ports 53. For a complete list of these default port assignments, visit the IANA Web site, www.iana.org/assignments/port-numbers.

The worm first surfaced at the turn of the century. In 2001, worms such as Code Red started to pop up at an alarming rate. This self-propagating worm began to infect Microsoft-based Web servers running Internet Information Server (IIS), and because so many such servers were in use, the virus spread extremely quickly. On various trigger dates, the infected machines would try to connect to TCP port 80 (used for Web services) on computers with randomly selected Internet Protocol (IP) addresses. When successful, the worm attempted to infect any remote system it could find and connect to. Some variations of the worm also defaced Web pages stored on the server as a form of digital graffiti. On other dates, the infected machine would launch a DoS attack against a specific IP address embedded in the code. CERT (www.cert.org) reported that Code Red infected more than 250,000 systems over the course of nine hours on July 19, 2001.

Then came Nimda—a newly created worm used to take advantage of known flaws within the Microsoft OS. In late summer 2001, the Nimda worm infected numerous computers running Windows 95/98/ME, NT, and 2000. The worm made changes to Web documents and executable files on the infected systems and created multiple copies of itself. Nimda spread via e-mail, across network shares, and via infected Web sites. It also exploited vulnerabilities in IIS versions 4 and 5 and spread from client machines to Web servers through the backdoors left by the Code Red II worm. Nimda allowed attackers to then execute arbitrary commands on IIS machines that had not been patched, and denials of service were caused by the worm's programmed payload.

As the IT community repaired systems at a feverish rate to recover from Code Red and Nimda, Klez reared its ugly head. In late 2001 and early 2002, the Klez worm spread throughout the Internet, primarily via e-mail. It propagated through e-mail mass mailings and exploited vulnerabilities in the unpatched versions of Outlook and Outlook Express mail clients, attempting to run when the message containing it was viewed or previewed in the preview pane. When Klez runs, it copies itself to the System or System32 folder in the system root directory, and modifies a Registry key to cause it to be executed when Windows is started. It also tries to disable any virus scanners and sends copies of itself to addresses in the Windows address book, in the form of a random filename with a double extension (for example, file.doc.exe). As though this wasn't harmful enough, the worm had a secret payload, which executed on the thirteenth day of every other month, starting with January, resulting in files on local and mapped drives being set to 0 bytes in length.

Worm outbreaks have become a cyclical plague for both home users and businesses, and have been eclipsed only recently in terms of damage by spyware. As they were from inception, today most worms are commonly written for the Windows OS, although a small number are also written for Linux and UNIX systems, such as 2005's Lupper, which was aimed at the growing use of Linux Web servers in the marketplace.

NOTE

The words *virus* and *worm* are often used interchangeably. Today some draw the distinction between viruses and worms by saying that a virus requires user intervention to spread, whereas a worm spreads automatically. Using this distinction, infections transmitted by e-mail or Microsoft Word documents, which rely on the recipient opening a file to infect the system, would be classified as viruses, not worms.

Trojan Horses

For a malicious program to accomplish its goals, it must be able to do so without being shut down by the user or administrator of the computer on which it's running. Concealment is a major goal of a malware creator. When a malicious program is disguised as something innocuous or desirable, users may be tempted to install it without knowing what it does. When reflecting on history, the documented first use of the Trojan horse was when the Greeks gave their enemies (the Trojans) a gift during the Trojan War. The gift (a gigantic wooden horse) was given in peace so that the Trojans would bring it into their stronghold, but at night, when the city slept, the Greek soldiers snuck out of the back of the horse and attacked and then captured the city of Troy.

This is how the Trojan horse exploit performs. The Trojan horse will appear harmless enough for the recipient to install, because it hides its true intention, which is based on malicious activity. The Trojan horse conceals a harmful or malicious payload within its seemingly harmless shell. The payload may take effect immediately and can lead to many undesirable effects, such as deleting all of the user's files, or more commonly, installing further harmful software on the user's system for future payloads.

Tools and Traps...

Rootkits, Backdoors, and Keyloggers

Malware can be very nasty, especially when it and its payload are concealed. For instance, consider the use of rootkits, backdoors, and keyloggers:

- **Rootkits** A rootkit is a form of malware that hides its presence on the target host. Now used as a general term, its original meaning was to define a set of tools installed by an attacker on a UNIX system, where the attacker had gained administrator (root) access. Today *rootkit* is used as a general term to describe any concealed malware on any type of system, such as UNIX or Windows. Rootkits act by modifying the host OS so that the malware is hidden from the user. Rootkits will remain undetected and can prevent a malicious process from being reported in the process table.

Continued

■ **Backdoors** A backdoor is a routine used to sidestep the normal authentication procedure found on most systems to keep them secure. Backdoors are just as dangerous as rootkits. Generally, backdoors are network-aware programs that allow access from an attacker into the target system without the target system's user knowing about it. A backdoor is a method of bypassing normal authentication procedures. Many software manufacturers preinstall backdoors on their products to provide technical support for customers. The malware version performs the same function, but is definitely not used to provide you with any help.

■ **Keyloggers** A keylogger is a form of malicious software that monitors what a user types on his keyboard. This will generally lead to the compromise of sensitive information, such as user credentials (usernames and passwords) and other sensitive data. Sometimes keyloggers are also implemented in hardware connected to the back of a PC or server without the user's knowledge.

Trojans can be very cleverly disguised as innocuous programs, utilities, or screensavers. A Trojan can also be installed by an executable script (JavaScript, a Java applet, ActiveX control, etc.) on a Web site. Accessing the site can initiate the program's installation if the Web browser is configured to allow scripts to run automatically. Trojans can use the default behavior of Windows to disguise their true nature. Because the file extension (the characters that appear after the last dot in a filename) are hidden by default, a hacker can name a file something such as harmless.jpg.exe and it will appear in Windows Explorer as harmless.jpg, seeming to be an innocent graphics file, when it is really an executable program. Of course, double-clicking it to open the "harmless picture" will run the program. Trojans that are designed to allow hackers to gain unauthorized access across a network, such as Back Orifice and NetBus, are sometimes called *remote access Trojans* (RATs). Back Orifice, Back Orifice 2000, NetBus, and SubSeven were the most commonly used Trojans of their time, although literally hundreds exist. Newer Trojan horses, such as Xombe and Dloader-L, both of which arrive as an executable attachment in spam e-mail messages claiming to come from windowsupdate@microsoft.com, are meant to wreak havoc by fooling you into thinking that the attachment legitimately came from Microsoft. Because the spoofed e-mail address "seemed" legitimate, many were fooled into executing the attachment, which can be thought of as any system administrator's nightmare.

NOTE

Hackers typically use backdoors to secure remote access to a computer, while attempting to remain hidden from casual inspection. To install backdoors hackers use either a Trojan horse or a computer worm, with the payload being the backdoor routine.

Trojan horses known as *droppers* are used to initiate a worm outbreak, by injecting the worm into users' local networks. Spyware is commonly distributed as a Trojan horse, bundled with a piece of desirable software that the user downloads from the Web, or from a peer-to-peer file-sharing network such as LimeWire (www.limewire.com). When the user installs the software, the spyware is installed alongside it. Spyware authors who attempt to act legally may include an End User License Agreement (EULA) which states the behavior of the spyware in loose terms, but with the knowledge that users are unlikely to read or understand it.

Spyware and Adware

Somewhere along the malware timeline, virus and exploit writers started to shift gears from attacking with a purpose, such as harm and damage, to just getting paid. Spyware and adware have become lucrative business ventures for those who have tried it and were successful at it. Spyware programs are designed to monitor users' Web browsing habits and then market relevant advertisements to these users based on their browsing history. Some spyware programs display unsolicited advertisements and then trick or force the user to click on them. Some are even self-activated. Other forms of spyware are intelligent enough to redirect affiliated marketing revenues to the spyware creator.

Spyware programs do not spread like viruses do; they are generally installed by exploiting known security holes or are packaged with software that the end user downloads and installs onto the target host. Spyware programs are usually installed as Trojan horses, meaning you believe you are installing software that does a specific function, but in the background, other functions are taking place. Spyware differs from standard viruses in that their creators present themselves openly as businesses, whether legitimate or not.

Spyware exploits are also used to obtain user information. Similar to how cookies help to aid your browsing experience, spyware does the same by analyzing what sites you go to and what your browsing habits are. However, it then invades your privacy further by not only using that information to market products to you, but also avoiding deletion or removal so that you cannot remove it. A cookie, on the other hand, is generally pretty easy to deny or delete, especially with Internet Explorer 7.

NOTE

A cookie is a very small text file that a Web server hosting a site deposits on your computer when you visit that site. A cookie contains information about the user, such as user IDs, preferences, and browsing history.

Some spyware can trick you by changing your search engine results to paid advertisements that benefit the spyware creator. Others change the affiliate marking codes so that all revenue goes to the spyware creator instead of to you. This is sometimes called *stealware*.

You can use spyware detection programs such as third-party vendor tools (e.g., Ad-Aware; www.lavasoftusa.com), or you can use Microsoft Defender in conjunction with SpyNet to help stop your spyware woes.

Similar to antivirus software, spyware removal programs compare a list of known spyware with files on your computer and then remove any that it detects. Antispyware programs can combat spyware from being installed, but the best strategy is to carefully examine and analyze what you choose to download and install.

WARNING

Most spyware programs present the user with a EULA that purportedly protects the creator from prosecution under computer contaminant laws. However, spyware EULAs have not yet been upheld in court. Stanford (http://cyberlaw.stanford.edu/packets003459.shtml) and Yale (http://research.yale.edu/lawmeme/modules.php?name=News&file=article&sid=1652) have both released data on how EULAs and law hold up when malware is a concern.

Botnets

Much like the DDoS attack, the botnet is a program that will facilitate an attack from coordinated systems. Software robots (or *bots*, for short) are controlled via a botnet.

In a botnet, the malware logs on to an Internet Relay Chat (IRC) channel or other chat-based system. The attacker can then give instructions to all the infected systems simultaneously. Botnets can also be used to push upgraded malware to the infected systems, keeping them resistant to antivirus and antispyware software or other security measures.

Tip

Attackers are using IRC as a main transport for their malware. IRC robots (*bots*) are used to execute commands unsuspectingly on host systems using IRC. IRC is a large-scale network of text channels used for communication. To learn more about botnets, IRC, and other malicious code, visit the forums at www.ryan1918.com and www.irchelp.org.

Prevention and Response

Before we get into how Microsoft's new products can help you reduce the threat of malware, it makes sense to discuss prevention and response first. As mentioned earlier, staying secure is a two-step dance. You need good software that protects you, and the mindset to protect your surfing habits. Protecting systems and networks from the damage caused by Trojans, viruses, and worms is mostly a matter of common sense. It's up to you to prevent harm by being aware of it, and then being able to respond to it and make the systems (or network) operational without any downtime, if possible. Although there are many ways to protect yourself and your system using Microsoft's tools, it always helps to practice some of the following general security practices as well:

- Periodically update every piece of software you install on your system, as well as the OS itself, which also needs to be updated periodically. You can do this by installing the latest updates, hotfixes, security patches, and SPs that are available for your software. Keep on top of when new patches come out, and try to test and then install the current patches to keep your system at its best.

■ When you are using your e-mail client, pay close attention to "who" is sending you e-mail and "where" the e-mail originates. Because e-mail can be spoofed, you may not always be able to do this, but in most cases, a spam filter can quickly identify unspoofed e-mail and send it right to the trash or automatically remove it.

■ If you receive files from sources that you do not recognize, it's wise not to execute them. Instead, delete them. In other words, if someone sends you a file such as harmless.jpg.exe, it's a good idea to delete the file and not execute it because it seems to fall into the characteristic of a typical malware hoax intended on getting you to launch it.

■ When using your e-mail client, make sure you turn off any preview pane functionality so that you do not open and, therefore, execute any attached scripts simply by opening your Inbox.

■ To prevent macro viruses, ensure that macro security is enabled in Office so that if you open a Word document, you won't necessarily run a malicious script that may also be contained within it.

■ Do not use floppy disks from untrusted sources. Also, pay attention to any file that enters your system from any source, whether it is a CD or DVD-ROM, USB flash device, or something similar.

■ Use host-based instruction detection/prevention (IDS/IPS) software if possible, as well as firewall software, antivirus software, and spyware removal software such as Microsoft Defender.

■ Harden your systems and disable unneeded or unwanted services.

■ Use a strong password policy. If malware does attempt to try to steal your credentials, having a strong password policy in place will help you if your system does become infected.

■ Configure your Web browser (such as Internet Explorer 7) to ignore or warn for cookies, and disable JavaScript and ActiveX, two commonly exploited scripting languages. Keep a close eye on sites that are not trusted and try to block sites that you know are malware-infected.

You may also want to make sure your network is also secure. Some more advanced practices include the following:

■ Configure your routers, switches, and other adjoining network hardware to be secure, which means locking down services, keeping the router or switch OS updated, and applying any security measures such as disabling broadcasts on certain interfaces, applying access control lists (ACLs), and so on.

- Disable the Simple Network Management Protocol (SNMP) and any other services that you do not need.

- Make sure any e-mail relays in use are protected and aren't being used to send spam.

- Use application gateway firewalls to protect against large-scale attacks.

- Apply defense in depth. Using a firewall alone is almost meaningless. You need to ensure that you have multiple levels of security in place, such as desktop policies, a firewall, and an IDS.

- Use a security policy and keep it updated. Security is upheld only when it's supposed to be, so make sure your company has a policy in place that dictates what needs to be secured and how it needs to be secured.

- Make sure you have an incident response plan ready, with detailed steps and a team that can carry it out. Your goal should be to prevent a crisis if you can, but your real responsibility when dealing with incident response concerns the response; in other words, taking care of the issue either while it is happening or after it has happened.

TIP

Creating backups of your important data is one place to start. Incident prevention and risk mitigation begin with your proactive planning. A great response to an attack that destroys your company's important data is data backup that restores that data to its original state.

Incident Response

Recognizing the presence of malicious code should be your first response step if the system does get infected. Administrators and users need to be on the alert for common indications that a virus might be present, such as missing files or programs; unexplained changes to the system's configuration; unexpected and unexplained displays, messages, or sounds; new files or programs that suddenly appear with no explanation; memory "leaks" (less available system memory than normal) or unexplained use of disk space; and any other odd behavior of programs or the OS. If a virus is suspected, a good antivirus program should be installed and run to scan the system for viruses and attempt to remove or quarantine any that are found. Finally, all mission-critical or irreplaceable data should be backed up on a regular basis in case all of these measures fail.

Remember that virus writers are a creative and persistent bunch and will continue to come up with new ways to do the "impossible," so computer users should never assume that any particular file type or OS is immune to malicious code. There is only one way to completely protect yourself against a virus, and that is to power down the computer and leave it turned off entirely.

Tip

You may want to consider creating an incident response plan as well as an incident response team for your future incident endeavors. You should also review "Creating a Computer Security Incident Response Team: A Process for Getting Started," released by CERT (www.cert.org/csirts/Creating-A-CSIRT.html).

Microsoft Vista and Security

The battle for malware wages on, but new weapons have been pushed to the front line. For Windows Vista, many new security features (as well as some updated ones) help to protect computer systems from past, present, and future malware threats of any class.

Vista includes many new features that help to thwart malware threats. Behind the actual making of the software was a major plan to shift the way Microsoft does business in the security sector. Now, making a secure, private, and reliable computing experience has become the company's top priority and has been dubbed "Trustworthy Computing." To preserve data confidentiality, integrity, and availability (CIA), Windows Vista brings a new level of confidence to computing through improved security, reliability, and management. It achieves this by establishing innovative engineering, applying best practices, and creating a system where the OS can be updated and maintained consistently to avoid intrusion or exploitation.

New features include:

- **Windows Service Hardening** (WSH) Windows Service Hardening limits the amount of damage an attacker can do if a service is compromised.

- **Network Access Protection (NAP)** Network Access Protection is used to prevent clients from connecting to the network if they are infected with malware.

- **Internet Explorer 7** Internet Explorer 7 comes with Windows Vista by default as the built-in Web browser. It includes many security enhancements that protect users from malware attacks such as phishing and spoofing, and it uses a new mode, called Protected Mode, to further secure the user's browsing experience.

- **Updated Windows Firewall** The new outbound filtering feature in the personal firewall helps to apply more granular control over traffic traversing it.

- **User Account Control (UAC)** This feature will allow a user to change computer settings while running as a standard user, instead of requiring administrator privileges to perform most tasks.

- **Windows Defender** The Windows Defender utility detects malware on your system and, when used in conjunction with SpyNet, can help to eliminate most spyware attacks and exploits.

Other features within Vista help to secure the system; however, these relate to the battle against malware.

Windows Service Hardening (WSH)

For a long time, malware seemed to be connected to Windows-based services. Because Windows services have always been an open door for malware creators, Microsoft took steps to ensure that this doesn't continue to be a problem. In the past, there has been a major issue with the number of critical services running as System, which basically gave an open door to anyone who could bypass the minimal security in place. The Sasser, Blaster, Slammer, and Code Red exploits targeted unprotected and easily exploited services. WSH is a new service released with Microsoft Vista that allows you to harden the security posture of your host system. It's not realistic to leave a PC powered down and not in use, because this goes against what a computer was originally designed to do, which is to help you be more productive. The computer was not meant to act as a 150-pound paperweight. Microsoft has raised the bar on system service hardening by releasing WSH.

A system service is normally a background process that runs to support specific functions, such as the Messenger service that is used to send and receive messages throughout the system. In the past, services have been able to be exploited because once they were breached they basically opened the door to the system for the malware creator. Now, WSH focuses on using the least-privileged account—for example, *LocalService*. To further understand how this works consider that the hardened service would be protected via service SID access via ACLs. The service would use an SID, an ACL, and a "write-restricted token" to further harden and protect the system from exploitation.

Microsoft's system services have been the base for many attacks because of the high level of privileges these services run with. If exploited, some services can give unfettered access to the entire system. The malware can then run with the highest possible system privileges, or *LocalSystem* privileges. Once the system has been exploited, the attacker can run exploits on the system with administrator privileges. Worms such as Slammer exploited known system service holes. System services are kept secure with Windows Vista through the use of *restricted services*. This is done by running the services used with the "least privilege" needed, which reduces the risk of a threat. Using restricted services minimizes the number of exploitable services that are running and helps to secure the ones that do run. Windows services are run under service profiles that help to classify the service further so that the Vista OS has full control over its own services, further limiting malware exploitation.

Used in conjunction with the newly updated Windows Firewall, inbound and outbound network ports that the services are allowed to use are now under Vista's control. If a system service attempts to send and receive network data on a specific port, the firewall will block access. The commonly exploited Remote Procedure Call (RPC) service is an example. When RPC is needed, it will be loaded and "restricted" to doing only certain things. No longer can it be used to replace system files and other data, modify the system Registry, and so on.

WSH is important to Vista's overall security because even if you cannot prevent your system from being infected by malware, at least now you have a good feeling that if the system does get infected, the payload will not be as extreme as it used to be with older versions of the Windows OS. WSH also opens the door for independent software vendors (ISVs) to develop components and programs that are secure and will not cause issues for Windows Vista.

WSH (in conjunction with other new security features) provides an additional layer of protection which builds on the defense in depth principle. Defense in depth is a general security term that means applying many levels of security to enhance your security posture. Do not rely on one form of security, such as a firewall, to protect you. Incorporate other forms of security so that you do not have all your eggs in one basket. With WSH, Vista adds another layer of security to the system, which can help thwart future attacks and exploits even further.

Network Access Protection (NAP)

NAP is used to prevent clients from connecting to the network if they are infected with malware. NAP is a policy enforcement platform incorporated into Windows Vista as well as Windows Server 2007 (codenamed Longhorn). By enforcing compliance with very specific system health requirements, Vista is able to help prevent malware from accessing the rest of the network and attached systems.

NAP can help verify that each computer connected to the network is malware-free; if it is not, it will not be allowed to connect to the network and further infect other systems. Until the system checks out as malware-free, it will not be allowed to use the network or its services.

WARNING

Vista supports NAP with limited functionality. You will need to use Windows Server 2007 to provide full network access protection because this is used as the NAP policy server.

 # Improvements in Internet Explorer 7

With the release of Windows Vista, you can expect to use the newest and most secure version of Microsoft's Web browser to date. New features in Internet Explorer 7 help to prevent the inception and spread of malware. To help protect a user's personal information and the security of Vista in general, Internet Explorer 7 comes with many new advances in security and tools to help prevent or limit damage from an attack. One simple change is with the Secure Sockets Layer (SSL) protection offered when using the browser. Commonly, a padlock icon will show up in the bottom of the browser indicating that you are entering a "secure" site that uses encryption technologies. Now, the new security status bar helps by showing you in clearer terms that a site you are visiting is safe. The padlock also appears closer to the top of the browser and is highlight blue when safe. This is but one very simple example of things that have changed to make your browsing experience easier and safer.

Basic Browser Behavior

When surfing the Internet, it's easy to visit sites that you think are safe, but are not. These sites can introduce malware when you click on the site itself, when you download a file from the site manually and install it, or worse, when you are conned into believing that the site you're visiting is a real site, but in fact is nothing more than a fake used to garner your personal information.

Browser Exploits

Web browsers are client software programs, such as Internet Explorer, Netscape, and Opera, that connect to servers running Web server software (such as IIS or Apache) and request Web pages via a URL, which is a "friendly" address that represents an IP address and particular files on the server at that address. The browser receives files that are encoded (usually in Hypertext Markup Language [HTML]) and must interpret the code or "markup" that determines how the page will be displayed on the user's monitor. Browsers are open to a number of attack types. The embedded scripts (and even some of the markup language) can be used to exploit your browser. With Internet Explorer 7, new tools such as the Phishing Filter help to thwart these attacks.

Early browser programs were fairly simple and could be exploited by using minimal techniques. Today's browsers are highly complex, signaling the need to secure them even further. These newer browsers are capable of not only displaying text and graphics, but also playing sound files and movies and running executable code. The browser software also usually stores information about the computer on which it is installed, as well as the user (via data stored as cookies on the local hard disk), which can be uploaded to Web servers—either deliberately by the user, or in response to code on a Web site. These characteristics serve useful purposes. Support for running code (as "active content" such as Java, JavaScript, and ActiveX) allows Web designers to create pages that interact with users in sophisticated ways. Cookies allow users to set preferences on sites that will be retained the next time they visit the site.

However, hackers and attackers can exploit these characteristics in many ways. For example, an attacker can program a Web site to run code that transfers a virus to the client computer through the browser, erases key system files, or plants a "backdoor" program that then allows the hacker to take control of the user's system.

Web Spoofing

Web spoofing is a means by which an attacker is able to see and even make changes to Web pages that are transmitted to or from another computer (the target machine). These pages include confidential information such as credit card numbers entered into online commerce forms and passwords that are used to access restricted Web sites. JavaScript can be used to route Web pages and information through the attacker's computer, which impersonates the destination Web server. The attacker can send e-mail to the victim that contains a link to the forged page, or put a link into a popular search engine. SSL doesn't necessarily prevent this sort of "man in the middle" attack; the connection appears to the victim to be secure, because it is secure. The problem is that the secure connection is to a different site than the one the victim thinks he is connecting to. Hyperlink spoofing exploits the fact that SSL doesn't verify hyperlinks that the user follows, so if a user gets to a site by following a link, he can be sent to a spoofed site that appears to be legitimate.

Web spoofing is a high-tech form of con artistry. The point of the scam is to fool the user into giving confidential information such as credit card numbers, bank account numbers, or Social Security numbers (SSNs) to an entity that the user thinks is legitimate, and then using that information for criminal purposes such as identity theft or credit card fraud. The only difference between this and the "real-world" con artist who knocks on a victim's door and pretends to be from the bank, requiring account information, is in the technology used to pull it off.

Certain clues may tip off an observant victim that a Web site is not what it appears to be, such as the URL or status line of the browser. You may think you are going to a Web site simply because it's listed in the URL field, while in another location on the browser, it's indicated that you are going to a different URL. An attacker can also use JavaScript to cover his or her tracks by modifying these elements from your view. An attacker can even go so far as to use JavaScript to replace the browser's menu bar with one that looks the same but replaces functions that provide clues to the invalidity of the page, such as display of the page's source code. Later versions of browser software have been modified to make Web spoofing more difficult. Older browsers are highly vulnerable to this type of attack. Improvements in Internet Explorer thwart spoofing attacks, because now you can check the validity of each site you visit.

Configuring Internet Explorer Securely

Now that you have a clear understanding of the types of malware in existence and the steps Microsoft has taken to prevent you from being exploited, let's discuss how to configure and use these tools and settings. With Internet Explorer 7, there are many ways to improve security. Internet Explorer 7 in Windows Vista represents a major step forward in browser security and privacy protection. All of Internet Explorer 7's security features revolve around making your computer and Web browsing experience all that it can—and should—be.

Protected Mode

Internet Explorer 7 has a new mode, called Protected Mode. When in Protected Mode, the browser will run without fear of malware taking over with elevated privileges. In addition to providing a more secure architecture in which to work, Protected Mode also assists with handling and verifying any scripted or automated action that would move data around the system, such as from the Temporary Internet Files folder, a haven for malware. Figure 2.1 shows the browser with Protected Mode enabled (or on) by default.

Figure 2.1 Internet Explorer's Protected Mode

ActiveX Opt-In

Internet Explorer 7 allows for tighter control and security when working with ActiveX components. Many attacks have exploited ActiveX in the past. ActiveX components can handle file download and installation for the computer user. Although this is handy, malware takes full advantage of it whenever it can. ActiveX runs only on Microsoft-based systems, as it is made and updated by Microsoft in a proprietary fashion.

A new feature called ActiveX Opt-In will disable all ActiveX controls that haven't been prescreened. In other words, if an ISV does not preset the control to work with Vista and Internet Explorer 7, it will not work. In fact, the security status information bar in Internet Explorer 7 will give you the option to work with each ActiveX control on a case-by-case basis. This allows the user to know exactly what each control is doing, what's being installed, and so on.

NOTE

ActiveX is a software technology developed by Microsoft that enables Internet Explorer to download applets and other tools and programs to be used with the browser to display pictures and video as examples. These programs are similar to Java applets, although Java is not constrained to using Microsoft-based products only.

Fix My Settings

Nothing could be easier than pressing one button to accomplish multiple tasks. Toward that end, Internet Explorer 7 has a new feature called Fix My Settings, which allows you to adjust the browser's default settings with just a single click. Used with the Security Status Bar, Fix My Settings helps users quickly determine whether a Web site is authentic and whether changes to their settings by a site are appropriate, and will even suggest settings for the user.

Figure 2.2 shows the Fix My Settings feature in action. If you visit a Web site that is questionable and Internet Explorer believes you may be at risk, the Security Status Bar will warn you of danger and give you options to fix or avert the danger. Here, you can see the **Fix Settings for Me** option, which will walk you through adjusting your settings so that you are not exploited.

Figure 2.2 Internet Explorer's Fix My Settings Feature

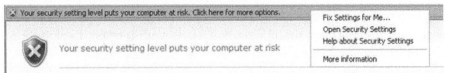

If you have issues with your browser, you can always reset it from within the Internet Options settings found in Internet Explorer, by going to the **Tools** menu and selecting either the **Security** tab (which will allow you to reset the zone directly) or the **Advanced** tab (where you can choose the **Restore advanced settings** option). Then, you can turn your browser back to the manufacturer's settings, as shown in Figure 2.3.

Figure 2.3 Internet Explorer's Restore Advanced Settings Option

Security Status Bar

As mentioned earlier, the new Security Status Bar used with Internet Explorer 7 keeps an eye out for you as you browse, and makes suggestions based on your browsing habits. In other words, if Internet Explorer feels you are at risk, it will warn you and suggest a way to protect yourself from the possible threat. The Security Status Bar operates by alerting you to issues that it believes may harm your system, and gives you options to help you navigate a potential issue. Users can now very quickly be warned about Web sites that are either authentic or spoofed/malicious in nature. By enhancing access to digital certificate information, which in turn helps validate the trustworthiness of e-commerce Web sites, you can now shop online with more confidence.

Windows Defender

Windows Defender enhances security and privacy protections when used with Internet Explorer 7. Although we will cover Windows Defender in more depth later in this chapter, it's important to know how it works with Internet Explorer 7 to secure your browsing experience.

Windows Defender is Microsoft's new spyware destroyer. When used with Internet Explorer 7, Windows Defender can help to scan all data traversing the browser for malware signatures. If it finds such a signature, it will work with Internet Explorer 7 and help you rid yourself of it. Defender will also keep an eye on spyware that is attached to (piggybacking onto) legitimate software which tries to install without your knowledge.

> **NOTE**
>
> Windows Defender is a powerful new tool and we will cover it later in this chapter. Be aware, however, of how it ties into Internet Explorer to provide security against malware threats.

Setting Internet Zones

One of the most important features of Internet Explorer 7 is the ability to configure zones. When you open Internet Explorer's properties, you will find the Security tab, which houses the **Internet**, **Local intranet**, **Trusted sites**, and **Restricted sites** zones (see Figure 2.4). You can configure these zones to allow for tighter security, or less-restrictive security, based on your browsing habits. For example, if you access the Internet and your local intranet simultaneously, you may need to configure security differently in each zone.

Figure 2.4 Setting Security Zones

As you can see in Figure 2.4, you can set each zone to the specific level of security you need. For instance, you may want to set the Internet zone to a very high level to avoid malware attacks (for the most part), even though it will reduce your browsing functionality severely, or you may want to set the Internet zone to a very low level so that you can do anything you want to do with your browser. You also can enable Protected Mode within this dialog.

If you need to configure more granular security, you can click on the **Custom level** button, which will open the Security Settings dialog for the zone you have selected. So, if you want to configure more granular levels of security on the Internet zone, select that zone and select **Custom level**, which will open the settings for that particular zone. Figure 2.5 shows advanced settings in which you can adjust for the Internet zone to include advanced cookies.

Figure 2.5 Setting Advanced Settings in the Internet Zone

Configuring Privacy

The next tab you can configure within Internet Options is your privacy level. In the **Internet Options** dialog box, select the **Privacy** tab. In the Privacy tab, you will find many settings to help secure your browser further. For example, you can select privacy settings based on a specific zone. In Figure 2.6, you can see privacy settings for the Internet zone. When configured correctly, you can either raise or lower the privacy settings you want based on your browsing habits. In Figure 2.6, the Internet zone is configured with a medium privacy rating. This makes sure that all third-party cookies are blocked from doing things you may not want them to do.

You can also select the **Sites** button, which will allow you to configure specific sites that you will either allow or not allow to use cookies, regardless of the privacy policy you select. In Figure 2.7, you can see that Internet Explorer 7 is always set to "allow" cookies from www.syngress.com. Although the privacy settings may disallow cookies altogether, this setting allows you to manually override Internet Explorer's privacy settings to allow any site you feel is not a threat.

Figure 2.6 Configuring the Privacy Tab

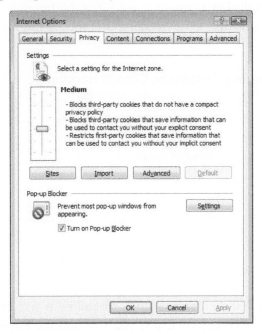

Figure 2.7 Setting per Site Privacy Actions

You can also use the **Advanced** button on the **Privacy** tab to specify how cookies should be handled in a particular zone. For the Internet zone, you can configure to override automatic cookie handling, and specify more granular settings, as shown in Figure 2.8.

Figure 2.8 Configuring Automatic Cookie Handling

Internet Explorer 7 also provides settings that allow you to control your security. On the bottom of the **Privacy** tab dialog you will find the **Pop-up Blocker**. Here, you can enable the Pop-up Blocker to block any pop up (or warn of a pop up) whenever you surf the Internet. By clicking on the **Settings** button, you can further control the Pop-up Blocker. You also can specify sites from which you will allow pop ups without the need to be prompted (see Figure 2.9), in case you visit sites often that have pop ups which are generally benign in nature.

Figure 2.9 Configuring the Pop-up Blocker

Other settings include a filter level, which can help you select a filtering level that makes sense for your browsing habits, as well as information bar settings and notifications such as sounds that will play when a problem occurs.

Advanced Security Settings

The last tab in the **Internet Options** dialog is the **Advanced** tab, as seen in Figure 2.10. Within this tab, you will find more than 100 settings that you can adjust. The best way to see what you can do is to scroll through all the options and read them one at a time, as they are very self-explanatory. In Figure 2.10, you can see a few settings that are crucial to applying security to Internet Explorer 7 and should not be overlooked.

For example, you can set more advanced security settings within the Security branch of the Advanced tab. Here you can adjust Internet Explorer's behavior by further controlling what it can and cannot do. For example, you can select to **Allow** software to run or install, even if the signature is invalid. Obviously, you would want to leave this unchecked because an invalid signature could lead to an exploited browser, depending on the nature of the site visited.

Figure 2.10 Setting Advanced Security Features

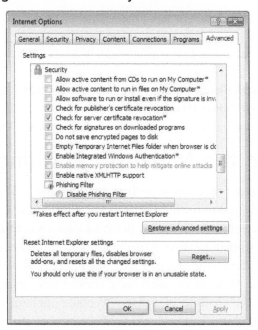

Figure 2.11 specifies more settings you can adjust to control Internet Explorer 7. Here you can adjust how the Phishing Filter behaves, as well as use of the SSL and Transport Layer Security (TLS) protocols.

Figure 2.11 Setting More Advanced Security Features

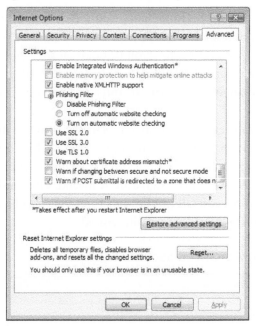

Once you have completed setting your Advanced security options, click on **OK** to close the dialog box. Some changes may require you to restart Internet Explorer. Simply close the browser and reopen it to continue working with your new settings.

Configuring the Microsoft Phishing Filter

The Microsoft Phishing Filter is new to Internet Explorer 7. It protects you from phishing attacks while you're surfing the Internet. Phishing is a technique that attackers use to trick you into giving up personal data, credentials, or other information by posing as legitimate businesses or operations. Phishing attacks are not new. For example, clever attackers in the past have spammed AOL users with spoofed e-mail purporting to be AOL. Many users were tricked into giving up their account information because they had no idea that a Web site operator could trick them into doing so with nothing but a similar-looking Web site that claimed to be something it wasn't. It wasn't until the end-user community started learning about spoofed Web sites and other ways attackers were getting people's personal information (sometimes without them even knowing about it) that AOL began to warn users against giving up their personal account information to anybody other than AOL, and to practice due diligence in checking for signs of phishing attacks by examining the URL to ensure that they were being approached by AOL and not by a spoofed site.

NOTE

Social engineering attacks are similar to phishing. With social engineering, an attacker will call someone on the phone, for instance, and trick her into giving up secure information by pretending to be someone he is not.

Phishing is the exploit hackers use to obtain personal information from unsuspecting users. It continues today, and you can find examples on the wildly popular site MySpace (www.myspace.com). MySpace has suffered from the same issues AOL worked through—malicious Web site operators pretended they were from MySpace when they were really gathering legitimate users' credentials and, inevitability, their personal information. MySpace owners posted the same types of warnings that AOL did years ago.

To take the security responsibility out of end users' hands, Microsoft designed and implemented the Phishing Filter into Internet Explorer 7. Now, if the end user wants to stay secure and not have to worry about checking his browser for clues that the site he is visiting is the real deal, he can simply turn on the Phishing Filter and it will ensure through verification steps that the site the end user is visiting is, in fact, legitimate.

When the Phishing Filter is turned on, it performs a few steps every time you visit a Web site. First, it verifies against a locally stored list that the Web sites you are trying to visit are not fraudulent. It will also analyze visited sites for suspicious behavior that is commonly associated with Phishing Web sites. Then, it will connect to an online service that constantly updates it with phishing attack sites that have been found and blacklisted.

TIP

By using the opt-in online service, you can update the Phishing Filter in Internet Explorer 7 to a more secure level.

You can adjust the Phishing Filter's settings from within Internet Explorer. When you open Internet Explorer 7, click on **Tools** and then **Phishing Filter**. Here you can turn the filter on or off (see Figure 2.12). Microsoft recommends that you used the filter at all times, as this will provide you with the highest level of security.

Figure 2.12 Using the Microsoft Phishing Filter

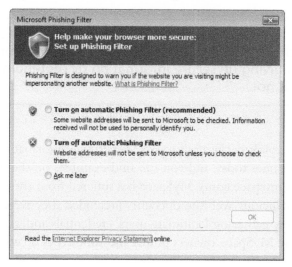

WARNING

You will notice that your Web surfing will become painfully slow as your browser verifies every site you visit. As always with security, you have to consider the trade-off between usability and security and find a happy medium. If you find that your surfing habits consist of visiting sites that are commonly spoofed, you may want to wait the few seconds it takes to verify that sites you are visiting are safe to visit.

To see the Phishing Filter at work, you can manually run a check on a suspicious Web site. To verify the validity of a site, click on **Tools**, then **Phishing Filter**, and then **Check This Website**. If the site is safe and legitimate, as in Figure 2.13, the Phishing Filter will report as such.

Figure 2.13 The Phishing Filter Reporting a Safe Site

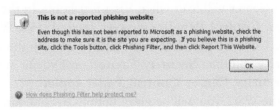

Internet Explorer 7 is the most secure version of the browser to date, and strides in programming to make it safer have been successful. In the next section, we will take a look at the Windows Security Center (WSC), which is used to keep your system's security centralized.

Windows Security Center

The Windows Security Center (WSC) is the brain and nervous system for Vista when it comes to security. The WSC, which debuted in Windows XP SP2, has been updated with new features, new tools, and more functionality. Through the WSC (see Figure 2.14), you can make sure that the four security essentials—the firewall, automatic updating, malware protection, and other security settings—are enabled to keep the system secure.

Figure 2.14 Viewing the Windows Security Center in Vista

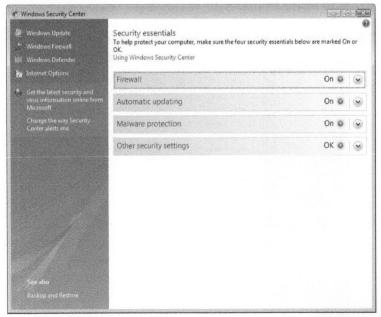

You can reach the WSC in several ways when you first load Windows Vista. By default, the Welcome Center will load when Vista first boots. In the **Welcome Center**, you can select **Control Panel** in the **Get started with Windows** section. Or you can open the **Control Panel** from the **Start** menu. In the Control Panel, you can select **Security** and then **Security Center**, or if you're in **Classic View**, you can select the **Security Center Control Panel applet**.

Once you open the WSC, you will be given options to configure Windows Firewall settings, Windows Update settings, malware protection, and advanced Internet Explorer settings. In Figure 2.14, Windows Vista is operating with a configured firewall, is configured for automatic updates, is running spyware software, and is using an updated antivirus software product. Any issues within any of these areas will result in the WSC alerting you to the issue, as well as recommending a possible solution.

Configuring a Firewall

To configure the firewall to allow or disallow specified traffic, first open the **Windows Firewall** settings by going to the **Control Panel**, selecting **Network and Internet**, and then clicking on **Windows Firewall**.

Here, you can turn the firewall on or off, as shown in Figure 2.15. It's recommend that you leave it on, especially if you do not have a third-party firewall application you would like to use in its place. Having multiple firewall products on one system is usually more of a configuration headache than it's worth. To further configure the Windows Firewall, click on the **Change** settings link within the **Windows Firewall** dialog box.

Figure 2.15 Configuring Windows Firewall

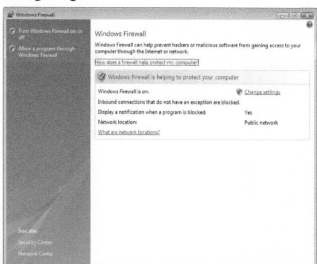

Here, you can adjust other settings, such as allowing or disallowing application-specific traffic to and from intended sources and destinations. In Figure 2.16, the General tab is selected. From here, you can turn the firewall on or off, as well as block all incoming connections if needed.

Figure 2.16 The General Tab in the Windows Firewall

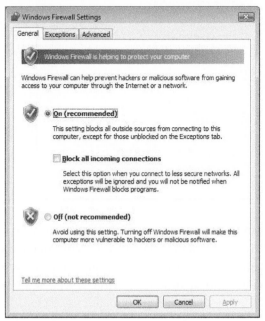

Click on the **Exceptions** tab, and you can configure how programs will communicate through the Windows Firewall. As shown in Figure 2.17, you can select a program that you want to block or unblock by its name or port number designation. Click on **Add program** to add a specific program you want to control access to, or use **Add port** to specify the application's port number. For instance, you could allow Secure Shell (SSH) and not Telnet for remote access. You can also specify the program (SSH or Telnet) or specify what ports to use (which in this case would be 22 and 21, respectively).

NOTE

The Vista version of the Windows Firewall is better than the Windows XP SP2 version because now you can set access control bidirectionally.

Figure 2.17 The Exceptions Tab in the Windows Firewall

The **Advanced** tab gives you options for selecting to which network connections you want to apply the firewall's security. It's recommended that if you are going to use a firewall, you protect all possible entry points into the system. Figure 2.18 shows how you can select a local area connection as well as a wireless network connection.

Figure 2.18 The Advanced Tab in the Windows Firewall

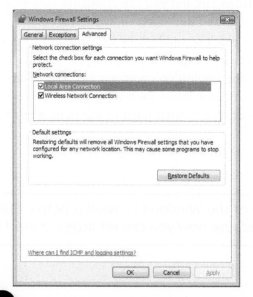

You can also set the Windows Firewall back to its default settings, by clicking on the **Restore Defaults** button.

Once your firewall is configured, you need to update it only if you want to restrict or allow access to new programs, or if you want to change settings. Otherwise, your firewall will alert you if any issues arise, and the WSC will alert you if there are any issues with your firewall.

WARNING

You need a security policy in place. Otherwise, your investment in security could be for naught. A security policy, as the term is used here, refers to a written document that defines an organization's approach to security or a specific security area. The policy is used to specify a set of rules to be followed in implementing the organization's security philosophy. Organizations may establish both written and unwritten rules pertaining to security matters, and may issue a number of different types of documents dealing with these issues.

Using Windows Update

Windows Update has been evolving every year since the late 1990s. When Microsoft first released its software offerings many hotfixes and service packs followed. At one time, you had to visit Microsoft's Web site, find the download you needed from the Downloads section, and then install it. Now, a centralized Web service hosted by Microsoft will work as the server-side function listening for the client side to contact it with its needs.

Updating Microsoft Windows and many other Microsoft programs (such as Microsoft Office products, Internet Explorer, and so on) is now quick and almost seamless. Also, now you don't have to visit Microsoft's Web site to get downloads, because once you turn on Automatic Updates, updates will be downloaded to your client at a specified time and will be ready for you to confirm and install the next time you are at your PC.

You can turn on Automatic Updates in the WSC or in the Control Panel. Once enabled, Automatic Updates will find and install updates for all of the Microsoft products you have installed.

TIP

You should add (and keep) Microsoft Update on your list of trusted Web sites within Internet Explorer.

To run Windows Update, click on the **Windows Update** link in the **WSC** on the top left-hand side of the dialog box. By clicking on this link, you will open the **Windows Update Wizard** seen in Figure 2.19. Once launched, the wizard will quickly scan your system's logs to verify what you have installed and what you currently need. Internet Explorer will work with Windows Update at Microsoft.com to produce a list of what you need to install and guide you through the install process.

Figure 2.19 Using Windows Update

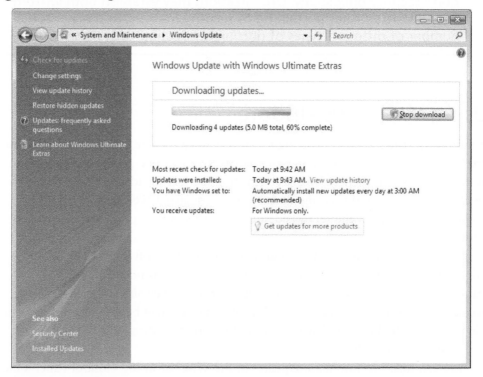

Figure 2.20 shows the available updates you can install on Vista. Here you can see the updates specific to Windows Vista (such as drivers, etc.) as well as the applications, such as Windows Defender. Click on **Install** to install the updates you would like to install. You can uncheck any update you do not want to install.

Figure 2.20 Viewing Available Updates for Your Computer

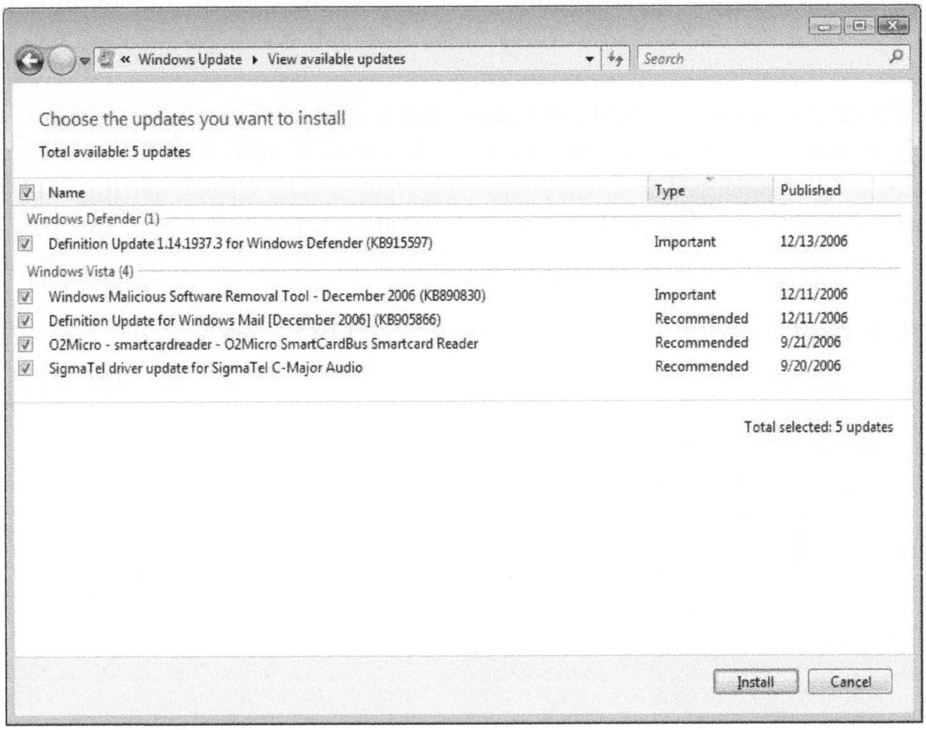

Using the Malicious Software Removal Tool

When running Windows Update, you will commonly find a download for the Malicious Software Removal Tool. This is a tool that will help to remove malware from your OS. Since January 2005, this tool has been run more than 3.2 billion times, on more than 270 million computers each month, to combat the spread and flood of malicious software over the Internet. Every month, Microsoft releases a new version of the tool through Microsoft Update, Windows Update, and the Microsoft Download Center.

The Malicious Software Removal Tool will also verify that your system is malware-free before you upgrade from, say, Windows XP to Windows Vista.

Configuring Malware Protection

When working within the WSC, you can configure **Malware Protection** so that your PC proactively looks out for exploits against which it is currently configured to guard. The WSC will periodically check to ensure that your system is kept updated.

It does this by checking that your antivirus software is on, is not damaged, and is updated with signatures and definitions, and by checking your spyware software to make sure is it updated and in working order as well. If nothing is installed, you will be warned that this is not recommended.

Figure 2.21 shows the WSC indicating that it couldn't find a valid antivirus application located on the system. Because this will most likely lead to infection or exploitation, it is flagged as an issue for you to resolve. The **Check settings** indicator (also colored yellow) indicates that no program is installed and/or that it is damaged.

Figure 2.21 Viewing Malware Protection within the WSC

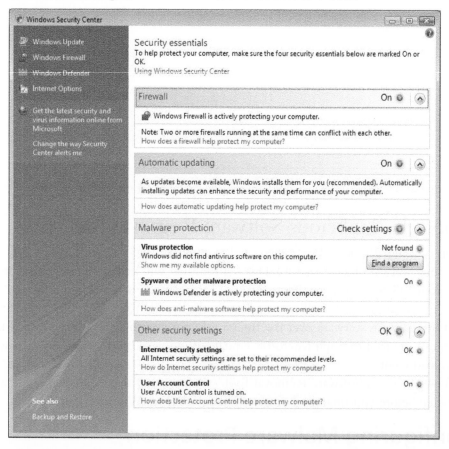

Be aware that if your antivirus software is installed but is out-of-date, you will be given a different indicator. You will still be asked to **Check settings**, but the indicator will be colored red (see Figure 2.22).

Figure 2.22 Viewing Out-of-Date Definitions in the WSC

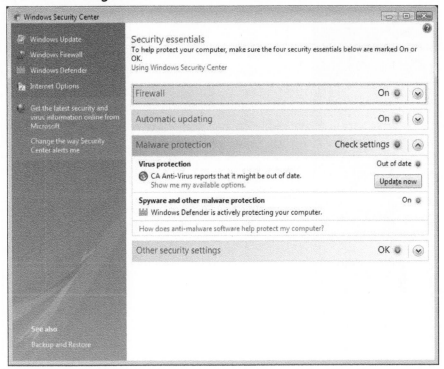

It is imperative that you keep your antivirus signatures, definitions, and engine updated; if you don't, the WSC will report a problem. In Figure 2.23, the WSC is reporting that malware protection is on and up-to-date.

Once you resolve all issues, the Malware Protection section of the WSC will return to its green indication status. This means your system is now ready to do battle with malware because it is completely updated and healthy, and is running optimally.

Microsoft Windows Vista is a brand-new product on the market so its important to consider your older software applications may not run on it at first., Third party vendor software generally do not have full version releases of heir software tested and ready to go, so its important to do some research on what is supported before you upgrade to Windows Vista.

Figure 2.23 The WSC Reporting That Malware Protection On and Updated

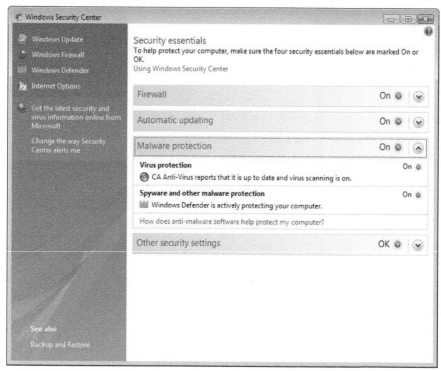

TIP

Most software applications and drivers written for Windows XP may also work with Windows Vista. You should always check regardless. Older programs may operate poorly or not at all. You can use the Program Compatibility Wizard to fix this problem. Open the Program Compatibility Wizard by clicking the **Start** button => clicking and opening the Control Panel => clicking Programs => clicking Use an older program with this version of Windows. The Windows Vista Hardware Compatibility List (also known as the HCL) is a hardware product list that has been verified by Microsoft. These products have passed a set of hardware compatibility tests that prove that the software installed works with genuine Windows products such as Vista. If hardware is purchased and not listed within the HCL, it is not guaranteed to work.

For software support:
http://windowshelp.microsoft.com/Windows/en-US/programs.mspx
For hardware support:

www.microsoft.com/technet/windowsvista/evaluate/hardware/defa
ult.mspx.
The Microsoft HCL:
www.microsoft.com/hcl/

Other Security Settings

In the WSC, you have a fourth area of configuration, called **Other security settings**. Here, you can check Internet Explorer's security settings, as well as use User
Account Control (UAC).

User Account Control

User Account Control (UAC) UAC is a new tool used with Windows Vista for preventing unauthorized changes. UAC is another level of security applied to the
defense in depth model. UAC (known in earlier Windows versions as Least-Privilege
User Account [LUA]) is responsible for warning you whenever Windows needs your
permission to continue with the use of a program or other application. LUA followed the concept that if the LUA account was jeopardized, it would not cause a
serious issue because it did not have administrator privileges. If the account was
compromised, there wasn't much you could do with it.

When a user now logs on to a Windows Vista computer, she is logged on by
default as a standard user. If she needs to perform a task in which administrator privileges are required, Vista (with the help of UAC) will prompt her for specific permission to perform the task. This helps to make sure that malware cannot manipulate
her account if jeopardized.

When an administrator needs to use her administrator privileges, she doesn't
have to use Run As, because Windows Vista can automatically prompt her for the
required credentials, as shown in Figure 2.24. In the past, accounts for standard users
contained too many available permissions. Now, standard user accounts are locked
down to allow for only the privileges that are needed; anything that requires administrator privileges (such as installing software on the system) will require that the user
log on with an administrator account. Because UAC is enabled by default, it will be
invoked whenever administrator logon is required. In past versions of Windows, such
as XP, you needed to use Run As to log on with administrator rights, although if the
user account had been jeopardized, it wouldn't matter anyway. UAC is a major
development in terms of giving only those privileges that users need to do their
jobs. As a result, if their accounts are compromised, the risk is lessened.

Figure 2.24 UAC Asking for Permission to Continue

Windows Vista automatically prompts you for administrator credentials when an application requests them. This way, another level of security is implemented to help ensure that the user isn't manipulated or that malware running silently doesn't infiltrate the system.

Tools & Traps…

Using the MBSA

The Microsoft Baseline Security Analyzer (MBSA) is a freely downloadable tool from Microsoft designed for IT professionals who need to check the security settings on host computers. With Windows Vista, you can still download and use this valuable tool. Figure 2.25 shows the MBSA in action.

The MBSA will check your computer locally (or a remote computer) for basic security settings and updates, report on their state, and make recommendations as to what you should do for specific issues. For example, if your system's updates are out-of-date, your passwords do not meet a minimum password length, and so on, you will receive a report on each section's status and what you need to do to ensure that your system is secure.

Continued

Figure 2.25 Using the Microsoft Baseline Security Analyzer

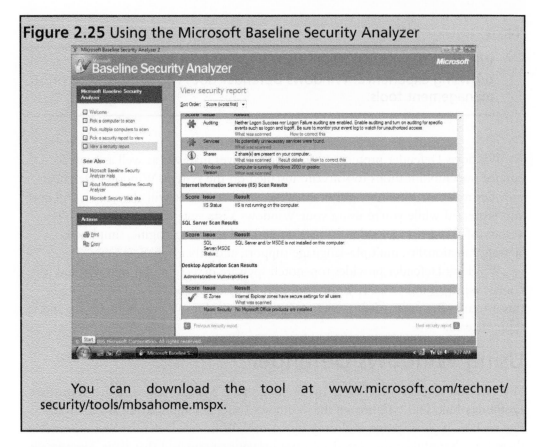

You can download the tool at www.microsoft.com/technet/security/tools/mbsahome.mspx.

Windows Defender

In December 2004, Microsoft acquired the Windows Defender security technology from GIANT Company Software, Inc. Windows Defender provides continuous security against malware, and if it detects anything suspicious, it will alert you of what it finds. It does this by using three specific tools:

- **Internet agents** Internet agents are used to monitor changes to Internet access settings, as well as to stop unauthorized connection attempts via the network.

- **System agents** System agents are used to monitor changes to your system's settings, such as passwords and permissions.

- **Application agents** Application agents are used to monitor changes to applications installed on your OS, such as Internet Explorer being modified by downloadable toolbar applications.

NOTE

Windows Defender is used locally to protect an end user's Web browsing experience. Windows Defender does not include enterprise management tools.

Windows Defender protects against and removes malware as well as provides control over modifications to software installed on the system. Windows Defender provides real-time monitoring functionality, which means it will always run and keep you protected while you're using your Windows Vista system. The Windows Vista version of Windows Defender features an updated scanning engine, simplified alerting functionality, multiple-language support, and other enhancements.

Windows Defender provides top-notch spyware detection and removal, and it is connected to an online service that will keep it updated and on top of the latest threat trends. Because malware constantly evolves, so does Windows Defender and its support team.

Using Windows Defender

You can find Windows Defender by opening the **WSC** and selecting the **Windows Defender** link. This will invoke the Windows Defender application, as shown in Figure 2.26. If your system is already up-to-date, Windows Defender will report that there is no harmful or unwanted software on your system and that your computer is running normally. If you have not run a scan yet, or your last scan was a while ago, you will be prompted with scan options.

Select the scan option that best suits what you want to do. If you want to perform a quick scan of the most common areas within your system affected by malware, check the **Quick scan** radio button. If you want to check your entire system, check the **Full system scan** radio button (note that a full system scan will take far longer to perform than a quick scan). You can also specify which drives or areas of your system you want Windows Defender to scan.

Figure 2.27 shows Windows Defender prompting you to begin a scan. Click on **Scan Now** to begin the scan.

Figure 2.26 Using Windows Defender

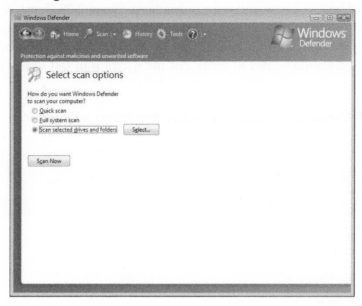

Figure 2.27 Starting a Scan with Windows Defender

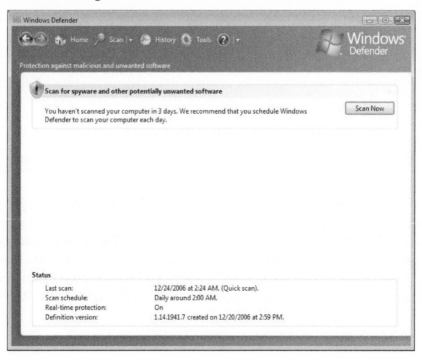

Once the scan is complete, you can view the report. If anything malicious is found, you will be asked how you want to handle it. Figure 2.28 shows Windows Defender completing a quick scan and not finding any malware on the system. (Because this was a quick scan, there still may be an issue with this system, however; a full system scan should be run to verify that the system is in fact free of malicious software.)

Figure 2.28 Viewing Windows Defender Reporting a Quick Scan Completed

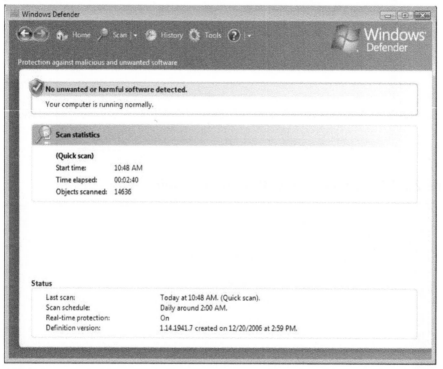

By clicking on **Tools** on top of the **Windows Defender** dialog box, you can adjust the settings for Windows Defender and select other tools to further secure your system. As shown in Figure 2.29, once you open the **Tools and Settings** configuration within Windows Defender, you can change the settings, use Microsoft SpyNet, view quarantined items, use the Windows Defender Software Explorer, set allowed items, and visit and use the Microsoft Windows Defender public Web site.

Figure 2.29 Setting Windows Defender Options

How to Use the Windows Defender Software Explorer

One of the newest and most helpful tools Microsoft has added to Vista and Windows Defender is Software Explorer. Software Explorer provides you with an unfettered view of the software that is currently running on your computer, along with details of each piece. It also helps you monitor programs that are set to start when the computer boots, programs that run in the background or as background processes, and programs that are used to perform low-level network functions (i.e., Winsock service providers).

> **NOTE**
>
> To use some Software Explorer options, you must be logged on as Administrator or be a member of the Administrators group.

Using Software Explorer

Changing how a program runs on your computer, such as blocking Internet or network connections and ending processes, can cause problems with Windows and other programs that you use. Use Software Explorer to change how a program runs on your computer only if you are certain the program is causing a problem. Once you open Software Explorer, you can select which category of programs you want to view or adjust. For example, in Figure 2.30, you can see Software Explorer in use. Here, the Startup Programs category is shown but blurred out to protect the identity of the system in use.

Figure 2.30 Using Software Explorer

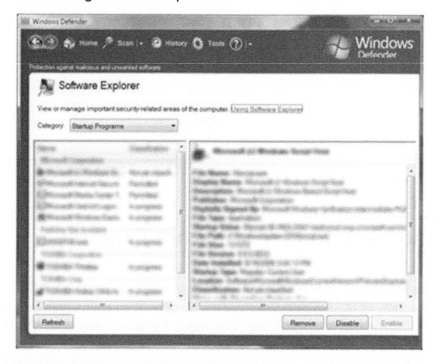

Other Related Tools

In the Tools and Settings dialog of Microsoft Defender, you can find links to more tools and settings. Here you will find SpyNet, a very useful Web site that helps you find information on malware as well as information on combating it and protecting yourself and your system from its threat of damage.

Using Microsoft SpyNet

Microsoft SpyNet is the network of Windows Defender users that helps determine which programs are classified as spyware. Because the face of malware constantly evolves, so does SpyNet and its hardworking team of security enthusiasts.

SpyNet works to build known signature files for commonly seen malware and to find malware that is new to the scene. It is recommended that you visit SpyNet to get acclimated with the site and the benefits it offers, and that you check back often for updates.

If you commonly surf the Internet and are worried about the effects of malware on your system, visiting SpyNet can give you an advantage, as you will be better educated on what can happen to your system, what is currently happening to others, and how you can support and better secure your OS, your browser, your identity, and your personal data.

Summary

Malware is a threat to computer systems, networks, and the public Internet. With the release of Windows Vista, Microsoft has developed new weapons in the battle against malware. Windows Vista, Internet Explorer 7, and associated software are hardened and ready for war.

Malware is any software product or program created with an intent to cause damage or harm. The most common forms of malware are viruses, Trojans, and worms. Viruses are malicious programs that are commonly installed on a target host with the intent to cause harm or damage. Common virus types include e-mail viruses, boot sector viruses, application viruses, and macro viruses. Worms are a form of malware that will propagate from host to host in order to spread and replicate across a network. A Trojan will appear harmless to the recipient, but actually contains a malicious payload. Trojans that contain a virus as a payload are called droppers. Spyware is the biggest malware issue to date. Spyware exploits include malicious scripts that do everything from rewriting browsers to perform malicious functions, to forcing payment for legitimate revenue streams to a secondary source (usually that of the attacker).

Windows Vista and Internet Explorer 7 were developed to thwart many common exploits and build a foundation in which new ones can be mitigated. New to Vista and Internet Explorer 7 is an updated Windows Firewall. The new outbound filtering feature in the personal firewall helps to apply more granular control over traffic traversing it, and is more flexible than previous versions. The new Phishing Filter is used to verify the validity of the sites you visit so that your personal information and data are not compromised. User Account Control (UAC) allows a user to change computer settings while running as a standard user, instead of requiring administrator privileges to perform most tasks. The updated Windows Defender utility detects malware on your system and, when used in conjunction with SpyNet, can help to eliminate most spyware attacks and exploits. The new Windows Security Center (WSC) is full of configurable options and tools to help you build a strong security posture so that you can safely surf the Internet without constantly worrying about your system. As you can see, there are many ways you can apply defense in depth for a more secure infrastructure.

Malware is definitely a threat, but these new tools and features help to provide a more secure experience. Microsoft Vista takes steps to ensure that the base OS is not jeopardized, and Internet Explorer 7 provides a secure framework in which to operate. Although the battle against malware continues, at least with Vista and Internet Explorer 7 you are well armed to fight that battle.

Solutions Fast Track

Malware Fundamentals

☑ Malware is any software product or program created with the intent to cause damage or harm. The most common types of malware are viruses, Trojans, and worms.

☑ A virus is a malicious program that is commonly installed on a target host with the intent to cause harm or damage. A virus (just like the medical version of the term) infects the host, usually by being installed by the end user of the target host. A virus is almost always executed by the end user without him knowing the true intention of the malware.

☑ An e-mail virus is transmitted via e-mail and contains a payload that is activated when the end user is provoked to activate it, or when something in the e-mail client and how it reads e-mail (and scripts) activates the payload upon delivery or viewing, without opening the e-mail (such as with an automatic reading pane found in most e-mail clients).

☑ Boot sector viruses are often transmitted via disk and are written to the master boot record on the hard disk. Application viruses are executable programs that infect your system when you run them, and macro viruses are commonly embedded in documents (such as Microsoft Word documents).

☑ Worms will propagate. They are programmed to "scan" the network from the infected target host to find other hosts with open and vulnerable services and ports.

☑ A Trojan horse will appear harmless enough for the recipient to install, but it contains a secret payload that usually is a virus or other form of malware.

☑ Malware can be very nasty, especially when it and its payload are concealed. For instance, consider the use of rootkits, backdoors, and keyloggers, all of which are secretly placed on your system for a future attack.

☑ Spyware exploits are also used to obtain user information. Spyware analyzes what sites you visit and what your browsing habits are, and then invades your privacy further by using that information to market products to you, as well as by preventing you from removing the spyware.

☑ You should periodically update every piece of software you install on your system. You can do this by installing the latest updates, hotfixes, security patches, and service packs. Keep on top of when new patches come out, and try to test and install them to keep your system at its best.

☑ Windows Service Hardening (WSH) limits the amount of damage an attacker can do if a service is compromised.

☑ Network Access Protection (NAP) is used to prevent clients from connecting to the network if they are infected with malware.

Improvements in Internet Explorer 7

☑ Internet Explorer 7 comes with Windows Vista by default as the built-in Web browser. New features in Internet Explorer 7 help to prevent the inception and spread of malware. To help protect a user's personal information and the security of Vista in general, Internet Explorer 7 comes with many advances in security, as well as tools that protect users from such malware attacks as phishing and spoofing. It also includes a new Protected Mode to further secure a user's browsing experience.

☑ The new outbound filtering feature in the Windows Firewall helps users to apply more granular control over traffic traversing the firewall.

☑ User Account Control allows a user to change computer settings while running as a standard user.

☑ The Windows Defender utility detects malware on your system and, when used in conjunction with SpyNet, can help to eliminate most spyware attacks and exploits.

☑ Phishing is the exploit that hackers use to obtain personal information from unsuspecting users. The Microsoft Phishing Filter is new to Internet Explorer 7. It protects you from phishing attacks while you surf the Internet.

Windows Security Center

☑ The Windows Security Center (WSC) is the brain and nervous system for Vista when it comes to security. Here, you can configure most (if not all) security functionality for the client system. In addition, it monitors your running systems and recommends ways to help mitigate risk and solve security-related issues.

☑ The WSC, which debuted in Windows XP SP2, has been updated with new features, tools, and functionality. With it, you can centrally control a personal firewall application, and make sure the OS and your antivirus software are up-to-date.

☑ In the WSC, you can configure four main security areas: the Windows Firewall, Automatic Updates, Windows malware protection, and other security settings, including Internet Explorer security settings.

☑ The updated Windows Firewall now scans traffic bidirectionally. Previous versions scanned in only a single direction.

☑ Once your firewall is configured, you need to update it only if you want to restrict or allow access to new programs, or if you want to change settings.

☑ You can turn on automatic updating in the WSC, which will allow Windows to monitor and download updates for you.

☑ The Malicious Software Removal Tool can help you to remove malware from your OS and is usually downloaded via Windows Update.

☑ User Account Control prevents unauthorized changes from taking place. Another level of security applied to the defense in depth model, UAC will warn you whenever Windows needs your permission to continue with the use of a program or other application.

☑ The Microsoft Baseline Security Analyzer (MBSA) is a freely downloadable tool from Microsoft. It is designed for IT professionals who need to check the security settings on host computers.

Windows Defender

☑ Windows Defender provides continuous security against malware. If it detects anything suspicious, it will alert you of what it finds.

☑ Windows Defender is composed of three separate agents. Internet agents are used to monitor changes to Internet access settings, as well as to stop unauthorized connection attempts via the network. System agents are used to monitor changes to your system's settings, such as passwords and permissions. Application agents are used to monitor changes to applications

installed on your OS, such as Internet Explorer being modified by
downloadable toolbar applications.

☑ Windows Defender is used locally to protect an end user's Web browsing
experience. Windows Defender does not include enterprise management
tools.

☑ Windows Defender features an updated scanning engine, simplified alerting
functionality, multiple-language support, and other enhancements.

☑ Changing how a program runs on your computer, such as blocking
Internet or network connections and ending processes, can cause problems
with Windows and other programs that you use. Use Software Explorer to
change how a program runs on your computer only if you are certain the
program is causing a problem. Once you open Software Explorer, you can
select which category of programs you want to view or adjust.

☑ Microsoft SpyNet is the network of Windows Defender users that helps
determine which programs are classified as spyware.

☑ SpyNet builds known signature files for commonly seen malware and finds
malware that is new to the scene. It is recommended that you visit SpyNet
to get acclimated with the site and the benefits it offers, and that you check
back often for updates.

Frequently Asked Questions

The following Frequently Asked Questions, answered by the authors of this book, are designed to both measure your understanding of the concepts presented in this chapter and to assist you with real-life implementation of these concepts. To have your questions about this chapter answered by the author, browse to **www.syngress.com/solutions** and click on the **"Ask the Author"** form.

Q: If a company has a good firewall installed, won't that protect it from all these attacks?

A: No. Firewall products are very useful for controlling what comes into or goes out of a network. But a firewall is like a computer (in many cases, a firewall is a specialized computer); it does only what the person who configures it tells it to do. Firewalls can recognize and stop some types of attacks, but certain attacks exploit the characteristics of the protocols commonly used for legitimate network communications, and a packet might appear to be nothing more than a benign bit of data destined for a computer on the internal network. Trojans, viruses, and worms piggyback into the network as e-mail attachments or through remote file sharing. Firewalls won't catch them, but a good antivirus program, frequently updated and set to scan all incoming e-mail, might be able to. Many companies seem to operate under the assumption that installing a firewall is akin to invoking a magic spell that casts a force field of protection around their networks, rendering them completely immune to attack. Even the best firewall won't protect against social engineering attacks, nor will it do any good against internal attackers who have physical access to the network. Studies have shown that a large number of network-related crimes are actually "inside jobs." Be sure to read Chapter 3, where we discuss how firewalls work, so that you understand why they are not the "cure-all" solution to network security that they're sometimes made out to be.

Q: I think I understand the differences between a virus, a Trojan, and a worm. But what are all these other types of viruses I hear about: stealth viruses, polymorphic viruses, armored viruses, and cavity viruses?

A: Stealth viruses are able to conceal the changes they make to files, boot records, and the like from antivirus programs. They do so by forging the results of a program's attempt to read the infected files. A polymorphic virus makes copies of itself to spread, like other viruses, but the copies are not exactly like the original.

The virus "morphs" into something slightly different in an effort to avoid detection by antivirus software that might not have definitions for all the variations. Viruses can use a "mutation engine" to create these variations on themselves. An armored virus uses a technique that makes it difficult to understand the virus code. A cavity virus is able to overwrite part of the infected (host) file while not increasing the length of the file, which would be a tip-off that a virus had infected the file.

Q: Can a rootkit be used for a good purpose, or is it always classified as malware?

A: The term *rootkit* was developed as a hacker term, although rootkits can also be used for what some vendors consider valid purposes. For example, if Digital Rights Management (DRM) software is installed and kept hidden, it can control the use of licensed, copyrighted material and prevent the user from removing the hidden enforcement program. However, such usage is no more welcomed than a rootkit that does damage or allows spyware to thrive without detection.

Q: I have an infected system and I cannot figure out what is wrong. Where can I look to find further information on the Internet?

A: Information about specific viruses and instructions on how to clean an infected system is available at www.symantec.com and www.mcafee.com. Both antivirus vendors provide detailed databases that list and describe known viruses. For more information on viruses, worms, and Trojans, see the article "How Computer Viruses Work," at www.howstuffworks.com/virus.htm.

Q: What are cookies and spyware? How are they different? Do some Web sites use cookies to exploit user information?

A: A cookie is just a bit of text in a file on your computer, containing a small amount of information that identifies you to a particular Web site, and whatever information that site wanted to retain about you when you were visiting. Cookies are a legitimate tool that many Web sites use to track visitor information. For example, you might go to an online computer store and place an item in your basket, but decide not to buy it right away because you want to compare prices. The store can choose to put the information about what products you put into your basket in a cookie stored on your computer. This is an example of a good use of cookies to help the user experience. The only Web sites that are supposed to be able to retrieve the information stored in a cookie are the Web sites that wrote the information in that particular cookie. This should ensure your privacy by stopping any site other than the one you are visiting from being able to read any cookies left by that site. Some Web sites do use cookies to exploit user information, however. Some also may deceive users or omit their policies. For example, they may track your Web surfing habits across many different Web sites without informing you, and then use this data to customize the advertisements you see on Web sites, which typically is considered an invasion of privacy. It is difficult to identify this and other forms of "cookie abuse," which makes it difficult to decide whether, when, and how to block them from your system. In addition, the acceptable level of shared information varies among users, so it is difficult to create an "anticookie" program to meet everyone's needs.

Q: Can spyware send tracked information to other people?

A: Some forms of spyware monitor a target's Web use or even general computer use and send this information back to the spyware program's authors for use as they see fit. To fight this kind of problem, a spyware removal tool is obviously helpful, as is a firewall that monitors outgoing connections from your computer. Other forms of spyware take over parts of your Web browsing interface, forcing you to use their own search engines, where they can track your browsing habits and send pop-up advertisements to you at will. The biggest concern regarding spyware is that most spyware is poorly written or designed. Many people first realize their computer is running spyware when it noticeably slows down or stops responding, especially when performing certain tasks such as browsing Web sites or retrieving e-mail. In addition, poorly written spyware can often cause your computer to function incorrectly even after it has been removed.

Q: Malware has completely taken over my PC and I cannot do anything to fix it. What is the best next step?

A: You used to be able to clean up most malware infections using various kinds of specialized antivirus and antimalware software. Sadly, this is no longer the case. Once upon a time, malware was written by amateurs and teenagers. But now, many very skilled programmers work on malware, because it is now a money-making business. Malware has become so insidious that it is often impossible to remove without expert or professional help.

You should first attempt to remove an infection with automated tools. If that fails (and most likely it will), there are two classes of antimalware software that you should use. The first is traditional antivirus software, which is very good at handling viruses and worms and not so great at handling newer styles of malware. The other kind of software is antispyware software, which is good at the newer sort of malware but not so good at the old kind. When attempting to clean up an infected system, you should run at least one of each. If you were running antivirus software when you became infected, you should see whether it was keeping itself up-to-date, or try running a different program. Proven antivirus software companies include Symantec (a.k.a. Norton), McAfee, Panda Software, Trend Micro, F-Secure, Eset (maker of NOD32), and Kaspersky Labs. Many of these companies have free Web-based scanners (ironically based on ActiveX) or downloadable tryout versions.

Antispyware software is a little more difficult. The various antivirus companies have been in business a long time, but antispyware is a new kind of software that was born at the same time as the modern age of malware. Therefore, many antispyware software companies are either incompetent or outright frauds.

It's been discovered that malware is very quickly outgrowing the capability for automated software to clean it. The automated tools you try may not work, even if you try multiple ones. Therefore, you will probably end up having to get help. Many local computer repair companies can clean infected computers. You may know an expert who is willing to help you. Sometimes the experts will tell you that the best or only way to take care of a really bad infection is to back up your personal data, clean out the computer completely, and start from scratch. They are not lying. Attempting to eradicate an infection by hand can be extremely time-consuming and is often unsuccessful, even for experts.

Q: Do I need additional antimalware and spyware tools, now that Vista and Internet Explorer are supposedly more secure and provide them?

A: With Windows Vista and Internet Explorer 7, you are definitely more secure than you were using older versions of the OS and Web browser. The fact is that you now get these applications with the base OS instead of having to pay for or download a third-party vendor's utility. Vista does not come with antivirus software, so you will need to acquire that separately. What Vista does have is a built-in spyware tool that helps prevent "some" malware exploits from taking place. Vista also has a built-in host-based firewall. Make sure that you add antivirus software for full protection.

Chapter 3

Microsoft Vista: Securing User Access

Solutions in this chapter:

- **Access Control Fundamentals**
- **Improving the Logon Architecture**
- **User Account Control**
- **Remote Assistance**
- **Network Access Protection**

☑ **Summary**

☑ **Solutions Fast Track**

☑ **Frequently Asked Questions**

Introduction

Windows Vista provides many security benefits, including enhancements to the Vista logon architecture, a new feature called User Account Control (UAC), smart card enhancements, and Network Access Protection (NAP). It also includes redesigned and redeveloped Remote Assistance functionality.

Although Microsoft designed Vista to be more secure, nothing really applies more security to your system than "defense in depth." Defense in depth is the technical term for a secure system that is applied in layers. Vista provides a new level of security with its enhancements. This is combined with ensuring that users handle their credentials properly; that they understand other concepts of physical security, such as limiting access to the systems you want to secure; and that they comply with these concepts. When correctly applied, a security policy and other security defenses create a secure multilayered "onion." If one layer is exploited or penetrated, others still stand guard.

Windows Vista is secure by design and offers many layers of security by itself. By following Microsoft's Trustworthy Computing initiative, the developers of Windows Vista have designed the software to eliminate the most common Windows-based attacks, such as buffer overflows. In addition, other known weaknesses to the logon subsystems have been reworked. User access has always been an issue and tough to secure within Microsoft's camp, but with Vista, secure advancements have been made to make these simple exploits a thing of the past. Because of the way Windows was initially designed, an attacker could exploit the OS's subsystems in many ways with Vista gaining access to the OS by sitting directly at the console, through malware and other subvert tactics to deploy rootkits, is very difficult. Administrative access using the Administrator account was considered gaining the keys to the castle, so use of it has been severely limited as well. Many exploits have been designed to thwart the system's access defenses, and many attacks have been developed to gain administrative access to the system. In the next section, we discuss the main updates to security user access within Vista and how to configure them. We also provide a brief overview of some of the most common attacks used to thwart a system's access defenses and controls.

Access Control Fundamentals

To protect system and network resources from theft, damage, or unwanted exposure, administrators must understand who initiates this risky behavior, why they do it, and how they do it. Obviously, hackers and those with ill intent are the ones trying to gain access, but the methods by which they do constantly evolve, as do the operating systems (such as Vista) themselves.

Understanding the concepts access control can be vital to keeping any system secure. Ensuring physical access control means you will attempt to control physical access to the servers, networked workstations, network devices, and cabling connections. You also must be aware of other security considerations when working with wireless media, portable systems such as laptops and personal digital assistants (PDAs), and removable media such as Universal Serial Bus (USB) stick drives, DVDs, CD-ROMs, and external hard disks. By limiting your exposure, using secure methods of authentication, and practicing general workstation security, you will also inherently limit your exposure to risk.

Limiting Exposure

An effective security plan does not rely on one technology or solution, but instead takes a multilayered approach. Compare this approach to a business's physical security measures; most companies don't depend on just the locks on the building's doors to keep intruders and thieves out. Instead, they might also have perimeter security (a fence), perhaps additional external security such as a guard or a guard dog, external and internal alarm systems, and, to protect special valuables, further internal safeguards such as a vault. Most administrators keep data backup copies off-site in a secure location in case of fire or some other natural disaster. For example an IT network and system security policy should be similarly layered.

For example, an effective IT security policy could incorporate the following:

- Firewalls at network entry points (and possibly a DMZ or screened subnet between the local area network [LAN] and the network interface connected to the Internet) that function as perimeter protection

- Password protection at local computers, requiring user authentication to log on, to keep unauthorized persons out, ensuring that all passwords used are limited by the user's ability to keep them simplified

- Access permissions set on individual network resources to restrict access of those who are "in" (logged on to the network)

- Encryption of data sent across the network or stored on disk to protect what is especially valuable, sensitive, or confidential

- Network and systems infrastructure (such as servers, routers, and switches) located in locked rooms with camera's to prevent people with physical access from accessing data without authorization

- Use of antivirus and other hardening applications such as host-based intrusion detection systems (IDSes), host-based firewalls, and spyware defenses such as Windows Defender

NOTE

Defense in depth is a concept in which all of the examples of security mentioned in the preceding list are applied simultaneously to create a multilayered security approach. This list is a sampling of some common areas where security is aplied. With the use of firewalls, access control with secure credentials, a security policy, and so on, you apply a layered security posture that is hard to unravel.

Understanding Attacks

Although there are many, some of the most common attacks to access control come in the form of attempts to bypass your secure credentials, or getting software on the host machine that can do it for you from the inside, also known as a *rootkit*.

Password Cracking

The best way to get into a system is to "trick" the system into thinking you're an authorized user. In many cases, you can do this simply by using a valid account name and password. This method is called *password cracking*. In this section, we will look at the tools and resources hackers use to obtain and/or crack passwords. Security administrators need to be aware of all the techniques and tools that can be used to impersonate a legitimate user, and how they work. Understanding how a crack was accomplished provides valuable clues to the cracker's skill level and how determined he is to get into a particular network, as well as other characteristics that can help track down the culprit.

In computer security, there are three basic ways to validate user identity: the "what you know" method (with the password being what you know); the "what you have" method mentioned, which requires physical possession of some object such as a smart card; and the "what you are" method, which uses biometrics data such as a fingerprint or retinal or iris scan.

It's important to know that the vast majority of networks rely solely on the first method, so anyone who knows or can guess the correct password that goes with a valid username can get in. Password cracking involves acquiring valid passwords. This can be done in several ways, including the following:

- **Brute force attacks** Brute force might not be the most elegant solution for a hacker in search of a password, but it can be very effective—especially if strong password policies aren't enforced. In its simplest form, a brute force attacker tries one possible password after another until she hits on the right one. Although someone can perform this process manually with a lot of time and patience, in practice it is usually done (much more efficiently) using a program that runs through all the words in a dictionary file, which is simply a large list of words (in what is sometimes called a dictionary attack) and other possible character combinations. Some of these cracking programs are very sophisticated and allow the cracker to implement rules or criteria. For example, if the cracker is able to obtain some information about the password—for example, the cracker knows that it consists of five alpha characters and three numeric—she can create a rule that will limit the program's attempts to passwords that fit the criteria (apple123, seven890, and so on). This strategy narrows the number of possible passwords and speeds the cracking process. Also note that newer password-cracking tools and programs grow more and more sophisticated—an entire attack can be launched from one program with multiple dictionary files, the program can intelligently append numbers and special characters to the equation in hopes of gaining access. Remember, Brute Force means just that—through brute force and nonstop checking, the password will eventually be cracked. The only way to defend against a brute force attack is to periodically change your password to a new and evenly secure one.

- **Interception of passwords** Another means of intercepting passwords is to use a keystroke logger. A keystroke logger is a hardware device or software program that captures and records every character that is typed—including passwords. It is often possible to detect an unauthorized packet sniffer on the wire using a device called a *time domain reflectometer* (TDR), which sends a pulse down the cable and creates a graph of the reflections that are returned. Users who know how to read the graph can tell whether and where unauthorized devices are attached to the cable.

- **Social engineering** Unlike the other attack types, social engineering does not refer to technological manipulation of computer hardware or software vulnerabilities, and it does not require much in the way of technical skills. Instead, this type of attack exploits human weaknesses—such as carelessness or the desire to be cooperative—to gain access to legitimate network credentials. The talents that are most useful to the intruder who relies on social engineering techniques are the so-called "people skills," such as a charming or persuasive personality or a commanding, authoritative presence. Social engineering is, in many cases, the easiest way to gain unauthorized access to a computer network.

Rootkits

Despite its name, a rootkit attack is not a method of obtaining root account privileges—at least, not directly. It is a group of programs that install a Trojan logon replacement with a backdoor, along with a packet sniffer, on UNIX systems as well as Windows systems. The sniffer can then be used to capture network traffic, including user credentials, thus giving the user access to the root account by logging on with legitimate credentials.

Rootkits come in all shapes and sizes. For example, a rootkit can be hidden within any Trojan horse, or other form of malware. Four types of rootkits can cause you numerous headaches: persistent, memory-based, user-mode, and kernel-mode.

Persistent rootkits are launched every time the system is rebooted. If your system has a rootkit on it, if it's persistent, every time you restart the system the rootkit will reappear, even after you think you may have cleaned it off your system. Persistent rootkits are commonly found deep within the file system or in the system Registry. Memory-based rootkits resides only in memory (RAM), and when the system is rebooted after it's cleaned, the rootkit should be gone. User-mode rootkits are very tricky because they try to evade detection by antimalware programs. By intercepting system calls, the rootkit is able to trick the system into believing that it is no longer installed. Kernel-mode rootkits are quite possibly the worst, because like user-mode rootkits, they evade detection and directly manipulate the system's kernel. This means that the rootkit could take itself out of a running process and not appear in the Task Manager, for example.

Using Encryption

Cryptography is a word derived from the Greek *kryptos* ("hidden"), and the use of cryptography predates the computer age by hundreds of years. Keeping secrets has long been a concern of human beings, and the purpose of cryptography is to hide information or change it so that it is incomprehensible to people for whom it is not intended. Cryptographic techniques are an important part of a multilayered security plan. Some security measures, such as implementation of a firewall and use of access permissions, attempt to keep intruders out of the network or computer altogether, much like fences and door locks attempt to keep burglars off the grounds or out of the house. Cryptography provides an inner line of defense. Like a wall safe that is there in case the burglars do make it inside your house—and to protect valuables from people who are authorized to come into your house—cryptography protects data from intruders who are able to penetrate the outer network defenses and from those who are authorized to access the network but not this particular data.

Cryptographic techniques concern themselves with three basic purposes:

- **Authentication** Verifying the identity of a user or computer.

- **Confidentiality** Keeping the contents of the data secret.

- **Integrity** Ensuring that data doesn't change between the time it leaves the source and the time it reaches its destination.

One or more of these goals may be a priority, depending upon the situation.

All three mechanisms can be used together, or they can be used separately when only one or two of these considerations are important. In the following sections, we look more closely at how each one works in relation to network security.

NOTE

The process of confidentiality, integrity, and authentication, is also known as *CIA*.

Cryptographic techniques include *encryption*, which involves applying a procedure called an *algorithm* to plain text to turn it into something that will appear to be gibberish to anyone who doesn't have the key to decrypt it. Encryption is a form of cryptography that "scrambles" plain text into unintelligible cipher text. Encryption is the foundation of such security measures as digital signatures, digital certificates, and the public key infrastructure that uses these technologies to make computer transactions more secure. Computer-based encryption techniques use keys to encrypt and decrypt data. A *key* is a variable (sometimes represented as a password) that is a large binary number—the larger, the better. Key length is measured in bits, and the more bits in a key, the more difficult the key will be to "crack."

Secure Protocols

The protocols used for authenticating identity depend on the authentication type. Some common protocols used for authentication include Kerberos and Secure Shell (SSH).

Kerberos

Kerberos is a logon authentication protocol that is based on secret key (symmetric) cryptography. It usually uses the DES or Triple-DES (3DES) encryption algorithm, although with the latest version, Kerberos v5, algorithms other than DES can be used. Kerberos uses a system of "tickets" to provide verification of identity to multiple servers throughout the network. Vista was also released with enhancements to the base Kerebos protocol so that it can now work with AES.

This system works a little like the payment system at some amusement parks and fairs where, instead of paying to ride each individual ride, customers must buy tickets at a central location and then use those tickets to access the rides. Similarly, with Kerberos, a client who wants to access resources on network servers is not authenticated by each server; instead, all the servers rely on "tickets" issued by a central server, called the Key Distribution Center (KDC). The client sends a request for a ticket (encrypted with the client's key) to the KDC. The KDC issues a ticket called a Ticket-Granting Ticket (TGT), which is encrypted and submitted to the Ticket-Granting Service (TGS). The TGS can be running on the same physical machine that is running the KDC. The TGS issues a session ticket to the client for accessing the particular network resource that was requested (which is usually on a different server). The session ticket is presented to the server that hosts the resource, and access is granted. The session key is valid only for that particular session and is set to expire after a specific amount of time. Kerberos allows mutual authentication; that is, the identities of both the client and the server can be verified.

SSH

SSH was designed to replace the use of Telnet, an IPv4 based protocol found on the application layer of the TCP/IP based OSI model. Telnet is used to gain remote access into systems and provide for a terminal in which text characters can be sent to and from a client to a server. Because this protocol is extremely old, it is easily exploited. Telnet sends data back and forth in cleartext. This includes the "credentials," such as the username and password. Because Telnet can be easily sniffed by a sniffer or acquired in a Man-in-the-Middle attack, using Telnet should be avoided at all costs.

SSH allows users to log on to UNIX systems remotely. Both ends of the connection (client and server) are authenticated, and data—as well as passwords—can be encrypted. 3DES, Blowfish, and Twofish are encryption algorithms that are supported by SSHv2, which also allows the use of smart cards.

Authentication Devices

Other hardware-based components of your network security plan may include devices that provide extra security for authentication, such as:

- Smart card readers
- Fingerprint scanners
- Retinal and iris scanners
- Voice analysis devices

These devices can be used in environments that require a high level of security for secure and reliable network authentication. Microsoft has acquired Biometric API (BAPI) technology from I/O Software and plans to incorporate support for biometrics authentication devices into future versions of its OSes. Windows Vista systems support smart card authentication as the main form of verifiable secure access into the system.

Smart Card Authentication

The term *smart card* has several different meanings. In a broad sense, it refers to any plastic credit-card-size card that has a computer chip (a memory chip and/or a tiny microprocessor) embedded in it to hold information that can be changed (as opposed to less "smart" cards that use a magnetic strip that holds static information). A smart card reader—a hardware device—is needed to write to and read the information on the card. Smart cards can be used for different purposes, but one of the most popular is for authentication. Satellite television services use smart cards in the SATV receiver to identify the subscriber and that subscriber's service level. Banks use smart cards for conducting transactions. These cards are especially popular in Europe.

Smart cards can also be used for network logon authentication. This provides an extra level of security, the "something you have" factor. The cards are generally resistant to tampering and relatively difficult for a hacker to compromise, because they are self-contained. They're also inexpensive in comparison with biometrics authentication devices.

Smart cards used for logon authentication generally store a digital certificate that contains user identification information, the user's public key, and the signature of the trusted third party that issued the certificate, as well as a time for which the certificate is valid. The certificates are stored on the cards by an authorized administrator. To log on with a smart card, a user must insert the card in the reader or swipe it through and enter a PIN that is associated with the card. If the PIN is compromised, an administrator can change it or issue a new card. To use smart cards for network logon, the computer must run an OS that supports smart card authentication, such as Windows 2000, Windows XP, or Windows Vista.

A number of companies manufacture smart cards and readers. Some vendors make keyboards that have built-in smart card readers, and there are combination fingerprint scanner/smart card readers for providing both card-based and biometrics security. Although smart cards provide for extra security, they (like all authentication methods) are not foolproof. Many cryptographers have been able to "break" smart card encryption. In general, there are two methods for defeating smart cards: logical and physical. An example of a logical attack is erasing parts of the data on the embedded microchip by raising or dropping the voltage; in some cases, this activity "unlocks" the security without deleting the data. A physical attack might involve actually cutting the chip out of the card and using a laser-cutter microscope to examine it. Although a determined attacker might be able to crack the smart card in this way, these methods are not easy and they don't always work.

Tools and Traps...

Windows Vista and Smart Cards

Windows Vista also offers easier smart card deployments because most of the logon architecture developments were focused on ensuring safer access control and attempting to make the smart and the safest option for anyone accessing a Vista system. Using a smart card reader with Windows Vista is about the most secure form of access control you can get today. Because smart cards offer two-factor authentication, it's a preferred method in use rather than just using credentials, which are usernames and passwords. Since Windows 2000 was released, smart cards have been supported, but not as well as they are now, with Windows Vista. Enhancements have been made to allow for new components, cryptographic modules, and more support for readers.

A smart card is an integrated circuit card (ICC) owned by an individual or a group, and it's used to provide physical access control. When used with a card reader, the card can help authenticate a user looking to gain access. The smart card is but only a portion of the subsystems used within Vista. Vista also uses a smart card common dialog box to help users select and use a smart card for authentication. A smart card database stores a list of known smart cards and a resource manager handles the resources within the database. A smart card subsystem is then used to provide a link between smart card readers and smart card-aware applications.

Windows Vista makes using smart cards easier. Now, a common cryptographic service provider (CSP) implements all the standard backend cryptographic functions that hardware and software developers need. Integrated third-party card modules make it easier to quickly deploy a smart card solution and enable secure communications between the CSP and other components within the smart card infrastructure.

Microsoft is also working closely with software and hardware developers so that if any module updates are needed for the smart card deployment, users can download them directly from Windows Update.

Biometrics Authentication

Biometrics authentication devices rely on physical characteristics such as a fingerprint, facial patterns, or iris or retinal patterns to verify user identity. Biometrics authentication is becoming popular for many purposes, including network logon. A biometrics template or identifier (a sample known to be from the authorized user) must be stored in a database for the device to compare to a new sample given during the logon process. Biometrics are often used in conjunction with smart cards in high-security environments. The most popular types of biometrics devices are the following:

- **Fingerprint scanners** These are widely available for both desktop and portable computers from a variety of vendors, connecting via a USB or Personal Computer Memory Card International Association (PCMCIA, or PC Card) interface.

- **Facial pattern recognition devices** These devices use facial geometry analysis to verify identity.

- **Hand geometry recognition devices** These are similar to facial pattern devices but analyze hand geometry.

- **Iris scan identification devices** Iris scanners analyze the trabecular meshwork tissue in the iris, which is permanently formed during the eighth month of human gestation.

- **Retinal scan identification devices** Retina scanners analyze the patterns of blood vessels on the retina.

Keeping Workstations Secure

Many network security plans focus on the servers but ignore the risk posed by workstations that have network access to those servers. It is not uncommon for employees to leave their computers unsecured when they leave for lunch or even when they leave for the evening. Often there will be a workstation in the receptionist area that is open to visitors who walk in off the street. If the receptionist manning the station must leave briefly, the computer—and the network to which it is connected—is vulnerable unless steps have been taken to ensure that it is secure. A good security plan includes protection of all unmanned workstations. A secure client OS such as Windows NT, Windows 2000, Windows XP, Windows Server 2003, and Windows Vista requires an interactive logon with a valid account name and password in order to access the OS (unlike Windows 9.*x* or ME). These systems allow users to "lock" the workstation when they are going to be away from it, so someone else can't just step up and start using the computer. Organizations must not depend on access permissions and other software security methods alone to protect the network.

If a potential intruder can gain physical access to a networked computer, he is that much closer to accessing valuable data or introducing a virus onto the network.

Many modern PC cases come with some type of locking mechanism that will help prevent an unauthorized person from opening the case and stealing the hard disk. Locks are also available to prevent use of the disk drive, copying of data to disk, or rebooting the computer with a disk.

Improving the Logon Architecture

When Windows Vista was initially on the drawing board, many efforts went into redesigning the logon architecture. The logon architecture is the grouping of systems and subsystems that will allow you to log on to your workstation. Based on the "architecture," it will provide a way to control the logon securely so that a security posture is maintained. If logon architecture was developed without security in mind, many exploits could be created (as they were in the past) to manipulate and exploit these subsystems and gain access to the system. Because Microsoft has to comply with C2 and other Orange Book standards, having a weak and crackable logon process is unacceptable.

With Windows Vista, the new logon architecture offers enhanced security benefits. Besides offering an improved, stable, and more reliable logon experience, Microsoft has completely rewritten the logon architecture to ensure that any services or functions not directly related to the logon process are now removed and used in other subsystems within Windows Vista.

The logon architecture has been completely redesigned to facilitate more secure forms of authentication, such as smart cards. Before Vista, many administrators and engineers held the responsibility of developing the Graphical Identification and Authentication (GINA) interface beyond what is was initially intended to do. Developers worked to supplement other forms of authentication, such as biometrics system, and other forms of security, such as one-time password tokens (OTPs).

With the redevelopment of the logon architecture for Windows Vista, Microsoft made sure that there was a stronger level of security that could (or should) be used when a user logged on to a system. Now, the primary form of authentication for Windows Vista is the use of a smart card. Because the logon architecture has been extended to meet new security demands, you can now work with new credential types easily by using the new Credential Provider, an application programming interface (API) that allows the Vista OS to remain secure, while still enabling users to write or develop code to interact with the OS. The Credential Provider API was created to support multiple credential types when logging on to the Vista system. Because Windows Vista doesn't support the use of a GINA, it's important that new Credential Providers handle this function—for instance, by allowing for multiple authenticating methods and devices, such as biometrics and smart cards. With the use of the

Credential Provider API, you can now choose or combine multiple authentication methods when logging on to Vista. The Credential Provider also allows developers to manipulate the existing architecture to build new or future methods of authentication into Windows Vista.

Notes from the Underground...

Understanding Winlogon and the GINA

The Windows logon architecture comprises two main components: Winlogon and the GINA dynamic link library (DLL). A DLL allows one library of information to serve multiple executable programs that may all share the same information or library.

With regard to Windows Vista and security, Winlogon has been completed updated. Winlogon is responsible for providing support for logon functions, starting the process for the secure attention key (SAK). They SAK, also known as the secure attention sequence (SAS), historically has been the Ctrl-Alt-Del key sequence. Winlogon is also responsible for interactive logon, which also controls the GINA DLL. In previous versions of Windows you can change, alter, replace, and customize the GINA DLL. In Windows Vista, the GINA DLL is no longer used.

The Windows Vista logon architecture has been completely redesigned in order to accommodate new security features that will make malware and other forms of exploitation almost nonexistent. When you log on to a Vista system, your logon request is handled by three separate sections: the Access Control services, the Cryptography services, and the secure OS. Within the Access Control module, you find Authentication services such as 2 factor authentication, logon, and identity controls. Authorization is handled by processes such as discretionary access control (DAC), mandatory access control (MAC), and Role-Based Access (RBAC), which is used to restrict system access based on authorized users. The Access Control module also handles auditing functions such as event logging. Credential management is handled within this module as well, so any use of a certificate server or smart card resides here, in the Access Control module.

Cryptography services are used to secure a user's logon experience. This is done by using X.509, or the cryptographic application programming interface (CAPI), which is the cryptographic library provided with Microsoft Windows Vista. Once the secure OS is reached, new features such as isolated desktop and kernel-mode signing are utilized.

Session 0

In Windows XP, Windows Server 2003, and earlier versions of the Windows OS, all services run in the same session as the first user who logs on to the console. This session is called Session 0. Running services and user applications together in Session 0 poses a security risk because services run at elevated privileges and therefore are targets for malicious agents who are looking for a way to elevate their own privilege level. Figure 3.1 shows how services and applications run within the same session. Each subsequent session is generated by a new logged-on user, as well as by remote users.

Figure 3.1 Older Versions of Windows Utilizing Session 0

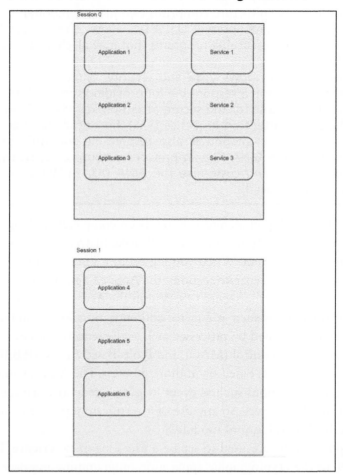

The Windows Vista OS mitigates this security risk by isolating services in Session 0 and making Session 0 noninteractive. In Windows Vista, only system processes and services run in Session 0, as shown in Figure 3.2.

Figure 3.2 Windows Vista and Session 0

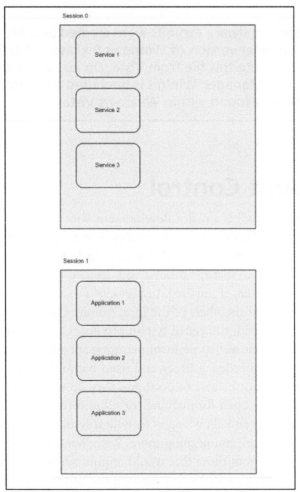

The first user logs on to Session 1, and subsequent users log on to subsequent sessions. This means that services never run in the same session as users' applications, and are therefore protected from attacks that originate in application code.

Within the session, you also have the Winlogon process, profile selection, the Shell, and the local security authority (LSA). The LSA is responsible for validation of credentials in Windows. This was the case with Windows XP and Windows Server

2003, but with Windows Vista, WinInit handles the LSA, Profiles, and Group Policy, and in other sessions, Winlogon handled each credential provider under the Logon User Interface (LogonUI).

WARNING

In the past, some malware exploits were created as a file called WinInit.exe. An older version of Windows 9.x also utilized a WinInit INI file. Do not delete this file from Vista. Do not try to kill the process listed within Task Manager. WinInit is now used to handle some of the logon functionality found within Windows Vista.

 # User Account Control

User Account Control (UAC) is a major development within access control and Windows Vista. For example, most of us remember how to use the Run As process. If you wanted to gain access to a process that required administrative privileges, you would have to use Run As so that the process you decided to use could be used with an administrative account if required. In previous versions of Windows, user accounts were configured as members of the local Administrator group, which in turn provided those users with unneeded system privileges and the ability to install and configure applications as well as perform management and administrative tasks on the workstation—all unneeded at times, and fixed within Windows Vista.

User accounts should not be able to do things they do not need to do. All that does is leave the door wide open for malware (or other forms of attack) that could compromise these accounts and allow access to system resources. Users should have only the privileges they need, and nothing more. With Windows Vista, UAC is used to separate user privileges from those that would require administrative rights and access. UAC defines access security by first limiting the surface area for attack. Accounts have been redefined so that if they are compromised, they will pose no security threat, but at the same time will allow for "nonthreatening" tasks to be functional, such as changing the clock's time, for example. When administrative privileges are needed (such as when installing an application), the user will be prompted for an administrator password. UAC makes user accounts safer for use by prompting the user for approval before allowing him to perform any administrative tasks.

TIP

Administrator accounts will run in Administrator Approval Mode by default, as will UAC. If changes need to be made, the "shield" icon will appear, which marks the use or need for administrative action. Unless turned off, UAC will be invoked when needed.

As we mentioned in Chapter 2, UAC will also help shield users from malware and other exploits by allowing each user to require an administrative password to be able to see and use content on the Web. As you learned in Chapter 2, with UAC and parental controls, users can now enjoy a safer Web surfing experience, and children will not be so easily duped into doing things that compromised security in the past.

UAC is also easier to understand. Now, when users are prompted for credentials, UAC more clearly defines what process is invoking it.

Using User Access Control

To use UAC, you simply need to boot your Vista system and use it, because it's enabled by default. UAC will pop up when administrative privileges are required. Figure 3.3 shows the UAC logon screen.

Figure 3.3 Viewing the UAC Logon Screen

When UAC is invoked, simply supply the credentials needed. Also, note the program icon, which shows the path to the program that invoked UAC to begin with. Sometimes, if a program is malicious, it will appear to be an unknown program or from an unknown publisher. To allow this program to run, you simply need to click the **Submit** button within the **Windows Security dialog**. You can also specify different accounts to use if you prefer to not use the Administrator account.

There are other ways to use UAC. For example, you can mark an application to run in an elevated fashion at all times, as well as set other advanced configurations. You also can disable UAC altogether. When you want to run a program as elevated, simply right-click the application to show the **Run as administrator** menu option, as shown in Figure 3.4. Here, we run Regedit, which is used to open and modify the contents of the Registry with administrative privileges.

Figure 3.4 Invoking UAC

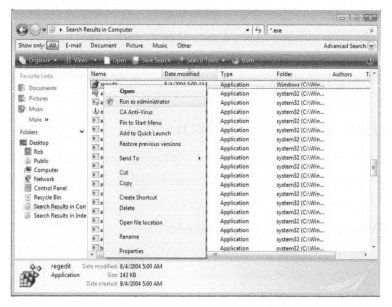

Marking an Application

You can mark applications to run in an elevated fashion very easily by finding the application in which you want to configure and right-clicking it, selecting the **Compatibility** tab from the **Properties** dialog box, and under **Privilege Level**, selecting **Run this program as an administrator**. In Figure 3.5, we view the elevation of Regedit by modifying the privilege level to allow the program to run as an administrator.

Figure 3.5 Setting Regedit's Privilege Level

Using the Local Security Policy to Configure UAC

You can disable Admin Approval Mode and UAC from prompting for credentials to install applications, and change the elevation prompt behavior, by changing the configuration within the Local Security Policy.

To disable Admin Approval Mode and UAC, click on the **Start** menu. When you open the menu, select **All Programs | Accessories | Run**. Type **secpol.msc** in the text area to open the **Local Security Policy Microsoft Management Console** (MMC), and click **OK**. The Local Security Policy MMC will open, as seen in Figure 3.6.

Figure 3.6 Opening the Local Security Policy MMC

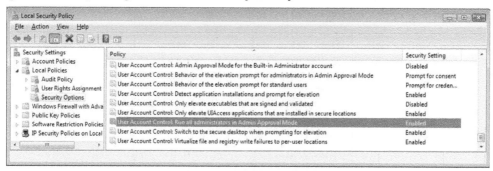

Once it is opened, drill down to the **Security Options** node in the MMC navigation pane. You can access this by going to **Local Policies**, and then clicking on the **Security Options** node. Scroll down until you find the **User Account Control** settings. Once there, you will find quite a few options you can adjust for UAC. Figure 3.7 shows disabling the Admin Approval Mode and UAC by selecting Disabled and clicking **OK**.

Figure 3.7 Disabling Admin Approval Mode and UAC

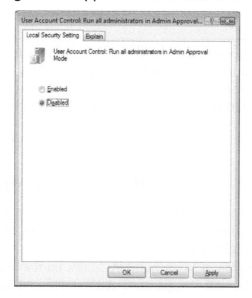

Disabling UAC When Installing Applications

You may want to disable UAC from prompting for credentials to install applications if you trust the users using the system to install applications without being prompted every time they do. For example, some users may be trusted to handle the installation of applications on their systems, or you may support a number of remote users that need to install applications remotely from time to time. In cases such as these, you may disable UAC from prompting each time someone needs to install an application.

From the **Local Security Policy MMC**, drill back down the UAC options in the **Security Options** node and select **User Account Control: Detect application installations and prompt for elevation**. As seen in Figure 3.8, you can enable or disable this option. Click **OK** for the settings to take place.

Figure 3.8 Changing How UAC Handles Application Installations

Changing the Prompt for UAC

You can also change how UAC will be invoked by changing the behavior of the elevation prompt for standard users. When standard users use the Vista system, either UAC can prompt them or you can configure it to automatically deny any elevation requests. You would do this to lock down the system completely and not allow users to even be prompted when privileges need to be elevated. The user can either be prompted for credentials (this setting requires username and password input before an application or task will run as elevated) or denied completely. Figure 3.9 shows the UAC settings you can adjust.

Figure 3.9 Changing How UAC Handles Standard Users

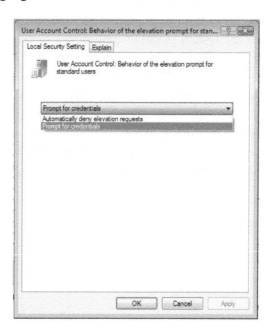

Remote Assistance

With the advanced development in Windows Vista access control, it is no wonder that Remote Assistance has been redesigned and redeveloped. Remote Assistance has historically been used (or not used) to access user desktops and interact with users through their systems. For example, why pick up a phone and call when you can use Remote Assistance just as quickly, and it comes with Vista? Many times, Remote Assistance is not used and is simply disabled, but with the Vista enhancements you may want to try it out again. One of the major enhancements to Vista is simply the redeveloped communication architecture, which enables Remote Assistance to work more quickly and efficiently than in past versions.

TIP

When using Remote Assistance, end users have to "grant" an administrator access and permission to connect to and manipulate their systems.

As it has been redesigned, Remote Assistance is now a stand-alone application (it is no longer a part of the Help and Support Center). In addition, it has advanced session logging to keep track of what assistance has already been given. Windows Vista's version of Remote Assistance has been limited to conserve bandwidth. Bandwidth is saved by disallowing the use of "voice" over the Remote Assistance session. Because Windows XP Remote Assistance supports voice sessions, it will not be compatible with Windows Vista's version.

A more important issue is that a person who is running Windows Vista will not be able to offer assistance to someone who is running Windows XP. Therefore, if your organization's help desk depends on Remote Assistance, you will probably want to make sure the help desk staff are the last ones upgraded to Windows Vista.

WARNING

When using Remote Assistance, XP SP2 will have incompatibility problems. For example, Windows Vista now allows you to pause a session, whereas XP does not.

To access Remote Assistance, click the **Start** button and select **All Programs | Maintenance | Remote Assistance**. You can also change Remote Assistance settings by opening the **Control Panel** and selecting **System and Maintenance**. When you click on **Allow remote access**, UAC will check your credentials and then allow you to change settings. Figure 3.10 shows the Control Panel.

Figure 3.10 Accessing Remote Access Settings via the Control Panel

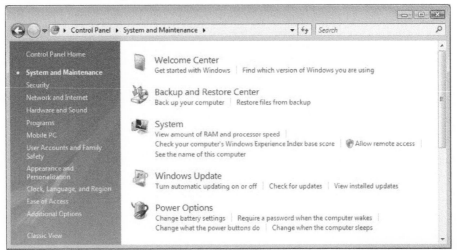

You can select the **Remote** tab in the **System Properties** dialog box, as seen in Figure 3.11. Here, you can allow Remote Assistance by selecting the checkbox. You can click **OK** to close the **System Properties** dialog box, or click on **Advanced** to change more settings.

Figure 3.11 Allowing Remote Assistance Connections

Figure 3.12 shows the advanced Remote Assistance Settings dialog box. Here you can adjust invitation settings and allow for remote control of the end-user system.

Figure 3.12 The Remote Assistance Settings Dialog Box

When launching Remote Assistance, you will see a screen that gives you the choice of either inviting someone to help you or offering to help someone. By selecting **Invite**, you are essentially saying that you trust that person to enter your system.

The newly developed Remote Assistance will allow for highly granular logging to an XML file stored on the local system. Although this version of Vista could have provided more information, it definitely provides more information than past versions of Remote Assistance.

Using Remote Assistance

To use Remote Assistance with Windows Vista, click on the **Start** button and then click on **Help and Support**. Under **Ask Someone**, click on **Remote Assistance**. Then click on **Invite Someone You Trust to Help You**. As you can see in Figure 3.13, two main parties are involved when working with Remote Assistance: experts and novices.

Figure 3.13 Using Remote Assistance

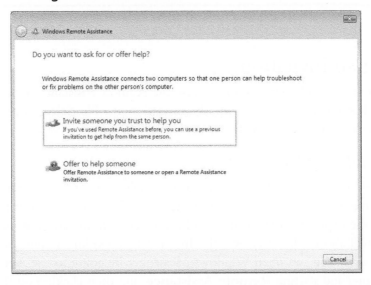

In order to use Remote Assistance, an expert will receive an invitation from a novice. The novice supplies the needed password to the expert and the expert can then connect using these credentials. The expert then initiates a session with the novice's computer. The novice's computer will also check to ensure that the expert used a valid invitation and that the invitation is still open. If the expert uses the correct password, the invitation is still open and valid, and the novice will receive a notification alert that the expert wants to start a Remote Assistance session.

Once the credentials are verified, the next step is for the novice to choose to start the session. Once this happens, the Novice Chat dialog box opens on the novice's system and the Expert Console opens on the expert's system. Now, the expert can control the user's desktop and see what is happening in real time. The expert can use the Expert Console to "Take Control" of the novice's system. This sends a message to the novice's system that the expert is now requesting to take control of the system.

There are three methods by which the novice can stop the expert's control of the novice's computer: Press the **Esc** key, hold down the **Ctrl** key, and then press the **C** key, or click **Stop Control** next to the novice's chat window.

TIP

It's better for the novice system to remain off the keyboard and mouse while control is in place. Because the keyboard and mouse are shared, any interference from the novice system will interrupt the expert's session.

Sending an Invitation

There are three available options for sending the Remote Assistance invitation: Windows Messenger, e-mail, or saving the invitation as a file. Select one of the three options to send an invitation to an end user.

Using Windows Messenger

You can use the Windows Messenger service to invite help. It's the preferred method because it's quick (it happens almost in real time), and an online indicator shows the novice that the expert is in fact online and can receive an invitation. Windows Messenger will also work better over the Internet by providing additional functionality and security. You can open Windows Messenger by going to the **Actions** menu, selecting and starting **Remote Assistance**, and then clicking on the desired contact. You can also right-click a Windows Messenger contact and select **Start Activities**, and then click on **Request Remote Assistance**.

Using E-mail

Another method in which a novice can send an invitation is through the use of e-mail. The e-mail will contain an attachment that includes the invitation from the novice to the expert. The expert will be prompted to provide a password when the attachment is opened.

Sending an Invitation As a File

In addition to Windows Messenger and e-mail, you can send an invitation in the form of a file. This option enables the novice to automatically save an invitation file to the local drive or to a network share. When the expert receives the file, she can double-click it to open the invitation and start the Remote Assistance session.

 # Network Access Protection

Microsoft has designed Windows Vista so that end-user access is secure, whether users realize it or not. With Vista, new security controls have been implemented to secure what accesses the system without the user's knowledge. For example, you might not know that malware has infiltrated your system until it unleashes its pay-load. With Vista's Network Access Protection (NAP), Vista has implemented a new level of security to secure access and control the spread of malware.

All Windows systems need security updates. To join a network, a system must comply with what's called a *health policy*. This is usually maintained on a health policy server. With NAP, if a client does not meet the rules of a healthy machine, the system will not be allowed to join the network until it has been updated. NAP is a network access control system that lets IT administrators ensure that only "healthy" machines connect to their networks, while enabling potentially "unhealthy" machines to be cleaned before they gain access.

The NAP client in Windows Vista simplifies the enforcement of network health policies and protects against malicious network attacks by enabling organizations to establish requirements for client health status (such as current software updates and up-to-date virus scanner signatures), and enforcing those requirements when the client connects to the network. If a client machine does not meet the health requirements, NAP can automatically update the machine or direct it to a separate "quarantine" area until the user or administrator can fix the situation.

NOTE

NAP requires functionality and support from the Windows Server 2007 (codenamed Longhorn) OS. Although the NAP client for Windows Vista is included in the OS, Microsoft also plans to release NAP client support in Windows XP SP2.

NAP is an extensible platform that provides an infrastructure and API for health policy enforcement. Independent hardware and software vendors can plug their security solutions into NAP, so IT administrators can choose the security solutions that meet their unique needs—and NAP helps ensure that every machine on the network makes full use of those solutions.

Notes from the Underground...

Microsoft and Cisco Collaborate

NAP with Windows Vista and Windows Server 2007 is now complemented by Network Admission Control (NAC), from Cisco Systems. Both NAC and NAP are now interoperable, which allows for defense in depth. With Windows Vista, a single agent handles the entire process.

The NAP client included with Windows Vista and Windows Server 2007 sends a list called a Statement of Health (SoH), also called a *health certificate*. Windows Vista or Windows Server 2007 will contain a client architecture that hosts a layer of System Health Agents (SHAs) as well as the NAP agent, the NAP client, and Extensible Authentication Protocol (EAP) supplicants. If the NAP client needs to obtain a health certificate, the NAP client will use the Health Certificate Enrollment Protocol (HCEP) to send a certificate request and its list of SoHs to the Health Registration Authority (HRA).

NAC-based network devices such as switches, routers, wireless access points, virtual private network (VPN) concentrators, and so on provide network access to clients and serve as network enforcement points. Cisco NAC will not allow infected systems to join the network, and NAP will make sure that systems that do not meet certain health requirements cannot join the network. Working together, NAP and NAC will enforce a deeper level of security on your network to disallow problems such as network worms from taking your systems down.

A Microsoft Network Policy Server (NPS) will perform the validation of a computer's system health and provides remediation instructions if needed. The HRA obtains health certificates on behalf of NAP clients from a public key infrastructure, if used.

Summary

Windows Vista provides many new security benefits to secure access to users' systems. User access control has always been a weak point for Windows systems, but with the creation of Windows Vista, those security issues have been addressed.

Microsoft created Windows Vista to eliminate the most common Windows-based attacks, such as buffer overflows and the manipulation and exploitation of service accounts. In addition, Vista provides secured user access. User access has always been tough to secure. Because of the way Windows was initially designed, an attacker could exploit the OS's subsystems in many ways.

Enhancements to the Vista logon architecture include a new feature called UAC, smart cards, and NAP. It also includes redesigned and redeveloped Remote Assistance functionality.

When using UAC, you will not allow a malicious attacker to bypass controls placed on standard user accounts, because if one is jeopardized, it will most likely not offer any kind of path to administrative privileges that could be used for harmful purposes.

Remote Assistance is used to offer help to remote users working on systems with remote assistance available, such as Windows XP SP2, Windows Vista, and Longhorn. With Windows Vista, Remote Assistance has been redeveloped to allow for better use of bandwidth and more security controls. Be aware that some functionality in Vista will not interoperate with Windows XP SP2.

NAP, or Network Access Protection, is new to Windows Vista and Longhorn. With NAP, a new level of security has been implemented to secure users' access to systems and control the spread of malware. NAP will ensure that your systems stay up-to-date. NAP keeps systems that are infected with malware or are not up-to-date from jeopardizing your network by not be allowing infected systems on to a network until they are updated.

Solutions Fast Track

Access Control Fundamentals

☑ Understanding access control is vital to keeping any system secure. Ensuring physical access control means you will attempt to control physical access to the servers, networked workstations, network devices, and cabling connections. You also must be aware of other security considerations when working with wireless media, portable systems such as laptops and personal digital assistants (PDAs), and removable media such as Universal Serial Bus (USB) stick drives, CD-ROMs, and hard disks.

☑ An effective security plan does not rely on one technology or solution, but instead takes a multilayered approach.

☑ Although there are many, some of the most common attacks to access control come in the form of attempts to bypass your secure credentials, or getting software on the host machine that can do it for you from the inside, also known as a rootkit.

☑ Defense in depth is a multilayered approach to network security. By using firewalls, access control with secure credentials, a security policy, and so on, you apply a layered security posture that is hard to unravel.

Improving the Logon Architecture

☑ The new logon architecture in Windows Vista offers enhanced security benefits. Besides offering an improved, stable, and more reliable logon experience, Microsoft has completely rewritten the logon architecture to ensure that any services or functions not directly related to the logon process are now removed and used in other subsystems within Windows Vista.

☑ The logon architecture has been completely redesigned to facilitate more secure forms of authentication, such as smart cards. Before Vista, many administrators and engineers held the responsibility of developing the GINA interface beyond what it was initially intended to do. Developers worked to supplement other forms of authentication, such as biometrics systems, and other forms of security, such as OTP.

☑ The Windows logon architecture provides two main components: Winlogon and the GINA DLL. A DLL allows one library of information to serve multiple executable programs that may all share the same information or library. Vista does not support a GINA; instead, Microsoft replaced it with Credential Providers.

☑ The Windows Vista logon architecture has been completely redesigned in order to accommodate new security features that will make malware and other forms of exploitation almost nonexistent. When you log on to a Vista system, your logon request is handled by three separate sections: the Access Control services, the Cryptography services, and the secure OS.

☑ In Windows XP, Windows Server 2003, and earlier versions of the Windows OS, all services run in the same session as the first user who logs on to the console. This session is called Session 0. Running services and user applications together in Session 0 poses a security risk because services run at elevated privileges and therefore are targets for malicious agents who are looking for a way to elevate their own privilege level. The Vista OS mitigates this security risk by isolating services in Session 0 and making Session 0 noninteractive.

☑ One of Windows Vista's main enhancements is the development and use of smart cards as a way to access the system securely.

User Access Control

☑ UAC is used to secure access to administrative privileges by allowing only standard accounts to have limited functionality.

☑ Administrator accounts will run in Administrator Approval Mode by default, as will UAC. If changes need to be made, the "shield" icon will appear, marking the use of or need for administrative action. Unless turned off, UAC will be invoked when needed.

☑ User accounts should not be able to do things they do not need to do. All that does is leave the door wide open for malware (or other forms of attack) that could compromise these accounts and allow access to system resources. Users should have only the privileges they need, and nothing more. With Windows Vista, UAC is used to separate user privileges from those that would require administrative rights and access.

☑ UAC defines access security by first limiting the surface area for attack. Accounts have been redefined so that if they are compromised, they will pose no security threat, but at the same time will allow for nonthreatening tasks to be functional. When administrative privileges are needed (such as when installing an application), the user will be prompted for an administrator password. UAC makes user accounts safer by prompting the user for approval before allowing him to perform any administrative tasks.

☑ UAC is also easier to understand. Now, when users are prompted for credentials, UAC more clearly defines what process is invoking it.

☑ UAC will also help shield users from malware and other exploits by allowing each user defined to require an administrative password to be able to see and use content on the Web. With UAC and parental controls, users can now enjoy a safer Web surfing experience, and children will not so easily be duped into doing things that compromised security in the past.

Remote Assistance

☑ Remote Assistance is used to offer help to remote users working on systems with Remote Assistance available, such as Windows XP SP2, Windows Vista, and Windows Server 2007 (codenamed Longhorn).

☑ Remote Assistance has historically been used (or not used) to access user desktops and interact with end users. One of the major enhancements to Vista is simply the redevelopment of the communication architecture, which enables Remote Assistance to work more quickly and efficiently than past versions.

☑ When using Remote Assistance, an end user has to "grant" an administrator access and permission to connect to and manipulate his system.

☑ Vista will not be able to offer full assistance to someone who is running Windows XP. Therefore, if your organization's help desk depends on Remote Assistance, you will probably want to make sure the help desk staff are the last ones upgraded to Windows Vista.

☑ When using Remote Assistance, XP SP2 will have incompatibility problems. For example, Windows Vista now allows you to pause a session, whereas XP does not.

☑ The newly developed Remote Assistance will allow for highly granular logging to an XML file stored on the local system.

Network Access Protection

☑ NAP is new to Windows Vista and Windows Server 2007. With NAP, a new level of security has been implemented to secure access and control the spread of malware.

☑ To join a network, a system must comply with a health policy, usually maintained on a health policy server. With NAP, if a client does not meet the rules of a healthy machine, the system will not be allowed to join the network until it has been updated.

☑ The NAP client in Windows Vista simplifies the enforcement of network health policies and protects against malicious network attacks by enabling organizations to establish requirements for client health status (such as current software updates and up-to-date virus scanner signatures) and enforcing those requirements when the client connects to the network. If a client machine does not meet the health requirements, NAP can automatically update the machine or direct it to a separate "quarantine" area until the user or administrator can fix the situation.

☑ NAP is an extensible platform that provides an infrastructure and API for health policy enforcement. Independent hardware and software vendors can plug their security solutions into NAP, so IT administrators can choose the security solutions that meet their unique needs—and NAP helps ensure that every machine on the network makes full use of those solutions.

☑ NAP requires functionality and support from the Windows Server 2007 OS. Although the NAP client for Windows Vista is included in the OS, Microsoft will also release NAP client support in Windows XP SP2.

Frequently Asked Questions

The following Frequently Asked Questions, answered by the authors of this book, are designed to both measure your understanding of the concepts presented in this chapter and to assist you with real-life implementation of these concepts. To have your questions about this chapter answered by the author, browse to **www.syngress.com/solutions** and click on the **"Ask the Author"** form.

Q: With all the computer and network security products currently on the market, why aren't all systems completely secured? How do I completely control access to a system?

A: Despite all the excellent products available, the only completely secure computer is one that is turned off. Computer and network security includes a balancing act of security and accessibility, and the two factors will always be at odds. The more secure your systems are, the less accessible they are, and vice versa. Because the very purpose of a computer network is accessibility, no network can ever be 100 percent secure.

Q: Does it matter which remote access authentication protocols are used? Are some more secure than others? Should access control authentication protocols be used?

A: The two most common authentication protocols used for dialup Point-to-Point Protocol (PPP) connections are Password Authentication Protocol (PAP) and Challenge Handshake Authentication Protocol (CHAP). PAP merely sends the user's name and password across the network to the server, in plain-text form. If the packets are intercepted in transit, the password can be read and stolen. CHAP uses symmetric encryption to protect the passwords that are sent over the network. However, the way CHAP works creates a new problem. The server generates a random key called *the challenge* and sends it to the client; the client uses the key to encrypt the password and sends the encrypted password back to the server. The server looks up the user's password in its database, uses the same key to encrypt it, and compares the result with the encrypted password sent by the client. Although the plain-text password never passes across the network with this method, the server must store a plain-text version of the user's password in its database in order to make the encryption for comparison. If an intruder accesses the server's database, the intruder will have the passwords for all the users. Remote Authentication Dial-in User Service (RADIUS) is a more secure alternative.

Q: Exactly how does social engineering work? Why would anyone reveal his password to a stranger? Does this really happen?

A: Yes, it really happens—and more often than you might think. Skilled social engineers are good con artists; they are masters at making other people trust them. In large companies, employees often aren't personally familiar with all other employees, so it's relatively easy for the social engineer to stroll in or even call on the phone and persuade a user that he is a member of the IT department and needs the user's password. The social engineer might have a convincing story, saying, for instance, that a hacker has gotten into the system and discovered all the password files, and now the IT department needs to know everyone's old password so that they can reset them and issue new ones to protect against the hacker. Like all con artists, the social engineer usually plays on common human emotions. For example, the engineer will play up the danger that the hacker can access and destroy all of the user's data if the "IT worker" doesn't get the password immediately and make the change. In other cases, the engineer might exploit other emotions, such as people's natural desire to help, claiming that the "IT worker" will get in trouble with the "big boss," maybe even lose his job, if he is unable to get the password information needed. Social engineers are not above appealing to the user's ego or pretending sexual/romantic interest in the user to get the password, either. Although some might not categorize it as social engineering, another technique involves simply spying on the user to obtain the password ("shoulder surfing," or looking over the user's shoulder as she types the password), or going through the user's papers to find a written record of the password. Infamous hacker Kevin Mitnik is quoted as saying "You can have the best technology, firewalls, intrusion-detection systems, [and] biometric devices. All it takes is a call to an unsuspecting employee who gives up the information needed."

Chapter 4

Microsoft Vista: Trusted Platform Module Services

Solutions in this chapter:

- **Understanding the TPM**

- **Configuring and Managing the TPM on a Stand-Alone System**

- **Configuring and Managing the TPM in an Enterprise Environment**

- **TPM Applications**

- **Understanding the Security Implications of the TPM**

- ☑ Summary

- ☑ Solutions Fast Track

- ☑ Frequently Asked Questions

Introduction

The Trusted Computing Group (TCG) was formed in 2003 with the goal of developing and promoting open standards for trusted computing. The group was founded by Advanced Micro Devices, Hewlett-Packard, IBM, Infineon, Intel, Lenovo, Microsoft, and Sun Microsystems, and currently has 135 members. The main product to come out of the TCG so far is the specification for the Trusted Platform Module (TPM), and the corresponding specification for the Trusted Computing Group Software Specification (TSS). The TPM is the key hardware component of a trusted computing platform and the TSS is the specification for an application program interface (API) that developers can use to create software that will interact with the TPM.

Windows Vista supports only version 1.2-compliant TPM devices natively, although third-party software, such as Wave's Embassy Trust Suite, is available that you can use to support some functionality of version 1.1b TPM devices. Version 1.2 of the TPM specification from the TCG was published in October 2003, and has since been revised. In this chapter, we will cover only the native Windows Vista support for version 1.2 TPM devices. In 2006, PC OEMs started to make a big push to incorporate TPM version 1.2 devices into their products. Laptops seem to be on the leading edge of this new technological wave, with Dell, HP, and Lenovo cranking up production of laptops.

Understanding the TPM

The TPM is a microchip for motherboards that is designed to create, store, and protect cryptographic keys, and the fact that the TPM is integrated into motherboards allows it to be used as a tool for strong authentication of devices as well. The TCG intends for the TPM to be the foundation upon which secure computing platforms are built. Because the TPM is a dedicated piece of hardware that creates a master encryption key which can be used to encrypt other keys that are created by user mode applications, keys are separated from software vulnerabilities that would directly jeopardize the security of keys protected only by software. A key protected by software is susceptible to disclosure the moment a buffer overrun or some other flaw in the software code is discovered. Protecting encryption keys with a hardware device such as the TPM can be seen as a direct response to many of the most prevalent and serious security issues facing information security professionals today, including rising numbers of software vulnerabilities, theft of equipment containing sensitive data including personally identifiable information (PII), and identity theft.

NOTE

Personally identifiable information (PII) is any information that may be used to uniquely identify a person, such as a Social Security number (SSN), credit card numbers, a person's health information (which the Health Insurance Portability and Accountability Act of 1996 [HIPAA] was enacted to protect), and the combination of a full name and address. It is critical to protect this information because it is useful to identity thieves.

However, cryptography is about more than just encrypting large amounts of data in order to keep it confidential. Cryptography is simply the process of taking a block of plain text and processing it to create cipher text. There are few limits as to what that plain text can be and what that cipher text can be used for. A lot of different applications for cryptography have been developed, including the following:

- A cryptographic algorithm can be applied to a file (or set of files) in order to create a hash or message digest which serves as a fingerprint of the file(s). This function is widely used for gauging the integrity of data, and is critical to the field of forensics.

- Digital signatures utilize public key cryptography and message digests in order to allow recipients to verify the integrity and authenticity of messages they receive.

- Sensitive user data can be processed using cryptographic algorithms in order to protect the confidentiality of the data.

The TPM and Windows Vista TPM services use all of these functions to implement the functions they provide, and in doing so they also support users' ability to securely utilize these cryptographic functions as well. Before getting into the technical details of how this works, we'll look at what a trusted platform is, who developed such an idea, and where the TPM fits in.

Are You 0wned?

Has Anyone Seen My Laptop?

In 2006, we witnessed a parade of news stories in which employees lost laptops that contained PII or other sensitive data:

- In April, Boeing announced that a laptop with PII of 3,600 of its employees had been stolen.

- In May, a U.S. Department of Veterans Affairs employee's laptop and external hard drive were stolen from his home. The laptop contained PII, including SSNs, on more than 26.5 million soldiers.

- In June, Hotels.com announced that an auditor from Ernst & Young Global Ltd. had his laptop stolen, exposing the names, addresses, and credit card information of nearly one-quarter of a million Hotels.com customers to thieves.

- In September, the U.S. Department of Commerce reported that 1,100 of its laptops were missing, and that 249 of the laptops contained PII.

- In November, Kaiser Permanente notified 38,000 members that their personal health information had been compromised when an employee's laptop was stolen out of his car.

- In December, we heard from Boeing again. This time it announced that a laptop theft had compromised the personal information of 382,000 employees.

These are just a handful of the highest-profile data loss stories from 2006, and the list of headlines for 2007 should be long as well. Not only are companies and government agencies relying more than ever before on laptops to serve their workforce, but more smartphones and personal digital assistants (PDAs) are in use as well. Even the iPods those employees are listening to on their way to and from work can be used to transport files. The location of sensitive data has never been more fluid.

The return on investment for erecting firewalls, virtual private networks (VPNs), proxies, and other perimeter protection devices in order to secure the data that is inside our networks is diminishing. What we as security professionals need is a perimeter that is as mobile as our data. Encryption may be the only security perimeter that is actually capable of moving with that data, and

Continued

provides a strong boundary between the data and the attacker. The TPM can help us build this new mobile perimeter by allowing us to use strong encryption while the cryptographic keys are protected in the TPM.

Trusted Platform Features

According to the TCG, a trusted platform must provide four features: protected capabilities, integrity monitoring, integrity storage, and integrity reporting. A trusted platform maintains certain storage locations, such as platform configuration registers (PCRs) and key storage slots in the TPM, where sensitive data is stored and processed. These locations may be accessed only by protected capabilities, which are the set of commands that are allowed to access and process the data.

The other three features of the trusted platform describe the system's trustworthiness. For instance, we would like to know whether the system has been in a secure state, or whether it has allowed some subject to access objects in an unsupported manner. It is actually acceptable (although undesirable) for the system to enter an insecure state. However, it is unacceptable for the system to lie about the states it has been in. Integrity monitoring is the collection of data on the state of the system, and other metrics which define the trustworthiness of the system for us.

These metrics are used to make judgments concerning the system's trustworthiness, so they must be adequately protected. The storage of integrity reporting measurements in protected locations is termed *integrity storage*. In addition to storing the actual data, integrity storage is used to store hashes of the integrity monitoring data. These hashes serve the same purpose as the hashes available with downloadable files and evidence collected for forensic analysis: They are used to ensure integrity of the data and they serve as proof that a third party has not tampered with the data. The metrics for integrity monitoring can be stored in a logfile, but the digests of the integrity monitoring data are stored in *PCRs*, which are volatile or nonvolatile data storage locations in the TPM itself. *Integrity reporting* is simply the process of vouching for the integrity of the data held in secure storage.

In the next section, you will see how the TCG trusted platform architecture supports and enables these features. It is important to understand how these features allow the trusted platform to start with a very small trust boundary that includes only a portion of the actual system. As the system loads, various pieces of code utilize these features to verify the integrity of other components in the system, and the trust boundary expands to include more and more portions of the system.

Trusted Platform Architecture

According to the TCG, the TPM is the base component of what it has labeled a *trusted platform*, which is a platform that provides users with a higher level of security than the traditional PC. When we discuss the TPM in this sense, we are discussing a somewhat abstract concept that is documented in specification materials developed by the TCG. However, the TPM is now also a part of real PCs.

Although the TCG is still in the process of developing the library of specifications which should be used together to form the trusted platform, we now have the real hardware for the TPM, Microsoft has implemented an operating system that provides a unified interface for the TPM in Windows Vista, applications within Windows Vista take advantage of the TPM, and we will soon see third-party applications that will run on the Windows Vista TSS and will take advantage of the TPM. Therefore, it is important to understand the TPM from two perspectives: We must look at it as a part of the architecture of the trusted platform as conceptualized by the TCG in its document, *TCG Specification Architecture Overview: Specification Revision 1.2*, found at www.trustedcomputinggroup.org/specs/IWG/ TCG_1_0_Architecture_Overview.pdf; and we must understand how Microsoft has implemented these specifications by examining the TPM services architecture in Windows Vista.

First, we will look at the TCG trusted platform architecture. It is important to cover this architecture first in order to understand what a trusted platform is and how it works, and to see how the TPM fits into that. Also, Microsoft and computer manufacturers have not simply ripped the TPM from this trusted platform architecture and used it in isolation for some unintended purpose. They are taking the initial steps in trying to implement this evolving design for a secure PC. Once we understand the trusted platform from the perspective of the TCG, we will take a look at the blueprint for Windows Vista TPM services.

The TCG Trusted Platform

The trusted platform needs to have *roots of trust*, which are parts of the system that must be trusted and must enable, at a minimum, the ability to verify the trustworthiness of the rest of the system. Generally, three roots of trust are required: the root of trust for measurement (RTM); the root of trust for storage (RTS); and the root of trust for reporting (RTR). The RTM is actually the normal computing engine for the platform (generally the CPU in the case of a PC) while it is controlled by the core root of trust for measurement (CRTM), which is the set of instructions the computing engine executes in performing its trusted measurement duties. This set of instructions is supposed to be either a portion of the basic input/output system (BIOS) (the BIOS boot block) or the entire BIOS.

A key concept in discussing the trusted platform is the Trusted Building Block (TBB), which is nothing more than the CRTM and the TPM working together. These two components are physically present on the motherboard, and they must be *immutable*. Every time the system is reset or booted, the CRTM must have first control of the system. In other words, no code may be executed before the CRTM is executed. Following that, the CRTM may not hand off control to another component until it has measured that component to determine its trustworthiness.

NOTE

An object whose state cannot be modified after it is created is considered *immutable*.

This assumes that trusted mechanisms are being used to boot and run the platform. It is important to remember that the TCG has explicitly stated in its specifications that using the TPM is not mandatory. Users take advantage of the TPM and Windows Vista TPM services on an opt-in basis. This means if the user of the platform wants her system to load just like PCs have loaded in the past—where no trust assurance is provided—she can do that. She can leave the TPM disabled in the BIOS, and not take advantage of TPM functionality.

However, assuming she has enabled the TPM and wants to boot into an operating system on a more trustworthy platform, the boot process starts by loading the CRTM into the CPU and the CRTM begins executing. This must always be the first thing that occurs in a trusted platform following a system reset. All trust in the platform is derived from the TBB, so we have to be absolutely certain that every other piece of code the platform runs comes after the TBB. Otherwise, if a malicious piece of code is inserted into the chain of execution at the beginning, nothing else following it can be trusted.

The system reset loads the CRTM, and it begins executing. At this point, we have a trusted platform. We are at a base state. Only our TBB is functioning, and at this point it is actually the only part of the platform that we trust. All other code that is loaded and executed becomes trusted when the piece of code executing before it takes an integrity measurement of it. No piece of code is allowed to transfer control to another piece of code until it has determined that the code is trustworthy. Once the CRTM is running, we can see the rest of the boot process, as shown in Figure 4.1.

Figure 4.1 The Trusted Platform Loading Process

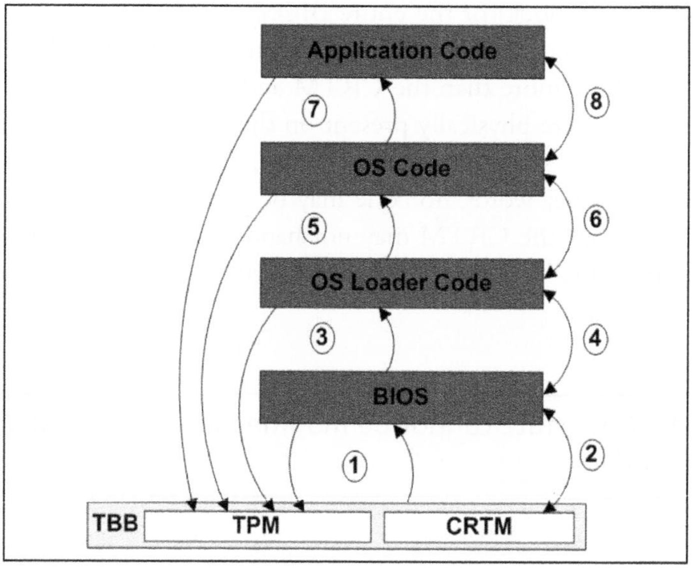

Here is an explanation of each step shown in Figure 4.1:

1. The CRTM takes integrity measurements of the remaining BIOS code. The measurements may be written to the Stored Measurement Log (SML) or recomputed whenever needed, and a digest of this measurement is created using the SHA-1 hashing algorithm. The SHA-1 digest is written to PCR[0].

2. If the CRTM determines that the measurement it has just taken is evidence of trustworthiness, it passes control of the platform to the remaining BIOS code.

3. The BIOS takes integrity measurements of the platform configuration settings, firmware code, and the code that loads the operating system (OS). The measurements may be written to the SML or recomputed whenever needed, and digests of these measurements are created using the SHA-1 hashing algorithm. The digests are written to the appropriate PCRs.

4. If the BIOS determines that the measurements it has just taken represent evidence of trustworthiness, it passes control of the platform to the remaining OS loader code.

5. Once the OS loader code executes, the next step is to pass control to the remainder of the OS. Before this can be done, the OS loader code must

establish trust in the OS code. Trust measurements are taken against this code, and again, a digest is written to the appropriate PCR in the TPM.

6. If the OS loader trusts the remainder of the OS based, again, on trust measurements, it passes control to the remainder of the OS code.

7. Once the OS is loaded and running, it will control the TPM. However, at times, other applications will need to utilize the TPM. Before the OS can transfer control to an application, it must establish that the application code is trustworthy. It can do this just as it did previously: It takes integrity measurements on the application code and writes a digest to the TPM.

8. Once trust in the application has been established, the OS may transfer control over to it.

You can see by the preceding steps that all trust in the trusted computing platform is based upon the ability to trust the CRTM and TPM. All other trust in the system is derived or induced from this initial TBB. The trusted platform is indeed built upon this relationship between the CRTM and the TPM, so calling them the trusted building blocks is very appropriate. This fact also speaks to the importance of ensuring that the TPM and CRTM are immutable and physically secured to the platform. If we are to rely on the TBB to vouch for the platform's trustworthiness, we must be sure that these two pieces are relatively impervious to modification. From this basis, the boundary of trust is extended to include more parts of the system. However, at any point during loading, if a piece of code does not pass muster during the integrity measurements, control is not transferred to that piece of code and the loading process stops.

Now that we understand how the trusted platform loads, we see the importance of the features of the trusted platform that we touched upon in the preceding section. Measurements are taken (integrity monitoring), they are stored in PCRs (integrity storage), the stored measurements must reliably be reported back to third parties that challenge the system's trustworthiness (integrity reporting), and secure commands (protected capabilities) are used to carry out these operations.

The Physical TPM Interface

Now that we understand the importance of being able to rely upon the physical connection of the TPM to the motherboard as a key assumption for the TBB, it is worth noting the characteristics of that physical connection. The TPM should utilize a Low Pin Count (LPC) bus interface to the motherboard chipset, and a TPM-write cycle and TPM-read cycle should be provided to the TPM. Only the TPM can use these cycles, and the LPC bus must be protected from interference by other devices.

Hardware manufacturers must implement these features. In addition, hardware manufacturers must implement secure firmware for the TPM, provide protection against dictionary attacks (often referred to as *antihammering protections*), and provide other countermeasures designed to combat hardware attacks.

Notes from the Underground…

As We Adapt, So Do the Attackers

As you read and learn about the powerful protection mechanisms that the TPM affords us, it is easy to be lulled into a false sense of security. Although the TPM allows us to avoid some vulnerabilities associated with software-only cryptographic solutions, this does not mean we are completely safe. It simply means that attackers will seek new avenues of attack. Many of these are more difficult and require more skill than what is currently required, though.

For a good briefing on penetration testing the TPM and Windows Vista TPM services, check out Doug MacIver's presentation from Hack in the Box 2006, "Penetration Testing Windows Vista BitLocker Drive Encryption," available at http://packetstormsecurity.org/hitb06/DAY_2_-_Douglas_MacIver_-_Pentesting_BitLocker.pdf.

Binding, Sealing, and Attestation

So far, we have been able to gain an understanding of what a trusted platform is and how it loads. We understand the boot process, and the method by which successive parts of the platform are incorporated into the trust boundary. We can see that each piece of code that controls the platform must not relinquish control to another until it collects metrics on that code and brings it into the trust boundary. All of these are critical functions, yet at the same time many services are available to the user or user mode applications that rely on the TPM. These rely on the capability of the TPM to carry out *binding*, *sealing*, and *attestation* functions.

Binding is essentially the process of encrypting an encryption key. As an example, Microsoft's BitLocker Drive Encryption must use a Volume Master Key (VMK), which encrypts the Full Volume Master Key (FVEK). The SRK, which is created when ownership of the TPM is taken and is stored in the TPM itself, is used to encrypt the VMK. This process is called *binding* or *wrapping*. Through binding or wrapping keys, users can be assured that the keys are secured even though they are not actually stored in the TPM, simply because the keys cannot be decrypted without a key that is stored in the TPM.

Sealing is the process of binding a key and tying it to certain platform characteristics. So, we know that binding is encrypting a key. Sealing goes one step further and associates the wrapped key to the state of the platform. For instance, it might check the software version, or it might check which versions of dynamic link libraries (DLLs) are loaded, and it will not unwrap the key it has sealed unless the platform has the same DLLs or software versions loaded.

Attestation is just a fancy name for the process of assuring that information is accurate. This is obviously a critical concept for the trusted platform, because as we have seen, all trust in the system is based on taking measurements and then checking those measurements. If the system cannot *attest* to the accuracy of that information, there can be no trust in the platform. An Attestation Identity Key (AIK) is a special 2,048-bit RSA key pair created and stored in the TPM that is used specifically for attestation. Numerous AIKs can be created after ownership of the TPM is taken, and they are used to digitally sign messages proving either the contents of the message or the authenticity of an entity (either a user or a platform). There are four types of attestation as far as the trusted platform is concerned:

- **Attestation by the TPM** The TPM uses an AIK to digitally sign some data that is held within the TPM itself, proving that the TPM is active and can verify itself.

- **Attestation of the platform** A set of PCRs are signed using an AIK so that the platform can report its integrity to a third party.

- **Attestation of the platform** The platform proves it can be trusted to report its integrity measurements by providing the credentials that were used to create an AIK credential.

- **Authentication of the platform** The platform uses a nonmigratable key, such as an AIK, to authenticate itself. This is strong device authentication.

Your Windows Vista PC

During the booting of a trusted computing platform based on Windows Vista, there is a point where the BIOS must transfer control to Windows Vista. We've covered the basics about what occurs before that transition and how the foundation of the trusted platform is established. We're mainly concerned with what happens after that transition occurs.

Figure 4.2 shows the TBB and BIOS in relation to the Windows Vista architecture. The first thing worth noting is that the TSS sits atop the TPM driver and the TPM Base Services (TBS). The TPM driver is provided by the TPM manufacturer, the TBS is a component of Windows Vista, and the TSS is the implementation of the TCG specification of the TSS. So, the TCG has defined the specs for a component at the bottom of your trusted computing platform, the TPM, as well as a component toward the top, the TSS.

Figure 4.2 The Windows Vista TPM Architecture

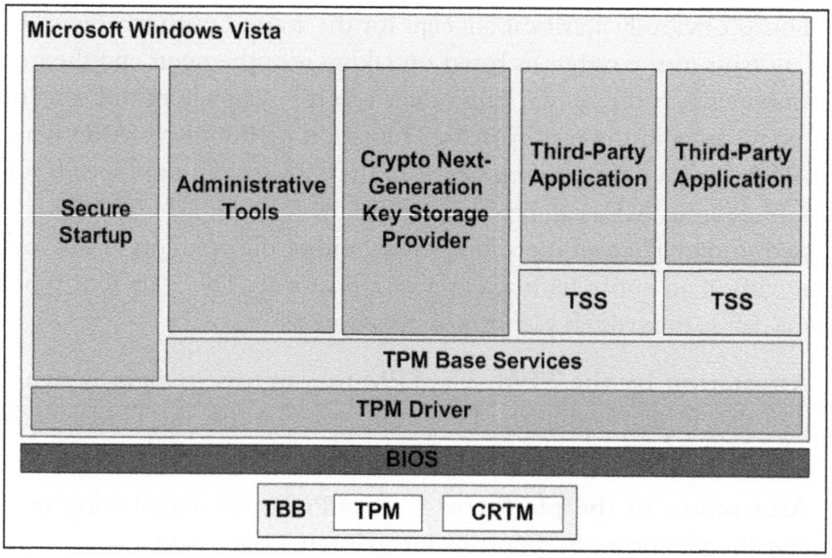

There are a few other important notes to consider with regard to the Windows Vista TPM architecture. It should not be surprising, but the TPM driver is required for the functioning of all other parts of the architecture above it. However, unlike most drivers, it is required before the OS loads because the OS loader needs to access the TPM if it is using a secure startup mechanism. Therefore, a TPM driver is also integrated into the BIOS code. Also, Microsoft has created the TBS in order to serve as a mediator between higher-level applications and the TPM driver, which is basically the TPM hardware itself, as far as these applications are concerned. Finally, for all non–Windows applications, the TSS provides a standard API for interacting with the TPM.

Currently, Windows Vista does not take integrity measurements of third-party applications, nor could it. Much like the BIOS, it is incumbent upon the third-party applications to provide measurements during a trusted state. If the applications could provide these metrics to Windows Vista, it can control whether those applications load depending on whether they have been corrupted, resulting in measurements that differ from the "trusted state" measurements. Any updates to these applications that would result in new integrity measurements need to be performed in a controlled manner, where this type of control of the application is shut off momentarily, the application code is updated, and then new measurements are provided.

That being said, the 64-bit version of Windows Vista is providing this level of protection for some pieces of code which it can control. Given that this sort of integrity checking would break most 32-bit applications which were developed with no security mechanisms such as this in place, Code Integrity has been implemented in only the 64-bit version of Windows Vista to prevent breaking already existing 32-bit applications. Code Integrity utilizes the processes and architecture of the trusted platform we covered in the previous sections in order to enable the following features:

- Verification of all drivers that are important to the boot process, including the Hardware Abstraction Layer (HAL) and the OS kernel, by the OS boot loader (which is now Winload)

- Verification of the integrity of all code that executes in a protected process

- Verification of the integrity of all kernel mode drivers

- Verification of the integrity of all user mode binaries that employ cryptographic functions

- Verification of the integrity of all user mode binaries that execute in a protected process used for high-definition media content

- Verification of the integrity of the kernel code itself

- Verification of the integrity of a specific set of user mode binaries

It is not too difficult to see how this Windows Vista architecture relates to the architecture we described when we talked about the more abstract features and functions of the TCG trusted platform. Let's revisit the trusted platform loading process, but this time we'll look specifically at our Windows Vista trusted platform (see Figure 4.3).

Figure 4.3 The Windows Vista Using BitLocker Secure Startup Loading Process

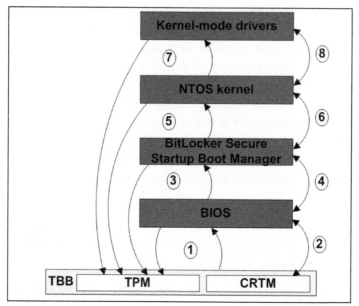

Here is an explanation of each step shown in Figure 4.3:

1. The CRTM takes integrity measurements of the remaining BIOS code. The measurements may be written to the SML or recomputed whenever needed, and a digest of this measurement is created using the SHA-1 hashing algorithm. The SHA-1 digest is written to PCR[0].

2. If the CRTM determines that the measurement it has just taken is evidence of trustworthiness, it passes control of the platform to the remaining BIOS code.

3. The BIOS takes integrity measurements of the platform configuration settings, firmware code, and the MBR. The measurements may be written to the SML or recomputed whenever needed, and digests of these measurements are created using the SHA-1 hashing algorithm. The digests are written to the appropriate PCRs. See Table 4.1.

4. If the BIOS determines that the measurements it has just taken represent evidence of trustworthiness, it passes control of the platform to the Windows Vista boot manager, which performs its own integrity checks as part of the secure startup process.

5. Once BitLocker's startup mechanism takes control, it takes integrity measurements of the New Technology File System (NTFS) boot sector and boot block, and it takes a measurement of the boot manager. These values are stored in PCRs 8 through 10, and PCR 11 is extended with a measurement after the VMK has been unsealed. BitLocker also looks back on the code that has already executed in a sense because the VMK it used for securing the drive has been sealed using PCRs 0, 2, and 4, in addition to 8 through 11.

6. So, once BitLocker's secure startup process has established trust in the code that preceded it, as well as in the code to which it is about to pass control, it unseals the VMK and decrypts the drive before passing control to the NTOS kernel.

7. Once Windows Vista is loaded and running, it will be responsible for validating the integrity of code that is to run. It does this just as it did previously: It takes integrity measurements of the code, and if it finds an inconsistency when compared to previous measurements, it will not allow the code to load.

8. Once trust in the code is established, Windows Vista allows it to load.

Table 4.1 Interesting PCR Usage Description

PCR Number	Description of Data Stored in PCR	Entity Writing to This PCR
0	An SHA-1 digest of the CRTM version ID, firmware for embedded devices, and remaining BIOS code to which the CRTM is going to transfer control.	CRTM
1	An SHA-1 digest of the motherboard configuration settings.	BIOS
2	An SHA-1 digest of the option ROM code.	BIOS
3	An SHA-1 digest of the option ROM configuration settings.	BIOS
4	An SHA-1 digest of the Initial Program Loader (IPL) code. This is the MBR.	BIOS
5	An SHA-1 digest of the IPL (MBR) configuration settings.	BIOS
6	An SHA-1 digest of state transition and wake events.	BIOS

Continued

Table 4.1 continued Interesting PCR Usage Description

PCR Number	Description of Data Stored in PCR	Entity Writing to This PCR
8	An SHA-1 digest of the NTFS boot sector.	Windows BitLocker
9	An SHA-1 digest of the NTFS boot block.	Windows BitLocker
10	An SHA-1 digest of the boot manager.	Windows BitLocker
11	An SHA-1 digest used for BitLocker access control.	Windows BitLocker

The Role of the TBS

The TBS is designed to serve as the scheduler and the TPM resource controller in Windows Vista. The TPM has scarce resources, with only a handful of key slots and session slots in volatile storage, so it is necessary to virtualize these resources and to queue access to them. The TBS accepts commands from higher-level software, performs some validation checks, and then routes the commands down to the TPM through the TPM driver. The TBS may even need to mediate resource requests from multiple instances of the TSS. The process of calling down through the TBS for usage of TPM resources goes like this:

1. A function of the application that requires the TPM is called down through the TSS.

2. The TBS mediates the request and manages the TPM resource.

3. A trust measurement is made of the code that is requesting control.

4. If the measurement reflects a trustworthy piece of code, control is transferred to the application.

5. Once the request is processed, the result is returned to the application.

6. The TBS is then free to process the next job in the queue.

The TBS processes commands based on priority, not on a simple first in, first out stack. When a resource, such as key slots, for example, runs out, the TBS finds the least recently used key slot, saves the key, and then places the new request in the freed slot. If the application or service that had originally requested the slot was evicted, the TBS recognizes this and again makes a least recently used decision in order to free another slot.

One last point of note about TBS is that this component sits at the bottom of the user mode TPM architecture in Windows Vista. At the top of the kernel mode is the TPM driver. The connection between these two components is the conduit between user mode and kernel mode operation as far as TPM is concerned.

Configuring and Managing the TPM on a Stand-Alone System

Configuring the TPM consists of two basic tasks. First, you must *enable* the TPM in the BIOS in order for Windows Vista to even recognize that the chip exists in your system. Second, you must *initialize* the TPM. During the initialization process, you set the TPM to *on*, which is the process by which Windows Vista starts the services provided by the TPM, and you *take ownership* of the chip, which is the process of setting the TPM owner password. The Storage Root Key (SRK) is also created and stored in the TPM at this time. First, we will look at what relevant BIOS settings you need to be worried about, and then we'll cover a few ways in which you can initialize the TPM within Windows.

Tools & Traps...

A TPM Term Quick Reference

As with any technical subject, it is impossible to communicate effectively and to understand the topic without first having a common language with which to communicate. The following is a quick reference of the terms commonly used in relation to TPM hardware and the TPM services within Windows Vista:

- **Enable** This refers to the setting in the computer BIOS where you set the TPM chip to be made available to the operating system by the BIOS.

- **Disable** This refers to the setting in the computer BIOS where you set the TPM chip to be made unavailable to the operating system by the BIOS.

- **Endorsement Key** This is an encryption key that the manufacturer has embedded in the TPM chip. It is composed of a private and public key pair, with the private portion of the key never being exported outside of the TPM chip. This private key can be used to hash data in order to verify that the data can be trusted. The

Continued

recipient of the data can use the public portion of the key to decrypt the data, and the recipient knows that only the TPM could have created the hash of the data. This plays an important part in the integrity monitoring, storage, and reporting functions we discussed earlier.

■ **Storage Root Key** The SRK is an encryption key that is created when you take ownership of the TPM, and it is stored in the TPM. When you clear the TPM this is erased, and when you take ownership of an already owned TPM it is replaced by a new SRK. The SRK is used as the master wrapping key. See the "Binding or Wrapping" entry, later in this list.

■ **Take ownership** Taking ownership of the TPM is simply the process of setting an owner password. Interestingly, access to the TPM is protected by only one-factor authentication. No username is required for authenticating to the TPM; only this ownership password. Effectively, anyone who knows the owner password is the TPM owner.

■ **Initialize** The TPM can be in four states: turned off and unowned; turned on and unowned; turned off and owned; or turned on and owned. When you first boot your Windows Vista system the TPM is turned off and unowned. Initializing the TPM is the process by which you turn on the TPM and take ownership of it.

■ **Turn off** Once the TPM is initialized, you may turn off the TPM without losing ownership information. Turning off the TPM simply allows you to stop using Windows Vista TPM services without losing ownership information.

■ **Turn on** If the TPM is currently in an off state you may turn the TPM on. Turning on the TPM provides access to Windows Vista TPM services. However, in order to use these services, you must have taken ownership of the TPM. If the TPM is already owned, turning it on allows the TPM services to function properly; if it is not already owned, you must take ownership of the TPM.

■ **Clear** When you clear the TPM you reset it back to its factory-default state. It will be off and unowned. This function is available within Windows, and is sometimes also available in the computer BIOS.

■ **Binding or wrapping** Encryption keys that the user (or applications and services acting on behalf of the user) creates can be encrypted by the TPM and stored outside of the TPM. This process is called *binding* or *wrapping* the key. Any request for those keys must be made to the TPM, which can unbind/unwrap the key, but

Continued

the private portion of the key is never exposed outside the TPM. The TPM uses the SRK to encrypt user keys.

- **Seal** In addition to simply encrypting keys, the TPM can tie those keys to certain metrics concerning the state of the platform, such as what software is installed. The TPM can decrypt the key only if the state of the platform is the same. When a key is wrapped/bound in this way it is called *sealing the key*.

- **Attestation** A trusted platform must be able to vouch for the accuracy and integrity of data. Attestation is the name for the process of vouching for data.

Configuring BIOS Settings

In order to use the TPM in Windows, as with most onboard hardware devices, you must *enable* it in the BIOS. We have been conducting tests on three different systems that contain a TPM chip, and some contain two BIOS settings that control the TPM. Your system should at least have a BIOS setting allowing you to *enable* or *disable* the TPM. This is a simple on or off function, like a light switch. If you leave this set to the Disable setting, the TPM chip is never made available to Windows. You will not see the chip in Device Manager. This setting must be set to **Enable**.

If you see a second setting concerning the TPM, it probably contains TPM options that can otherwise be controlled within Windows. One of the settings for this second TPM option usually allows you to *clear* the TPM, which erases all of the ownership information and cryptographic keys, including the SRK. It may also allow you to activate and deactivate the TPM. These settings are the equivalent of Turn TPM On and Turn TPM Off in the TPM Management Console. If this set of options is available to you, set the TPM to **Activated** here.

WARNING

When you are configuring the TPM in the BIOS, in tpm.msc, or through scripting, make sure you are careful. For instance, if you used Microsoft BitLocker Drive Encryption to protect a partition and you accidentally clear the TPM, you have just made it very difficult to get your data back. Even if you reinitialize the TPM using the same owner password, it will not contain the same SRK, and it is the SRK that encrypts the keys that were actually used to encrypt your data.

Using the TPM Microsoft Management Console

For anyone familiar with Microsoft Windows computers, the Microsoft Management Console (MMC) should be second nature. It should also be no surprise that Microsoft has built an MMC for configuring and managing the TPM. The consoles continue to be named with the .msc extension, thus invoking the TPM MMC is most handily done by opening the **Run Dialog Box**, typing **tpm.msc**, and then pressing **Enter**.

The TPM MMC has three panes. On the left are just two nodes: the TPM Management on Local Computer node and the Command Management node. When the TPM Management on Local Computer node is selected the center pane displays information specific to the TPM chip in the local computer, and the right pane displays the actions you can perform on the TPM chip, such as clearing the TPM, turning it on or off, and changing ownership of the TPM. Figure 4.4 shows this view of the TPM MMC.

Figure 4.4 The TPM MMC Before Initializing the TPM

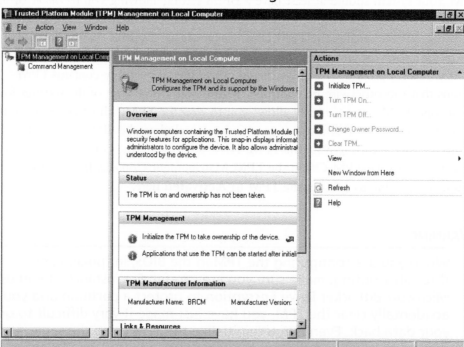

The TPM Management on Local Computer node is very straightforward. You can perform five actions on the TPM from this node, and they are shown in the right pane. You can tell the state of the TPM by seeing which actions are grayed out and inaccessible. In Figure 4.4, it is apparent that the TPM is in a factory-default state because the only action available to us is **Initialize TPM**.

When the Command Management node is selected on the left, the full list of TPM commands is displayed in the center pane, and the command-related actions that may be performed are displayed in the right pane. Figure 4.5 shows this view of the TPM MMC.

Figure 4.5 The TPM MMC Command Management Node

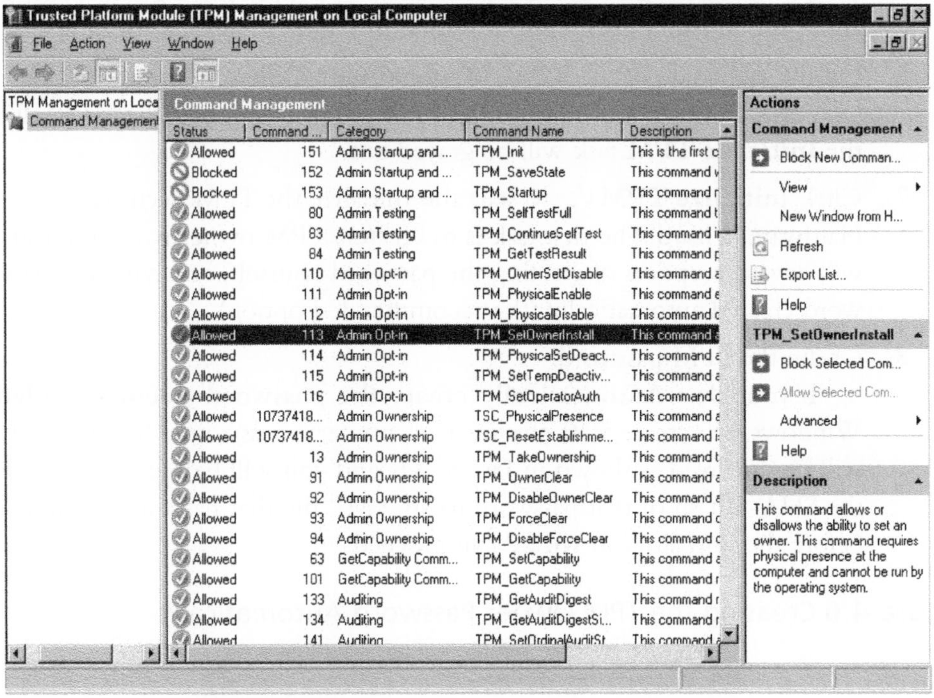

Initializing the TPM

The first thing you need to do, before you can take advantage of any TPM-enabled applications, is to initialize the TPM. During the initialization process, you take ownership of the TPM. This means you create an owner password, and a hash of that password is stored in the TPM itself. This owner authorization hash value can also be stored in an XML file, and the credential is needed to perform many of the other TPM management functions, so you want to make sure that it is backed up somewhere. However, considering that this value is the key to getting into the TPM, it should be protected from disclosure. This means that you should not save it to a Universal Serial Bus (USB) device and then carry that USB device around in the same bag with your laptop.

In order to initialize the TPM, follow these steps:

1. Enter the BIOS and enable the TPM chip.

2. Click **Start | All Programs | Accessories | Run**.

3. Type **tpm.msc** and click **OK**.

4. Click **Continue** to allow the management console to open.

5. The **TPM Management Console** should open, displaying information about the installed TPM chip, as shown in Figure 4.4.

6. On the right side of the **TPM Management Console**, common TPM tasks will be listed, and because the TPM has not been initialized yet, all but the **Initialize TPM** task will be grayed out.

7. Click **Initialize TPM** . . . to start the Initialize the TPM Security Hardware Wizard. The first task is to create a TPM owner password. You will have the option of creating the password yourself, or having the password created automatically (the recommended option).

8. Create the TPM password.

   If you select **Automatically create the password (recommended)**, Windows will create a 40-character, all-numeric password. The password will be displayed as shown in Figure 4.6, and you will be required to save the SHA-1 hash of that password to an XML file that has a .tpm extension before the initialization wizard can proceed.

Figure 4.6 Creating the TPM Owner Password Automatically

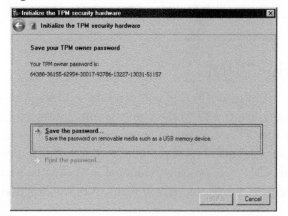

If you choose the **Manually create the password** option, Windows will ask you to enter a password that is a minimum of eight characters. Using the manual password creation option, you are expected to remember the password (or write it down on a sticky note and attach it to your monitor).

9. Click **Initialize**.

10. After a moment, the wizard will finish and display a message notifying you that it has completed successfully, and that TPM-enabled applications may be used.

Whether you have Windows create the password for you or you create it yourself, you can always store the owner authorization value in a TPM file. Figure 4.7 shows a sample TPM file. Notice that the hash of the owner password is contained between the ownerAuth tags.

Figure 4.7 The Contents of a TPM File

```
<?xml version="1.0" encoding="UTF-8"?>

<!--

This page is a backup of Trusted Platform Module (TPM) owner

authorization information. Upon request, use the authorization information
to prove ownership of the computer's TPM.



IMPORTANT: Please keep this file in a secure location away from your
computer's local hard drive.

-->

<tpmOwnerData version="1.0" softwareAuthor="Microsoft Windows [Version
6.0.6000]" creationDate="2006-12-25T16:56:45-05:00"
creationUser="SYNGRESS\mshepherd" machineName="SYNGRESS">

        <tpmInfo manufacturerId="1112687437"/>

        <ownerAuth>hVOA6LhVpQ8FOZsrKuxyZVgNy5U=</ownerAuth>

</tpmOwnerData>
```

Turning the TPM On

You may turn on the TPM only if it is already in the off state, but you can complete the task regardless of whether you have the password. The following steps lead you through turning the TPM on when you have the password:

1. Click **Start | All Programs | Accessories | Run**.

2. Type **tpm.msc** and click **OK**.

3. Click **Continue** to allow the management console to open.

4. In the **TPM Management Console**, make sure you have the **TPM Management on Local Computer** node selected, and then click **Turn TPM On** in the right pane.

5. When the first screen of the wizard is displayed, select **I have a backup file with the TPM owner password** if you have a TPM file with the password in it, or **I want to type the TPM owner password** if you want to type it in manually.

6. If you opted to type the password manually, the next screen of the wizard requires you to type in the password, and then you can click **Turn TPM On**. If you opted to load the password from a backup file, the next screen will allow you to type or browse to the location of the file, and then you can click **Turn TPM On**.

7. The wizard will turn off the TPM, and then close.

Use these steps in order to turn on the TPM if you have lost the password:

1. Click **Start | All Programs | Accessories | Run**.

2. Type **tpm.msc** and click **OK**.

3. Click **Continue** to allow the management console to open.

4. In the **TPM Management Console**, make sure you have the **TPM Management on Local Computer** node selected, and then click **Turn TPM On** in the right pane.

5. The first screen of the wizard asks you to select whether you have the password in a TPM file, whether you will type it in manually, or whether you do not have the password at all. Select **I do not have the TPM password**.

6. The next screen of the wizard provides some basic instructions, as shown in Figure 4.8. You will need to click the **Restart** button in order to proceed.

Figure 4.8 Turning On the TPM: Final Instructions from the TPM Management Wizard

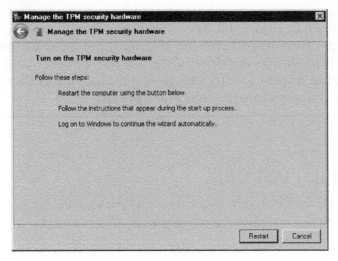

7. When the machine restarts, right after the BIOS loads and before the Windows boot manager has control of the machine, you should see a message telling you that a request to change the TPM configuration has been received (see Figure 4.9). Select **MODIFY** and then press **Enter** to allow the machine to turn the TPM on, and the machine will finish booting.

Figure 4.9 The Computer BIOS Confirmation Message

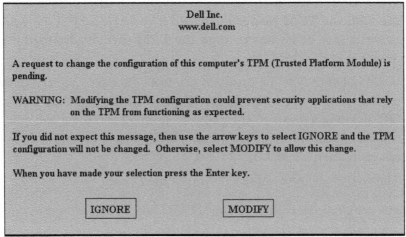

NOTE

The message you see may be different from the one described in step 7 and shown in Figure 4.8. The BIOS produces this message for the specific platform upon receiving the input provided by the wizard we just ran from within Windows Vista. So, don't expect your Lenovo ThinkPad to display exactly the same message, but it should provide basically the same information and options.

 ## Turning the TPM Off

You may turn off the TPM only if it is already in the on state, but just like turning the TPM on, you can complete the task regardless of whether you have the password. The following steps lead you through turning the TPM off when you have the password:

1. Click **Start | All Programs | Accessories | Run**.

2. Type **tpm.msc** and click **OK**.

3. Click **Continue** to allow the management console to open.

4. In the **TPM Management Console**, make sure you have the **TPM Management on Local Computer** node selected, and then click **Turn TPM Off** in the right pane.

5. When the first screen of the wizard is displayed, select **I have a backup file with the TPM owner password** if you have a TPM file with the password in it, or **I want to type the TPM owner password** if you want to type it in manually.

6. If you opted to type the password manually, the next screen of the wizard requires you to type in the password, and then you can click **Turn TPM Off**. If you opted to load the password from a backup file, the next screen will allow you to type or browse to the location of the file, and then you can click **Turn TPM Off**.

7. The wizard will turn off the TPM, and then close.

Follow these steps in order to turn off the TPM if you have lost the password:

1. Click **Start | All Programs | Accessories | Run**.

2. Type **tpm.msc** and click **OK**.

3. Click **Continue** to allow the management console to open.

4. In the **TPM Management Console**, make sure you have the **TPM Management on Local Computer** node selected, and then click **Turn TPM Off** in the right pane.

5. The first screen of the wizard asks you to select whether you have the password in a TPM file, whether you will type it in manually, or whether you do not have the password at all. Select **I do not have the TPM password**.

6. The next screen of the wizard provides some basic instructions, as shown in Figure 4.10. You will need to click the **Restart** button in order to proceed.

Figure 4.10 Turning Off the TPM: Final Instructions from the TPM Management Wizard

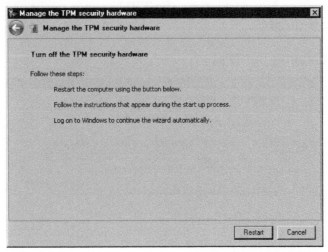

7. When the machine restarts, right after the BIOS loads and before the Windows boot manager has control of the machine, you should see a message telling you that a request to change the TPM configuration has been received (see Figure 4.9 again, and read the note just below the graphic). Select **MODIFY** and then press **Enter** to allow the machine to turn the TPM on, and the machine will finish booting.

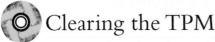 Clearing the TPM

You may clear the TPM only if it has already been initialized (enabled and an owner has been set), but as with the preceding two tasks, you can clear the TPM regardless of whether you have the password. The following steps lead you through clearing the TPM when you have the password:

1. Click **Start | All Programs | Accessories | Run**.

2. Type **tpm.msc** and click **OK**.

3. Click **Continue** to allow the management console to open.

4. In the **TPM Management Console**, make sure you have the **TPM Management on Local Computer** node selected, and then click **Clear TPM** in the right pane.

5. When the first screen of the wizard is displayed, you will be presented with a justifiably menacing warning message, and options with regard to the TPM owner credentials (see Figure 4.11). Select **I have a backup file with the TPM owner password** if you have a TPM file with the password in it, or **I want to type the TPM owner password** if you want to type it in manually.

Figure 4.11 Clearing the TPM

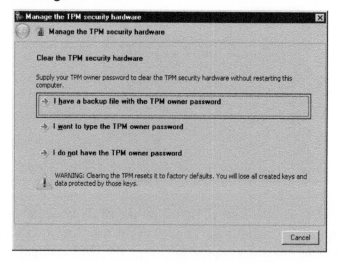

WARNING

Please take this warning seriously. If you do not have a backup of the keys created or protected by the TPM, any data encrypted with those keys is gone forever!

6. If you opted to type the password manually, the next screen of the wizard requires you to type in the password, and then you can click **Clear TPM**. If you opted to load the password from a backup file, the next screen will allow you to type or browse to the location of the file, and then you can click **Clear TPM**.

7. The wizard will clear the TPM, and then close.

Follow these steps in order to clear the TPM if you have lost the password:

1. Click **Start | All Programs | Accessories | Run**.

2. Type **tpm.msc** and click **OK**.

3. Click **Continue** to allow the management console to open.

4. In the **TPM Management Console**, make sure you have the **TPM Management on Local Computer** node selected, and then click **Clear TPM** in the right pane.

5. The first screen of the wizard asks you to select whether you have the password in a TPM file, whether you will type it in manually, or whether you do not have the password at all. Select **I do not have the TPM password**.

6. The next screen of the wizard provides some basic instructions. You will need to click the **Restart** button in order to proceed.

7. When the machine restarts, right after the BIOS loads and before the Windows boot manager has control of the machine, you should see a message telling you that a request to change the TPM configuration has been received (see Figure 4.9). If you allow the machine to make the change, the TPM will be cleared and the machine will finish booting.

For each of the preceding tasks, you were allowed to perform the task without knowing the owner password. This may seem like a security flaw, but it is not. In order to perform these commands, the following must be true:

■ The machine booted successfully, meaning that initial integrity measurements were taken and found to be consistent.

■ If the machine uses any secure startup mechanism such as that which comes with BitLocker Drive Encryption, the system was able to verify the integrity of the boot volume, and the TPM successfully unsealed the key used to seal the volume.

- The person logging on was required to present logon credentials to Windows Vista, and these credentials were valid.

- The user that logged on had the appropriate permissions to run the TPM MMC.

- The user was physically present at the system.

Based on these prerequisites, Windows Vista is trusting that it is safe to allow you to turn the TPM on or off or to clear it, even though you do not have the TPM owner credentials. In order for an attacker to use this to his advantage, he would have already had to steal your computer as well as your logon credentials. On top of that, if your computer was protected by a secure startup mechanism, he may have had to steal your PIN, USB storage device, or smart card as well. In addition, the attacker would be able to do nothing more than turn the TPM on, which would basically have no effect on you; turn it off, which would disable any TPM-dependent applications (you could remedy this easily by turning the TPM back on, and these applications would again function properly); or clear the TPM, resulting in a loss of the SRK which is required to access any data that was encrypted using the TPM.

Clearing the TPM has to be considered the worst-case scenario, given that it could lead to a loss of data. It does not provide the attacker with access to your data, though; he already has it by virtue of the fact that he is logged on to Windows. Furthermore, if you (or your organization, if we are discussing a scenario where this is part of an enterprise deployment) are using best practices procedures, you should have the BitLocker Drive Encryption keys backed up to a secure location stored away from the computer, and you can still perform emergency recovery procedures to get the data back.

Also, we should note here that in most cases, the system BIOS provides these functions. So, lacking the protections we mentioned in the five bullets shown earlier, an attacker can just access the BIOS and perform any of these functions much more easily than Windows is allowing him to. Even if you protect your BIOS with a password, this should be considered a much easier attack target than getting into Windows Vista and using the TPM MMC to perform these functions.

These three functions are executed using the *SetPhysicalPresenceRequest* method of the *Win32_Tpm* class, which is described in Table 4.3, later in this chapter. This means that the operation cannot be processed unless the user is present at the platform and authorizes the operation to complete. So, allowing you to turn the TPM on or off without the owner authorization value is not a security flaw. As we shall see in the next section, you are required to provide the owner authorization information in order to change the owner password. This function differs from the previous in that it:

- Provides the attacker with full control of the TPM
- Cannot be performed from outside the OS

Changing the Owner Password

Follow these steps to change the owner password:

1. Click **Start | All Programs | Accessories | Run**.
2. Type **tpm.msc** and click **OK**.
3. Click **Continue** to allow the management console to open.
4. The **TPM Management Console** should open, displaying information about the installed TPM chip, as shown in Figure 4.12.

Figure 4.12 The TPM MMC with an Owner Set and the TPM Turned On

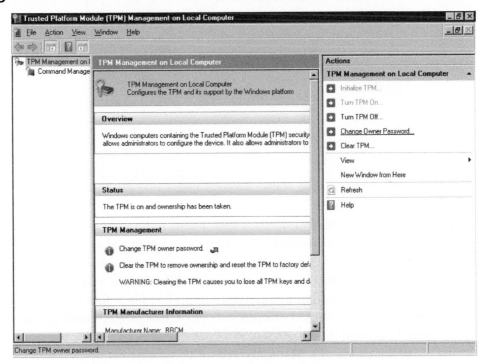

5. In the **TPM Management Console**, make sure you have the **TPM Management on Local Computer** node selected, and then click **Change Owner Password** in the right pane.

6. When the first screen of the wizard is displayed, select **I have a backup file with the TPM owner password** if you have a TPM file with the password in it, or **I want to type the TPM owner password** if you want to type it in manually.

7. If you opted to type the password manually, the next screen of the wizard requires you to type in the password, and then you can click **Create New Password**. If you opted to load the password from a backup file, the next screen will allow you to type or browse to the location of the file (see Figure 4.13), and then you can click **Create New Password**.

Figure 4.13 Select the Backup File with the TPM Owner Authorization

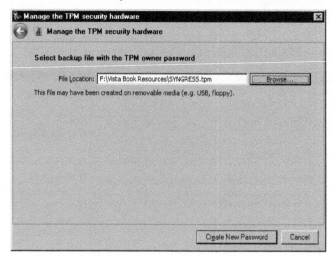

8. Create the TPM password.

    If you select **Automatically create the password (recommended)**, Windows will create a new, 40-character, all-numeric password. The password will be displayed as shown in Figure 4.2, and you will be required to save the SHA-1 hash of that password to a TPM file before the Change Owner Password Wizard can proceed. The **Change Password** button is grayed out until the file is saved.

    If you choose the **Manually create the password** option, Windows will ask you to enter a password that is a minimum of eight characters. Using the manual password creation option, you are expected to remember the password, but you can save the authorization value (a hash of that password) to a TPM file if you wish.

9. Once the new owner authorization information has been saved, you can click the **Change Password** button to finish the process (see Figure 4.14).

Figure 4.14 Finishing the Process of Changing the Owner Password Using an Automatically Created Password

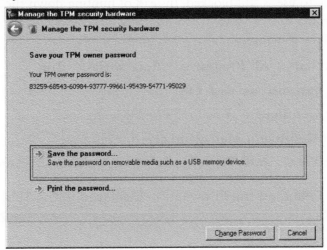

 Blocking and Allowing Commands

Blocking and allowing commands allows granular control over the secure operation of the TPM within your Windows Vista system. Currently, 125 commands are listed in the TPM MMC, and they are organized into 26 categories of functionality. Each is represented by an ordinal value, which is the value you will pass to the block and unblock functions.

There are three possible lists of blocked commands: the default list provided with Windows Vista; a list maintained on the local machine and managed by local administrators; and the list of commands controlled by Group Policy Objects (GPOs). If a TPM command exists in any of the lists, it will be blocked by the entity that controls command execution, the TBS. The TBS checks all three lists before passing the attempted command down to the TPM driver for processing. If the command exists in one of the lists, the TBS prevents the execution and returns an error to the service or application that sent the command.

The default list is evidenced by the fact that on a fresh Windows Vista install, some commands are already listed as blocked in the TPM MMC. In Figure 4.4, you can see that commands 152 (*TPM_SaveState*) and 153 (*TPM_Startup*) are blocked, but no administration of the command blocking list has occurred yet. Those are blocked by default.

There is more than meets the eye when it comes to the Command Management node in the TPM MMC. When you are managing the TPM on a system and you have these three lists to worry about, it can be difficult to figure out why a command is being blocked or allowed. Perhaps you've set the default block list to ignore (not recommended, by the way), but one command that you need to be able to use is still blocked. Instead of hunting down the lists in various places, you can use the TPM MMC to display which block list a command is on. To do that, follow these steps:

1. Click **Start | All Programs | Accessories | Run**.

2. Type **tpm.msc** and click **OK**.

3. Click **Continue** to allow the TPM MMC to open.

4. Select **Command Management** in the left pane.

5. Click **View | Add/Remove Columns**, as shown in Figure 4.15.

Figure 4.15 Changing the Information Displayed in the TPM MMC

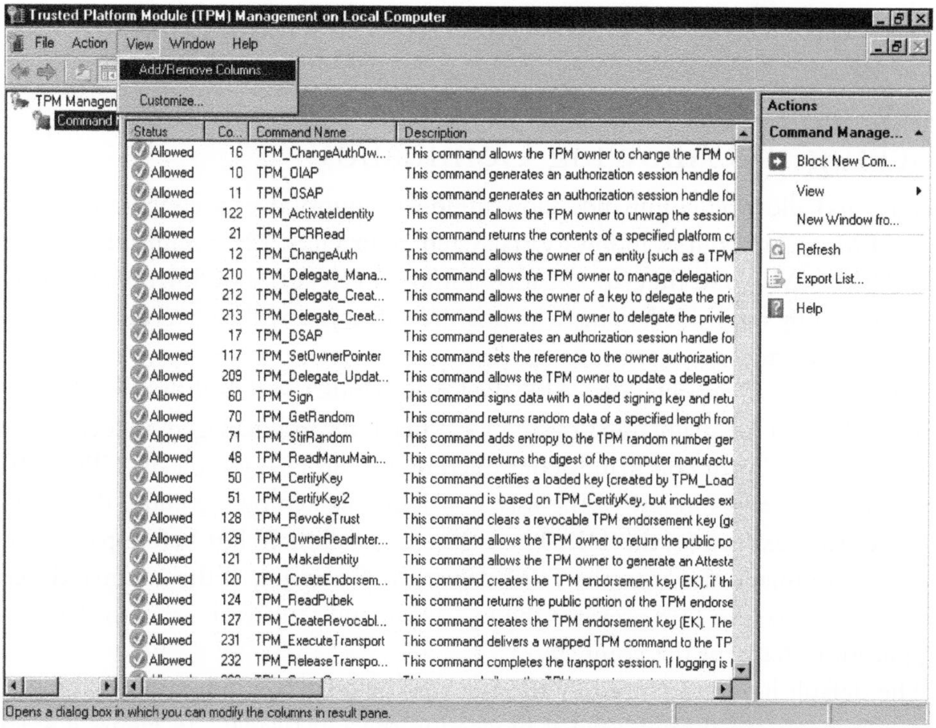

6. Use the **Add/Remove Columns** dialog box to add the On Default Block List, On Group Policy Block List, and On Local Block List columns, and remove any unwanted columns (here we have removed Category and Description), as shown in Figure 4.16.

Figure 4.16 The Add/Remove Columns Dialog Box for the Command Management Node

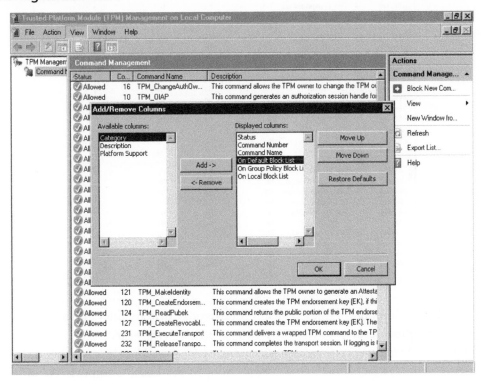

7. Click **OK** and the Command Management node will appear as it does in Figure 4.17.

Now that we can actually see what commands are on which lists, let's take a look at how you manage them. Commands that are on the default block list cannot be allowed through the TPM MMC unless you set the Local Computer Policy to ignore the default list. We would caution at this point that in a stand-alone system, the default block list should always be used. The commands are on the default list because they are either deprecated or can compromise privacy.

Figure 4.17 The TPM MMC Command Management Node Displaying the Block List Columns

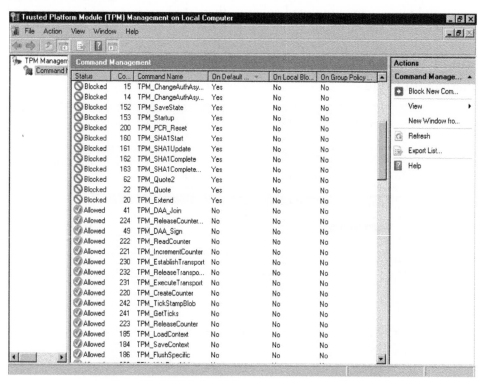

The Local Computer Policy contains four settings that are relevant to the TPM. You can find these settings in the *Local Computer Policy\Computer Configuration\Administrative Templates\System\Trusted Platform Module Services* node, and the settings are described in Table 4.2. You can open the Local Computer Policy using the following steps:

1. Click **Start | All Programs | Accessories | Run**.

2. Type **gpedit.msc** and click **OK**.

3. Click **Continue** to allow the management console to open.

Table 4.2 TPM Group Policy Settings for Stand-Alone Systems

Setting Name	Description	Possible Configurations	Result
Turn on TPM backup to Active Directory Domain Services	This setting controls whether the hash of the TPM owner password is backed up to Active Directory.	Not Configured Disabled Enabled	TPM owner credential is not backed up to Active Directory. TPM owner information is silently backed up to Active Directory when the owner credential is changed.
		Enabled – Require backup to Active Directory Domain Services	TPM owner information is silently backed up to Active Directory when the owner credential is changed; if the backup fails, the owner credential is not changed in the TPM.
Configure the list of blocked TPM commands	This is the Group Policy block list. You may enable it and add blocked commands.	Not Configured Disabled Enabled	The Group Policy block list is not used. The Group Policy block list is used, and any commands added to the list using the **Show**	**Add** function of this setting will be blocked.
Ignore the default list of blocked TPM commands	Controls whether the default list of blocked TPM commands is used.	Not Configured Disabled Enabled	The default list is used to block TPM commands. The default list is ignored, and commands on this list are allowed.
Ignore the local list of blocked TPM commands	Controls whether the local list of blocked TPM commands is used.	Not Configured Disabled Enabled	The local list is used to block TPM commands. The local list is ignored, and commands on this list are allowed.

Because we are managing the TPM on a stand-alone system, we think the best practice for managing the TPM is to leave the default block list in place, and to use the local list to add other commands we may want to block. There is no reason to add another layer of confusion to the scenario by utilizing both the Group Policy list and the local list to set our own blocked commands. Also, because we are managing a stand-alone system, we do not have an Active Directory infrastructure to which we can back up the owner authorization credentials. So, basically the best method for managing the TPM is to leave all the Local Computer Policy settings in their default states, and to utilize only the TPM MMC to block and allow commands. Here is the easiest method for blocking/allowing commands within the MMC (these directions assume you already have the TPM MMC opened to the Command Management node):

1. Select the command you want to block/allow, as shown in Figure 4.18.

Figure 4.18 The TPM MMC Command Management Node before Blocking a Command

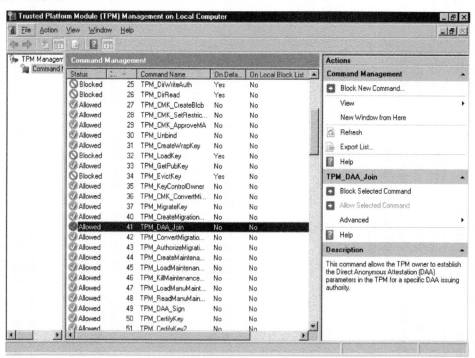

2. If the command is currently blocked and you want to allow it, click **Allow Selected Command**. If the command is currently allowed and you want to block it, click **Block Selected Command**.

3. If you blocked the command, the MMC will add the command to the local block list. If you allowed the command, the MMC will remove the command from the local block list. The new status will immediately be reflected in the MMC, as shown in Figure 4.19 (make note of the Status and On Local Block List columns for command 41).

NOTE

You'll notice that in Figure 4.19, the command status displays as Blocked, but the icon shown is still the Allowed icon. If you click **Refresh** in the right pane, the icon is updated. Consider this a very minor bug in this prerelease of Windows Vista.

Figure 4.19 The TPM MMC Command Management Node after Blocking a Command

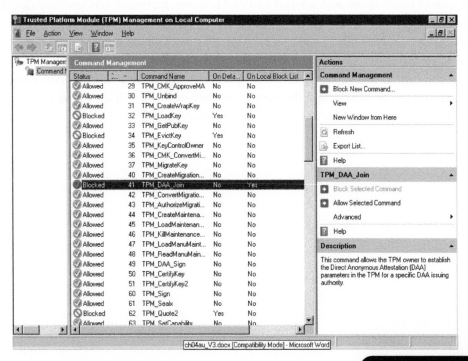

> **NOTE**
>
> If you enjoy doing things the hard way and need a way to really screw something up on your machine, you should know that the default block list, Group Policy block list, and local block list are stored in the Registry. You could avoid the ease of use the TPM MMC provides and edit the Registry, and risk deleting some critical Registry key in the process. You can find the default block list in *HKEY_LOCAL_ MACHINE\Software\Microsoft\Tpm\BlockedCommands\List*. You can find the local block list at *HKEY_LOCAL_MACHINE\Software\ SYSTEM\ControlSet001\SharedAccess\Parameters\Tpm\ BlockedCommands\List*. The Group Policy block list is stored in *HKEY_ LOCAL_MACHINE\Software\Policies\Microsoft\Tpm\BlockedCommands\ List*.

You have probably noticed that a Block New Command function is provided in the right pane as well. This does not provide the same functionality as the Block Selected Command function we just covered, and in fact, you cannot use it to block any of the commands listed in the TPM MMC at this point. All TPM commands agreed upon by the TCG at the time Vista is released are listed in the MMC, and you should block them as described earlier. However, hardware vendors may decide to implement commands that are not a part of the TPM specification, or the TCG may add new commands to the specification. Microsoft implemented the Block New Command function to provide coverage for both of these situations. In order to test the function, just pass it a number that does not correspond to a command that appears in the MMC, and the new command number will appear in the list. In Figure 4.20, you can see that we have blocked command 270.

Figure 4.20 Blocking New TPM Commands

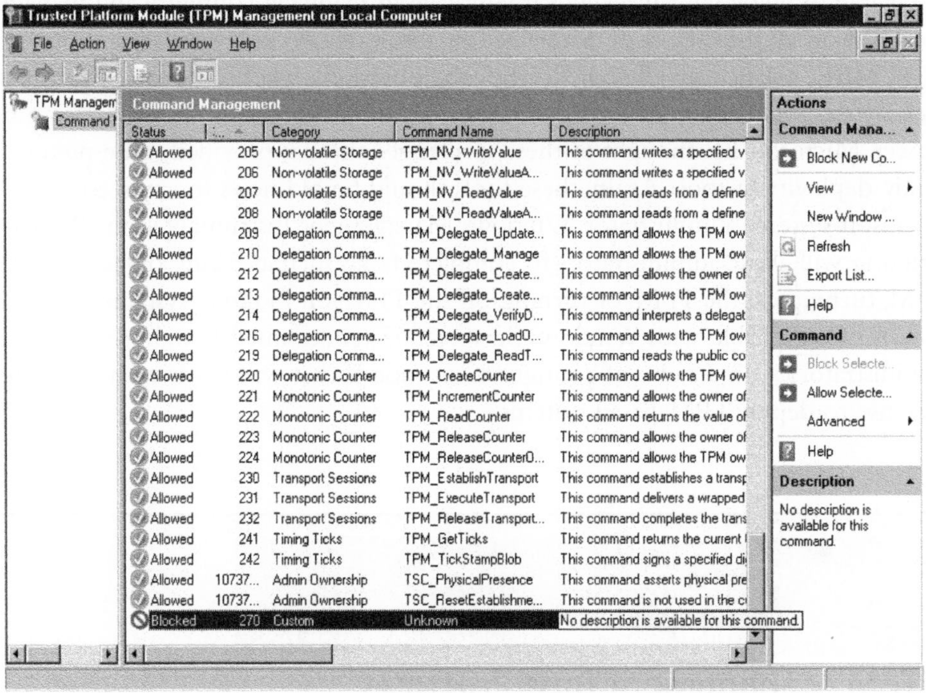

Configuring and Managing the TPM in an Enterprise Environment

The TPM MMC provides a familiar interface for Windows system administrators to manage the TPM on a local machine. However, you cannot use the MMC to perform remote TPM management, and it does not allow for the batch processing of management tasks across multiple machines at once. In the enterprise environment, you're going to need to deploy numerous systems all at once instead of just one. Even in the enterprise where you will not be utilizing the TPM and the services Microsoft has built on it, it is still a good idea to lock users out of being able to manage the TPM locally. Otherwise, your help desk phones are likely to start ringing with calls from users who read about the cool new TPM features somewhere, tried to enable BitLocker Drive Encryption themselves, and in the end lost all the data on their hard drives when they cleared the TPM. Regardless of whether you plan to use the TPM right away, it is now a resource in your organization that needs to be managed.

This presents a whole new slew of challenges, and you know you are not going to be able to enjoy your weekends if you have to manually configure and manage the TPM on all these devices manually. You absolutely do not want to be using the TPM MMC to manage all your devices, and you don't want to be saving the hash of each owner password to one USB key which you'll then toss into your bottom desk drawer. Microsoft has thought of these challenges and has provided some pretty handy deployment tools. Again, these tools should be old news to any seasoned Microsoft systems administrator. Windows Management Instrumentation (WMI) scripting will allow administrators to complete tasks, such as taking ownership of the TPM, turning on the TPM, or turning off the TPM, on multiple systems at the same time. GPOs available with Windows Server 2007 (codenamed Longhorn) provide administrators with a cadre of configuration options that will work with the scripts they use to deploy TPM-based systems.

Tools & Traps...

TPM Management Best Practices

You should use the following best practices to help ensure a secure and manageable deployment of TPM hardware and Windows Vista services within your enterprise:

- First, you need to ensure that you are purchasing systems with TPM chips that comply with the TCG TPM version 1.2 specification.

- Second, make sure that any applications you plan to use comply with version 1.2 of the TCG TSS specification, and have been developed to work with TBS.

- Use WMI scripts to initialize the TPM on multiple systems, if possible, before you deploy hardware to users.

- Use WMI scripts to take ownership of the TPM if you need to do it remotely, or if you are performing the task on multiple systems.

- Store TPM-related data in Active Directory.

- Use unique owner passwords on all systems in the enterprise.

- Never give TPM owner passwords or authorization information to system users.

- If system users need to perform tasks that require TPM owner credentials, it is best to delegate permissions to the users to perform

Continued

---

the tasks. This will depend on whether the software supports delegation of duties.

- Maintain the list of blocked TPM commands using restrictive policies.

- Do not store the owner password or authorization information on local system media.

Using GPOs and Active Directory

The next version of Windows Server, codenamed "Longhorn," will include Active Directory schema extensions that support both TPM management and BitLocker Drive Encryption management. (The latter is covered in more detail in Chapter 5). The main thing you need Active Directory to do for you is provide a place to store the hashes of TPM owner passwords so that each TPM may have a unique owner password, and you can store the hashes in a central, secure location. The same goes for the BitLocker Drive Encryption keys. You can store those keys in Active Directory in the event you need to enact emergency recovery procedures. The Active Directory attribute where the TPM owner authorization value is stored is *ms-TPM-OwnerInformation*. Keep this in mind for when you need to run a script, and you need to have the computer's owner authorization information to call the *Win32_Tpm* method you want.

Preparing Your Pre-Longhorn Domain Controllers

These schema extensions come with Windows Server 2007 by default, but if you are running a domain that utilizes Windows Server 2003 and/or Windows 2000 Server domain controllers, you do not have the necessary objects and attributes in Active Directory to take advantage of these central management and key storage features. In order to extend your Active Directory schema, all of your domain controllers must be running Windows Server 2003 Service Pack (SP) 1 or later because the Active Directory schema version in this release contains the ability to set certain attributes in Active Directory as confidential, which protects them from being read by unauthorized personnel. The TPM and BitLocker Drive Encryption keys should be stored in confidential attributes for obvious reasons.

There is a version of the Microsoft schema preparation utility, adprep, which comes on the Windows Vista and Windows Server 2007 DVDs in *sources\adprep*. This is not a new utility, and anyone who has been through the Active Directory upgrade process should be familiar with it. However, the official word from Microsoft is that this should not be used. This folder is included for informational purposes only, to demonstrate what schema changes will take place. The scripts did work for us on a Windows Server 2003 for Small Business Server SP1 system, but because you are not supposed to be using them at this time, you'll have to run them at your own risk. Once Windows Server 2007 is actually released, official support for using these is sure to come with it.

It is suggested that you make sure you use the latest version of adprep anytime you perform an upgrade of Active Directory. You'll need to be able to access the entire adprep folder (adprep needs those .ldf files too) from your Windows Server 2003 SP1 flexible single master operations (FSMO) server in order to perform the required schema upgrade. When the folder is available, execute the following command from a command prompt (the location of the files is assumed to be *C:\adprep* in the following example):

```
C:\adprep>adprep /forestPrep
```

After a lengthy warning from the utility, if you choose to continue you should see something such as the following:

```
Opened Connection to DC1
SSPI Bind Succeeded
Current Schema Version is 30
Upgrading schema to version 39
Connecting to "DC1"
Logging in as current user using SSPI
Importing directory from file "C:\WINDOWS\system32\sch31.ldf"
Loading entries . . . . . . . . . . . . . . . . . . . . . . . . .
139 entries modified successfully.

The command has completed successfully
Connecting to "DC1"
Logging in as current user using SSPI
Importing directory from file "C:\WINDOWS\system32\sch32.ldf"
Loading entries . . . . . . . . . . . . . . . . . . . . . . . . .
18 entries modified successfully.

The command has completed successfully
Connecting to "DC1"
Logging in as current user using SSPI
```

```
Importing directory from file "C:\WINDOWS\system32\sch33.ldf"
Loading entries . . . . . . . . . . . . . . . . . . . .
17 entries modified successfully.
```

This continues until you've reached version 39 of the schema. After this, just run:

```
C:\adprep>adprep /domainPrep
```

At this point, you will have an Active Directory schema capable of accommodating the new features of Windows Vista. The downside is that you will not have the proper administrative templates installed to see the corresponding Group Policy settings. However, you can add the following text to your System administrative template, stored in *%systemroot%\SYSVOL\Policies\<varies>\Adm\system.adm*, in the section where the policy categories are defined, in order to have the same template available as Windows Server 2007 users will have:

```
CATEGORY !!TrustedPlatformModuleServices
      #if version >= 4
            EXPLAIN !!TrustedPlatformModuleServices_Help
      #endif
      POLICY !!ActiveDirectoryBackup
            #if version >= 4
                   SUPPORTED !!SUPPORTED_WindowsVista
            #endif
            EXPLAIN !!ActiveDirectoryBackup_Help
            KEYNAME "Software\Policies\Microsoft\TPM"
            VALUENAME "ActiveDirectoryBackup"
            VALUEON NUMERIC 1
            VALUEOFF NUMERIC 0
            PART !!RequireActiveDirectoryBackup_Name CHECKBOX
                  VALUENAME "RequireActiveDirectoryBackup"
                  DEFCHECKED
                  VALUEON NUMERIC 1
                  VALUEOFF NUMERIC 0
            END PART
      END POLICY
      POLICY !!BlockedCommandsList
            #if version >= 4
                   SUPPORTED !!SUPPORTED_WindowsVista
            #endif
```

```
            EXPLAIN !!BlockedCommandsList_Help
            KEYNAME "SOFTWARE\Policies\Microsoft\Tpm\BlockedCommands"
            VALUENAME "Enabled"
            VALUEON NUMERIC 1
            VALUEOFF NUMERIC 0
            PART !!BlockedCommandsList_Ordinals2 LISTBOX
                 KEYNAME
"SOFTWARE\Policies\Microsoft\Tpm\BlockedCommands\List"
               END PART
       END POLICY
       POLICY !!IgnoreDefaultList
            #if version >= 4
                 SUPPORTED !!SUPPORTED_WindowsVista
            #endif
            EXPLAIN !!IgnoreDefaultList_Help
            KEYNAME "Software\Policies\Microsoft\TPM\BlockedCommands"
            VALUENAME "IgnoreDefaultList"
            VALUEON NUMERIC 1
            VALUEOFF NUMERIC 0
       END POLICY
       POLICY !!IgnoreLocalList
            #if version >= 4
                 SUPPORTED !!SUPPORTED_WindowsVista
            #endif
            EXPLAIN !!IgnoreLocalList_Help
            KEYNAME "Software\Policies\Microsoft\TPM\BlockedCommands"
            VALUENAME "IgnoreLocalList"
            VALUEON NUMERIC 1
            VALUEOFF NUMERIC 0
       END POLICY
END CATEGORY ; TrustedPlatformModuleServices
```

In the *[strings]* section at the bottom of the file, include the following text:

```
ActiveDirectoryBackup_Help="This policy setting allows you to manage the
Active Directory Domain Services (AD DS) backup of Trusted Platform Module
(TPM) owner information. \n\nTPM owner information includes a cryptographic
hash of the TPM owner password. Certain TPM commands can only be run by the
TPM owner. This hash authorizes the TPM to run these commands. \n\nIf you
enable this policy setting, TPM owner information will be automatically and
silently backed up to AD DS when you use Windows to set or change a TPM
owner password. \n\nIf you select the option to "Require TPM backup to AD
```

DS", a TPM owner password cannot be set or changed unless the computer is connected to the domain and the AD DS backup succeeds. This option is selected by default to help ensure that TPM owner information is available. Otherwise, AD DS backup is attempted but network or other backup failures do not impact TPM management. Backup is not automatically retried and the TPM owner information may not have been stored in AD DS during BitLocker setup. \n\nIf you disable or do not configure this policy setting, TPM owner information will not be backed up to AD DS. \n\nNote: You must first set up appropriate schema extensions and access control settings on the domain before AD DS backup can succeed. Consult online documentation for more information about setting up Active Directory Domain Services for TPM. \n\nNote: The TPM cannot be used to provide enhanced security features for BitLocker Drive Encryption and other applications without first setting an owner. To take ownership of the TPM with an owner password, run "tpm.msc" and select the action to "Initialize TPM". \n\nNote: If the TPM owner information is lost or is not available, limited TPM management is possible by running "tpm.msc" on the local computer."

BlockedCommandsList_Help="This policy setting allows you to manage the Group Policy list of Trusted Platform Module (TPM) commands blocked by Windows. \n\nIf you enable this policy setting, Windows will block the specified commands from being sent to the TPM on the computer. TPM commands are referenced by a command number. For example, command number 129 is TPM_OwnerReadInternalPub, and command number 170 is TPM_FieldUpgrade. To find the command number associated with each TPM command, run "tpm.msc" and navigate to the "Command Management" section. \n\nIf you disable or do not configure this policy setting, only those TPM commands specified through the default or local lists may be blocked by Windows. The default list of blocked TPM commands is pre-configured by Windows. You can view the default list by running "tpm.msc", navigating to the "Command Management" section, and making visible the "On Default Block List" column. The local list of blocked TPM commands is configured outside of Group Policy by running "tpm.msc" or through scripting against the Win32_Tpm interface. See related policy settings to enforce or ignore the default and local lists of blocked TPM commands."

ActiveDirectoryBackup="Turn on TPM backup to Active Directory Domain Services"

BlockedCommandsList_Name="Configure the list of blocked TPM commands"

IgnoreDefaultList_Help="This policy setting allows you to enforce or ignore the computer's default list of blocked Trusted Platform Module (TPM) commands. \n\nIf you enable this policy setting, Windows will ignore the computer's default list of blocked TPM commands and will only block those TPM commands specified by Group Policy or the local list. \n\nThe default list of blocked TPM commands is pre-configured by Windows. You can view the default list by running "tpm.msc", navigating to the "Command Management" section, and making visible the "On Default Block List" column. The local list of blocked TPM commands is configured outside of Group Policy by running "tpm.msc" or through scripting against the Win32_Tpm interface. See the related policy setting to configure the Group Policy list of blocked TPM

commands. \n\nIf you disable or do not configure this policy setting, Windows
will block the TPM commands in the default list, in addition to commands in
the Group Policy and local lists of blocked TPM commands."

IgnoreDefaultList="Ignore the default list of blocked TPM commands"

IgnoreLocalList_Help="This policy setting allows you to enforce or ignore
the computer's local list of blocked Trusted Platform Module (TPM) commands.
\n\nIf you enable this policy setting, Windows will ignore the computer's
local list of blocked TPM commands and will only block those TPM commands
specified by Group Policy or the default list. \n\nThe local list of blocked
TPM commands is configured outside of Group Policy by running "tpm.msc" or
through scripting against the Win32_Tpm interface. The default list of
blocked TPM commands is pre-configured by Windows. See the related policy
setting to configure the Group Policy list of blocked TPM commands. \n\nIf
you disable or do not configure this policy setting, Windows will block the
TPM commands found in the local list, in addition to commands in the Group
Policy and default lists of blocked TPM commands."

IgnoreLocalList="Ignore the local list of blocked TPM commands"

TrustedPlatformModuleServices="Trusted Platform Module Services"

TrustedPlatformModuleServices_Help="The Trusted Platform Module is a
microchip that supports trusted computing services in Windows Vista. These
settings control the functioning of the device."

BlockedCommandsList="Configure the list of blocked TPM commands"

BlockedCommandsList_Ordinals2="The list of blocked TPM commands:"

RequireActiveDirectoryBackup_Name="Require TPM backup to AD DS"

SUPPORTED_WindowsVista="At least Microsoft Windows Vista"

Now your Windows Server 2003 SP1 or later domain controller will provide
the same functionality as a Windows Server 2007 domain controller does with
regard to TPM management. It should be noted that you can use the Group Policy
Object Editor (GPOE) or Group Policy Management Console (GPMC) that comes
with Windows Vista and Windows Server codenamed "Longhorn" to manage your
Windows Server 2003 environment.

Preparing Your Longhorn Domain Controllers

The process of preparing your Windows Server 2007 domain controllers in an all-
Longhorn environment is much simpler. There is no need to upgrade the Active
Directory schema. The only things missing from these domain controllers are the
administrative templates that display the relevant Group Policy settings in the Group
Policy Management MMC. Actually, they're not missing entirely. They are installed in
the *%systemroot%\PolicyDefinitions* folder on both Windows Vista and Windows
Server 2007 systems where the Local Computer Policy reads them from.

All we need to do is copy them to the central store which is part of *SYSVOL* so that they are replicated to all domain controllers and are available for domain GPOs. We need to make sure we copy both the administrative templates and the language-specific files. For English, execute the following commands from a command prompt:

```
C:\>xcopy C:\WINDOWS\PolicyDefinitions\*
C:\WINDOWS\SYSVOL\domain\policies\PolicyDefinitions\

C:\>xcopy C:\WINDOWS\PolicyDefinitions\EN-US\*
C:\WINDOWS\SYSVOL\domain\policies\PolicyDefinitions\EN-US\
```

When the files have been copied, you may need to wait for replication to distribute this change throughout your network. However, on the domain controller on which you just performed the copy, you can start using the Group Policy Object Editor to create a GPO right away.

Blocking Commands

In order to block TPM commands, you don't actually need to meet the requirements set forth in the section on preparing Windows Server 2003 domain controllers. The GPO used to block commands simply pushes changes to the Registry on domain computers. The schema upgrades we covered are necessary only for storing the TPM owner authorization hash and other cryptographic keys related to the TPM (such as BitLocker Drive Encryption keys) in Active Directory. Technically, you could make the changes to your administrative template that were shown on any domain controller in an enterprise running Active Directory, and you'd still be able to utilize the settings related to command blocking. Just be absolutely sure you don't enable the **Turn on TPM backup to Active Directory Domain Services** setting. If you do this, you will require the computer to back up the TPM owner authorization values to Active Directory, but there will be no place for the keys to be stored in Active Directory. The result is that no attempts to set ownership on any TPM devices in your organization will be able to succeed.

Table 4.2 contains a listing of the settings you can implement in your domain using GPOs. Table 4.3 contains the suggested settings you should use.

Table 4.3 Suggested Group Policy Settings in an Active Directory Domain

GPO Setting	Suggested Setting	Explanation for Setting
Turn on TPM backup to Active Directory Domain Services	*Enabled; Required*	You should definitely be backing up the owner authorization values dispersed throughout the systems in your organization to Active Directory to ensure that any required recovery procedures or management tasks requiring owner authorization go smoothly. Make sure the backup is required to ensure that you don't end up with systems for which you don't have the owner authorization values handy due to a change owner task completing without the Active Directory backup completing as well.
Configure the list of blocked TPM commands	*Enabled*; Configure list of commands	We're assuming you have commands you want to block with this one. If not, leave it as **Not Configured**. You cannot enable this setting and leave the list blank. Once you enable it, you must add at least one command.
Ignore the default list of blocked TPM commands	*Disabled*	You may want to add the default list of blockedcommands to your Group Policy list, but you should not use this as a replacement for the default list. No coverage would be provided if a user logged on to a local account. If set to *Not Configured*, users can set the default list to be ignored using the Local Computer Policy.
Ignore the local list of blocked TPM commands	*Enabled*	Ensure that users cannot configure the local list of blocked commands.

Deploying TPM-Equipped Devices with Scripting

Once you've configured GPOs to handle your TPM settings, you can move on to using scripts to deploy the devices containing version 1.2 TPMs. We strongly suggest you get everything else in place before moving on to actual device deployment. Update your Active Directory schema if necessary, build your administrative template if necessary, and set the Group Policy settings. This will ensure that once you start taking ownership of TPM chips, the owner authorization values will get backed up to Active Directory. Finally, refer to the section earlier in the chapter where we covered the BIOS settings you need to configure.

Your TPM WMI Primer

It wouldn't be appropriate to simply dive into chunks of script code here without providing a basic explanation of WMI and how you will be able to interact with the TPM using scripts. So, let's start with a WMI primer. We think it will be valuable for all but advanced programmers/scripters.

Microsoft implemented WMI with Windows 2000 in order to serve as a uniform and consistent way to monitor and manage Windows platforms. Not only does it standardize access to components of the systems you need to manage, but it also provides greater access to those components than were previously supported. In other words, administrators were tired of having to manually manage their Windows systems through graphical user interfaces (GUIs) or other kludgy means. There was a strong outcry to be able to script everything, just like those UNIX guys have been doing for the past 30 or so years. In previous versions of Windows, we could use a few command-line interface (CLI) utilities and various scripting languages to hack solutions together, but scripted system management was limited with these tools. Microsoft answered with WMI, which administrators generally rely on VBScript to access.

With WMI, every piece of the system is an object, including files, user accounts, and hardware resources. There is a WMI Class (WMIC) for each type of resource, and each WMIC has methods and properties. You can use scripts to read or modify the properties of an object, and to invoke the methods of the object. WMI remains the consistent interface that exposes those properties and methods to you. The TPM is no different.

Win32_Tpm is the class representing the TPM hardware in your system. Table 4.4 shows some of the more basic and useful methods available with the *Win32_Tpm* class.

Table 4.4 Some Useful Win32_Tpm Methods

Method	Description
AddBlockedCommand	Add a TPM command to the list of commands not permitted to be run by the platform. The command to be blocked is sent with this method as an ordinal value.
Clear	This is the equivalent of a pressing a reset button for 5 seconds. It clears all information in the TPM, resetting it back to its factory-default state.
Disable	Disables the TPM chip.
Enable	Enables the TPM chip.
IsActivated	Shows whether the TPM chip is activated.
IsCommandBlocked	Shows whether the command queried with this method is listed as blocked.
IsEnabled	Shows whether the TPM chip is enabled.
IsOwned	Shows whether the TPM chip is owned.
RemoveBlockedCommand	Removes a TPM command from the list of commands not permitted to be run by the platform. The command to be removed from the blocked list is sent with this method as an ordinal value.
ResetAuthLockOut	Manufacturers implement a lockout period for the TPM to protect against dictionary attacks. This command resets that timeout.
TakeOwnership	Sets the ownership information for the device.
SetPhysicalPresenceRequest	This method performs functions that require physical presence. The specific command executed depends on the ordinal value sent with the method. This method does not avoid the physical presence requirement for executing the commands. This method sets a device operation as pending, and a reboot is required at which time the platform will display a screen asking the user to accept or reject the operation (see Figure 4.8).

> **NOTE**
>
> Although you can accomplish a lot with the methods listed in Table 4.4, you should familiarize yourself with the full list of methods and properties in the *Win32_Tpm* class. This will allow you to write more robust scripts. For example, you may want to check whether the device is owned before you go ahead and execute the *TakeOwnership* method. The *Win32_Tpm* class is not overly complex, so you should be able to gain an understanding of the full range of functions fairly quickly. The full *Win32_Tpm* class reference is available at http://msdn2.microsoft.com/en-us/library/aa376484.aspx.

Scripting the TPM Deployment

The first task you need to perform when deploying a TPM-equipped platform is to initialize the TPM. This means enabling, activating, and taking ownership of the device. The unfortunate thing when working with TPM-equipped devices is that some tasks require that you be physically present at the machine. This is part of what makes us trust these trusted platforms. So, when you run a script, you still need to be present at the system to provide input when the BIOS requires it with interfaces such as that shown back in Figure 4.8.

In order to initialize the TPM, we suggest that you first use the *SetPhysicalPresenceRequest()* method of the *Win32_Tpm* class. *SetPhysicalPresenceRequest()* allows you to perform a lot of different tasks depending on the numeric value you pass to the method. This method sends a command request to the TPM which is processed on the next reboot. Table 4.5 shows just a handful of these.

Table 4.5 Parameters for the SetPhysicalPresenceRequest Method

Parameter	Description
1	Enable the TPM.
3	Activate the TPM.
5	Clear the TPM.
10	Enable, activate, and allow an owner to be installed on the TPM.

You probably want to use the *SetPhysicalPresenceRequest()* method as the leadoff in your TPM deployment script. Go ahead and call the method using parameter 10. When the system reboots, you will, as we mentioned, need to be physically present at the device. You should see the screen shown in Figure 4.8 twice before Windows will actually start, and you need to select **MODIFY** for both. Once that is complete, you only need to set an owner for the device. For this, you want to create an SHA-1 hash for the owner authorization value using the *ConvertToOwnerAuth()* method, and then set that value in the device using the *TakeOwnership()* method:

```
'Generate a random number to use as the owner password
Dim num1, num2, pword
num1 = (100000000 * rnd())
num2 = (10000000 * rnd())
pword = (CDbl(num1) * CDbl(num2))


' Create the Win32_Tpm object
Set oTpmService = GetObject("winmgmts:{impersonationLevel=impersonate," _
                    &  "authenticationLevel=pktPrivacy}!\\" _
                    & "." _
                    & "\Root\CIMV2\Security\MicrosoftTpm")
Set oTpm = oTpmService.Get("Win32_Tpm=@")


oTpm.IsActivated isactv          'Test if the TPM is activated
oTpm.IsEnabled isenabled         'Test if the TPM is enabled
oTpm.IsOwnershipAllowed isownable      'Test if ownership of the TPM is
allowed
oTpm.IsOwned isowned             'Test if the TPM is owned


If isowned = False And isenabled = False Then
   oTpm.SetPhysicalPresenceRequest(10)        'Enable, activate, and allow the
installation of an owner
   Wscript.Echo "The TPM has been initialized.  The system will now reboot
to complete this operation.  When the system reboots a screen will ask if
you want to modify the configuration of the TPM.  You will need to allow this
operation twice, and then Windows will load."
   CreateObject("Wscript.Shell").Run "shutdown /r /t 5"       'Reboot the
machine
ElseIf isowned = False And isactv = True And isenabled = True And isownable
= True Then
   oTpm.ConvertToOwnerAuth pword, ownerauth      ' Create a SHA-1 hash of a
password
```

```
    oTpm.TakeOwnership(ownerauth)                    ' Take ownership
End If
```

Add this command as the logon script for yourself (or a special user account you use to initialize TPM devices), and then start booting and logging on to machines. If these commands complete successfully, the first time you boot you'll get the first set of logical tests. They should indicate that the system needs to be enabled, or activated, or set to allow ownership, and the *SetPhysicalPresenceRequest* call will make it happen. After you answer the BIOS' questions and log on again, the first set of logical tests will fail. The second set will then call the *ConvertToOwnerAuth* and then the *TakeOwnership* methods. After a brief wait, you'll have a TPM that is ready to perform all of the functions that other services and applications that rely upon it need. If your Group Policy is configured as we mentioned earlier, you have all of those TPM owner authorization values stored in Active Directory as well. You may need those if you want to perform further management operations on the TPM.

We won't cover all of the methods of the *Win32_Tpm* class here. You can head to the Microsoft Web site to find references on the class, at http://msdn2.microsoft.com/en-gb/library/aa376484.aspx. In this section, we did cover the methods you'll need to deploy TPM systems in your enterprise, however. Just remember that if you need to call a method that utilizes the owner authorization information stored in Active Directory, you need to perform a Lightweight Directory Access Protocol (LDAP) search for *ms-TPM-OwnerInformation* using its LDAP display name, *msTPM-OwnerInformation*. Also, keep in mind that you want to be sure you set up a secure connection to send this information. Do not pass the owner authorization value across your network in plain text.

NOTE

You can rely on the *Win32_Tpm* class alone to perform all your administrative functions, but if you like to have options, there's no need to feel locked in. A script called manage-bde.wsf is included with Windows Vista for managing BitLocker Drive Encryption from the command line, and it includes some basic TPM management functions, including the ability to set an owner. So, you could use this script to set an owner by issuing the following command in a command prompt: *cscript manage-bde.wsf –tpm –o owner_password*. The *owner_password* is any string of at least eight characters which the script will automatically hash for you.

TPM Applications

Now that we have seen how the TPM works and we know what sort of capabilities it provides to us, it is time to discuss some of the applications that are using that functionality. Microsoft has made good use of the TPM for some applications in Windows Vista, and some third-party applications that utilize the TPM are already on the market. However, as this is an emerging technology, and because the scope of usefulness of the TPM is so broad, we are likely to see an explosion of applications implementing TPM-based features in the coming years.

Digital Rights Management

The TPM is a part of what Microsoft is calling its Next-Generation Secure Computing Base (NGSCB), or System Integrity, which was originally codenamed Palladium. Many saw the initiative as a way for Microsoft to implement, and to allow others to implement, very strong Digital Rights Management (DRM) protections. This has not changed much in the years since it was first announced, and at this time, there is a great deal of skepticism and an outcry against the NGSCB.

You'll notice that we have not mentioned DRM in this chapter until now, and we've done that for a reason. The TPM, Windows Vista's TPM Services, and the NGSCB overall, provide a great deal of functionality. You can use some of that functionality to implement DRM techniques that are stronger than anything media pirates have come up against thus far. That is sure. However, as you have seen throughout this chapter, the TPM is not about DRM. It is a device centered on cryptography, providing key storage locations, cryptographic functions, and hashing functions. Yes, you can use those cryptography features to implement DRM applications, but you can also use them to implement a great number of security features and applications.

Therefore, we could have spent the entire chapter participating in the flame war that rages on the Internet about the TPM and Microsoft's NGSCB, or we could have a productive discussion about how the TPM works, what it can be used for, and how Windows Vista takes advantage of it. If we had taken the first route, you'd end up with some gross misconceptions about the TPM and everything related to it, and you wouldn't be equipped to implement Windows Vista on TPM-equipped devices.

However, it would be just as misleading if we did not mention DRM at all in the chapter. So, keep in mind that there are DRM applications for the TPM as well. One TPM feature that will be especially useful to those who want to implement DRM is the device authentication feature the TPM provides. You may buy a song via download with a usage right that limits playback of the song to that device alone. The TPM can seal a key that will be used to encrypt the song, and the song cannot be decrypted and played back from another system.

Microsoft Applications

Currently, Microsoft has implemented a good base of functionality in Windows Vista using the TPM. It has built BitLocker Drive Encryption and its secure startup mechanism around the TPM. It has built a very nice, easy-to-use set of management tools for the TPM in both the TPM MMC and the *Win32_Tpm* WMI class. However, there is a whole set of TPM-based functionality, called Code Integrity, that is available only in the 64-bit version of Windows Vista.

When we discussed the TCG trusted platform, we mentioned that the TPM could be used to extend trust to higher-level components that run on the OS. Code Integrity takes advantage of this by implementing the following protections:

- Verifies the integrity of all code that loads into a protected process.

- Winload verifies the integrity of all drivers that are critical to the boot process, including the HAL and the Windows kernel.

- Verifies the integrity of all kernel-mode drivers.

- Verifies the integrity of all user-mode binaries that implement cryptographic functions.

- Verifies the integrity of all user-mode binaries that load into a protected process used for the playback of high-definition media.

- Verifies the integrity of a specific set of user-mode binaries using page hashes in nt5ph.cat and ntpe.cat.

- Verifies kernel code.

These functions are generally carried out just as we discussed in the beginning of the chapter: Code integrity measurements are taken, and the TPM can be used to attest to these measurements. This protects the system from running any of the areas of code mentioned earlier if intentional or unintentional corruption occurs. If a rootkit successfully loads into the kernel on your Windows Vista 64-bit system, it will be detected, and it will be prevented from executing. Obviously, this does not necessarily protect your system from being compromised by a rootkit, but it does ensure that the compromise is brought to light when integrity measurements uncover it.

Third-Party Applications

Some third-party applications that rely on the TPM have already begun to emerge. Probably the best example of this is Wave Embassy Suites. This software package was originally developed to take advantage of version 1.1 TPM chips, but it now supports version 1.2 chips as well. This is a very popular application that OEMs are deploying with devices they sell that include biometric hardware. The TPM will be utilized by applications such as this which enable strong biometric authentication measures by securing the biometric data that the application relies upon. Just as the TPM assists BitLocker Drive Encryption by sealing the VMK, the TPM can seal the user's biometric data that the application is using.

Another important application for TPM-enabled devices that will emerge will be remote access solutions. Given the strong device authentication possible with the TPM, you can be sure that remote access will appeal to a segment of the software market that turns toward implementing TPM support. In this way, you can think of the user needing an RSA SecureID or smart card to authenticate to the remote access solution, and the device he or she is connecting from will also need to present its credentials using the TPM. This can help network administrators eliminate remote security breaches due solely to compromised user authentication tokens such as passwords, RSA SecureIDs, or smart cards. Now the attacker will also need to have the user's laptop as well.

This is really only the tip of the iceberg as far as TPM-based applications go, however. Some implementations we are likely to see are as follows:

- Users are provided with the ability to wrap the cryptographic keys they use for secure connections over the Internet, such as logging into their bank accounts via a Web browser and using secure e-mail applications.

- Web servers can use the TPM's sealing functionality to provide assurance to connecting nodes that they are trustworthy, including assurance that the server-side software and settings are the same as when the node connected previously, when the trust relationship was established.

- DRM will likely emerge as a popular way to use the TPM. Media applications such as iTunes can use the TPM's sealing functions to lock down access to media if tampering takes place.

Understanding the Security Implications of the TPM

One of the main implications of the TPM is that it will require massive hardware expenditures in order to take advantage of it. In most cases, when a new version of Windows is released, every enterprise has some systems that need to be upgraded in order to run the new version, but many of their existing systems already support it. So, the rollout does not require sweeping hardware upgrades across the board. However, the TPM is a new piece of hardware that is still included in only certain product offerings from OEMs, with market penetration of these devices only really getting started within the past 12 months, and it is required in order to take advantage of the TPM services in Windows Vista. This means enterprises that want to take advantage of the TPM will need to budget for widespread replacements of desktop and mobile systems, which can be expensive.

Aside from the budgetary implications, the TPM and TPM support in Windows Vista solve many security problems, and at the same time there is a lot of nonsense about the TPM being a magic bullet. These issues are worth discussing so that we, as information security professionals, can make informed decisions about what countermeasures are worth implementing, and so that we can accurately assess the security posture of our systems and our enterprise as a whole.

Encryption as a Countermeasure

Let's start by first mentioning cryptography in a general sense. After all, the TPM device and TPM services in Windows Vista are obviously focused on encryption. The TPM is mainly designed to create, store, and protect encryption keys, password hashes, and digital certificates.

The first thing we should say here is that no single countermeasure will fully protect digital assets from attack. In fact, there is probably not a combination of countermeasures that can ensure 100 percent protection from attack. Cryptography is no exception to that rule. Consider this as you read vendor product claims, white papers, and other industry articles that tout TPM as the end of your search for a secure enterprise.

Several sources are currently touting media sanitization as a feature of the TPM. The argument goes that you can clear the TPM in a matter of seconds, and your data is gone. No more spending money on and waiting hours for National Security Agency (NSA) media sanitization procedures to work. Just clear the TPM and your data is gone forever. There are two important points here:

1. When you clear the TPM your data is *not* gone. Only the key that was used to wrap the key that was used to encrypt that data is gone. The data, in encrypted form, still exists on the drive.

2. Encryption can be defeated by brute force attacks.

This is not meant to argue that encryption is insecure. The fact of the matter is that with current computing power, it would take a state-of-the-art desktop machine more than 100 trillion years to brute force your data if it is encrypted using the 128-bit Advanced Encryption Standard (AES)! Obviously, if it takes trillions of years to crack into your data, it's safe. We raise this issue only because a lot of talk is circulating about using the clearing of the TPM as a media sanitization method, when *technically speaking*, the data is not destroyed and it can be attacked using brute force. Now those brute force attacks may very well remain infeasible for the next 2,000 years. However, there is a chance that leaps in the power of computers over the next two decades or a flaw discovered in the AES algorithm could make brute forcing a 128-bit AES encryption seem as easy as cracking the Data Encryption Standard (DES) is today.

Tools & Traps...

Media Sanitization

The most important thing to consider when using encryption is how long the data you are protecting needs to remain confidential. If you have information on your hard drive that you expect to remain sensitive for the next six months (maybe it is a proposal you are working on, and you must turn it in within that six-month time frame), you can expect the AES algorithm with a 128-bit key to do the job for you. On the other hand, if you are storing a full portfolio of personal information which you need to keep confidential for the next 50 years, you might want to consider how quickly a computer can chug through those keys 35 years down the road. What is the shelf life of your data?

Even the good folks at the National Institute of Standards and Technology (NIST) seem to be riding the fence on this media sanitization issue. In the recently released Special Publication 800-88, "Guidelines for Media Sanitization," found at http://csrc.nist.gov/publications/nistpubs/800-88/NISTSP800-88_rev1.pdf, NIST added and then removed the following text:

Continued

"Encryption is not a generally accepted means of sanitization. The increasing power of computers decreases the time needed to crack cipher text and therefore the inability to recover the encrypted data [cannot] be assured."

You'll also find a lot of good debate on the topic throughout the Internet. We don't usually disagree with what comes out of NIST, and we won't start here. Just remember that this method of sanitization does not destroy the data or the media. Encryption is a method of ensuring that it takes a long time to get to sensitive data, and for most data this method of sanitization will probably buy us enough time. However, in some applications, this will not be an adequate sanitization method. The important point is that you know how sensitive your data is and how long it must remain confidential before it becomes useless, and that you apply the proper methods given those facts.

You should also note that NIST did not go so far as to add cryptographic destruction anywhere in its list of sanitization methods.

Now that we've addressed that caveat, let's look at the power at our fingertips. Where the TPM and its capability to give us a more robust encryption platform help the most is simply in the fact that the data we are protecting is increasingly moving outside the walls of the enterprise. As we mentioned before, employees are going ever more mobile, with laptops replacing desktops, and cell phones, PDAs, and even MP3 players providing more and more storage and remote connectivity features. Those firewalls, proxies, DMZs, and other layered perimeter protection rings we designed and built in the past are doing a great job at keeping the bad stuff out. What we have increasingly less ability to do is keep the assets we protect in.

This is where encryption and the trusted platform come to the rescue. Encrypting data, especially when we utilize full-disk encryption technologies such as BitLocker Drive Encryption, allows us to create an environment where employees are carrying our security perimeter with them wherever they go. That encryption creates a boundary wherever the device and the data are between the data and the outside world. There are, of course, already software-only solutions for full-disk encryption, but the TPM provides better protection of encryption keys because key recovery techniques that may have worked fairly well against keys held in software are not likely to work against keys protected by the TPM.

Our protection is strengthened even more by the fact that many normal attacks which involve subverting the system software will not work. As soon as part of the system has been modified, the chain of trust will cease to extend to that part of the system. The platform will not load, and the data will not be able to be recovered by simply creating a backdoor in some poorly coded software. The only piece of software we have to rely upon is the tiny bit of code known as the CRTM. Because this code is small and relatively simple, it is easier to ensure that there are no vulnerabilities in it. Buffer overflows and backdoors tend to get lost in a program of tens of thousands of lines of code.

Either brute force cracking methods or attacks on the hardware itself will be required. As long as the data was encrypted using large keys and a secure algorithm, brute force attacks will prove to be a fruitless endeavor, and hardware attacks require a lot more skill and resources than running the canned attack code available on the Internet which is used against software.

Notes from the Underground...

Mandating Full-Disk Encryption

On June 23, 2006, the Office of Management and Budget (OMB) issued Memoranda M-06-16, "Protection of Sensitive Agency Information." This was a direct response to many of the data loss problems that afflicted the federal government during the first half of 2006. The memoranda requires a blend of technical, management, and operational controls defined in the NIST Special Publication (SP) 800-53, "Recommended Security Controls for Federal Information Systems," to be implemented, but one specific requirement leading off the memoranda requires that all sensitive data on mobile devices be encrypted.

In rapid response to the memoranda, the U.S. Air Force posted a request for a full-disk encryption solution on the Federal Business Opportunity Web site. The U.S. Department of Agriculture (USDA) also posted a request for quotes (RFQ) on www.fbo.gov in relation to mobile device encryption. In an article for *Government Computer News* found at www.gcn.com/online/vol1_no1/42640-1.html?topic=mobile-wireless, Mary Mosquera wrote that the USDA's requirements for the encryption solution include the following:

- It must be Federal Information Processing Standards (FIPS) 140-2 compliant.
- It must integrate with a Microsoft Active Directory infrastructure.
- It must be invisible to users.
- It must be scalable.
- It must provide automated deployment tools.
- It must provide adequate recovery processes.

Continued

As we have seen throughout this chapter, devices containing version 1.2 TPM chips and Windows Vista TPM services fulfill all of these requirements. They go beyond the requirements by securing encryption keys with TPM hardware instead of relying on a software-only solution. Whether Windows Vista becomes the solution of choice for most federal agencies remains to be seen.

This is the leading edge of a widespread change in the way that both the public and the private sectors protect their digital assets on mobile devices. As the federal government leads this process of carefully identifying all PII, controlling which mobile devices that the PII. It is just unfortunate that the compromise of the PII of millions of people has been the impetus required to effect this change.

Here are some references for more information on this issue:

- You can find OMB Memoranda M-06-16 at www.whitehouse.gov/omb/memoranda/fy2006/m06-16.pdf.

- You can find information about the U.S. Air Force procurement at www.fbo.gov/spg/USAF/AFMC/ESC/FA8771-07-R-0001/Attachments.html.

- You can find NIST SP 800-53 Revision 1 at http://csrc.nist.gov/publications/nistpubs/800-53-Rev1/800-53-rev1-final-clean-sz.pdf.

Can I Really Trust These People?

We must rely on trustworthy BIOSes, TPM drivers, the TBS, and TSS implementations from myriad sources in order to be sure that our trusted platforms are actually trustworthy. More important, as we saw in discussing the trusted platform architecture, the platform builds by evaluating the trustworthiness of each component one at a time, and then relying on that component to evaluate the next component, and so on. In this way, trust in one component is derived from the trust we had in each preceding component. Therefore, if one component in the chain is suspect, all components that derived their trust from that piece are also suspect.

How much can we really trust these platforms, then? We can be sure that there will be numerous problems with code security in the coming years. BIOSes, drivers, OSes, and third-party applications will all be susceptible to attack. What we rely upon is the capability of the trusted platform to provide reliable metrics about itself—in fact, the TCG has defined *trusted platform* as "a computing platform that can be trusted to report its properties," in its glossary of terms at www.trustedcomputinggroup.org/groups/glossary. So, the idea is not that the trusted computing platform is impervious to attack, nor that it can detect when it has been compromised. As we discussed at the beginning of this chapter, the trusted platform can enter insecure or unstable states. However, it must provide reliable measurements of itself. Other parties then challenge the system to produce these measurements when they need to decide whether they trust the platform, and in this way, communication with an untrusted system can be avoided.

The TPM Only Enables Technical Security Controls

Any good information security program relies upon technical, operational, and management security controls. The TPM and Windows Vista TPM services provide us with an incredibly powerful and flexible set of technical controls. However, they do not help us to implement operational or management controls, and therefore they can never be touted as the end game in information security. So, be wary of any claims of that nature.

What the TPM and TPM services in Windows Vista do allow us to do is to implement a range of controls based on encryption and device authentication to greatly improve enterprise security. However, as with many of the technical controls we currently have, holes still exist. For the most part, people are either using or implementing those technical controls, and we have management and operational controls to which those people are supposed to adhere. Whether they do adhere to them is the issue.

For example, we read in the sidebar about best practices for TPM management that the TPM owner password should never be stored to local media. However, when we initialized the TPM and set the TPM owner password using the automatically created password, we were required to save the password to local media in an XML file with a .tpm extension (refer to the section on initializing the TPM, and to Figure 4.2). From Microsoft's perspective, this required save is understandable. There is simply no way that anyone will remember a 48-digit password, so in order to ensure that the owner authorization information is available when required, Microsoft requires that automatically created authorization information be saved.

This is exactly where a good operational control is necessary. That file should be stored in a secured location away from the device on which it was created as soon as the initialization process completes. This will eliminate the chance that the owner authorization information is stolen along with the asset to which the owner authorization information pertains. However, those TPM files will invariably be saved to USB keys which will then be carried around in the laptop bag or backpack that contains the laptop on which they were created. So, basically, we have a tool that allows us to provide a high level of security for a platform if we use it correctly, but in all likelihood, a simple mistake such as this will invalidate any security that the TPM can provide.

This is not a weakness of the TPM or of Windows Vista's TPM services. This should be considered a weakness of an immature security program that does not provide a broad range of controls, and instead foolishly counts on a single magic bullet to provide protection. With an already robust security program, the TPM could be just what is needed to help the organization implement an even stronger security posture.

Are You 0wned?

I Wonder How Much My Social Security Number Costs

If you believe that technical security controls are superior to management and/or operational controls, please revisit the "Are You 0wned?" sidebar that kicked off this chapter. Note that ChoicePoint *sold* PII on more than 160,000 people to identity thieves just a few years ago. ChoicePoint was not hacked. There was no missing laptop. Identity thieves were able to breach very weak management and operational controls. They portrayed themselves as private companies that required the information for various credit and background checks, and ChoicePoint sold them the information despite the fact that policies and procedures for performing basic checks would have revealed the fraud. The following quote is from an MSNBC.com article on the data breach, found at www.msnbc.msn.com/id/11030692:

"The FTC's complaint against ChoicePoint paints a picture of a firm that was selling data to all comers, even after obvious signs of trouble. Law enforcement agencies began to warn ChoicePoint of fraudulent activity back in 2001, the complaint alleges. ChoicePoint continued to sell data to companies with expired business licenses, with canceled telephones and after employees signaled them out as suspicious. The firm even continued to supply credit reports to the crime ring after the fake accounts it had set up were suspended by ChoicePoint for non-payment, the complaint says."

Existing Attacks

The main problem people may have with Windows Vista TPM services is incorrect usage of it. As we discussed, many people see clearing the TPM as a valid method of wiping your drive if the drive is encrypted using the TPM. The flip side to that is that it takes only one small mistake to eliminate all of someone's data. So be careful with the TPM MMC. Do not run the Clear TPM wizard if you have data that you need that was encrypted with the TPM and be careful with those scripts. When you issue a *SetPhysicalPresenceRequest(5)* call on a machine, you had better mean it, or you had better be able to get on the machine and prevent the configuration modification from completing after reboot.

By the same token, this may become a popular form of denial of service (DoS) attack for the bad guys. If they cannot get to your data, it may simply be enough to prevent you from getting to it. This means organizations are going to make sure they enable the backup of recovery keys so that they can enact emergency recovery procedures. This makes protecting the Active Directory infrastructure more important than ever, but we already have ways to protect what is inside the perimeter. We need to have a tool that could help us extend the security perimeter outside the walls of the office, and that is where we can leverage the TPM to great effect.

What we will see is how effective and easy hardware attacks can become. We know this is a weakness, now that we are relying on hardware to provide some security functions. These sorts of attacks generally require more skill and are harder to implement than software attacks, though, and attackers will always take the path of least resistance.

Summary

The TPM is the cornerstone of the TCG trusted platform, which is a computing platform that can provide reliable integrity metrics on itself. The TPM itself does not prevent virus attacks, theft of equipment, theft of data, or hacking attempts. However, it does allow software developers to outfit security professionals, administrators, and even users with a wide range of tools that can protect their systems. Windows Vista includes some of these tools, including BitLocker Drive Encryption, a secure startup mechanism within BitLocker, and Code Integrity features. The TPM and Windows TPM services also support strong device authentication, which gives network administrators a reliable means for controlling connectivity throughout their networks.

It is interesting to see that although Microsoft has certainly spent a lot of development time on implementing TPM services and applications in Windows Vista, it also has spent a very large amount of time and effort on penetration testing Windows Vista's TPM implementation. We included a link to the Doug MacIver presentation earlier in the chapter. Microsoft used BitLocker penetration testing as a way to provide feedback to the developers, and apparently this has had an important impact on the choices of which PCRs are used to seal the VMK.

This is an emerging technology, in terms of both the hardware and the software that takes advantage of it. At this point, it seems as though Microsoft has built a very robust and secure platform around the TPM, but given the wide-ranging possibilities for TPM applications, we have seen only the tip of the iceberg. Although Microsoft has even taken a whole new approach to system architecture in controlling what processes may operate in kernel mode, and implementing Code Integrity to provide integrity monitoring for all of that code, Code Integrity could very well be extended to provide this integrity checking for other parts of the system. As Tom Petty once sang, "the future was wide open."

However, it's good to bring at least a small degree of skepticism anytime you examine something. As we pointed out throughout this chapter, as old attack surfaces vanish, attackers will find new ones. Hardware attacks such as those that are currently possible against smart cards will emerge as a popular target. Although the TPM is just emerging, some lessons are being incorporated into chip design, such as under- and over-volting protection mechanisms. Despite any weaknesses, the TPM and Windows Vista's TPM services provide security professionals with a very useful tool to secure their data.

Solutions Fast Track

Understanding the TPM

- ☑ The Trusted Computing Group is an industry standards organization that is developing specifications for the trusted platform architecture. The TPM is at the core of the trusted platform.

- ☑ Trusted platforms are based on two trusted components: the TPM and CRTM, which are called the Trusted Building Blocks. Trust in the rest of the platform is derived from these two basic components. The trust boundary gradually extends to include other components, such as the OS and applications.

Configuring and Managing the TPM on a Stand-Alone System

- ☑ Use the TPM MMC console to configure the TPM on your stand-alone system. This MMC provides all the functionality you should need in a familiar interface that is easy to use.

- ☑ Always back up your TPM owner authorization information to an external storage device, and make sure you do not keep this device with the system for which it contains the owner authorization information.

Configuring and Managing the TPM in an Enterprise Environment

- ☑ Make sure you are requiring that the TPM owner authorization information is backed up to Active Directory, if at all possible. This backup functionality requires (1.) that all your domain controllers are running Windows Server 2003 SP1 or later and (2.) that you have upgraded your Active Directory schema using the adprep utility that comes with the Windows Server 2007 and Windows Vista DVDs.

- ☑ Utilize the Group Policy settings covered earlier in this chapter to lock down users' ability to tamper with the TPM command block lists, and to configure your central block list. If you need to have the Group Policy settings available with Windows Server 2007 on your Windows Server 2003 domain controllers, you can use the code included in this chapter and on the CD that comes with this book to modify your administrative templates.

☑ Use scripting to take advantage of the *Win32_Tpm* WMI class to ease your TPM device deployments. You can refer to Microsoft's reference documentation on this class at http://msdn2.microsoft.com/en-gb/library/aa376484.aspx in order to familiarize yourself with the class.

TPM Applications

☑ Microsoft has built several key TPM-related components into Windows Vista. The TBS has been implemented to serve as an agent that mediates access to the TPM. The TCG has outlined an architecture whereby a trusted platform relies on the BIOS and the OS boot manager to implement a trusted boot process in order to maintain system integrity through to the OS. BitLocker Drive Encryption implements this trusted boot process. See the coverage of BitLocker Drive Encryption provided in Chapter 5.

☑ A small number of applications rely on the TPM, and there should be large growth in these types of applications once Windows Vista is officially released and begins to gain a foothold in desktop deployments.

☑ To the dismay of music and movie lovers everywhere, the TPM will enable content providers to implement more robust DRM techniques.

Understanding the Security Implications of the TPM

☑ The TPM and Windows Vista TPM services are powerful tools for securing the enterprise. They can provide very strong device authentication, powerful protection of encryption keys, and assurance that code running on the system is trustworthy. However, the TPM and services that depend on it cannot ensure security. In order to provide security, we as security professionals must implement strong technical, management, and operational controls. The TPM can help us to implement strong technical controls, but it does not address the other control areas.

☑ As small devices include ever-increasing storage capacity, information security professionals have two problems to solve as users become more mobile. First, we must understand the data we protect so that we know where any sensitive data is, and we must provide policies and training on how the data is to be stored and handled. Second, we must implement a mobile security perimeter to protect that data when it leaves the walls of the enterprise, and the way to do this is to use cryptography.

Frequently Asked Questions

The following Frequently Asked Questions, answered by the authors of this book, are designed to both measure your understanding of the concepts presented in this chapter and to assist you with real-life implementation of these concepts. To have your questions about this chapter answered by the author, browse to **www.syngress.com/solutions** and click on the **"Ask the Author"** form.

Q: Can I protect sensitive data by storing it in the TPM in my computer?

A: No, the TPM is used only to create and store the private portions of keys, and certain platform metrics. Those keys may then be used to encrypt the contents of a disk or other data storage locations. So, you would use the TPM to protect your data, but not by directly storing the data in the TPM.

Q: If I want to use Microsoft's new BitLocker Drive Encryption, do I need to have a TPM?

A: No, you can take advantage of BitLocker Drive Encryption by storing the encryption key on a USB storage device. However, using the TPM to store the key is preferred, and it is strongly recommended that you utilize the TPM if one is present in your system. For more information on BitLocker Drive Encryption, see Chapter 5.

Q: Does the TPM mean that Windows Vista is hack-proof?

A: No, nothing can make a computer hack-proof. Even if a system is unplugged and powered off it is susceptible to physical attacks. However, the TPM and Windows Vista TPM services have provided coverage against a lot of the most popular current attack vectors, and using them together will provide better security than an otherwise identical system that does not take advantage of them can provide. In the meantime, attackers are going to be looking for new attack surfaces through which they can gain access to the system and the data stored on it. Implementing layers of defense across the spectrum of technical, management, and operational security controls is a necessary supplement to a security program that leverages the powerful countermeasures that Windows Vista's TPM services provide.

Q: Are there any differences between the TPM features included in the 32-bit version and 64-bit version of Windows Vista?

A: Yes, there are. Only the 64-bit version of Windows Vista includes Code Integrity features, which include:

- Verification of the integrity of all code that loads into a protected process

- Winload verification of the integrity of all drivers which are critical to the boot process, including the HAL and the Windows kernel

- Verification of the integrity of all kernel-mode drivers

- Verification of the integrity of all user-mode binaries that implement cryptographic functions

- Verification of the integrity of all user-mode binaries that load into a protected process used for the playback of high-definition media

- Verification of the integrity of a specific set of user-mode binaries using page hashes in nt5ph.cat and ntpe.cat

- Verification of kernel code

Chapter 5

Microsoft Vista: Data Protection

Solutions in this chapter:

- **USB Devices**

- **Rights Management**

- **Encrypting File System**

- **Whole-Disk Encryption**

- **PatchGuard**

☑ **Summary**

☑ **Solutions Fast Track**

☑ **Frequently Asked Questions**

Introduction

Windows Vista introduces many new elements that allow for greater protection of your data—protection against loss, protection against theft, protection against outsiders and insiders. Vista offers new Universal Serial Bus (USB) policy controls, a built-in rights management software engine, drive encryption, and protection against kernel modifications. Vista also offers some updates to time-tested features that have already worked well for data protection, such as the Encrypting File System (EFS).

USB Devices

Only a few versions of Windows ago, USB devices were completely unknown and new. Today they are ubiquitous. Every other desk now has a USB hub, whether it's in the shape of a mouse pad, a mug warmer, a snowman, or for the really wacky, a hub that doesn't do anything cute. Every USB hub has a rat's nest of wires leading to other devices: a lamp to light your keyboard, a fan to keep you cool, a charger for your batteries, and so on.

None of the devices we've described is typically a security concern, though, because all they do to your computer is consume power. What's truly disconcerting to IT management in any company with significant amounts of data to protect from theft is the threat presented by the simple USB storage device. Known by any of a number of names—flash drives, thumb drives, memory sticks, and more than a few brand names—USB storage devices get simultaneously smaller and larger every year; smaller in physical size, and easier to conceal or lose, and larger in capacity so that more data—purloined or authorized—can be stored inside them.

There's also a wide range of other devices that use USB as a peripheral connection standard. Printers, scanners, keyboards, cameras, music players, mice, CD and DVD writers; IT managers may want to allow users to connect some of these devices without intervention by a system administrator, and prevent access to others.

With Windows Vista, Microsoft has added a number of different features targeting USB devices. ReadyBoost is a performance improvement, using a USB storage device as an external memory device; BitLocker can use a USB storage device to hold an external key or a recovery key for decrypting or controlling access to an encrypted drive; Group Policy gains several settings to control how users can, or cannot, install and access drivers for all classes of USB devices.

ReadyBoost: Plug In to Speed

ReadyBoost isn't strictly a security feature, but it's important for the security professional to be able to answer some inevitable questions about the technology, to assure
others that it is safe to use in a restricted environment.

What ReadyBoost does is quite simple. Because external USB storage devices
are fast, they can be used as an adjunct to the system's onboard memory, providing
an extra gigabyte or two of boost to a starved system. We've been using it while
writing this book to help with our word processor's incessant demands on our
system for more, more, more, and although we haven't evaluated scientifically the
gain in speed, the presence of the thumb drive makes our use of the word processor
just that little bit more comfortable.

But we're not here to tell you about its performance. We're here to tell you
about how it holds up to security analysis. After all, it is a copy of some of your
memory contents on a small, easily stolen or lost device. It is, in essence, your "page
file on a stick." If you've ever investigated in depth the use of the EFS to protect
files, you'll have come across articles describing how EFS protects the data "at rest"
on the disk, but doesn't protect it in memory, or in page files (until Vista). The page
file contains clear-text copies of parts of whatever you've been working on since you
last booted your computer.

What about the contents of this "page file on a stick"? It's made safer in a couple
of ways. First, it's holding only the discardable contents of your memory—those that
can be read back from disk if they fall out of memory. This is a reliability measure;
you can remove the ReadyBoost drive without losing any of your memory contents. Discardable memory will consist mostly of program code and other read-only
memory-mapped files. These can still contain valuable information, though, if
someone finds your discarded/lost/stolen ReadyBoost drive, so the Windows Vista
developers made sure that all data stored on the ReadyBoost drive is encrypted
using AES-128, an appropriate combination of speed and strength.

A rough and completely unscientific demonstration of ReadyBoost's performance enhancement occurred in actual use. While we were defragmenting the hard
drive on our system, we opened the Reliability and Performance Monitor (from the
Administrative Tools menu), and we could see that the CPU was bouncing up and
down to 100 percent, the hard drive was getting a lot of throughput, there was no
network traffic, and the number of hard page faults (swapping information back into
physical memory from the page file or hard drive) was oscillating at around 50 hard
faults per second. We plugged in our ReadyBoost USB drive and went to make a
pot of tea. By the time we got back, the CPU was still bouncing about as much as it

ever was, and the hard drive was still being accessed at a good speed, but the rate of hard page faults had dropped close to zero.

What does that mean? It means that all the CPU and hard drive traffic was concentrated on actually handling the defragmentation process, rather than on swapping portions of Windows and the defragmentation program into memory from the hard drive.

Amazingly enough, even with ReadyBoost using an external drive, and encrypting and decrypting everything that goes to or from the drive, it still provides a performance improvement that makes it worth sacrificing (temporarily—you can always disable ReadyBoost on the drive or delete the cache file) a gigabyte or two of USB. And now you have the information to prove that it's a secure way to give yourself that performance.

USB Group Policy Settings

Most IT departments have been asked, at one time or another, to prevent the theft of secret data by employees, whether that secret data is intellectual property, legal confidences, business strategy, or customer data. As we discuss later in this chapter, Rights Management Services can prevent some copying of application-specific content, but as far as USB devices are concerned, there are some special challenges, and some targeted solutions from Microsoft in Windows Vista.

In many organizations, you'll want to disable writeable USB storage devices, but still allow users to access printers, CD-ROM drives, and the like. You may even want users to be able to install new devices, including their new drivers. You couldn't do that in Windows XP without handing out administrator accounts, but you can in Windows Vista, with the right Group Policy templates applied in your domain/forest.

Tools & Traps…

Think Before Applying Schema Changes

Windows Vista's installation media includes an adprep.exe utility, designed for upgrading an existing Active Directory Domain Services installation to support the extra Group Policy settings that apply to Windows Vista.

Various sources have described whether or not you should apply the schema changes that these LDF files contain—some have suggested that these

Continued

schema changes are for information only and that they will not be finalized until Windows codename "Longhorn" ships. Others have suggested that these files would not be put on the disk if they were not already finalized and point to the fact that these changes are to support existing Group Policy-controlled features in Windows Vista's release. Microsoft has made no public statement on the matter, however, so domain administrators should be cautious in deploying these changes—ideally, deploying them to a test domain until a public statement of support or otherwise comes from Microsoft. Remember always that schema changes can not be removed, except by restoring your domain controllers to an earlier version.

Controlling Device Installation

Because a number of Group Policy settings allow or deny operations on a USB device, it's important to draw a picture (see Figure 5.1). Notice that you can clarify the confusing array of Group Policy options when you break it down into the following questions:

- Are local administrators going to have the ability to add devices?

- Are you going to allow removable devices at all?

- Do you want to list as exceptions those devices you allow ("deny by default"), or those devices you refuse ("allow by default")?

- Are you going to specify accepted devices by device class (storage, scanner, printer, etc), or by hardware/compatible ID (the vendor's identification for a specific device, or a device ID that this device is compatible with)?

As security professionals, we hope that your immediate response to the third question in the preceding list is "deny by default." The "allow by default" setting has very few uses when considering Group Policy-based security. If pressed to say why the feature is there, we arrive at two arguments, the weak and the less-weak: The weak argument is that this provides a symmetry to the process; the less-weak argument is that you may use this as a reliability measure—if a device gains popularity despite causing numerous reliability problems, you would want to prevent this particular device from being installed on machines that you control.

Figure 5.1 Group Policy Controlling Device Installation

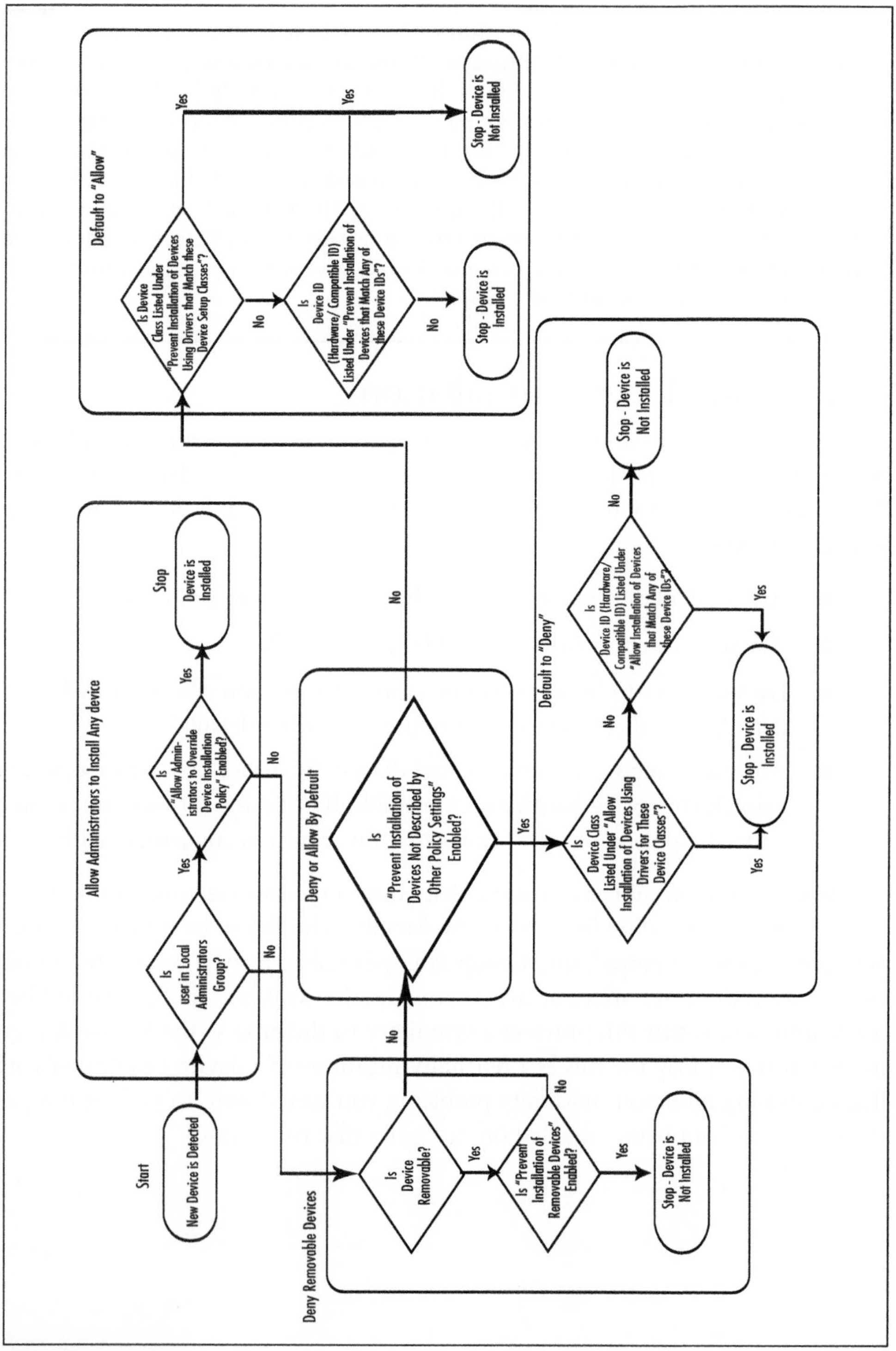

A possible third argument for using "allow by default" centers on the idea that there may be specific classes that you want to prevent—storage drivers, or cameras and scanners, for instance—while allowing all others.

For those of you who prefer tables to flowcharts, Table 5.1 describes the device installation Group Policy Objects that you can set.

Table 5.1 Group Policy Objects Controlling Device Driver Installation

Policy Name	Effect
Allow administrators to override Device Installation policies	Enabled: Local administrators may install devices at will. Disabled (default): Local administrators are subject to other device installation policies.
Prevent installation of removable devices	Enabled: Any device marked by its manufacturer as "removable" will not be installed. Disabled (default): Removable devices may be installed, dependent on other policy settings.
Prevent installation of devices not described by other policy settings	Enabled: Operate in a "deny by default" mode. Disabled (default): Operate in an "allow by default" mode.
Allow installation of devices using drivers for these classes	List of device classes that are to be allowed in an otherwise "deny by default" environment.
Allow installation of devices that match any of these device IDs	List of device IDs (hardware IDs or compatible IDs) that are to be allowed in an otherwise "deny by default" environment.
Prevent installation of devices using drivers for these classes	List of device classes that are to be prevented in an otherwise "allow by default" environment.
Prevent installation of devices that match any of these device IDs	List of device IDs (hardware IDs or compatible IDs) that are to be denied in an otherwise "allow by default" environment.

Continued

Table 5.1 continued Group Policy Objects Controlling Device Driver
Installation

Policy Name	Effect
Display a custom message when installation is prevented by policy	Balloon title: The title to be used in the "balloon" message when a disallowed device is inserted. Balloon text: The text to be used in the "balloon" message.

You can find the Group Policy Objects controlling device driver installation at
Computer Configuration | Administrative Templates | System | Device Installation
| Device Installation Restrictions. There is no matching Group Policy setting under
the User Configuration tree.

Tools & Traps...

You Can't Install It, but You Can Use It!

A device that you prevent, for whatever reason, from installing may still be
able to work on your systems. It may even be a security risk for you to prevent
a device from being installed.

This seems hugely counterintuitive, but here's the explanation. This set of
policies applies only to devices (or updates to devices) that have not yet been
installed. If a device has been installed on your system prior to your deployment of this Group Policy Object or a compatible driver that recognizes and
operates on the device, that driver will quite happily be used by the operating
system (OS) to talk to your device. There's another risk with devices that exist
on a system prior to its receiving a Group Policy Object that prevents further
installation: The term *installation* also covers updates.

If you prevent a device because it has a flakey, exploitable driver, for
instance, all you prevent are future installations of that device. A machine that
has the driver already installed will continue to run the exploitable driver. And
when the manufacturer releases an upgrade to the driver, fixing the
exploitable flaw, your users are prevented from upgrading to the fixed, stable
version, from the flawed version of which you are rightly afraid.

A Real-World Scenario of Device Installation

You are supporting a team of pharmaceutical sales representatives who travel from town to town. As these representatives travel to different cities, they stay at a wide range of hotels. Even when they can find one with an in-hotel office setup, every hotel has a different printer, and the representatives have asked to be able to connect to these printers.

With Windows XP on their laptops, you would have two choices. One is to make all these representatives the local administrator on their laptops. The other is to leave the representatives as restricted users, and tell them that they can't print.

For Windows Vista, you can have your cake and eat it too. Now your road warriors can plug in any USB printer and have the device installed and ready for use, without giving the keys to their laptop kingdom. Here's how you do it.

1. Create a Group Policy object for your road warriors (it is best to edit the default Group Policy object only rarely, if at all, since you may need a 'baseline' to return to when things go wrong).

2. Open it for editing in the **Group Policy Object Editor**.

3. Navigate to **Computer Configuration | Administrative Templates | System | Device Installation | Device Installation Restrictions** as shown in Figure 5.2.

Figure 5.2 Navigating to Device Installation Restrictions

4. The first setting that you will likely want to enable denies access to install any new device drivers. Enable **Prevent installation of devices not described by other policy settings**.

5. Then move to **Allow installation of devices using drivers that match these device setup classes**. Enable this setting also, but note that there is

more user interface than just **Disable**, **Enable** and **Not Configured**, as you can see in Figure 5.3.

Figure 5.3 Choosing Which Device Setup Classes to Allow to Install

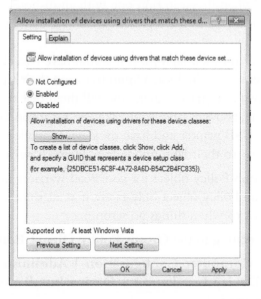

6. Click the **Show** button, which only becomes active when you have enabled this policy, so that you can enter the device class that you want your users to be able to install.

7. You'll see a list of device class GUIDs—initially empty—that are allowed for installation. Click the **Add** button, and you will be prompted for a new class GUID.

8. For printers, that class GUID is **{4d36e979–e325–11ce–bfc1–08002be10318}**—enter it with the surrounding curly brackets included. You can see this in Figure 5.4.

9. Click **OK**, and **OK** again. Click **OK** a third time, and you're back to the Group Policy Object Editor.

Figure 5.4 Adding the Printer's Device Setup Class to Allow Installation

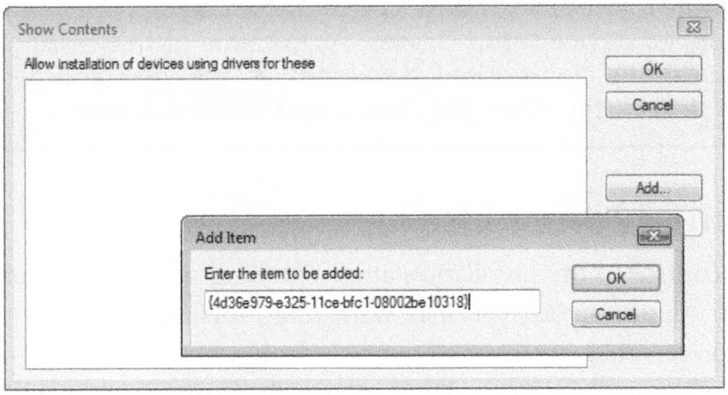

We're almost there—just one more setting to concern ourselves with. Although the user can now install the device, he may not yet be able to install the driver if it (or a compatible driver) is not already on the laptop.

If you want to allow users to install drivers for this printer, you will need to navigate to **Computer Configuration | Administrative Templates | System | Driver Installation**. You can see here that there is a setting for this, **Allow non-administrators to install drivers for these device setup classes**. Again, you will need to click **Enable**, then **Show**, then **Add**, then enter the GUID for your device setup class, and then click **OK** three times to return to the Group Policy Object Editor.

Finally, let's not forget that the Group Policy Object doesn't apply to anyone until we link it to one or more organizational units (OUs), set Filter Groups on it, and wait for the computers to update the Group Policy.

Tools & Traps…

And You Found This GUID How?

Device setup class GUIDs are documented in the Windows Driver Development Kit. Fortunately, you don't have to install this esoteric set of developer tools just to find the right class GUID.

We found the device setup class GUID list at http://msdn.microsoft.com/library/en-us/DevInst_d/hh/DevInst_d/setup-cls_f7544122-69a3-4b34-85f5-

Continued

db3714408026.xml.asp. That's a lot to remember or to copy out of a book, so the simple way is just to visit www.microsoft.com, and in the **Search** box, type **system-supplied device setup classes**. At the time of this writing, this search term produces the appropriate document as the first and second search matches. It should still return the right pages when you search.

Controlling Device Use

Once you've controlled the installation and upgrading of device drivers for your users and your administrators, you may want to go further and control the use of those device drivers that you have allowed to deploy.

The "big whammy" setting is **All Removable Storage classes: Deny all access**. Enable this setting and (after a reboot if the devices are currently in use) all removable storage is inaccessible to the OU—computer or user—on which you enable it.

None of these settings applies to processes running in the SYSTEM context, such as the aforementioned ReadyBoost technology.

All of the settings listed in Table 5.2 reside under the Group Policy subtree, **Computer Configuration | Administrative Templates | System | Removable Storage**. You can also apply these settings to users under **User Configuration | Administrative Templates | System | Removable Storage**.

Table 5.2 Group Policy Objects Controlling Device Use

Policy Name	Effect
All Removable Storage classes: Deny all access	Enabled: All removable storage devices are inaccessible, for write or read. Disabled (default): Removable storage devices are subject to class-specific settings.
All Removable Storage classes: Allow direct access in remote sessions	Enabled: Removable storage devices can be accessed by remote sessions. Disabled (default): Removable storage devices may not be accessed by remote sessions.
CD and DVD: Deny read access	Enabled: Read access to CD/DVD storage devices is denied. Disabled (default): CD/DVD storage devices may be read from.

Continued

Table 5.2 continued Group Policy Objects Controlling Device Use

Policy Name	Effect
CD and DVD: Deny write access	Enabled: Write access to CD/DVD burning devices is denied. Disabled (default): CD/DVD burning devices are writeable.
Custom Classes: Deny read access	Enabled: A list of class GUIDs must be provided; read access to devices matching the listed classes is denied. Disabled (default): There is no custom list of GUIDs for which read access is denied.
Custom Classes: Deny write access	Enabled: A list of class GUIDs must be provided; write access to devices matching the listed classes is denied. Disabled (default): There is no custom list of GUIDs for which read access is denied.
Floppy Drives: Deny read access	Enabled: Floppy drives may not be read from. Disabled (default): Floppy drives may be read from.
Floppy Drives: Deny write access	Enabled: Floppy drives may not be written to. Disabled (default): Floppy drives may be written to.
Removable Disks: Deny read access	Enabled: Removable disks may not be read from. Disabled (default): Removable disks may be read from.
Removable Disks: Deny write access	Enabled: Removable disks may not be written to. Disabled (default): Removable disks may be written to.
Tape Drives: Deny read access	Enabled: Tape drives may not be read from. Disabled (default): Tape drives may be read from.

Continued

Table 5.2 continued Group Policy Objects Controlling Device Use

Policy Name	Effect
Tape Drives: Deny write access	Enabled: Tape drives may not be written to. Disabled (default): Tape drives may be written to.
WPD Devices: Deny read access	Enabled: Devices marked as "Windows Portable Devices" (WPD) may not be read from. This includes mobile phones, media players, cameras, and so on (i.e., devices that do more than simply provide storage). Disabled (default): WPDs may be read from.
WPD Devices: Deny write access	Enabled: WPDs may not be written to. Disabled (default): WPDs may be written to.
Time (in seconds) to force reboot	Enabled: The time spent waiting for a resource currently being accessed before rebooting the system to force a change in this set of policies to be applied. Disabled (default): If a removable storage device is currently in use, and policy changes cannot be applied as a result, the policy change will not take effect.

Tools and Traps…

Group Policy Restrictions Don't Apply at Boot Time

Group Policy restrictions such as those in Table 5.2 apply only to access from within Windows. If you disable read access to CD and DVD drives, you have not protected your systems against being booted from a CD-ROM or DVD-ROM. To do that, you must alter the basic input/output system (BIOS) settings, and protect those BIOS settings with a BIOS password.

Real-World Usage: Our Road Warrior Returns

You've just been asked to make sure that road warriors are able to give corporate presentations while they are on the move, but that they can't save them, or the confidential information they carry, to removable storage devices.

No problem; we'll simply revisit our Group Policy Object from before, navigate to **Computer Configuration | Administrative Templates | System | Removable Storage**, and enable every policy that includes the words *Deny write access* (except, of course, for the option to deny write access to custom classes, because we don't know which custom classes those might be, so our list would remain empty).

Notes from the Underground...

You Can't Ban What You Don't Know

Because device usage policies listed here work from an "allow by default" model, the only way to ban writes to all removable storage devices is to ban all access to all removable storage classes, using the **All Removable Storage classes: Deny all access** setting. Because this bans read access as well, you will probably be reluctant to do this.

In our opinion, this is a misstep on Microsoft's part, because it means that as soon as a new device class is created, you're going to have to add it to your **Custom Classes: Deny write access** list, or run the risk that confidential information can be copied over.

For us, this means that it may be possible to find a device that you haven't considered blocking, and that we can use to copy off large amounts of your business secrets, whether that's customer data, business intelligence, legal and contract information, and so on.

Rights Management

Digital Rights Management (DRM) is a tricky topic, particularly when couched in the common terms of the movie makers versus the general public. Because that discussion is intensely personal and very controversial, we want to steer clear of making any statements that endorse or condemn DRM. It is your decision whether to use it. This chapter will discuss the Rights Management System as it is implemented in

Windows Vista (you can also download it as an add-on for other versions of Windows at www.microsoft.com/downloads/details.aspx?FamilyID=02da5107-2919-414b-a5a3-3102c7447838&DisplayLang=en) to provide DRM services to Windows applications.

Rights Management Is Bad—No, Good—No, Bad...

Many people in the press and on Web logs have expressed the opinion that DRM in general is a bad thing, because it prevents content consumers from accessing content to which they should have access, whether it's because the content is provided for free, or because they have paid for access to the content.

This is, quite clearly, true: If you have paid for access, or if access is provided for free, it seems strange that someone would prevent you from accessing content just because of the way you plan to access the content, or what you plan to do with it.

But it's not a binary argument. For instance, a person may paint a mural on the side of his house, which makes it "publicly readable"; he has not given implicit permission, by doing that, for anyone walking by with a paintbrush to make additions to the mural. That would be vandalism, because he didn't approve of it.

Historically, content providers' rights have been protected by copyright law, and there's a huge amount of legislation and precedent in the direction of protecting the rights of both the content producer and the content consumer.

With DRM, content consumers intend to make sure that their wishes are met when producing and distributing content—and it's hard to argue with that goal. If you write the next Great American Novel, or you've painted "What the Mona Lisa Did Next", you're justified in releasing it only for what you consider to be appropriate recompense, or withholding it from the public until you are satisfied with your remuneration.

The objection to DRM (except from those who insist that all information, all art, all content, "wants to be free") comes from putative content consumers who are concerned that their own ability to consume the content is unnecessarily restricted. They may want to view the movie they purchased on a different screen, or add subtitles to it so that they can watch it with a deaf relative.

Too much DRM protection on content means the content is no longer acceptably usable by your targeted consumers. If your goal is to sell content to those consumers, clearly this is a losing proposition. You don't make money by killing piracy, unless you make money by selling more product as a result.

For publicly available content, however, some protection may remind otherwise-honest consumers that the content they are viewing is not completely licensed to them—distribution rights have not been granted, and the content is intended to be accessed only through the method and media that have been purchased. This is disappointing for the consumer who bought a DVD, intending to watch it on a remote device, but not totally unsurprising (if there is a market for watching movies on remote devices, maybe a smart company will come along and exploit it by licensing content for distribution in that way).

Rights Management Is Doomed to Failure

Wow, that didn't sound inflammatory, did it?

Seriously, perfect DRM is not physically possible. There's always what's known as the "analog path"—even if that's only from the loudspeaker to your ear, from the monitor to your eyes. A movie can always be videotaped; a radio program can always be recorded by placing a microphone from a tape recorder next to the speaker, as we used to do in our youth; a protected document can be forwarded to someone by opening an e-mail client on a nearby computer, and simply typing the message in as you read it on the other screen.

Our favorite story of the mistaken belief in the perfection of Rights Management comes from a time when we were asked to give a quote for developing a solution for a software house that wanted to prevent its developers from stealing code. The quote we gave was "you can only achieve this solution by killing or lobotomizing your development staff before you let them go home."

Particularly when it comes to protecting against theft by the people who create your content, technology doesn't—can't—help, and you need to start consulting with your lawyers and human resources specialists, to make sure that sufficient policies and contractual protections are in place to punish anyone found to have broken your trust.

This is not an old problem. In his first job, one of the authors of this book signed the British Official Secrets Act, and as a result he is forbidden from reading some of the things he wrote as a teenager. That doesn't mean he doesn't know those things anymore, and couldn't write them again—just that he can't read the document to which he contributed work. Similarly, the software house's developers could not prevent the developers they employ from creating similar works for others, except by writing punitive measures into their contracts should they do so, and watching them to make sure that they don't.

Rights Management Can Only Succeed

So, let's swing the argument in the other direction—having argued that it can never be perfect we're now going to argue that DRM can be a good and worthwhile thing.

Where DRM truly comes into its own is in private environments—generally within a corporate enclave, as an adjunct to the legal and social (human resources) protections you should already have in place.

If we send an e-mail to you, and prohibit it from being printed or forwarded, you can certainly use your cell phone to take a photo of the e-mail, and print that photo on your own time and on your own equipment. But as soon as we find that you have done that, any pretense that you didn't know the e-mail was not to be printed is voided, because of the effort you have undergone in order to print the message and the warning that was displayed to you when you tried to print it in any usual way.

NOTE

We are not lawyers, and this is not legal advice. As far as we are aware, this assertion has not been tested in court; it is merely the technical person's answer to "how can I make it easier to punish those who break their agreements with me?"

As with many "security" solutions, like a lock on your bicycle, Rights Management presents a reminder to the "mostly honest" that the content owner has particular wishes regarding his content, and will likely take action against you if you try to subvert those wishes. Someone with the right technology and sufficient reason to break the protection is going to do so.

Clearly, then, DRM is going to work only in an environment where the content provider has the ability to take punitive action against the content consumer. That's why DRM is less useful in the public sphere, but close to essential in private.

DRM's closest cousin in security theory is the concept of "Mandatory Access Control," wherein documents can be marked—for instance, "Public", "Secret", "Top Secret", and "For Your Eyes Only". The merging of information in two documents leads to the merged document receiving at least the higher of the two ratings, unless it is specifically declassified to a lower level. Despite this process having obvious flaws and means of subversion, Mandatory Access Control has been in use in many military and government circles for decades, both in the online computer world and in the manual world of paper files.

Are You 0wned?

Media License Acquisition

In 2006, there was a brief period where it seemed to be in vogue among hackers to distribute media that was "protected" by DRM in Windows Media Player. Most often, this was found in pornographic movies and popular music downloads. The media itself was nothing special, and may even have contained the content it claimed to. But the license acquisition process would take you to a Web site that installed any number of malware components through your Web browser, usually through the vulnerability of the time in Internet Explorer.

Remember, when you see an advisory that says the workaround is to avoid browsing to untrustworthy sites, there are many ways in which you can be taken to an untrustworthy site in your Web browser. Make sure that any media requiring license acquisition comes from a reputable, trustworthy source, or get the media elsewhere. If you can't trust the license acquisition process or its source, you can't trust the media.

Windows Rights Management Services (RMS) has several required components. Although this book focuses on Windows Vista, and therefore limits itself to the documentation of the client side of Windows RMS, it's important to realize that deploying Windows RMS is not a simple procedure. You need to deploy an authoritative RMS server for your forest domain—currently, this would be a Windows Server 2003 system, which needs to run ASP.NET 1.1, IIS 6, and MSMQ, and needs access to a local or remote SQL Server instance (this can be an MSDE instance, if run locally).

Your RMS server will be able to effectively limit what can be done with documents throughout your domain, and in other trusted domains, so long as those documents are created or distributed by applications that interface with RMS. These may also be described as "IRM"-capable applications (IRM stands for Information Rights Management). In order to protect documents, RMS encrypts them at the point at which IRM is enabled on the document. Make sure to distribute the protected version of the document!

There is no client-side user interface or administrative task for Windows RMS—your RMS server is discovered through Active Directory settings, and each application chooses to apply its own user interface to the RMS application program interface (API). An example of the way in which you would create an RMS-protected document in Microsoft Word would be to choose **File | Permission**, and then select the permission type, as defined at your RMS server under **Rights Policy Templates**.

When you use an RMS client application, such as Microsoft Word, or Microsoft Outlook, to open a protected document, it will use Active Directory to locate the forest's RMS server. It will verify your credentials at the RMS server, using your e-mail address, and verifying that you have been given permission to access the document for some purposes. The RMS server will grant a "use license" (that's "use" with a soft *s*, meaning it's a license for a use), which contains a decryption key allowing the software to display the protected content.

Although it would certainly be possible for a malicious programmer to write a program that used the RMS API in Windows to access use licenses and decrypt protected documents, because you are in a forest/domain and you are using RMS to enforce business policies, it is possible for you to do something about a breach when you detect it. On the RMS server itself, you can disable any programs that you do not trust to access RMS-protected documents. You can also disable access from any OS versions that you do not trust to access protected documents. Disabled software will not be granted a use license and, as a result, will not be able to decrypt content.

Encrypting File System

The Encrypting File System (EFS) has been a component of the New Technology File System (NTFS) since Windows 2000. It's a reliable technology and implementation, and is strongly recommended in environments where private information is easily identified by information owners and administrators. For environments where private information moves around from place to place, where there isn't as much oversight ability, or where the risk is considered greater (particularly in mobile computers such as laptops and Tablet PCs), whole-disk encryption, which we discuss later in this chapter, may be considered a better threat mitigation.

A Little Crypto Theory

Cryptography is all about taking data that you can read and turning it into mush that you can't—and sometimes, it's about taking that mush and turning it back into data that you can read. One of this book's authors studied mathematics at Cambridge University, and the mathematics that get used in cryptography make his head hurt. He understands them enough to trust them, and we suggest that you do as he does: trust the mathematicians, and believe in the operation of cryptography as voodoo magic, as though someone had shown you that not only can she turn a crank handle on a side of beef and turn it into burgers, but also that she can turn it the other way and turn your dollar value meal into a cow's rump, a tomato, and a few chaffs of wheat.

For EFS and BitLocker, we're mostly concerned with this ability to perform encryption and decryption—specifically, the use of asymmetric and symmetric encryption. Asymmetric encryption is also known as public key cryptography. For asymmetric encryption to work, there have to be two keys: a public key and a private key. The public key is used to encrypt, and the private key is used to decrypt. Symmetric encryption, by contrast, uses one key, and it uses that key to encrypt and decrypt—hence the name *symmetric encryption*.

Symmetric encryption is fast, but isn't quite as secure as asymmetric encryption, partly because the two parties have to share a key (and when two parties share a secret, it's no longer a secret), but mostly because the mathematics are less tricky. It takes a significantly shorter time (a few dozen years, say, in the case of EFS) to crack a symmetric encryption key, than it takes to crack an asymmetric encryption key (on the order of a few billion years). Because of this, encryption schemes usually follow the procedure whereby a large symmetric key is created, and then is exchanged between the two parties through encryption by the public key of the recipient.

This is exactly how BitLocker and EFS accomplish their magic (BitLocker's use of asymmetric encryption is limited to decryption of the Volume Master Key held by the Trusted Platform Module [TPM]).

Ancient History: What You Should Already Know

Given that information about the application of cryptography, EFS works in the only way that makes any sense. EFS uses both Asymmetric Key Encryption and Symmetric Key Encryption (also referred to as Public/Private Key Encryption) versus Shared Key Encryption. When a file has EFS enabled on it, a random symmetric key is generated, and this key is used to encrypt and decrypt the file for as long as the file exists. This symmetric key is itself encrypted using the public key of every user who is defined in EFS to have access to the file. (Note that this does not mean that those users also have rights to access the file. NTFS access control lists [ACLs] are always checked first, and if you have no access granted through NTFS ACLs, you won't be able to read the file's cipher text in order to decrypt it.)

Now, when you want access to the EFS-protected file, your usual NTFS access rights are checked first, to see whether you have access to the file's cipher text (the encrypted, otherwise meaningless, contents of the file on disk). If you don't have access, the usual "Access Denied" message will be displayed. If you do have access, the EFS certificates in your certificate store are compared against the list of public keys that have been used to encrypt the file's symmetric key. If you possess a certificate whose public key matches one that was used to encrypt the file's symmetric key, and you have a private key for that certificate, this private key will be used to decrypt the symmetric key so that you can read and/or write to the file. Otherwise, you will see "Access Denied".

Backup programs use a special set of APIs so that they will simply back up the cipher text of the file (along with the encrypted copies of the symmetric key); the backup operator's account does not need to be granted EFS access to a file. When an EFS-encrypted file is restored, it is useless unless someone has access to a private key that will decrypt the file!

Enabling Encryption on a File or Folder

We sometimes like to describe administrators as *clickies* and *clackies*—a *clicky* will want to find every possible way to use the mouse to accomplish an administrative goal; a *clacky* will generally use commands at the command prompt. Which type are you? Coming out of the world of software development, the author of this chapter is very much a clacky, although he does appreciate the power of a well-designed graphical user interface (GUI). We hope we can accommodate both kinds of administrators in the following instructions.

The GUI way to enable encryption on a file or folder in Windows Vista is as follows:

1. Right-click on the file, select Properties, and on the General tab, click the Advanced... button, as in Figure 5.5.

2. Check the box that reads Encrypt contents to secure data, click OK and then Apply or OK.

3. You will be prompted to choose between encrypting just the file (or files) selected, or the file and its parent folder, as shown in Figure 5.6. If you selected a folder to encrypt, you will be asked if you want to encrypt just the folder, or the folder, its subfolders and files. Selecting to encrypt folders and subfolders, rather than files, is a good security measure, as it reduces the chance that a temporary copy of the file will be made and stored unencrypted in this folder.

Figure 5.5 Using Advanced Attributes to Encrypt Important Documents

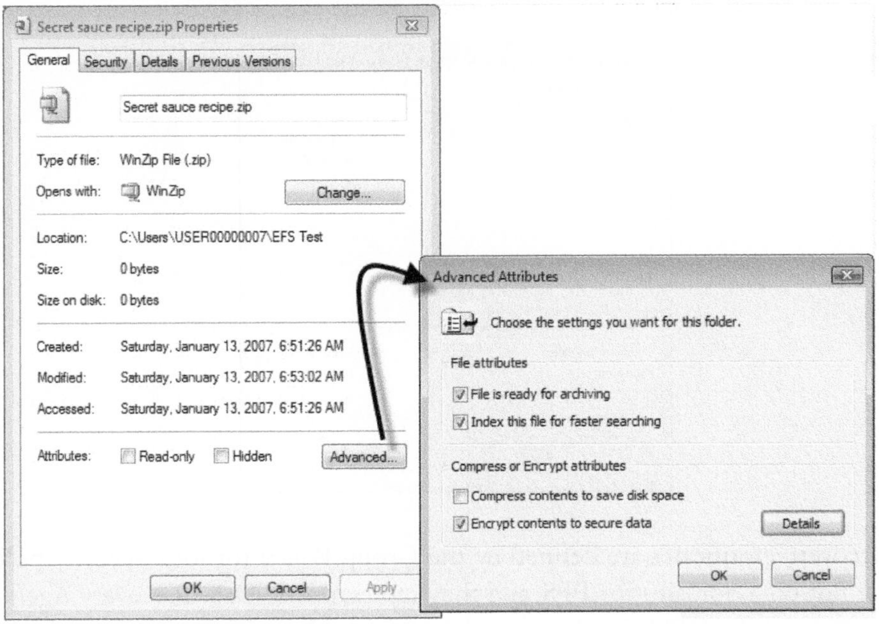

Figure 5.6 Encrypting a File and Choosing to Encrypt Its Parent Folder

(You can, of course, enable encryption using the command line *cipher /e <file>* or *cipher /e /s:<directory>*.)

If you were paying attention on the **Advanced Attributes** dialog, you will have seen a grayed-out (disabled) **Details** button. This button is now enabled, because you now have some encryption details that you can view and modify. Clicking this takes you to the **User Access** dialog for this EFS file, as you can see in Figure 5.7. The User Access dialog displays the list of users who are given access to decrypt (read) and encrypt (modify) the file, their certificates, and the list of recovery certificates.

Figure 5.7 Listing the Users and Recovery Certificates for an EFS-Protected File

Recovery certificates are defined by the Group Policy (or local security policy if you are not on a domain) for EFS, and they represent the Data Recovery Agent (DRA). You need a DRA for those scary moments when the original owner of a file is no longer available to decrypt the file, and no one else has been given access through EFS.

Tools & Traps...

Jumping without a Backup Parachute

At one point, encryption in the hands of mere users was considered so dangerous and scary that Windows would not allow you to create an EFS-encrypted file that didn't have a DRA, but now those of you who like to live on the edge can change your EFS policy to remove the requirement for a DRA on encrypted files.

Encryption is already a double-edged sword: If you lose your password, you're not going to get your files back without brute force cracking your own password, or begging the owner of the DRA account. If you fly without a DRA, you're saying "if I forget my password, I'm comfortable forgetting all possibility of getting my data back."

If you don't use a DRA, at the very least you should back up your keys (you can do this from the User Access dialog) to a removable storage device.

Continued

Because the keys are exported in a PFX file that has password protection, you should also write down the password for the PFX file, and store the password and file in a physically secure location.

If you can't back up your keys, back up your data.

Or, simply accept the risk that you will lose your files' contents completely.

Splat.

Depending on where you apply EFS policy in the Active Directory structure, you may wind up with several DRAs enacted on users who encrypt documents. This is not necessarily a bad thing, as different DRAs may be used for different purposes—an all-powerful, overarching DRA might be used to decrypt files for forensic investigation by a compliance team, whereas a DRA local to a particular team might be used to provide "oops" recovery for that team in the event of occasional slip-ups.

Exporting Your EFS Encryption Keys

You can export your EFS encryption keys at the GUI or at the command prompt. The command-prompt way to export a user's EFS encryption keys is via *cipher /x <backup.pfx>*. This will prompt you for a password—twice—and will use that to encrypt the private key information within the PFX. You can also export an EFS encryption key pair used for a particular file, using *cipher /x:<file> <backup.pfx>*. This is useful in case you have changed encryption keys since encrypting that file, but still have access to the keys used for the file in question.

Through the GUI, you can also export your EFS encryption keys for a file, or your current user. To export the keys from a file:

1. Locate the file in Windows Explorer, and right-click it.

2. Select Properties, and on the General tab, click Advanced… | Details, to give the User Access dialog shown in Figure 5.7.

3. Select the user whose keys you wish to back up – this should generally be you, as you will not have access to another user's keys – and click on Back up keys as described previously.

4. This takes you to the **Certificate Export Wizard**, with the only option available being to export to a PFX file.

To export your current EFS certificate from the GUI, it's probably easiest to choose a file you have recently encrypted, and select the **Back up keys** button as described previously. You could also export your keys from the Certificate Manager, but using the EFS dialog allows you to avoid picking the wrong certificate.

Adding Users to EFS-Protected Files

To add a user to an EFS-protected file, the command-line method is a little tricky. First, you have to find the user's certificate hash or CER file. Then, you specify one of these in the command *cipher /adduser /certhash:<hash> <file>* or *cipher /adduser /certfile:<cert-file> <file>*—as with the *cipher* command to begin encryption, you can also use */s:<directory>* to apply the command to an entire tree.

The GUI version of this operation is far easier. From the **User Access** dialog for the file, simply click **Add** and select the user from a list. Note that you will only be presented with a list of users who have already created EFS encryption key pairs. It would be rather useless to create an encryption key pair for someone else simply so that you could add her to an access list for a file. A key pair works only if the private key is known only to the owner of the key pair.

Removing users from EFS-protected files is a similar operation: Either click the **Remove** button, or use the *cipher /removeuser /certhash:<hash> <file>* command.

Creating a Nondefault EFS Policy

By default, every file that you encrypt using EFS is backed by a DRA, and the account whose certificate is chosen (and created, if necessary) for this purpose is that of the administrator. For a workgroup machine or a standalone machine, this is the built-in administrator account; for a domain-joined machine, it is the administrator account on the first domain controller.

Other defaults are also present on Vista relating to EFS. EFS is allowed, by default, and although smart cards are allowed, they are not required. Where smart cards are in use, the system will create a user-cacheable key from the information on the smart card (allowing you to remove your smart card but still access encrypted files). Files that can be encrypted by policy, but aren't by default, include the user's Documents folder and the system page file.

You can see all of these settings at the EFS policy setting at **Computer Configuration | Windows Settings | Security Settings | Public Key Policies**. Right-click on **Encrypting File System** and you'll see the policies window shown in Figure 5.8.

Figure 5.8 Investigating the Default EFS Properties

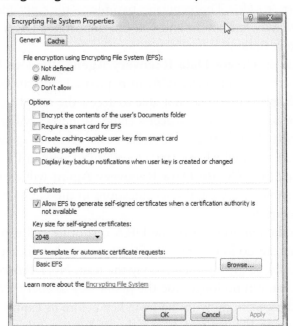

There are, of course, some parts of the default settings that you may want to change. Our favorite change is to assign a different DRA; the built-in administrator account has so much to do already (especially because it is disabled in Windows Vista by default), that it seems to be too much to ask that it also be the keeper of the last resort in encrypted file recovery.

So, again, right-click on the **Encrypting File System** element under **Computer Configuration | Windows Settings | Security Settings | Public Key Policies**, and you'll see that you have the option to **Add Data Recovery Agent** or **Create Data Recovery Agent**. The former is what you will do if you already have created an EFS encryption key pair and stored it to a PFX file, and the latter is so that you can create an EFS encryption key pair associated with your account. The former is the safest option to use, as it does not tie the EFS encryption keys to a specific logon account, meaning that you can lock them away safely until you need them. You should treat EFS recovery as an exceptional process—one that does not happen frequently. For everyday access to encrypted files, after all, you can simply add a user on your team to the list of users with access to the secret key protecting the file.

To create a self-signed encryption key pair for a recovery agent so that you can use the Add Data Recovery Agent option and then save the resulting PFX file without its private key ever entering your certificate store, the simplest way is to run the command *cipher /r:<file>*. This generates two files: <file>.pfx and <file>.cer. The first is to be locked away, and the second you can import as a DRA, using the Add Data Recovery Agent option.

When you click on **Create Data Recovery Agent**, Windows Vista will contact the domain's certificate authority (CA) to request a certificate based on the EFS Recovery Agent template. If you are not able to access the template, either because it does not exist or because you have no access rights, Windows will give you an error message with the text "Windows cannot create a data recovery agent."

If you have a CA from which you are allowed to request an EFS Recovery Agent certificate, selecting **Create Data Recovery Agent** will create a new DRA certificate in your name, following the specifications in the CA's EFS Recovery Agent certificate template.

One default in the template is that the DRA certificate will expire in two years. Does this mean you can no longer recover files that were last encrypted two years or more ago? That would be inconvenient, to say the least. No, DRA certificate expiry simply means that you can no longer use the public key to encrypt files in EFS unless you renew the certificate with the same key before its expiration date. You can recover old files with an old key pair, even if the PFX file you have on backup says that the certificate has already expired.

Once you have created the DRA, you will notice that none of your existing EFS-protected files has changed to reflect this. Changes to EFS policy take place only with regard to files created after the policy is changed and has taken effect. This is why it is very important to consider your EFS recovery policies before allowing EFS throughout your organization. It does you no good to declare that "all encrypted files may be recovered by calling the help desk" if someone has already encrypted an important spreadsheet with a now-defunct DRA, and then leaves the company.

NOTE

Again, we cannot overemphasize that if you do not have the keys to an EFS-protected file, the data within that file is irretrievably lost.

Exporting and Deleting EFS Private Keys

The first thing you should do when creating a DRA is to export the key pair and delete the private key from your certificate store. That way, the private key is no longer sitting on an active system. The exported key pair, in a PFX file, can now be saved to a well-labeled floppy or a USB stick, and locked in a secure cabinet. Because PFX files with private keys are encrypted with a password, you will need to securely store the passwords for your private keys so that you can recover them later.

By locking away the keys to the DRA account like this, you make it easier to treat DRA recovery requests as exceptional occurrences, and you can educate users that they can use EFS encryption to share files among their teammates, just as they can use it to keep others out of the files.

Viewing your certificates is the first step to exporting them. To view your certificates, you will open the Certificate Manager Microsoft Management Console (MMC) snap-in. The easiest way we find to do this is via **Start | Run | certmgr.msc**. The tool doesn't appear on the Start menu by default, but you can always create your own shortcut to it if you find that you use it frequently enough.

> ## NOTE
>
> Running Certificate Manager this way shows you your certificate store. You can view other accounts' certificate stores, including those of the local computer and system services to which you have access, by adding the Certificate Manager snap-in to an MMC session, at which point you will be asked to choose which account to view.

The certificates that belong to you are listed under **Certificates – Current User | Personal | Certificates**. Because all of these certificates may be issued to you, and therefore will have similar-sounding names, it's often worth using the **Friendly Name** setting to distinguish them. You can edit any certificate's Properties to add a Friendly Name that will be displayed in your personal certificates store.

The DRA certificate will have a value of **File Recovery** in its **Intended Purposes** column. Double-clicking on the certificate will show its properties (see Figure 5.9) so that you can check that this is the certificate you are expecting.

Figure 5.9 Viewing the Properties for an EFS File Recovery Certificate

Click **OK** to close this dialog box.

To export the key pair and certificate to a PFX file, right-click on the certificate and select **All Tasks | Export**. You will then see the **Certificate Export Wizard** start up.

Click **Next** after reading the introductory page of the wizard. You will be asked whether you want to **Export Private Key**. Click the button that reads **Yes, export the private key**, and then click **Next**. Because you are exporting the private key, the next dialog only allows you to choose to export as a Personal Information Exchange file, also known as a PFX file, or a PKCS #12 file.

Because you are exporting this certificate and key pair in order to remove them from the machine, you will also want to check the box marked **Delete the private key if the export is successful**. Then click **Next** again. You will need to supply a password that protects the private key. You will need this password when you import the certificate again to recover files, so make sure that you keep a record of it in a secure place. You must type the password in twice, as a protection against mistyping it (check that Caps Lock and any other key locks are not set). Then click **Next** again. You can now provide the filename and path onto which you will be exporting this key. Ideally this would be a floppy or a removable USB stick that you will later be storing in a locked cabinet.

Once you have entered the filename or browsed to its location, click **Next** again, and you will see a summary screen as in Figure 5.10. Click **Finish**, and you will see a dialog box that reads **The export was successful**. Click **OK**, and you are returned to the Certificate Manager, where you can verify that the private key has been deleted from your certificate store, by opening the Properties of the certificate. It should no longer display the message "You have a private key that corresponds to this certificate."

Figure 5.10 Completing the Certificate Export

Recovering EFS-Protected Files

Recovering an EFS-protected file is a simple matter of importing the DRA private key and certificate from the PFX file that you saved earlier, using the password with which it was created; then opening the file and copying it to an unencrypted location, simply removing the encryption, and possibly then moving to another encrypted location for which active users do have keys.

To begin importing the key, you can simply open the PFX file—either from Explorer or from the command prompt. This will start the **Certificate Import Wizard**; read the explanatory text and then click **Next**. You will be presented with the path to your PFX file that you have chosen to install; click **Next** again. You are now asked to enter the password. This time, you have to type it correctly only once. Pay careful attention to the checkboxes on the page shown in Figure 5.11.

Figure 5.11 Importing a PFX Certificate for a DRA

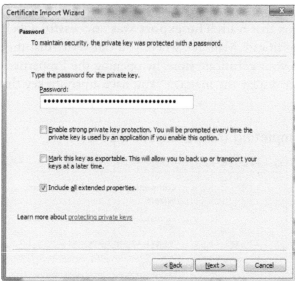

(As you can see, our usual password for certificates is a long string of circles.) Consider the ways in which you might use any of these settings:

■ **Enable strong private key protection** With this setting, anytime you use the certificate, you will be asked to confirm the use by entering a password. This way, you aren't surprised by your certificate being used behind your back.

■ **Mark this key as exportable** You usually don't want this. You have previously stored the private key into the PFX file that you are importing, and you don't want to find people using the certificate that you import in order to create their own PFX files that they can carry around with them for later use.

■ **Include all extended properties** We leave this checked. If the certificate had extended properties when we created and exported it we would probably want to keep them here.

Click **Next** and you will be prompted to choose a certificate store into which the certificate will be placed. The option to **Automatically select the certificate store based on the type of certificate** is usually sufficient. Click **Next**.

You will now see the summary screen of the Certificate Import Wizard, detailing that the import action will take place, where the certificate comes from, and where it will go to. Click **Finish** to begin the import process. You will be prompted that **The import was successful**. It is a good idea to check everything by opening the Certificate Manager (remember, **Start | Run | certmgr.msc**) to see your certificates. Double-click the newly imported certificate, and make sure that **You have a private key that corresponds to this certificate**.

Now, you can recover the files simply by copying them to somewhere that encryption doesn't apply, or by unchecking the box **Encrypt contents to secure data** in the **Advanced Attributes** dialog, or (for those of you who like the command prompt) by using the command *cipher /d <file>* to decrypt the file in place.

New EFS Features with Windows Vista

New to Windows Vista, you can now encrypt and decrypt files and folders by using a key held on a smart card, whether that's for a user's own access to those files and folders or for a DRA's access to recover encrypted files.

Also new to Windows Vista is the ability to use EFS to encrypt the page file—this is carried out using a randomly generated key that is held in memory for the duration of the boot cycle—so that the page file is not readable after a reboot.

You can also encrypt your Offline Cache files—changed in Windows Vista is the fact that this encryption is carried out using the user's public key, rather than a system key—so that only the files' owner can access them later.

A new Group Policy setting for Windows Vista EFS support is under **Computer Configuration | Administrative Templates | Windows Components | Search**, and sets whether to index encrypted files so that they can be searched quickly. The default is not to attempt to index encrypted files, because it is likely that you do not want contents of these files to be held in the index store. Of course, the indexing service cannot possibly make up a key that it does not have access to, so this setting does not allow you to "backdoor" your way into an encrypted file through the indexing service. But it may allow you to accidentally expose your own encrypted files through the indexing service. You can see most of these settings in Figure 5.8.

Whole-Disk Encryption

Unless you've been holed up in a bunker somewhere and this is the first book you picked up on escaping into the outside world, you've seen numerous reports of widespread data theft. Maybe even your own data has been stolen. Sometimes what's stolen is a simple USB flash drive, and other times it's a whole system—laptop or desktop.

Notes from the Underground...

Why Am I Stealing Your Laptop Anyway?

The majority of laptop theft is opportunistic—someone with a criminal bent notices you have left your laptop unattended, or arms up and visits the local coffee shop with intent to grab the first laptop he sees.

As a result, the aim is merely to steal a chunk of hardware that can be sold to the next person.

Most criminals are not going to care about the data on the laptop because, quite frankly, if they had the skills necessary to extract it, they'd be gainfully employed by organized crime instead.

But consider the thrifty entrepreneur who goes to his local pawnbroker with the intent of acquiring an inexpensive laptop—given that the criminal, the fence, and the pawnbroker each have minimal computer skills, if any, it is entirely likely that the laptop this entrepreneur receives still has retained all of its data.

It's for that reason that the technology journalist with too much time on his hands and not enough ideas for a story will often visit the local second-hand vendors of ill repute and purchase all the secondhand computers that his editor's corporate credit card can afford. Then he'll spend a few hours with a boot disk and his steno pad, noting all the secret information on these machines so that he can do a big exposé.

Do you want your name splashed across that story?

Although we've talked about using EFS to protect your data, it's a little ... fiddly. You have to specify which folders and/or files are protected, and who has access to each one. You have to maintain access through private and public key pairs and certificates, and you're constantly faced with that nagging doubt of "did I really find and lock all of my secret files?"

If only there was a "sledgehammer" to crack this particular nut—something that would encrypt everything on the entire machine! Well, now there is, and it's in the Ultimate and Enterprise SKUs of Windows Vista. This whole-disk encryption tool is called BitLocker.

It's Been a While Coming

A number of different third parties have provided whole-disk encryption, under various names, on a number of different platforms. Windows Vista is the first version of Windows to innately support whole-disk encryption, and there is no indication that it will be available for other versions of Windows. It's a little surprising that it has taken this long to arrive from Microsoft and that it is not available for other versions of Windows, because when you think about it, whole-disk encryption is little more than a disk driver that does a little extra mathematical work on the data being read and/or written.

If the truth is told, it's probably that "little more" that has made for much of the delay. As we mentioned when talking about EFS, encryption protects your information from anyone who doesn't have the key—and that can just as easily be you, the owner of the data, as anyone you'd normally like to keep out. So, Microsoft has taken great pains to ensure that BitLocker has a thoroughly complete set of key maintenance and recovery tools at its disposal, and Microsoft has limited BitLocker's dispersal to the top two tiers of Windows Vista's product SKUs—Windows Vista Ultimate and Windows Vista Enterprise.

Tools & Traps...

How Dangerous Can BitLocker Be?

When we were initially testing BitLocker during the Beta test cycle of Windows Vista, we were a little reckless in our choice of key stores: We chose to encrypt with a USB flash drive as our key store, and we thought we could get away without saving our recovery password.

Only when the system booted after initial encryption had begun, did we find that the system we were testing on could not recognize a USB flash drive at boot time, and hence the BitLocker boot loader could not read our key and could not unlock our disk.

If this should happen to you and you did not save your recovery key, the only thing you can do is reinstall over the top of your now-randomized disk, and chalk it up to experience.

Remember that you should use encryption in an environment where you accept that the "live" data to be encrypted may be lost if you are careless, or if you are unfamiliar with what you are doing. As long as you spend some time testing beforehand and figuring out how to work BitLocker on a discardable test machine, you will not find any significant problem in using BitLocker.

(The day job of one of this book's authors involves working with one of the third-party whole-disk encryption products, and his negative opinions about this product center on the fact that, although the encryption works really well on laptops, the recovery and enterprise management features leave a lot to be desired. He is hugely pleased to say that this is not the case with BitLocker, where the management features begin even before you start to encrypt a drive.)

Group Policy is, of course, where you'll find the management features showing up—to allow these settings to be deployed to your domain (and particularly, to allow recovery passwords to be stored in Active Directory), you will need to download Microsoft's suite of scripts and documentation for "Configuring AD to Back up BitLocker and TPM Recovery Information", which you will find at www.microsoft.com/downloads/details.aspx?FamilyID=3a207915-dfc3-4579-90cd-86ac666f61d4.

These Group Policy settings will appear under **Computer Configuration | Administrative Templates | Windows Components | BitLocker Drive Encryption**. Table 5.3 lists all these settings.

Table 5.3 Group Policy Settings Controlling BitLocker Protection

Policy Name	Effect
Turn on BitLocker backup to Active Directory Domain Services	Enabled: BitLocker recovery information is backed up to Active Directory Domain Services. You can further require the backup be performed before BitLocker may be turned on, for enhanced reliability, and you can choose to back up a recovery password only, or the recovery password and recovery keys, to aid in specialized restoration. Disabled: BitLocker recovery information is not backed up to Active Directory Domain Services. Note: Backup of recovery information to Active Directory Domain Services requires schema modifications to Active Directory that will be shipped with Windows Server 2007 (code-named Longhorn); you can install them from an adprep.exe tool shipped with Windows Vista, but it is imperative that you take great care, as outlined in the section on USB device policy.

Continued

Table 5.3 continued Group Policy Settings Controlling BitLocker Protection

Policy Name	Effect
Control Panel Setup: Configure recovery folder	Enabled: Allows you to specify where the recovery password will be stored automatically. Disabled: Leaves the decision on where to store the recovery password entirely up to the user. Note: Whether this setting is enabled or disabled, the user will still be able to store the recovery password where he chooses.
Control Panel Setup: Configure recovery options	With this setting enabled, you can configure whether to require or disallow the creation of either a 48-digit recovery password or a 256-bit recovery key. Microsoft has required that some form of recovery capability be enabled, so if you disable both of these settings, you must have backup to Active Directory Domain Services enabled; if you disable all three recovery storage methods, BitLocker will fail to encrypt, and you will receive a policy error.
Control Panel Setup: Enable advanced startup options	Allow BitLocker without a compatible TPM: If your system does not have a compatible TPM chip (or indeed, any TPM chip), you can enable this setting in order to allow BitLocker to proceed. For all of Microsoft's dire warnings, BitLocker even without TPM is a significant advance, for those of us who have data we don't want to be made available to anyone willing to walk off with a laptop. Configure TPM startup key option: You can choose whether to require or prevent the use of a USB startup key, or leave the decision to the user. Configure TPM startup PIN option: You can choose whether to require or prevent the use of a startup PIN, or leave the decision to the user. Note: You cannot require both the startup key and the startup PIN. For reasons we'll discuss later, you should not rely on the TPM alone.

Continued

Table 5.3 continued Group Policy Settings Controlling BitLocker
Protection

Policy Name	Effect
Configure encryption method	For serious gear-heads, you can choose between the 128-bit and 256-bit Advanced Encryption Standard (AES), and whether to apply Microsoft's "Diffuser" technology. (Diffuser protects against a relatively obscure cryptographic attack.)
Prevent memory overwrite on restart	Enabled: This will slightly improve your restart time, but will leave memory contents intact when you restart. An attacker with some ability to read residual memory (perhaps by booting to an external device) might be able to read the contents of memory and deduce where the keys for your hard drive are being stored. Disabled: Protects you against this memory attack, by forcing the memory to be cleared when you restart your computer.
Configure TPM platform validation profile	This policy applies only if you enable it before enabling BitLocker on your system drive. Changes to this policy have no effect on a system that is already protected by BitLocker. The contents of this policy are a checklist of which items are to be scanned by TPM prior to allowing BitLocker. This setting is way beyond the scope of this chapter. For most administrators, it's worth considering only if and when you have to call support on an overactive system scan, if it keeps complaining incorrectly that the system is being modified.

Preparing a New Installation of Vista for BitLocker

BitLocker in Windows Vista is designed on the premise that you will encrypt your boot drive—the one that contains your system (as opposed to the system drive, which is the one from which you boot; seriously).

If you encrypt your boot drive, the BIOS on your system will be unable to recognize it and will refuse to boot. As a result, you will need to make sure that your boot drive and your system drive are separate partitions.

If you haven't installed Windows Vista yet, it's an easy task to prepare your system for BitLocker. You can simply create two partitions: one sized at least 1.5 GB, and the other taking up the remainder of the disk. You can do this via the following procedure.

Click the **System Recovery Options** button in the **Install Windows** screen. Deselect any operating systems listed, click **Next**, and then click **Command Prompt** in the **System Recovery Options** dialog box. This presents you with a command prompt, at which you can run the *diskpart* command to start designing your system's partitions.

In response to the *diskpart* prompt, enter the following commands:

- *list disk* This lists the disks present in your system. The main hard drive should be disk 0. Check that its size is as you would expect so that you know the subsequent instructions refer to the right disk.

- *select disk 0* This selects the first drive in your system. Use a different number if *list disk* suggests it.

- *clean* This wipes the partition table. It effectively destroys access to data currently on the disk, so please make sure that you really wanted to do so!

- *create partition primary size=1500* This creates the primary partition of 1.5 GB.

- *assign letter=D* This will be your new D drive. Choose another letter if you prefer.

- *active* This sets this partition to be the one from which the system will be booted.

- *create partition primary* This creates a new partition, using the remaining space.

- *assign letter=C* We are all accustomed to using C as our system drive, right? You can make it something else if you choose to, maybe because you're the type that likes to prevent malware from writing to C:\Windows.

- *list volume* This lets you see the results of your handiwork. Check your work, because it'll be a long time before you can change it.

- *exit* This lets you leave the diskpart utility.

Because we're at the command prompt, we want to format the two drives here, and because we want to leave the system unattended during the format operation, we can use a dual command:

```
format C: /y /q /fs:ntfs & format D: /y /q /fs:ntfs
```

This command will format both the C and the D drive without stopping to ask for directions. The single & character in between the two commands indicates that they should operate one after the other; a double ampersand character, as &&, would run the second command only if the first succeeded.

Once the drives have been formatted and you have come back from your break, type **exit** to leave the Command Prompt window, and then close the System Recovery Options dialog. You could restart, but then you'd have to wait to press a key to boot from the DVD-ROM, and then reenter your installation language, time zone, and keyboard layout. Now you can click on **Install Now**, and proceed through a normal Windows Vista installation to the C drive. The Windows Vista installation is smart enough to tell that it should install the boot files on the system drive that we marked as **active**.

Preparing an Upgrade of Vista for BitLocker

If you're lucky, as we were, you'll already have a Windows XP system with two drives: a smaller system drive and a larger boot drive. Why is this here? This is a result of OEMs putting a "recovery partition" on your system. To do this, they created a bootable partition with recovery material, separate from your system partition. If this is the case, you can simply upgrade Windows XP to Windows Vista, and your system is ready for BitLocker to be enabled.

If this is not the case, upgrade to Windows Vista anyway, and step straight into the instructions for preparing an existing installation of Vista for BitLocker.

Preparing an Existing Installation of Vista for BitLocker: The Hard Way

If you've already installed Windows Vista on a single partition, don't panic: The instructions aren't that much more complicated, if any, than those for preparing for BitLocker on a new installation.

WARNING

If you've been using your Windows Vista computer for anything serious, of course, the margin of error is somewhat smaller, so please make a backup of your system and data files before proceeding. This process may render all of your data unusable if you, or we, get it wrong. After it works well the first few dozen reboots, you'll be more comfortable trusting BitLocker and can return to your original backup schedule.

As with the instructions for preparing a new installation for BitLocker, you will need to boot from the DVD.

Click the **System Recovery Options** button in the **Install Windows** screen. Deselect any operating systems listed, click **Next**, and then click **Command Prompt** in the **System Recovery Options** dialog box. This presents you with a command prompt, at which you can run the *diskpart* command to start designing your system's partitions.

In response to the *diskpart* prompt, enter the following commands:

- *list disk* This lists the disks present in your system. The main hard drive should be disk 0; check that its size is as you would expect so that you know the subsequent instructions refer to the right disk.

- *select disk 0* This selects the first drive in your system. Use a different number if *list disk* suggests it.

- *list partition* This lists the partitions on this disk, to verify that your existing partition is number 0.

- *select partition 0* This selects the main partition on your disk.

- *shrink desired=1500* This shrinks the partition to create an extra 1.5 GB of space.

- *create partition primary* This creates the primary partition of 1.5 GB.

- *assign letter=D* This will be your new D drive. Choose another letter if you prefer.

- *active* This sets this partition to be the one from which the system will be booted.

- *list volume* This shows you the results of your handiwork. Check your work, because it'll be a long time before you can change it.

- *exit* This lets you leave the diskpart utility.

We now want to format this drive:

```
format D: /y /q /fs:ntfs
```

This command will format the D drive without asking whether you really want to.

Once the drives have been formatted and you have come back from your break, you will need to copy the boot files from the old system partition to the new one. The commands to do this are as follows:

```
xcopy C:\bootmgr D:\bootmgr /h
xcopy C:\boot D:\boot /e /h
```

Now, type **exit** to leave the Command Prompt window, and restart. All being well, your system should now boot from the new D drive, but store all your data on the old C drive as before.

Preparing an Existing Installation of Vista for BitLocker: The Easy Way

While we were writing this chapter, we heard that Microsoft will be releasing a Windows Ultimate Extra download called the Windows BitLocker Drive Preparation Tool. This will do all the "heavy lifting" of disk partition resizing for you.

The other Windows Ultimate Extra download that has been announced is the Secure Online Key Backup, allowing you to store your BitLocker recovery password, or EFS recovery certificate, on a free Microsoft Web site called Digital Locker.

For more details on these, and on upcoming Windows Ultimate Extras, visit the Windows Vista Ultimate Web site at http://windows.ultimate.com. Windows Ultimate Extra downloads will be available after January 30, 2007.

Enabling BitLocker to Protect Your Laptop's Data in Case of Loss

Enabling BitLocker is simple: Open the **Control Panel**, and find **BitLocker Drive Encryption**. If you're using the Classic View, you will see this close to the top; if you prefer the Category View, you can find this under **Security**.

Because the preceding chapter went into some detail about the purpose of TPM and how to enable it, we're not going to cover that ground again.

BitLocker requires elevation, so it will prompt you if you have the user agent client (UAC) still turned on (you do still have UAC turned on, don't you?).

BitLocker shows the volumes that it will allow you to encrypt. In Windows Vista, this is only the boot volume, but in Windows Server 2007, you will be able to use the GUI to encrypt any volume other than the system volume. Underneath each volume label is the text "Turn On BitLocker" or "Turn Off BitLocker," depending on the state of that volume.

Depending on Group Policy settings that you have enabled for BitLocker, you will see a dialog box that presents a number of choices for startup protection: a USB key, a PIN, or simply using the TPM. For whatever reason, Microsoft has prevented the choice of combining a USB key and a PIN, or using a PIN without the TPM. If you have no compatible TPM on your system, you will see the dialog shown in Figure 5.12.

Figure 5.12 Choosing to Use a USB Startup Key on a Non-TPM Machine

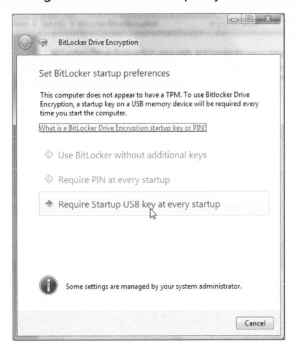

Use External Keys, or I'll Come Hack Your System

Whatever choices are offered to you for startup protection, it is important that you choose a method that keeps the startup protection—or some part of it— away from the computer when it's not currently being booted.

Continued

A startup PIN offers the best protection, because unless you write it on a sticky note and plaster it on the top of your keyboard, you can't accidentally leave it in the machine.

A startup key on a USB stick is a good protection too, but be careful to choose a stick on which you keep *only* your startup key. If you keep the stick in the machine's USB slot, when someone steals your laptop that person also has stolen your startup key.

If someone has your laptop and with it all of the keying material used to encrypt and decrypt it, you almost might as well not have encrypted it at all. This is particularly true if you are careless enough to leave your recovery password on the unencrypted portion of your drive, or on the USB stick that you left in the USB slot, or on the piece of paper in your laptop bag.

Top-class hackers can break into your system—encrypted though it is—if they have physical access to it in its booted, unlocked state, even if they can't immediately log on.

As you can see from Figure 5.12, we're demonstrating this on a system without a compatible TPM—we're obviously in an environment where the Group Policy setting **Allow BitLocker without a compatible TPM** has been enabled. Our only choice, therefore, is to use a USB startup key. Because we're disciplined enough to remove that key every time we boot (it's a "Hello Kitten" USB fob in bright pink, so we don't want to leave it in there where someone might notice it), we are very comfortable with that choice. So, if you're following along, click on **Require Startup USB key at every startup**.

You will now be prompted to **Save your Startup Key**, and a list of USB removable drives pops up. Choose the one you will always have with you for booting your system; ideally one that will fit in your pocket or your purse, or that you can carry somewhere other than in your laptop bag. If a malicious person steals your laptop bag, you don't want him to have your laptop and the keys to start it up.

Click **Save** to put the startup key onto your USB drive.

You are now prompted with the cornucopia of options for saving your recovery password (see Figure 5.13). In addition, if Active Directory Domain Services has been updated with the current scheme, and your policy requires the recovery password to be saved there, the recovery password will already have been stored there. The wide-ranging choice of options should be a colossal hint to you that you should choose as many of these as makes sense; especially if you use a TPM chip, the recovery password is the one thing that you absolutely, positively must keep safe. If something goes wrong, and your system won't boot (for instance, if the TPM boot process thinks the system has been tampered with), your recovery password can be used to recover and decrypt all the data in your drive, without the TPM cooperating on giving up its key. This is how you sleep at night, knowing that even if your CEO drives his Enzo Ferrari over his Acer Ferrari, as long as the disk is intact, you can get back his collection of "classic collector movies" as well as the business plan that he has been working on all week.

Figure 5.13 Choosing All the Places You Want to Save the Recovery Password

As we said earlier, don't pick just one of these places to save the recovery password—pick them all. Save one copy on a USB drive that you lock in your safe deposit box at the bank; save another in a folder on your network, protected by ACLs and EFS; print three copies, giving one to your grandmother to keep safe, one to put under the USB drive in the safe deposit box, and one to slide under the mattress (they'll never look there!).

If you do print out the password, you'll notice it comprises 48 digits of random numbers. If you ever have to use this in anger, you will have to type it out on the Function keys at the top of your keyboard. Why? Because these were the only keys Microsoft could reasonably guarantee would give the same key codes no matter what keyboard arrangement you use. Some other third-party encryption products are able to use regular pass phrases because they support only a limited number of keyboard layouts. Microsoft is suffering here from the results of serving the whole world's demands.

NOTE

Because there was so much response to this restriction of "Function keys only" in the Windows Beta test community, Microsoft changed the boot loader for BitLocker so that if it can recognize numeric keys as being present on the keyboard, BitLocker will allow you to use those ordinary numbers, either across the top of the keyboard or on the number pad. If your number keys are not recognized, of course, use the function keys F1 through F10.

Another key point to note on the Save the Recovery Password dialog is that there is no Next button. This is another hint to you that the recovery password is important to the safe operation of BitLocker. You will get a Next button from this dialog only after you have saved the recovery password to at least one location. With this, Microsoft is telling you "it isn't worth trying BitLocker unless you have a recovery password stashed away." We don't think we can overemphasize how important the recovery password is.

Once you feel you have saved the recovery password enough times, click on **Next**, and you will be prompted to encrypt the volume (see Figure 5.14).

Figure 5.14 Encrypting the Volume Begins Right after This Dialog

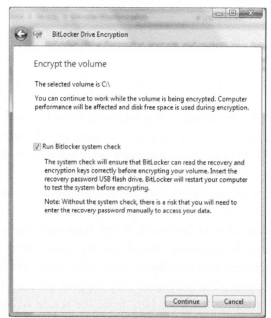

The checkbox **Run Bitlocker system check** (they miscapitalized BitLocker) should remain checked. Although it does require a restart to run this system check, what the system check does is go through a test boot with the USB startup key, prior to encrypting a single byte on your hard drive. If it fails this test, you will not be able to boot your drive once it is encrypted, and it will be difficult to recover; for this reason, we advise that even if you're pretty certain that you've run the test before on this system, you should run it again every time you go through this process. It adds a few minutes to an operation that takes several hours (on our test machine, it took around five hours to encrypt the drive during normal use), and provides immeasurably better reliability.

Click **Continue** to proceed to the dialog in Figure 5.15 so that you can restart to perform this test.

Figure 5.15 Testing the System through One Boot Cycle

Did you notice that? The prompt is asking for the startup key, not the recovery password, as was offered in the preceding dialog. What's being checked for is indeed the startup key, so you should have that handy. If you have media in your CD/DVD drive, you will be prompted to remove it.

After a restart, you will see the first instance of the Windows BootLocker startup screen, with the message **Windows BitLocker drive encryption key loaded**, and underneath, **Remove key storage media**. That same message will flash by every time you turn on the power to this computer. Sometimes it will flash by so fast that you don't manage to read it in time. This page in this book doesn't have that problem, so please read it again: **Remove key storage media**. To make this very clear, that is a suggestion to you that the BitLocker process has read the key from the USB drive, and that you should remove the USB key and stick it safely in your pocket or purse. It's such an important habit that you should start getting practiced with it now.

Your boot process from here on in should be just as usual: Once you log on, you'll get a new System Tray icon and its associated balloon text, as shown in Figure 5.16.

Figure 5.16 Encrypting the C Drive: The Start of a Long Road

If you click in the balloon, you'll get a dialog that continues to show you the progress of your encryption task and offers you the ability to **Pause** the progress (see Figure 5.17). This is useful if you want to run a disk-intensive task, or squeeze out a little bit more performance or battery life. After all, right now BitLocker is reading every sector of your disk, encrypting it, and then writing it back to the disk. That operation is taking place in the background while you use your computer, and although it doesn't take a whole lot of performance away from you, it does use up battery, and it may slow you down sufficiently so that time-critical tasks, such as game playing and video editing, may suffer noticeably. Actual work doesn't seem to be affected any by the encryption process.

Figure 5.17 BitLocker Encrypting the Drive

Eventually—and again, remember, this process is not broken if it takes several hours—the encryption process will complete, and you are able to continue in the assurance that your data is safe. Figure 5.18 shows the notification message that Windows Vista displays at this time.

Figure 5.18 BitLocker, Finished with Its Arduous Task, Now Sits in the Background

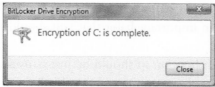

At this point, BitLocker behaves less like an application and more like a disk driver that knows how to do a bit of simple mathematics. Every time a sector is read from the disk, it passes through BitLocker to be decrypted; every time a sector is written to the disk, it passes through BitLocker to be encrypted. At this point, BitLocker is a small piece of code, and it can be trusted to do its work reliably.

Performance is often a concern of people who have never used drive encryption software before—a moment's thought on this should reassure you that the time when drive encryption is likely to cause performance issues is in a long write or read operation (a disk-bound process). Although the disk-bound portion of the process takes just as long as always, the CPU is called upon to decrypt the data as it is read, before it can be made available, or encrypt the data on its way out, before it can report that the write operation has succeeded. However, because the CPU is generally sitting idly by, waiting for something to do while the disk is reading or writing, it should have the spare cycles to decrypt or encrypt that data without noticeably affecting the speed with which your system feels like it is operating.

Using manage-bde.wsf to Protect Volumes other Than the Boot Volume

The clackies reading this (see earlier) will by now be asking whether there's only a GUI way to operate Windows BitLocker.

Of course, there's a command-prompt way to work with BitLocker. You can use scripts and commands to do absolutely *anything*. Almost.

In Windows Vista, the command to manage BitLocker is actually a script, called manage-bde.wsf. It lives in the *C:\WINDOWS\System32* directory or, if you prefer, in *%windir%\System32*.

Running *cscript manage-bde.wsf* with no parameters leads to a usage message:

```
Microsoft (R) Windows Script Host Version 5.7
Copyright (C) Microsoft Corporation. All rights reserved.


manage-bde[.wsf] -parameter [arguments]


Description:
    Configures BitLocker Drive Encryption on disk volumes.


Parameter List:
    -status     Provides information about BitLocker-capable volumes.
    -on         Encrypts the volume and turns BitLocker protection on.
    -off        Decrypts the volume and turns BitLocker protection off.
```

```
-pause      Pauses encryption or decryption.

-resume     Resumes encryption or decryption.

-lock       Prevents access to BitLocker-encrypted data.

-unlock     Allows access to BitLocker-encrypted data.

-autounlock Manages automatic unlocking of data volumes.

-protectors Manages protection methods for the encryption key.

-tpm        Configures the computer's Trusted Platform Module (TPM).

-ForceRecovery or -fr

            Forces a BitLocker-protected OS to recover on restarts.

-ComputerName or -cn

            Runs on another computer. Examples: "ComputerX", "127.0.0.1"

-? or /?    Displays brief help. Example: "-ParameterSet -?"

-Help or -h Displays complete help. Example: "-ParameterSet -h"
```

```
Examples:

    manage-bde -status

    manage-bde -on C: -RecoveryPassword -RecoveryKey F:\

    manage-bde -unlock E: -RecoveryKey F:\84E151C1...7A62067A512.bek
```

Let's examine the examples briefly (for this, you will need to be running the command prompt as an administrator):

```
C:\Windows\system32>cscript manage-bde.wsf -status
Microsoft (R) Windows Script Host Version 5.7
Copyright (C) Microsoft Corporation. All rights reserved.


Disk volumes that can be protected with
BitLocker Drive Encryption:
Volume C: []
[OS Volume]


    Size:               67.12 GB
    Conversion Status:  Fully Encrypted
    Percentage Encrypted: 100%
    Encryption Method:  AES 128 with Diffuser
    Protection Status:  Protection On
    Lock Status:        Unlocked
    Key Protectors:
        External Key
        Numerical Password
```

As you can see, this is following our successful run through the preceding GUI encryption process. Our drive is fully encrypted, just as it says (and the *Percentage Encrypted* value fortunately agrees). We use the default encryption method, *AES 128 with Diffuser*. Protection is on, which means that we have BitLocker protecting our boot process (with the Root of Trust Measurement enabled if we have TPM), and that the key is not stored in clear text between boots (we'll talk about this a little more, later).

Lock Status: Unlocked may surprise you—after all, isn't BitLocker supposed to be locking your bits away?

Okay, the explanation is simple enough. By *Unlocked*, it really means that the running instance of BitLocker (that *manage-bde* is managing) has in memory a key that goes with this drive. When you turn off your system, and until you boot it with the startup key in place, the boot drive is locked. Once the startup key or recovery password has been provided, the boot drive is unlocked. You can lock and unlock drives other than the boot drive.

The next sample requires that we start with a volume that has not yet been encrypted. Wouldn't it be really useful if we could encrypt a USB drive? The bad news is that you cannot use BitLocker to encrypt those little flash drives that you stick in your pocket. But you can encrypt external hard drives, as well as internal partitions. Let's try it on a small partition created just for this purpose:

```
C:\Windows\system32>cscript manage-bde.wsf -on t: -RecoveryKey d:\ -
RecoveryPassword
Microsoft (R) Windows Script Host Version 5.7
Copyright (C) Microsoft Corporation. All rights reserved.


Volume T:
[Data Volume]
Key Protectors Added:

    Recovery Key:
      ID: {E99378CE-6121-4716-9C19-1AB1E373608E}
      External Key File Name:
        E99378CE-6121-4716-9C19-1AB1E373608E.BEK


    Saved to directory d:\


    Numerical Password:
      ID: {85ABF671-1201-4A6E-80A5-F9CB05838758}
      Password:
```

```
         417912-292853-484946-440374-185801-705738-553927-434995


ACTIONS REQUIRED:



    1. Save this numerical recovery password in a secure location away from
    your computer:

    417912-292853-484946-440374-185801-705738-553927-434995


    To prevent data loss, save this password immediately. This password
helps
    ensure that you can unlock the encrypted volume.
Encryption is now in progress.
```

Don't worry, that's not our recovery password anymore.

Note those options to store the recovery password and the recovery key; they're a lot to type, so you can abbreviate them to *–rp* and *–rk*, respectively.

If we query for status again, we see the current state of encryption on all drives. Here's the information for the new T drive:

```
Volume T: [Encryptable]
[Data Volume]


    Size:                 0.44 GB
    Conversion Status:    Encryption in Progress
    Percentage Encrypted: 28%
    Encryption Method:    AES 128 with Diffuser
    Protection Status:    Protection Off
    Lock Status:          Unlocked
    Automatic Unlock:     Disabled
    Key Protectors:
        External Key
        Numerical Password
```

It is important to note that the BitLocker GUI in Windows Vista is designed to encrypt only the boot drive (that's the one with the system on, remember), so encrypting a second drive such as this is something you can do only from the command line using *manage-bde.wsf*. That's a point in favor of learning how to use the command prompt. Once you have encrypted external volumes, they show up in the

BitLocker GUI, so those of you out of your comfort zone in the command prompt don't have to stay there long.

Here's something you can't do with the boot drive:

```
C:\Windows\system32>cscript manage-bde.wsf -lock t:
Microsoft (R) Windows Script Host Version 5.7
Copyright (C) Microsoft Corporation. All rights reserved.


Volume T: is now locked


C:\Windows\system32>dir t:
This volume is locked by BitLocker Drive Encryption. Return to the control
panel to unlock volume.
```

So now, we have a partition on our system—or on an external drive—that we have locked away from access. Even if you can log on to our PC, you can't get at this partition unless you have access to the key. And we can take this drive, if it's an external drive, to another PC, along with our recovery key, and unlock it there so that we can use this securely locked drive. We can't lock this drive through the GUI either, though the GUI will tell us that we have locked it, by changing the "keys" icon from a pair of keys to a golden padlock.

But, following the samples in the help text, we can unlock the drive:

```
C:\Windows\system32>cscript manage-bde.wsf -unlock t: -rk d:\E99378CE-6121-
4716-9C19-1AB1E373608E.BEK
Microsoft (R) Windows Script Host Version 5.7
Copyright (C) Microsoft Corporation. All rights reserved.


The file "d:\E99378CE-6121-4716-9C19-1AB1E373608E.BEK" successfully unlocked
volume T:.
```

The obvious command will also start decryption of this partition:

```
C:\Windows\system32>cscript manage-bde.wsf -off t:
Microsoft (R) Windows Script Host Version 5.7
Copyright (C) Microsoft Corporation. All rights reserved.


Decryption is now in progress.
```

Recovering a BitLocker
System after Losing Your Startup Key or PIN

Recovering a BitLocker system is relatively simple (if tedious), and if you've booted your system once or twice without the startup key, you probably already know how this will start.

Before we start, we hope you have printed out the recovery password, because you are going to have to type it in now. If you haven't printed it out, but you have saved it to another folder, it's simple enough to print using Notepad; it's just an ordinary text file. Here's an example of the contents you should expect:

```
The recovery password is used to recover the data on a BitLocker protected
drive.


Recovery Password:


372471-482163-719576-220528-253462-701118-651761-248523


To verify that this is the correct recovery password compare these tags with
tags presented on the recovery screen.
Drive Label: BENNEVIS C: 1/10/2007.
Password ID: {D4E562EC-749F-4B06-93FA-0D2F4B8BE796}.
```

(Of course, this is not our recovery password now; by decrypting and re-encrypting our drive, we have already changed that.)

Now, if you boot our laptop without the startup key and without a PIN being set, you will see the following message on boot (other recovery scenarios include the TPM chip being reinitialized):

```
Windows BitLocker Drive Encryption key needed.
Insert key storage media.
Press ESC to reboot after the media is in place.
Drive Label: BENNEVIS C: 1/10/2007
Key Filename: 8A3556DD-8116-44BE-9F18-A09348CD51B4.BEK
ENTER=Recovery                    ESC=Reboot
```

You don't have the startup key on hand, so you press **Enter** to enter recovery. Now the screen shows this message:

```
Windows BitLocker Drive Encryption Password Entry
Enter the recovery password for this drive.
```

```
_____  _____  _____  _____

_____  _____  _____  _____
Drive Label: BENNEVIS C: 1/10/2007
Password ID: D4E562EC-749F-4B06-93FA-0D2F4B8BE796
Use the function keys F1-F9 for the digits 1 - 9.  Use the F10 key for 0.
Use the TAB, SHIFT-TAB, HOME, END and ARROW keys to move the cursor.
The UP and DOWN ARROW keys may be used to modify already entered digits.
ENTER=Continue                                          ESC=Exit
```

Those underscored characters are input blocks in which you should enter the recovery password that you printed out. Whereas the password is printed on one line in the recovery password file, you will need to enter the first half of the password on the top line and the second half of the password on the bottom line.

A weak checksum is in place on each group of digits, so if you make a typing mistake (and it's easy to do so, using the F keys instead of the number keys just beneath them), that block will be highlighted and a message will display at the foot of the screen, reading "Invalid group of digits entered. Please correct the highlighted group." This is not intended to prevent you from making up your own code, as you can easily demonstrate for yourself. But if you do make up your own code, the recovery will fail and you will have to enter the code again.

Once you have given BitLocker the right recovery password, press **Enter** as suggested, and your system will boot as normal.

Removing BitLocker Protection Temporarily to Install a BIOS or System Update

To remove BitLocker protection temporarily, open the **BitLocker Control Panel** as before, and under the drive on which you want to disable protection click the label that reads **Turn Off BitLocker**. You will be prompted what kind of "Turn Off" you are considering, as shown in Figure 5.19.

Figure 5.19 Turning BitLocker Off

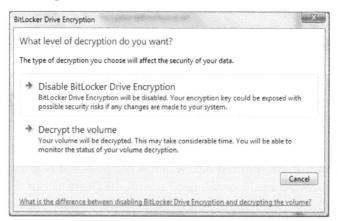

Tools & Traps...

When You Decrypt the Volume...

If you choose to start decrypting your drive, you have started a process that takes several hours (depending on the size of your hard drive, its speed, and your processor speed) to conclude.

Although you can pause this process, you cannot reverse it until it has finished.

Once you start decrypting, if you want to put BitLocker back onto the system, you have no choice but to continue all the way through decrypting your hard drive. When the drive is fully decrypted you can start encrypting it again, at which point new keys will be created: a new recovery password, a new recovery key, and a new boot key.

You will probably do this only once accidentally. We know that's eight hours of our computer's life we'd like back.

Choose **Disable BitLocker Drive Encryption**. This is what you would do if you were making changes to your system and didn't want BitLocker to "get in the way"—for instance, if you're handing your PC over to your company's desktop services team for them to add software or hardware. That way, you don't need to hand them your key.

Disabling BitLocker in this manner is also necessary if you have a TPM chip and you are going to make any changes that would alter the Core Root of Trust Measurement (CRTM) components—the BIOS, the boot components of the OS, CMOS settings, and so on. Disable BitLocker, make the change, and then reenable BitLocker again.

As the prompt says, there are a number of ways in which this could cause exposure of your system's encryption key.

Are You 0wned?

Did You Give Up Your Keys?

If you disable BitLocker and feel like you may have given out the keys to the wrong person, it takes a little effort to rekey your system. Some third-party whole-disk encryption tools have a single "re-encrypt" command that will cause a new key (equivalent to the Volume Master Key in BitLocker) to be generated, and will re-encrypt each sector on the disk.

To achieve the same effect on Vista—for instance, if you wanted to keep a laptop secure after dismissing a technically talented employee—you will need to decrypt the drive entirely and then encrypt it again from scratch.

Once you have completed any tasks that caused you to disable BitLocker, enabling it again is as simple as opening the **BitLocker Drive Encryption Control Panel** and clicking **Turn On BitLocker**.

BitLocker with TPM: What Does It Give You?

BitLocker with TPM is an impressive achievement. Microsoft has worked with its Trustworthy Computing Initiative and the members of the Trusted Platforms Group to ensure that new systems are provided with a piece of serious cryptographic hardware on board: the Trusted Platform Module (TPM). With the TPM, you can essentially guarantee that the OS you boot today is the same as the OS you shut down or hibernated yesterday—that nothing has added itself to the boot loader, or altered the OS in between your last shutdown and your next startup.

As with so many security features, we have to ask the question: What is the risk against which the technology protects you, and do you realistically face that risk?

The risks that BitLocker with TPM protects you against are as follows:

- Someone steals your machine's hard drive and wants to mount it on his own system to read it

- Someone borrows your machine, boots to another OS (with a CD or a USB drive), and uses that OS to alter your OS so that it runs his code

What BitLocker with TPM surprisingly does not protect you against is an attack wherein an attacker steals your entire system. Once she has your system, she can plug it in, turn it on, and boot it up, sailing straight through BitLocker's TPM protection.

Okay, that sounds needlessly alarmist, but it's true. The attacker can boot the system through all of BitLocker and TPM's protection, to the point where the OS has mounted its drives and is sitting at the logon prompt waiting for a user to log on.

Now, we don't know about your system, but we know that our laptop system has a lot of little holes on the outside that let the rain come in. In addition to that, at various times in the past, they have been known to let attackers in too. Particularly that one labeled "Network"—that has been the target of many different forms of attack. How certain are you that the person who stole your laptop and wants to get at your data will not wait until a network vulnerability is discovered in one of the networking services you run on your laptop? Or that all the known network holes in your laptop's software have already been discovered and plugged?

Then there's USB; each USB device has a window into your system's memory and can read from or write to the memory more or less as it sees fit. Could an attacking group build an exotic USB device to use this memory openness to gain access to your laptop's files?

For this reason, we strongly recommend that you do not use just TPM as a key store for your BitLocker-protected drives. At the very least, use a PIN—and don't write it down on the laptop. We use a USB startup key, and we keep that with us at all times, except when we're actively booting our laptop.

BitLocker with EFS: Does It Make Sense?

At first glance, it would seem like BitLocker with EFS falls afoul of one of our personal "golden rules" of cryptography: Double encryption is usually a sign that you don't understand what you're doing.

Usually, that golden rule holds. After all, you generally encrypt content with a symmetric key and encrypt the symmetric key with the public keys of all the intended recipients. Two keys, two encryptions, but each piece of data (the data and the symmetric key) is encrypted only once.

BitLocker has already encrypted your system drive, and perhaps some of your other drives, so why use EFS as well?

BitLocker, as we described it earlier, is very much a broad-brush approach. It encrypts either the whole partition, or nothing. As such, if you have a key to the drive, you have a key to everything on the drive. EFS allows you to fine-tune the encryption of files and folders that are accessible to people who do have the keys to boot your system. EFS also allows you to protect access across the network from others who may have access to your network shares.

So, yes, BitLocker with EFS does make sense, but it is going to compound the performance hit that encryption causes to your machine.

BitLocker for Servers

Another nonsense-sounding application of BitLocker is to protect volumes on a server, as will happen in Windows Server 2007.

After all, a server requires that there be no human presence when it boots, and BitLocker requires either that you use TPM, which is little protection on the drive, or that you use a startup key or PIN, which each require the user's presence. What point is there having a server with the USB startup key always plugged in?

As it turns out, there's quite a significant point in that. If you are planning a move of servers from one facility to another, but you want to protect them in transit, what better way than to spend the preparation time enabling encryption on the drive, using a cheap USB stick to hold the key and provide continued operation, and then when move time comes, unplug the USB stick, ship the stick and the server in two different convoys, and when they both reach the other end, reunite them. Your servers will be ready to run again, and they will not be in any risk of successful interception by thieves interested in stealing your data en route. You could, of course, do the same thing with a recovery password, by disabling BitLocker while the server is at rest and reenabling it while it is in transit.

BitLocker on a server would also be useful for those remote branch offices that cannot be adequately physically secured after business hours, and where the domain controller needs to be protected against theft. Simply removing the USB startup key at the end of the day, locking it in the safe, and then shutting down (or hibernating) the server provides excellent protection against theft.

Using BitLocker to Decommission a System

If your company is like many, when a computer has reached the end of its serviceable life, as many parts of it as possible are donated to charity to get a tax write-off. Even if you don't donate old computers to charity, it's likely that you don't want the data on those computers to be available to anybody outside the company who may receive them, whether it's finding them in a landfill, or taking them as a returned lease product.

Even if the data is not important, the OS is your purchase, and you may not be legally entitled to pass it on to the next owner of the computer.

Before BitLocker, the best thing you could easily do without third-party tools was to mount the drive on another machine, format it, and then run *cipher /w* (cryptographically wipe the free space) to clear the drive.

With BitLocker, you don't even have to do that—just make sure that BitLocker is turned on and that the encryption has completed, and then wipe the startup key, forget the PIN, and destroy any copies of the recovery password that you printed out. Now that drive contains only random bytes—it contains nothing that could be used to write a big exposé about how careless you have been with customer secrets. Journalism schools may need to rewrite their classes.

 # PatchGuard

In 2002, Microsoft announced its Trustworthy Computing Initiative. Unless you were living in your Y2K fallout shelter at the time, you were well aware of the numerous security issues that Microsoft was facing on a daily (if not hourly) basis. In a paper by Craig Mundie (et al.), trust from a user perspective was broken down into four areas: Business Integrity, Privacy, Reliability, and Security.

Reliability and Business Integrity are straightforward; users should expect that the products be reliable and that vendors shall act in a reasonable manner. In Security, users are believed to expect the traditional "CIA triad" of security: confidentiality, integrity, and availability (see Figure 5.20). The belief was that users should be confident that their systems will be able to withstand an attack. Likewise, with Privacy, Microsoft's belief was that at no time should user data be vulnerable to outside forces.

These principles were to be a key component of Windows 2003, which was supposed to be much more secure than previous Windows releases. To be fair, the number of patches specifically for Windows 2003 (not including Internet Explorer or Media Player) was greatly reduced from those of Windows 2000. Microsoft also did a much better job of being proactive as opposed to reactive to security flaws. The introduction of Windows Update, Software Update Services (SUS), and later, Windows Server Update Services (WSUS), helped remove some of the black cloud from Microsoft with relation to security. Unfortunately, there continue to be enough security updates needed that Microsoft had to do something to counteract this problem.

Figure 5.20 The CIA Triad

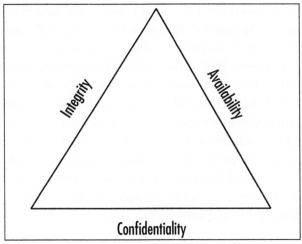

With the announcement of Windows Vista, Microsoft also began pushing the feature known as PatchGuard. In the following sections, we will explore how PatchGuard works, and what it means to the future of Microsoft's security initiative, as well as third-party security products.

What Is PatchGuard?

If you've been following the trade magazines, you know that PatchGuard (a.k.a. Kernel Patch Protection or KPP) has been a very controversial feature in Windows Vista. What you might find surprising is that KPP has been available in the 64-bit edition of Windows 2003 since SP1 was released. Likewise, KPP was available for the 64-bit edition of Windows XP. Before we start throwing around too many new terms and concepts, let's take a step back and review what the kernel does and why it's an issue.

The "kernel" of the OS essentially is the "brains of the operation." It has a variety of responsibilities, including resource management and hardware/software communication. On a high level, it is what allows an application to request hardware resources such as memory, processor time, and other hardware devices (disk drives, etc.). The issue that arose with previous versions of the Windows kernel is that software development companies began using unsupported interfaces in the applications they were developing. In many companies, it became commonplace to practice "kernel patching," which directly modified the way the system would behave. Kernel patching (or "hooking") was a quick and dirty way to avoid some of the built-in checks-and-balances of the OS. Although it was initially intended for nonmalicious purposes, it became a "backdoor" to causing many a malicious event.

In the white paper "Microsoft® Windows Vista™: An Inflection Point for Kernel Security and 64-Bit Computing," Microsoft is quick to point out that a great example of "good code gone bad" is the Audio CD copyright protection that was implemented in 2005. These CDs essentially installed a "rootkit" onto the computer, without the consent of the user. Rootkits are typically seen as a form of Trojan horse, embedding themselves into the system and tracking user activity, and indeed, they do make system modifications without owner consent or knowledge. The Audio CD rootkits were intended to track the behavior of users playing these audio CDs. When it was discovered that this practice was occurring, a number of security vulnerabilities were also detected. Some were so serious that they actually allowed malicious access to the protected kernel area.

Are You 0wned?

Play That Funky Music

You're checking your CDs right now, aren't you? Well, if you somehow missed this event in late 2005, fear not. As long as you have patched your PC in the past 12 months and have up-to-date antivirus software running, chances are you are safe. In case you are curious, the rootkit that used this vulnerability was called **Stinx-E** (Sophos) or BKDR_BREPLIOBOT.C (Trend). You can read more about this at www.pcpro.co.uk/news/79728/virus-targets-sonybmg-rootkit-drm.html.

So, you're probably thinking "great refresher on the kernel and kernel patching, but tell us about PatchGuard!" Well, PatchGuard basically monitors whether kernel resources (or the actual kernel code) have been changed in any way. If Windows determines that an unauthorized patch has been installed, it will cause the system to shut down. This may seem a bit extreme, but think about it: If your system is under attack from malicious code, and your antivirus, spyware, and other malware software has missed the intruder, do you really want to keep your system online and susceptible? Now, this does pose an interesting problem: How do we address legitimate software that uses these coding shortcuts? Well, that actually leads us into our next topic: why only 64-bit support for PatchGuard?

Why Only 64-Bit?

So, the question is, why did Microsoft decide to incorporate PatchGuard into only the 64-bit edition of Windows? When you think about it, the answer is pretty obvious. Many of the third-party applications that you use today were built specifically for the 32-bit platform, meaning they may or may not work under the 64-bit OS. Because the adoption rate of Windows 2003 and Windows XP 64-bit editions had been fairly slow, it also meant that software developers were generally still writing code for the 32-bit platform. Therefore, Microsoft saw limited risk in introducing this to the 64-bit world, as opposed to forcing end users to replace existing 32-bit software with a PatchGuard-compatible version. Because Microsoft offers Vista in both 32-bit and 64-bit flavors, everyone is happy. Right? Well, not exactly….

Why Third-Party Security Companies Don't Want to Use PatchGuard

For many third-party security software developers (Symantec, McAfee, etc.), PatchGuard is seen as more of a burden than a feature. Many of these companies have complained that because of the inability to perform kernel-hooking, Host Intrusion Protection Software (HIPS) is unable to perform as expected. If you are unfamiliar with HIPS, it is touted to be the next generation of host-based security software. Whereas today's antivirus and antimalware programs depend on signature files to detect malicious code, HIPS products (such as Cisco's CSA program) are intended to analyze the behavior of an application and determine whether the intent is malicious.

The argument these third-party companies are making is that a number of "white hat" and "black hat" hackers have already been able to circumvent PatchGuard's security. The larger concern is that in order to make their software packages work properly, these companies will have to begin to use the same tactics these hackers employ. Likewise, many of these companies have cried foul, stating that this is just another attempt by Microsoft to push one of its own security packages: Forefront.

Notes from the Underground…

Bypassing PatchGuard

Although the intent of this book is not to teach you how to get around Microsoft's new security features, it is our responsibility to educate you on exactly how hackers can get around PatchGuard. Luckily for us, the process has been documented quite well. In 2005, Matt Miller and Ken Johnson published a very lengthy paper on how to bypass PatchGuard. You can read their findings at www.uninformed.org/?v=3&a=3.

Interestingly, companies such as Authentium (www.authentium.com) have already begun developing software that essentially works around the PatchGuard feature. Authentium claims that it has successfully developed a 64-bit version of its ESP Enterprise platform, which offers virus protection, antispyware, data recovery, firewall, and transaction security capabilities. It claims that it has developed its application in such a way that it does not set off the PatchGuard alarms we discussed earlier. Although it's purely speculation, these types of tactics effectively forced Microsoft to do something about this problem. Microsoft's solution was to grant vendors access to new APIs which would give much more flexible access to the kernel. Indeed, Microsoft's previously documented firewall API already gives enough capabilities to write a HIPS package without resorting to kernel-hooking techniques.

Notes from the Underground…

Choosing Sides

Curiously enough, not all security companies are against Microsoft's PatchGuard initiative. For example, Sophos has applauded Microsoft's decision to secure the kernel as much as possible (www.informationweek.com/news/showArticle.jhtml?articleID=193401506). It claims that it has been able to develop its HIPS product in such a way that it functions as expected, without the need for kernel hooking. This may be because Microsoft designed a

Continued

number of "filter APIs" that allow applications such as virus scanners to insert themselves into the chain of access to file contents, network traffic, and so on. Sophos also blames the other third-party vendors for not having enough foresight to begin developing to PatchGuard instead of trying to fight it. It will be interesting to see how this ends.

An interesting occurrence to come out of the annual Black Hat Conference was an admission from a malware researcher that a previous vulnerability in PatchGuard had already been, well, patched! This same person ultimately praised Microsoft for its efforts with PatchGuard, saying in her blog that "PG is actually a very good idea. PG should not be thought as of a direct security feature. PG's main task is to keep legal programs from acting like popular rootkits. Keeping malware away is not PG's main task. However, by ensuring that legal applications do not introduce rootkit-like tricks, PG makes it easier and more effective to create robust malware detection tools" (http://theinvisiblethings.blogspot.com/2006/10/vista-rc2-vs-pagefile-attack-and-some.html).

Basically, the jury is still out on PatchGuard. Only time will tell whether it is one of Microsoft's great innovations in computing, or if it is just the next Microsoft Bob.

Summary

Windows has been updated for the Vista release to include several highly valuable data protection measures.

You can now block USB devices down to the individual type (or class) of device, and you can block devices broadly across a range of classes to allow or disallow access, and to allow or disallow installation.

Rights Management Services has been included in the OS, meaning that all users are ready to operate against your RMS server as soon as you enable it.

The Encrypting File System has been augmented with dialogs that are easier to use, and policy settings that allow you to encrypt the page file against subsequent attack, to offline files against other system users, and to use encryption keys maintained on a smart card, making it unlikely that you will lose the key or accidentally expose it to a third party.

BitLocker is a must-have feature for laptop users, and it even serves a purpose for desktop users who may want to keep a partition of their drive—or an external, portable hard drive—inaccessible to others.

PatchGuard is a paradigm-shifting attempt by Microsoft to reestablish control over what programs get to run in kernel space. Some antimalware vendors who are used to editing the kernel for themselves are upset that they will have to change their method of operation; others say it's a brilliant move that will improve system stability.

Solutions Fast Track

USB Devices

☑ ReadyBoost securely provides the speed advantage of USB flash drives as a "page file on a stick" for read-only, discardable data such as programs.

☑ Device Installation Group Policy settings allow you to control which devices and device classes may be installed, either by regular users or by local administrators.

☑ Removable Storage Group Policy settings allow you to deny read and/or write access to individual classes of removable storage devices.

☑ For the truly paranoid, Removable Storage Group Policy settings can disable all access to all removable storage devices.

Rights Management

☑ Discussion of Digital Rights Management software is generally highly controversial and usually resolves down to personal opinion.

☑ Digital Rights Management approaches work effectively only in situations where punitive measures can be taken against content consumers when they skirt the DRM prohibitions on content use.

☑ Windows Rights Management Server is difficult to install, and it requires many components on Windows Server 2003, plus a Client Access License for each content consumer.

☑ Windows Rights Management Services Client is an API that is accessed by application software, each with its own user interface to present Rights Management to the user.

Encrypting File System

☑ The Encrypting File System allows you to encrypt individual files, or all files within a folder.

☑ Windows Vista adds support for EFS keys held on smart cards; page file encryption; offline file encryption based on the user's key; and policies to control the indexing of encrypted files.

☑ Always set up a Data Recovery Agent to allow you to recover files after the user who encrypted them has left your domain; export the DRA keys into a PFX file so that the DRA's private key is not resident on the system.

Whole-Disk Encryption

☑ BitLocker provides whole-disk encryption features for Windows Vista's boot drive.

☑ BitLocker with TPM enabled provides protection based on the Static Root of Trust Measurement, to prevent out-of-OS modification of boot components.

☑ BitLocker's command prompt control script, manage-bde.wsf, allows whole-disk encryption of partitions other than the system partition (which should never be encrypted).

☑ You can store BitLocker's recovery password in a number of ways: to Active Directory Domain Services, printed, stored to a network folder, or saved to a USB key.

PatchGuard

☑ PatchGuard, formerly known as Kernel Patch Protection, is a means to prevent modification of the OS kernel by unauthorized third parties (including Microsoft's own application developers).

☑ PatchGuard is available only for 64-bit versions of Windows Vista, because applying it to 32-bit versions of Windows would likely break too many applications that rely on hooking into the OS kernel.

☑ There is a controversial debate among different antimalware vendors as to whether PatchGuard is a beneficial reliability measure, or an anticompetitive measure designed to freeze them out of the market.

☑ Microsoft has provided filtering and firewall APIs that allow antimalware vendors to operate the same kinds of activities they are used to doing through patching of the kernel. Because these APIs are documented and maintained, they will be far more reliable than trusting your network to hooks into a kernel that may change with any patch.

Frequently Asked Questions

The following Frequently Asked Questions, answered by the authors of this book, are designed to both measure your understanding of the concepts presented in this chapter and to assist you with real-life implementation of these concepts. To have your questions about this chapter answered by the author, browse to **www.syngress.com/solutions** and click on the **"Ask the Author"** form.

Q: I've tried to enable ReadyBoost on my Windows Vista system, but even my newest drives don't seem to be fast enough. What could be causing that?

A: Most often, the speed measurements on ReadyBoost are hampered by ongoing activity on your system. Attach a new ReadyBoost-capable USB drive when the system is quiet, not during the first few seconds after logon or when you are running software you know to be a processor hog. Also, ReadyBoost will not work on a USB 1.0 device. And when you plug a USB 2.0 device into a USB 1.0 hub, it acts like a USB 1.0 device with regard to speed. Try plugging your USB drive into the computer directly.

Q: What's the difference between a device setup class, a hardware ID, and a compatible ID?

A: Device setup classes are groupings of kinds of device, so "removable disks" might be one grouping and "printers" would be another. As with so many things in Windows, device setup classes are GUIDs—long strings of hexadecimal digits inside braces. Hardware IDs and compatible IDs are slightly more descriptive, and describe the hardware in terms ranging from generic to the class all the way up to specific for the revision number of the device. Each device contains a list of hardware IDs and compatible IDs, and each driver is installed with a list of compatible IDs and hardware IDs that it supports. Windows decides which driver to use on a device by matching IDs—first by hardware ID, from the most specific to the least specific, and if no match has been found, then the comparison is made by compatible ID.

Q: Where do I find hardware and compatible device ID information?

A: In Device Manager (from the Control Panel), you can view any device's properties. The Details tab lists a number of different details about the device, including its hardware IDs and compatible IDs. The driver's list of hardware IDs and compatible IDs is in the INF file for that driver, usually located in *%systemroot%\inf*.

Q: How can I add Rights Management Services to documents produced by other programs?

A: Rights Management Services requires that you trust the application that displays content; otherwise, there would be no management of the rights. You will need to contact the application vendor and ask them to add RMS support.

Q: If I am violently opposed to the use of DRM technologies, can I remove RMS from my system?

A: No, but you can simply not use it. Remember, RMS requires that you access a Rights Management Server. As long as you do not install an RMS in your domain, or subscribe to another party's RMS, you should be fine.

Q: I encrypted a file, forgot to back it up, and now I've installed a new copy of Windows over the old one. Can I get the file back?

A: Only if you saved your (or your DRA's) encryption keys in a PFX file using the Certificate Export Wizard. Some tools are available from third parties that will try to crack your old password and fetch your keys for you, but they will work only if you did not overwrite the Registry of the old version of Windows.

Q: Does Microsoft have a backdoor into EFS, allowing it to decrypt my files if the FBI, NSA, or other government organization requires it to?

A: No; the technology has been analyzed by a number of different people, some of them remarkably well skilled. No such backdoor has been found. It would be a commercially bad move for Microsoft to allow a backdoor, because it would prevent the various other governments and companies with whom it does business from trusting its OSes.

Q: Can my system administrator read my encrypted files?

A: No, but your system administrator can set a policy detailing who can, by choosing a certificate to use for DRA purposes. If a file you encrypt has no DRA, or has a DRA that you know is someone outside of your administrative structure, administrators cannot read from or write to that file.

Q: I don't want the system administrator to see that this encrypted file is called "World Domination Plans." Can I prevent her from seeing that such a file exists?

A: No; EFS does not encrypt the name of the file, or its size. If these are to be kept secret, you will need to use some other form of protection. At some point, you have to choose between trusting your system's administrators or not using the systems they administer.

Q: What's the difference between a certificate, a public key, and a private key?

A: Technically, a certificate is a statement of record tying a public key to an identified party—an individual, a Web server, and so on—and is signed by a trusted third party called a certificate authority (CA). A public key is one-half of a key pair, and has a matched private key. A PFX file may contain a certificate (which includes the public key) and its associated private key; a CER file, another certificate format, may contain only a certificate, which does not include a private key. Your certificate store may hold certificates and their associated private keys.

Q: Does Microsoft have a backdoor into the encryption used in BitLocker?

A: No, for the same reasons as outlined earlier. BitLocker's protection, as EFS, uses AES encryption, with a 128-bit or 256-bit key (dependent on your policy settings). There are currently no known attacks on this, other than the brute force guessing of keys at random until one works. Although you could make a lucky guess, on average that takes more time than the universe has existed, with current computer technology.

Q: Is BitLocker fast enough and reliable enough for general use?

A: Yes. We use it on our personal laptop and our work laptop. We have not noticed any perceptible decrease in their speed. But we do make a nightly backup.

Q: Which is better, command-line or GUI control for BitLocker?

A: It depends on what you need. The command-line tool offers more features and functionality, but you make fewer mistakes with the GUI prompting you every step of the way and making sure that you store your recovery password somewhere safe.

Q: How does BitLocker's protection compare with other third-party tools?

A: AES encryption is the de facto standard for storage encryption at present, so the protection is the same as other tools. Remember that the strength of protection is governed as much by how safe you keep your keys (and in the case of a PIN, how long and complex it is), as by the strength of the encryption algorithm.

Q: Why isn't BitLocker available for Windows Vista Home Edition, or other SKUs than Enterprise and Ultimate?

A: Sometimes there have to be advantages to paying more for a higher SKU. This is one such advantage. If you need BitLocker, you can always upgrade to Windows Vista Ultimate. Another possible reason for restricting BitLocker from the Home Edition could be to reduce the number of calls from people who have encrypted their family photos and videos away, and have now lost the USB startup key or forgotten their PIN.

Q: Why doesn't PatchGuard work on 32-bit versions of Windows Vista?

A: Because too many applications abuse the system by patching into the kernel; all of these would break. Because those applications have to be reworked a little, and tested, on Windows Vista 64-bit, those application breaks are not a significant concern to 64-bit Windows Vista.

Q: If antimalware vendors hate PatchGuard, doesn't that mean malware producers will love it?

A: On the contrary, malware authors are going to be just as prevented from overwriting the system kernel as the vendors of antimalware software. Attacking PatchGuard requires beating BitLocker's system protection prior to boot, or stealing a private key from Microsoft, or finding a bug in PatchGuard itself. At least the antimalware vendors have an API that will allow them to inspect drive traffic, network traffic, and so on.

Q: If some vendors say that PatchGuard prevents them from enacting malware protection, and others say that they have no such problems, how do I choose whom to trust?

A: As always, try the products, investigate the technical truth of their claims, and ask the vendors to defend themselves against criticism from other vendors against their statements. Pick industry experts whom you feel you can trust, and listen to what they have to say.

Chapter 6

Microsoft Vista: Networking Essentials

Solutions in this chapter:

- Not Your Father's TCP/IP Stack
- Using the Network and Sharing Center
- Using the Network Map
- Working with the Windows Firewall

☑ Summary

☑ Solutions Fast Track

☑ Frequently Asked Questions

Introduction

Microsoft Windows Vista includes a number of significantly improved networking technologies that are designed to enhance productivity and security for end users and the corporate environment, as well as simplify the administration process for system administrators. In this chapter, we'll take a look at some of the new networking technologies in Windows Vista, as well as technologies that have been significantly improved over previous versions of the Windows operating system (OS).

We begin with a discussion of Internet Protocol (IP) version 6, or IPv6. Windows Vista is the first Microsoft OS to provide full support for IPv6 straight out of the box, while still allowing complete interoperability with existing IPv4 networking technologies. We'll discuss the origins of IPv6, its advantages over IPv4, and how Windows Vista has deployed IPv6 support.

Next, we'll move on to the new "home" for Windows Vista networking, the Network and Sharing Center. This new interface provides much more streamlined and intuitive access to configuring Windows Vista networking components, and it includes new options for displaying a graphical view of your network infrastructure using the Network Map.

We'll then spend a good deal of time looking at the Windows Firewall, which has undergone a significant overhaul in Vista, even from the improvements that Microsoft made in Windows XP Service Pack (SP) 2. The Vista Firewall addresses a number of limitations that were present in the XP Windows Firewall, including the ability to monitor and restrict both incoming and outgoing traffic, as well as combining the administration of IP Security (IPSec) and the Windows Firewall to allow the two technologies to work together more smoothly.

Not Your Father's TCP/IP Stack

Although support has been available for IPv6 in previous versions of the Microsoft OSes, Windows Vista is the first OS to turn on IPv6 straight out of the box. Microsoft did this as part of a belief that IPv6 will begin to play a much greater role on the Internet as more and more devices and applications become a part of the so-called "connected world." Deploying IPv6 offers a number of benefits for consumers, administrators, developers, and Internet service providers (ISPs) alike. But to fully appreciate these benefits, it's necessary to take a step back and compare IPv6 against the current de facto IPv4 standard.

NOTE

In previous versions of Windows, you could enable IPv6 support by manually installing it from the Network Control Panel.

Limitations of IPv4

The current implementation of the Transmission Control Protocol/Internet Protocol (TCP/IP), IPv4, has been in use on the Internet since the early 1980s. Although this makes IPv4 something of a dinosaur by technology standards, the current implementation has nonetheless held up quite well under the demands of an exploding Internet population of high-speed consumer connections and e-commerce sites aplenty. However, IPv4 has a number of limitations that we will discuss next. The IPv6 standard has specifically addressed these limitations to improve the security, manageability, and scalability of TCP/IP networks.

Limited Address Space

IPv4 has a much more limited address space than the IPv6 standard. IPv4 has a 32-bit address space, which most of us are familiar with seeing in *dotted decimal notation*, written like this: **192.168.2.168**. What this actually represents is a binary string that is 32 digits long (and thus a 32-bit string), where each of those four numbers is translated into binary. So, an IP address that is expressed using dotted decimal notation as **192.168.2.168** would be represented in binary as follows: **11000000101010000000001010101000**.

By using a 32-bit address space, IPv4 has a theoretical upper bound of 4,294,967,296 possible IP addresses. However, the actual number of available IPv4 addresses is limited by some implementation decisions that were made in the early days of IPv4's use as a protocol. The most striking example of this is the *loopback address range*, where all IPv4 addresses in the 127.*x.x.x* space have been reserved for troubleshooting and testing purposes: By making the familiar 127.0.0.1 address available as a troubleshooting tool, the originators of the IPv4 standard eliminated 16,777,216 IP addresses in one fell swoop.

The number of available IPv4 addresses has also been limited by some early decisions in doling out IPv4 IP addresses to various organizations that were early adopters of the Internet. For some historical perspective on this, remember the following: Before the mid-'90s, the Internet was primarily an educational tool that was funded by the National Science Foundation and populated only by large research universities and corporations such as MIT and Bell Labs. Not foreseeing the commercial explosion that would take place with the rise of e-commerce many years later, IP addresses were doled out quite generously to early Internet residents because there seemed no danger of ever running out: A single research university in the United States might have more IP addresses assigned to it than an entire European nation, for example. For both of these reasons, the actual number of available IPv4 addresses is closer to a few *million* rather than upward of 4 *billion*.

IPv4 has thus far staved off being relegated to legacy status by the active use of a network address translator, or NAT. This has allowed latecomers to Internet society to conserve the available reserves of IP addresses by relying on *private IP addresses* for the majority of their networking needs. RFC 1918 defines the following private IP address ranges that have been reserved from the IPv4 space for use by private organizations:

- 10.0.0.1 through 10.255.255.255
- 172.16.0.0 through 172.31.255.255
- 192.168.0.0 through 192.168.255.255

This RFC defined private IP addresses to meet both of the following needs (as noted at www.faqs.org/rfcs/rfc1918.html):

- "Hosts that do not require access to hosts in other enterprises or the Internet at large; hosts within this category may use IP addresses that are unambiguous within an enterprise, but may be ambiguous between enterprises."

- "Hosts that need access to a limited set of outside services (e.g., e-mail, FTP, netnews, remote login) which can be handled by mediating gateways (e.g., application layer gateways). For many hosts in this category an unrestricted external access (provided via IP connectivity) may be unnecessary and even undesirable for privacy/security reasons. Just like hosts within the first category, such hosts may use IP addresses that are unambiguous within an enterprise, but may be ambiguous between enterprises."

In other words, private IP addresses are intended for use by both personal and business computers that don't necessarily need to possess a public IP address all their own. These will typically be desktop computers that are being used to access Internet resources such as e-mail, the World Wide Web, and so on, using a NAT device that can provide Internet connectivity under these conditions without expending a public IP address for each connected computer.

NAT to the Rescue?

Devices configured with private IP addresses can communicate on the Internet by using a NAT device such as a router or proxy server. A NAT device will take packets sent from a device configured with a private IP and then, as the name suggests, *translate* those packets using a public IP address assigned to the NAT device. For example, say that you have a workstation on a corporate network that is configured with the private IP address of 192.168.0.155. This workstation wants to communicate with a Web server on the Internet that is configured with an IP address of 151.4.5.7. When the private computer transmits packets to the destination Web server, the source and destination addresses read as follows:

- Destination address: 151.4.5.7
- Source address: 192.168.0.155

The private computer does not transmit these packets directly to the destination Web server, however; the traffic is instead transmitted to a NAT device configured with a public IP address of 217.8.6.5. The NAT device then removes the private source address, replaces it with a public IP address, and then retransmits the packets to the destination host as follows (the NAT device maintains a translation table to keep track of inbound and outbound traffic that it is translating for multiple hosts on the private network):

- Destination address: 151.4.5.7
- Source address: 217.8.6.5

When the destination Web server transmits information back to the 192.168.0.155 workstation, the destination address is not the private IP address, but rather the *public* address of the NAT device. (The destination Web server typically does not even realize that a NAT device is involved in the conversation.) So, the return headers will look like this:

- Destination address: 217.8.6.5
- Source address: 151.4.5.7

Based on the information that it recorded in its translation table, the NAT device will receive this information and then translate the destination address to that of the computer on the private network:

- Destination address: 192.168.0.155
- Source address: 151.4.5.7

Although the use of NAT has been a boon for conserving available addresses within the IPv4 32-bit space, it is not the panacea that it might seem at first glance. The use of NAT for network applications can create performance issues as packets are bottlenecked into a single NAT device on one or both ends of the communication, and certain applications and protocols do not function reliably (or sometimes at all) if they are required to transmit through a NAT device. For example, many devices are unable to route IPSec-secured traffic (such as that used for a virtual private network [VPN]) through a NAT device because the headers are encrypted, thus rendering NAT unable to modify the source and destination addresses without breaking the encryption process. This has largely been addressed by the use of NAT-Traversal (NAT-T), but this is unfortunately not a universal solution because not all NAT devices conform to a single standard. This "NAT Traversal" problem has also reared its head in the case of peer-to-peer applications used for file sharing and Voice over IP that cannot always communicate through NAT devices.

Notes from the Underground...

Calling It "Private" Doesn't Necessarily Make It So...

These IP address ranges are considered private because they are not typically passed along beyond the boundary of a router; however, that doesn't mean that they *can't be*. The key point to remember here is that an RFC is a standard, not a technical requirement; an attacker can choose to not "play by the rules" of the RFC if that works to his advantage in attacking a network.

Although most routers and other Internet-connected devices will not pass traffic to or from the RFC 1918 address spaces by default, these devices can often be manually configured to allow an attacker to do so. Either through maliciousness or through someone misconfiguring an Internet-connected device, you can often find routes to so-called private address spaces being advertised to and from routers attached to the Internet. And although this provides an attack vector that a malicious user can exploit, it's an attack vector that can be fairly easily mitigated. Particularly if you are protecting Internet-facing machines that are configured with public IP addresses, your border router can quite easily assist you in some of the "heavy lifting" associated with Internet security if you configure it with the following set of (fairly simple) rules:

- **Drop any inbound traffic that is not destined for a host on the internal network** For example, if your router is in front of computers with IP addresses ranging from 216.1.5.4 to 216.1.4.25, why would you accept any traffic that had been addressed to 151.6.6.4? This seems like common sense when it's spelled out, doesn't it? But many routers can be configured with an inbound routing rule of "Accept *all* inbound traffic," rather than "Accept inbound traffic destined for IP addresses within my network."

■ **Drop any outbound traffic that does not originate from a host on the internal network** This is the preceding rule in reverse: If my router is in front of computers with IP addresses from 216.1.5.4 through 216.1.4.25, why would I want to transmit any outbound traffic that originated from a computer with an IP address not in that range?

■ **Drop any traffic (inbound or outbound) destined for the RFC 1918 ranges** As we've been discussing, these IP ranges should not be routed across the Internet under any circumstances; any traffic that your router receives that is destined for these IP addresses was sent through either maliciousness or misconfiguration. Please note here that we're not referring to dropping NAT traffic if your network is configured for it: We're not talking about traffic that is destined for a NAT device that will then be retransmitted to an internal computer on your network. We're referring to traffic that actually has a Destination Address field within one of the three RFC 1918-defined address ranges.

Security and Quality of Service

Another limitation of IPv4 is a lack of support for built-in security and quality of service (QoS) functionality. Although one can use security measures such as IPSec to secure IPv4 traffic, these technologies are not mandatory and were often vendor-specific or shoehorned onto the IPv4 standard after the fact; this can create havoc in terms of deploying and troubleshooting these security measures, particularly when dealing with heterogeneous networks connected by many different vendor devices.

Another limitation of IPv4 is that it has no built-in mechanism to support QoS. The idea behind QoS is fairly simple: It is a matter of granting priority to certain types of traffic in limited-bandwidth environments. An example here might be found in trying to optimize bandwidth utilization at a research university: As a network engineer, would you rather give priority to Internet traffic being used by a scientist to perform cancer research, or to the resident of an undergraduate residence hall who is downloading a pirated copy of *The Matrix 7: Can't Kill Neo!* from a peer-to-peer file-sharing network? (The undergraduate in question might have a different answer to that query than the university network engineer, but that's another matter.) Similar to security measures for IPv4, QoS is not mandatory for IPv4 traffic, and many current QoS solutions are vendor-specific and are not scalable across the whole of the Internet.

Host and Router Configuration

IPv4 requires quite a bit of manual labor in configuring both host computers and routers on an IPv4 network. In order to communicate over an IPv4 network, all hosts either require a statically assigned IPv4 address or must be able to contact a Dynamic Host Configuration Protocol (DHCP) server to obtain their IPv4 configuration information. To transmit traffic between hosts IPv4 routers require cumbersome methods to "learn" where other routers on the Internet are located; these methods will often involve route advertisements being broadcast across an entire IPv4 subnet.

Introduction to IPv6 and Dual Layer

To alleviate the issues created by the current reliance on the IPv4 standard, the updated IPv6 was introduced in the mid-1990s and was defined in RFC 2460 (www.faqs.org/rfcs/rfc2460.html). IPv6 has thus far had a slow adoption rate for one simple reason: IPv6 is *not* backward-compatible with IPv4. This means any organization that wants to use IPv6 has had one of the following three fairly unappealing choices:

- Perform a "hard cut" in which all networked resources were converted from IPv4 to IPv6.

- Maintain a separate network infrastructure for IPv6-enabled network devices.

- Invest in network hardware that was both IPv4- and IPv6-capable.

The first two options would be about as welcome as a root canal under any circumstances (particularly because the first option would not address the need to communicate beyond one's own local network), and hardware that supported both TCP/IP versions was either unavailable or prohibitively expensive in the early days of IPv6. As time has gone on, however, IPv6 has come into broader usage so that supporting a "dual stack" environment is far less distasteful.

In the following sections, we will examine how IPv6 addresses the limitations that were present in the IPv4 implementation of TCP/IP.

Increased Address Space

The most noticeable difference between IPv4 and IPv6 is the massive disparity in the number of available IP addresses. As we mentioned previously, IPv4 uses a 32-bit address space which allows for a theoretical maximum of around 4 billion IP addresses. IPv6, by contrast, uses a 128-bit address space; this allows for 2^{128} total IP addresses, or $3.4 * 10^{38}$ possible IP addresses. This figure represents the scientific notation shorthand for 2^{128}; the exact number is *340,282,366,920,938, 463,463,374,607,431,768,211,456* possible IP addresses. Even allowing for future growth, this address space seems nigh-inexhaustible; there are enough available IP addresses in the IPv6 space to assign multiple IP addresses to every man, woman, and child currently living on the planet Earth.

IPv6 addresses contain eight groups of hexadecimal characters separated by colons—for example, 4DAB:FFFF:0000:3E3A:02AA:00FF:DA72:9C5A. You'll often see the leading zeros in a section suppressed to save space; we could have written the preceding example as 4DAB:FFFF:0:3E3A:02AA:00FF:DA72:9C5A. In cases where more than one hexadecimal grouping consists of all zeros, we can cut these out entirely and replace them with a double colon; so, we could abbreviate fe80:0:0:0:2aa:ff:fe9a:4ca2 as fe80::2aa:ff:fe9a:4ca2.

TIP

So, how do you know how many groupings have been replaced by a double colon? Just remember that every IPv6 address contains eight groups of hex characters. In the case of fe80::2aa:ff:fe9a:4ca2, only five such groupings are written out. This means that there are (8 – 5), or 3, groupings of all zeros that were replaced by the double colon.

Built-in Security and QoS

Unlike IPv4, in which security and QoS measures were optional portions of the protocol that were often added in later as protocol extensions, IPSec and QoS are built right into IPv6 and are a mandatory component of each packet. Quality of Service information is encoded into the Flow Label Header field of IPv6 packets, as defined in RFC 3697 (www.faqs.org/rfcs/rfc3697.html).

WARNING

This does not mean that all IPv6 traffic is IPSec-encrypted or QoS-configured by default; it simply means that these two features have been written directly into the IPv6 standard so that all IPv6-capable devices can interoperate and support IPSec and QoS in a standards-based fashion.

Windows Vista Support for IPv6

Windows Vista is the first Microsoft OS to support IPv6 natively; it is installed and enabled by default when the OS is first installed. This includes support for a number of IPv6 features, including the following:

- **IPSec support** In both Vista and Longhorn, IPSec support under IPv6 is the same as it is for IPv4, including support for the Internet Key Exchange (IKE) protocol as well as IPSec encryption using 128-, 192-, or 256-bit Advanced Encryption Standard (AES) encryption. You can configure IPSec for IPv6 using the IPSec Microsoft Management Console (MMC) snap-in, as well as the new Windows Firewall applet.

- **Link-Local Multicast Name Resolution (LLMNR)** The IPv6 RFC defines a number of different classifications of IPv6 IP addresses. Global Unique Addresses, for example, are analogous to public IP addresses in IPv4. But rather than force network administrators to rely only on the public/private classification, IPv6 includes multiple types of local-use addresses that can be used under various circumstances. Site-local addresses correspond most closely to private IP addresses under IPv4; they are not reachable outside of a private site and are not forwarded by any IPv6-capable router. In addition to these two address types, IPv6 also defines link-local addresses, which can be used by nodes on a single network that are not separated by a router. LLMNR allows link-local addresses on a single subnet to resolve each other's names even without the use of domain name system (DNS) or NetBIOS; this is accomplished by sending a name resolution query to a multicast address to which any LLMNR-capable hosts will respond.

- **IPv6 over PPP** The Windows Vista remote access client allows you to configure a Point-to-Point Protocol (PPP) connection using IPv6, as well as providing support for creating L2TP-based VPN connections over IPv6.

- **GUI configuration** In Windows XP and Windows Server 2003, you were only able to configure IPv6 from the command line using the *netsh* command. Windows Vista allows you to configure IPv6 settings through the Properties sheet of a network connection in the Network and Sharing Center, just as you would an IPv4 connection.

Understanding the Dual-Layer Architecture

From the standpoint of the underlying network architecture, Windows Vista's IPv6 support is fundamentally different from what was implemented in Windows XP and Windows Server 2003. In XP and 2003, IPv6 was implemented in a *dual-stack archi-tecture* alongside IPv4. This meant that IPv4 and IPv6 were deployed as two entirely separate networking protocols, each with their own Transport and Data Link (framing) layers. This meant, for example, that IPv4 and IPv6 each had their own implementations of the Transmission Control Protocol (TCP) and the User Datagram Protocol (UDP) and never the twain would meet. This also made it more difficult to implement any sort of TCP/IP filtering, because a separate mechanism needed to be implemented for each separate TCP/IP stack. Finally, developers had to do double-duty to write applications that took advantage of both IPv4 and IPv6 because they were implemented using two separate drivers: tcpip.sys and tcpip6.sys.

Windows Vista has completely reengineered this model, replacing the "dual-stack" architecture of XP and 2003 with a much improved dual-layer architecture. This means that IPv6 and IPv4 are supported in Windows Vista using a single driver—tcpip.sys—and the two protocols share a common Transport and Framing layer. This allows developers to write applications that can take advantage of both protocols, and it allows network administrators to use the Windows Firewall and IPSec to control both IPv4 and IPv6 traffic simultaneously.

Configuring IPv6 Using the GUI

You can view and modify your computer's IPv6 settings through the graphical user interface (GUI) by following these steps:

1. Open the **Network and Sharing Center**.

2. Click on **View Status**, and then click on **Details** to see a screen similar to Figure 6.1. As you can see, this computer has been automatically configured with an IPv6 link-local address, even though it is not connected to an IPv6-capable network.

Figure 6.1 Viewing Details of TCP/IP Properties in Windows Vista

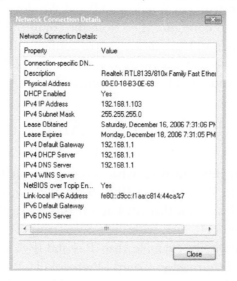

3. Click **Close** to return to the **Connection Status** screen. To modify the properties of the IPv6 protocol, click on **Properties**. If you have **User Account Control** enabled, you'll see an additional prompt before being taken to the screen shown in Figure 6.2.

Figure 6.2 Viewing Installed Network Components in Windows Vista

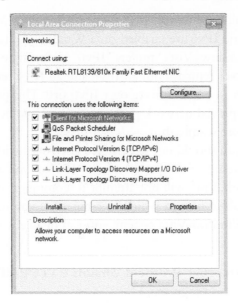

4. To modify the IPv6 configuration, highlight the **Internet Protocol Version 6 (TCP/IPv6)** option and select **Properties**. You'll see the screen shown in Figure 6.3.

Figure 6.3 Modifying the IPv6 Settings on a Windows Vista Computer

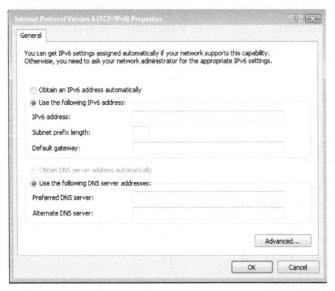

Disabling IPv6 Using the GUI

You do not have the ability to uninstall IPv6 from a Windows Vista computer. In addition, if both IPv4 and IPv6 are enabled on a Windows Vista system, Vista will attempt to use IPv6; Windows Vista "prefers" IPv6. An example of this preference is as follows: If a DNS server returns both an IPv6 and an IPv4 record for the same query, Vista will attempt to communicate over IPv6 first. This preference of IPv6 over IPv4 allows for improved network performance in Vista by allowing IPv6 technologies to function more seamlessly.

For the most part, you should not experience any issues with your existing network connectivity as a result of this preference for IPv6; if you are communicating on an IPv4-only network, Vista will not attempt to communicate using IPv6 unless you specify an IPv6-enabled host to which to connect. If you do experience any issues with IPv6 on a Windows Vista system, you can disable it in one of the following ways:

- Uncheck the **Internet Protocol Version 6 (TCP/IPv6)** checkbox on the screen shown in Figure 6.2.

- Modify *HKEY_LOCAL_MACHINE\SYSTEM\CurrentControlSet\Services\tcpip6\Parameters\DisabledComponents* using one of the values listed in Table 6.1.

Table 6.1 Disabling Individual IPv6 Components in Windows Vista

To Disable the Following Feature(s)...	...Enter the Following Value for ~\DisabledComponents
Disable all tunnel interfaces	0x1
Disable 6to4 support	0x2
Disable ISATAP	0x4
Disable Teredo	0x8
Disable Teredo and 6to4	0xA
Disable all LAN and PPP interfaces	0x10
Disable all LAN, PPP, and tunnel interfaces	0x11
Prefer IPv4 over IPv6	0x20
Disable IPv6 over all interfaces and prefer IPv4 to IPv6	0xFF

Configuring IPv6 from the Command Line

Similar to IPv6 in Windows XP and Windows Server 2003, Vista offers you the ability to configure IPv6 at the command line using the *netsh* command. *Netsh* has several subcommands that you can use to configure an IPv6 IP address, add an IPv6 gateway, and configure IPv6 DNS servers, as well as other configuration options. Let's look at some of the more common subcommands.

Configuring an IPv6 IP Address

To configure an IPv6 address using *netsh*, use the following syntax:

```
netsh interface ipv6 add address "Local Area Connection"
1045:CA8:260C:1291:5AB2:D
```

To delete an IPv6 IP address, simply repeat the preceding command, replacing the *add* subcommand with *delete*.

Configuring an IPv6 Default Gateway

To add a default gateway for an IPv6 command, you use the *add route* subcommand, which takes the following syntax (we explain the various subcommands in Table 6.2):

```
netsh interface ipv6 add route [prefix=]::/0
[interface=]Interface_Name_or_Index [[nexthop=]IPv6_Address]
[[siteprefixlength=]Length] [[metric=]Metric_Value]
[[publish=]no|yes|immortal] [[validlifetime=]Time|infinite]
[[preferredlifetime=]Time|infinite] [[store=]active|persistent]
```

Table 6.2 Netsh Options for Adding IPv6 Gateways

Subcommand	Explanation	Default Value
prefix	The IPv6 address prefix and prefix length for the default route	Use ::/ for the default route.
interface	The name of the interface or connection that you're configuring	N/A
nexthop	The next-hop IP address (if a nonlocal link)	N/A
siteprefixlength	Specifies the prefix length for the site if the destination is on the local link	N/A

Continued

Table 6.2 continued Netsh Options for Adding IPv6 Gateways

Subcommand	Explanation	Default Value
metric	Specifies a preference if more than one route is available to a particular destination	Routes with a lower metric will be used before routes with a higher one.
publish	Specifies whether this route will be included in router advertisements	N/A
validlifetime	The lifetime for which a route is preferred	Infinite
store	Specifies whether the route is *active* (is removed from memory when the system restarts) or *persistent* (remains in memory after a system restart)	Persistent

At its simplest, the following command will add a default gateway using default values:

```
netsh interface ipv6 add route ::/0 "Local Area Connection"
FE80::5226:ff:12A9:56CA
```

Adding IPv6 DNS Servers

Configuring an IPv6 DNS server is very similar to configuring an IP address. To add an IPv6 DNS server, use the *netsh interface ipv6 add dnsserver "Local Area Connection" <IPv6 Address>* command. Likewise, you'll use the *netsh interface ipv6 delete dnsserver...* command to remove a DNS server entry.

Using the Network and Sharing Center

One of the new features in the Windows Vista GUI is the Network and Sharing Center, which replaces the Network Connections applet in the Windows XP Control Panel. The Network and Sharing Center acts as a kind of "one-stop shop" to control many aspects of networking within Windows Vista: configuring and troubleshooting network locations, providing access to network diagnostics, and even providing a graphical Network Map of your existing network layout. (We'll discuss the Network Map further in the next section.) You can see a typical view of the Network and Sharing Center in Figure 6.4.

Figure 6.4 Introducing the Windows Vista Network and Sharing Center

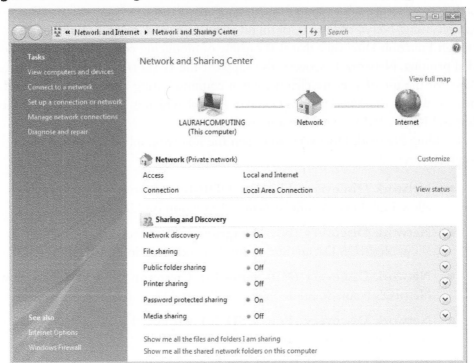

Working with Network Sharing and Discovery

To help improve network security, particularly for home-based users, Vista introduces the notion of *network locations* to help you apply preconfigured security settings to a particular network connection. Network locations help you to configure security for your network by bundling together configuration settings for the networking options discussed in the following sections.

Network Discovery

When Network Discovery is enabled, Vista opens up a number of ports on the Windows Firewall to allow other computers on a network to browse to resources on your computer. Enabling Network Discovery allows you to access files and devices (such as shared printers) on other computers, and allows other network users to access files and devices on your computer. At first glance, this may seem analogous to the Network Browser service in previous versions of Windows. Windows Vista, however, has significantly updated the Network Discovery process and includes a number of new features for resource discovery. One of the most promising is the

Function Discovery feature, which is a programming interface that will allow hardware vendors to advertise what type of function a particular device can perform. For example, using Network Discovery might allow a network printer to advertise through Function Discovery that it is capable of producing color output or double-sided printing. Network Discovery also supports the *WSDAPI framework*, which allows for the use of a secure channel when communicating between a device and a client, as well as the *Simple Service Discovery Protocol*, which is used to detect Universal Plug and Play (UPnP) devices on a network.

Enabling Network Discovery will open the following inbound ports in the Windows Firewall:

- **Network Discovery (LLMNR-UDP-In)** Creates an inbound rule to allow Link Local Multicast Name Resolution on UDP port 5355.

- **Network Discovery (NB-Datagram-In)** Creates an inbound rule to allow NetBIOS Datagram transmission and reception on UDP port 138.

- **Network Discovery (NB-Name-In)** Creates an inbound rule to allow NetBIOS Name Resolution on UDP port 137.

- **Network Discovery (Pub-WSD-In)** Creates an inbound rule to discover devices via Function Discovery on UDP port 3702.

- **Network Discovery (SSDP-In)** Creates an inbound rule to allow use of the Simple Service Discovery Protocol on UDP port 1900.

- **Network Discovery (UPnP-In)** Creates an inbound rule to allow use of Universal Plug and Play on TCP port 2869.

- **Network Discovery (WSD Events-In)** Creates an inbound rule to allow WSDAPI Events via Function Discovery on TCP port 5357.

- **Network Discovery (WSD EventsSecure-In)** Creates an inbound rule to allow Secure WSDAPI Events via Function Discovery on TCP port 5358.

- **Network Discovery (WSD-In)** Creates an inbound rule to discover devices via Function Discovery on UDP port 3702.

Because the new Windows Firewall in Vista can also monitor and control outbound connections, enabling Network Discovery will enable the following outbound ports in addition to the inbound ports just discussed:

- **Network Discovery (LLMNR-TCP-Out)** Creates an outbound rule to allow Link Local Multicast Name Resolution (LLMNR) on TCP port 5355.

- **Network Discovery (LLMNR-UDP-Out)** Creates an outbound rule to allow Link Local Multicast Name Resolution on UDP port 5355.

- **Network Discovery (NB-Datagram-Out)** Creates an outbound rule to allow NetBIOS Datagram transmission and reception on UDP port 138.

- **Network Discovery (NB-Name-Out)** Creates an outbound rule to allow NetBIOS Name Resolution on UDP port 137.

- **Network Discovery (Pub WSD-Out)** Creates an outbound rule to discover devices via Function Discovery on UDP port 3702.

- **Network Discovery (SSDP-Out)** Creates an outbound rule to allow use of the Simple Service Discovery Protocol on UDP port 1900.

- **Network Discovery (UPnPHost-Out)** Creates an outbound rule to allow the use of Universal Plug and Play over TCP (all ports).

- **Network Discovery (UPnP-Out)** Creates a second outbound rule to allow use of Universal Plug and Play over TCP (all ports).

- **Network Discovery (WSD Events-Out)** Creates an outbound rule to allow for WSDAPI Events via Function Discovery on TCP port 5357.

- **Network Discovery (WSD EventsSecure-Out)** Creates an outbound rule to allow for Secure WSDAPI Events via Function Discovery on TCP port 5358.

- **Network Discovery (WSD-Out)** Creates an outbound rule to discover devices via Function Discovery on UDP port 3702.

NOTE

To minimize the impact of enabling this feature incorrectly, all of these firewall exceptions are scoped to the local subnet only.

Working with File and Printer Sharing

The basic file- and printer-sharing functionality in Windows Vista has not changed substantially from earlier versions of Windows; enabling File Sharing in the Network and Sharing Center allows other computers to be able to access files and folders that are stored on your local hard drive. Enabling File Sharing will configure the following inbound port exceptions in the Windows Firewall:

- **File and Printer Sharing (Echo Request - ICMPv4-In)** This exception allows PING messages to be sent to the local computer from any computer attached to the network using ICMPv4, including those attached to the Internet or other remote networks.

- **File and Printer Sharing (Echo Request - ICMPv6-In)** This allows IPv6-enabled computers to send PING messages to the local computer using ICMPv6. This exception is enabled for all network-attached computers, regardless of location.

- **File and Printer Sharing (NB-Datagram-In)** This creates an inbound rule to allow NetBIOS Datagram transmission and reception over UDP port 138 from machines on the local subnet.

- **File and Printer Sharing (NB-Name-In)** This creates an inbound rule to allow NetBIOS Name Resolution over UDP port 137 from machines on the local subnet.

- **File and Printer Sharing (NB-Session-In)** This creates an inbound rule to allow NetBIOS Session Service connections from the local subnet on TCP port 139.

- **File and Printer Sharing (SMB-In)** This creates an inbound rule to allow Server Message Block (SMB) transmission and reception via Named Pipes over TCP port 445 from machines on the local subnet.

- **File and Printer Sharing (Spooler Service - RPC)** This creates an inbound rule to allow the Print Spooler Service to accept dynamic Remote Procedure Call (RPC) connections over TCP from machines on the local subnet.

- **File and Printer Sharing (Spooler Service - RPC-EPMAP)** This creates an inbound rule to allow RPC-EPMAP connections over TCP from the local subnet.

The Windows Firewall also enables the following outbound exceptions when File and Printer Sharing is enabled:

- **Outbound PING traffic, both ICMPv4 and ICMPv6** Outbound Internet Control Message Protocol (ICMP) connections are enabled to all network-connected devices.

- **Outbound NetBIOS and SMB traffic** Creates outbound rules for UDP ports 137 and 138, and TCP ports 139 and 445, to machines on the local subnet.

Enabling Printer Sharing

The Network and Sharing Center lists File Sharing and Printer Sharing as two separate options. However, both options enable the same Windows Firewall exceptions, and enabling Printer Sharing automatically enables both File Sharing *and* Network Discovery. In addition, enabling Printer Sharing creates a *\\<computername>\print$* hidden share that maps to *~\Windows\system32\spool\drivers*. This share is *not* removed when Printer Sharing is disabled in the Network and Sharing Center. Additionally, if you turn off Printer Sharing, Network Discovery and File Sharing remain turned on unless you disable them separately.

Introducing Public Folder Sharing

Public Folder Sharing is a new construct within Windows Vista. Not to be confused with Exchange Public Folders, which are an entirely different entity, Public Folder Sharing creates a single shared document repository on a Vista workstation. This is intended to allow easier shared file access among multiple users of a single computer, as well as users across a small office, home office (SOHO) or other peer-to-peer network. When you enable Public Folder Sharing in the Network and Sharing Center, the following takes place on the local computer:

- The *C:\Users\Public* folder is shared out as *\\<computername>\Public* (you can grant the Everyone group either Read or Full Control permissions).

- The Network Discovery and File and Printer Sharing exceptions are enabled in the Windows Firewall.

You can see an example of Public Folder Sharing configured with read-only network access in Figure 6.5.

Figure 6.5 Enabling Public Folder Sharing in the Network and Sharing Center

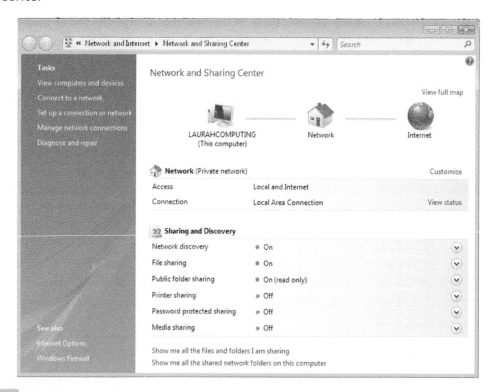

WARNING

If you enable Public Folder Sharing and then subsequently disable it, the Windows Firewall exceptions for Network Discovery and File and Printer Sharing *remain enabled*! Remember to disable these exceptions manually after disabling Public Folder Sharing.

Password-Protected Sharing

Password-protected sharing is another new feature in Vista network sharing. This feature does not open any new exceptions within the Windows Firewall; rather, it limits network access to the Public Folder to only users who have a configured username and password on the local computer.

Media Sharing

Enabling the Media Sharing option in the Network and Sharing Center configures the Windows Media Player Network Sharing Service, which requires the following ports and services:

- Windows Media Player Network Sharing Service (HTTP-Streaming-In) accepts inbound connections on TCP port 10243 from the local subnet.

- svchost.exe accepts inbound QoS traffic on TCP and UDP port 2177 from the local subnet.

- The Simple Service Discovery Protocol accepts inbound traffic on UDP port 1900 from the local subnet.

- wmpnetwk.exe is configured to accept inbound TCP and UDP connections on all ports from the local subnet.

- The Windows Media Player Network Sharing Service (UPnP-In) accepts inbound TCP traffic on port 2869 from the local subnet.

Working with Network Locations

When Vista detects that you've connected to a new network, such as when you first install or upgrade to Vista or connect to a new wireless network, you will be prompted to select from a set of preconfigured network locations. Vista offers the following preconfigured locations to allow users to quickly configure their network settings in a secure fashion:

NOTE

These options are not configurable on Vista computers that are attached to an Active Directory domain.

- **Home or Work (Private network)** In a private network, Vista enables Network Discovery and Password-Protected Sharing within the Network and Sharing Center, because the assumption is that this is a trusted network that is being protected by a firewall, proxy server, or similar device.
- **Public (Public network)** Choose this option for airports, coffee shops, and other public locations, or if you are directly connected to the Internet.

Under this option, only Password-Protected Sharing is enabled; Network Discovery, File and Printer, Public Folder Sharing, and Media Sharing are all disabled.

NOTE

To be as secure as possible, you can certainly choose the Public configuration settings even if you are connected to a private network.

To quickly reconfigure a network connection from Public to Private or vice versa, do the following:

1. Open the **Network and Sharing Center**.

2. Click **Customize**. You'll see the screen shown in Figure 6.6.

Figure 6.6 Changing the Network Location Type

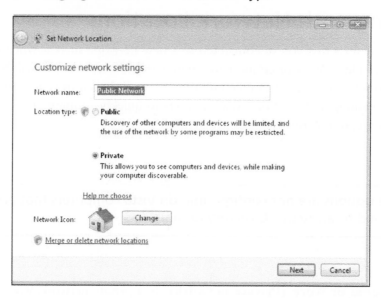

3. Next to **Location type**, select the radio button corresponding to a **Public** or **Private** network, and then click **Next**, followed by **Close**.

NOTE

As you can see by the shield that's next to the **Location type** menu option, User Account Control will prompt you to make any changes to the configuration of your network location.

Using the Network Map

Another new feature in the Network and Sharing Center is the Network Map, which provides a graphical view of your local computer's relative position on the network, as well as indicates any networked computers that have been configured for Network Discovery and/or File and Printer Sharing. For example, Figure 6.7 shows the Network Map on a single-computer network, the kind you might see on a home computer that's attached to a high-speed Internet connection such as a cable modem.

Figure 6.7 Viewing a Simple Network Map

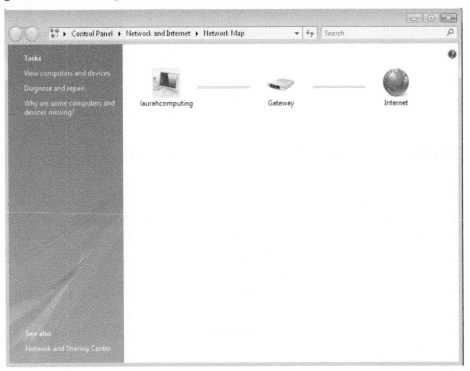

In Figure 6.8, you can see how the Network Map changes if multiple computers are configured for Network Discovery from a private network location. (The Network Map function is not available if the network location is configured as a public network.)

Figure 6.8 A More Complex Network Map

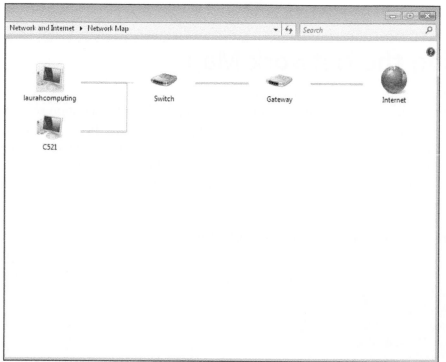

Troubleshooting with the Network Map

Another useful feature of the Network Map is its capability to provide a graphical interpretation of various issues that you may encounter when working with networking in Windows Vista. If a particular network segment becomes disconnected, it will be displayed on the Network Map with a red *X* over the segment. This can be a great help in troubleshooting, as the Network Map can often indicate *where* a particular fault has occurred. For example, look at the Network Map in Figure 6.9, in which the network cable for the LAURAHCOMPUTING computer has become unplugged from the switch. You can clearly see by the location of the red *X* that the fault lies in the connection between the LAURAHCOMPUTING computer and the Internet.

Figure 6.9 Viewing a Network Fault with the Network Map

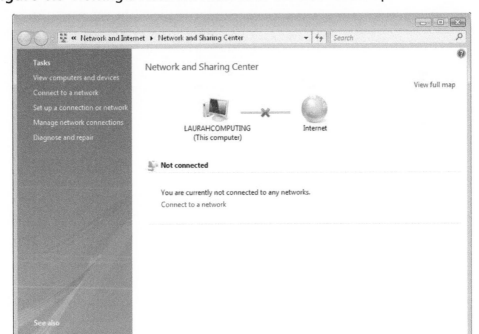

Now let's look at another troubleshooting scenario and how it is displayed in the Network Map. In this case, we have two computers configured in a peer-to-peer network behind a SOHO router, but the router has lost its connection to the outside world. Figure 6.10 shows you how this might look in the Network Map; you can see that LAURAHCOMPUTING and C521 have connectivity with one another, but that there is a fault somewhere between the local switch and the outside world.

The Network and Sharing Center also offers options to diagnose and repair issues with network connectivity, such as those shown in Figures 6.9 and 6.10. Say, for example, that Internet connectivity has been restored to the network in Figure 6.10, but the LAURAHCOMPUTING machine is still unable to connect to the Internet. Simply click on **Diagnose and Repair** from the Network and Sharing Center, and quite often Windows Vista will offer a suggestion to correct the issue—not to mention the ability to perform the fix automatically. In this case, Figure 6.11 indicates the cause of the continued connectivity issue and offers to implement a solution.

Figure 6.10 Viewing a More Complex Troubleshooting Scenario

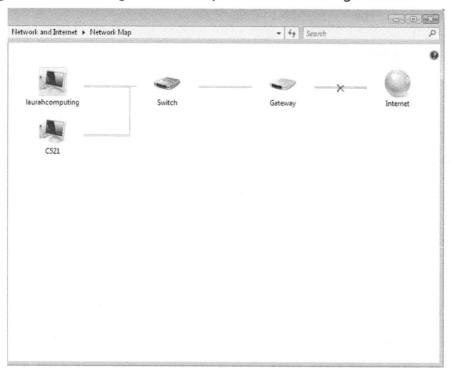

Figure 6.11 Troubleshooting with the Network and Sharing Center

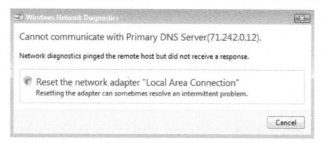

If the troubleshooting measure was successful, you'll be greeted with the screen shown in Figure 6.12.

Figure 6.12 A Problem Successfully Resolved!

Working with the Windows Firewall

You can find another significant update to Windows Vista within the Windows Firewall, in which Microsoft has taken the improvements made in Windows XP SP2 and improved upon them even further. Before we examine the new firewall features available with Vista, though, let's take a moment to look at the introduction of the Windows Firewall within the Windows XP OS.

With the release of Windows XP SP2, information technology (IT) professionals saw a huge leap forward in Microsoft's desktop security strategy with the addition of the Windows Firewall. In some ways, the Windows Firewall was a natural progression from the Internet Connection Firewall (ICF) that had been bundled into XP since its original release, but in most respects, the Windows Firewall was a huge departure from earlier Microsoft desktop security mechanisms. The ICF was turned off by default on new XP installations, so many users didn't even realize it existed. And those people who manually enabled ICF often found that it was difficult to use and configure. This was particularly the case for system administrators because the ICF was not configurable across an enterprise; the only Group Policy setting associated with ICF was the ability to disable it en masse.

The release of the Windows Firewall in XP SP2 presented a much broader range of options for securing the Windows desktop, particularly for Active Directory administrators who wanted to deploy a consistent firewall configuration across an enterprise. Most prominently, the SP2 upgrade process would prompt the user to turn on the Windows Firewall when the install was completed, and the Windows Firewall was turned on out of the box on computers that were preinstalled with SP2. This configuration eliminated many instances of the "My computer got compromised in the time it took me to go out to Windows Update and get my patches" phenomenon that had previously plagued end users and system administrators. The Windows Firewall also added dozens of configurable settings within Group Policy. For example, administrators can use Group Policy to specify which applications or ports to open and whether connections to those resources must be secure, all within the new Windows Firewall with Advanced Security Group Policy node. Group Policy allows administrators to exert granular control of its configuration across an entire organization or a single subset of users. Windows Vista takes this a step further by introducing the Windows Firewall with Advanced Security.

NOTE

For brevity's sake, we will continue to refer to the Vista firewall as the *Windows Firewall* through the remainder of this chapter, except where we are referencing new features specific to the new Windows Firewall with Advanced Security interface.

Configuring the Windows Firewall

Similar to the Windows XP firewall, the Windows Firewall with Advanced Security is a stateful, host-based firewall that you can configure to allow or disallow traffic that is generated by either a particular executable file, such as C:\Program Files\Microsoft SQL Server\sqlserver.exe, or traffic that is destined for one or more TCP or UDP ports, such as TCP port 80 for Hypertext Transfer Protocol (HTTP) traffic. You'll find that basic firewall configuration tasks haven't changed much between Windows XP and Windows Vista; you'll continue to make these changes using the Windows Firewall Control Panel applet. But even this piece has been updated to make it more intuitive and informative for the end user: When you open the Windows Firewall applet, the first thing you see is a summary of your current Windows Firewall settings, as shown in Figure 6.13.

As you can see, this provides an at-a-glance summary of the current state of the firewall; whether it is turned on or off, how exceptions and notifications are being handled, and the network location to which the computer is currently connected. By clicking on **Change settings**, you'll be taken to a familiar-looking interface that will actually allow you to make changes, as shown in Figure 6.14.

Figure 6.13 A New Look for the Windows Firewall Control Panel Applet

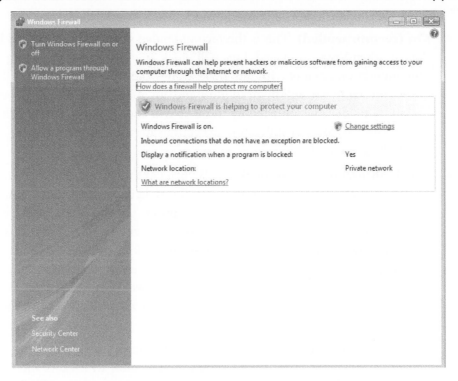

Figure 6.14 Configuring Basic Windows Firewall Settings

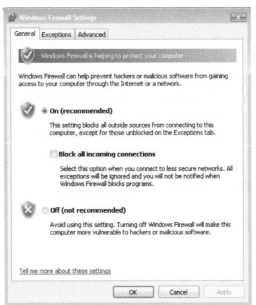

Similar to Windows XP, we define the three settings on the General tab as follows:

- **On (recommended)** This is the recommended setting and is enabled by default when Vista is installed. This will block any unsolicited incoming communication attempts that are made against the Vista workstation. All outbound traffic will still be permitted, and any inbound responses to outbound traffic that was initiated by the user will also be permitted. On the Exceptions tab, you can still define exceptions for inbound traffic that should be permitted.

- **Block all incoming connections** By placing a checkmark here, you will instruct the Windows Firewall to block all unsolicited connection attempts even if exceptions are defined on the Exceptions tab. You should select this option if you are connected to a public or otherwise insecure network such as one in a hotel, airport, or coffee house, or if a known virus or worm is spreading across the Internet and you want to be extra careful until the threat has largely run its course. When you remove the checkmark next to this option, any traffic defined on the Exceptions tab will once again be permitted to connect to the Vista workstation.

- **Off (not recommended)** Microsoft does not recommend this setting for obvious reasons, as it leaves the workstation vulnerable to hackers and malicious software. The only reason you might want to turn off the Windows Firewall would be if you or your organization has already standardized on a third-party software firewall such as the ones offered by Symantec, McAfee, and others.

The Advanced tab in the Control Panel applet has had most of its functionality removed relative to Windows XP SP2. In XP SP2, the Advanced tab allowed you to configure settings for firewall logging, allowing or disallowing inbound ICMP traffic, and creating exceptions on a per-interface basis. As you can see in Figure 6.15, the Advanced tab in the Vista firewall only allows you to do the following:

- Enable or disable the firewall on each installed network interface
- Restore the Windows Firewall to its default settings

NOTE

The functions that were formerly found on the Advanced tab, as well as a number of new features in the Vista firewall, have been moved to the Windows Firewall with Advanced Security MMC snap-in, which we'll discuss in the following section.

Figure 6.15 The Advanced Tab in the Windows Vista Firewall

Working with Built-In Firewall Exceptions

In Figure 6.16, you can see the Exceptions tab of the Windows Firewall Control Panel applet. Windows Vista has improved this tab by offering a much wider array of preconfigured firewall exceptions, including the following:

- **BITS Peercaching** Allows workstations in the same subnet to locate and share files from the Background Intelligent Transfer Service (BITS) cache using the WSDAPI framework.

Figure 6.16 Viewing the List of Windows Firewall Exceptions

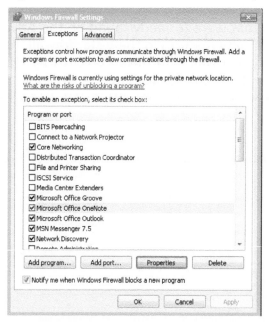

- **Connect to a Network Projector** The Windows Firewall allows users to easily connect to projectors over wired or wireless networks using WSDAPI.

- **Core Networking** This allows for basic inbound and outbound network connectivity over wired and wireless connections.

- **Distributed Transaction Coordinator** Coordinates transactions that update transaction-protected resources such as databases, message queues, and file systems.

- **File and Printer Sharing** Used for sharing local files and printers with other users. File and Printer Sharing still relies on NetBIOS, SMB, and RPC to communicate.

- **iSCSI Service** Used for connecting to iSCSI target servers and devices.

- **Media Center Extenders** Allows Media Center Extenders to communicate with a computer running Windows Media Center.

NOTE

The exceptions for the Microsoft Office and MSN Messenger products that you see in Figure 6.16 are not default exceptions that come with Windows Vista; these exceptions were configured automatically by the Office and Messenger installation routines.

- **Network Discovery** As we discussed earlier in this chapter, this feature allows a Windows Vista device to discover other devices and be discovered by other devices on the network using SSDP, Universal Plug and Play, NetBIOS, and LLMNR.

- **Remote Administration** This allows administrators to connect remotely to the local computer using interfaces such as the Computer Management MMC snap-in, as well as familiar administrative hidden drive shares such as \\computername\c$.

- **Remote Desktop** Allows a remote user to connect to the Vista desktop using the Remote Desktop client over TCP port 3389.

- **Remote Event Log Management** Allows remote viewing and management of the local event log using Named Pipes and RPC.

- **Remote Scheduled Task Management** Allows remote management of the local task scheduling service over RPC.

- **Remote Service Management** Allows remote management of local services using Named Pipes and RPC.

- **Remote Volume Management** Provides the ability to manage software and hardware disk volumes remotely over RPC.

- **Routing and Remote Access** Creates exceptions to allow incoming VPN and Remote Access Server (RAS) connections.

- **Telnet and Telnet Server Remote Administration** Creates a firewall exception to allow remote administration using telnet on TCP port 21.

- **Windows Collaboration Computer Name Registration Service** Allows other computers to locate and communicate with the local computer using the Peer Name Resolution Protocol and SSDP.

- **Windows Firewall Remote Management** Allows for remote management of the Windows Firewall over RPC.

- **Windows Management Instrumentation (WMI)** Allows system administrators to retrieve and modify configuration information about the local PC using a standard set of classes and components.

- **Windows Media Player** Allows users to receive streaming media using UDP.

- **Windows Media Player Network Sharing Service** Allows users to share media using UPnP and SSDP.

- **Windows Meeting Space** Creates an exception to allow users to share desktops, programs, and documents over the network.

- **Windows Peer to Peer Collaboration Foundation** Creates a common framework to allow various peer-to-peer application traffic to pass through the Windows Firewall.

- **Windows Remote Management** Allows remote management of a Vista system using WS-Management, which is a Web services-based protocol that allows for remote management of operating systems and devices.

- **Wireless Portable Devices** Allows users to transfer media from a networked camera or other media device using the Media Transfer Protocol (MTP). This exception relies on UPnP and SSDP to function.

Creating Manual Firewall Exceptions

In addition to the built-in firewall exceptions we just discussed, you can also create additional firewall exceptions to allow inbound traffic to pass through the Windows Firewall. In many cases, these manual exceptions will be created automatically by the installer for a particular program, or else you'll need to manually specify them from the Exceptions tab. The two types of exceptions you can create are as follows:

- **Port exceptions** These exceptions allow all incoming traffic destined for particular TCP or UDP ports; for example, you can create an exception to allow incoming traffic on TCP port 80 for HTTP traffic, or on UDP port 69 for Trivial File Transfer Protocol (TFTP) traffic.

- **Program exceptions** These exceptions allow all incoming traffic that is destined for a particular executable file running on the local workstation, which will typically correspond to a service running on the local computer. To understand the difference between a port exception and a program exception, let's look at the example of creating an exception for sqlserver.exe, the executable file associated with Microsoft SQL Server, versus opening an exception for TCP port 1433, which is the default TCP port that SQL Server uses. By creating an exception for sqlserver.exe, the Windows Firewall will allow incoming traffic only when the SQL Server service is actually running; if you stop the service to perform an application upgrade or database maintenance, the Windows Firewall will not accept incoming Structured Query Language (SQL) traffic while the application is not running. By contrast, creating a port exception for TCP 1433 will create an "always on" exception; the Windows Firewall will accept traffic from port 1433 regardless of whether the SQL Server service is running.

To create a program exception, click on **Add program** from the **Exceptions** tab. You'll see the **Add a Program** screen shown in Figure 6.17. Click on **Browse** to select the executable file for which you want to create an exception and then select **Open**.

Figure 6.17 Creating a Program Exception

By default, any new exception that you create will be accessible by any computer, including those on the Internet. To restrict the scope of an exception that you've created, click on the **Change scope** button. You'll be presented with the screen shown in Figure 6.18, which will allow you to set one of the following three scopes:

- **Any computer (including those on the Internet)** This scope will allow any computer on any network to access this program, including computers located anywhere on the Internet.

■ **My network (subnet) only**   For example, if your workstation has an IP address of 192.168.1.100 and a subnet mask of 255.255.255.0, the exception will be accessible by a machine with an IP address of 192.168.1.1 through 192.168.1.254.

■ **Custom list**   Here you can specify a list of individual IP addresses or ranges and their associated subnet masks; separate multiple entries with commas. For example, you can allow an exception for an entire range of clients plus an administrative workstation as follows: 192.168.1.146/255.255.255.255, 192.168.2.0/255.255.255.0. Unfortunately, there isn't a good way to specify a range of addresses that does not correspond to a subnet mask; if you want to allow an exception for 192.168.1.152 through 192.168.1.159, you will need to specify each IP address individually.

Figure 6.18 Configuring the Scope of an Exception

WARNING

Use the **My network (subnet) only** scope with care if you are creating an exception for a computer that is attached to a home-based ISP using a cable modem or DSL connection. Depending on the way in which your ISP has configured its network, using this exception on a home network might open up the firewall exception not just to every machine on your home network, but to every machine in a much larger portion of the ISP's customer base.

To create a port exception, you'll likewise click the **Add port** button when creating the exception; you'll see the screen shown in Figure 6.19. Creating a port exception requires the following information:

- **Name** A descriptive name for the exception, such as "HTTP", "WSUS Administration Port", and so on.

- **Port** The port number of the exception.

- **TCP/UDP** Whether the exception corresponds to a TCP port or a UDP port.

- **Scope** By clicking the **Change scope** button, you'll specify the scope of the exception just as you would for a program exception.

Figure 6.19 Creating a Port Exception

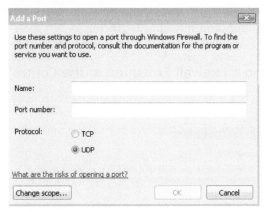

 ## Advanced Configuration of the Windows Firewall

Unlike the Windows Firewall in XP SP2, you cannot modify the scope or properties of the preconfigured Windows Vista exceptions from the Control Panel applet, as you can see in Figure 6.20. However, there is a new interface for more advanced configuration of the firewall through an MMC snap-in, called Windows Firewall with Advanced Security. This new snap-in provides a number of new features that were not previously available in the XP firewall, including the following:

- Controlling outbound as well as inbound traffic. The inability to control outbound traffic was a major criticism of the Windows Firewall in XP SP2, which was limited in functionality to controlling inbound traffic only.

- Configuring the Windows Firewall on remote computers. This feature allows you to attach to a remote computer and configure the firewall from within the Windows Firewall with an Advanced Security snap-in.

- Integrating Windows Firewall functionality with IPSec. You can now control and administer both of these features from within the same MMC snap-in to avoid conflicts between them.

- Configuring Authenticated IPSec Bypass, a feature that allows IPSec-authenticated computers to bypass firewall rules that would otherwise block incoming or outgoing connection attempts.

- Creating and configuring separate firewall profiles based on whether a computer is attached to a private network or a corporate domain versus attaching to a public network in an airport, coffee shop, and the like. The XP SP2 firewall allowed for only two profiles—Domain and Standard—which did not allow the level of granularity that is often required for mobile computers and traveling workers.

Figure 6.20 Viewing a Firewall Exception in the Control Panel

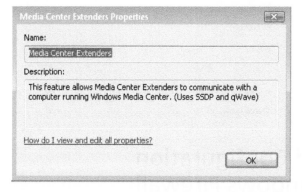

You can access the new Windows Firewall with Advanced Security applet from the Administrative Tools menu, or by opening a blank MMC console and clicking on **File | Add/Remove Snap-In**. You can see the opening screen of the new snap-in in Figure 6.21. As you can see, this snap-in provides a very different view of the Windows Firewall. The left-hand and right-hand panes provide you quick access to perform common tasks and to access different portions of the snap-in, such as viewing inbound rules, outbound rules, connection security rules, and firewall monitoring.

Figure 6.21 Viewing the Windows Firewall with Advanced Security MMC Snap-In

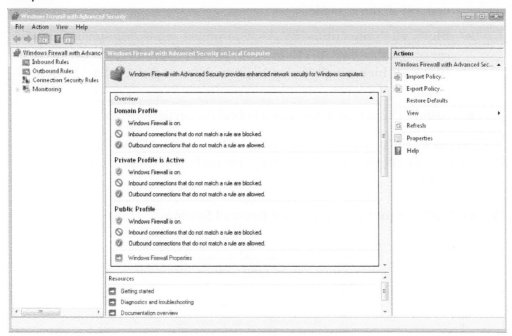

The main screen of the snap-in provides an at-a-glance view of the three available firewall profiles, as well as a visual indicator of which profile is active. The Vista firewall allows you to create different firewall settings for the following profiles:

- The Domain Profile is active whenever the computer is attached to a corporate Active Directory domain.

- The Private Profile is active when the computer is attached to a private network.

- The Public Profile is active when the computer is attached to a public network.

As you can see from Figure 6.21, the default Windows Firewall settings are similar for all three profiles: The Windows Firewall is turned on, inbound connections that do not have a defined exception are blocked, and all outbound traffic is permitted. To customize this default behavior for one or more profiles, click on the **Windows Firewall Properties** link; you'll see the screen shown in Figure 6.22. From here, you can change the firewall state from on to off, and change the behavior for inbound and outbound connections. You can change the behavior for inbound connections to one of the following:

- **Block** Blocks any inbound connection attempt that doesn't have an exception associated with it. This is the default setting for inbound connections on all three profiles.

- **Block all connections** Blocks all incoming connection attempts regardless of whether there is a rule associated with them; this corresponds to the **Block all incoming connections** checkbox in the Windows Firewall Control Panel applet.

- **Allow** This setting allows any inbound connection attempt.

You can set the behavior for outbound connections to **Allow** (the default for all three profiles) or **Block**, which will block outbound traffic unless a rule has been created to allow it.

Figure 6.22 Customizing Windows Firewall Settings

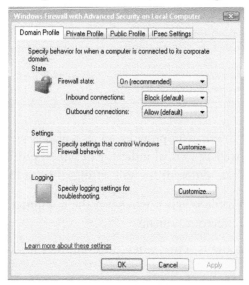

Clicking **Customize** under the **Settings** header will allow you to configure the following:

- Whether to display a notification when Windows Firewall blocks an incoming connection. By default, notifications are enabled in all three profiles.

- Whether to allow a unicast response to broadcast or multicast traffic. This is permitted by default in all three profiles. Disabling this feature will not interfere with the operation of a DHCP server, as the Windows Firewall will always permit responses to DHCP messages. However, disabling this feature will interfere with many network discovery protocols, such as NetBIOS, SSDP, and WSDAPI.

Clicking **Customize** under the **Logging** header will allow you to configure these settings:

- The name, size, and location of the Windows Firewall logfile. By default, this file is located at *%systemroot%\system32\LogFiles\Firewall\pfirewall.log* and has a maximum size of 4,096 kilobytes.

- Whether to log dropped packets and/or successful connections within the Windows Firewall logfile. By default, neither dropped packets nor successful connections are logged within the Domain, Public, and Private profiles.

NOTE

If you change the location of the Windows Firewall logfile, be sure that the Windows Firewall service account has Write permissions to the new directory.

Modifying IPSec Defaults

The final tab that you see in Figure 6.22 is the **IPsec Settings** tab; this tab allows you to configure the settings IPSec uses to establish secured connections, as well as whether ICMP traffic should be exempted from IPSec rule processing. These advanced options allow you to configure the default manner in which IPSec handles key exchange, data protection (integrity and encryption), and authentication settings to meet the needs of your network.

NOTE

You can still create connection security rules (discussed in the next section) that deviate from these defaults; this simply creates the baseline that all rules will follow unless you specify otherwise.

By default, IPSec exemptions for ICMP are turned off; however, you may want to enable these exemptions to allow for troubleshooting of network connectivity by allowing PING and TRACERT traffic to pass through the Windows Firewall. By clicking **Customize** from the **IPsec Defaults** header, you can customize the default behavior of IPSec from the screen shown in Figure 6.23.

Figure 6.23 Viewing the Default IPSec Settings

From here, you can customize IPSec's default behavior in several areas, as we discuss in the following sections.

Key Exchange (Main Mode)

IPSec key exchange is used to establish authentication and data encryption between two computers. This process is divided into two phases: *Main Mode* and *Quick Mode*. In Main Mode, the two computers that are communicating use the IKE protocol to set up a secure, authenticated channel between them. This process creates a Main Mode security association (SA). You'll sometimes also hear this referred to as a *Phase I SA*. The settings that you define here will apply to all IPSec connection security rules that you create (we'll discuss connection security rules next); the default settings that are used to create a Main Mode SA are as follows:

- **Key lifetime (minutes)** 480 minutes.

- **Key lifetime (sessions)** 0. Having a key lifetime of zero sessions forces any new keys to be issued in accordance with the **Key lifetime (minutes)** setting only.

- **Key exchange algorithm** Diffie-Hellman Group 2.

- **Security methods (integrity)** IPSec security methods include both integrity algorithms and encryption algorithms. You can use any combination of these algorithms in order to secure the key exchanges. You can have as many of these combinations as you want, arranged in whatever order you want. These combinations of integrity and encryption algorithms will be attempted in the order that you've specified; the first combination that is supported by both peer computers will be the one that is used. If the computers are not capable of using any of the combinations that you've defined for IPSec, the two computers will not be able to communicate using IPSec. The default security method used for data integrity is SHA-1.

- **Security methods (encryption)** AES-128 is the primary method, and 3-DES (Triple DES) is the secondary method.

Either you can accept the defaults for Main Mode key exchange, or you can select **Customize** to manually specify any of the settings we've described here. Figure 6.24 illustrates the **Properties** screen where you can modify any of these settings.

Data Protection (Quick Mode)

Phase 2 of the IKE process provides for the integrity and/or encryption of the data that's being transmitted between two computers that have established a Main Mode SA. The default settings for IPSec Quick Mode are as follows:

Figure 6.24 Customizing Advanced Main Mode Settings

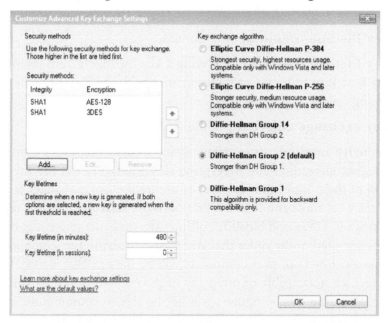

- **Data Integrity** To provide data integrity only within Quick Mode (instead of providing both integrity and encryption), IPSec will first attempt to use the Encapsulating Security Payload (ESP) combined with the SHA-1 data integrity protocol to protect each packet. If ESP protection fails, IPSec will then use the Authentication Header (AH) protocol combined with SHA-1 to protect each packet. When using this method, IPSec does not incorporate any encryption algorithms such as AES or 3-DES. In both cases, the Quick Mode key lifetime is 60 minutes or 100,000 kilobytes of data transmitted, whichever comes first.

- **Data Integrity and Encryption** To provide for both data integrity and encryption, IPSec will first attempt to communicate using ESP combined with SHA-1 for data integrity and AES-128 for data encryption. If this connection attempt fails, IPSec will attempt to communicate using ESP, SHA-1, and 3-DES encryption. The key lifetime is the same as before: 60 minutes/100,000 KB.

Again, you can either accept the defaults for IPSec Quick Mode, or select **Customize** to manually specify any of the settings we've described here. Figure 6.25 illustrates the **Properties** screen where you can modify any of these settings.

Figure 6.25 Customizing IPSec Quick Mode Settings

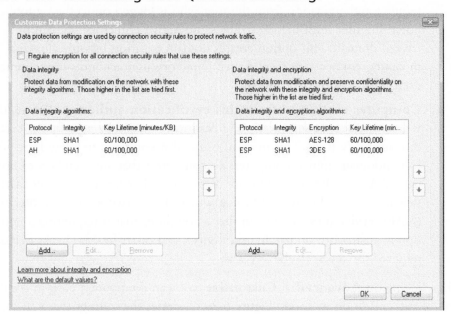

Authentication Method

The authentication method settings that you select here will determine how two computers will authenticate one another in order to create an IPSec SA. The default authentication method is Computer (using Kerberos V5), but you can choose any of the following preconfigured methods:

- **Computer and User (using Kerberos V5)** This authentication method requires both computer and user authentication, which means that both the user and the computer must authenticate successfully in order for the two computers to communicate. You can use this option to configure domain isolation, which will create a requirement that any incoming connections to the local computer originate only from domain-joined computer or user objects.

- **Computer (using Kerberos V5)** This method requires only the computer account to authenticate before communication can take place; the computer must be a part of the same Active Directory domain or in a separate domain that has a trust relationship configured. This option creates domain isolation by only allowing incoming connection attempts from domain-joined computers.

■ **User (using Kerberos V5)** Similar to the preceding method, this method requires authentication from the user who is logged on to the remote computer; the user must belong to the same Active Directory domain or a trusted domain. This option creates domain isolation by only allowing incoming connections from Active Directory user accounts in the same domain or in a trusted domain.

■ **Computer certificate from this certification authority** This method will authenticate computers using certificates issued by a particular certificate authority (CA). This method is useful if you need to allow IPSec traffic to nondomain-joined computers or computers that are members of nontrusted Active Directory domains. You can further specify that this method will accept only health certificates, which the Network Access Protection (NAP) service uses to confirm that a computer that is requesting a connection is up-to-date on patching, antivirus, and other health checks that are required for access to the network.

By clicking on **Advanced | Customize**, you can configure a custom combination of authentication methods; Figure 6.26 illustrates the settings that you can configure in this way.

Figure 6.26 Creating a Custom Authentication Method

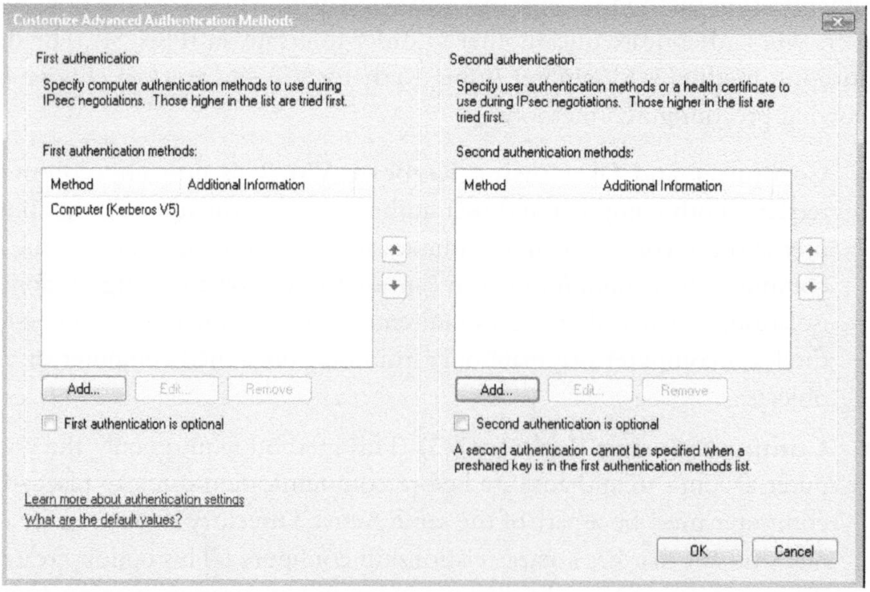

The **First authentication** method describes how the computer account is authenticated, and the **Second authentication** method describes user authentication. As you can see, you can specify that one of these steps is optional; user-only authentication would use Second authentication only, for example. When you click **Add** within the **First authentication** section, you see the screen shown in Figure 6.27.

WARNING

Although it is technically possible to make both First authentication and Second authentication optional, this is not recommended because doing so effectively disables IPSec authentication within your environment.

Figure 6.27 Customizing Computer Authentication

When creating a custom method for computer authentication, you can select from one of the following options:

- **Computer (Kerberos V5)** This is the default method for First authentication and will authenticate a computer in the same or in a trusted domain using Kerberos V5.

- **Computer (NTLMv2)** This method is used for backward compatibility and to provide authentication for nondomain-joined PCs or PCs joined to untrusted domains.

- **Computer certificate from this certification authority (CA)** This method will authenticate computers using certificates issued by a particular CA. You can further control this method by selecting one or both of the following:

  Accept only health certificates This will accept only certificates that the NAP process utilizes.

  Enable certificate to account mapping This allows you to map a certificate to one or more computer accounts within Active Directory, thus allowing you to use a single certificate for a group of computers.

- **Preshared key (not recommended)** This is the least secure authentication method and Microsoft does not recommend it; it is present only for backward compatibility and to ensure compliance with the RFC standards for IPSec. If you configure a preshared key as the First authentication method, you cannot use any method for Second authentication.

Figure 6.28 illustrates the options available when creating a custom method for Second authentication. Similar to First authentication, you can create a custom user authentication method by selecting one of the following:

- **User (Kerberos V5)** This is the default method for Second authentication and can authenticate any user in the local domain or in any trusted domain.

- **User (NTMLv2)** This method exists for backward compatibility and to authenticate nondomain-joined users.

- **User certificate from this certification authority (CA)** This method will authenticate users using certificates issues by a particular CA. You have the option to enable certificate-to-account mapping in order to use a single certificate to authenticate one or multiple users.

- **Computer health certificate from this certification authority (CA)** Allows you to authenticate using computer health certificates used by the NAP service. You again have the option to enable certificate-to-account mapping of NAP health certificates.

Figure 6.28 Customizing User Authentication

Creating Connection Security Rules

Once you've configured the default IPSec behavior for your individual computer or for an entire network, you can create connection security rules that will define how the Windows Firewall with Advanced Security will enforce authentication require-ments for different situations. You can view any existing rules by clicking on **Connection Security Rules** from the main screen of the MMC snap-in. If you right-click on **Connection Security Rules**, you can view only a subset of these rules, filtered in one of two ways:

- **Filter by Profile** will show only those rules that have been configured for the Domain, Private, or Public profile. Selecting **Show All** will remove any filters.

- **Filter by State** will show only those rules that are currently enabled or disabled. Again, selecting **Show All** will remove any filters and display all defined rules.

To create a new rule, right-click on **Connection Security Rules** and select **New Rule**. You'll see the screen shown in Figure 6.29. You can create one of the following types of connection security rules; we will discuss each one in turn:

- An isolation rule will restrict connections to one or more computers based on authentication criteria, by using domain memberships, certificates issued by a CA, or network health certificates issued by NAP.

- An authentication exemption rule will allow a connection to take place without attempting to authenticate the two computers involved.

- A server-to-server connection security rule will authenticate a connection between two specific computers.

- A tunnel connection security rule will authenticate connections between two gateway computers—for example, two computers that are being used to configure a site-to-site VPN.

- A custom connection security rule will allow you to define the exact parameters that the rule should abide by, if one of the preconfigured choices is not appropriate.

Figure 6.29 Creating a Connection Security Rule

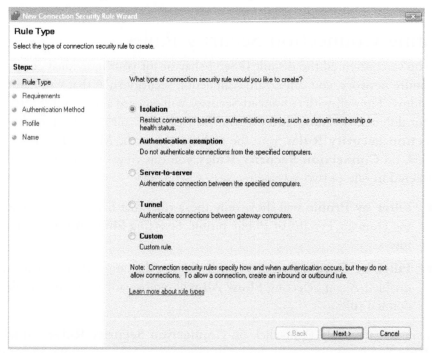

Configuring an Isolation Rule

To configure an isolation connection security rule, select **Isolation** from the screen shown in Figure 6.29 and then click **Next**. You will then be prompted to select one of the following three authentication requirements for the new isolation rule:

- Request authentication for inbound and outbound connections
- Require authentication for inbound connections and request authentication for outbound connections
- Require authentication for inbound and outbound connections

Once you have made your choice, click **Next**. You will then be prompted to select the authentication method that this rule should use. Choose among the following:

- **Default**.
- **Computer and User (Kerberos V5)**.
- **Computer (Kerberos V5)**.
- **Computer Certificate**. If you select this option, you will be prompted to enter the name of a CA on your network. You will also have the option to accept only NAP health certificates.
- **Advanced**. If you select this option, you will be prompted to configure a custom authentication method as described in the "Authentication Method" section, earlier in this chapter.

Once you have made your choice, click **Next**. You will then be prompted to select which Windows Firewall profile will apply this rule: Domain, Public, and/or Private. You can configure this rule to be enforced under one, two, three, or none of the Windows Firewall profiles.

Click **Next** to continue. You'll be prompted to enter a name and an optional description for this rule. Click **Finish** when you're done. You'll be returned to the main MMC snap-in window, where you will see the newly created rule listed in the main window. From here, you can right-click on the rule to disable or delete it, or you can select **Properties** to modify any of the settings that you configured in the wizard.

Configuring an Authentication Exemption Rule

To create an authentication exemption rule, perhaps for a destination computer that does not support IPSec or that needs to be made available to public-facing clients, select **Authentication Exemption** from the screen shown in Figure 6.29 and click **Next**.

Click **Add** to configure the list of computers that should be exempt from IPSec authentication; you'll see the screen shown in Figure 6.30. You can configure exemptions for one or more single IP addresses, for a range of IP addresses, or for one of the following predefined sets of computers:

- Default gateway.

- Windows Internet Name Service (WINS) servers.

- DHCP servers.

- DNS servers.

- Local subnet. This includes all computers available to the local computer, except for any that are configured with public IP addresses (interfaces). This includes both local area network (LAN) and wireless addresses.

Figure 6.30 Defining a List of IP Addresses

When you've added all of the IP addresses or devices that should be exempt from IPSec authentication, click **Next**. You will then be prompted to select which Windows Firewall profile will apply this rule: Domain, Public, and/or Private. You can configure this rule to be enforced under one, two, three, or none of the Windows Firewall profiles. Click **Next** to continue. You'll be prompted to enter a name and an optional description for this rule. Click **Finish** when you're done. You'll be returned to the main MMC snap-in window, where you will see the newly created rule listed in the main window. From here, you can right-click on the rule to disable or delete it, or you can select **Properties** to modify any of the settings that you configured in the wizard.

Configuring a Server-to-Server Connection Security Rule

To configure a connection security rule that defines how authentication should take place between a specific set of servers or devices, select **Server-to-Server** from the screen shown in Figure 6.29 and click **Next**. You'll see the screen shown in Figure 6.31.

Figure 6.31 Configuring a Server-to-Server Rule

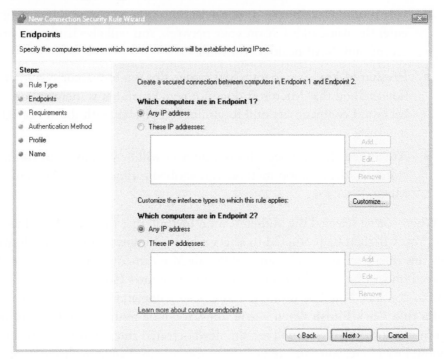

To specify individual devices to which this rule should apply, click **Add**. You'll be taken to the **IP Address** screen shown in Figure 6.30, where you'll be able to specify one or more single IP addresses, a range of IP addresses, or one of the predefined sets of devices discussed in the "Configuring an Authentication Exemption Rule" section. You can also select **Customize** to specify the type of interface to which the rule should apply: LAN, remote access, or wireless. The rule can be applied to one, two, or all three of these interface types; it will be applied to all interface types by default.

Click **Next** once you have specified the endpoints to which this rule should apply. You will then be prompted to select one of the following three authentication requirements for the new isolation rule:

■ Request authentication for inbound and outbound connections

■ Require authentication for inbound connections and request authentication for outbound connections

■ Require authentication for inbound and outbound connections

Click **Next** once you've made your selection. You can then choose from one of the following three authentication methods:

■ **Computer Certificate** If you select this option, you will be prompted to enter the name of a CA on your network. You will also have the option to accept only NAP health certificates.

■ **Preshared key** As we discussed earlier, this is a low-security authentication method that Microsoft does not recommend; it is included only for backward compatibility and to ensure compliance with the IPSec RFC standards.

■ **Advanced** If you select this option, you will be prompted to configure a custom authentication method as described earlier, in the "Authentication Method" section.

When you've selected the authentication method that this rule should use, click **Next**. You will then be prompted to select which Windows Firewall profile will apply this rule: Domain, Public, and/or Private. You can configure this rule to be enforced under one, two, three, or none of the Windows Firewall profiles. Click **Next** to continue. You'll be prompted to enter a name and an optional description for this rule. Click **Finish** when you're done. You'll be returned to the main MMC snap-in window, where you will see the newly created rule listed in the main window. From here, you can right-click on the rule to disable or delete it, or you can select **Properties** to modify any of the settings that you configured in the wizard.

Configuring a Tunnel Rule

To create a tunnel connection security rule, most commonly in the case of a site-to-site VPN, select **Tunnel** from the screen shown in Figure 6.29 and then click **Next**. You'll be presented with the screen in Figure 6.32.

Figure 6.32 Configuring a Tunnel Connection Security Rule

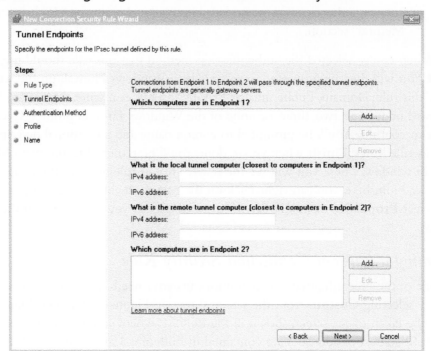

Use the **Add** button to specify the computers that are being protected by each tunnel node; you'll be taken to the **IP Address** screen shown in Figure 6.30, where you'll be able to specify one or more single IP addresses, a range of IP addresses, or one of the predefined sets of devices discussed in the "Configuring an Authentication Exemption Rule" section. Then specify the IP address of the tunnel gateway node for each endpoint; you can specify the IPv4 and IPv6 addresses if they are available.

Click **Next** once you've specified the IP addresses and tunnel endpoints for each end of the connection. You can then choose from one of the following three authentication methods:

- **Computer Certificate** If you select this option, you will be prompted to enter the name of a CA on your network. You will also have the option to accept only NAP health certificates.

- **Preshared key** As we discussed earlier, this is a low-security authentication method that Microsoft does not recommend; it is included only for backward compatibility and to ensure compliance with the IPSec RFC standards.

- **Advanced** If you select this option, you will be prompted to configure a custom authentication method as described earlier, in the "Authentication Method" section.

When you've selected the authentication method that this rule should use, click **Next**. You will then be prompted to select which Windows Firewall profile will apply this rule: Domain, Public, and/or Private. You can configure this rule to be enforced under one, two, three, or none of the Windows Firewall profiles. Click **Next** to continue. You'll be prompted to enter a name and an optional description for this rule. Click **Finish** when you're done. You'll be returned to the main MMC snap-in window, where you will see the newly created rule listed in the main window. From here, you can right-click on the rule to disable or delete it, or you can select **Properties** to modify any of the settings that you configured in the wizard.

Creating a Custom Connection Security Rule

If none of the preconfigured rule definitions fits your needs, you can create a custom rule by selecting **Custom** from the screen shown in Figure 6.29 and clicking **Next**. You'll be taken to the screen shown in Figure 6.31, where you'll need to specify which IP address or addresses are contained in Endpoint 1 and Endpoint 2. To specify individual devices to which this rule should apply, click **Add**. You'll be taken to the **IP Address** screen shown in Figure 6.30, where you'll be able to specify one or more single IP addresses, a range of IP addresses, or one of the predefined sets of devices discussed in the "Configuring an Authentication Exemption Rule" section. You can also select **Customize** to specify the type of interface to which the rule should apply: LAN, remote access, or wireless. The rule can be applied to one, two, or all three of these interface types; it will be applied to all interface types by default.

Click **Next** once you have specified the endpoints to which this rule should apply. You will then be prompted to select one of the following three authentication requirements for the new isolation rule:

- Request authentication for inbound and outbound connections
- Require authentication for inbound connections and request authentication for outbound connections
- Do not authenticate

Click **Next** once you've made your selection. You will then be prompted to select the authentication method that this rule should use. Choose among the following:

- **Default**.

- **Computer and User (Kerberos V5)**.

- **Computer (Kerberos V5)**.

- **Computer Certificate**. If you select this option, you will be prompted to enter the name of a CA on your network. You will also have the option to accept only NAP health certificates.

- **Advanced**. If you select this option, you will be prompted to configure a custom authentication method as described earlier, in the "Authentication Method" section.

Once you have made your choice, click **Next**. You will then be prompted to select which Windows Firewall profile will apply this rule: Domain, Public, and/or Private. You can configure this rule to be enforced under one, two, three, or none of the Windows Firewall profiles.

Click **Next** to continue. You'll be prompted to enter a name and an optional description for this rule. Click **Finish** when you're done. You'll be returned to the main MMC snap-in window, where you will see the newly created rule listed in the main window. From here, you can right-click on the rule to disable or delete it, or you can select **Properties** to modify any of the settings that you configured in the wizard.

Creating Firewall Rules

In addition to configuring connection security rules, you can use the Windows Firewall with Advanced Security MMC snap-in to exert far more granular control over inbound traffic rules than is available within the Control Panel applet. You can view any existing inbound rules by clicking on **Inbound Rules** from the main screen of the MMC snap-in; likewise, you can view any existing outbound rules by clicking on **Outbound Rules**. If you right-click on either of these nodes, you can view only a subset of these rules, filtered in one of three ways:

- **Filter by Profile** will show only those rules that have been configured for the Domain, Private, or Public profile. Selecting **Show All** will remove any filters.

- **Filter by State** will show only those rules that are currently enabled or disabled. Again, selecting **Show All** will remove any filters and display all defined rules.

- **Filter by Group** will only show rules that are associated with a particular predefined rule set, such as BITS Peercaching or Connect to a Network Projector, or you can display only those rules that are not associated with a group. Selecting **Show All** will remove any filters.

To create a new rule, right-click on **Inbound Rules** and select **New Rule**. You'll see the screen shown in Figure 6.33. You can create one of the following types of inbound rules; we will discuss each one in turn:

- Program creates a rule that is associated with a particular executable file, similar to the Add Program option on the Exceptions tab of the Windows Firewall Control Panel applet.

- Port creates a rule associated with a network port, similar to the Add Port option in the Windows Firewall Control Panel applet.

- Predefined creates a rule associated with one of the services that have been predefined within the Windows Vista firewall, such as BITS Peercaching or Network Discovery.

- Custom creates a custom rule when none of the preconfigured choices is appropriate for your needs.

NOTE

The GUI screens used in creating an inbound rule and an outbound rule are nearly identical; we will be creating an inbound rule in the following example and we'll point out any differences as needed.

Figure 6.33 Creating a New Firewall Rule

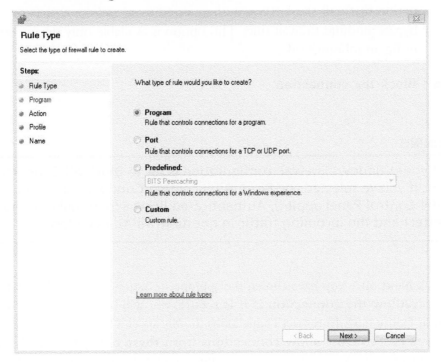

Creating a Program Firewall Rule

To configure a firewall rule associated with a particular application, select **Program** from the screen shown in Figure 6.33 and click **Next**. You can create a rule that applies to one of the following:

- **All programs** affects all programs that are installed on the local computer.
- **This program path** allows you to click **Browse** to select an individual .exe file.

Click **Next** when you have made your selection. You'll be prompted to select one of the following **Actions** that should be taken when an executable is found that matches this rule:

- **Allow the connection**.
- **Allow the connection if it is secure**. If you select this option, you can select one or both of the following additional options:
  Require the connections to be encrypted.

Override block rules. This enables the Authenticated IPSec Bypass option that will allow IPSec-authenticated users and computers to bypass inbound firewall rules. This option is available only when configuring an inbound rule.

■ **Block the connection**.

WARNING

If your Windows Firewall configuration is set to **Block All Connections** (or if you've selected the **Block All Incoming Connections** option from the Control Panel applet), Authenticated IPSec Bypass will have no effect and the incoming traffic in question will still be blocked.

Click **Next** once you have chosen the appropriate action for this rule to take. If you select **Allow the connection if it is secure**, you will be taken to the screen shown in Figure 6.34. To restrict connections to only specific computers, place a checkmark next to **Only allow connections from these computers**; click **Add** to add one or more Active Directory computer accounts to the firewall rule. To restrict inbound connections to specific Active Directory user objects, place a checkmark next to **Only allow connections from these users**; click **Add** to specify one or more Active Directory user or group objects. Both of these checkboxes are optional; you do not need to restrict the rule to specific users or computers if you do not want to do so.

NOTE

When creating an outbound rule, the wizard will read **Only allow connections to these computers**. In addition, the option to restrict connections according to user accounts will not be available.

Figure 6.34 Restricting Firewall Connection by User or Computer

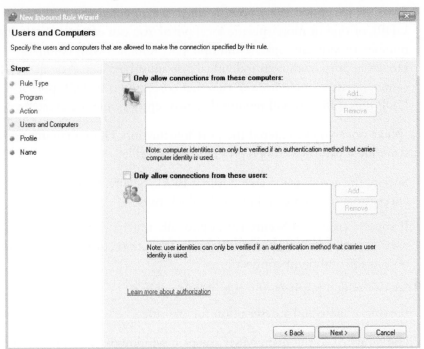

If you were taken to the **Users and Computers** screen shown in Figure 6.34, click **Next** once you have made the appropriate selections. Once you have made your choice, click **Next**. You will then be prompted to select which Windows Firewall profile will apply this rule: Domain, Public, and/or Private. You can configure this rule to be enforced under one, two, three, or none of the Windows Firewall profiles.

Click **Next** to continue. You'll be prompted to enter a name and an optional description for this rule. Click **Finish** when you're done. You'll be returned to the main MMC snap-in window, where you will see the newly created rule listed in the main window. From here, you can right-click on the rule to disable or delete it, or you can select **Properties** to modify any of the settings that you configured in the wizard.

Creating a Port Firewall Rule

To configure a firewall rule associated with a particular network port, select **Port** from the screen shown in Figure 6.33 and click **Next**. You'll need to specify the following information:

- Is the exception being created for a TCP port or a UDP port?

- Does the exception correspond to all port numbers (whether TCP or UDP), or one or more specific local ports? You can enter an individual port number, or you can separate multiple port numbers with commas. However, ports within an individual rule must be all TCP or all UDP. You cannot create a single firewall rule that corresponds to TCP port 138 and UDP port 138; this will require that two separate rules be created.

Click **Next** once you've entered the port information. The remaining steps in the wizard are identical to creating a program firewall rule:

- Specify the action to be taken: Allow, Block, Secure, Secure and require encryption, or Secure and override block rules.

- If you are creating a Secure rule, optionally restrict connections to specific user or computer objects for inbound connections, or to specific computer objects for outbound connections.

- Specify which profile(s) the rule should apply to.

- Provide a name and a description for the rule.

You'll be returned to the main MMC snap-in window, where you will see the newly created rule listed in the main window. From here, you can right-click on the rule to disable or delete it, or you can select **Properties** to modify any of the settings that you configured in the wizard.

Configuring a Predefined Firewall Rule

To modify the rules associated with one of the predefined Windows Vista exceptions, choose **Predefined** from the screen shown in Figure 6.33. (You should select this option with care, because you will be overwriting the predefined firewall rules that were installed with Windows Vista.) Select the exception that you want to modify and click **Next**. For this example, we have selected the **Connect to a Network Projector** exception. You will see the screen shown in Figure 6.35.

Figure 6.35 Modifying a Preconfigured Exception

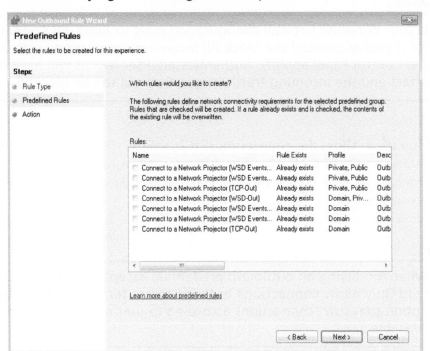

Place a checkmark next to as many individual rules as you want to modify, and then click **Next**. Again, select this option with care, because you will be overwriting the existing rule set. You'll be prompted to select one of the following actions that should be taken when an executable is found that matches this rule:

■ **Allow the connection**.

■ **Allow the connection if it is secure**. If you select this option, you can select one or both of the following additional options:
   Require the connections to be encrypted.
   Override block rules. This enables the Authenticated IPSec Bypass option that will allow IPSec-authenticated users and computers to bypass inbound firewall rules. This option is available only when configuring an inbound rule.

■ **Block the connection**.

WARNING

If your Windows Firewall configuration is set to **Block All Connections** (or if you've selected the **Block All Incoming Connections** option from the Control Panel applet), Authenticated IPSec Bypass will have no effect and the incoming traffic in question will still be blocked.

If you select **Allow the connection if it is secure**, you will be returned to the screen shown in Figure 6.34 to specify which user and/or computer accounts to allow connections to or from. Otherwise, your only option will be to select **Finish** to save your changes.

NOTE

When modifying an outbound predefined exception, the wizard will read **Only allow connections to these computers**. In addition, the option to restrict connections according to user accounts will not be available.

Creating a Custom Firewall Rule

Configuring a custom firewall rule allows you the greatest amount of flexibility in configuring the Windows Firewall. To begin configuring a custom rule, select **Custom** from the screen shown in Figure 6.33 and then click **Next**.

Your first configuration step will be to define the program to which this exception applies. Select one of the following:

- **All programs** This rule will apply to all connections to the local computer that match any other properties defined within the custom rule.

- **This program path** Select this option and browse to the specific executable file to which the custom exception refers.

Also on this screen, you'll need to configure which services and processes this exception will refer to. Click **Customize** to select one of the following options:

- **Apply to all programs and services**.

- **Apply to services only**.

- **Apply to this service.** This option allows you to select a specific Windows service.

- **Apply to service with this service shortname.** This option allows you to specify the shortname of the service in question, such as eventlog or w3svc.

Click **Next** once you've defined the program to which this exception applies. You'll be taken to the screen shown in Figure 6.36, which will allow you to specify the following information about any specific port to which this exception refers:

- **Protocol type** Most commonly TCP, UDP, or ICMPv4, but other options such as IGMP and GRE are available.

- **Protocol number** This field is automatically populated based on your choice of protocol type.

- **Local port** You can choose **Any** port or specify one or more specific ports from which this traffic will originate, with multiple port numbers separated by commas. All ports that you specify must be of the same protocol type: TCP 135 and TCP 139, for example, but not TCP 21 and UDP 22.

- **Remote port** Similar to the local port, you can choose **Any** port or specify one or more ports of the same protocol type.

- **Internet Control Message Protocol (ICMP) settings** If you select ICMPv4 or ICMPv6 as the protocol type, you can allow this rule to apply to all ICMP traffic, or you can specify one or more of the following ICMP message types.

  For ICMPv6:

  1. Destination Unreachable

  2. Packet Too Big

  3. Time Exceeded

  4. Parameter Problem

  5. Echo Request

  6. Multicast Listener Query

  7. Multicast Listener Report

  8. Multicast Listener Done

9. Router Solicitation

10. Router Advertisement

11. Neighbor Discovery Solicitation

12. Neighbor Discovery Advertisement

13. Redirect

14. Multicast Listener Report v2

And for ICMPv4:

1. Packet Too Big

2. Destination Unreachable

3. Source Quench

4. Redirect

5. Echo Request

6. Router Advertisement

7. Router Solicitation

8. Time Exceeded

9. Parameter Problem

10. Timestamp Request

11. Address Mask Request

Once you've defined any relevant port and protocol settings, click **Next**. You'll then need to define both the local and remote IP addresses to which this exception refers. For both the local and remote addresses, you can select either **Any IP Address** or **These IP Addresses**. To specify the IP addresses to which this rule should apply, click **These IP Addresses** and then click **Add**. You'll be taken to the **IP Address** screen shown in Figure 6.30, where you'll be able to specify one or more single IP addresses, a range of IP addresses, or one of the predefined sets of devices discussed in the "Configuring an Authentication Exemption Rule" section. You can also select **Customize** to specify the type of interface to which the rule should apply: LAN, remote access, or wireless. The rule can be applied to one, two, or all three of these interface types; it will be applied to all interface types by default.

Figure 6.36 Configuring a Custom Port Definition

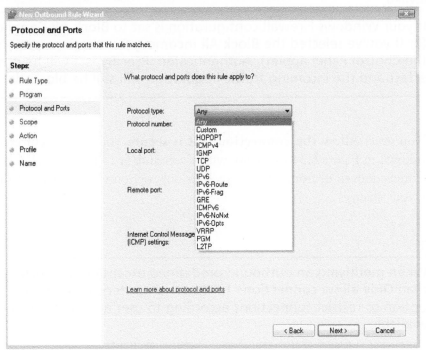

Click **Next** once you have specified the local and remote IP addresses to which this rule should apply. You'll be prompted to select one of the following actions that should be taken when a packet is found that matches this custom rule:

- **Allow the connection**.

- **Allow the connection if it is secure**. If you select this option, you can select one or both of the following additional options:
  Require the connections to be encrypted.
  Override block rules. This enables the Authenticated IPSec Bypass option that will allow IPSec-authenticated users and computers to bypass inbound firewall rules. This option is available only when configuring an inbound rule.

- **Block the connection**.

WARNING

If your Windows Firewall configuration is set to **Block All Connections** (or if you've selected the **Block All Incoming Connections** option from the Control Panel applet), Authenticated IPSec Bypass will have no effect and the incoming traffic in question will still be blocked.

If you select **Allow the connection if it is secure**, you will be returned to the screen shown in Figure 6.34 to specify which user and/or computer accounts to allow connections to or from. Otherwise, your only option will be to select **Finish** to save your changes.

NOTE

When modifying an outbound predefined exception, the wizard will read **Only allow connections to these computers**. In addition, the option to restrict connections according to user accounts will not be available.

If you were taken to the **Users and Computers** screen shown in Figure 6.34, click **Next** once you have made the appropriate selections. Once you have made your choice, click **Next**. You will then be prompted to select which Windows Firewall profile will apply this rule: Domain, Public, and/or Private. You can configure this rule to be enforced under one, two, three, or none of the Windows Firewall profiles.

Click **Next** to continue. You'll be prompted to enter a name and an optional description for this rule. Click **Finish** when you're done. You'll be returned to the main MMC snap-in window, where you will see the newly created rule listed in the main window. From here, you can right-click on the rule to disable or delete it, or you can select **Properties** to modify any of the settings that you configured in the wizard.

Tools & Traps...

Configuring the Windows Firewall from the Command Line

In addition to the GUI configuration options we've outlined thus far, you can also administer the Windows Firewall using the *netsh* command-line utility. *Netsh* allows you to configure and monitor the Windows Firewall by creating rules, monitoring connections, and displaying the status of the Windows Firewall.

To access *netsh* simply go to the command prompt and enter **netsh advfirewall**. From this context, you will have the following subcommands available:

- **export** Exports the current firewall policy to a file.
- **help** Displays a list of available commands.
- **import** Imports the firewall configuration from a particular file.
- **reset** Restores the Windows Firewall to its default configuration.
- **set file** Copies the console output to a file.
- **set machine** Denotes the computer that should be configured.
- **show allprofiles** Displays the firewall properties for all three profiles.
- **show domainprofile** Displays the firewall properties for the domain profile.
- **show privateprofile** Displays the firewall properties for the private profile.
- **show publicprofile** Displays the firewall properties for the public profile.

You can also access the following additional subcontexts to configure additional aspects of the Windows Firewall:

- **consec** View and configure connection security rules.
- **inbound** View and configure inbound firewall rules.
- **outbound** View and configure outbound firewall rules.
- **monitor** View and configure monitoring information.

Continued

> And of course, you can obtain help from any *netsh* menu by simply typing **?** and pressing **Enter**.

Monitoring the Windows Firewall

Using the Windows Firewall with Advanced Security MMC snap-in, administrators now have access to real-time firewall configuration information that can be invaluable in troubleshooting connectivity issues on Vista workstations. Simply open the MMC snap-in and select **Monitoring** in the left-hand pane, as shown in Figure 6.37.

Figure 6.37 Monitoring the Windows Firewall

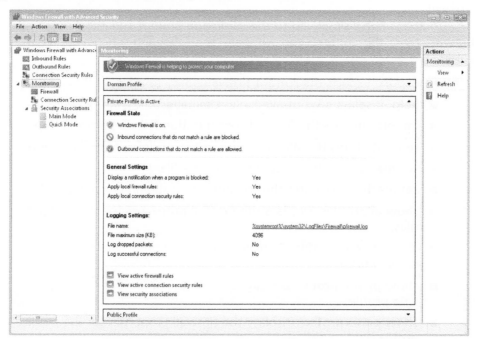

From the main **Monitoring** screen shown in Figure 6.37, you will see an at-a-glance summary of your current firewall settings, describing the overall state of the firewall, which profile is active, as well as notification and logging settings. You also have the ability to drill down to a detailed view of any of the following:

- Active firewall rules
- Active security connection rules
- Active IPSec SAs

In Figure 6.38, you can see the information that is displayed when you drill down to the Firewall node: which firewall rules are currently active, as well as specific details on each rule, including the name of the rule, the action associated with that rule (allow, secure, block), and whether it is an inbound or outbound firewall rule.

Figure 6.38 Monitoring Active Firewall Rules

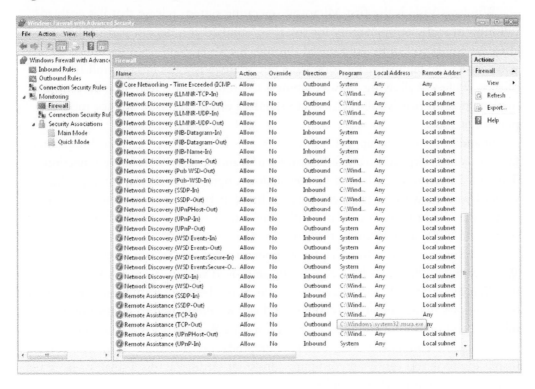

Summary

As you've seen throughout this chapter, Windows Vista has made numerous improvements in the way that it handles network communications with other computers on a local area network or on the Internet. These changes have been designed to enhance both the security and usability of the new Microsoft operating system for both end users and corporate administrators.

Windows Vista is the first Microsoft operating system release that has enabled full support and interoperability for the IPv6 standard as a default part of the operating system. IPv6 can be configured through the Vista graphical user interface, or you can use the familiar *netsh* command-line utility. Vista has enabled full IPv6 compliance while still allowing Vista computers to communicate using the current IPv4 implementation that is still the de facto standard on the Internet and for most corporate networks.

In addition to IPv6 support, Vista offers a greatly improved graphical user interface for configuring and troubleshooting wired and wireless network connections. The new Network and Sharing Center includes options for displaying a graphical view of your network infrastructure using the Network Map, as well as providing a simple way to configure a new network connection as either a public or private network with the security settings that are appropriate to each.

In the second half of this chapter we spent a great deal of time examining the Windows Firewall, which has been greatly improved within Windows Vista. The new Windows Firewall with Advanced Security has been more fully integrated with the Windows implementation of IPSec, and it now allows you to control both inbound and outbound connections to and from a Windows Vista computer. These settings can be configured using the Vista graphical user interface or the *netsh* command-line tool. You can even configure consistent settings across a small or large network by using Group Policy Objects.

Solutions Fast Track

Not Your Father's TCP/IP Stack

☑ IPv6 was designed to address numerous shortcomings in the IPv4 standard, including a lack of built-in security measures and an inefficient addressing system.

☑ Windows Vista is the first Microsoft OS to provide IPv6 support out of the box.

☑ You can configure IPv6 from the Windows Vista Control Panel, as well as from the command line using the netsh tool.

Using the Network and Sharing Center

☑ Windows Vista introduces the concept of network locations, allowing you to configure different settings for public, private, and office networks.

☑ Windows Vista introduces a new protocol for Network Discovery, which uses the WSDAPI framework as a secure channel when communicating between a device and a client, as well as the Simple Service Discovery Protocol.

☑ You can use Public Folder Sharing to allow for easier shared file access between multiple users of a single computer, as well as users across a SOHO or other peer-to-peer network.

Using the Network Map

☑ The new Network Map provides a graphical view of your local computer's relative position on the network, as well as indicating any networked computers that have been configured for Network Discovery and/or File and Printer Sharing.

☑ The Network Map can be used for network troubleshooting: If a particular network segment becomes disconnected, it will be displayed on the Network Map with a red X over the segment.

☑ The Network and Sharing Center also offers options to diagnose and repair issues with network connectivity.

Working with the Windows Firewall

☑ The Windows Firewall with Advanced Security is a stateful, host-based firewall that can be configured to allow or disallow traffic that is generated by an executable file or by one or more TCP or UDP ports.

☑ Windows Vista offers numerous preconfigured Windows Firewall exceptions to allow traffic for common Vista networking scenarios, such as using BITS Peercaching or connecting to a network projector.

☑ Connection security rules can be used to define how devices should authenticate with one another before communication can take place.

Frequently Asked Questions

The following Frequently Asked Questions, answered by the authors of this book, are designed to both measure your understanding of the concepts presented in this chapter and to assist you with real-life implementation of these concepts. To have your questions about this chapter answered by the author, browse to **www.syngress.com/solutions** and click on the **"Ask the Author"** form.

Q: What does the Windows Firewall do if it is configured with two conflicting rules: one that disallows a particular type of traffic and one that allows it?

A: Block rules will be given precedence over allow rules; if Windows Vista encounters a firewall rule that blocks a particular type of traffic, that traffic will be blocked even if other allow rules are in place.

Q: I would like to configure Windows Firewall settings across my entire organization. Does Vista allow for this?

A: If you are working in an Active Directory environment, you can use Group Policy to apply consistent settings across an entire organization for numerous Windows Vista features, including Internet Explorer, Windows Defender, and the Windows Firewall.

Q: You've mentioned Network Access Protection several times in this chapter. What is it?

A: Network Access Protection, or NAP, is a new service that will be offered in the new version of Windows Server currently codenamed Longhorn. NAP is a policy enforcement mechanism that can monitor the health of your Windows Vista and Windows XP SP2 workstations and limit their network access if their health falls out of compliance with your corporate standards. For example, if a traveling user's laptop has become infected with a virus or worm, NAP can quarantine the network connection when the user attempts to connect to the corporate network so that the virus does not spread to other computers on the corporate network.

Q: I have numerous Windows XP computers on my network that are not being displayed in the Network Map. Is the Network Map available only for Vista computers?

A: Not at all; however, you need to install an update on the Windows XP computers so that they can be displayed on the Network Map. Check out Knowledge Base article 922120 on the Microsoft Web site for more information.

Chapter 7

Microsoft Vista: Wireless World

Solutions in this chapter:

- **What's New with Wireless in Vista?**
- **Wireless Security**
- **Network Group Policy Enhancements**
- **Configuring Wireless Security in Vista**

☑ **Summary**

☑ **Solutions Fast Track**

☑ **Frequently Asked Questions**

Introduction

Unlike traditional wired networks in which communications travel along a shielded wire cable, wireless radio frequency signals traverse the open air. As such, a wireless signal is exposed to anyone within the signal's range. Therefore, we must take proper security measures so that potential attackers or anyone within a wireless signal's range does not have the ability to view, steal, or manipulate what we send through the open air.

Security is one of the biggest concerns in any network infrastructure. A public security breach of a business network can scare away current and potential clients, causing a company to lose millions of dollars in revenue. Today, network architectures built without security components are unacceptable.

Wireless local area networks (WLANs) are changing the way business is conducted. The use of remote devices such as phones, laptops, and personal digital assistants (PDAs), along with a demand for continuous network connection without having to "plug in," is driving the wireless revolution and the adoption of WLAN.

In this chapter, we will review general network security and the best practices for understanding and protecting your wireless network. We will go over new capabilities and enhancements present in Microsoft Vista wireless networking, and changes from previous versions, such as Windows XP and Windows Server 2003. At the end of the chapter, we will configure an actual secure wireless network using both the new Vista wireless commands in the command-line prompt and the newly developed wireless user interface (UI).

What's New with Wireless in Vista?

Microsoft Vista includes many new enhancements to the Institute of Electrical and Electronics Engineers (IEEE) 802.11 wireless standards. The following is a list from Microsoft describing some of these changes:

- Native wireless architecture
- User interface improvements
- Wireless group policy
- Wireless auto configuration
- WPA2 support
- Integration with network access protection (NAP) when using 802.1x
- EAP host infrastructure

- Microsoft Vista network diagnostics
- Command-line support
- Network location awareness and profiles
- Next-generation TCP/IP stack
- Single sign-on

Native Wireless Architecture

In older Windows versions, such as Windows XP and Windows 2003, the software infrastructure that supported wireless connections was built to emulate wired Ethernet configurations. In Vista, the software infrastructure for 802.11 wireless connections has been redesigned to provide independent hardware vendors (IHVs) with more flexibility over 802.11-specific settings and configurations. In Microsoft Vista, wireless 802.11 now has its own independent architecture and a media type that no longer emulates the wired 802.3 Ethernet media type. Vista's independent media type for 802.11 wireless allows IHVs to use advance 802.11 settings such us sending larger frame size data compared to the old Ethernet emulated media type.

The new architecture performs authentication, authorization, and management of wireless connections, thus reducing the burden on IHVs to build these functions into their wireless adapters and drivers. Because these functions are included inside the Windows software, it's much easier for IHVs to develop drivers and network adapters. With this new Windows architecture, you can configure all of your authentication mechanisms, including Wi-Fi Protected Access/Wi-Fi Protected Access 2 (WPA/WPA2), 802.1x, and the Extensible Authentication Protocol (EAP), without needing to install the additional vendor-specific applications that come with your wireless network adapter. By using one standard architecture and application to configure your wireless capability, regardless of the vendor hardware you use, you make it easier to support and understand your application. By reducing the burden on IHVs to build additional functions into their wireless adapters and drivers, you leave less room for incompatibility issues between IHVs and Windows. Standardizing architecture and support in Vista reduces the number of potential errors in IHV application code.

The new architecture supports the application program interface (API) for wireless networking. The API allows independent software vendors (ISVs) and IHVs to extend and build customized wireless additions and services on top of the core software. Vendors can now build custom configuration boxes and wizards and attach them to wireless APIs.

UI Improvements

For improved manageability, Microsoft has integrated the wireless connectivity configuration from the properties of a wireless network adapter in older versions of Microsoft into the new Network and Sharing Center in Vista. You can manage, set up, and connect using wireless connectivity from the Network and Sharing Center. Figure 7.1 displays the new Network and Sharing Center where wireless connectivity is managed.

Figure 7.1 The Network and Sharing Center in Vista

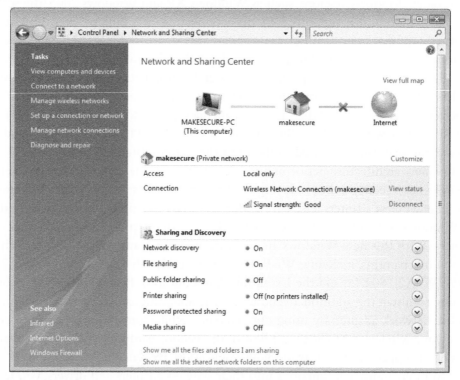

You can configure wireless network profiles on a per-user basis. In the Manage Wireless Networks folder inside the Network and Sharing Center, you can configure wireless network profiles that you can apply to all users on your computer or to a specific user. The per-user profile policy is initiated when a user logs on to the computer, and is disconnected when the user logs off or changes to a different username.

The advantage of configuring per-user wireless profiles is that administrators can restrict network security policy based on the user currently logged on to the system. For example, multiple users can share your corporate wireless workstation. A user from the engineering group that logs on will be allowed access to the internal network via its wireless connectivity, as well as to the Internet. However, a guest user that logs on to the same workstation will only be allowed to wirelessly connect to the Internet and surf the Web. Per-user profiles allow wireless workstations to be shared among multiple security policy groups.

In Vista, you can configure a nonbroadcast wireless network. A nonbroadcast wireless network is a wireless network that does not advertise its network name, or Service Set Identifier (SSID). (For further details on SSIDs and broadcasting, refer to the "Wireless Security" section, later in this chapter.) In Windows 2003 and Windows XP, you could not configure a preferred wireless network as a nonbroadcast wireless network. This feature limited users from being able to automatically prefer and connect to wireless networks that had SSID broadcasting disabled.

Nonbroadcast networks are displayed as "Unnamed Network" when scanning for wireless networks. You will have to pick the name when connecting to an unnamed nonbroadcast network.

Vista will now prompt you when you try to connect to an unsecured wireless network before it automatically connects you (see Figure 7.2). This feature helps users be aware of possible wireless security threats before they connect to networks; for example, connecting to a wireless network that does not support encryption.

When connecting to a wireless network, the Network Connection Wizard will list all security methods that the wireless adapter supports. This allows you to pick the best security method available for your wireless adapter.

Figure 7.2 Security Warning in Vista When Connecting to an Unsecured Wireless Network

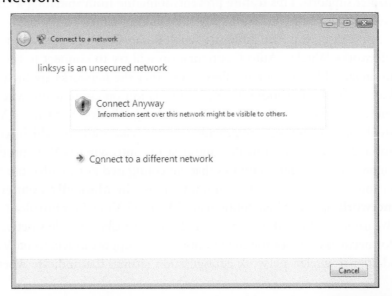

Wireless Group Policy

Microsoft also has added to Vista enhancements in wireless Group Policy, such as WPA2 authentication options and lists of allowed and denied wireless network names. We will discuss some of these changes in detail later in this chapter, in the "Network Group Policy Enhancement" section.

Wireless Auto Configuration

Wireless Auto Configuration is a Windows service that dynamically selects a wireless network and automatically connects to it. This service includes the ability to connect to a preferred wireless network as soon as it is within reach.

In Windows XP and Windows 2003, if a preferred wireless network could not be connected to and the wireless client was configured to not connect to any other wireless networks other than the preferred one, Wireless Auto Configuration would create a random wireless network name and would place the network adapter in it, in infrastructure mode. This feature proved to be insecure, because the random wireless network name would have no security features enabled, thus allowing an attacker to connect to the client using the randomly picked name.

In Microsoft Vista, when preferred networks are out of reach and the wireless settings are configured to not connect to any other wireless networks, Wireless Auto Configuration will still create a random name to which it adds the wireless adapter. However, this time, the random name includes a security configuration consisting of a 128-bit random encryption key and the strongest encryption method that the wireless adapter supports. This feature prevents someone from initiating a connection to the wireless client just by guessing only the random name.

In Microsoft Vista, you can configure wireless networks as broadcast or non-broadcast networks. Wireless Auto Configuration will try to connect to the wireless network in preferred list order, regardless of whether the networks are broadcast or nonbroadcast networks. For more detailed information on configuring wireless broadcast networks, refer to the section "Configuring Wireless Security in Vista," later in this chapter, where we will provide a sample case study in which we will list the steps for adding a wireless broadcasting network into wireless Vista profiles.

For nonbroadcast wireless networks that are configured not to advertise themselves to surrounding wireless users, you must choose the **Manually connect to a wireless network** option when configuring Microsoft Vista. Nonbroadcast wireless networks by nature will not show up on the list of "available" wireless networks when you scan for networks. Part of the new nonbroadcast support in Microsoft Vista includes additional wireless network configuration settings that indicate whether a wireless network is a broadcast or a nonbroadcast network. You can configure these additional settings through the **Manually connect to a wireless network** dialog box (see Figures 7.3 and 7.4), through the **Wireless Network** properties menu (see Figure 7.5), via the command line using *netsh wlan*, or through Group Policy. In Figure 7.5, the **Connect even if the network is not broadcasting** checkbox on the **Connection** tab is selected, indicating that the wireless network you have config-ured will not broadcast its SSID. In this case, Wireless Auto Configuration will send probe requests to discover whether the nonbroadcast network is in range. Microsoft Vista wireless client adopters will send probe requests only for wireless networks that are configured for automatic connection (in other words, only when the **Connect automatically when this wireless network is in range** checkbox on the **Connection** tab is checked) and for nonbroadcast networking. This behavior allows Microsoft Vista wireless clients to detect nonbroadcast networks when they are in range. Therefore, even though the wireless routers are not broadcasting the name (SSID) of their wireless network, they will still show up in the list of available wireless networks when they are in range when manually configured.

Figure 7.3 Setting Up a Connection by Manually Connecting to a Wireless Network

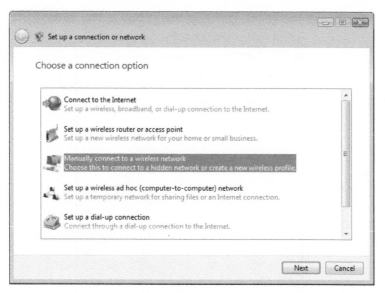

Figure 7.4 Connecting Even If the Network Is Not Broadcasting

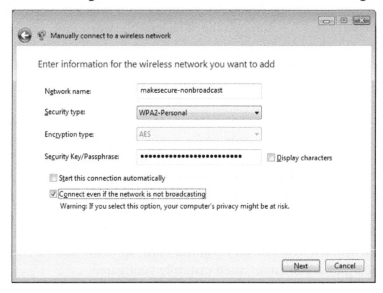

Figure 7.5 The Nonbroadcast Option in the Wireless Network Properties Page

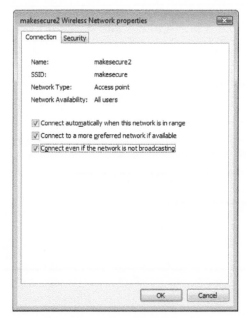

WPA2 Support

Microsoft Vista includes built-in support for configuring WPA2. Figure 7.6 shows the WPA2-supported security type and other settings in Vista's network properties. WPA2 is a product certification available through the Wi-Fi Alliance that certifies wireless equipment as being compatible with the IEEE 802.11i standard. Microsoft Vista supports WPA2-Personal and WPA2-Enterprise modes. For more details on WPA, refer to the section "Wireless Security," later in this chapter.

Figure 7.6 WPA2 Support in the Vista Network Properties

Integration with NAP When Using 802.1x

WPA2 in Enterprise mode using 802.1x authentication can leverage the NAP platform to prevent wireless clients that do not comply with system health settings and requirements (for example, clients that are not running antivirus software) from gaining full access to the wireless network. NAP in Microsoft Vista provides policy enforcement components that help ensure a computer's health prior to connecting to a network with administrator-defined requirements. Some of the health components that can be automatically checked with NAP on a client's PC prior to allowing connectivity to the network may include whether the latest patch level is applied, whether a firewall is installed and running, whether antivirus software is running, and whether proper passwords are set and configured. If the client's PC fails to pass these administer-defined health policy requirements, it will be alerted with administrator-configured instructions on how to comply before full network connectivity is granted.

NOTE

For more details and steps for configuring a NAP environment within your organization, visit www.microsoft.com/technet/network/ nap/default.mspx.

EAP Host Infrastructure

For easier development of EAP authentication methods for IEEE 802.1*x* wireless connections, Microsoft Vista supports the new EAP host infrastructure.

The default EAP authentication method has changed in Vista. In Windows XP, the default EAP method is EAP-TLS, and in Vista the default is PEAP-MSCHAP v2. With the Transport Layer Security (TLS) protocol, where the public key infrastructure (PKI) is required to distribute, revoke, and renew user certificates, MSCHAP is a password-based authentication method.

Microsoft Vista Network Diagnostics Framework

The Network Diagnostics Framework (NDF) is an extensible architecture that helps users recover from and troubleshoot problems with network and wireless connectivity. The NDF architecture in Vista prompts the user through a series of options in an effort to automatically eliminate possible network connectivity causes until the root cause of the problem is identified or all other possibilities are eliminated. The NDF architecture helps users with limited detailed knowledge of networking and wireless communications to resolve small issues by themselves.

During network connectivity issues, NDF will investigate why the task has failed and present a solution to the problem or a probable list of causes and corrections, allowing you to take action to fix the problem. Figure 7.7 shows an example of the Windows Network Diagnostics dialog box. In this example, we tried to connect to a *network12* wireless network. The security settings we configured in our Microsoft Vista workstation did not match our *network12* wireless security settings. Windows Network Diagnostics automatically picked up on this misconfiguration and prompted us with possible error suggestions and solutions.

Figure 7.7 Windows Network Diagnostics

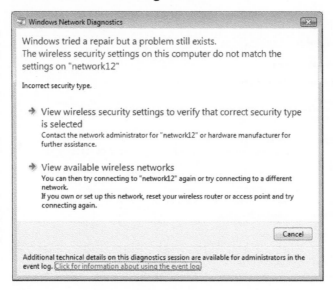

More detailed and technical information on network diagnostics is saved in the event logs. You can use the Event Viewer to further analyze connectivity problems or help interpret error messages. To access the Event Viewer, select **Start | Control Panel | Administrative Tools** or simply click on the link from the **Windows Network Diagnostics** dialog box shown in Figure 7.7. The Network Diagnostics event logs are saved as system events in the Windows Logs folder with an event ID of 6100. Figure 7.8 shows the Event Viewer and all of its Network Diagnostics events. Double-click on an event within the Event Viewer in order to view its properties and details. Figure 7.9 shows the properties details of our last event log in which we misconfigured our wireless security settings for *network12*.

Figure 7.8 The Event Viewer

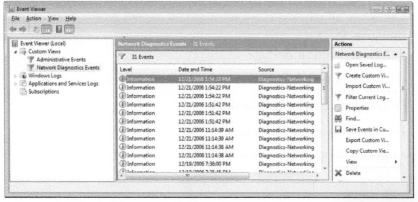

Figure 7.9 Event Properties Details in the Event Viewer

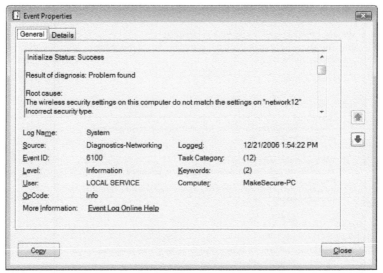

Command-Line Support

Unlike in Windows XP, where there are no command lines that allow you to configure wireless settings and connections, Microsoft Vista includes a new command, *netsh wlan*, which allows you to configure your wireless settings.

Having commands available for configuring your wireless settings allows you to support automated scripts for wireless settings without using Group Policy. Wireless network policy settings apply only in Active Directory domains. In environments that do not have Active Directory, a script can automate the process of configuring wireless settings.

Some of the things you can do with the *netsh wlan* command include the following:

- Configure all wireless client settings in a named profile, such as one indicating an SSID, the type of authentication, the type of encryption, and the 802.1x authentication type

- Configure a list of allowed and denied wireless networks

- Display wireless configurations

- Remove wireless configurations

- Migrate settings among wireless clients

Figure 7.10 shows the primary commands in the *netsh wlan* context. You add a *?* to the end of each command to display a list of parameters and examples of how to use the command. Examples of the *?* commands include */?*, *add /?*, and *delete profile /?*. Figure 7.11 displays the output following the *netsh wlan add /?* and *netsh wlan add profile /?* commands. As you can see, details of specific parameters and examples of how to use the command are shown. The *add* command in Figure 7.11 adds a configuration entry to a table, such as filters to allow or deny specific wireless networks.

Figure 7.10 The netsh wlan Command and Its Main Options

Figure 7.11 The netsh wlan add /? and netsh wlan add profile /? Commands

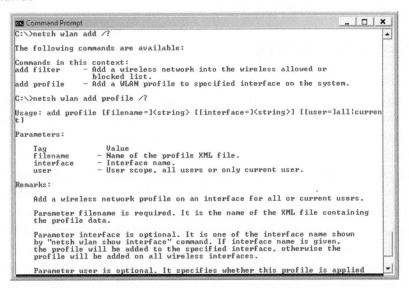

For more details on how to configure and use the *netsh wlan* command, refer to the "Configuring Wireless Security in Vista" section, later in this chapter.

Network Location Awareness and Profiles

Lots of applications are not network-aware and cannot automatically adjust their behavior based on network changes. Network awareness APIs in Microsoft Vista provide network information to the application and to developers so that applications can automatically adapt based on changes in network connectivity.

Next-Generation TCP/IP Stack

The new next-generation Transmission Control Protocol/Internet Protocol (TCP/IP) stack in Vista includes support for new TCP algorithms that optimize network throughput by recovering packet loss and detecting spurious retransmissions. Fast recovery from packet loss improves wireless networking and the overall user experience.

Single Sign-on

The single sign-on feature in Microsoft Vista allows a user to enter her logon name and password credentials through the integrated Windows logon capability. You can use Group Policy settings or the new *netsh wlan* command to configure your single sign-on feature. After single sign-on is configured, 802.1x authentication will precede the computer's logon to the domain. This feature ensures that wireless connectivity is established prior to domain logon.

Wireless Security

Wireless is all around us; data is constantly flowing through the air. The right person with the right tool set can tap into the air where wireless communication and data are sent and view, steal, and even manipulate that data. It's important that we are aware of these wireless weaknesses and that we do our best to secure our data that we're sending across the air.

On the next few pages, we will discuss in detail the topic of general wireless security and possible threats that expose our wireless data. The first step in security is to be aware of a potential threat before you secure your network. Therefore, when it comes to wireless security, you need to be familiar with two main topics: access and privacy. *Access* concerns making sure that only authorized individuals can have access to your wireless network and its data. *Privacy* deals with encryption and with making sure that whatever you send through the air cannot be read by anyone else within the signal's range.

Wireless Ranges

As technology evolves, wireless networks will continually improve to enhance their footprint. You might be surprised to learn how far the signal from your laptop or your home wireless network can reach. The current standard we all have—known as 802.11b or 802.11g—has a default reach of up to one football field (~ 350 feet). This measurement depends, of course, on your antenna's strength and any other interference or configuration settings. The new 802.11n standard, which is currently in draft status, can send signals up to a distance of three football fields (~ 1,000 feet) (Table 7.1 provides a detail range and throughput comparison of different wireless standards). Imagine that you are using your wireless network at home to shop online (you're paying by credit card). Or perhaps you are sending an e-mail to your spouse with details regarding the two-week vacation you'll be taking in Hawaii next month (revealing that no one will be home during that time). Or maybe you are doing something seemingly as harmless as surfing the Internet. That data, or the signal you are sending from your wireless-enabled laptop in your living room to your wireless router or access point in the next room, is being sent far beyond the walls of your home. Your neighbors, or perhaps a potential attacker within reach, could see this transmitted data. Following proper access and privacy practices will keep your data private and out of the hands of nosy bystanders or the neighborhood geek who taps into unprotected signals to view, steal, or manipulate your data.

Notes from the Underground...

802.11n

In 2004, the IEEE formed the new 802.11 Task Group n (TGn) to develop new 802.1x standards. The real throughput of the new 802.11n standard is expected to reach 540 Mbps. The new standard should be 50 times faster than 802.11b and up to 10 times faster than 802.11g and 802.11a. The signal range of 802.11n is expected to be three times the range of 802.11b and 802.11g and five times the range of 802.11a. Some vendors, such as Linksys, have already started selling products supporting the new 802.11n technology, even though the official standard is not expected to be finalized and signed until early 2007.

Table 7.1 Wireless Ranges

Protocol	Data Rate (Max)	Range (Indoor)
802.11a	54 Mbps	~ 180 feet
802.11b	11 Mbps	~ 350 feet
802.11g	54 Mbps	~ 350 feet
802.11n	540 Mbps	~ 1,000 feet
Bluetooth	1 Mbps	~ 32 feet

Why We Need Security

The Internet and WLANs are rapidly changing the economy, the way we do business, and the way we live. Rapid growth and endless new discoveries constantly improve wireless technology. Business and government leaders recognize the strategic role of the Internet and WLANs and realize how important it is to be competitive in this new electronic century.

For consumers and businesses to accept wireless networks, they need guaranteed secure methods of communicating, sharing data, and performing electronic commerce. Unfortunately, many existing wireless networks are not taking advantage of recently improved security measures and are vulnerable to many different attacks. As with any security implementation, businesses face the daunting security issue of how to implement and constantly update new and improved defensive practices, and thereby reduce their vulnerability to attacks.

Over the past two years, wireless networking standards have improved security measures and finalized some of the long-awaited security technology that is now available in every new product line. These new security standards in wireless networks allow businesses and organizations to deploy new wireless environments without worrying about being attacked.

The Two Main
Security Threats: Access and Privacy

As we mentioned previously, the two primary threats are access and privacy. To review, access is implemented when we want to make sure that only authorized individuals can have access to our wireless network and its data. Privacy is implemented when we deal with encryption and making sure that whatever we send through the air cannot be read by anyone else within the signal's range. In the next few sections, we will examine these threats in detail and outline their importance.

Access

To allow access to only those who are authorized that access is a key security measure. Some access control methods include the following:

■ Changing defaults

■ Employing Media Access Control (MAC) filters

■ Decreasing signal strength

■ Changing and broadcasting the SSID

■ Enabling WPA or WPA2

■ Patching devices on the wireless network

■ Turning off your wireless network

Changing Defaults

Nearly all devices are preconfigured with default configuration settings. These settings are well known to the public and are shared among similar devices. For example, every device has an administrator super-user logon name and password that you use to gain access to and configure your device. These administrator logon names and passwords are not secret; they are available to anyone. Changing the default administrator password on your wireless device will prevent an attacker from attempting to log on and view/change your wireless network settings. The username is often simply the word *administrator* and the password is typically set to empty (none), or the word *administrator, admin*, *password*, or *public*. The following sidebar provides examples of super-user passwords set by manufacturers by default.

Tools & Traps...

Vendor-Specific Default Superuser Passwords

The following list includes some publicly known administrator accounts from various vendors that are configured on your wireless access point by default:

3Com User: admin; Password: comcomcom

3Com Office Connect Wireless 11g Cable/DSL User: (none); Password: admin

Continued

ACCTON User: none; Password: 0

Actiontec User: admin; Password: password

Advantek Networks User: admin; Password: (none)

Amitech User: admin; Password: admin

Bausch Datacom User: admin; Password: epicrouter

Cisco AP1200 User: Cisco; Password: Cisco

Cisco AP1200 User: root; Password: Cisco

Cisco AP1100 User: (none); Password: Cisco

Cisco WLSE User: root; Password: blender

Cisco WLSE User: wlse; Password: wlsedb

E-Tech User: (none); Password: admin

Intel Wireless AP 2011 User: (none); Password: intel

Intel Wireless Gateway User: intel; Password: intel

Linksys User: admin; Password: admin

Motorola Wireless Router User: admin; Password: Motorola

Topcom User: admin; Password: admin

In addition to changing your default administrative logon name and password, you should disable unwanted services on your access point. Disable unwanted services, such as the Network Time Protocol (NTP), the Cisco Discovery Protocol (CDP), the Hypertext Transfer Protocol (HTTP), Telnet, and the Simple Network Management Protocol (SNMP), if you do not plan to use them. These services, when not disabled, act as doors into your wireless device. An attacker could find and use vulnerabilities in these service ports to gain unprivileged access.

MAC Filters

MAC is the unique assigned address that is programmed into a network adapter at the time of manufacture. The MAC address is unique to every network device. It is used to communicate on Layer 2 of the Open System Interconnection (OSI) model. Because MAC addresses are uniquely assigned, the same MAC address will never be assigned to two different network adapters.

Wireless access points or routers allow you to configure MAC filter control lists. Such a control list specifies the addresses that are allowed to connect to the network. Anyone using a wireless network adapter that does not match the list of allowed MAC addresses will be denied access.

Security issues exist with MAC filters. An attacker can spoof your network adapter's MAC address. In other words, the attacker can program his network adapter MAC address to look like yours. Figure 7.12 shows an attacker spoofing a MAC address in Linux from 66:55:44:33:22:11 to AA:BB:CC:DD:EE:FF. Figure 7.13 shows a similar utility, called SMAC, which allows attackers to change MAC addresses in Microsoft Windows.

Figure 7.12 Changing a MAC Address in Linux

Figure 7.13 Changing a MAC Address in Windows

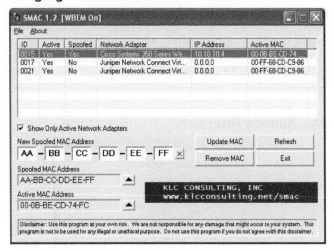

When you implement security, do so in layers. Although it is easy to spoof a MAC address, you should still use MAC address filters when configuring your access controls for wireless networks wherever possible. Not everyone will know how to spoof a MAC address, nor will everyone want to. There are so many unprotected wireless networks out there that an attacker will likely move on to his next target if he finds that you've configured security on your network. Implementing security in layers allows you to protect yourself from a variety of attacks.

Figure 7.14 shows a Linksys wireless router and its MAC filter configuration window. As you can see, we have set up a MAC filter list to allow only the network device with AA:BB:CC:DD:EE:FF to connect.

Notes from the Underground...

Finding MAC Addresses

Every manufacturer programs a unique MAC address into its network card; this MAC address is 48 bits long. The IEEE controls the first 24 bits (three octets) of the address. These first three octets are called the Organizational Unique Identifier (OUI). OUIs are given to corporations that produce network devices such as network cards. These corporations must use these unique three octets assigned to them in all of their network devices. The second 24 bits of the 48-bit-long MAC address are controlled by the manufacturer. If the manufacturer runs out of unique addresses for the second half of the MAC address, it requests a new three-octet address from the OUI. To look up a MAC address and its manufacturer, visit the OUI database at http://standards.ieee.org/regauth/oui/index.shtml. As an example, we entered the first half of our wireless network card's MAC address, 000CCE, and clicked **Search**. The OUI database revealed that the MAC address belongs to Cisco Systems.

Figure 7.14 MAC Address Filter List

Signal Strength

Wireless signals travel a long way. As we discussed previously, the signals we send from our wireless devices can go as far as three football fields. These long ranges impose potential vulnerability threats as signal/data can be tapped into by an attacker within range.

Decreasing your signal strength in your wireless networks at home or at work will limit your exposed perimeter. If you have a wireless network at home and the farthest room is 30 feet away from your wireless gateway, there is absolutely no reason why you need to send your signal up to 1,000 feet away. By lowering the strength of your signal, you will keep it within the protected range of your home's walls, thus minimizing opportunities for attack.

Changing and Broadcasting the SSID

The SSID is a wireless network identifier that your wireless router broadcasts into the air every second to notify surrounding users of its presence. This feature is designed to allow clients to automatically discover wireless hot spots and to provide for easy roaming.

SSIDs are not encrypted; they are sent in clear text over the air, allowing anyone within range to capture them. Knowing your network's SSID brings hackers one step closer to attacking your network.

In home use, you should disable the SSID broadcast feature because you do not have multiple access points at home; therefore, you do not need to roam, and you do not need to advertise to your neighborhood that you have a wireless network. It is a recommended security practice that you disable your SSID broadcasting feature on your home wireless gateway.

Hackers' tools such as Network Stumbler are designed to specifically sniff the air for broadcast SSIDs of wireless networks that they can potentially attack. Figure 7.15 shows Network Stumbler in action, scanning for all unencrypted broadcasting networks within its signal range. Within one hour, we were able to find hundreds of broadcasting networks, of which 45 percent were not using any encryption or security measures.

Figure 7.15 Network Stumbler Scanning for Broadcasting Networks

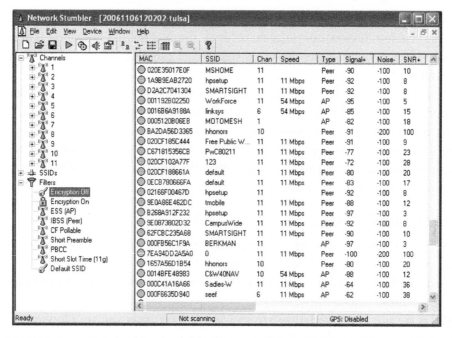

Even though you disabled the SSID broadcasting feature on your wireless device, SSIDs are still sent with wireless data when a client is present on the network. More sophisticated tools can be used to sniff the air and still find the SSID, even though you disabled broadcasting.

Changing your SSID string will make it harder for an attacker to direct specific attacks. If you leave a vendor-default SSID configured, an attacker will know what type of hardware device you have and will be able to better direct his attack against it. Changing the default SSID string to something random will make it harder for the attacker to determine what type of wireless hardware you have. Figure 7.16 shows a Linksys wireless router and its SSID configuration. In this scenario, we changed the SSID to *to be or not to be* and disabled broadcast of the SSID.

Figure 7.16 Changing the SSID and Broadcast Features

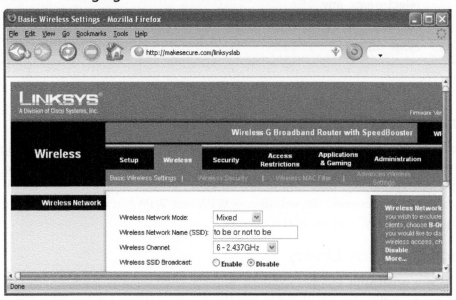

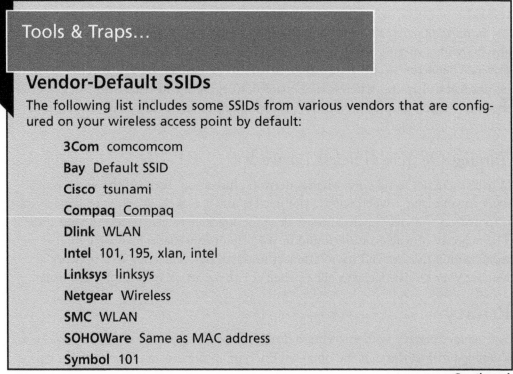

Tools & Traps…

Vendor-Default SSIDs

The following list includes some SSIDs from various vendors that are configured on your wireless access point by default:

   3Com comcomcom

   Bay Default SSID

   Cisco tsunami

   Compaq Compaq

   Dlink WLAN

   Intel 101, 195, xlan, intel

   Linksys linksys

   Netgear Wireless

   SMC WLAN

   SOHOWare Same as MAC address

   Symbol 101

Continued

www.syngress.com

> **Telectronics** any
> **Zcomax** any, mello, Test
> **Zyxel** 1234

Enabling WPA/WPA2

The WPA and WPA2 standards are mainly used for encryption. However, configuring encryption on your wireless network and prohibiting anyone without the proper encryption keys from connecting to your network allows you to control access into your network. We will discuss WPA and WPA2 in more detail in the upcoming "Privacy" section of this chapter.

Patching Wireless Devices

Just as you patch your PC every month with the latest security fixes, you should patch your wireless devices. Wireless vendors release security patches for network adapters, wireless routers, and other devices. All of your security configurations could be put at risk if your wireless device has a serious vulnerability that you have failed to patch.

In mid-2006, researchers found that they could gain unauthorized access into any PC with a specific wireless adapter using a vulnerability inside the adapter's drivers. The victim in this attack did not have to be connected to a wireless network; he just had to have his wireless card enabled. Keeping up-to-date with patches, even for your wireless adapter in your PC, is a very important security task that many of us tend to overlook.

Turning Off Your Wireless Network

When you're not using your wireless network, turn it off. Turn off the wireless network in your laptop when you do not need to use it as well. When your wireless card is turned on, it merely opens another door for attackers to gain access to your data. The majority of wireless cards found in your laptop automatically search wireless networks within the area and try to connect to them. By connecting to a network without your knowledge, you put yourself at risk for attack or possible legal issues.

Privacy

You achieve privacy with encryption. Encryption allows you to send your data in a scrambled format through the open air. Encryption prevents an attacker from tapping into the air and reading your data. Privacy is the second main security threat you must be aware of and know how to properly configure. In this section, we will discuss three standards that enable network privacy:

- WEP
- WPA
- WPA2

WEP

Wired equivalent privacy (WEP) is defined as the 802.11 standard for a mechanism to encrypt data moving through the air. WEP works at the data link layer of the OSI model. It was originally designed with a 40-bit key to avoid conflicts with U.S. control of exporting strong encryption. It is now available in 40-bit and 104-bit keys.

The WEP static key and its implementation have been exploited and exposed by security engineers. It is possible to crack a WEP key in as little as 30 minutes. WEP uses the RC4 stream cipher, invented by Ron Rivest of RSA Data Security Inc., for encryption. The RC4 algorithm is a symmetrical stream cipher whereby both parties share the same key to encrypt data between them. The Initialization Vector (IV) is a component used with the encryption key to create the ciphered text. The added IV is used to randomize the encryption and to ensure that the same plain-text data will not generate the same ciphered data. Figure 7.17 shows the WEP encryption process and its standards.

Figure 7.17 WEP Encryption Process and Standards

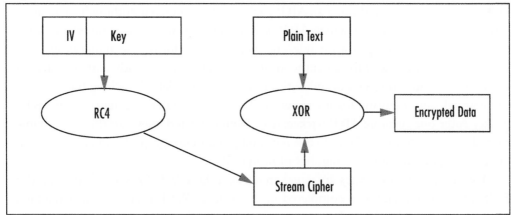

XOR is a mathematical function that combines the resulting cipher stream with plain text to produce encrypted data. IVs that consist of a random 24-bit value must be sent to the receiver. The IV is sent in clear text, attached to an 802.11 frame.

The IV being sent in clear text is vulnerable to attackers that can capture the encrypted frames and derive their content. An IV is 24 bits long and provides 16,777,216 possible values. An engineer at the University of California at Berkeley found that when the same IV was used on two different packets, also called a *collision*, an attacker could capture both packets, attack them, and break the key (for more information, refer to www.isaac.cs.berkeley.edu/isaac/wep-faq.html).

Another vulnerability in the RC4 key-scheduling algorithm that can expose static WEP keys was discovered by Fluhret, Martin and Shamir (FMS). Due to RC4 implementation in WEP and its use of 24-bit IVs, different methods can be used in this static pattern to derive a secret WEP key. This so-called FMS attack uses between 100,000 and 1 million encrypted packets, using the same static key to derive the WEP key.

The biggest roadblock that attackers face when trying to expose WEP keys is that collecting enough packets can be quite time-consuming. Fortunately, whether an attacker is trying to collect weak IVs or just unique IVs, you can lengthen this process even further. For instance, you can inject traffic into the network, thereby creating more packets. This is usually accomplished by collecting one or more Address Resolution Protocol (ARP) packets and retransmitting them to the wireless access device. ARP packets are a good choice because they have a predictable size (28 bytes). The response will generate traffic and increase the speed at which packets are collected. Collecting the initial ARP packet for reinjection can be problematic. You could wait for a legitimate ARP packet to be generated on the network, but again, this can take a while, or you could force an ARP packet to be generated. Although there are several circumstances under which ARP packets are legitimately transmitted, one of the most common in regard to wireless networks occurs during the authentication process. Rather than wait for an authentication, if a client has already authenticated to the network, you can send a deauthentication frame, essentially knocking the client off the network and requiring reauthentication. This process will often generate an ARP packet. After one or more ARP packets have been collected, they can then be retransmitted or reinjected into the network repeatedly until enough packets have been generated to supply the required number of unique IVs.

Figure 7.18 demonstrates an actual attack of a static WEP key cracked using the FMS attack. This attack was completed in 55 minutes. WEP is an old and vulnerable standard that you should no longer use when you implement wireless privacy.

Figure 7.18 Cracking the WEP Key

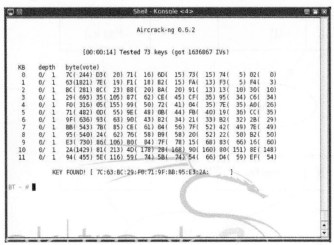

WPA

Due to WEP vulnerabilities and studies that showed that intruders equipped with proper tools could break a WEP key in a few minutes and gain access to wireless networks, in 2003 the wireless community introduced WPA as a strong standards security specification for wireless networks. WPA provides assurance to wireless networks that their data will remain protected.

WPA replaces WEP with strong, new data encryption, called Temporal Key Integrity Protocol (TKIP) encryption. WPA is a subset of the IEEE 802.11i specification. In addition to privacy, WPA provides a scheme of mutual authentication using either IEEE 802.1x/EAP authentication, or pre-shared key (PSK) technology. As we discussed previously, most of the attacks against WEP are due to poor implementation in the IV and its use of the same key per packet. By using different keys per packet, you can eliminate some of that threat. TKIP is used to enhance WEP with a per-packet keying mechanism. As shown in Figure 7.19, the temporary key derived from a hash function is used to encrypt packets, instead of the static WEP key.

By implementing TKIP, you do not eliminate the vulnerability of deriving a WEP key. Instead, the intruder attacking your network has to deal with multiple sets of keys (280 trillion possible keys, in fact) that are randomly generated from the master static key and are used to encrypt data. This is different from WEP, in which one key is used to encrypt all the traffic. WPA protects your privacy by generating multiple random WEP keys.

Figure 7.19 WPA Using TKIP

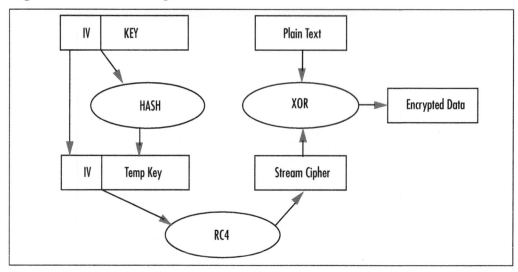

You can implement WPA inexpensively. Software for firmware upgrades for most existing wireless devices is available free for download from several manufacturers. Before purchasing new hardware, check with your manufacturer for the latest patches and software updates available for your device.

WPA2

The wireless alliance community launched WPA2 in September 2004. WPA2 is the certified interoperable version of the full IEEE 802.11 standards. Just like WPA, WPA2 supports 802.1x/EAP authentication or PSK technology. However, WPA2 also includes a new encryption standard that uses the Advanced Encryption Standard (AES) algorithm.

The U.S. Department of Commerce and the National Institute of Standards and Technology (NIST) have adopted AES as an official government standard. WPA2 may require you to purchase new hardware, whereas with WPA you can apply a simple patch to your existing wireless device.

WPA and WPA2 Modes

There are two setup modes for WPA and WPA2:

- Personal
- Enterprise

Both modes provide encryption and authentication solutions. Enterprise mode uses an extra set of features to authenticate users in larger environments, and personal mode is mainly used in home and small-office environments.

WPA and WPA2 Personal Modes

In personal mode, designed for home as well as small office, home office (SOHO) wireless networks, WPA and WPA2 operate by using a PSK for authentication. This key is statically configured in network devices and must be shared with other users connecting to the network. The PSK in WPA is then used with TKIP (described earlier) to generate random keys used to encrypt data. Personal mode supports per-user, per-session, and per-packet encryption via TKIP with WPA, or AES with WPA2. Figure 7.20 displays a Linksys wireless router and its WPA personal mode configuration. When choosing your PSK, make sure it's longer than 21 characters and not easily guessed with dictionary words.

Figure 7.20 WPA with AES on Linksys

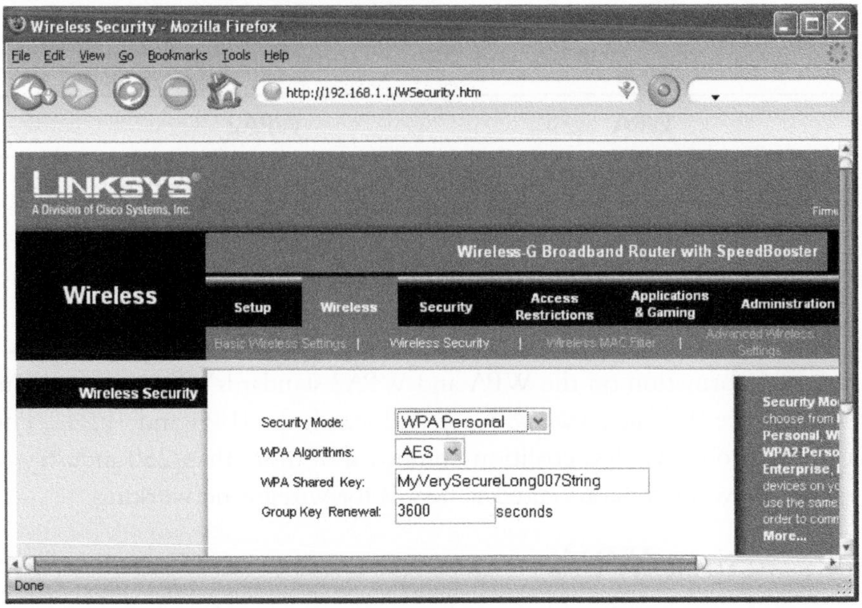

WPA and WPA2 Enterprise Modes

In enterprise mode, designed for larger wireless networks with multiple users, WPA and WPA2 leverage the IEEE 802.1x authentication mechanism using EAP. EAP is used with an authentication server, which provides strong mutual authentication between the client and the wireless network via the access point. Unlike in personal mode, where the master key is configured and shared with other users, the authentication server in enterprise mode allows for per-user security policy. Again, TKIP encryption is used with WPA, and AES encryption is used with WPA2. Figure 7.21 shows a typical enterprise mode hardware setup. Table 7.2 summarizes the authentication and encryption types of personal and enterprise modes.

Figure 7.21 WPA2 Enterprise Mode Hardware Setup

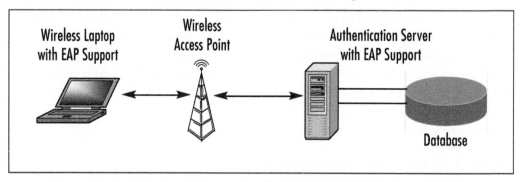

Table 7.2 A Summary of WPA and WPA2 Mode Support

Mode	WPA	WPA2
Enterprise	Authentication: IEEE 802.1x/EAP Encryption: TKIP	Authentication: IEEE 802.1x/EAP Encryption: AES
Personal	Authentication: PSK Encryption: TKIP	Authentication: PSK Encryption: AES

For more information on the WPA and WPA2 standards and configurations, visit the Wi-Fi Alliance Web site, www.wi-fi.org, and search for *WPA* and *WPA2*. The Wi-Fi Alliance is a global wireless coalition composed of more than 250 industry members pushing for worldwide-accepted standards for wireless networking.

Attacks against WPA

Unlike attacks against WEP, which we discussed earlier in this chapter, attacks against WPA do not require a large number of packets to be collected. In fact, most attacks can actually be performed without even being in range of the targeted wireless network.

Attacks against WPA are currently successful only when WPA is used in a personal PSK and the key is less than 21 characters long. This means that if you are running WPA-PSK at home, you need to make sure that your PSK is hard to guess and that it's more than 21 characters long.

To successfully accomplish an attack against WPA-PSK, you have to capture the four-way Extensible Authentication Protocol Over LAN (EAPOL) handshake. You can wait for a legitimate authentication to capture this handshake, or you can force an association by sending deauthentication packets to clients already connected to the wireless network, forcing them to reauthenticate. After capturing the handshake, each dictionary word the attacker uses to try to guess the master PSK must be hashed with 4,096 interactions of the Hashed Message Authentication Code-Secure Hash Algorithm 1 (HMAC-SHA1) and two *nonce* values, along with the MAC address of the supplicant and the authenticator.

For this type of attack to have a reasonable chance of success, the PSK (passphrase) should be shorter than 21 characters, and the attacker should have an extensive word list at her disposal.

Rogue Access Points

A *rogue access point* is an unauthorized access point. Unauthorized access points can pose a significant threat by creating a backdoor into sensitive corporate networks. A backdoor allows access into a protected network by avoiding all front-door access security measures. As we discussed in previous chapters, wireless signals travel through the air and, in most cases, have no boundaries. They can travel through walls and windows, reaching potentially long distances far outside of a corporate building's perimeter.

These radio signals outside of the secure perimeter can represent either rogue or valid wireless access gateways. Both could be carrying the same data, some of which may be sensitive and confidential. The difference between the radio frequencies from these two wireless gateways is that the rogue unauthorized access point was installed by an employee with limited security protection, often leaving it at its default Plug and Play unsecured configurations, and the authorized access was installed by a skilled engineer with full security support.

The bottom line is that rogue access points installed by employees pose a significant threat because they provide poor security measures while extending a corporate network's reach to attackers from the outside, without going through any security measures.

Are You Owned?

Audit against Rogues

Audits to detect rogue wireless access points should be required in all corporate network environments, even if they do not provide wireless access.

Detecting and Protecting against Rogue Access Points

Protecting against rogue access points is an ongoing task for security engineers. You never know when an employee will plug a wireless device into the network and expose it to attackers. Following are some techniques you should take to detect and protect against rogue access points:

- Follow corporate policy and be aware
- Insist on mutual authentication
- Employ sniffers and WIDS
- Employ central management and detection
- Employ physical detection
- Employ wired detection

Corporate Policy and User Awareness

Employees that install access points often do not understand the security risks of their actions. To avoid this and enforce your security policy you must implement a wireless security policy that mandates that all employees obey proper security measures, and coordinate with your information technology (IT) department the installation of any network equipment. You must audit and communicate this policy to your employees on a regular basis. A security policy works only if employees are aware of it and obey it.

Mutual Authentication

Mutual authentication of the user and the authenticator eliminates the ability of a corporate user authenticating with a rogue access point planted by an attacker to steal another user's credentials.

Sniffers and WIDS

You can use sniffer tools and a Wireless Intrusion Detection System (WIDS) to continually watch the air for any wireless signals and data passing through. Then you can match detected signals against a list of valid wireless devices to determine whether any rogue access points are present.

Central Management and Detection

Vendors such as Cisco Systems provide central management solutions for enterprise network clients to manage their wireless security. One feature of such solutions is the ability to detect rogue access points. Access points as well as wireless clients are turned into an army of scanners and auditors. This army then reports to the central management server any security findings within the signal area. For example, say a client with a wireless laptop is walking around campus using his wireless connection and he detects two other access points nearby. He reports these two access points to his wireless gateway router, and that information is then passed to the central management server. The central management server compares the detected access points against its access list to determine whether rogues have been found. If it determines that the detected access points are rogues, the server calculates the rogues' position using the wireless network within the area and sends an alert to the security administrators that rogues have been detected.

Physical Detection

Sometimes all you have to do is to walk around the office, looking for unauthorized devices and access points plugged into wired ports at users' desks. If you find an unauthorized access point plugged into a wired network, you should turn it off and inform the user of your corporate security policy against unauthorized network devices.

Wired Detection

You can scan your wired network with an application such as Nmap to detect what is plugged into it and where. Each network device has its own set of signatures, which define the way it acts and reacts to certain probes. These detected signatures are used to detect the types of devices plugged into your network. For example, say you have a network that is dedicated to user desktops against which you run your Nmap scanner, and you notice that five of the desktop Internet Protocol (IP) addresses are running HTTP (port 80) and Telnet (port 23) services. There is no reason a desktop should be running these services; hence, this immediately raises a red flag, and a reason for you to investigate.

Tools & Traps...

Nmap

Nmap (Network Mapper) is a free, open source utility for network exploration and security auditing. It was designed to rapidly scan large networks, although it works fine against single hosts. Nmap uses raw IP packets in novel ways to determine what hosts are available on a network, what services (application name and version) those hosts are offering, what operating systems (and operating system versions) they are running, what type of packet filters/firewalls are in use, and dozens of other characteristics. Nmap runs on most types of computers and both console and graphical versions are available. For more information, visit http://insecure.org/nmap.

Security Enhancements Using 802.1x/EAP

The original 802.11 authentication and security components proved to be a security risk in one way or another. Therefore, the 802.1x standard was developed to provide a better authentication mechanism for wireless environments. One of the underlying characteristics of 802.1x components is EAP, which was originally created for the Point-to-Point Protocol (PPP). EAP-Transport Layer Security (EAP-TLS), Protected EAP (PEAP), Cisco's LEAP, and EAP-TTLS/MCHAPv2 are part of EAP and the 802.1x standards that are used separately or together based on the required wired/wireless design.

EAP

The 802.1x protocol is based on the EAP formally created and specified in RFS 2284. EAP supports multiple authentication methods. The advantage of this dynamic protocol is that it does not specify an authentication method; rather it allows the authentication process to request a specific authentication method before it completes. This allows administrators to pick different extensions and methods for EAP, and use third-party devices such as the Remote Authentication Dial-in User Service (RADIUS) to manage such requests. Figure 7.22 displays EAP and its use in many different link and physical solutions. EAP's dynamic nature makes it popular and well adopted.

Figure 7.22 EAP

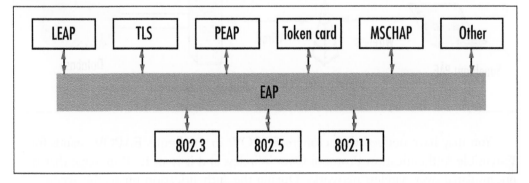

802.1*x*

802.1*x* is a port authentication control protocol used to translate messages from a variety of different authentication types into their appropriate frame formats. You can use 802.1*x* in other 802-based technologies such as Ethernet (802.3) and Token Ring (802.5). For the purposes of this chapter, we will refer to 802.1*x* and its use for wireless (802.11) networks.

802.1*x* supports the requirements for per-user authentication and settings. It supports mutual authentication methods between the access point and the wireless client that is authenticating. Allowing the wireless client to authenticate the wireless gateway just as the wireless gateway authenticates the client user helps improve security by preventing the possibility of clients authenticating to a possible rogue device or, perhaps, a planted attacker's access point. 802.1*x* also supports dynamic per-user keying. Dynamic creation of encryption keys and per-user capability create robust security for enterprise networks.

Although 802.1*x* does not choose what authentication and algorithm types it will use, it does work with EAP to provide such information.

The three common components of 802.1*x* are the *supplicant* Port Access Entity (PAE), the *authenticator* PAE, and the *authentication server*. The supplicant is the client end user trying to authenticate and connect to the wireless network resources. The authenticator is normally the access point that enforces authentication before it allows access to the resources. The authentication server is used to verify end-user credentials against a local or remote database. Figure 7.23 shows the relationship among the three components.

Figure 7.23 802.1*x* Components and Their Relationship

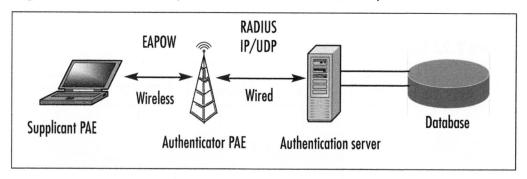

You may have noticed the acronym EAPOW in the figure. EAPOW stands for Extensible Authentication Protocol Over Wireless and it is an EAP message that is encapsulated over wireless networks. During the authentication phase, the access point will only allow EAPOW traffic through to the wired network from the end user trying to establish connectivity. This mechanism prevents the authenticating user from sending anything but its credentials into the wired network. After a successful authentication completes, an EAP message is sent from the authentication server to the access point telling the access point that the authentication has passed. At this point, the access point lifts the EAPOW access-only filter and opens up other communications specified by the security policy for the authenticating user.

Network Group Policy Enhancements

Microsoft Vista wireless clients support several enhancements that can be configured through Group Policy settings and supported by domain controllers. The following are network Group Policy enhancements:

- Mixed security mode
- Allow and deny lists for wireless networks
- Extensibility
- Wired LAN settings

NOTE

Note that the updated Wired and Wireless policies may require a forestwide schema update. For more information on this requirement, visit http://microsoft.com/technet/itsolutions/network/wifi/vista_ad_ext.mspx.

Mixed Security Mode

One of the enhancements in Microsoft Vista and its Group Policy is that you can now configure per-user wireless security policy using the same wireless network. For example, a user connecting to a corporate network with the latest and greatest wireless network adapter with WPA2 capability will have a different policy setting than a user with the older WPA capability. The same SSID wireless network can build different user policies based on logon credentials. Another example of per-user policy settings is two users sharing the same computer with different wireless security setting requirements. Your corporate network might have several WLANs configured for different users. You might have a guest WLAN that only allows users to connect to the Internet and not any corporate servers. You can associate this guest WLAN wireless profile policy with a unique user that will be applied as soon as the user logs on.

Allow and Deny Lists for Wireless Networks

The new wireless Allow and Deny feature in Microsoft Vista Group Policy settings enables you to control whether specific users or groups are allowed to connect to wireless networks. This new feature allows you to prohibit a user's PC from connecting to unknown wireless access point networks. Connecting to an unknown wireless network exposes your PC to possible threats from other connected individuals on that network. The new deny wireless policy setting also helps with rogue access point control. The policy will prohibit an individual from installing a rogue access point and connecting to it. Having the ability to police users to which wireless networks they are allowed to connect increases control and overall security of your environment.

Figure 7.24 displays a screenshot of actual configuration settings from a wireless Group Policy that was configured to allow the wireless network *makesecure* and deny the wireless network *network12* from users. When a user logs on to a workstation, he will download the wireless policy along with the allowed and denied list of networks he is allowed to view and connect to. This will prevent the user from installing his wireless access points and connecting to them. For more details on rogue access points refer back to the "Wireless Security" section of this chapter.

Figure 7.24 Denying Wireless Networks in Group Policy

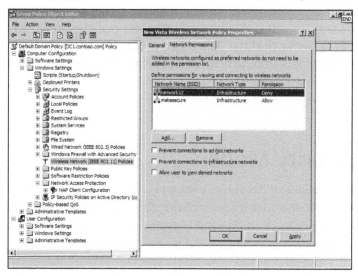

Extensibility

You can import profiles that have the specific connectivity and security settings of wireless vendors, such as different EAP settings and types, into your Group Policy. Figure 7.25 shows the extensibility of the new wireless Group Policy in Vista and its capability to import and export profiles custom to unique vendor settings.

Figure 7.25 Importing Wireless Profiles into Group Policy

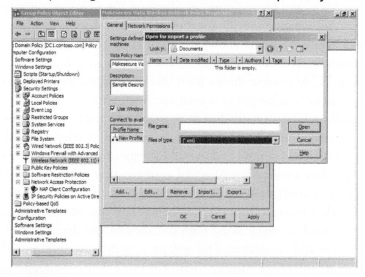

Wired LAN Settings

In Microsoft Vista, you can now support configuration settings of 802.1*x* authentication standards, which we discussed earlier in this chapter. Support for 802.1*x* through Group Policy in Vista is different from that in Windows XP and previous releases. The 802.1*x* protocol configuration allows administrators to control who connects to your wireless networks, and where. This 802.1*x* authentication, together with EAP, allows administrators to check user credentials and computer health prior to allowing access to the network.

Network Awareness

The new, updated Microsoft Vista Group Policy is smart enough to know about network connectivity in real time, unlike Group Policy in previous Windows versions. The main change is that the Group Policy server now takes advantage of the Network Location Awareness (NLA) 2.0 handler in Vista. The NLA service also alerts the Group Policy server whenever a domain controller is available, and if a Group Policy refresh is needed. In previous versions of Windows, such as Windows XP and Windows 2000, a user could connect to the network, check his e-mail, and disconnect immediately afterward, all without getting a Group Policy refresh.

Prior to Vista, the Group Policy engine would try to figure out how fast your network connection was to determine whether it was connecting over a slow link or a fast link. The engine server used this knowledge to help pick which policy settings it would apply based on this information. If you had a slow link the Group Policy server would not send the whole set of policy settings to your computer, as this could take a long time to download and would decrease the user experience. Microsoft has incorporated improvements into Vista concerning how current network bandwidth is calculated. Previously, Internet Control Message Protocol (ICMP) (ping) packets were used to determine the latency between the user and the Group Policy engine, which proved to be insufficient because many ICMP messages were blocked by filtering devices such as firewalls.

Error Messages and Troubleshooting Improvements

The Group Policy server leverages the new Windows event log, which splits events into two logs:

- **The system log** Now known as the administrative log, this log is used for Group Policy error events. If an error occurs with Group Policy, it will appear in the system log, and it will be listed as coming from the Group Policy service engine.

■ **New applications and services logs** Now known as the operational log, this log is used for Group Policy operational events. This new log essentially replaces the cumbersome *userenv.log* troubleshooting file and make it more manageable and cleaner to administrators.

Configuring Wireless Security in Vista

Microsoft Vista includes many improvements in terms of configuring and connecting to a wireless network. We have outlined many of these improvements in previous sections of this chapter. A few additional improvements for configuring wireless connectivity are support for nonbroadcast wireless networks; a new set of UIs that make it easier to configure wireless connectivity; and an option for configuring wireless connectivity and settings using the *netsh wlan* command from the command prompt.

In this section, we will apply wireless security measures that we learned earlier in this chapter. We will configure and secure our Microsoft Vista wireless workstation connecting to a wireless network. First, we will configure and secure our Vista workstation using its new UI within Windows. We will then look at the same configuration using the *netsh wlan* commands and configure our wireless network. Figure 7.26 shows this scenario. In addition, we will configure our wireless access point with WPA2 Personal Mode, and we will use *makesurethiskeyisatleast21char* as our WPA2 key and *makesecure* as our SSID. Figure 7.27 shows the actual configuration of the access point.

Figure 7.26 A Typical Home Network Configuration

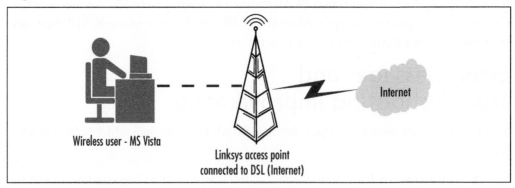

Figure 7.27 Access Point Configuration

Configuring Wireless Security
Using the Connect to a Network Dialog Box

The **Connect to a network** dialog box is the most popular method among users for configuring wireless network connectivity. You can access the **Connect to a network** dialog box in different ways. Here are two methods you can use in Microsoft Vista:

1. Click **Start** and then click **Connect to** from the desktop menu.

2. Click **Start | Control Panel | Network and Sharing Center**, and then click **Connect to a network** (Figure 7.28 displays the network and Sharing Center with connect to a network as one of it's options in the left menu).

Figure 7.28 Accessing the Network and Sharing Center

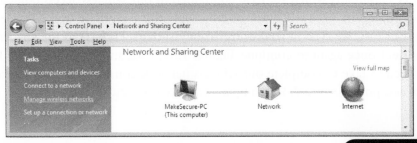

At this point, the **Connect to a network** dialog box opens on the screen. Figure 7.29 shows the actual **Connect to a network** dialog box. Notice that the screenshot displays three networks. Scrolling your mouse over the networks will display details of each network's settings. Notice that the first network on the list is *makesecure*, with WPA2-PSK-enabled security. This is the network we have configured in our scenario and the network we will want to connect to with our secure WPA2 option.

Figure 7.29 The Connect to a Network Dialog Box in Microsoft Vista

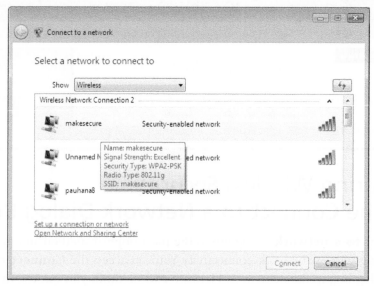

This new **Connect to a network** dialog box is a redesign from the **Choose a wireless network** dialog box in Windows XP. In this scenario, we chose to show **Wireless** networks only. By default, **All** networks are displayed (including dial-up and virtual private network [VPN] connections).

Next, we click on our *makesecure* network and then on the **Connect** icon in the lower-right corner. Figure 7.30 shows a screenshot of the next configuration window, after we clicked on the **Connect** icon. In this window, we need to type in our security passphrase, which we have configured in our wireless access point as the WPA2 key. Microsoft Vista will automatically apply this passphrase to the wireless profile. In our case, we type in **makesurethiskeyisatleast21chars** as the key and click **Connect** once again to continue. Figures 7.31, 7.32, and 7.33 display the last steps we need to take to complete our wireless network connectivity to a *makesecure* wireless access point. Figure 7.31 prompts us to save our newly created wireless profile and gives us the option of automatically connecting to this wireless network whenever it's within reach.

Figure 7.30 Typing In Our WPA2 Key

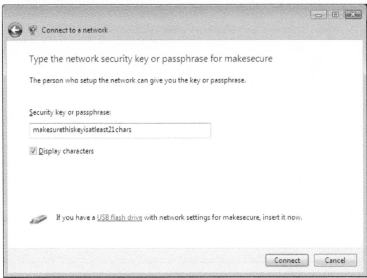

Figure 7.31 Saving the Wireless Network

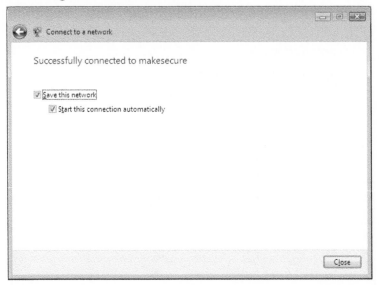

Figure 7.32 Saving the Configuration As a Home Network

Figure 7.33 Successfully Setting Network Settings

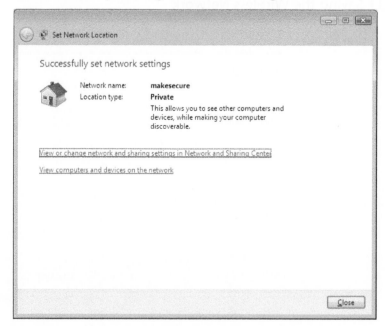

Now that we've configured our wireless network, to manage our wireless profiles and delete profiles we created we need to go back to the **Network and Sharing Center** dialog box and click on **Manage wireless networks** (see Figure 7.34). By default, if more than one wireless profile exists, Microsoft Vista will try to connect to the listed networks in the order they are listed. To change the preferred order, drag a network up or down in the list. You can also add or remove network profiles to or from this list. In this configuration dialog box, you can control all your security settings and wireless network settings for each specific profile.

Figure 7.34 Managing Wireless Networks

To manage the properties and security settings of our wireless network profile, we need to right-click on the profile and select **Properties** (see Figures 7.35 and 7.36). In the **Connection** tab, we can change a variety of settings to reflect whether we want to automatically connect when the network is in range, connect to a more preferred network if available, and connect even if the network is not broadcasting. In the **Security** tab, we can change our security type, encryption type, and actual encryption security key. The encryption types that are supported in Vista are WPA2 Personal, WPA Personal, WPA2 Enterprise, WPA Enterprise, and 802.1x (as discussed earlier in this chapter).

Figure 7.35 The Connection Tab of the makesecure Wireless Network Properties Profile

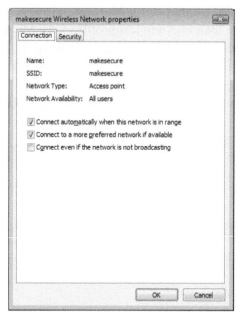

Figure 7.36 The Security Tab of the makesecure Wireless Network Properties Profile

This concludes our configuration of secure wireless connectivity in Microsoft Vista using the UI. In this demonstration, we used a Cisco wireless adapter card with a Vista laptop. As you might have noticed, we did not need Cisco's client utility in order to configure the wireless security settings. One of the enhancements in Microsoft Vista is that it now supports all the latest security measures by default, which you can configure without needing third-party support applications.

Configuring Wireless Security from the Command Line

In this section, we will configure our wireless security and configuration profiles using the *netsh wlan* command from the command prompt. We will use the same scenario we used in the preceding section. Our wireless network SSID will be *makesecure*, our security authentication/encryption will be WPA2-PSK, and our key for WPA2 will be *makesurethiskeyisatleast21chars*.

To enter the command prompt we click **Start | Run,** type **cmd**, and then click **OK**. Before we can use *netsh wlan* commands to configure our wireless network, we must build a profile that we need to attach to our wireless interface. Figure 7.37 shows a sample profile for WPA2-PSK taken from Microsoft. Coding wireless *.xml* profiles for use with the *netsh wlan* command is a topic outside the scope of this chapter. For sample profiles and detailed information on how to build your own personal profile, visit http://msdn2.microsoft.com/en-gb/library/aa369853.aspx (sample profiles) and http://msdn2.microsoft.com/en-gb/library/ms706965.aspx (*wlan_profile* scheme elements).

Figure 7.37 Sample WPA2-PSK Profile from Microsoft

```
makesecure2 - Notepad
File  Edit  Format  View  Help
<?xml version="1.0"?>
<WLANProfile xmlns="http://www.microsoft.com/networking/WLAN/profile/v1">
    <name>makesecure2</name>
    <SSIDConfig>
        <SSID>
            <name>makesecure</name>
        </SSID>
    </SSIDConfig>
    <connectionType>ESS</connectionType>
    <connectionMode>auto</connectionMode>
    <autoSwitch>true</autoSwitch>
    <MSM>
        <security>
            <authEncryption>
                <authentication>WPA2PSK</authentication>
                <encryption>AES</encryption>
                <useOneX>false</useOneX>
            </authEncryption>
            <sharedKey>
                <keyType>passPhrase</keyType>
                <protected>false</protected>
                <keyMaterial>makesurethiskeyisatleast21chars</keyMaterial>
            </sharedKey>
        </security>
    </MSM>
</WLANProfile>
```

As you can see from the profile, we have modified our sample WPA2-PSK profile to match our wireless configuration settings. The profile name is *makesecure2*, the authentication type is listed as WPA2PSK, and the key inside *<keyMaterial>* matches the security key we configured on our wireless access point.

Next, we use the *netsh wlan add profile* command to attach our profile to a specific wireless interface. The syntax of this command is *add profile filename=PathAndFileName [[interface=]InterfaceName] [[user=]{all | current}]*. Figure 7.38 shows the actual command using our profile filename. The interface parameter is one of the interface names shown by the *netsh wlan show interface* commands. After we successfully add our profile, it appears in our UI inside the dialog box, as we saw in Figure 7.33.

Figure 7.38 Adding a Profile to a Specific Wireless Interface with the netsh Command

Next, we connect to our wireless network using the *netsh wlan connect* command. The syntax for this command is *connect[[ssid=]SSIDName] name=ProfileNameinterface=InterfaceName*. Figure 7.39 shows the actual command we used to match our wireless network settings.

Figure 7.39 Connecting to a Wireless Network with the netsh Command

Now that we are successfully and securely connected to our wireless network, let's explore some of the *show* commands available with the *netsh wlan* command. First, let's view our detailed profile settings for the *makesecure2* profile we added earlier. To accomplish this, we use the *netsh wlan show profile makesecure2* command. If you are not sure of the names of your profiles, simply type **netsh wlan show profile**, which will display all available profiles. Figure 7.40 shows our *makesecure2* profile.

Figure 7.40 Showing the makesecure2 Profile with the netsh Command

For more details and help with the *netsh wlan* command you can always add a *?* after each command to display proper syntax and examples of how to use the command.

Summary

To fully understand and implement security measures in networks, you need to understand all of the different available technologies and their functions. Security fundamentals and principles are built around confidentiality, integrity, and availability.

Security is a never-ending cycle that needs continuous testing, constant auditing, and immediate remediation. It's easy to forget about patching your wireless networks when you are running the latest and greatest security configuration. Keep in mind that vulnerabilities found in wireless drivers or a wireless gateway could undermine your entire security posture.

Microsoft Vista presents a variety of new wireless security enhancements, most of which we have reviewed in this chapter. WPA2 support allows users to configure the best security measures currently available. Microsoft Vista provides security support for both home and enterprise-level environments.

Solutions Fast Track

What's New with Wireless in Vista?

- ☑ In Vista, the software infrastructure for 802.11 wireless has been redesigned from the original Ethernet emulation.

- ☑ The new architecture supports APIs for wireless networking. APIs allows ISVs and IHVs to extend and build customized wireless additions and services on top of the core software.

- ☑ Wireless network profiles can be configured on a per-user basis.

- ☑ In Vista, you can configure a nonbroadcast wireless network as part of your preferred and wireless configuration profiles.

- ☑ Enhancements in wireless Group Policy, such as WPA2 authentication options and lists of allowed and denied wireless network names, have been added to Vista.

- ☑ In Microsoft Vista, when preferred networks are out of reach and the wireless settings are configured to not connect to any other wireless networks, Wireless Auto Configuration will create a random name that it adds to the wireless adapter with a 128-bit random encryption key and the strongest supported encryption method.

☑ Microsoft Vista now includes built-in support for configuring WPA2.

☑ Unlike Windows XP, where there are no command lines that allow you to configure wireless settings and connections, Microsoft Vista introduces a new command, *netsh wlan*, that allows you to configure your wireless settings.

Wireless Security

☑ The two main security threats are access and privacy. Access concerns making sure that only authorized individuals are allowed access to your network, and privacy concerns encrypting communication so that attackers cannot capture it in mid-air.

☑ Security measures applied on your access point as part of your wireless access controls should include changing your default administrative passwords, changing your default SSID, disabling SSID broadcast, keeping up-to-date with patches, using MAC address filters, configuring WPA/WPA, and lowering your signal strength whenever possible.

☑ Signal reach could cause potential security issues by extending signal reach to unwanted areas. The new 802.11n standard beams wireless signals up to 1,000 feet away.

☑ Recent flaws found in wireless network adapter drivers allowed attackers to gain access to unpatched PCs. PCs running unpatched drivers are vulnerable even if they are not connected to wireless networks.

☑ WEP is vulnerable; it takes 30 to 60 minutes to crack a WEP key. You should use WPA and WPA2 in its place. Furthermore, you should use keys longer than 21 characters when configuring WPA-PSK mode.

☑ Rogue access points are unauthorized wireless devices installed on a network. They pose a serious security threat to corporations because they extend wired networks to possible attacks from the outside.

Network Group Policy Enhancements

☑ Mixed Security Mode is one of the enhancements in Microsoft Vista and its Group Policy. With it, you can configure a per-user or group wireless security policy.

☑ The new wireless allow and deny features in Microsoft Vista Group Policy settings enable you to police specific users or groups to which wireless networks they are allowed or denied connectivity.

☑ The Group Policy server in Microsoft Vista takes advantage of the NLA 2.0 handler in Vista. The NLA service also alerts the Group Policy server whenever a domain controller is available, and if a Group Policy refresh is needed.

Configuring Wireless Security in Vista

☑ The Network Sharing Center available in the Control Panel is the main UI dialog box from which you configure and manage your wireless networks.

☑ By default, wireless networks that you configure are set up to automatically connect to the network whenever it's within reach.

☑ In addition to configuring your wireless network via the UI, you can also use the *netsh wlan* command from the command line.

Frequently Asked Questions

The following Frequently Asked Questions, answered by the authors of this book, are designed to both measure your understanding of the concepts presented in this chapter and to assist you with real-life implementation of these concepts. To have your questions about this chapter answered by the author, browse to **www.syngress.com/solutions** and click on the **"Ask the Author"** form.

Q: In Windows XP and Windows 2000, in order to connect to a network that supports only WPA2-PSK authentication/encryption settings, I have to install a vendor-specific application to configure my wireless card. Will I still have to do this in Vista?

A: No. Microsoft Vista supports WPA2 modes such as WPA2-Personal and WPA2-Enterprise. These are prebuilt inside the operation system so that you do not have to install external third-party client applications.

Q: What is one of the benefits of having command-line support when configuring wireless connectivity and security?

A: Having commands available for configuring wireless settings allows you to support automated scripts for wireless settings without using Group Policy.

Q: What security measures changed in the way Wireless Auto Configuration is configured in Vista?

A: In Microsoft Vista, when preferred networks are out of reach and the wireless settings are configured to not connect to any other wireless networks, Wireless Auto Configuration will create a random name that it adds to the wireless adapter and will include a security configuration consisting of a 128-bit random encryption key and the strongest encryption method supported by the wireless adapter.

Q: I'm using WEP security in my wireless network. Is this enough?

A: An attacker can crack WEP in less than an hour, so you should consider using WPA or WPA2 instead. If your older access point doesn't support these options, check with your vendor because many times simple application upgrades are available for you to apply.

Q: I've heard that WPA is vulnerable to attacks as well. Is this true?

A: Yes. WPA is vulnerable to brute force dictionary attacks. Therefore, when choosing your master key, make sure you choose a key that is at least 21 characters long and is not a dictionary word or anything easily guessed.

Q: What is a rogue access point?

A: A rogue access point is an unauthorized wireless device that an employee or attacker attaches to a wired network. It is highly insecure and provides serious risk to corporations because it extends networks outside of the corporate control perimeter.

Q: What are some of the Group Policy enhancements in Vista for wireless networks?

A: Per-user wireless policy and security settings, as well as the ability to permit access to specific wireless networks in the environment, are two major security enhancements in Group Policy for Vista.

Q: How can I get help on syntax as well as examples of how to use the new command-line commands to configure my wireless network?

A: When inside the command prompt, add a *?* after each command. For example, *netsh wlan show ?* will list all available options under the *show* option.

Chapter 8

Microsoft Vista: Windows Mail

Solutions in this chapter:

- Comparing Windows Mail with Outlook Express

- Phishing Filter

- Junk Mail Filter

- Instant Search

☑ Summary

☑ Solutions Fast Track

☑ Frequently Asked Questions

Introduction

Windows Mail is fundamentally a new application. Though it is clearly perceived as a successor to Outlook Express and even maintains some of the look and feel, beneath the hood nearly everything is different. Microsoft has taken its built-in mail client and converted it into a JET database-driven application that is so tightly integrated with the operating system (OS) that messages and news posts are treated the same way as system files. Even the security of identities has given way to the Windows profile, and the much-anticipated functionality of Instant Search within Vista is showcased within the new mail client.

Taking full advantage of the newer features of Internet Explorer, Windows Mail arrives with a heightened focus on security. Features relegated only to Outlook or Internet Explorer are now a part of the application and are even enabled by default. The powerful SmartScreen filter used by Exchange is at work within Windows Mail, making the filtering capabilities of the application extend far beyond those of simple filters, and the Phishing Filter recently introduced in the latest Internet Explorer delivers up-to-date security checks from the blacklists maintained at Microsoft.

More than just another version of Outlook Express, Windows Mail delivers robust features and a usability that will be a "first" for many users. In this chapter, we'll take a look at some of these structural changes to the built-in mail client of Windows Vista, and we'll compare these to the shortcomings of Outlook Express. We'll also examine the powerful security tools incorporated to secure the Windows Mail experience.

Comparing Windows Mail with Outlook Express

When Microsoft released Outlook Express in November 1997, the user community had just undergone a seismic shift brought about by the earlier release of Microsoft's first graphical-based OS, Windows 95. For more than two years, personal computers, thought to be forever tied to their owners' drab and dreary cubicles for tasks limited only to work, were now making their way into homes and dormitories at an exponential rate. The Internet was also growing at an exponential rate, and the tools shipping with each revision of Windows needed to be tailored to this exploding home-based population. So, with the release of Internet Explorer 4.0 in Windows 95 OSR 2.5 came the successor to Internet Mail and News: Outlook Express.

Although Internet Mail and News was a simple freeware add-on client available to users of Internet Explorer 3.0, Outlook Express was built into Internet Explorer

4.0. Every user who purchased a Windows 95 OSR 2.5 and subsequent Windows 98 machine would get this new application as part of his Internet-browsing arsenal. In fact, Outlook Express was built with the integration of Internet Explorer in mind, something that would be both a blessing and a curse for users of the application. With the advent of Hypertext Markup Language (HTML)-based e-mail came the exposure of myriad security holes for Outlook Express users. Because Internet Explorer managed its content and security by "zoning" different Web sites, Outlook Express was relegated to the same approach. Outlook Express rendered mail through Internet Explorer, and the behavior and "trusts" of Internet Explorer were passed along to its news and mail counterpart. Because Internet Explorer traditionally ran all code and scripts it encountered in an effort to streamline the user's browsing experience, Outlook Express followed the same behavior. Executable files could be attached to messages received by earlier versions of Outlook Express and rendered only as harmless picture attachments. Even worse, insidious virus architects found that they could launch harmful scripts in the background of a user's session without her knowledge. Because the default behavior of Outlook Express is to automatically open the first message in the Inbox, regardless of the preview pane settings, multitudes of viruses emerged to exploit this threat. Unfortunately for many, a number of these efforts were met with great success (Nimda, anyone?).

Nevertheless, Outlook Express has always maintained a solid following. As a news and mail application, it is easily a favorite among home and small-office users for managing mail for Post Office Protocol 3 (POP3) and Internet Message Access Protocol (IMAP). Outlook Express had a wizard-driven introduction to usher a new user down the road of configuration and quickly provided users an "Outlook" experience for free. As Outlook Express continued to be refined, the application began to incorporate the functionality of supporting multiple mail and user accounts, which solidified its place in the home PC used by the entire family. It was not long before Lightweight Directory Access Protocol (LDAP) and Secure/Multipurpose Internet Mail Extensions (S/MIME) were added to the list of supported protocols. Even Mac users found the opportunity to explore the utility in a version free for download when Microsoft chose to support the application for those running classic Mac OSes (8.1 to 9.x). Aside from this sidestep into the Mac world, Outlook Express has remained an application built into the Microsoft OSes and browser, something you could expect to find answering every hyperlink with an @ symbol as you browsed with Internet Explorer.

> **NOTE**
>
> The integration of applications such as Outlook Express and Internet Explorer has been both a blessing and a curse for Microsoft. Although considered a sacred cow for Microsoft in the States, the European Union charged that Microsoft's "bundling" of software presented an unfair and almost impossible challenge for vendors of competing software. Although a version of Windows XP was released that did not include Media Player (Windows XP N), the EU required the software giant to pay an initial fine of $613 million.

Windows Mail is the next iteration of this product. Although it is absolutely a "version" of Outlook Express, carrying with it many visual similarities to the Outlook product, Windows Mail is fundamentally a different application. Although Outlook Express is tied to Internet Explorer, Windows Mail is more tightly integrated into the OS. This may well be serving the purpose of delineating the product from its predecessors as well as making it more difficult for antitrust lawsuits to be filed against Microsoft for "bundling" products into its OS. Windows Mail is not designed as a plug-in or addition to Internet Explorer, and though it is very much its own application, it is now a fundamental component of the OS itself.

 # Database Architecture

At its core, Windows Mail runs with a completely different architecture than Outlook Express. Outlook Express presented a set of direct database files to both the user and the OS. At least four default folders are created with each "identity" in Outlook Express. These are:

> *C:\Documents and Settings\<user>\Local Settings\Application Data\Identities\{GUID}\Microsoft\Outlook Express\Folders.dbx*
>
> *C:\Documents and Settings\<user>\Local Settings\Application Data\Identities\{GUID}\Microsoft\Outlook Express\Outbox.dbx*
>
> *C:\Documents and Settings\<user>\Local Settings\Application Data\Identities\{GUID}\Microsoft\Outlook Express\Inbox.dbx*
>
> *C:\Documents and Settings\<user>\Local Settings\Application Data\Identities\{GUID}\Microsoft\Outlook Express\Offline.dbx*

Outlook Express utilizes the single database file, Folders.dbx, as the master index for the entire messaging store. It holds the tree structure for all mail folders, the newsgroups on each news account, and even the options for the synchronization of "subscribed" folders. It is ultimately in this design that Outlook Express begins to fall short of many hopes and expectations. All mail items reside within each of these folders, meaning that the corruption of any of the folders results in the loss or corruption of all the mail stored within. Even worse, there are functional capacity limits for each of the individual files. If any of these files gets too large, typically near 2 GB, searching for mail and even opening Outlook Express becomes slow or even impossible.

For these reasons, the Windows Mail design team did away with the single storage-file design. Instead, Windows Mail utilizes a JET database, the same database engine in use for Exchange and Active Directory, and the very same instance in use in the Vista OS on which Windows Mail is installed. The database file tree structure that existed in Outlook Express now exists only as folders within the OS. All of these folders, as well as the pointers to the actual messages, are located in a single folder for each user (see Figure 8.1).

Figure 8.1 The Windows Mail Folder Structure

If you were paying attention, you may have noticed our use of the term *pointers* regarding messages. Via JET, Windows Mail now stores each piece of mail and each news post as a separate file within the OS. Mail files are given the .eml file extension and news posts receive an .nws file extension. Each of these files is composed of two streams. For messages, the primary stream of the file is the RFC standard MIME. This is the portion of the message that is easily read by opening an .eml file in Notepad.exe (see Figure 8.2).

Figure 8.2 An E-mail File Opened in Notepad

The secondary stream is actually XML. Because JET is part of Vista and Vista supports even more metadata in the file's file system than earlier OSes, this stream is populated with flags, account information, state information, and filter handlers that get promoted up into JET for categorization. This allows for the integration of the new Windows Search, which we'll cover more in the section "Instant Search," later in this chapter.

The utilization of the JET database on the OS provides myriad benefits. The most noticeable is easily the improvement in performance. Searching for mail, opening mail, and ultimately running the application is markedly faster due to the flatness of the file structure within the OS. A flatter file structure means it's easier to grab data from the application level. In Vista, e-mail messages and news posts are found and displayed even as the user is typing criteria into the search engine, eliminating the extra actions of initiating a search and then perusing the search results for the appropriate mail content as opposed to only the filename. The use of JET also provides a self-cleaning mechanism from within the OS. As files are added and deleted, garbage collection processes within the OS groom the disk and ultimately the database in a very natural way that is transparent to the user and even the application. The result is a lighter application, a faster data store for mail, and a simpler organization of files and folders.

Loss Prevention and Identities

Windows Mail takes a significant step forward when it comes to addressing the shortcomings of Outlook Express in the area of mail corruption and loss. Once again, the chief contributor to that effort is the major player of the new architecture: JET.

Because the JET database enables the storage of e-mails as individual files, a major point of failure is avoided. In Outlook Express, the corruption of the single Inbox.dbx file typically meant the loss of everything in it. Now, however, the corruption of any single mail file doesn't mean the loss of integrity of any and all mail, but rather only the single message.

Or does it?

A few surprise bells and whistles are working in the background of Windows Mail to keep order in the area of disaster recovery. In fact, there is a layered approach to the mitigation of corruption and loss. First, there is the fact that the new database is fully transactional. This means when messages are deleted, you can play back the transaction logs to re-create the full picture. For example, if you're about to save a message and you lose power, the transaction logs will roll back to the point of failure. Second, the database can be reconstructed from the files themselves, so the loss of the database is only a minor hit. Lastly, an actual backup database is kept up-to-date with everything that takes place within the primary mail database. This database file is an exact replica of the primary one, and is located at C:\Users\<USER>\AppData\Local\Microsoft Windows\Windows Mail\Backup.

In the event of corruption to any of the three sources (primary message database, backup database, or log files), the OS uses the other two to rebuild the third automatically. This establishes a very sound and stable environment for users, even those in business settings where locally stored mail cannot be lost to corruption.

Now, if you've been in the business of mail management, you know the obvious problem with the preceding statement is that corruption is only one way to lose data; disk loss is another. How does Windows Mail handle the backing up and restoring of mail and associated accounts? The answer is "much differently than Outlook Express."

In Outlook Express, the account information that tied the .dbx files to real users was kept in the Registry. This presented two problems. First, there were now two groups of data to back up: a series of .dbx files, and then a series of Registry entries for both the mail and news accounts that are stored in the Registry key *HKEY_CURRENT_USER\Software\Microsoft\Internet Account Manager.*

At the point of a restore to a second machine or new profile, the user accounts had to be re-created first. This meant dealing with the backups of the Registry key, the importing of the Registry key, and the configuring of the profile prior to even touching mail database files. The second challenge is in the actual backup: If a user wanted to export or import his mail data he needed to be logged onto Outlook Express to run the utility in a neat and easy fashion. This was also true of managing the Address Book, which is a subset of the Windows Address book that held all contacts on the machine.

The Windows Mail design team moved the account data from the Registry into XML files that are associated with each Inbox in the Windows Mail folder. This means that to back up the totality of mail and profile information for a user, all you need to do is copy the Windows Mail folder under that user's profile. If that folder is then copied to a new profile, all account and mail data is effectively moved and will come online when Windows Mail is launched.

There is one caveat to this new approach: Although it is more efficient to administer, it does require that Outlook Express users who had multiple accounts or "identities" converge their data into one user profile. Windows Mail does not support identities. Strangely, you are never informed of this when you configure multiple POP3 accounts within Windows Mail. In fact, there is a very deceptive menu item seemingly labeled just for the management of your identities, at **File | Identities**.

If you select this menu option, you will actually launch a wizard that both announces this change in identity support and offers to consolidate your "identities" into a single user profile (see Figure 8.3). Here you are given the opportunity to learn a bit about the change from Identities to Windows Profiles by clicking a built-in link to a Help and Support article. If you are upgrading from Outlook Express, this wizard will start automatically every time Windows Mail is launched until all Identities are imported, unless you choose the "Do not show this again" box.

Figure 8.3 The Identity Import Wizard

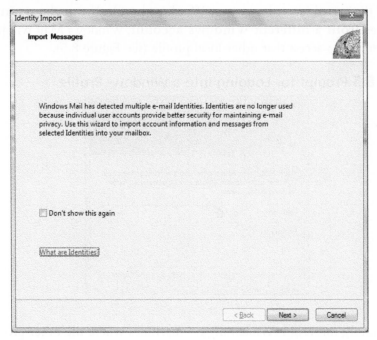

After clicking **Next**, you are brought to the import options page (see Figure 8.4).

Figure 8.4 Import Path Choices

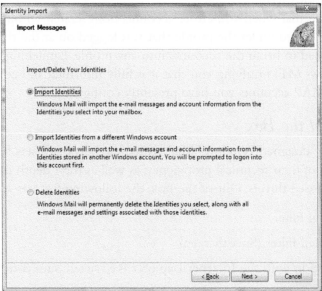

If you choose **Import Identities**, Windows Mail will search for and allow you to select the varied identities in your Windows profile. If you choose **Import Identities from a different Windows account**, Windows Mail will prompt you for credentials to access that other local profile (see Figure 8.5).

Figure 8.5 Prompt for Logging into a Windows Profile

Obviously, this tool is viable only on machines where the other profiles are local. Typically this will be home-based machines and shared workstations in smaller offices.

Lastly, if you choose the **Delete Identities** option, you are presented with a list of accounts that Windows Mail already knows about and you can elect to remove them from Windows Mail.

Keep in mind that when you create accounts from scratch within Windows Mail they are already placed under the profile that was logged on at the time of creation, so there is no need to bring the accounts into any profile. Launching the tool will result in Windows Mail notifying you that it is fully informed and content with all the POP and IMAP accounts you have presently configured.

 Secure Out of the Box

Microsoft clearly designed Windows Mail with awareness that users have become savvier in terms of their technical proficiency, as well as their depth of knowledge about Internet-based threats. Out of the box, the following features are enabled:

- Phishing Filter
- Junk Mail Filter (SmartScreen)
- Integration with the Internet Explorer Restricted Sites zone

- A trigger to warn the user when an application attempts to send mail "as" the user

- Threat attachment filtering

These options can be viewed and managed via the Security tab under Tools | Options (see Figure 8.6).

Tools & Traps…

Management through Group Policy

Shockingly, as of this writing, only one of the settings in the preceding list is available to Group Policy: threat attachment filtering. The Group Policy Object, "Block attachments that could contain a virus," is located under the User Configuration node of Group Policy within an Administrative Template for Internet Explorer. If that were not confusing enough, you expose the setting within Internet Explorer by double-clicking the **Configure Outlook Express** selection.

Figure 8.6 The Security Settings Tab

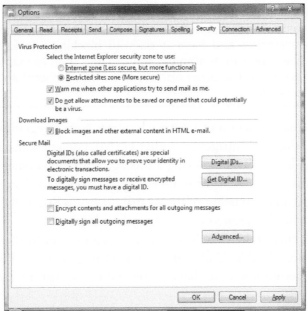

Although the Phishing and Junk Mail filters receive dedicated attention later in this chapter, the other options enabled by default are worthy of description. The Integration with the Internet Explorer Restricted Sites zone means that the ActiveX and Java settings from Internet Explorer are inherited and used to filter mail. As such, mail with this content is not displayed unless the user takes specific action to enable that content or disable this default setting.

The "send as" trigger is often a function of antivirus software, but Windows Mail enables this functionality by managing its own sensitivity to Trojans and other malware that may initiate the creation of a message. When this effort is made and detected, a Security pop-up from within Windows Vista will notify you of the effort.

Dangerous attachments are typically those that have executable extensions. By default, these attachments are blocked, in that the e-mail will be received and displayed (assuming there is no other insecure content like ActiveX), but the attachment will not be downloaded from the mail server. Windows Mail will notify you that the application has been stripped.

Tools & Traps...

Attachment Blocking, Not Filtering

Windows Mail will block all attachments with certain extensions, such as .exe, .vb, .prg, and so on. There is no way to allow a "friend" to send an attachment with such an extension and have it pass all blocking checks when this is enabled. However, you can disable the feature and then reenable it after you receive the attachment. The other option, as is often the workaround, is to Zip the file prior to receipt.

Despite the similar function of Internet Explorer zone integration, automatic downloading and display of images and other HTML content is managed separately and is enabled by default. Right-clicking a message with such content and choosing to display images is all that is required, unless a user chooses to change the setting here. This setting is a continuation of the security that was originally lacking in Outlook Express and that created enormous vulnerabilities.

Although not enabled by default, a number of options for further securing the transport of mail are available. Under the Secure Mail section, any Vista user now has the ability to use certificates for authentication and to encrypt messages during transfer. The bottom two checkboxes detail these options, but the top two options for Digital IDs (certificates) are what we'd like to focus on for a moment.

If you choose the **Get Digital IDs** option, Windows Mail opens an Internet Explorer page at the Microsoft Office Web site that details various sources for obtaining digital certificates. These are not provided for free; rather, Microsoft provides the less savvy user a directory of providers.

Tools & Traps…

Preinstalled Certificates

Although Microsoft will kindly guide you to a site where you can obtain additional certificates, most Vista clients will have a plethora of certificates already installed on the machine. You can view these from within Windows Mail by selecting the **Trusted Root certificates** tab in the **Certificate Import Wizard**. Figure 8.7 shows this window as it is seen by default during an import, but selecting any of the other tabs will reveal a whole world of digital authenticity already built into Windows Vista and available to Windows Mail.

Once you have a digital certificate, you can import it into Windows Mail via the following steps:

1. Within **Windows Mail**, navigate to **Tools | Options**.

2. Choose the **Security** tab.

3. In the bottom section of the **Security** page (refer to Figure 8.6), find the section labeled **Secure Mail** and select the button for **Digital IDs**.

4. The next window is labeled **Certificates** (see Figure 8.7). Here there are six tabs for organizing and displaying the type of digital certificates already installed and available. To continue importing a new certificate, click **Import**.

5. The next window is the welcome screen for the Certificate Import Wizard (see Figure 8.8). Click **Next**.

Figure 8.7 The Certificates Page (Default)

Figure 8.8 The Welcome Page for the Certificate Import Wizard

6. The next window requires that you browse to the certificate you want to use. In this case, we are importing a certificate from Equifax that is located on our desktop (see Figure 8.9).

Figure 8.9 Browsing for a Certificate

7. The next step is to choose the method for storing the certificate you import within Vista. The default is to **Place all certificates in the Private store** (see Figure 8.10). We ultimately chose to let Vista decide based on the type of certificate. After making your choice, click **Next**.

Figure 8.10 The Certificate Store

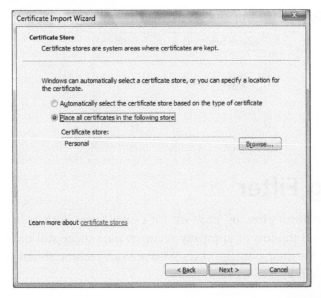

8. To complete the import, you must agree to click **Finish** at the **Completing the Certificate Import Wizard** page (see Figure 8.11).

Figure 8.11 Completing the Certificate Import Wizard

At this point, Windows Mail will complete the action and, if successful, will display the completion notification (see Figure 8.12).

Figure 8.12 Successful Import Notification

 # Phishing Filter

Phishing has become a growing problem for e-mail users both at home and at work. Administrators feel the loss of company security via a successful phishing scam; home users fear for their poor mothers who are not technically savvy and may fall into a trap that will lead to identity theft.

In short, "phishing" is when an e-mail is sent with the intent of extracting personal information from the recipient. Typically, the information being sought is both personal and financial. As such, the authors of these phishing efforts typically disguise the e-mail as a very professional and courteous correspondence from a trusted source such as a bank, insurance company, or even educational institution. Within the body of the e-mail is a hyperlink to a fraudulent Web site which will present a similarly trusting face to the ensnared victim and then require perhaps two or three pieces of information to "update their database" or "process their re-enrollment." In addition to posing as a familiar face to the victim, these Web sites portray themselves as extremely security-conscious and require great levels of "authentication" before continuing. It is in the information provided for validation that the scammers reach their goal in gaining passwords, Social Security numbers (SSNs), and account numbers. Their ploy is to present themselves as everything that they're not; secure, professional, and out for your best interests.

Windows Mail now boasts an additional tool to the typical arsenal of antimalicious mail weaponry, and that is the integration of Microsoft's Phishing Filter. Initially a part of Internet Explorer and the MSN toolbar, the Phishing Filter automatically analyzes URLs presented to and clicked by the user in Windows Vista and compares them to a local copy of the blacklists maintained at Microsoft (these local copies are updated as part of Microsoft Update). Windows Mail can take the Phishing Filter service even further by analyzing incoming messages to not only see whether the URLs listed in the body of the message are known for phishing, but also whether the actual links in HTML messages are the same as the URLs displayed to the user. Messages caught by the Phishing Filter can be accepted or rejected.

Scanning from the Start

In accordance with Microsoft's continued effort to provide applications and platforms that are secure out of the box, the Phishing Filter built into Windows Mail is enabled by default. In fact, very few settings are available to the user. The only place to adjust settings for the filter is within the settings for the Junk Filter. You can access these settings via **Tools | Junk E-mail Options**.

Five tabs are exposed for configuring all junk-mail-related options, the last of these being the Phishing Filter (see Figure 8.13).

Figure 8.13 The Phishing Tab

By default, the Phishing Filter is set to protect the user's Inbox against "phishing," though not to move the mail in any way out of the Inbox. The options available to the user are to accept this protection, remove the protection altogether, or choose to have the protection enabled and all detected e-mails moved into the Junk E-mail folder.

Because the updates for the Phishing Filter take place within Windows Update and have little to do with human interaction, there are no settings to modify this within the Windows Mail user interface. Rather, Windows Vista handles the security and the updating for the utility on behalf of the user. It is important to understand that the default behavior of the Phishing Filter is not regulated by Windows Mail, but by Internet Explorer. If the Phishing Filter is not set to automatically check in with Microsoft's blacklists (which is the default setting), the filter (which is enabled automatically within Windows Mail) checks URLs in messages only against the local copy of the blacklist.

A point for clarification is the distinction between junk e-mail and phishing e-mail. Junk e-mail is mail identified as having a certain level of content that is sinister, erroneous (smart speak for "bogus"), advertisement-related, and so on. Phishing, on the other hand, is very specific and typically requires that the user take action to be forwarded to a Web site or form. Windows Mail handles these two types of electronic garbage differently. If a message has a high probability of being junk mail and is considered to be only "potentially" fraudulent, that message will be moved over to the Junk E-mail folder. The settings for junk e-mail on the Options tab take precedence as the e-mail is not actually considered to be a phishing attempt. A message is classified as a phishing attempt if the sender, subject, or content/URL in the body of the e-mail is verified with the local copy of the Microsoft blacklist. The Phishing Filter service performs these checks in real time, allowing for a very high degree of security before messages are even opened.

Working with Filtered Mail

When Windows Mail receives a potentially malicious message, it immediately scans the message for any fraudulent links. If it does not detect such a link, Windows Mail will determine whether the message should go to the Inbox or to the Junk E-mail folder.

The first action that is actually visible to the user is the pop-up security window (see Figure 8.14), where the user is given the opportunity to navigate to the Junk E-mail folder (where the message resides), navigate to the Junk E-mail Options page, or set Windows Mail such that it will never prompt on such an occurrence again.

Figure 8.14 A Suspicious E-mail Alert

Unless told to no longer display the message (via the "Please do not show me this dialog again" checkbox), Windows Mail will display this alert at every instance of suspicious mail. If the user chooses the default option (Close), he is redirected to the Junk E-mail folder where the suspect message is awaiting review (see Figure 8.15).

Figure 8.15 The Junk E-mail Folder Populated with a Suspicious Message

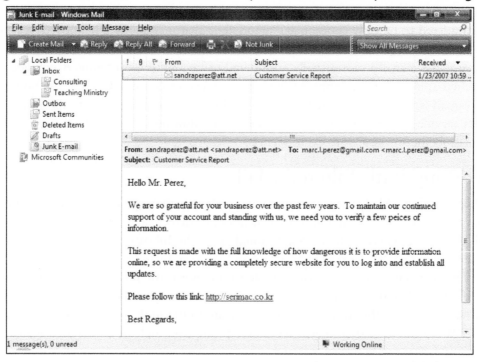

At this point, the user can fully view the "suspect" message and give it a "not Junk" status.

If the Phishing Filter confirms that a message is malicious, it behaves slightly differently. First, it does not move the message to the Junk E-mail folder. Second, it displays it in the Inbox with a red header/banner that provides the user with a very clear warning that the link or sender is known for phishing (see Figure 8.16). The message header information is set to a bold red font and the now familiar Security Shield (first introduced in Windows XP) is appended to the message displayed in the Inbox.

Lastly, Windows Mail removes all images and hyperlinks, further shielding the user who chooses to investigate the e-mail from the dangers of accidental enabling or browsing. Although this may initially seem somewhat restrictive, consider that many unwise users may not be up-to-date on matters such as antivirus, leaving them very vulnerable to the threats brought about by accidentally launching a Web site.

Figure 8.16 Notification of a Confirmed Phishing Threat

Program Improvement

It is only a matter of time before a Windows Mail user receives a message that contains a link to a Web site that is fraudulent and wonders why the great and powerful Phishing Filter has not caught it. The answer has less to do with a deficiency in Microsoft code and more to do with today's electronic culture.

At the time of this writing, Microsoft has averaged an addition of 17,000 URLs per month to the Phishing Filter service. These are updates provided by the users of Hotmail and Live Mail who sent suspicious URLs to Microsoft for research. Since the release of Internet Explorer 7, users of the program have reported close to 4,500 potential phishing sites per week. Needless to say, the rate at which new scams and forms of spam are released into the Internet is truly staggering, and there are simply no applications that can boast 100 percent effectiveness at providing security and detection.

To ensure that the Phishing Filter can continue to provide you with accurate information, you have the option to report suspicious Web sites to Microsoft. This feature, however, is not on by default, and you must configure it from within Internet Explorer. In fact, to ensure that your Phishing Filter is checking more than just the local copy of the Microsoft blacklist, you need to enable the full function-ality of the feature. To do this, simply go to **Internet Explorer** and choose **Tools | Phishing Filter** (see Figure 8.17).

Figure 8.17 Adjusting the Phishing Filter via Internet Explorer Tools | Phishing Filter

The options available to you are:

- **Check This Website** This establishes a connection to Microsoft's blacklist to query the URL for the Web site you are presently on. If the Web site is found, you will be alerted that the site is known for phishing.

- **Turn ON/OFF Automatic Website Checking** This option must be set to On to ensure that the Phishing Filter goes beyond the local copy of the Microsoft blacklist. With this setting off, Windows Mail can incorporate fil-tering only against your local copy of the Microsoft which is updated only on occasion.

- **Report This Website** This is where you can send Microsoft a notification that the Web site you are currently visiting seems suspicious and request that the site be researched. Microsoft does not offer a guarantee of when you can expect to find the site you've reported on its list.

- **Phishing Filter Settings** This brings you to Internet Explorer's traditional Advanced Settings window, where you can toggle Automatic Website Checking on or off or disable the Phishing Filter altogether (see Figure 8.18).

Figure 8.18 The Advanced Tab of Internet Options for the Phishing Filter

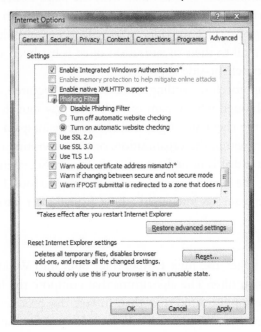

It has taken a great deal of "group" effort for perpetrators of phishing campaigns to become as successful as they have. It stands to reason, then, that the user community will need to meet the effort with as solid a unifying effort to combat their assault. The Microsoft Phishing Filter is a phenomenal tool, but one that is only as good as its updates. Taking the time to enable the feature and the communication is definitely worthwhile.

Although the Phishing Filter offers you little granular control over the application and virtually none via Windows Mail, it is still an incredible tool for securing the e-mail experience for Microsoft Vista users. Now, the security once regulated only to Microsoft's Hotmail and MSN servers is available for free to Windows Mail users, and this means fewer add-ons, no third-party applications, and a more streamlined experience for all.

Junk Mail Filter

It would seem that everyone on planet Earth has received spam. In fact, it is probably not unrealistic to think that spam has been somehow transmitted across the wireless waves in space to our yet undetected cosmic neighbors who can only conclude that we are obsessed with online meetings, free prescription refills, and miraculous growth enhancers. Indeed, the Internet is as much a place of "dodging" unwanted material as it is "searching" for the content of choice.

No network administrator is unfamiliar with the pains associated with spam filtering. Many enterprises turn to a third-party solution out on the perimeter, and yet others opt for a separate service provider who will accept and filter all their mail for them and then relay mail to their organization once it has been sanitized. Few organizations rely solely on client-side applications.

Often, a layered approach to battling spam is what is required, one that utilizes each of the avenues through which spam can make its way into the organization's e-mail system. As such, the client-side fight will always remain; spam or virus-generated mail could come from within the organization, or from a visiting consultant or a poorly protected laptop that is brought into the company. So, taking yet another step forward in improving the e-mail experience for former Outlook Express users, the Windows Mail design team has integrated a Junk E-mail filter into Windows Mail.

SmartScreen

Contrary to popular belief, the Junk E-mail filter built into Windows Mail is not simply another Bayesian filter. The algorithms that compose the learning engine for this product are more sophisticated than that. In fact, this product is not a client-side application; what ships with Windows Mail's Junk E-mail filter are filters derived from the Microsoft SmartScreen spam-filtering solution that has been refined over the past few years at the enterprise level.

First deployed to its Hotmail servers, the SmartScreen technology leveraged learning algorithms against large sets of data (hence Hotmail and eventually Windows Live Mail). The design team that is focused exclusively on the antispam effort at Microsoft found higher levels of "learning" with a broader user base and deeper concentration of mail. Based on user input, the algorithms adjust their detection settings and then generate filters accordingly. This approach has provided SmartScreen with such a high success rate at the identification of spam (95 percent, according to Microsoft) that the product was eventually incorporated into the Exchange 2003 and Outlook 2003 products, as well as their respective 2007 versions.

Because of the nature of the algorithms, the application does not learn at the client level, that is, no "personal" settings or adjustments are made to tailor the filtering to a user's preference. To do so would be to take these finely tuned enterprise-level algorithms and point them at a ridiculously small subset of data, which would essentially stunt the learning process. However, like in Outlook, the Windows Mail Junk E-mail filter is set to pull filter updates from Microsoft via the Microsoft Update service. In this way, the filter settings in use for Exchange are at work on your local machine from the first use of Windows Mail.

Configuring Junk E-Mail Options

Enabled by default, the Junk E-mail filter sits silently; in effect, watching all e-mail. Virtually no setup is required. In fact, when a user first launches Windows Mail and sets up the account information for either a POP or an IMAP account (the only two account types the Junk E-mail filter supports), there is neither an indication that junk e-mail filtering is enabled nor a prompt to configure settings.

Once you are up and running with an account, any new mail is run through the filter. If a message is identified as spam, it is moved immediately to the Junk E-mail folder, which notifies you that there are messages waiting there for your review, just like your Inbox (see Figure 8.19).

Figure 8.19 Default View of Windows Mail with a Detected Message in the Junk E-Mail Folder

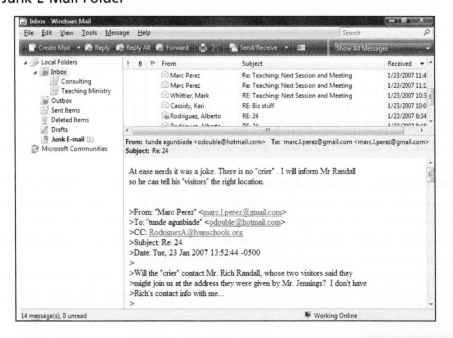

Although the Junk E-mail filter functionality is on by default, some settings are available to the user. You can access these settings in the main menu in **Windows Mail** via **Tools | Junk E-mail options**.

A five-tab window is opened (see Figure 8.20) where you can finely tune the Junk E-mail filter to your liking.

Figure 8.20 The Junk E-mail Options Tab

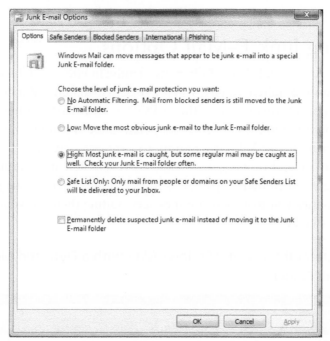

The first tab offers you the ability to manage the level of sensitivity that the application will apply to messages. This essentially amounts to a degree of filtering. By default, the Junk E-mail filter is set to "Low: Move the most obvious junk e-mail to the Junk E-mail folder." Adjusting the sensitivity is as simple as choosing a radio button.

During testing, we found that the High setting provided the best results. Certain companies that we have received e-mail from saw fit to send us advertisements for related products, even on behalf of their partners. On the High setting, these less personal e-mails were moved to the Junk E-mail folder, allowing us to quickly discern what we cared for and what was likely irrelevant mail.

The first and last radio button options under "Choose the level of junk e-mail protection you want" provide the opposite ends of the spectrum. The No Automatic

Filtering and Safe List Only settings rely not on the SmartScreen algorithms, but simply on block or allow lists. These lists specify who is allowed to send mail to the recipient, and who is not. In Windows Mail, these lists are Safe Senders and Blocked Senders, respectively.

Let's take a moment to discuss the Blocked Senders and the Safe Senders lists, both of which are easily administered through dedicated tabs. The Safe Senders and Blocked Senders tabs are fairly straightforward. Both allow you to add, remove, and edit entries. When "Add" an entry is chosen, Windows Mail provides you with a simple interface for data entry (see Figure 8.21).

Figure 8.21 The Address or Domain Prompt for the Senders List

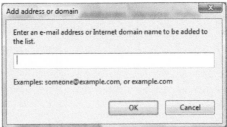

As is clearly stated, you add not only e-mail addresses, but also entire domains. This is both a good and a bad thing. You can add entire organizations in one fell swoop by choosing to place a domain (Syngress.com, for example) into the Safe Senders list. Now, everyone from the editor-in-chief to the cafeteria janitor can e-mail you, allowing you to avoid the administrative nightmare of having to add each and every employee.

Obviously, there is a flip side to this coin. If you choose to block an entire domain because a very odd employee of that company seems to have taken a particular interest in you, don't be surprised when your friend in Marketing can't e-mail you to inform you that the new company beach balls are in. If the entire domain is blocked, the entire domain is blocked, right?

Not really. If you block an entire domain from sending e-mail by listing the domain in the Blocked Senders list, individuals within the domain can still receive e-mails if they are specified on the Safe Senders list. The Safe Senders list has priority over the Blocked Senders list, enabling just this very thing.

Before leaving the Safe Senders and Blocked Senders tabs, let's look at one more set of options found only on the Safe Senders tab, the auto-trust features.

At the bottom of the Safe Senders tab (see Figure 8.22) are two options for adding users to the Safe Senders list automatically. By default, anyone in your Windows Contacts is allowed to send mail to you. They are "trusted," but not actually on your Safe Senders list. This means the list can be disposed of and their ability to e-mail you will remain. In fact, their names and e-mail addresses will never appear on the Safe Senders list.

Figure 8.22 The Junk E-mail Safe Senders Page

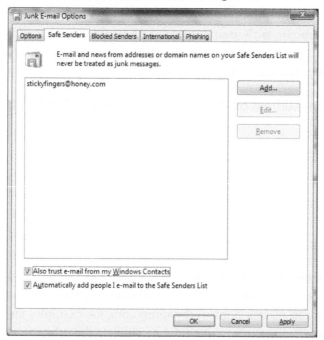

The "Automatically add people I e-mail to the Safe Senders list" option is different in that entries for every e-mail address you send to from Windows Mail is added to the Safe Senders list when this option is checked. A message does not have to be successfully delivered or even have to leave the Outbox for this entry; it is added as soon as you click Send.

Now, if we consider the settings available to us for junk e-mail filtering given this information about the Safe Senders and Blocked Senders lists, we can make more informed decisions. Let's review our options again:

- **No Automatic Filtering** Mail from blocked senders is still moved to the Junk E-mail folder.

- **Low** The most obvious junk e-mail is moved to the Junk E-mail folder.

- **High** Most junk e-mail is caught, but some regular mail may be caught as well. Check your Junk E-mail folder often.

- **Safe List Only** Only mail from people or domains on your Safe Senders list will be delivered to your Inbox.

If a sender's address is on the Blocked Senders list and the option for No Automatic Filtering is selected, any message he sends will be received and compared to the Blocked Senders list (which is essentially a local blacklist) and, when his address is matched, moved to the Junk E-mail folder. The true junk e-mail filters are never put into practice. Consequently, mail from any and all other sending addresses, no matter how obviously spam, will be delivered to the Inbox.

If a sender's address is on the Safe Senders list and the Safe List Only setting is chosen, all mail from that sender, and that sender only, will be accepted. Obviously, no further filtering is applied or even required. Although this is a highly secure setting, it is one that places a great deal of administrative burden on the user because enabling any sort of e-mail communication from a new contact requires that the Windows Mail user take action to update the Safe Senders list.

A last option remains on the first tab of the Junk E-mail Options window, and that is to "Permanently delete suspected junk e-mail instead of moving it to the Junk E-mail folder". Although this may sound like a fairly reasonable choice, keep in mind that "suspected" junk e-mail is just that. In addition, the level of suspicion is adjustable based on the Low/High options, which means legitimate mail can be moved and deleted without your consent.

Working with Junk Mail

When a message is detected as junk e-mail, it is placed within the Windows Mail Junk E-mail folder. This means the message is in the Windows Vista file system and is still very much accessible. By clicking on the Junk E-mail folder, you can actually see the message which, depending on its content, has been filtered or blocked from full display (see Figure 8.23).

In this particular example, Windows Mail detected both the potential for a spam advertisement and the presence of images. As a measure of protection, the images have been blocked, as is described in the warning banner posted within the header information bar.

Figure 8.23 Junk E-mail Displayed

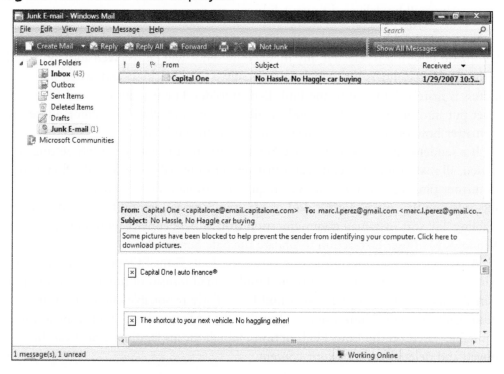

From here, you have several options. From the messaging toolbar, you may delete the message or mark the message as "Not Junk."

Although choosing to delete the message rids your Junk E-mail folder of the suspect message, marking the message as "Not Junk" automatically moves the message into the Inbox. This is a one-step process that allows you to quickly recover any message erroneously identified as spam.

In addition to the toolbar, you may simply right-click a message in the Junk E-mail folder (see Figure 8.24) and select any one of the five options available to you.

From the right-click message menu, you may add either the sender or the sending domain to the Safe Senders list or to the Blocked Senders list. In addition, you may also mark the e-mail as "Not Junk" here. You cannot, from this menu, delete the message.

As with the Phishing Filter, some messages that are truly junk in their core will arrive unscathed through our Junk E-mail filter. Although this is a nuisance, it is not the end of the world. And although not quite a one-click process as was deleting or releasing a message from the Junk E-mail folder, the steps for marking an e-mail as junk are still familiar. To mark an e-mail as junk, simply right-click the message, navigate to the Junk E-mail menu item we saw earlier, and choose again from the options presented (this time there are only four, because "Mark as Not Junk" is unavailable to us for messages already in the Inbox).

Figure 8.24 Junk E-mail Options at the Message Dropdown Menu

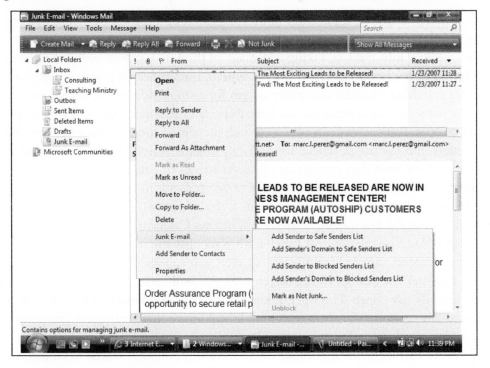

 # Instant Search

Without question, one of the great accomplishments that Microsoft was able to unveil with the release of Windows Vista is the Instant Search technology. If you had any experience on a newer Mac in recent years (OS X), you know the great envy that belonged to every Windows user who found himself selecting searchable file extensions, entering portions of names and folders, and even rerunning searches with refined criteria in hopes of finding a particular file quickly.

Windows XP, with all of its advances from Windows 98 and Windows 2000, left a great void when it came to data management. Though it is a fine solution for hosting applications, Windows has never been a great OS for data retrieval. In fact, most Windows users would probably say that data retrieval is for database servers. When Apple released OS X with a built-in search tool that would provide near-immediate results for searches of all kinds, Microsoft was pressed to provide a solution to really enhance the browsing experience of the local machine. To this end, Windows Instant Search has been deployed in Windows Vista and integrated into Windows Mail.

Basic Functionality

Instant Search is not an application to be configured or a feature to be enabled by only the technically savvy user. Rather, Microsoft has released Vista with this powerful tool built into the OS. Taking advantage of the JET database within Vista and the increased level of metadata in the file system, Instant Search provides a Web-like tool for searching an entire computer system for a single document, entry, line of text, or name. Search criteria do not have to be full filenames, extensions, or prepositional phrases. Rather, you can begin a search literally as soon as you enter the first few letters into the search wheel. Immediately, Instant Search begins to populate a results window with data containing whatever strings of data match what you entered, be it filenames, text within a file, or an application.

Instant Search is exposed to the user in several places within the OS: Start Search, Search (within the Start menu), Explorer, Windows Calendar, Windows Contacts, Windows Mail, and the Control Panel. Each place that the search tool is exposed places some restriction or "focus" on what areas you can search. For instance, if you are in Explorer and you go to the Search tool, you will be searching within the folder you currently have open. This open folder from which you launched Instant Search becomes the "context" for the search tool: It will search neither beyond that particular folder nor above it. Likewise, with the application-based Search tools, deep searches are enabled in an application-wide focus or context: A search in Contacts provides a search of the Contact database, not of any other folders.

There are obvious reasons why Microsoft placed the Search tool within the bounds of "contexts." Imagine a creative writing student is in her My Documents folder and is looking for a document she had written about a cab driver she met and with whom she had the most interesting conversation. A simple search in My Documents for the text string *cab*, with the new and powerful Instant Search tool, would provide her with results, would it not? You bet! In fact, without any context, it would not only find her Noble Prize-worthy essay, but also tell her that she has instant access to TokenAPI.cab, ACEAgentBrowserPlugin.cab, AdminTool.cab, DefaultHelpFiles.cab, DefaultProgram.cab, ExplorerPlugin.cab, LoginAutomation.cab, NetscapePlugin.cab, a few Excel documents with the string *cab*, and a handful of other unrelated texts. Think we're kidding? Figure 8.25 shows what we get when we run a search on *cab* in the Start Search.

Figure 8.25 Search Results for "Cab" within Start Search

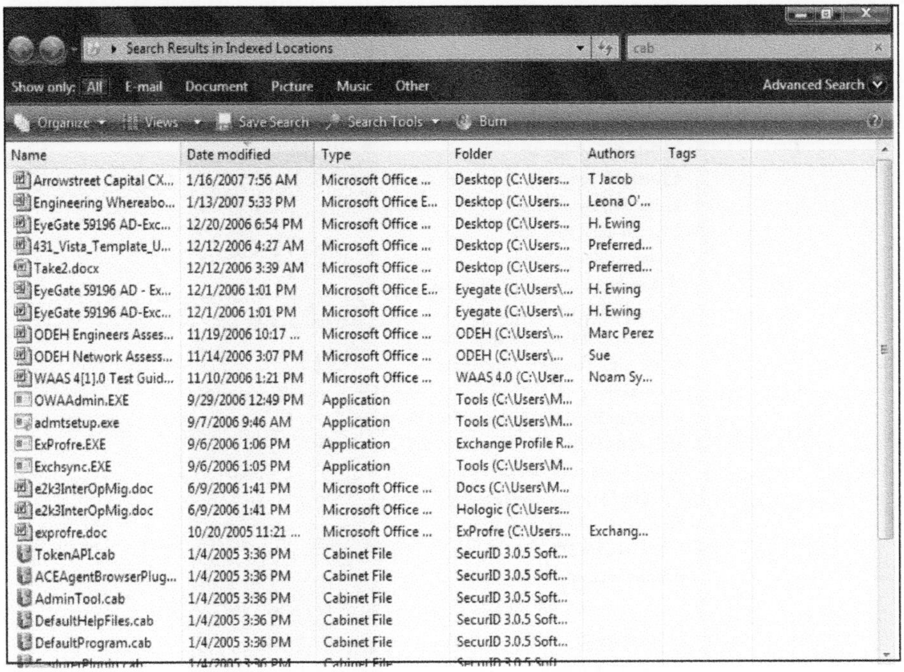

For the sake of usability, Microsoft has to place the Instant Search tool within "contexts." These contexts restrict the scope of the search to a specific "focus." If you search for something within My Documents, you get only data within My Documents.

If you're thinking that the system-wide search is a good thing, fear not; Microsoft thought so too. We derived the search results in Figure 8.25 from a search we ran from the Start Search wheel (see Figure 8.26).

The Start Search box allows you to find literally any file on the system, including e-mails, applications, and documents. The results pane is populated almost immediately after you type the text.

Figure 8.26 The Start Search Wheel

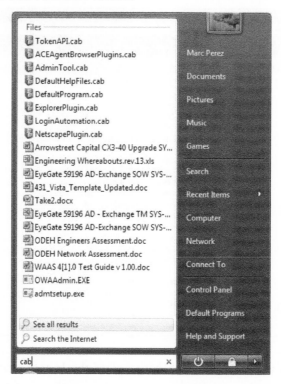

Searching from within Instant Mail

The Mail Search word wheel is always visible and accessible in Windows Mail. It lives in the upper-right corner of the user interface on the same level as the toolbar and is easily identifiable by the icon of a magnifying glass that has become the sign for Search (see Figure 8.27).

Windows Mail places a "focus" on Instant Search that regulates its phenomenal searching power to mail-related items. This is a very good thing. In fact, the flat architecture of Windows Mail's mail database enhances the tool's speed, or better yet, enables its function within the application.

Figure 8.27 The Search Wheel As Seen in the Default Windows Mail View

Because all mail messages are stored as individual files within the file system and certain filter handlers are promoted into JET, Instant Search (using the APIs within Vista) has fast and thorough access to not only message headers, but also ultimately body text. The search is not restricted to one folder within Windows Mail, nor does Instant Search perform its seek-and-find routine one folder at a time (that wouldn't be "instant," would it?). Rather, Instant Search within Windows Mail searches all of your mail at almost the same time. This means you can search for a word or even a phrase in an e-mail and not have to strain your brain for the "most likely folder" of residence for your message. Instead, you simply begin to type your text and let Windows Mail go forth and conquer (see Figure 8.28).

Figure 8.28 Search Results in the Default View of Windows Mail for the Word "Account"

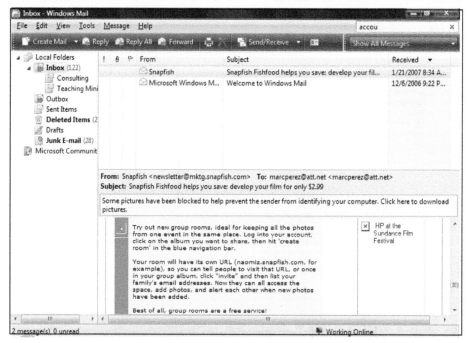

In the example in Figure 8.28, we typed the word *account* into the word wheel. Although we have more than two messages in our Inbox, only two are returned to us. If you're paying attention, you'll observe that the word *account* is nowhere to be found in the header information of either e-mail. Rather, you can find it in the body of the text in both.

You may have noticed that the display of our Inbox has been replaced with the results pane. This is behavior that was also in Outlook's Find utility: Search results were always placed to the forefront of the user interface. Windows Mail now allows you a cool feature to streamline the user experience. To toggle back to our Inbox, we can simply press the **Esc** key. Doing so blanks out the word wheel and represents our Inbox as it was prior to searching. Even better, if we want to quickly switch back to the search and its results, we have only to press the **Esc** key again and then we're back to the window in Figure 8.28.

Searching for Messages outside of Windows Mail

Because the redesigned Outlook Express database for Windows Mail places the actual message files out on the file system, Instant Search can search for and retrieve messages outside of Windows Mail. In fact, Windows Mail doesn't even need to be running for you to search for and even read mail.

Utilizing Start Search, we entered three letters into the Instant Search engine that we knew to be both in e-mails and in a folder. The results were not only instantaneous, but thorough (see Figure 8.29).

Figure 8.29 Mail Results at the Start Search (OS) Level

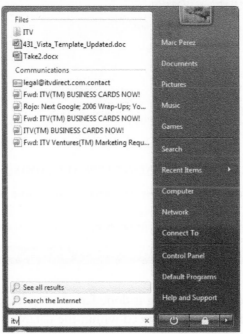

Instant Search displays not only that it found files containing the criteria, but also what type of files they are. It found and identified a folder within My Documents and displayed that for us under the classification of "files." Instant Search also found two e-mails with the search criterion "ITV" in the messages. In one e-mail, the search criterion is clearly in the header of the e-mail. In the other, we don't see the search criterion because it is in the message body. Regardless, Instant Search found it immediately and presents it to us with clear identification.

If you click the messages that Instant Search finds, they open. Now, that may not sound like a great feat, especially if you're used to seeing Outlook Express open automatically every time you accidentally click a link with an @ symbol. However, this is different. If you click a message found in the OS and Windows Mail is closed, the message is displayed … and Windows Mail stays closed (see Figure 8.30).

Figure 8.30 Mail Opened at the OS without the Windows Mail Interface

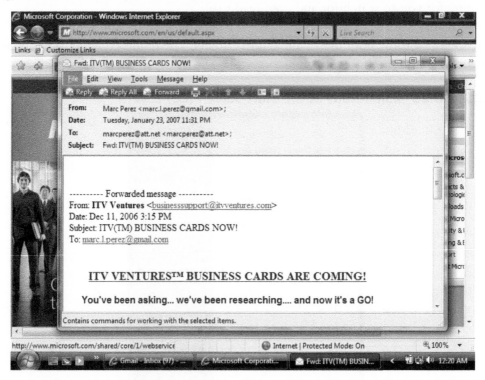

Remember that message rendering is done far more quickly because the data streams for each message are split for speed within the databases and the file system. So, you can read a message in full without launching Windows Mail. Even more, you can actually reply to or forward the message without ever having to open Windows Mail. This results in a faster, more streamlined experience for users who are looking for better performance and fewer application interfaces to deal with as they work.

Summary

If you were an Outlook Express user, you're likely as surprised as we are. Typically, the Microsoft applications related to Office morph and change by degrees. Windows Mail, however, is a completely different animal from its predecessors, one that is unique in ways that go beyond mail handling. The GUI aside, Windows Mail has little in common with Outlook Express. Nearly everything under the hood is either reengineered or completely new, and this time the application is built with security in mind.

If you fear that the new API is so different that there is no backward compatibility, rest easy. The old APIs are still present in the file system and application. This means that calls to the old APIs are received by the old APIs and are then forwarded to the new ones. Ultimately, the new database does all the work, which is ideal, but the old API-driven tools can still serve you and their associated applications. For the network administrator, this may not mean very much, but for application developers, this means code written for Outlook Express plug-ins will work on Windows Mail without much tailoring. Microsoft has provided via TechNet a collection of schema attributes just for this purpose, along with attributes new to Windows Mail so that developers can take advantage of more of the OS-based mail platform while still being confined to the Windows profile-based security structure.

The tight integration with Vista's file system raises some interesting questions. What is the future of messaging applications? Do users need a separate application to handle their mail? Windows Mail raises these heretical and ludicrous ideas as it presents Windows users the first opportunity, via Vista, to access and utilize mail functions without launching a mail application. The utilization of Instant Search and the ability to read and write messages outside of the Windows Mail user interface create a "never before" moment for every user. These functions, along with the enterprise-level Phishing and Junk E-mail filters, elevate this built-in application from the status of an add-on restricted to home users to that of a secure by default enterprise client.

Solutions Fast Track

Comparing Windows Mail with Outlook Express

☑ At its core, Windows Mail runs with a completely different architecture than Outlook Express. Now, all mail files and system resources are a part of the JET database that the Vista OS uses, providing improved performance in Windows-integrated security and redundancy.

☑ The Windows Mail design team moved the account data from the Registry into XML files that are associated with each Inbox in the Windows Mail folder. In addition, "identities" are no longer managed, but mail is regulated to specific Windows profiles. This means that to back up the totality of a user's mail and profile information, all you need to do is copy the Windows Mail folder under that user's profile.

☑ In Vista, e-mail messages and news posts are found and displayed even as the user is typing criteria into the search engine, eliminating the extra actions of initiating a search and then perusing the search results for the appropriate mail content as opposed to only the filename. You can actually open and read messages without starting a separate application.

Phishing Filter

☑ Initially a part of Internet Explorer and the MSN toolbar, the Phishing Filter automatically analyzes URLs presented to and clicked by the user in Windows Vista, and compares them to a local copy of the blacklists maintained at Microsoft.

☑ Windows Mail can take the Phishing Filter service even further by analyzing incoming messages to see not only whether the URLs listed in the body of the message are known for phishing, but also whether the actual links in HTML messages are the same as the URLs displayed to the user.

☑ The Phishing Filter built into Windows Mail is enabled by default.

Junk Mail Filter

☑ The Windows Mail design team has integrated the SmartScreen Junk E-mail filter into Windows Mail.

☑ As in Outlook, the Windows Mail Junk E-mail filter is set to pull filter updates from Microsoft via the Microsoft Update service. In this way, the filter settings in use for Exchange are at work on your local machine from the first use of Windows Mail.

☑ A five-tab options window enables you to fine-tune the Junk E-mail filter to your liking.

Instant Search

- ☑ Instant Search is not an application to be configured or a feature to be enabled by only the technically savvy user. Rather, Microsoft has released Vista with this powerful tool built into the OS.

- ☑ Instant Search is exposed to the user in several places within the OS: Start Search, Search (within the Start menu), Explorer, Windows Calendar, Windows Contacts, Windows Mail, and the Control Panel. Each place that the search tool is exposed places some restriction or "focus" on what areas can be searched.

- ☑ Windows Mail places a "focus" on Instant Search that relegates its phenomenal searching power to mail-related items. Mail and news items are found and displayed as the user types search criteria, allowing for a much more efficient use of "old" or unsorted mail.

Frequently Asked Questions

The following Frequently Asked Questions, answered by the authors of this book, are designed to both measure your understanding of the concepts presented in this chapter and to assist you with real-life implementation of these concepts. To have your questions about this chapter answered by the author, browse to **www.syngress.com/solutions** and click on the **"Ask the Author"** form.

Q: Will upgrading from Outlook Express be possible with Windows Mail?

A: Absolutely. The application is designed with backward compatibility in mind. In fact, many of the old APIs are in use, allowing for a more seamless integration with add-ins and custom applications constructed for use with Outlook Express. Wizard-driven import tools will bring and consolidate mail identities from Outlook Express into mailboxes within Windows profiles.

Q: How is mail kept secure if messages and news posts are now "part of the OS"?

A: By making the messages a part of the OS, Microsoft increased security. With New Technology File System (NTFS) permissions, everything within a user's profile is accessible only to that user (and to the Administrator). To access messages requires logging in "as the user," making a shared kiosk computer a secure source for individuals' mail.

Q: Will users who don't know all about the new security features of Windows Mail have a hindered e-mail experience? Are these really for the technically savvy?

A: Almost all of the new security-focused features within Windows Mail are enabled by default and are at work in the background. The Junk E-mail filter updates itself via Windows Update, and the Phishing Filter manages its searches against the Microsoft blacklists. As such, a less-than-savvy user can maintain a secure environment with little action required of him.

Q: How is mail protected against corruption and loss?

A: Unlike Outlook Express, Windows Mail utilizes the JET database functionality of the OS, which allows it to function with two databases: a primary database and a backup database. If a message is corrupt or lost in one database, the pointers within the OS will direct the OS or application to the other. In addition, the database is fully transactional, making for a robust point-in-time restore solution. If databases are lost, the OS can replay transaction logs to re-create the messages.

Q: How can administrators more efficiently manage the application and its deployment?

A: As with nearly everything built into the OS, Microsoft has continued to refine Group Policy to be able to effect aspects of the products deployed with an OS. With regard to Windows Mail, however, currently only one Group Policy setting is published in TechNet for Windows Mail: "Block attachments that could contain a virus." Aside from actually building an "image" for mass deployment that already has the settings of your choice, this represents the only real option for managing Windows Mail settings via policy at this time.

Q: How does Instant Search compare with Google Desktop search?

A: The Instant Search technology is very similar to that of the Google Desktop or MSN Desktop search products. Depending on how you view it, there is an obvious advantage/disadvantage: The solution is built into applications such as Windows Mail, allowing you to not get every file in the OS matching your criteria, but only files relevant to mail and news, for example. However, if you're someone who wants to be able to access everything from anywhere, you may be frustrated in having to remember which search does what.

Chapter 9

Microsoft Vista: Update and Monitoring Services

Solutions in this chapter:

- **Using Windows Update**

- **Using Windows Server Update Services (WSUS) and Vista**

- **Using Systems Management Server (SMS) and Vista**

- **Using Microsoft Operations Manager (MOM) and Vista**

- **Using Third-Party Tools with Vista**

☑ **Summary**

☑ **Solutions Fast Track**

☑ **Frequently Asked Questions**

Introduction

Regularly updating the applications, operating system (OS), and drivers on your desktop and server systems is an essential part of being a system administrator. If you have ever been in the position of having to administer a large group of desktop and server systems, you know that patch management is one of the most tedious and frustrating pieces to the security puzzle. It is also one of the most important and, unfortunately, overlooked pieces.

We need to be diligent in patching the systems we manage throughout our organization, but individual users also need to make sure they are keeping their home systems up-to-date and secure. Although it seems like we've got all the assets we need to worry about within the walls of our office, those home systems are an important aspect of organizational security, the security of individuals' personal information, and the security of the Internet in general. If those systems are left open to be compromised, a great deal of personal data is at risk. Also, those in charge of the security of an enterprise risk being attacked by home systems. We give the attacker a valuable starting point toward breaking into our work environment if we leave our PC systems at risk. How many of us have a laptop that we bring home from work and plug directly into our home network, and then link back to our work network with a virtual private network (VPN)? If the system at home is compromised, and an attacker is able to start logging passwords used on that machine, the attacker will quickly build a bank of working credentials to use in attacks. We quickly begin to see the importance of keeping our systems patched and why there has been such a push toward building a better software update system.

Microsoft has long held a majority of the market share for desktop OSes, and because of widespread use of its software, it finds itself under constant attack by evildoers and under constant scrutiny from users, administrators, and security research groups. Windows Update was brought into existence to provide an easy way to apply updates, but several problems with the system are now evident. The first problem lies with the home users who should be updating their systems on a regular basis, but in reality rarely check the Windows Update site for patches. The second problem lies with the system administrators who are in the awful position of either setting the system to automatic updates and hoping a patch doesn't incapacitate their users' systems, or spending a lot of manpower to manually update the systems under their control. It took events such as SQL Slammer to expose the flaws in enterprise patch management systems. What good is a security update for a known vulnerability if most of the population doesn't go to the Windows Update Web site to install it?

Notes from the Underground...

A History Lesson

Table 9.1 shows some of the more destructive worms in recent history and the amount of time users and administrators had to patch their systems. We can't decide which is more disheartening—the fact that some of these worms were in the wild in such a short amount of time, or the fact that users had four to six months to patch their systems prior to the release of the worms.

Table 9.1 Destructive Worms

Worm	Worm Public Discovery	Bulletin Date	Days to Patch
Sasser	April 30, 2004	April 13, 2004	17 days
MS Blaster	August 11, 2003	July 16, 2003	26 days
SQL Slammer	January 24, 2003	July 24, 2002	**184 days**
Nimda	September 18, 2001	May 16, 2001	**125 days**
Code Red	July 16, 2001	June 18, 2001	28 days

The landscape of the software update world looks much different from how it looked just a few years ago. We have a refined Windows Update, and now Microsoft Update, which provides automatic updates for products other than the core Windows OS. We also have the very robust Windows Server Update Services (WSUS), which provides central control over the systems in our organization and their software update needs, with the second version of the free software package. Not far off we see a very impressive WSUS 3 that will provide administrators with a very robust, easy-to-use update system that is administered through the familiar (and itself recently updated) Microsoft Management Console (MMC) 3.0. When we look at enterprise-level update and monitoring packages, we see Systems Management Server (SMS), which can provide software updates for Microsoft products and third-party software, as well as provide centralized monitoring of our networked systems. Microsoft Operations Manager (MOM) is a product that is focused on monitoring our data center and other network systems. MOM also allows us to install

Management Packs (MPs) for Microsoft servers and technology as well as third-party devices. The field of third party update packages also continues to grow and mature. ScriptLogic and Altiris both provide a set of modular software products enabling administrators to manage and update their enterprise systems. Ecora also provides a patch management system to go along with their auditing and compliance focused products.

Moving forward even further we look at the System Center line of products that Microsoft is releasing, and we see that these products have become very robust management and monitoring tools for not only a homogeneous Microsoft-based network, but also the real-world, heterogeneous, diverse networks that we actually design and administer. In this chapter, we will look at three System Center offerings, all of which are currently provided as Beta or release candidate-level products. Systems Management Server (SMS) v4, otherwise known as System Center Configuration Manager (SCCM) 2007, is the evolution of SMS v3 and provides enterprises with the ability to monitor, manage, and update their systems. System Center Essentials (SCE) 2007 is provided for the mid-size business as a sort of hybrid between SMS, WSUS 3, and MOM. SCE will provide monitoring, remote management, software updates, and software installation services. MOM has evolved into System Center Operations Manager (SCOM) 2007 and will provide a robust monitoring and management infrastructure for large enterprises. Several other products in the System Center family focus on things such as data protection management and virtual server management.

We will also take a look at one of the third-party enterprise-level management solutions available, Altiris Client Management Suite. Altiris has an incredible software catalog and its products are designed to work well together as well as work in homogeneous environments. Client Management Suite can be seen as a rival to Microsoft's SMS, and it includes very robust, yet easy-to-use software update, software installation, monitoring, and management tools.

Using Windows Update

Microsoft provides the user with a very capable OS update system that is built into the OS, through Windows Update. Using this system to apply patches is like applying kernel patches to a Linux system. The Windows Update system provides updates for the Windows kernel, as well as any number of userland applications that are considered part of the base OS: Internet Explorer, Windows Media Player (WMP), and so on. Windows Update mostly provides security and other critical updates, but new versions of WMP and Internet Explorer are pushed out through the system as well. Microsoft will also push Service Packs (SPs), Update Rollups, and

Feature Packs through the Windows Update system. In addition, we can, if we are so inclined, update signed hardware drivers.

Windows Update has been around for many versions of Windows, but the earlier versions were rarely used by home users and were reserved mostly for use in the corporate world. If a home user's computer had patches applied it was either immediately after the initial install or because an SP was released. SP2 for Windows XP was released and Microsoft began to force Windows Update on all XP users by implementing a notification system to inform users when automatic updates and other security software weren't enabled, as well as notifying users when new updates were available for download or installation.

Windows Update Settings

The Windows Update mechanism in Vista operates very similarly to XP SP2, but with a few differences. Vista will give you a choice of three options during installation. These options not only relate to update settings, but also encompass error reporting, driver installation, and antispyware protection. Table 9.2 is a matrix of the options available, and the ultimate outcome of your choice.

Table 9.2 Security Settings during Windows Vista Installation

Setting	Description
Use recommended settings	Windows will download and install important as well as recommended updates. Windows Defender Anti-Spyware will be enabled and the user will be automatically enrolled in Microsoft SpyNet. Windows will also automatically check for drivers when new hardware devices are installed and, when errors occur, will send error reports to Microsoft and check for solutions online.
Install important updates only	Windows will download and install security and other important updates only.
Ask me later	Neither of the preceding options will be set and automatic updating will be turned off. Windows will ask you what you'd like to do once installation is completed and you have logged in for the first time.

After installation, or on an existing installation, you can change these settings through the Windows Update Control Panel applet, as shown in Figure 9.1.

Figure 9.1 Accessing the Windows Update Control Panel Applet

You can reach the Windows Update Control Panel applet by following these steps:

1. Go to **Start | Control Panel**.

2. Select **Classic View** on the right.

3. Double-click **Windows Update**.

Alternatively, you can reach the Windows Update Control Panel applet through the new Windows Vista Control Panel layout in the Security Center. The new layout is nice, because it groups related items together, such as the security-related items under the Security Center. But using the new layout will add an extra click when you're trying to reach specific items, such as Windows Update. In the end, it becomes a personal choice, but we prefer a more familiar layout with fewer clicks.

You may notice that the Windows Update Control Panel applet is very different from what Windows XP offered. First, you now have access to all aspects of updating from one main screen. In previous versions, the Windows Update Control Panel applet was reserved for one task: to set whether you wanted to use automatic updating and on what schedule you wanted the service to operate. Gone are the days of visiting the Windows Update Web site and dealing with installing ActiveX controls and browser settings in order to apply updates manually. We also gain the ability to view our update history and, possibly the greatest addition of all, uninstall updates.

You can change Windows Update settings by selecting **Change Settings** from the main **Windows Update** screen. You will be presented with the **Change Settings** window (see Figure 9.2), where you'll see familiar automatic update choices.

Figure 9.2 Changing Windows Update Settings

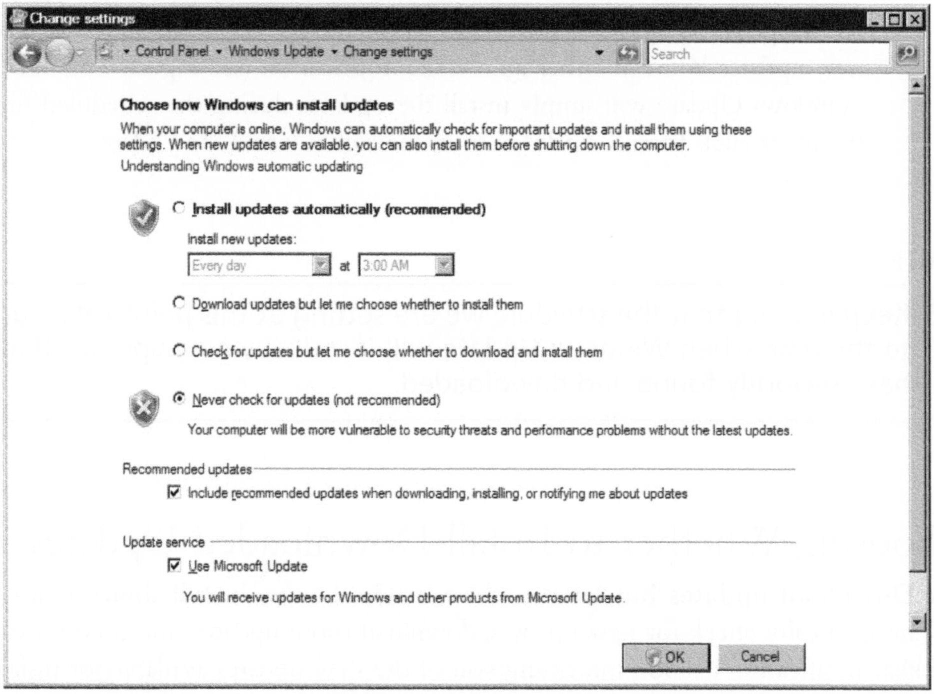

Installing Updates Automatically

The **Install updates automatically (recommended)** option will automatically check for new updates, download those updates that are pertinent to your system, and, according to the schedule you specify, install those updates. To use this option, follow these steps:

1. Select the **Install updates automatically (recommended)** radio button
    (refer to Figure 9.2). The scheduling options will no longer be grayed out.

2. Choose **Every day** at **Specified Time (12 AM to 11 PM)** to install new
    updates every day, or choose **Every (Specific Day)** to install new updates
    only once a week (refer to Figure 9.2).

3. Select the **Include recommended updates when downloading,
    installing, or notifying me about updates** checkbox, under the
    Recommended updates section, if you want recommended updates to
    be included (refer to Figure 9.2).

4. Click **OK**.

5. Click **Continue** on the **User Account Control** dialog box to save the
    settings and return to the main Windows Update screen.

6. At this point, Windows Update will automatically check for and download
    new updates. You can either ignore the notification (see Figure 9.3) and
    Windows Update will simply install the updates during the scheduled time
    frame, or click **Install updates** to immediately install the updates.

NOTE

Keep in mind that the schedule we are setting at this point refers only
to the time when Windows Update will *install* any new updates that it
has previously found and downloaded.

Choosing Whether to Install Downloaded Updates

The **Download updates but let me choose whether to install them** option
will automatically check for new updates, download those updates, and then provide
a taskbar notification balloon informing you of the new updates available for installation. To use this option, follow these steps:

1. Select the **Download updates but let me choose whether to install
    them** radio button (refer to Figure 9.2).

2. Select the **Include recommended updates when downloading,
    installing, or notifying me about updates** checkbox, under the
    Recommended updates section, if you want recommended updates to
    be included (refer to Figure 9.2).

Figure 9.3 Installing or Deferring Updates

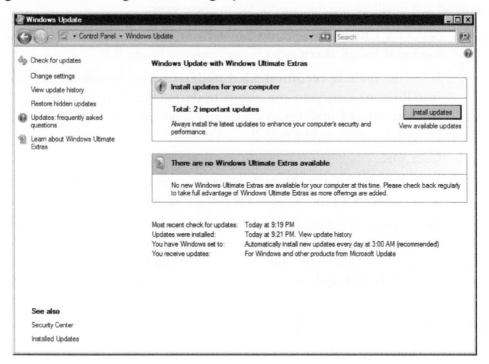

3. Click **OK**.

4. Click **Continue** on the **User Account Control** dialog box to save the settings and return to the main Windows Update screen.

5. At this point, Windows Update will automatically check for and download new updates. You can either ignore the notification (refer to Figure 9.3) and you will receive the taskbar notification balloon until you install the updates, or you can click **Install updates** to immediately install the updates.

Checking for Updates but Choosing Whether to Download and Install Them

The **Check for updates but let me choose whether to download and install them** option will automatically check for new updates and then provide a taskbar notification balloon informing you of the new updates available for installation. This option works in an identical manner to the preceding option, but it provides the benefit of conserving bandwidth until you determine exactly which updates to download and install. To use this option, follow these steps:

1. Select the **Check for updates but let me choose whether to download and install them** radio button (refer to Figure 9.2).

2. Select the **Include recommended updates when downloading, installing, or notifying me about updates** checkbox, under the **Recommended updates** section, if you want recommended updates to be included (refer to Figure 9.2).

3. Click **OK**.

4. Click **Continue** on the **User Account Control** dialog box to save the settings and return to the main Windows Update screen.

5. At this point, Windows Update will automatically check for new updates. You can either ignore the notification (refer to Figure 9.3) and you will receive the taskbar notification balloon until you install the updates, or you can click **Install updates** to immediately install the updates.

Never Checking for Updates

The **Never check for updates (not recommended)** option will turn off all Windows Update automatic features and allow the user to manually check, download, and install new updates. Microsoft lists this choice as "not recommended," and it is correct in labeling it as such for the majority of users. There will always be exceptions, though, and through this option any user can choose to manually manage her updates through Windows Update, or use some other Microsoft-based or third-party update service. If you do choose this option, you will receive a rather persistent notification from the Windows Security Center. To disable the notification, follow these steps:

1. Click on the **Security Center** taskbar icon or go to **Start | Control Panel | Classic View | Security Center**.

2. Click **Change the way security center alerts me**.

3. Choose from one of these two options: **Don't notify me, but display the icon** or **Don't notify me and don't display the icon (not recommended)**.

Using Microsoft Update

Microsoft Update is the expanded software update service from Microsoft that encompasses many of its product lines and server technologies. It works identically to Windows Update and is actually just a simple update to the Windows Update mechanism. We have not been able to find a good answer as to why Microsoft is "marketing" Microsoft Update as something entirely new instead of rolling it out as an update to the Windows Update service. All in all, the Microsoft Update service is a welcome enhancement and we tend to use it on all our systems, including servers. Microsoft Update can provide updates for the following Microsoft products in addition to the Windows OS family:

- Microsoft SQL Server 2000 and later
- Microsoft Exchange Server 2000 and later
- Microsoft Visual Studio
- Microsoft Internet Security and Acceleration Server
- Microsoft Data Protection Manager
- Microsoft Office System XP and later
- Windows Defender
- MSN

Installing Microsoft Update

After installing Microsoft Update, you will be able to utilize the new features and receive updates for the previously mentioned Microsoft products, all through the Windows Update Control Panel applet. To install Microsoft Update, follow these steps:

1. Click **Get updates for more products** on the main **Windows Update** applet screen. This will open Internet Explorer, displaying the Windows Vista-specific Microsoft Update installation Web page.

2. Select **I accept the Terms of Use** and click **Install**.

3. Click **Continue** on the **User Account Control** dialog box.

4. Once the installation is complete, a Web page instructing you to "use your Start menu to check for updates" and confirming the successful installation of Microsoft Updates with a large green check is displayed.

Enabling and Disabling Microsoft Update

If you decide at some point to disable or reenable Microsoft Update features, Windows Vista greatly improves on the options you had in previous versions of Windows. Here's how to enable and disable Microsoft Update:

1. Go to **Start | Control Panel | Classic View | Windows Update**.

2. Click **Change Settings**.

3. Under the **Update service** heading (refer to Figure 9.2), select or deselect the **Use Microsoft Update** checkbox.

4. Click **OK**.

5. Click **Continue** on the **User Account Control** dialog box to save the settings and return to the main Windows Update screen.

Managing Updates

Windows Update has provided us the ability to see our update history, view update details, hide and unhide certain unwanted updates, and read about methods to uninstall problematic updates. However, it has suffered from a few critical drawbacks associated with being served as a Web application from the Microsoft site. Windows Vista has all of these same functions available to the user, but as we have seen, it takes the entire Windows Update service and integrates it into the Control Panel. This seems trivial at first, but the bonuses to this are that we don't need to rely on Internet Explorer to get updates, there is no need to install ActiveX controls, and we do not need to worry about users getting tricked into going to a spoofed Windows Update Web site.

Checking for Updates

Checking for updates is as easy as navigating to the **Windows Update Control Panel** applet and clicking **Check for updates**. You will see a status bar and the system will inform you that it is checking for available updates. Once Windows Update is done checking for updates, it will ask you to download and install the updates that are pertinent to your system (see Figure 9.4).

Figure 9.4 Checking and Installing New Updates

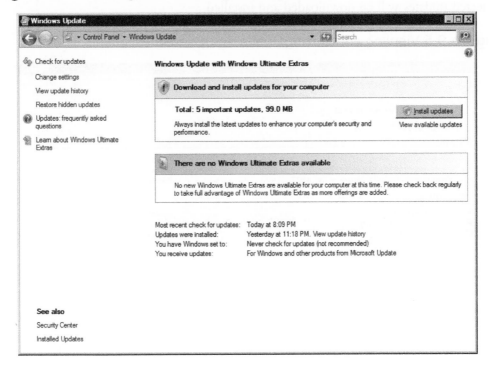

Installing Updates

At this time, you can simply accept that Windows Update knows best and click **Install updates**, or you can delve a little deeper to make choices about the updates available by clicking **View available updates**. The **View available updates** screen (see Figure 9.5) shows you what updates are currently available for your system. At the time of this writing, only three updates were available, but as time passes more and more updates will inevitably become available and new installs of Vista will begin to require quite a few updates to be patched properly.

In our example, we have handy filter options that work just like any other Windows Explorer-based mechanism. Updates are initially grouped and sorted by the name of the program or system component to which the update is related. Clicking the **Type** heading will sort the updates according to their classification: Important, Recommended, and so on. Clicking the **Published** heading will sort the updates by the date that Microsoft published them. Toggling the checkbox in the header will select or deselect all the updates at once. Toggling the individual check-boxes next to each update will let the user choose which updates to install. Clicking

Install at this point will return you to the main Windows Update screen and the selected updates will be downloaded and installed.

Figure 9.5 Viewing and Sorting Available Updates

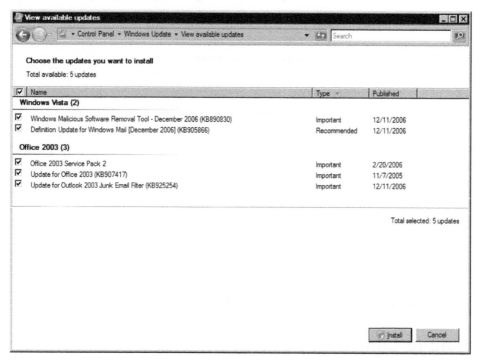

The **View available updates** screen also allows you to view the details of an update by right-clicking and choosing **View Details**. The **Windows Update Details** dialog box shows information about the specific update, such as size, type, description, Microsoft Knowledge Base code, a link to an informational Web page, and a link to a help and support Web page that is specific to that update (see Figure 9.6).

Figure 9.6 Viewing Update Details

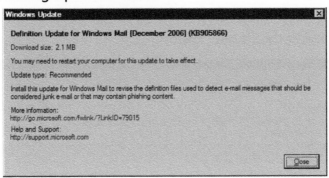

You can also hide unwanted updates by right-clicking on the specific update and choosing **Hide update**. The update will then be deselected and grayed out. The update will also no longer appear in the list of available updates when checking for updates.

Viewing the Update History

Viewing your update history may be valuable, although in the current implementation, it has limited usefulness. It is useful to see a history of what updates were installed and when they were applied, however. For instance, if your network is attacked and a system is compromised, you would want to search for other internal systems that may have been compromised if the first system was used as the staging area for further attacks. The problem is that a lot of exploits are available for an attacker to use. How do you efficiently search for evidence of an exploit?

One way to narrow your search is to check your list of known exploits against your update history to see which ones you can eliminate because the patch for that exploit was applied prior to the system compromise. This sounds great in theory, and it will work in most instances, but it seems that Vista does not update your history when an update is uninstalled from the system. The only other things you can do from this window are sort updates and view the details of an update, which you can do by following these steps:

1. Go to **Start | Control Panel | Classic View | Windows Update**.

2. Click **View update history**.

3. Click **Installed Updates** to uninstall an update, click **Name**, **Status**, **Type**, and **Date Installed** to sort the list of updates by attribute, or right-click on the specific update and choose **View Details** to access the details dialog for that update (see Figure 9.7).

4.   Click **OK** to return to the main Windows Update screen.

Figure 9.7 Viewing the Update History

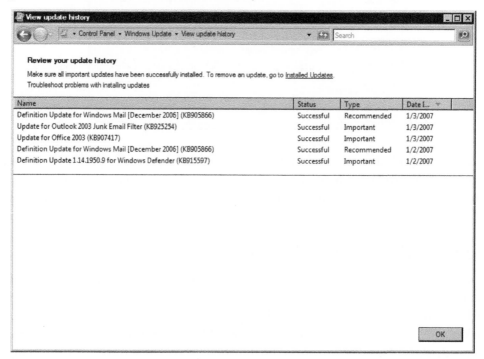

Restoring Hidden Updates

If you have previously hidden certain updates for your system that you later decide to install, you will need to restore those previously hidden updates. To do so, follow these steps:

1.   Go to **Start | Control Panel | Classic View | Windows Update**.

2.   Click **Restore hidden updates**.

3.   Select the checkboxes next to the updates you want to restore, or select the checkbox in the header to select all the updates (see Figure 9.8).

4.   Click **Restore** and then click **Continue** on the **User Account Control** pop-up dialog box. This will return you to the main Windows Update Control Panel applet screen and automatically trigger the system to check for new updates.

Figure 9.8 Restoring Hidden Updates

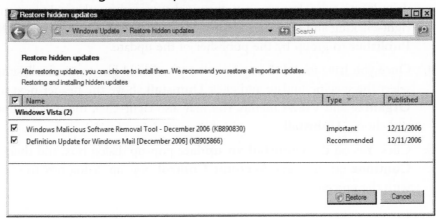

Uninstalling Updates

We have all been in the situation where we need to uninstall a previously installed update, and if you haven't been in that position and you work in IT, you will most likely run into that situation at some point. In previous versions of Windows, the updates were placed under Add and Remove Programs in the Control Panel. Windows Vista separates the user-installed programs and the installed updates for easier viewing and manageability. Vista also makes the Installed Programs and Installed Updates screens part of the new Windows Explorer interface (see Figure 9.9), which means that you get familiar file-sorting and searching functionality. The Installed Updates screen also has a customized header which allows for quick sorting by name, related program, publisher, and when the update was installed. You can also customize the header to show any number of update-specific attributes, such as the update ID and update info link. To uninstall updates, follow these steps:

1. Go to **Start | Control Panel | Classic View | Windows Update**.

2. Click **Installed updates** in the bottom left-hand corner of the main **Windows Update Control Panel** applet, under the heading **See also**. This will display the **Installed Updates** screen, which you can also reach through **Start | Control Panel | Classic View | Programs and Features | Uninstall an update**.

3. At this point, you can customize the header and list additional attributes, or you can sort the list of installed updates by clicking any of the attributes listed on the header. You can also right-click in the **Installed Updates** window to bring up a menu allowing you to change how the items are

viewed, sorted, and grouped. The default grouping for updates is to group them by program, but you can change that to a chronological grouping by right-clicking and choosing **Group By | Installed On**, or **Group By | Publisher** to group by the publisher of the update.

4. Once you have found the update that you would like to uninstall, simply select the specific update and click **Uninstall** above the header next to the **Organize** and **Views** menus. You may also right-click the specific update and choose **Uninstall**.

5. Click **Yes** on the **Uninstall an update** pop-up dialog box, and then click **Continue** on the **User Account Control** pop-up dialog box to continue with the process.

Tools & Traps...

Uninstall What Now?

During our use and testing of Windows Vista, we found that the Installed Updates window shows only certain updates. At first, when we did some preliminary research, we thought that maybe only updates marked as Recommended (in other words, updates not marked Important) would show up and be available for us to uninstall. (This, after all, makes a bit of sense. You've got people to patch; you shouldn't give them or an attacker the ability to uninstall updates that patch security holes. If they really need to, they can roll the system back using a restore point.) After further testing, we found that important updates available for Office 2003 would show up in the Installed Updates screen, so we thought that maybe the important Office 2003 updates were available for uninstall because they were attached to a user program and not to the base OS itself. That theory also failed after we right-clicked on one of the Office 2003 updates (Update for Office 2003: KB907417) and didn't receive any right-click menu. The Uninstall button also did not appear when we highlighted the update. We could uninstall the other available update for Office 2003 (Update for Outlook 2003: Junk E-mail Filter KB925254). At that point, we decided to accept the fact that some updates can be uninstalled and some can't, and that the criteria that are used to make this decision are not available to the user.

Continued

Remember, not all updates will be available for a simple uninstall from the Installed Updates screen, and even some updates that show on the Installed Updates screen will not be able to be uninstalled. In order to remove an update that you can't uninstall from the Installed Updates screen, you will have to refer to the update history to see when the update was installed and roll the system back using a system restore point. The unfortunate outcome of having to use the system restore point is obviously that any other changes made between the installation of that update and when you roll the system back will be lost.

Figure 9.9 Uninstalling Updates

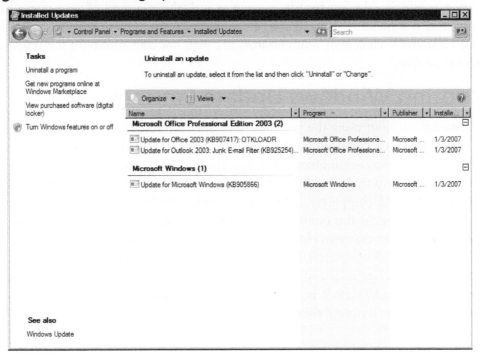

Microsoft releases scheduled patches on the second Tuesday of every month, although it has been known to skip a scheduled patch day in the past. Microsoft will also rarely release extremely critical patches on-the-fly, so to speak. The reality of patching is that most users will choose one of the initial security settings (refer to Table 9.1) during installation, or leave the setting as the factory-installed default and never think about the security of their system again. Because the default setting is usually the Microsoft recommended setting that may be sufficient for most home users. However, for some home users, and for systems in a corporate environment, this may not be the be-all and end-all of software update services. A lot of users will simply choose **Install important updates only**, which means they will only receive security updates and other important updates. This setting sounds like a valid choice, especially from the perspective of this book, because after all, we are talking about security and Windows Vista. Unfortunately, this fails to take into account other Microsoft products and their security updates. Microsoft Office and other Microsoft-produced applications are not included in the default update process without first installing Microsoft Update, and third-party user applications aren't included without a completely separate update service. Windows Update, Microsoft Update, and Windows Vista go a long way toward increasing the security of work and home systems alike, but security awareness and taking control of your own security posture is something that can't be forced. Unfortunately, there will always be home users and even system administrators that will not take control of the systems under their care.

Scripting Windows Update Settings

We have talked about using the graphical user interface (GUI) tools in Vista to control Windows Update, and although using these tools will work for home users, administrators in very small offices, and masochistic administrators in large organizations, they really won't work for the majority of system administrators in offices with more than 10 or 15 computers, unless they are using the "set and forget" method of automatic updating. At this point, our advice is to get WSUS up and running and control your system that way. However, maybe your office is sitting on that threshold—10 to 15 computers, but no spare servers—or maybe you have outsourced all your server roles and don't even have an old computer somewhere that you can use to run WSUS. Who knows, maybe you're one of those administrators that just really likes scripting everything.

TIP

Great primers for Windows scripting and scripting Windows Update are Tales from the Script, by The Scripting Guys on Microsoft TechNet (www.microsoft.com/technet/community/columns/scripts/default.mspx), and the Script Center Script Repository (www.microsoft.com/technet/scriptcenter/scripts/default.mspx?mfr=true). You can find more information on the Windows Update Agent API on MSDN (http://msdn2.microsoft.com/en-us/library/aa387099.aspx).

Tales from the Script gives a good run-down of common tasks that you, as an administrator, would want to accomplish. We will look at and expand on a few of those scripts. First, we want to take a look at changing Windows Update settings. The unfortunate reality of scripting Windows Update is that a lot of these scripts cannot be run against a machine remotely. This means that you can run a lot of the functionality that you would want to run on a machine only if you are logged onto that machine. For example, if we wanted to determine whether the Automatic Updates service was installed, we could do that remotely, but if we wanted to determine what the Automatic Updates notification level was, we would have to run the script locally. You can create the script and have it run upon logon via Group Policy, but all that does is report the notification level on the screen. These scripts can also be useful when first setting up a machine, or when you find that a user with too many privileges has gone in and changed these settings, and you would like to return to the correct settings with one command.

Enabling and Scheduling Automatic Updates

First, we want to enable automatic updates:

```
Set objAutoUpdate = CreateObject("Microsoft.Update.AutoUpdate")
Set objSettings = objAutoUpdate.Settings
objSettings.NotificationLevel = 4
objSettings.Save
```

The value of *objSettings.NotificationLevel* is set to the notification level that you want to use, and it maps directly to the settings shown on the **Change Settings** screen (refer to Figure 9.2). Those settings are as follows:

- **1** Never check for Updates. Automatic Update is essentially disabled.
- **2** Check for updates, but let me choose whether to download and install them.
- **3** Download updates, but let me choose whether to install them.
- **4** Install updates automatically. This installs updates per the user-defined schedule.

Using that script by itself will allow you to determine what level of automation and required user interaction you want, and it will let you set it via the command line. If you choose a notification level of 4, you can either accept the default schedule, or set a schedule that you choose using the following script:

```
Set objAutoUpdate = CreateObject("Microsoft.Update.AutoUpdate")
```

```
Set objSettings = objAutoUpdate.Settings
objSettings.ScheduledInstallationDay = 4
objSettings.ScheduledInstallationTime = 2
objSettings.Save
```

The value of *objSettings.ScheduledInstallationDay* is set to the day you want installations to occur every week, and it maps directly to the schedule settings shown on the **Change Settings** screen (refer to Figure 9.2). Those settings are as follows:

- **0** Every day.

- **1** Sunday.

- **2** Monday.

- **3** Tuesday.

- **4** Wednesday.

- **5** Thursday.

- **6** Friday.

- **7** Saturday.

The value of *objSettings.ScheduledInstallationTime* is set to the hour during the day that you want installations to occur, and again it maps directly to the schedule settings shown on the **Change Settings** screen (refer to Figure 9.2). A value of 0 represents 12:00 AM, 1 represents 1:00 AM, and 23 represents 11:00 PM.

Finally, we can combine these snippets of code into a finished script that, when run from the local machine, will set the machine to automatically download and install updates every Wednesday at 2:00 AM (see Figure 9.10). In the figure, the *NOTIFICATION_SETTING* constant is the *NotificationLevel* you want to set. You can alter the *EVERY_WEDNESDAY* and *TWO_AM* constants to suit your desired installation day and time.

Figure 9.10 Setting Automatic Update Notifications and Schedule

```
Const NOTIFICATION_SETTING = 4
Const EVERY_WEDNESDAY = 4
Const TWO_AM = 2
Set objAutoUpdate = CreateObject("Microsoft.Update.AutoUpdate")
Set objSettings = objAutoUpdate.Settings
objSettings.NotificationLevel = NOTIFICATION_SETTING
objSettings.ScheduledInstallationDay = EVERY_WEDNESDAY
```

```
objSettings.ScheduledInstallationTime = TWO_AM
objSettings.Save
```

Opt In to Microsoft Update

Now we want to set the computer to use Microsoft Update. If we were doing this on a Windows 2003 or Windows XP machine, we would first want to determine that the current version of the Windows Update Agent (WUA) was 5.8.0.2469 or later. Because we are doing this on Windows Vista, we don't need to deal with determining the WUA version, as the default version of WUA already meets that requirement. To opt in to Microsoft Update we need to have muauth.cab downloaded and stored in an accessible location.

> **NOTE**
>
> You can download the muauth.cab file from http://download.windowsupdate.com/v6/windowsupdate/redist/standalone/muauth.cab.

Next, we run our opt-in script:

```
Set ServiceManager = CreateObject("Microsoft.Update.ServiceManager")
Set NewUpdateService = ServiceManager.AddService("7971f918-a847-4430-9279-
4a52d1efe18d", "C:\muauth.cab")
ServiceManager.RegisterServiceWithAU "7971f918-a847-4430-9279-4a52d1efe18d"
```

Again, it's easy to integrate this last code snippet into the script in Figure 9.10, place the script and muauth.cab file on a flash drive, network share, or other accessible location, and then run it as needed.

You can do a lot more with WUA through scripting, but much of what you can do is beyond the scope of this book; searching, downloading, and installing updates, updating the WUA, uninstalling individual updates, and viewing update history are a few of the many tasks you can script through this interface.

Using Windows Server Update Services (WSUS) and Vista

Microsoft released Software Update Services (SUS) 1.0 in 2003 to the delight of many in the Windows IT world. SUS gave us the ability to have a central update server controlling the automatic update behavior of clients, and to conserve a lot of bandwidth by effectively acting as a mirror of the content on the Windows Update site. It also had many shortcomings; first, it had no reporting or inventory, and second, you needed to run the Microsoft Baseline Security Analyzer to see what updates were needed on which machines before you could approve those updates on the SUS server. SUS also lacked the capability to update anything other than the Windows OS.

Windows Server Update Services 2

In early 2005, Microsoft released the much-anticipated second version of SUS, rebranded as Windows Server Update Services (WSUS) 2. WSUS 2 made up for many of the shortcomings of SUS by adding a reporting and inventory mechanism that allows you to see what updates computers need or already have installed. It also added the ability to use Microsoft Update to integrate updating for many of the products in the Microsoft line, including Office, Exchange, and SQL Server, to name a few. Today WSUS 2 includes the ability to provide updates for the following products:

- Exchange 2000, 2003, 2007, and 2007 Anti-Spam

- Forefront Client Security

- Internet Security and Acceleration Server 2004, 2006, and the Firewall Client for ISA Server

- Microsoft Core XML Services

- Microsoft System Center Data Protection Manager 2006

- Office 2002/XP and 2003

- SQL Server 2000 and 2005

- System Management Server 2003

- Visual Studio 2005

- Windows Live Mail Desktop and Windows Live Toolbar

- Windows Defender

- Windows 2000

- Windows Small Business Server 2003

- Windows 2003 x64, x86, and Itanium versions of Standard, Enterprise, and Datacenter Editions

- Windows XP x64 and x86

- Windows Vista, Vista Dynamic Installer, Vista Ultimate Language Packs, and Ultimate Extras

SP1 for WSUS 2 was released in July 2006 and includes the ability to use SQL Server 2005 as the database backend, as well as support for Vista.

The mechanism that WSUS 2 uses for updating on the client is the Windows Automatic Update (AU) client, and although it works almost identically to Windows Update and Microsoft Update, it is a different product. AU utilizes the Background Intelligent Transfer Service (BITS) 2.0 to go up to the WSUS server to which the client has been directed, and download the updates that the administrator has approved through the WSUS administration Web site.

Bandwidth conservation is an important part of the benefits WSUS provides to an organization. WSUS acts as a concentrator for the Windows Update service; the local WSUS server synchronizes to the WSUS update servers on the Internet and retrieves the update metadata information for the products and classifications that you have set. During this synchronization, WSUS pulls only the necessary metadata for an update and then later uses that metadata to determine the status of that update on each system that has reported to it. WSUS downloads and stores only a local copy of the updates that are needed. Those updates are then offered to the systems that contact the server through the AU mechanism, and each update that has been approved for installation is then downloaded from the local repository and installed. Considering that WSUS can support thousands of clients in an organization, the bandwidth conservation benefit becomes very obvious. Do you want 1,000 client machines downloading 150 MB of updates over a slower wide area network (WAN) line, or over a 100 MB or 1,000 MB local area network (LAN) connection?

WSUS is flexible in how it can be deployed, it does not require that the Active Directory schema be extended, nor does it require Active Directory at all. Furthermore, you can manage the client settings using a local Group Policy Object, the Registry, or an Active Directory Group Policy Object. We will discuss the different possibilities for managing the client AU settings in the following sections.

TIP

We will not be discussing WSUS deployment in this book. You can find ample documentation on WSUS deployment in the following sources:

www.wsuswiki.com
http://blogs.technet.com/wsus
http://technet2.microsoft.com/windowsserver/en/technologies/featured/wsus/default.mspx

http://technet2.microsoft.com/WindowsServer/en/library/29733254
-b3e2-43d6-aaa6-4ba5df50e9611033.mspx?mfr=true
www.microsoft.com/windowsserversystem/updateservices/default.
mspx
How to Cheat at Managing Windows Server Update Services
(Syngress Publishing, 2005)

WSUS 2 Stand-Alone Installation

If you are using WSUS 2 for your update service needs currently and you want to add several Windows Vista machines to your organization, you need to make sure that you have SP1 for WSUS 2 installed. If you are starting from scratch or you plan to move to WSUS 2 for your update needs, logically you should be installing WSUS 2 with SP1 from the outset. SP1 for WSUS 2 added support for Windows Vista, bundled the latest version of Microsoft SQL Server 2000 Desktop Engine: Windows (WMSDE), and added support for using SQL Server 2005.

Once your WSUS infrastructure is in place, all you need to do is use a local Group Policy Object or edit the Registry settings on the Windows Vista machine so that it will direct the machine to the WSUS server. Editing the local Group Policy Object is the preferred method for most users in this situation, but you can also edit the settings through the Registry.

Controlling WSUS Settings through Local Group Policy

We will be covering local Group Policy before delving into the Registry settings because the Registry key is created when the client machine contacts the local WSUS server for the first time and downloads and installs the AU client. The settings are located in *Local Group Policy/Computer Configuration/Administrative Templates/Windows Components/Windows Update.* To control WSUS settings through local Group Policy, follow these steps:

1. Go to **Start | Run**, enter **gpedit.msc** in the box, and press **Enter**.

2. Go to **Computer Configuration | Administrative Templates | Windows Components**.

3. Go to **Windows Update**.

4. Select the **Specify intranet Microsoft update service location Properties** policy setting, and specify the location of your WSUS server (e.g., http://util1:8530 for both values).

NOTE

If your WSUS server is installed on the default IIS Web site, you don't need to specify a port number. However, if WSUS was installed on anything other than the default IIS Web site, you must specify the port number in both values.

5. Next, select the **Configure Automatic Updates** policy setting and specify the type of automatic updating you desire. Remember to set the installation schedule if you choose **4 – Auto download and schedule the install**.

These are the only settings necessary to configure Windows Vista to operate with a WSUS server, but many other settings are available. Table 9.3 lists a few of these values and the effect they have on the AU client.

Table 9.3 Windows Update Group Policy Settings

Setting	Description	Enabled	Disabled
Configure Automatic Updates	This setting directly relates to the four available settings on the Windows Update Change Settings window (refer to Figure 9.2). It specifies whether the computer will use the AU mechanism to receive security and other important updates, how the user will be notified if updates are found, and, if the updates are set to be automatically installed, when the installation will take place.	When enabled, AU will check for updates every 22 hours. You will also need to set one of the following four choices: 2 – *Notify for download and notify for install.* 3 – *Auto download and notify for install.* 4 – *Auto download and schedule install.* 5 – *Allow local admin to choose setting.* If you choose option 4, you must set *Scheduled install day* and *Scheduled install time* to the desired installation schedule.	This is equivalent to disabling AU from the Windows Update Change Settings screen (refer to Figure 9.2).
Specify intranet Microsoft update service location	This setting allows the administrator to specify the location of a WSUS server on the internal network. The AU client will contact this server to locate updates. This setting requires two server name values: The first is the server from which the AU client retrieves updates, and the second is the server to which the AU client reports update statistics.	This setting, when enabled, requires that you set two values. The first is *Set the intranet update service for detecting updates*, and the second is *Set the intranet statistics server.* The format for these settings is *http:// servername*, and you must set both settings to the same value for them to be valid.	The AU client will connect directly to the Windows Update site on the Internet.

Continued

Table 9.3 continued Windows Update Group Policy Settings

Setting	Description	Enabled	Disabled
Enable client-side targeting	This setting allows the administrator to specify the name of a computer group for this machine. This setting takes effect only when an intranet WSUS server is specified and the server is set to enable client-side targeting.	The *Target group name for this computer* value specifies the target group information that is sent to the WSUS server.	When this is set to Disabled or Not Configured, no target group information will be sent and the machine will be placed in the *Unassigned Computers* group.
Allow non-administrators to receive update notifications	This setting allows an administrator to specify whether nonadministrative users will receive update notifications.	AU will send notifications to nonadministrative users if they are logged on to the machine. This setting is useful because in most environments, you don't want to allow standard users to have administrative privileges, but if you have configured AU to notify before download or installation, the AU client cannot proceed with update download or installation until an administrative user logs on to the machine.	The AU client will notify only logged-on administrative users. This also applies when set to *Not Configured*.
Automatic Updates detection frequency	This setting specifies the duration of time that Windows will wait before checking for available updates. The wait time is determined by taking the value set and subtracting zero percent to 20 percent of the hours specified.	Windows will check for available updates using the specified wait time.	Windows will check for available updates using the default wait time, which is 22 hours.

Continued

Table 9.3 continued Windows Update Group Policy Settings

Setting	Description	Enabled	Disabled
Turn on recommended updates via Automatic Updates (Vista Only)	This setting is specific to Windows Vista Group Policy and specifies whether the AU client will deliver both important and recommended updates.	The AU client will install recommended as well as important updates. This is equivalent to the Recommended Updates checkbox available on the Windows Update Change Settings screen.	The AU client will no longer deliver recommended updates.
Enabling Windows Update Power Management to automatically wake up the system to install scheduled updates (Vista Only)	This setting allows the user to specify whether Windows Update will use Windows Power Management features to wake the system from hibernation to install scheduled updates.	Windows will automatically wake the system if it is configured to automatically install updates and the system is in hibernation during the scheduled install time and updates are available. The system will also wake up if an install deadline occurs. The system will wake up from hibernation only if there are updates to install. If the system is on battery power, no updates will be installed and the system will automatically return to hibernation in 2 minutes.	If this is set to Disabled or Not Configured, Windows will not use the Windows Power Management feature to wake the system.

Tools & Traps…

Incorporating Vista Policy
Settings in a Windows 2003 Domain

The two "Vista Only" policy settings in Table 9.3 are new to Vista and do not have any effect on other versions of Windows. If you would like to control these settings through a domain Group Policy Object, you will either need to wait for Windows Server 2007 (codenamed Longhorn) to be released so that you can simply copy the new .ADMX policy template from Vista to Longhorn and load it into your domain Group Policy Object, or create a custom .ADM policy template and load it into the Group Policy Object on your existing domain controller. We have created a .ADM file named wuau2.ADM and have included it on the accompanying CD for your use. To use the new .ADM file, follow these steps:

1. Copy **wuau2.ADM** to an accessible location on your domain controller.

2. Go to **Start | Administrative Tools | Active Directory Users and Computers**.

3. Right-click on your domain **contoso.org** and select **Properties**.

4. Click the **Group Policy** tab and select your **WSUS GPO**. Ours is aptly named WSUS. You are using a separate Group Policy Object that holds only Windows Update policy settings and not the Default Domain Policy; aren't you?

5. Click **Edit**. This will open the **Group Policy Object Editor**.

6. Right-click on **Administrative Templates** under the **Computer Configuration** section. Click **Add/Remove templates**. This will open the **Add/Remove templates** dialog box.

7. Select **wuau** and click **Remove**. This will remove the old wuau.adm file so that you don't have duplicate policy settings listed.

8. Click **Add** and browse to where you put the wuau2.ADM file on your domain controller. Double-click **wuau2.ADM**.

9. Click **Close**. This will load the template. Now you can browse to **Administrative Templates | Windows Components | Windows Update** to view and edit the new policy settings.

Controlling WSUS Settings through the Registry

If you want to drill down as far as possible when it comes to setting up WSUS, editing the Registry is probably the most fine-grained method. Editing the registry is also the most dangerous and cryptic, so you'll need to refer to the TechNet resources available at the link at the end of this section. These resources break down most of the keys and their values for you so that when you do mess with your Registry, you will know what you're doing.

Once you have pointed the AU client at your WSUS server, you will find a newly created Registry key at *HKEY_LOCAL_MACHINE\Software\Policies\Microsoft\Windows\WindowsUpdate*. At this point, do the following:

1. Go to **Start | Run**, enter **regedit** in the box, and press **Enter**.

2. Go to the **WindowsUpdate** Registry key.

Many settings are available, all of which match up to the Group Policy settings. You can find a full description of the Registry settings on Microsoft's TechNet Web site, at http://technet2.microsoft.com/WindowsServer/en/library/75ee9da8-0ffd-400c-b722-aeafdb68ceb31033.mspx?pf=true.

WSUS 2 Active Directory Integration

WSUS operations are the same regardless of whether you are using WSUS in a stand-alone configuration or in an Active Directory environment. The only differences concern where the administration of the service takes place. When we operate in an Active Directory environment, the client computers can be members of either the domain or a workgroup. If the client is a member of the Active Directory domain, we begin to see the advantages that running WSUS in an Active Directory environment brings us over simply using local Group Policy or Registry settings to administer the AU client.

When we set up a Group Policy Object on the domain controller, we simply specify the same settings we specified in the local Group Policy. There is no difference in the settings; the domain Group Policy Object simply overrides the local Group Policy Object. Why, then, is a domain Group Policy Object better than a local Group Policy Object? When we use a domain Group Policy Object, the settings are applied to all the machines in the scope of that Group Policy Object, and there is no need for us to perform the repetitive task of traveling to each machine to set its local Group Policy Object.

Targeting Updates via Group Policy

We mentioned the scope of a Group Policy Object; this is an important and valuable tool when we have decided to target certain updates to specific computers or groups. An example of this would be if we put different machines in different organizational units (OUs) in our Active Directory and then applied specific Group Policy Objects to each OU. For instance, if we had a group of lab computers set up, we could put them in a separate computer group on our WSUS server by enabling **Client-side targeting** on the server and in the Group Policy Object. Then we would set a different value for **Target group name for this computer** for our lab computers than what we would set for our production computers. We can also separate our servers from our end-user machines this way.

We can even direct a certain group of computers to an entirely different WSUS server. This is helpful in larger environments where computers are geographically separated or where we have a large number of clients and want to spread out the workload among different servers.

Administering WSUS

We have our WSUS server set up and our clients configured to use that server for their updating needs. Now we need to look at the WSUS Web administration interface, where we will approve and deny updates for our newly added Windows Vista clients. To reach the WSUS administration Web site, in your Web browser go to http://servername:port/WSUSAdmin. For example, in our domain we would go to http://util1:8530/WSUSAdmin to reach the administration site.

From the main administration page, we can see the status of our WSUS server, the last time it synchronized with the Microsoft Update Internet servers, the number of updates, the number of approved, not approved, and declined updates, and some basic reporting about the number of updates needed by computers. We can also initiate a manual synchronization from this page, and perform many common administrative tasks (see Figure 9.11).

Figure 9.11 WSUS Administration Site Home Page

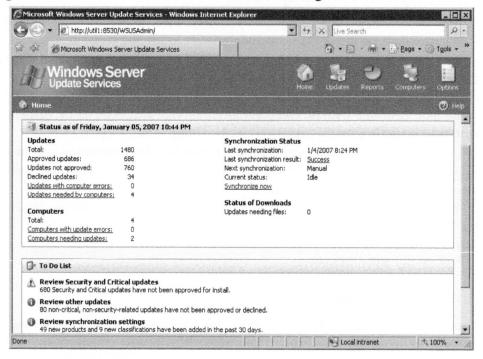

Managing Updates

As you can see, we have two computers that need updates, one of those being the Vista machine that we just added to our domain. The Vista machines in our domain are placed in the Vista computer group under WSUS so that we can get a clearer picture of the status of those machines. To view the updates that our Vista machine needs, we followed these steps:

1. First we clicked **Reports | Status of Computers**.

2. On the left side of the page, under **View**, we chose the **Vista** computer group from the drop-down box.

3. Next, we selected the status that we wanted updates to match. For the purposes of this example, we chose **Installed**, and then **Needed**.

4. Then we Clicked **Apply**. This rendered a report showing our single Vista machine, named vista01.contoso.org.

5. We clicked the **plus sign** next to the VISTA01 machine to expand the list of updates that matched our criteria.

6. At this point, we saw four updates listed. Three of the updates were already installed and one update was needed, meaning that it was approved for detection but not for automatic installation (see Figure 9.12).

Figure 9.12 Filtering to Show Installed and Needed Updates

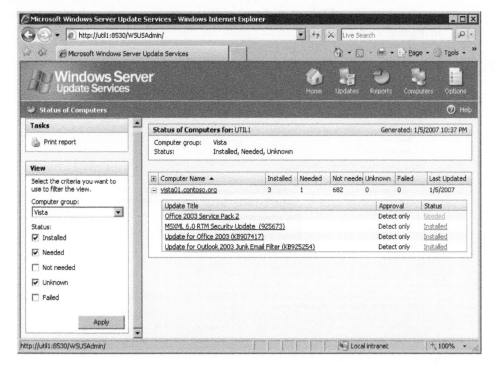

7. Clicking on any of the **underlined update titles** provided us with the **Update Properties** pop-up window. The **Update Properties** window provided us with all the pertinent update information, such as title, description, update ID, Knowledge Base article number, classification, and related products. It also provided detailed installation information, such as whether the update was removable, required user input, required a reboot, or needed to be installed exclusively.

8. Clicking the **Status** tab on the **Update Properties** dialog window showed us the status of this update on other machines.

9. If we had decided that we wanted this update to move from **Detect only** to **Install** and have it installed automatically, we would need to click **Change Approval** and choose the appropriate approval for the various computer groups (see Figure 9.13). However, we decided to approve the

Office 2003 SP2 update for installation on the machines in our Vista computer group. So, we clicked **Same as All Computers group** in the Approval column, which matched up with the Vista computer group, and selected **Install** from the drop-down box. The rest of the computer groups will continue to use the same approval as the All Computers group, which currently is set to **Detect only**, as you can see in the main drop-down box in Figure 9.13.

Figure 9.13 Approving Updates for Specific Computer Groups

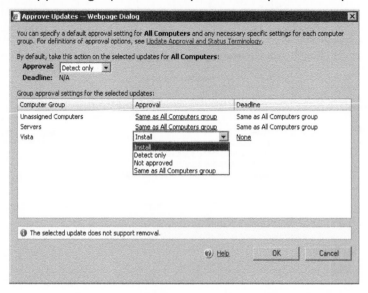

10. At this point, you can set a deadline for the installation, or you can leave it to update based on the installation schedule. To set a deadline, simply click **None** and the **Edit Deadline Webpage Dialog** will appear (see Figure 9.14).

11. Choose **Install updates by the selected date and time** to override the client settings and set your deadline for installation. Click **OK**.

12. Click **OK** again on the **Approve Updates Webpage Dialog** and click **Close** on the **Update Properties Webpage Dialog**.

Figure 9.14 Setting a Deadline to Override the Default Client Install
Schedule

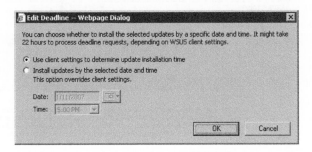

Synchronizing WSUS

WSUS synchronizes to the Microsoft Update Internet servers and downloads meta-data information for updates and software, but WSUS doesn't pull all the information for all the updates and software available on the Microsoft Update servers. The list of products at the beginning of this section is extensive, but rarely would one organization have all of the software products in that list in use at the same time. Thankfully, WSUS gives us the ability to choose the products and classifications for which we want to retrieve metadata. To do that, follow these steps:

1. Click **Options** at the top of the **WSUS administration page**.

2. Click **Synchronization Options**. On this page, you can define a synchronization schedule, proxy server settings, and the update source if you have multiple WSUS servers, and you can specify where to store downloaded files and which update languages to download.

3. We are concerned with the **Products and Classifications** section of this page (see Figure 9.15). Under the list of products, click **Change**, which will open the **Add/Remove Products Webpage Dialog**.

4. On the **Add/Remove Products Webpage Dialog** (see Figure 9.16), choose the products you use in your organization and be sure that the **Windows Vista, Windows Ultimate Extras, Windows Vista Dynamic Installer**, and **Windows Vista Ultimate Language Packs** checkboxes are selected to receive the proper updates for your Windows Vista machines. It would also be wise to check **Windows Defender, Windows Internet Explorer 7.0 Dynamic Installer**, and **Windows Media Dynamic Installer**.

Figure 9.15 Changing the Synchronization Settings

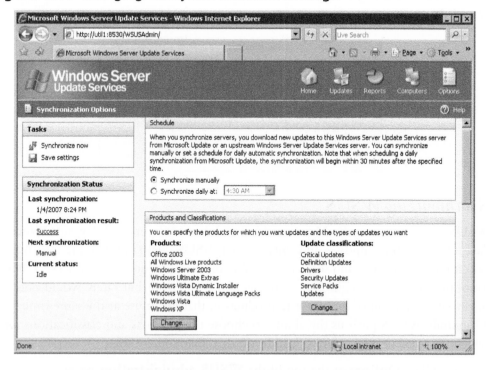

Figure 9.16 Choosing Products to Synchronize

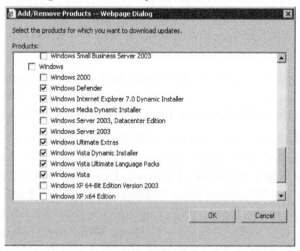

5.   Click **OK** to save your changes.

6. Under the list of classifications, click **Change**, which will open the **Add/Remove Classification Webpage Dialog**.

7. On the **Add/Remove Classification Webpage Dialog** (see Figure 9.17), choose the classifications of software updates that you want to synchronize from the Microsoft Update servers for each specified product. The default is to synchronize only critical and security updates.

Figure 9.17 Choosing Update Classifications to Synchronize

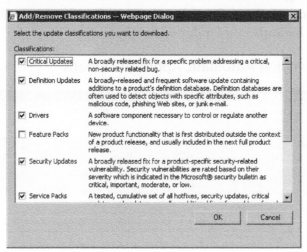

8. Click **OK** to close the **Add/Remove Classifications Webpage Dialog**, and then click **Save Settings** on the left side of the **Synchronization Settings** Web page.

Managing Automatic Approvals

We looked at changing the approval of specific updates, but we can also choose entire classifications to automatically approve for detection or installation. This way, we can specify that all critical and security updates are automatically approved for installation for all computer groups. We can also exclude certain computer groups from the automated process—for instance, we would probably want to exclude our server group so that updates could first be tested. To choose entire classifications to automatically approve for detection or installation, follow these steps:

1. Click **Options** at the top of the **WSUS administration page**.

2. Click **Automatic Approval Options**. On this page, we have the ability to specify how to handle update revisions, automatically approve updates for

WSUS itself, and set the automatic approval settings for update classifications.

3. We are concerned with the **Updates** section of the page (see Figure 9.18). We have decided to approve critical, definition, and security updates, service packs, feature packs, update rollups, and updates for automatic detection for all our computers. Click **Add/Remove Classifications**, which will open the familiar **Add/Remove Classifications Webpage Dialog** (refer to Figure 9.17), where we will select the **Critical Updates**, **Definition Updates**, **Security Updates**, **Service Packs**, **Feature Packs**, **Update Rollups**, and **Updates** checkboxes.

Figure 9.18 Changing Automatic Approval Options

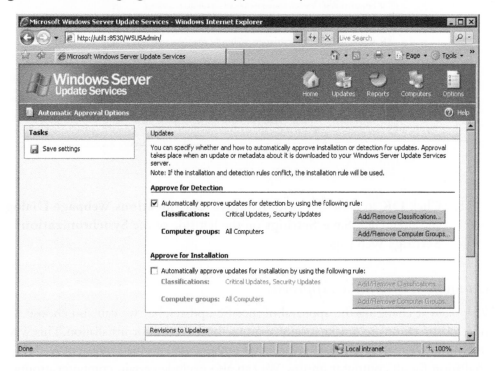

4. Click **OK**, and then click **Save Settings** to continue. You can also define which classifications to automatically approve for installation from this page.

Windows Server Update Services 3

WSUS 2 was a huge improvement over SUS 1, and SP1 for WSUS 2 added much-needed Vista and SQL Server 2005 functionality. WSUS 2 also has a very mature update catalog derived from the Microsoft Update catalog. So, why is WSUS 3 on the horizon if SP1 for WSUS 2 was released a short seven months ago, and WSUS 2 was released only two years ago, in early 2005? WSUS 3 brings several new features to the table; it includes SQL Server 2005 Embedded Edition in the install package, and it runs a setup wizard upon initial installation to set synchronization options and proxy settings, and to choose products and classifications. WSUS 3 also breaks away from the somewhat clumsy Web interface of WSUS 2 and uses the new MMC 3.0 for administration. MMC 3.0 is available for download and comes with Windows 2003 R2.

> **NOTE**
>
> As of the writing of this book, WSUS 3 Beta 2 has a downloadable add-on to support Windows Vista Release Candidate 1 (RC1). That add-on will not support Windows Vista Release to Manufacturing (RTM), and the WSUS 3 team has stated that support for Vista RTM won't be in until they release WSUS 3 RC1 in early 2007.

WSUS 3 Stand-Alone and Active Directory Installations

WSUS 3 uses the same methods as WSUS 2 to control the behavior of the AU client. All the local Group Policy and domain Group Policy settings operate the same and have the same effect as they do when directing clients to a WSUS 2 server. Please refer back to the WSUS 2 section for this information.

WSUS 3 MMC 3.0 Administrative Interface

The new MMC-based interface is much easier to use and much more familiar for administrators used to using MMC snap-ins for all their administration of Windows-based servers. WSUS 3 also uses the Microsoft Report Viewer 2005 for its reporting, and what a welcome change this is in comparison with the limited reporting interface in WSUS 2. You can even author your own reports and save them for later use.

Remember the somewhat confusing, approve-for-detection mechanism in WSUS 2? That mechanism has been removed and a new rule-based mechanism has been added to allow administrators to create rules to approve updates for installation and target them to specific computer groups and update classifications. Another important addition is the ability to manage multiple servers from a single MMC. In WSUS 2, having multiple servers meant administering each server from a different Web interface. Now, you can add all your servers to a single MMC and administer them from any computer that has the WSUS 3 MMC console installed.

You can install the WSUS 3 MMC on any Windows 2003 machine, or on any Windows XP machine with MMC 3.0 installed. You can download the redistributable MMC 3.0 packages for various versions of Windows from www.microsoft.com/downloads/results.aspx?pocId=&freetext=MMC%203.0&DisplayLang=en.

Once MMC 3.0 is installed, simply run the WSUS 3 Beta 2 installation package with the *Console_install* command-line switch:

```
C:\>WSUSSetup-x86.exe Console_install=1
```

When you have the WSUS 3 console installed on your administrative machine, you can administer all the WSUS 3 servers in your organization by following these steps:

1. Go to **Start | Administrative Tools | Microsoft Windows Server Update Services v3.0**.

2. Right-click the **Update Services** node and select **Connect to server**. This will open the **Connect to Server** dialog box (see Figure 9.19).

3. Enter the **Server name** and **Port** number of the server you want to add to the console. Also be sure to select the **Do not use Secure Sockets layer (SSL) to connect to this server** checkbox if you are not using SSL on your WSUS 3 server.

4. Click **Connect** to add the server.

Now that you are connected to the WSUS server, you can expand the **UTIL3** node to administer the server. From this view (see Figure 9.20), you can access the settings, computer groups, update views, reports, and other WSUS tasks.

Figure 9.19 Connecting to a WSUS 3 Server

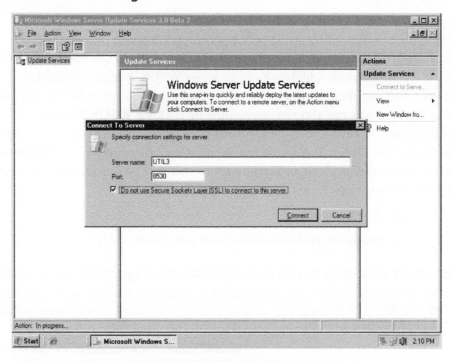

Figure 9.20 WSUS 3 Administrative Console

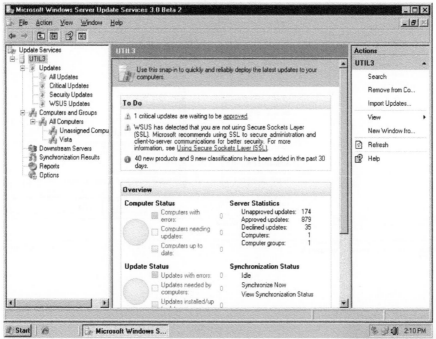

Synchronizing WSUS

The process of synchronizing WSUS 3 is very similar to that of synchronizing WSUS 2, but the administration interface is entirely different. You still choose product categories and update classifications that you want to synchronize, and you still set a synchronization schedule. You can access WSUS 3 options from the **Options** node, and there is an initial setup wizard that runs when WSUS 3 is first installed but that you can also run at any time by clicking **WSUS Server Configuration Wizard** under the **Options** node. You also can access all the settings in the wizard and change them individually from the other links in the **Options** node. To change the products and classifications that will be synchronized by your server, follow these steps:

1. Click the **Options** node.

2. Click **Products and Classifications** (see Figure 9.21).

Figure 9.21 Changing Products and Classification Synchronization Settings

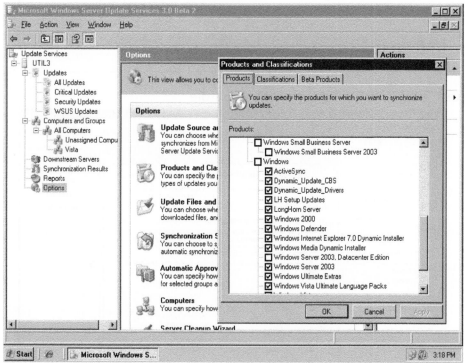

3. Choose the products you want to synchronize from the Products list. You will notice that the list of products is slightly different in WSUS 3 compared to WSUS 2. Because this is a Beta version, the product catalog is not as robust as the WSUS 2 product catalog. Once WSUS 3 moves into the RC and RTM stages, the catalog will come up to par with the WSUS 2 catalog.

4. Click the **Classification** tab and choose the appropriate classifications. If you want to receive updates for the Microsoft Beta products you are testing, you can click the **Beta Products** tab, which will ask you to enter your Beta ID.

5. Click **OK** to save the settings and continue.

Managing Updates

You manage updates in WSUS 3 through the Updates node. The node has several predefined filters that list certain classifications of updates. Right-clicking on the **Updates** node will allow you to **Search** for updates using the search function, **Import Updates** directly from the Windows Update Web site, and create a **New Update View**. By creating a new view of the updates on your server, you're simply applying a filter to the updates and displaying the results of that filter. The mechanism WSUS 3 uses to build these filters is very robust, giving you much more control over the updates on your server. One of the most frustrating things about WSUS 2 was that it provided a very valuable function but lacked in key areas such as reporting and inventorying. To view and manage your updates, follow these steps:

1. Expand the **Updates** node and select one of the update views, such as **Critical updates**.

2. Change the **Approval** and **Status** options at the top of the middle panel to display the critical updates that meet the necessary criteria. We have chosen to view updates with an **Approval** of **Any Except Declined** and a **Status** of **Any**. Click **Refresh** to apply the new filtering options. The middle panel will now display updates that meet those criteria (see Figure 9.22).

Figure 9.22 Filtering Updates

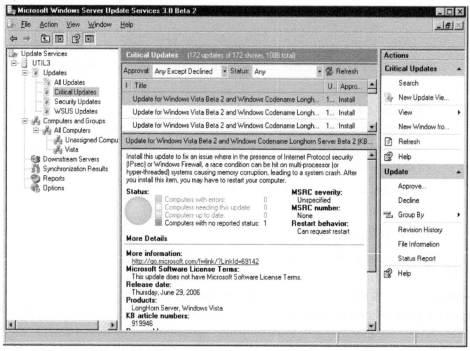

   This window displays the update title, up-to-date and unknown percentage, and approval status. You can edit the header, and you can add other properties by right-clicking on the header and choosing the properties from the right-click menu. After you choose a specific update from the top section of the updates view section, the bottom section will display the various update details.

   The right-hand section of the console shows the context-sensitive **Actions**. The top section relates to the overall **Critical Updates** node, and the lower **Update** section applies to the selected update. Right-clicking on a specific update will bring up an identical right-click menu, allowing you to **Approve** or **Decline** the update. Selecting **Group By** allows you to change the organization of the updates by grouping them based on **Title**, **Classification**, **MSRC severity**, and **Approval**. Clicking **Revision History** brings up the **Revision History** window, showing previous versions of the update, the date it was released, and any changes made to the update. Clicking **File Information** brings up the **File Information** window, showing the various files packaged in the update, the release date, the file size, and the filename. Clicking **Status Report** opens the report viewer and renders a status report for the specific update. The status report contains the same update detail information displayed in the bottom half of the **Critical Updates** section of the

console, but provides you the added benefit of being able to print the report or
export it to PDF or Excel format. To change the approval of a specific update, follow
these steps:

1. Right–click a specific update and select **Approve**. This brings up the
   Approve Updates window (see Figure 9.23).

Figure 9.23 Changing Update Approvals

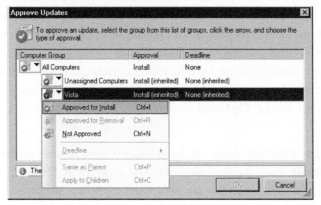

2. Clicking the icon next to the **Vista** computer group brings up a drop-
   down menu showing the approval options. Because computer groups are
   nested, changing the approval of this update for the Vista computer group
   will cause it to stop inheriting the Approval and Deadline settings from the
   All Computers computer group.

TIP

One of the big changes in WSUS 3 is the addition of nested computer
groups. Using nested computer groups gives an administrator fine-
grained control over update approval and deadline settings.

---

3. Once you have altered the approval settings to suit the needs of your organization, click **OK** to save the settings and close the Approve Updates
   dialog.

Managing Automatic Approval Rules

Another cool new feature in WSUS 3 is the way automatic approval of updates is handled. Microsoft has adopted a rule-based method for automatic approvals. This allows much more control over what classification of updates are automatically approved, and for which computer groups the approval applies. In WSUS 2, we were limited to one rule that automatically approved updates for detection, and one rule that automatically approved updates for installation. This provided administrators with very little flexibility. In WSUS 3, we can create as many rules as we need, and thankfully the somewhat odd process of approving updates for detection has been removed to simplify the process even more.

Automatic approval rules are easy to write, concise, and very clear about to which updates and computer groups they apply. To set up automatic approval rules we are going to revisit the **Options** node of the WSUS 3 console (refer to Figure 9.20):

1. Click the **Options** node of the WSUS 3 console and select **Automatic Approvals** from the middle pane. The **Approval Rules** window appears (see Figure 9.24), and we are presented with one generic automatic install rule. The rule is not enabled by default, so the checkbox is normally deselected and the **Run Rule** button is grayed out.

Figure 9.24 Setting Automatic Approval Rules

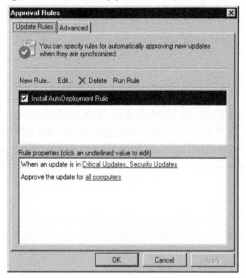

2. Selecting the **Install AutoDeployment Rule** checkbox and clicking **Apply** will enable the rule, but the rule will apply only to future updates. As is stated at the top of the window, "You can specify rules for automatically approving new updates when they are synchronized." This means any updates that are already synchronized and in the system will not abide by the rule.

3. In order to have the rule run against existing updates, simply click **Run Rule**, at which point you will see a pop-up box with a status bar as the rule runs against your update catalog. Once it is done, you will also see the results of running the rule.

When setting up a new rule, you can apply three groups of criteria for the rule to match against: the update classification, product group, and computer group. Rules always apply to, at the very least, one computer group, but whether they leverage update classifications and product groups is up to you. In the following tutorial, we will create a rule that automatically approves critical updates, security updates, and service packs that belong to the Windows Vista product group for computers in the Vista computer group:

1. Begin by setting up a new rule, which you do by simply clicking **New Rule**. This will display the **Add Rule** dialog (see Figure 9.25).

Figure 9.25 Creating a New Rule

2. Select both the **When an update is in a specific classification** and **When an update is in a specific product** checkboxes. In the **Step 2 portion** of the window, two properties corresponding to classification and product will appear.

3. Click the blue **classification** text and the familiar **Add/Remove Classification** window dialog will appear. Choose only the **Critical Updates**, **Security Updates**, and **Service Packs** checkboxes. Click **OK**.

4. Click the blue **product** text and the familiar **Add/Remove Product** window dialog will appear. Choose only the **Windows Vista** checkbox. Click **OK**.

5. Specify a descriptive name in the Step 3 text box and click **OK** to save and continue.

6. Now the rule is added and the checkbox next to the new rule should already be selected. Click **Apply** to confirm the settings.

7. Finally, select the new rule so that it is highlighted in blue, and click **Run Rule** to apply the update retroactively.

8. Click **OK** to close the **Approval Rules** dialog.

All in all, WSUS 3 is shaping up to be a very robust and feature-rich product. Compared with WSUS 2, which was a huge improvement over SUS 1.0, WSUS 3 is a welcome tool in a marketplace full of costly or complicated update management systems. Microsoft seems to have listened to its user base and improved or added the features that WSUS 2 was lacking.

Currently, WSUS 2 with SP1 will fully support Vista clients and the administration of Vista and non-Vista clients is identical. WSUS 3 Beta 2, on the other hand, does not support the RTM version of Vista and supports only the RC version of Vista with an add-on pack. This, of course, will change with the soon-to-be-released WSUS 3 RC milestone. If you are trying to decide between WSUS 2 and WSUS 3 Beta 2, and you currently have Vista machines in your environment, we suggest that you go with WSUS 2 and perform an upgrade when the WSUS 3 RC is released. Once the RTM version of WSUS 3 is released, you will be able to move from the RC version easily. Microsoft, however, does not support moving from Beta versions to RC or RTM versions of its products.

Using Systems Management Server and Vista

Systems Management Server (SMS) 2003 is the current version of the Microsoft enterprise-level configuration monitoring software. SMS was designed to be the powerhouse Microsoft product for managing network clients, and it accomplishes that goal in most situations. It can easily handle many thousands of clients in each site, and it has a very flexible architecture in that it allows the site designer to spread out the different SMS server roles among a group of SMS servers. The problem with SMS is that it is almost overly complicated in design and implementation. It does have many strengths, but those strengths don't seem to balance out the product's extremely steep learning curve.

SMS 2003 and Vista

Microsoft has released two SPs for SMS 2003, and SP3 is on the horizon for the first or second quarter of 2007. If you would like to use SMS 2003 SP2 to manage your Vista clients, you will either have to wait for SP3 or try your luck with SP2. Unfortunately, there is no official document from Microsoft that details what works and what doesn't, and most of the information has to be tested or extrapolated from different sources.

Shitanshu, a blogger who works as a technologist on the SMS Infrastructure team at Microsoft, talks about Vista and Longhorn support at http://blogs.msdn.com/shitanshu/archive/2006/11/27/sms-2003-sp2-compatibility-with-vista-and-longhorn-server.aspx. Once again, it is a case of pre-RTM support in the current release and full Vista RTM support in the next release. If you would like to attempt to use SP2, be forewarned that even getting the SMS client installed on your Vista machines will be quite a task. You must install it manually by connecting to the share on an SMS server and running the setup. At that point, cross your fingers and hope the installation completes successfully. We also found that even when the installation did complete successfully, the SMS site server wouldn't recognize the system as an agent-managed resource.

If you are already invested in SMS 2003 for your client management and software deployment tasks, you should sit tight and wait for SP3 to be released before managing any Vista clients on your network. If you are thinking about using SMS 2003 or SMS version 4, we suggest you think twice and look at some of the other third-party options available to your organization.

We found that installation of SMS 2003 was wrought with difficulties. Just getting the proper prerequisites was difficult because the Microsoft documentation of

SMS is vague in many areas. The difference between what is supported in SP1 and SP2 is not presented in a way that is easily decipherable. We read in one document that SP2 supported SQL Server 2005, and we already had a SQL Server 2005 machine available in our lab, so we decided to use that box to support our SMS 2003 installation. Unfortunately, we quickly found out that there was no version of SMS 2003 available with SP2. SP2 was an update that we needed to install once we had installed SP1. After setting up a version of SQL Server 2000 and patching it up to SP4, as the documentation stated, we tried the installation again. At this point, we found out that SMS doesn't support named instances. The list of errors we encountered just during the installation phase of SMS goes on and on.

We did finally complete the installation and were able to test some of the Vista support in SMS 2003. Remote management tools that are reported to work are Resource Explorer, Windows Diagnostics, Performance Monitor, and Remote Desktop. We tested those tools and were able to get them to operate properly with our Vista machine. Event Viewer, Remote Assistance, and Hardware Inventory failed to work, however. The word is that Event Viewer in Vista underwent a complete overhaul, and this would explain why the older version of the client agent was unable to access it. Software deployment, OS deployment, and patch management worked in Vista, although the OS deployment features were troublesome with certain types of hardware, and the current version of the feature pack doesn't include the new WinPE 2.0. As for Microsoft-based patch management, we concur with the community of SMS administrators and insist that you run WSUS alongside your SMS server.

System Center Configuration Manager 2007 Beta 1 and Vista

SMS 4, or System Center Configuration Manager 2007 (SCCM for short), is the new version of SMS and is currently in the Beta 1 release stage. A quick look at some of the SCCM release notes reveals that the new version of SMS has a lot of the same problems with Longhorn and Vista clients that SMS 2003 did. We're not quite sure why the Microsoft team didn't begin SMS 4 development with Vista and Longhorn in the forefront of their minds, but the reality is that we have yet another product that isn't Vista-ready, and at the time of this writing, Vista was scheduled to ship at the end of January 2007.

SMS 4 is another product that we will need to look forward to in order to see the benefits. Some of the more interesting features Microsoft hopes to introduce in this version of SMS are Network Access Protection (NAP), built-in Operating System Deployment (OSD), and a new MMC 3.0 console.

The OSD feature isn't necessarily new, because a feature pack is available for SMS 2003. The current iteration of OSD is still using WinPE 1.0 instead of the newer WinPE 2.0. WinPE 2.0 has many improvements over 1.0; ultimately one of the most important is the updated hardware driver support.

NAP looks like a promising addition to the features of SMS, though, with the ability to limit network access for clients that don't meet software update requirements. NAP is built into Vista and Longhorn, and it uses Dynamic Host Configuration Protocol (DHCP) enforcement, VPN enforcement, 802.1x enforcement, Internet Protocol Security (IPSec) enforcement, or all four, depending on the needs of your network. For anyone who struggled with the old method of creating a VPN quarantine using Microsoft's Routing and Remote Access server, this looks like a very powerful feature. Unfortunately, a quick look at the release notes for SMS 4 Beta 1 shows us that the NAP feature in SMS does not yet work with Vista and Longhorn.

Some other improvements at first glance are to the Administration Console, via MMC 3.0 and the much improved searching, filtering, and sorting features. Reporting also looks to be improved, and possibly even more so if used with Microsoft's Report Viewer 2005, although we were unable to test this. Also, there are a lot of new wizards, for everything from initiating a client push installation to the initial installation, although this is not to say that successfully setting up an SMS site has gotten any easier. If you haven't had the pleasure of planning an SMS deployment, thank your lucky stars, because it continues to be one of the more difficult Microsoft technologies to set up.

The long and short of it is that Microsoft is a bit behind its own curve when it comes to supporting Vista and Longhorn in its systems management, patch update, and monitoring software packages. In SMS 2003 and SMS 4, Vista and Longhorn work with the Performance Monitor, most of the System Information view, most of the Resource Explorer, and OSD—sometimes. We will be waiting for SMS 2003 SP3 and future Beta releases of SMS 4 to see how the Vista and Longhorn support comes along. It has to get better than it is now, and fast. The Vista release is right on top of us, and Longhorn should be out sometime around mid-year if we are lucky. Microsoft cannot afford to fall behind with support for its own products.

Using Microsoft Operations Manager and Vista

Microsoft Operations Manager (MOM) 2005 and its successor, System Center Operations Manager (SCOM) 2007, provide administrators with advanced network monitoring abilities. They both utilize MPs to provide support for network devices, network-aware software products, and various OSes and servers. The power of MOM comes from the capability to support a wide variety of objects that exist on the corporate network. Some of the currently available MPs support the following:

- Microsoft Forefront Security for Exchange 10

- Microsoft Exchange 2000 and 2003

- Microsoft SharePoint 3

- Microsoft Host Integration Server 2006

- Microsoft Antigen 9

- Microsoft ISA Server 2000, 2004, and 2006

- Microsoft SQL Server 2000 and 2005

- Microsoft Virtual Server 2005

- nWorks VMware Events

- Windows Terminal Services 2000 and 2003

- VERITAS Storage Foundation for Windows

- Citrix Presentation Server

- Virtual Agent for IronPort, NetBotz, TrendMicro, and ProofPoint

This is far from a complete list of the available MPs and device connectors that you can use with MOM. For a complete list, go to www.microsoft.com/technet/ prodtechnol/mom/mom2005/catalog.aspx.

System Center Operations Manager 2007 RC2

It seems that with the development of the System Center product line, Microsoft has decided to drive us mad with extremely long names and acronyms. Aside from the name, SCOM RC2 is a very nice solution for those looking to monitor the various clients, servers, and devices on their networks. Microsoft did several things right with the development of MOM from the outset. Our favorite feature of MOM, and now SCOM, is the ability for anyone to author an MP. This means that anyone, any-where, can create an MP using the authoring tools built into the MOM console. These MPs can support any number of network clients, devices such as routers, switches, and firewalls, and anything else you can plug into your network. Another feature is transparent integration with Active Directory. SMS wanted to be able to extend your Active Directory schema to enable advanced features. MOM doesn't require something that serious, and if you aren't using Active Directory or you want to manage devices outside of Active Directory, that is supported as well.

SCOM is due out very soon; an exact date wasn't available at the time of this writing, but because Microsoft is currently in the RC2 stage of the product, an RTM can't be far behind. If you are looking at a new MOM 2005 deployment, we suggest you wait for SCOM. We also suggest you download the SCOM RC2 evaluation from www.microsoft.com/mom/evaluation/beta/opsmgroverview.mspx, install it at your organization, and begin getting familiar with the way it operates. If you are currently using MOM 2005, we suggest you do the same thing; don't forget to put the money in your budget to upgrade when it is released.

SCOM installation was very simple, and once we had made sure our machine met the prerequisites, the installation process went off without a hitch. SCOM requires that SP1 for SQL Server 2005 is installed if you are using SQL Server 2005. It also requires .NET 3.0, which is currently still in Beta, and Windows Powershell 1.0. As you can tell from the prerequisites, SCOM 2007 uses the very latest technologies from the Microsoft catalog, and although this means that a lot of shops will be waiting until all the required products are out of Beta before deploying SCOM, it also means that SCOM leverages the latest innovations available from Microsoft.

Monitoring Clients and Servers

The name *System Center Operations Manager* doesn't really give users an idea of what the product can do for their organization, and the reality of the situation is that a lot of users are turned off by this. When we went to the Microsoft site to see whether it had any good descriptions or examples of exactly what could be accomplished with SCOM (or MOM, for that matter), we were sorely disappointed. We found very technical white papers, deployment and planning guides, and documents that just contained a lot of marketing.

SCOM and MOM alike provide administrators with a platform for monitoring the health of their networked systems by watching for predefined events and incidents. SCOM then goes a step further and notifies the necessary personnel when problems do arise. Now here comes the good part: SCOM also allows for the definition of diagnosis and repair tasks that occur when the health of a system degrades. These tasks are basically commands that are run against the system to try to diagnose and repair the situation. All the pieces that go into monitoring, diagnosing, and repairing the different systems on your network are what make up MPs. An MP is a set of predefined conditions that allow the system to determine the health of the monitored client. The MP also defines what commands are run when the health of the system degrades.

After installation, we added the clients on which we wanted to install the agent, by simply running a wizard that allowed us to choose the clients from Active Directory. We then ran a network discovery task to verify the existence of the clients, after which the agent was installed. Installation of the client agent on our Vista machine went flawlessly, and immediately after the task was complete we were able to browse to the VISTA01 computer in the SCOM console, view the machine's health, and perform some basic management tasks.

Monitoring Vista

To monitor Vista, follow these steps:

1. Open the **SCOM console** by going to **Start | All Programs | System Center Operations Manager 2007 | Operations Console**.

2. The SCOM console will launch and you will be presented with the home screen. Click **Computers** in the left-hand navigation pane.

3. The middle pane will give you the **Computers** pane with a **Detail View** of the selected computer object directly below the list of managed systems. Click the **Vista machine** to view various details about the system.

4. On the right-hand side of the console you will see the **Actions** pane. From here, you can perform various tasks on the selected system. Click **Computer Management** to launch the familiar Computer Management MMC console.

NOTE

The Computer Management console does not support the Event Viewer, Performance Monitor, or Device Manager when connecting to Vista machines.

5. Click **Remote Desktop** to connect to the selected computer via the Remote Desktop Protocol (RDP). Clicking **Remote Desktop (console)** will launch an RDP connection that connects directly to the console.

TIP

If you want to launch RDP connections that connect directly to the console of the machine you are connecting to, use this command: *mstsc /v:SERVERNAME /console*.

System Center Essentials 2007 Beta 2

System Center Essentials (SCE) 2007 is the next big thing for small and mid-size businesses. SCE uses the SCOM framework and integrates WSUS 3 to handle software updates, and even has the capability to distribute software. The pricing information was not released for SCE at the time of this writing, but Microsoft is marketing it heavily to the little guy. The underlying structure and operation of the system will be very familiar to MOM users, and it performs the same health monitoring, diagnosis, and repair tasks as MOM. It even uses a similar MP structure to extend its features.

SCE is currently available as a beta 2 product, and the RC1 milestone should be released shortly. The client-server support numbers is one area where SCE and SCOM will differ greatly. As of January 16' 2007, Microsoft announced that SCE will support 30 servers and 500 clients, a significant rise from the previous 15-server limit. This enhanced support makes SCE a very strong competitor in the management and update market, and one must wonder where SCOM fits in the System Center family of products. Looking at the current Microsoft product lineup, we see MOM 2005 and MOM 2005 Workgroup Edition. MOM 2005 Workgroup Edition eliminated a few of the higher end reporting and integration abilities of MOM 2005 while also limiting it to 10 servers. Similarly, SCE will support a lot less servers and clients compared with the number that SCOM supports. SCE also includes built-in updates with WSUS 3 and software distribution through a software push setup similar to SMS.

Using Third-Party Tools with Vista

Network device management tools have been a hot topic in the industry for a long time. With the addition of update management to the list of features that system administrators want included in the management solutions they purchase, we imagine management solutions will continue to be a hot topic for a long time. We've looked at some of the tools available to manage updates from Microsoft products, and some of the tools available to manage and monitor our Vista clients. Now we will look at what the independent software vendors (ISVs) have to offer in the way of converged client management, monitoring, and update management solutions.

Altiris

Altiris develops a vast array of management, monitoring, auditing, virtualization, and update management solutions. Its catalog has an extensive list of the available products and various bundles it offers. Don't expect to stroll right up to its Web site and purchase 50 licenses for your small business, though, Altiris seems to be squarely aimed at large enterprises. Small and midsized business IT professionals are probably better off looking for another solution. Altiris clients include the U.S. Army, General Motors, and the Dutch Ministry of Defense.

In order to test the Altiris solution, we had to get a trial version of the software. At first, we thought this was going to be troublesome because some of the larger solution providers don't like to provide users with trial versions without first acquiring plenty of personal information so that their salespeople can call and e-mail the users in perpetuity. Altiris couldn't have been easier, though. We simply followed the download link on the site and were directed to enter some basic information about our company and our position there. Then it let us download the installer package. We had decided to test the Client Management Suite, which is basically a bundle of the various software products Altiris develops and is aimed at managing clients and handheld devices. Some of the key features of the suite include:

- OS deployment and migration
- Hardware and software inventorying
- Web-based reporting
- Automated patch management
- Software license compliance
- Active Directory integration
- Cross-platform management support

At this point, we decided to investigate exactly what Altiris would cost to deploy at a smaller organization. We have purchased plenty of software, and we always seem to run into strange problems when dealing directly with a software vendor, especially one this size. We called the sales number for our region and expected to have to deal with the runaround for quite some time, but to our surprise we were given a per-client price within 30 seconds of being on the phone with the sales representative. The real surprise is that even though the Altiris product is used by some of the largest organizations in the world, it is still an affordable solution, especially when you consider the features it offers. The Client Management Suite has three levels: Level 1 provides the most commonly used features; level 2 and level 3 each add more features, with a small bump in price. Level 1 will be sufficient for most administrators, because it includes the patch management, hardware/software inventory, reporting, license compliance, Active Directory integration, and OS deployment and migration features.

Installing the Altiris Client Management Suite

Installing the Client Management Suite was simple enough, but the whole process took a long time. The initial download was only 5 MB, but we soon found out that the initial download simply started the full download, which was 650 MB. After the download was complete, the install process began by checking our prerequisites. The prerequisites were common to most of the other management suites available. We used SQL Server 2000 SP4 as our database backend, IIS 6.0 with .NET 1.1, although Altiris required only IIS 5.0 or higher. The database server was recognized easily and Altiris created a database.

NOTE

We mention that Altiris recognized the database server and created a database for itself, which doesn't sound like much of an accomplishment for an installer at this point in time. However, we would like to point out that SMS 2003 was unable to recognize our database server until we discovered that SMS 2003 doesn't support named instances. Surprisingly, it also would not create a database automatically. We had to manually create the database for use by SMS 2003. These may seem like small complaints of lazy sys admins, but in our mind, if we are paying top dollar for a product, the installer and setup process in general should *just work*. SMS 4 does improve on this portion of the setup a bit by automatically creating its database.

The install then asked which management features to enable. These features were listed in plain English and related to the features listed earlier (see Figure 9.26). We chose all the available features for the sake of testing, and clicked **Next**, at which point we were pleasantly surprised to see that Altiris now wanted to know which devices on our network we wanted to manage with the Client Management Suite. Again, this does not seem like a killer feature for management software, but SMS 2003 and SMS 4 certainly did not offer this ability in the installation wizard, and completing the task of installing the client agent after installation in SMS was far from intuitive.

Figure 9.26 Enabling Management Features

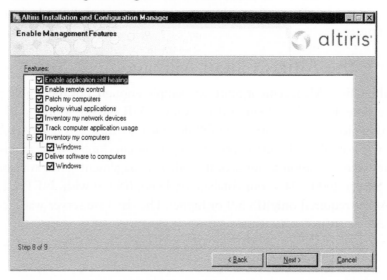

After choosing the clients on our network that we wanted to manage, the process proceeded to install 59 components. This part of the installation went through without a hitch, and at the end of the installation we were presented with a notice that the installation had completed and we should proceed with the initial configuration of the system. Altiris uses a Web-based console for administration but also includes several non-Web-based wizards for performing tasks such as software and OS deployment. We are not extremely fond of Web-based consoles for anything and everything, but the Altiris console works well, and its layout makes sense.

Managing Vista Clients

We immediately skipped the recommendation to perform the initial configuration tasks and went in search of our Vista client. When we spoke with Altiris sales, we were told that Vista support would be released in the next month or so. We were disappointed, to say the least, but we found that the client agent installed successfully on our Vista machine. Not only was it installed successfully, but it also recognized the OS and version information successfully. Again, this is something we had problems with in both versions of SMS. A little more digging and we found that most of the management features in Altiris already worked with Vista.

Using the Real-Time Consoles

Altiris does a lot of data collection about resources and stores that information in the database. You can then access this information from a variety of reports to view information about your clients. Altiris also includes something called *real-time consoles*, which simply means that when you access these consoles, the client is polled for the information that is displayed. To see how well these real-time consoles work with Vista, follow these steps:

1. Open the **Altiris administration console** and click **View | Resources**.

2. Expand the **Collections | Computer Collections** nodes and select the **All Computers** collection (see Figure 9.27).

Figure 9.27 Viewing Resource Collections

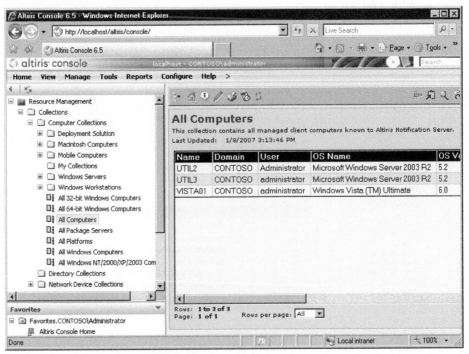

NOTE

Collections in Altiris are very similar, if not identical, to collections in SMS, and they are basically predefined filters. You can also create your own collections for all sorts of resources. The overall structure of Altiris and the processes and constructs it uses are very similar to SMS. If you are an SMS user or are familiar with SMS, you will have a very short learning curve with Altiris.

3. Right-click on the machine you want to manage (e.g., **VISTA01**, in this case), and select **Real-time System Manager | Manage**.

4. This will bring up the VISTA01 Altiris Resource Manager and will load the General Information | Summary on the Real-Time tab (see Figure 9.28). From this tab, you can access any of the various real-time consoles provided by Altiris.

Figure 9.28 Managing Computers with Real-Time Consoles

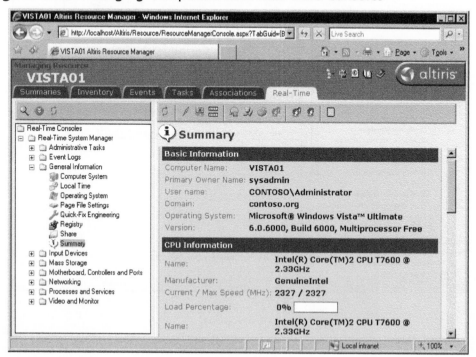

The Summary console shows basic computer information, CPU information and usage, memory usage, disk usage, network connectivity, and antivirus status. The majority of consoles here provide extensive resource information, including hardware information down to the basic input/output system (BIOS) level, running processes and services, and network settings and active connections both to and from the client. We could change some of the time zone information, the computer description, the workgroup membership, and the maximum allowed size of the Registry. We couldn't access a few consoles at all, including the Page File Settings console.

What we could do was access running processes and kill them. We could also view the services on the system and start, stop, pause, resume, and set the services to automatically start, start as needed, or become completely disabled. Under the Networking node, we were able to modify IPv4 route information. Printer management didn't work under the VISTA01 resource, but it worked great when we managed one of our Windows Server 2003 resources. All in all, printer management and page file settings were minor losses, and hopefully, when full Vista support is released in the next few months, these features will work as intended.

Another concern of ours was whether we would be able to view the Event Logs from the Vista machine. This feature did not work in SMS, and from everything we've read, it was because the underlying event reporting service in Vista is vastly different. Clicking on the **Event Logs** node and then on the **Application**, **System**, or **Security Log** brought up the appropriate log information. A quick look at the Event Viewer in Vista shows much more than the standard three logs we are all used to seeing, though, and these extra logs were not available through Altiris. Hopefully, this is something that gets added in the near future, but just having the Application, System, and Security logs is helpful and much more sensible than having absolutely no event viewing support for Vista, which is the case with the current releases of SMS.

Using Carbon Copy for Remote Control

Altiris uses a proprietary product called Carbon Copy for remote control of clients. Carbon Copy is an ActiveX-based program that allows administrators to view and interact with the remote console session of a system. It operates similarly to VNC and Microsoft's Remote Assistance functionality. It allows you to view the current console session only, meaning that you can't remotely control RDP or Terminal Server sessions. Carbon Copy, like any other remote session control technology, is extremely useful for servicing help desk requests and any task that requires interaction with the local computer console to complete. The bad news is that as of this writing, Carbon Copy doesn't support Vista clients, but again, we imagine that when Altiris mentioned "full Vista support," this is part of what the company meant.

Software Delivery Methods

Altiris can deliver software for Windows and Macintosh alike, and it uses a straight-forward wizard to walk the administrator through the steps necessary to create a Software Delivery task. Once the task is created and assigned to a specific computer or collection of computers, either it is run without user intervention or, depending on the software package, the user is notified that new software is available by the Altiris Agent System Tray icon. The System Tray icon notifies the user of the available software and allows him to run the task (see Figure 9.29). You can also schedule the task to run at certain times so that users can't just ignore the notifications.

Figure 9.29 Delivering Software to End Users

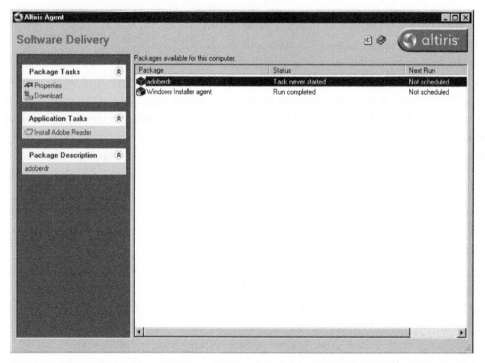

We created a task to deploy Adobe Reader 8.0 for Vista and assigned the task to our VISTA01 machine. The task immediately became available and we were able to successfully run the installation. After installation was complete, the Altiris Agent prompted us to reboot the system, which we did, and Adobe Reader installed successfully. One of the nice features of delivering software through the Altiris Agent is the ability to designate the credentials to use when the task is run. This means you can set up software delivery tasks to run and the system will notify your users when the task is launched. Even if it requires user intervention, it will run using privileges of the account you specified.

Managing Software Updates

Altiris not only allows administrators to patch and monitor Windows and other Microsoft products, but it also supports patching non-Microsoft products. Altiris uses an extensible repository to house OS, software, and hardware vendor patches. The Altiris patch management product also integrates with its recovery solution, which allows administrators to roll back machines that encounter problems with patches.

In order to start using Altiris Patch Management to roll out software updates, you need to first enable the Software Update Agent installation task. Once the task is enabled, the agent will be rolled out to computers that need the agent. To enable and begin rollout of the Software Update Agent, follow these steps:

1. From the **Altiris Console**, click **Manage | Software**.

2. Expand the **Configuration | Patch Management | Windows | Software Update Agent Rollout** nodes.

3. Click **Software Update Agent Install** and select the **Enable (currently disabled)** checkbox at the top of the frame on the right-hand side.

4. Click **Apply**.

Once you have done this, the installation should occur without user intervention. To verify that the agent has been installed, from the **Software Update Agent Rollout** node click **All Windows Computers without Software update Agent Installed**.

This is the collection of computers that should have received the agent rollout from the previous task. This collection should eventually empty as your managed client computers have the agent pushed to them. We took a quick glance at this list prior to enabling the installation task and our VISTA01 machine was listed. After we enabled the task, it was no longer on this list. Because this was the first time we attempted the installation on a Vista machine, we also physically logged onto the box and right-clicked on the **Altiris Agent** System Tray icon. The right-click menu showed a new option, **Software Updates**. Upon clicking **Software Updates**, the Altiris Agent window opened on the Software Updates tab and gave us the error "The Software Update Agent is not ready." A quick reboot solved that problem, and once we were logged back onto our VISTA01 machine, we had the full Software Update interface available.

Even though we had installed the Software Update agent and it was operating properly, we were not seeing any available updates for our Vista machine. If this happens to you, you need to make sure your Altiris server has downloaded and imported the PMIimport.CAB file. When you enable software updates, this file is supposed to be downloaded and imported. Our system was having a bit of trouble showing that it had successfully completed the import, something we blame on the condition of our lab machines. Again, after a reboot, we found that the file had been downloaded and imported properly. The PMIimport.CAB file is downloaded from an Altiris server according to the default schedule. You can change this schedule, but for our purposes, we left it alone. The file itself is about 790 KB and contains the most recent Microsoft Security Bulletins. Once it is imported, you can view the available bulletins, search for specific bulletins, and view bulletin details. In order to apply bulletins, you will need to create new Software Update Tasks, which are very similar to Software Delivery Tasks.

All in all, the Altiris solution is a very powerful management tool for an organization, although we weren't thoroughly impressed with its ability to handle Microsoft-based software updates. The good thing about the way Altiris handles software updates is that it is extensible, and you can use it to update non-Microsoft products. Considering the fact that WSUS 3 is a free product, though, if we were using Altiris for our management needs, we would still include WSUS 3 in our organization to handle Microsoft-based software updates.

Other Third-Party Tools

There are, of course, many more enterprise management solutions out there for Windows and non-Windows clients alike. The increasing size of data centers and IT resources in general makes the market for centralized management technologies one of the fastest growing in the industry right now. Also, the increased focus on security and patch management means that ISVs are offering all-inclusive solutions, allowing administrators to invest in a solution that provides all the pieces to the puzzle. Some of the other patch management and system management solutions available from ISVs include:

- ScriptLogic, which is similar to Altiris in that it offers a vast array of technologies and then provides packages and bundles of those technologies to companies of varying sizes. For more information, visit www.scriptlogic.com.

- Ecora, which focuses more on auditing and compliance than on full systems management, but as a part of its compliance and auditing, it does provide a very capable patch management solution. For more information, visit www.ecora.com.

Summary

Windows Update and Microsoft Update both continue to improve, and the versions available for use in Windows Vista are no exception. Microsoft has taken these tools and closely integrated them with the OS, and in doing so it has removed some of the security concerns of the Windows Update Web site. Users no longer need to navigate to a Web site in Internet Explorer in order to receive security updates that patch potential vulnerabilities in Internet Explorer. This change in the overall process also removes the negative effect on user behavior caused by the use of the Windows Update Web site. Other changes in the WUA allow users to receive recommended updates in addition to important security updates. Administrators are also given greater control over the WUA through additional Group Policy settings.

WSUS provides administrators with a centralized patch management solution for Microsoft-based products. WSUS 2 is currently the only patch management product from Microsoft that fully supports patching Vista RTM. WSUS 3, which is still in Beta 2, is an extremely strong product and will be a very valuable upgrade for any organization. Another key benefit of WSUS is its ease of use. WSUS uses Group Policy settings to control clients. These are the same Group Policy settings administrators use to control the behavior of the WUA.

SMS is a powerful systems management tool, but it requires a lot of specialized knowledge and training to successfully install and use in your environment. If you are looking for a tool with similar constructs but a much shorter learning curve, Altiris Client Management Suite or one of ScriptLogic's products might be right for your organization.

Altiris provides a very robust systems management solution that is also flexible and relatively easy to use. The Client Management Suite includes the tools necessary to patch, monitor, and remotely manage clients and other devices on your network. It goes a step further by including OS and software deployment features as well.

Microsoft Operations Manager, and its successor, System Center Operations Manager, provide organizations with the ability to monitor, diagnose, and repair networked devices, clients, and even distributed software products. The power of MOM and SCOM is that they let you plug in MPs that provide specific support for the devices and software present on your network. Because anyone can author MPs, administrators are presented with a large community of ISVs and independent developers providing MPs for their needs. SCE, which is a hybrid of SCOM, WSUS 3, and software deployment via Group Policy, provides small to mid-size businesses with an affordable monitoring and management product.

Solutions Fast Track

Using Windows Update

- ☑ The Windows Update Agent in Vista is completely integrated with the Windows Update Control Panel applet and you can now accomplish all update tasks without having to go to the Windows Update Web site.

- ☑ Vista adds the ability to automatically download and install recommended updates, in addition to important and critical updates. This ability, combined with an expanded Microsoft Update catalog, allows users to fully automate their update services.

- ☑ Uninstalling Microsoft updates has always been a problematic process. Vista improves on this process by providing a better view of the updates that have been installed. Unfortunately, you cannot uninstall the majority of updates, and you need to use the System Restore feature in Windows OS instead.

Using Windows Server
Update Services (WSUS) and Vista

- ☑ You can use client-side targeting through local or domain Group Policy to automatically place computers in specific computer groups on your WSUS server. This allows for fine-grained targeting of available updates.

- ☑ Bandwidth conservation is an important part of the benefits WSUS provides to an organization. WSUS acts as a concentrator for the Windows Update service; the local WSUS server synchronizes to the WSUS update servers on the Internet and retrieves the update metadata information for the products and classifications that the administrator has chosen.

- ☑ WSUS 3 improves upon its predecessor by utilizing the newest technologies available from Microsoft. Improved reporting, custom reports, granular control over update approval, and an MMC 3.0 administration console top the list of new features and improvements.

Using Systems Management Server (SMS) and Vista

☑ SMS is a powerful management tool, but the complexity of the initial deployment is overwhelming. If you decide to use SMS to manage your network, we suggest that you have previous experience working with the product or that you seek outside resources in the initial planning and implementation phase of the process.

☑ The next version of the OS Deployment feature pack will support WinPE 2.0, which will support a host of new hardware devices and will include full support for creating and deploying Vista images.

☑ Network Access Protection (NAP) is one of the widely anticipated features available in SMS v4. NAP gives administrators the ability to leverage the NAP features in Vista and Longhorn in order to limit network access for clients that don't meet software update requirements.

Using Microsoft Operations Manager (MOM) and Vista

☑ System Center Operations Manager 2007 is the next version in the Microsoft Operations Manager line of software products, which provide enterprises with the ability to monitor and maintain the health of clients, servers, and devices on their networks.

☑ MOM allows administrators to not only utilize MPs from Microsoft and ISVs, but also author new MPs based on their network needs.

☑ SCOM is purely a network monitoring and management tool, and although WSUS 3 has an available MP, you cannot manage software updates with SCOM directly. System Center Essentials, on the other hand, integrates SCOM and WSUS 3 to provide small and mid-size businesses with a monitoring, management, and software update solution.

Using Third-Party Tools with Vista

☑ Altiris Client Management Suite is the combination of several Altiris software products which provide enterprises of all sizes with a comprehensive client monitoring and management, software deployment, software update, and OS deployment and migration solution.

☑ Altiris includes Carbon Copy, a software product which allows administrators to connect to a remote computer's console, and view and interact directly with the computer and the user that is currently logged on to the machine.

☑ The Software Delivery Service in Altiris allows administrators to define a set of available products and advertise the availability of those software products to end users. The end users can then select which pieces of software are necessary for them to accomplish their tasks and install those pieces as needed without administrator intervention.

Frequently Asked Questions

The following Frequently Asked Questions, answered by the authors of this book, are designed to both measure your understanding of the concepts presented in this chapter and to assist you with real-life implementation of these concepts. To have your questions about this chapter answered by the author, browse to **www.syngress.com/solutions** and click on the **"Ask the Author"** form.

Q: What happened to the Windows Update Web site in Vista?

A: Microsoft has done away with having to use Internet Explorer to navigate to the Windows Update Web site in order to receive updates. Now the Windows Update and Microsoft Update agents are integrated into the Windows Update Control Panel applet.

Q: What can I do to keep my users from changing AU settings or ignoring installation notifications?

A: All the AU settings are available through local or domain Group Policy. Use gpedit.msc or edit the domain Group Policy Object to set the policies to your desired configurations, and your users will no longer be able to change the settings. Use the wuau2.ADM file included on the CD to update your Windows 2000/2003 Group Policy Object so that you can access the Vista-specific policy settings.

Q: How can I automatically set my new Vista installs to use Microsoft Update instead of the standard Windows Update catalog?

A: Simply script the process. Using the muauth.CAB file along with this three-line script, you can easily set your machines to automatically use the Microsoft Update catalog:

```
Set ServiceManager = CreateObject("Microsoft.Update.ServiceManager")
Set NewUpdateService = ServiceManager.AddService("7971f918-a847-4430-9279-
4a52d1efe18d", "C:\muauth.cab")
ServiceManager.RegisterServiceWithAU "7971f918-a847-4430-9279-4a52d1efe18d"
```

Q: I need to centrally manage updates for Vista clients immediately. What are my choices?

A: WSUS 2 is probably the best choice, and currently it is the only Microsoft-based product that fully supports Vista. Altiris and SMS can also provide updates for Vista clients, but it is not officially supported.

Q: Where can I find the download for MMC 3.0 so that I can start using WSUS 3?

A: The download is available at www.microsoft.com/downloads/results.aspx? pocId=&freetext=MMC%203.0&DisplayLang=en.

Q: I currently run WSUS 2 for my Microsoft-based software update needs. Why should I migrate to WSUS 3 when it is released?

A: WSUS 3 offers several improvements over WSUS 2. The administration interface has moved from a Web-based solution to an MMC 3.0 console-based solution. Reporting is greatly improved, and you get more granular control over update approval and targeting.

Q: Which version of SMS currently supports Microsoft Vista or Longhorn?

A: None of them does, unfortunately. But this is due to change very soon, with the release of SP3 for SMS 2003. There is currently no word on when or how Microsoft will release support for Vista and Longhorn in the SMS v4 Beta product, but it will most likely appear in the next milestone release, Beta 2.

Q: Is it possible to test the new NAP features in Vista with System Center Configuration Manager 2007?

A: Currently the NAP features in SCCM do not support Vista or Longhorn.

Q: Do SMS 2003 and SMS 4 provide patch management for third-party software products, or only for Microsoft-based updates?

A: Both SMS 2003 and SMS 4 will support the ability to deploy patches for both Microsoft-based and non-Microsoft software products.

Q: Can I deploy software updates with MOM or SCOM?

A: No, MOM and SCOM are purely monitoring and health management products. They do, however, support monitoring SMS and WSUS 3 with the addition of the appropriate MPs. SCE, on the other hand, incorporates the powerful features of MOM with the ability to deploy software and software updates.

Q: I am using WSUS 2 to provide software updates to clients on my network and MOM 2005 to provide monitoring for my network. Is an MP available for MOM so that I can monitor my WSUS 2 server?

A: No, there is no WSUS 2 MP, but an MP is available for MOM 2005 that supports the WSUS 3 Beta.

Q: Where does System Center Essentials fit in the network management puzzle?

A: System Center Essentials is Microsoft's new monitoring and management tool for small to mid-size businesses. It includes the monitoring capabilities of MOM and the Microsoft-based patch management capabilities of WSUS 3, with software deployment features thrown in for good measure.

Q: I can't seem to connect to my Vista clients using the Altiris Carbon Copy agent. What am I doing wrong?

A: Carbon Copy, unfortunately, does not currently support Vista clients. There is no official word on when Carbon Copy will fully support Vista clients, but hopefully we will see an update in the next couple of months.

Q: The hardware and software inventory reports are excellent, but I want to view this information and be able to make changes to the system in question. Does Altiris give me the ability to do this?

A: The real-time consoles in Altiris give an administrator the ability to perform some management tasks, such as changing service state and startup options, rebooting or powering off a system remotely, killing processes, and running commands.

Q: Does Altiris support updating non-Microsoft software products?

A: Yes! Altiris, like Microsoft's own SMS and many other third-party patch management tools, supports updating both Microsoft and non-Microsoft software.

Chapter 10

Disaster Recovery with Exchange Server 2007

Solutions in this chapter:

- Backing Up Exchange 2007 Using Windows 2003 Backup

- Restoring Exchange 2007 Storage Groups and Databases Using Windows 2003 Backup

- Repairing a Corrupt or Damaged Exchange 2007 Database Using Eseutil

- Restoring Mailbox Data Using the Recovery Storage Group Feature

- Recovering an Exchange 2007 Server Using the RecoverServer Switch

- Recovering an Exchange 2007 Cluster Using the RecoverCMS Switch

- Restoring Mailbox Databases Using the Improved Database Portability Feature

Introduction

The messaging and collaboration servers are mission critical, being perhaps the most vital servers in our datacenters today. It's therefore of the utmost importance that these servers be up and running all the time. Most service level agreements today require more than 99.99 percent uptime when it comes to the messaging and collaboration servers in the organization. Even if you have HA solutions such as CCR-based mailbox servers available, a disaster can still strike in your environment, and if this happens, you better be prepared since downtime typically means lost productivity and revenue. In this chapter, we'll go through the steps necessary to back up the different Exchange 2007 Server roles in your organization, and, just as important, look at how you restore Exchange 2007 servers and data should it be required.

Backing Up Exchange 2007 Using Windows 2003 Backup

Frequent backups of the Exchange 2007 servers in an organization are important operational tasks that, though a bit trivial, should be taken very seriously. I can only imagine one thing worse than a complete failure of an Exchange 2007 server, and that's a complete failure of an Exchange 2007 server without any backups to restore from. In the first section of this chapter, we'll take a look at what you must back up, depending on which Exchange 2007 Server roles were deployed in your organization.

Backing Up an Exchange 2007 Mailbox Server

One of the most important things to back up regarding Exchange 2007 Mailbox Servers are the databases, which hold user mailboxes and public data. Exchange 2007 provides a new continuous replication functionality that keeps a second copy of one or more databases in a storage group in sync with the active versions of the databases using log file shipping and replay. This provides an extra level of protection for Mailbox and Public Folder databases. However, although the new functionality allows you to make less frequent backups of your databases, it doesn't eliminate the *need* for database backups. In this section, I'll show you how to perform a backup of the databases on an Exchange 2007 server.

NOTE

Another reason why it's crucial to conduct frequent full backups of your Exchange databases with an Exchange-aware backup application is to commit and delete any transaction log files generated since the last full backup. If these log files aren't committed, they will take up more and more space on your disks, and when there's no more disk space for the log files, the database will be dismounted.

Since Exchange 2007 databases still use ESE, you can (just as with previous versions of Exchange), back them up using the Exchange-aware native Windows 2003 backup tool. Exchange 2007 supports two different backup methods. The first is a legacy streaming backup method based on the ESE application programming interface (API), which allows you to back up one or more storage groups at the same time. However, only one backup job can run against a specific storage group. Most of us are familiar with this type of backup since it's the one we have used for ages when referring to Exchange databases. The ESE API backup method is supported by the Windows 2003 backup tool, as well as most third-party backup products.

Then we have the Volume Shadow Copy Service (VSS) backup method, which some of you may know from Exchange 2003 where it was first introduced. The interesting thing about VSS is that this method, in addition to what the legacy streaming backup method offers, can also make an online backup of the copy database when using either Local Continuous Replication or Cluster Continuous Replication in your setup. This means you can schedule the backup windows anytime you want since taking a backup of the database copy has no performance-related impact on the active database. Unfortunately, this method isn't supported by the Windows 2003 backup tool when speaking Exchange databases (only file level backups), and Microsoft doesn't offer any products capable of using VSS, at least not at the time of this writing.

NOTE

The Data Protection Manager (DPM) v2 product will support VSS backups, however. DPM is a server software application that enables disk- and tape-based data protection and recovery for file servers, servers running Microsoft Exchange, and servers running Microsoft SQL Server in an Active Directory Domain Services (AD DS) domain.

DPM performs replication, synchronization, and recovery point creation to provide reliable protection and rapid recovery of data for both system administrators and end users.

Let's go through the steps necessary to back up an Exchange 2007 Mailbox and Public Folder database on an Exchange 2007 Mailbox Server. The first thing you need to do is launch the Windows 2003 backup tool, which can be done by clicking **Start | Run** and typing **NTBackup**. Now click **Switch to Advanced Mode** and then click the **Backup** tab shown in Figure 10.1.

Figure 10.1 Windows 2003 Backup Tool

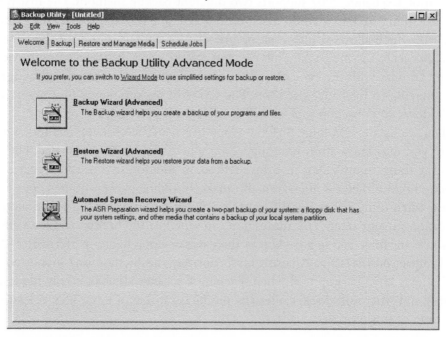

Under the **Backup** tab expand **Microsoft Exchange Server | Mailbox Server | Microsoft Information Store** and check the storage group(s) containing the **Mailbox** and **Public Folder** database (Figure 10.2). Now specify the backup media or filename you want to perform the backup to, and then click **Start Backup**.

Figure 10.2 Selecting the Storage Groups to Be Backed Up

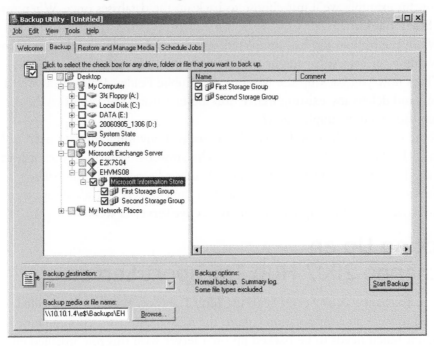

As you can see in Figure 10.3, you now have the option of entering a description for the respective backup job, as well as specify whether the backed-up data should be appended to an existing backup. In addition, you can create a scheduled backup job so it runs, let's say, every day at midnight. By clicking the **Advanced** button, you also have the option of having the backed-up data verified when the job completes.

Figure 10.3 Backup Job Information

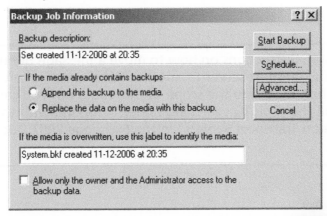

Typically, you should set up an automated backup job schedule, but for the purpose of this example we'll just choose to back up the databases once. When ready, click **Start Backup**.

When the backup job has completed, you can view a report, which will contain any warnings or errors that might occur during the backup.

That's how you back up the Mailbox and Public Folder databases, as well as commit and delete any existing transaction log files using the Windows 2003 Backup tool. Sounds simple, right?

Some of you might wonder whether there isn't anything else you need to back up on an Exchange 2007 Mailbox Server? The answer is no critical files at least since you can always recover an Exchange 2007 Mailbox Server using the *Setup /Mode:RecoverServer* command (shown later in the chapter), but it's always a good idea to back up the System State of the respective server as well.

Backing Up an Exchange 2007 Hub Transport Server

Since an Exchange 2007 Server with the Hub Transport Server role installed was designed to store all configuration data in the Active Directory configuration container, not much needs to be backed up on a server with this role installed either. But just as with the Mailbox server role, you should back up the System State.

Some of you may be wondering why I haven't mentioned anything about backing up the message queues stored in an ESE database on an Exchange 2007 Hub Transport Server... Well, there shouldn't be any need to do so since you can mount the message queues on another existing, or newly installed, Hub Transport server if required. You just need to retrieve the mail.que (which, by default, is located under C:\Program Files\Microsoft\Exchange Server\TransportRoles\data\Queue) from the failed Hub Transport server.

NOTE

Step-by-step instructions on how to move a message queue from a failed Hub Transport server to another Hub Transport server in the organization is outside the scope of this book, but you can find information on the topic by searching under "Working with the Queue Database on Transport Servers" in the Exchange 2007 Documentation Help file.

One thing you might want to back up regarding an Exchange 2007 Hub Transport Server is the Message Tracking and Protocol logs which, by default, are located under C:\Program Files\Microsoft\Exchange Server\TransportRoles\Logs. These files can be backed up using a file level backup.

Author: changes above ok? Mike

As is the case with a Mailbox Server, you can recover a Hub Transport server using the *Setup /Mode:RecoverServer* command.

Backing Up an Exchange 2007 Client Access Server

When using Exchange 2007 Server with the Client Access Server role installed, there are several files you should back up. The first, and perhaps most important, to back up is the IIS Metabase, which among other things is used to store OWA Virtual Directory configuration data. You can back up the IIS configuration on a CAS using the following command:

get-owavirtualdirectory "owa (default web site)" | export-clixml owa.xml -depth 1

In order to restore the IIS configuration from the owa.xml file, you need to use a Windows PowerShell script similar to the following (save it as Restore-OWA.PS1 or use some other meaningful name):

```
$ErrorActionPreference = 'stop'
$savedprops = @(
'DirectFileAccessOnPublicComputersEnabled',
'DirectFileAccessOnPrivateComputersEnabled',
'WebReadyDocumentViewingOnPublicComputersEnabled',
'WebReadyDocumentViewingOnPrivateComputersEnabled',
'ForceWebReadyDocumentViewingFirstOnPublicComputers',
'ForceWebReadyDocumentViewingFirstOnPrivateComputers',
'RemoteDocumentsActionForUnknownServers',
'ActionForUnknownFileAndMIMETypes',
'WebReadyFileTypes',
'WebReadyMimeTypes',
'WebReadyDocumentViewingForAllSupportedTypes',
'AllowedFileTypes',
'AllowedMimeTypes',
'ForceSaveFileTypes',
'ForceSaveMimeTypes',
```

```
'BlockedFileTypes',
'BlockedMimeTypes',
'RemoteDocumentsAllowedServers',
'RemoteDocumentsBlockedServers',
'RemoteDocumentsInternalDomainSuffixList',
'LogonFormat',
'ClientAuthCleanupLevel',
'DefaultDomain',
'FormsAuthentication',
'BasicAuthentication',
'DigestAuthentication',
'WindowsAuthentication',
'GzipLevel',
'FilterWebBeaconsAndHtmlForms',
'NotificationInterval',
'DefaultTheme',
'UserContextTimeout',
'ExchwebProxyDestination',
'VirtualDirectoryType',
'RedirectToOptimalOWAServer',
'DefaultClientLanguage',
'LogonAndErrorLanguage',
'UseGB18030',
'UseISO885915',
'OutboundCharset',
'CalendarEnabled',
'ContactsEnabled',
'TasksEnabled',
'JournalEnabled',
'NotesEnabled',
'RemindersAndNotificationsEnabled',
'PremiumClientEnabled',
'SpellCheckerEnabled',
'SearchFoldersEnabled',
'SignaturesEnabled',
'ThemeSelectionEnabled',
'JunkEmailEnabled',
'UMIntegrationEnabled',
'WSSAccessOnPublicComputersEnabled',
```

```
'WSSAccessOnPrivateComputersEnabled',
'ChangePasswordEnabled',
'UNCAccessOnPublicComputersEnabled',
'UNCAccessOnPrivateComputersEnabled',
'ActiveSyncIntegrationEnabled',
'AllAddressListsEnabled',
'InternalUrl',
'ExternalUrl'
)

$vdir = import-clixml $args[0]

'Recreating "' + $vdir.name + '"' + ' owa version: ' + $vdir.owaversion
if ($vdir.owaversion -eq 'Exchange2007') {
new-owavirtualdirectory -website $vdir.website -internalurl
$vdir.internalurl -externalurl $vdir.externalurl
}
else {
new-owavirtualdirectory -website $vdir.website -owaversion $vdir.
owaversion -name $vdir.displayname -virtualdirectorytype $vdir.
virtualdirectorytype
}
$new = get-owavirtualdirectory $vdir.name
'Restoring properties'
foreach ($prop in $savedprops) {
if ($prop -eq 'ExchwebProxyDestination' -or $prop -eq
'VirtualDirectoryType') {
continue
}
$new.$prop = $vdir.$prop
}
$new | set-owavirtualdirectory
```

To restore the IIS configuration data that were saved in the owa.xml file, type **Restore-OWA.PS1 owa.xml**.

In addition to the IIS metabase, you should back up the System State and the files listed in Table 10.1.

Table 10.1 Files Needed to Restore the IIS Configuration

Data	Location
Microsoft Office Outlook Web Access Web site, and Web.config file	C:\ProgramFiles\Microsoft\Exchange Server\ClientAccess\Owa
IMAP4 and POP3 protocol settings	C:\Program Files\Microsoft\Exchange Server\ClientAccess\
Availability service	Active Directory configuration container and file system, including the Web.config file C:\Program Files\Microsoft\Exchange Server\ClientAccess\exchweb\ews
Autodiscover	IIS metabase
Exchange ActiveSync	Active Directory configuration container File system, including the Web.config file in the \ClientAccess\Sync folder IIS metabase
Outlook Web Access virtual directories	Active Directory configuration container and file system C:\Program Files\Microsoft\Exchange Server\ClientAccess\
Web services configuration	IIS metabase

Like a Mailbox or Hub Transport Server, a Client Access Server can be restored using the *Setup /Mode:RecoverServer* command.

Backing Up an Exchange 2007 Unified Messaging Server

Exchange 2007 servers with the Unified Messaging (UM) role installed store most of the configuration data in the Active Directory, which means it's very limited what you need to back up on the UM server itself.

Table 10.2 lists the files you need to back up.

Table 10.2 Files to Back Up on Unified Messaging Server

Data	Location
Custom audio prompts: Custom audio files (.wav) for UM Dial Plans and UM Auto Attendants Custom audio files (.wav) for telephone user interface (TUI) or Voice Access	C:\Program Files\Microsoft\ Exchange Server\UnifiedMessaging\ Prompts
Incoming calls: .eml and .wma files for each voicemail	C:\Program Files\Microsoft\ Exchange Server \ UnifiedMessaging\temp

In addition, you should back up the System State.

The rest of the configuration data is, as mentioned previously, stored in Active Directory, which makes it possible to restore using the *Setup /Mode:RecoverServer* command.

Backing Up an Exchange 2007 Edge Transport Server

An Exchange 2007 Server with the Edge Transport Server role installed can be restored by using a Cloned Configuration (employing the ImportEdgeConfig.ps1 script). In addition to cloned configuration, you should back up System State as well as the Message Tracking and protocol logs, which are located in C:\Program Files\Microsoft\Exchange Server\TransportRoles\Logs. The message queues that are stored in an ESE database just like message queues on a Hub Transport server can be mounted on another Edge Transport server.

Restoring Exchange 2007 Storage Groups and Databases Using Windows 2003 Backup

So now that you have seen how to back up Mailbox and Public Folder databases, you should of course also be aware of how you restore these databases properly should you experience a database corruption or find them unusable in some other way. In this section, I'll show you how to perform a restore of a Mailbox database from the backup set we created earlier in this chapter. When you restore a Mailbox or Public Folder database from a backup set, any associated transaction log files are restored as well. It's important you understand that a restore of a Mailbox database will copy the database file (.EDB) into its original location on the disk, and thereby overwrite any existing .EDB file. In addition, any transaction log files will be copied to a temporary location, which can be specified when doing the actual restore. Upon the restore's completion (hopefully without any serious warnings or errors!), the log files will be replayed into the restored version of the database. In addition to the log files, a file called Restore.env will also be copied to the specified temporary folder. This file keeps control of which storage group the log files belong to, as well as the database paths and range of log files that have been restored.

In order to restore the aforementioned Mailbox database, we need to perform the following steps. First, open the **Exchange Management Console**, expand **Server Configuration**, and then select the **Mailbox** subnode. Now choose the respective Mailbox server in the **Result** pane, and then dismount the Mailbox database, as shown in Figure 10.4.

Figure 10.4 Dismounting the Mailbox Database

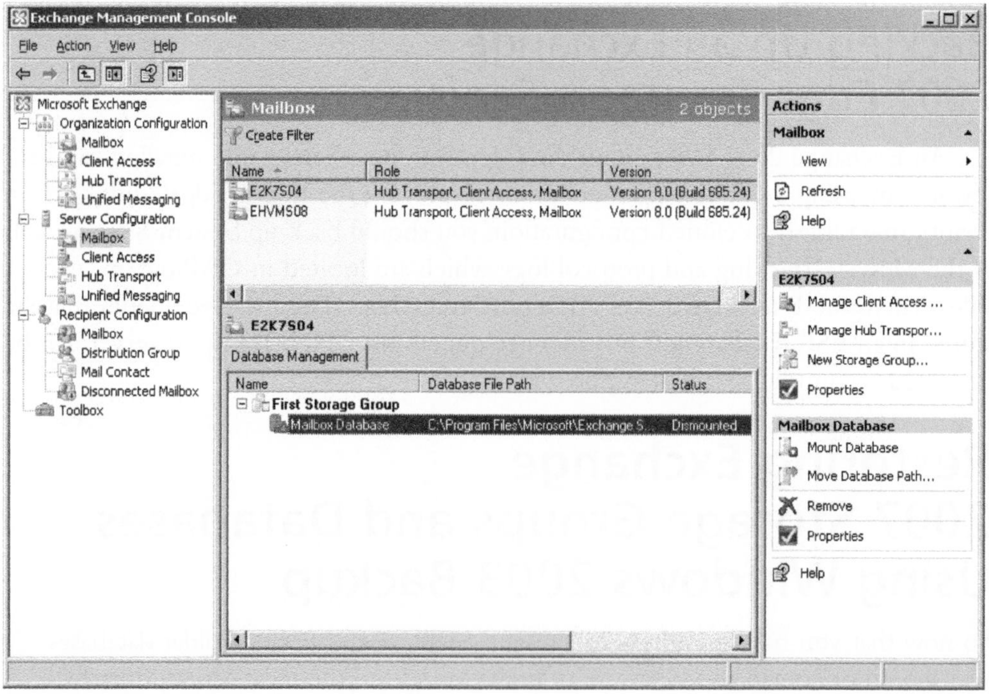

Now open the properties page for the Mailbox database. Check **This database can be overwritten by a restore** (Figure 10.5) and click **OK**.

Figure 10.5 Allowing the Mailbox Database to Be Overwritten by a Restore

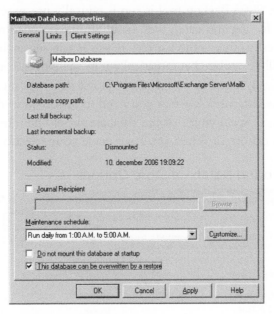

We're now ready to restore the databases using the Windows 2003 Backup tool, so let's launch this tool by clicking **Start | Run** and typing **NTBackup**, and then selecting the **Restore and Manage Media** tab. Expand the desired media item and backup set, then check the **log files** and **mailbox database**, as shown in Figure 10.6. We can then click **Start Restore**.

Figure 10.6 Restoring the First Storage Group

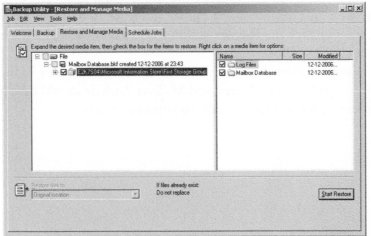

You'll be faced with a screen similar to the one shown in Figure 10.7. Here, you need to specify the server you want to restore the database to (the local server on which the Windows 2003 Backup tool is run is typically pre-entered here), and the temporary location for log and patch files. In addition, you need to specify whether the restore you're performing is the last restore set. If you select this option, all the restored log files will be replayed automatically into the database after the restore has completed. You typically want to do this if you don't have any incremental or differential backups of the database's log files you need to restore after this restore. Finally, you have the option of specifying that the database should be mounted automatically after the restore has occurred. When you have made your selections, click **OK**.

Figure 10.7 Restoring Database Store Options

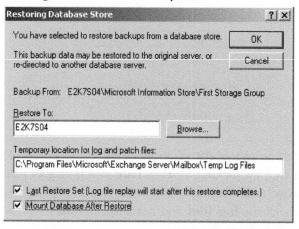

The restore will now begin. Depending on the size of the database, it will take some time to complete. Since the database in this example is under 11MB, the restore took less than a second, as you can see in Figure 10.8. When the restore has completed, you can click the **Report** button to see a detailed log of the restore process. When ready, click **Close**.

If your restore completed successfully, you can now switch back to the Exchange Management Console, where the restored Mailbox database should have been mounted automatically, and we can call the restore a success.

Figure 10.8 Restore Completed Successfully

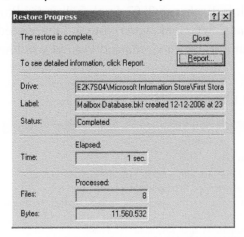

NOTE

It's beyond the scope of this book to show the steps necessary to restore a database to its last good known state using a combination of a full backup set and incremental or differential backups.

Repairing a Corrupt or Damaged Exchange 2007 Database Using Eseutil

There may be situations where you either don't have a proper backup set to restore a particular database from, or perhaps you found out that the database you just restored to replace a corrupt or damaged database is also corrupt or damaged. This is where Extensible Storage Engine Utilities for Microsoft Exchange Server (Eseutil) comes in. Eseutil is a command-line utility that can be used to perform a range of database tasks including repair, offline defragmentation, and integrity checks. Eseutil hasn't changed much from Exchange 2003 since Exchange still uses ESE databases when speaking Exchange 2007. This means that pretty much all of the switches and parameters available in Eseutil are the same as in previous versions. Since there are plenty of books and online documentation describing how you should approach fixing a corrupt database using Eseutil, I won't include comprehensive information on how to use this utility in this book. Instead, I'll provide you with the most common Eseutil switches, as well as a few examples.

Eseutil, as in previous versions, is located in the Bin folder under your Exchange installation path, which in Exchange 2007, by default, is C:\Program Files\Microsoft\Exchange Server. However, you no longer need to run the tool from that path; you can just open a Command Prompt window and type **Eseutil**, as shown in Figure 10.9.

Figure 10.9 Eseutil Modes

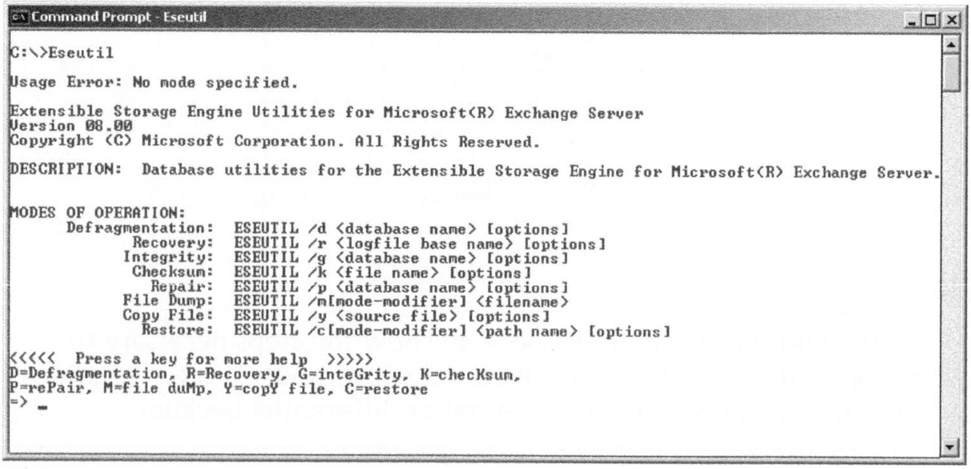

NOTE

You can also run Eseutil directly from the Exchange Management Shell.

Before we move on, we want to stress that it's very important you always try to restore your databases from a backup if possible, since there's a good chance you will lose some data when performing a repair of a database. The reason for this is that Eseutil often needs to discard rows from tables or even entire tables. In addition, you should have a repaired database running in your production environment only for a temporary period, which means that after you have repaired a database, you should move all mailboxes from the database to a new one. Needless to say, you should also be sure to make a copy of the database before performing a repair using Eseutil.

NOTE

Did you know that when a database corruption occurs, 99.9 percent of the time it's caused by the underlying hard disk drive subsystem? Yes, it's true! This means there's a pretty good chance the database corruption experienced is caused by an I/O issue on the disk set in your Exchange 2007 server. You should therefore always examine the Application and System logs, searching for any events that might indicate this to be the problem.

Eseutil /P can, in addition to the Mailbox and Public Folder databases, also be run against the ESE database-based message queues on either a Hub Transport or Edge Transport server in your Exchange 2007 organization.

To repair a corrupted or otherwise damaged database, run Eseutil with the /P switch. So, to repair a database called Mailbox Database.edb located in E:\Program Files\Microsoft\Exchange Server\Mailbox\First Storage Group, you would need to type:

Eseutil /P "E:\Program Files\Microsoft\Exchange Server\Mailbox\First Storage Group\Mailbox Database.edb"

After pressing **Enter**, you would receive the warning message shown in Figure 10.10.

Figure 10.10 An Eseutil Repair Warning

NOTE

You must have the necessary amount of free space (equal to 110 percent of the database file size) on the disk containing the database before you can run Eseutil /P and Eseutil /D.

Click **OK** to proceed, and then wait until Eseutil has repaired the database. If the database is completed successfully, it's highly recommended you perform a full backup of the database, since restoring a backup made before the repair would roll the database back to the state it was in at the time of the backup, which wouldn't be very smart.

After you have run Eseutil /P against a database, also run Eseutil /D in order to fully rebuild indexes and defragment the database. In order to run Eseutil /D against the database, type:

Eseutil /D "E:\Program Files\Microsoft\Exchange Server\Mailbox\First Storage Group\Mailbox Database.edb"

When an offline defragmentation has been completed, there's one additional thing to do: repair the database at the application level (repair information and relationships between mailboxes, folders, items, and attachments) by running the Information Store Integrity Checker (Isinteg) utility with the *-fix* parameter. Figure 10.11 shows the parameters and syntaxes available for the Isinteg utility.

Figure 10.11 Isinteg Switches

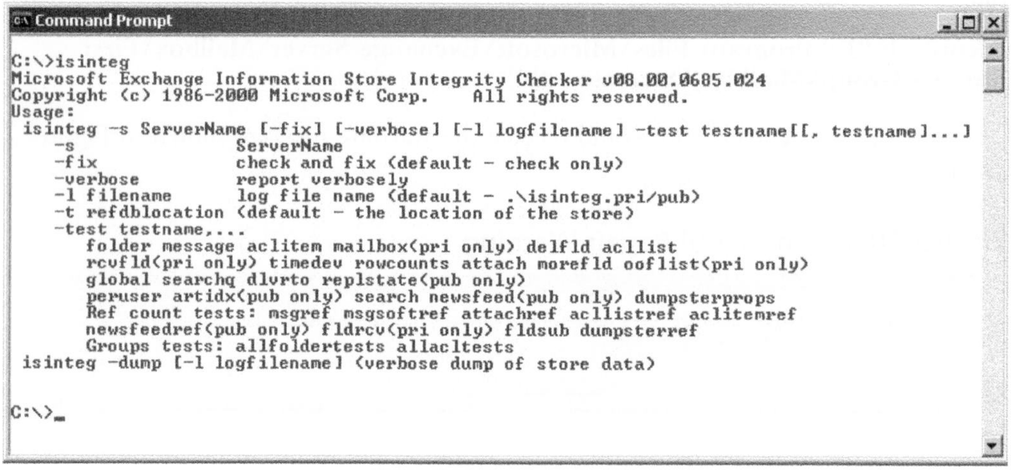

If you aren't comfortable running the Eseutil and Isinteg utilities manually on your databases, you also have the option of performing a repair using a wizard-driven interface. This is where the new Disaster Recovery Management tool, a sibling of tools such as the Exchange Best Practices Analyzer Tool (ExBPA), comes into play. To invoke this tool, click the **Toolbox** work center node in the navigation tree in the **Exchange Management Console**, then open the tool by selecting it in the Result pane and clicking **Open Tool** in the **Actions** pane (Figure 10.12).

Figure 10.12 Disaster Recovery Management Tool

   The tool will now check if there is any tool or configuration file updates available on Microsoft.com, and if so, apply them without requiring a restart. Once any updates have been applied, click the **Go to Welcome Screen** link, then enter an identifying label for the activity, and click **Next**. When the tool has connected to the Active Directory, you will be presented with the task list shown in Figure 10.13. Here, you should select the **Repair Database** task.

   Now select the storage group that contains the database you wish to repair, click **Next**, and on the **Select Databases to Repair** page, check the respective database, as I did in Figure 10.14. Then, click **Next**.

Figure 10.13 Exchange Troubleshooting Assistant Tasks

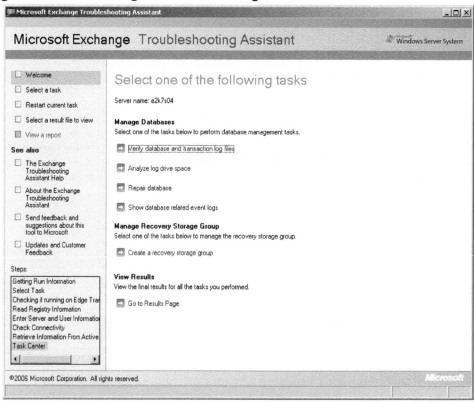

Figure 10.14 Selecting the Database to Repair

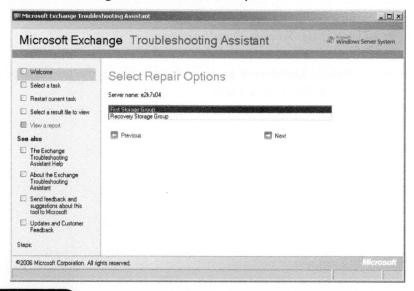

You will now need to read a repair task warning. I suggest you read it carefully. When you have done so, choose **Continue to Perform Repair Task**, and then click **OK** in the confirmation dialog box shown in Figure 10.15.

Figure 10.15 ExTRA Confirmation

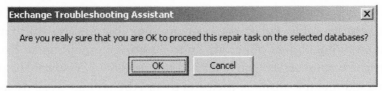

The tool will now run Eseutil /P and then Eseutil /D, followed by Isinteg –fix –test alltests against the respective database, just like we did manually earlier in this section. After a while, depending on the size of the database, you will be taken to a Report Repair Results page where you can see if the actions completed without any issues, and if not, it will show an explanation why it didn't.

Restoring Mailbox Data Using the Recovery Storage Group Feature

The Recovery Storage Group (RSG) feature, which was originally introduced back in Exchange 2003, gives you, the Exchange administrator, the option of mounting a second copy of a mailbox database (typically a mailbox database restored from backup) so you can extract data from one or more mailboxes in the respective database during working hours without affecting the production databases.

Depending on how much you have used the new Exchange 2007 Management Console (EMC), you may have noticed you can no longer create an RSG from within the EMC. With Exchange 2007, this is instead done using the new Database Recovery Management tool, which as you saw in the previous section, is found under the Exchange Toolbox work center, or by using the Exchange Management Shell (EMS).

When mounting a copy of a Mailbox database to an RSG, you can extract the data from a mailbox and then merge the data with another mailbox located in a mailbox database in a production storage group. You can also extract the data and copy it to a specific folder in another mailbox. With Exchange 2003 RTM, the data was extracted, copied, and merged with another mailbox or mailbox folder using the Microsoft Exchange Server Mailbox Merge Wizard (ExMerge) tool, but in Exchange 2003 SP1 the process was integrated into the Exchange 2003 System Manager GUI.

There are a few things you should be aware of when dealing with RSGs. First, they cannot be accessed by any protocols other than MAPI, and although they can be accessed using MAPI, this doesn't mean you can connect to a mailbox stored in a recovery database using an Outlook MAPI client. MAPI is strictly used to access mailboxes using the Exchange Troubleshooting Assistant and the respective Exchange Management Shell cmdlets. In addition, you should be aware that you still cannot use RSGs to restore Public Folder data, only mailbox data. It's also worth mentioning that even though you can create up to 50 storage groups on an Exchange 2007 Enterprise edition server, you're limited to one RSG per server. However, it's supported to add multiple mailbox databases to an RSG as long as all databases belong to the same storage group. Finally, you should note that although it's possible to add a restored mailbox database to an RSG on another Exchange 2007 server, it's important you understand that the Exchange 2007 server must belong to the same Active Directory forest.

With the preceding in mind, let's move on and see how you manage RSGs.

Managing Recovery Storage Groups Using the Exchange Troubleshooting Assistant

You can create a Recovery Storage Group (RSG) either by using the Disaster Recovery Management tool, which is based on the Microsoft Exchange Troubleshooting Assistant (ExTRA), or by running the *New-StorageGroup* cmdlet with the *–Recovery* parameter in the Exchange Management Shell.

To create the RSG using the Disaster Recovery Management tool, you should first launch it from beneath the Toolbox work center in the navigation tree of the Exchange Management Console (EMC). Let the tool check for any tool or configuration file updates available, and then click the **Go to Welcome** screen link. Enter an identifying label for this activity (such as Create RSG), and then click **Next**. In the **Tasks** list that appears, click **Create a Recovery Storage Group**, and then select the storage group you want to link with the recovery storage group, as shown in Figure 10.16. Then, click **Next** once again.

Figure 10.16 Selecting the Storage Group to Link with the RSG

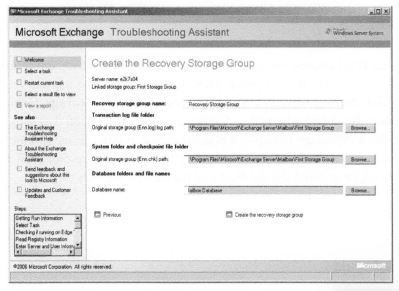

Now it's time to create the RSG, but before doing so you need to give it a name (the default name is Recovery Storage Group, which should be okay in most situations). When you have entered an appropriate name, click **Create the recovery storage group** (Figure 10.17).

Figure 10.17 Creating the RSG

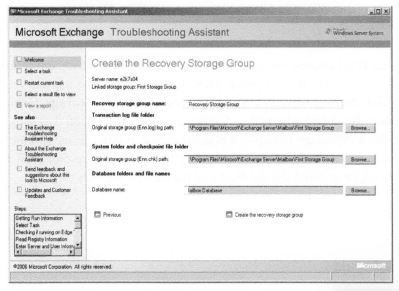

After a little while, you will be presented with a screen similar to the one in Figure 10.18, and the RSG for the respective Mailbox database has now been created.

Figure 10.18 RSG Result

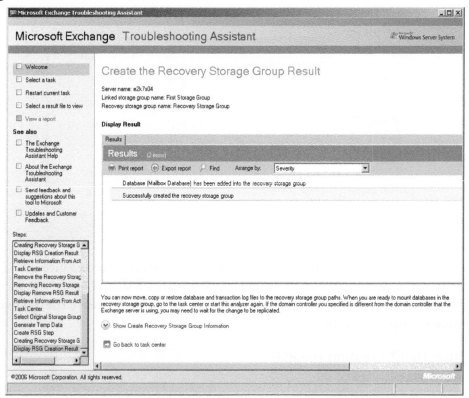

With the RSG created, we can move, copy, or restore database and transaction log files to the recovery storage group paths. To see the path for the recovery storage group log and database files, click **Show Create Recovery Storage Group Information**. By default, the path is C:\Program Files\Microsoft\Exchange Server\Mailbox\<Storage Group>\RSG*xxxxxxxxx*, as you can see in Figure 10.19. The RSG*xxxxxxxxx* folder will appear empty in Windows Explorer until you have moved, copied, or restored the database and transaction log files to it.

Figure 10.19 Storage Group and Recovery Storage Group Paths

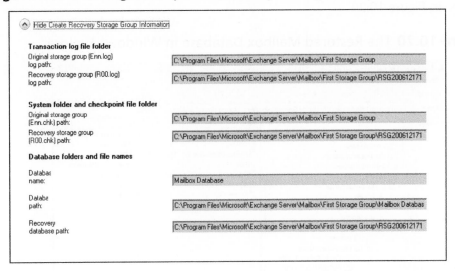

For the purpose of this example, we will restore a Mailbox database from a backup using the Windows 2003 Backup tool. So let's launch the Windows 2003 Backup tool in advanced mode, and then click the **Restore and Manage Media** tab. Here we need to select the Mailbox database and log files we want to restore. When you have done so, click the **Start Restore** button.

> **NOTE**
>
> Note that the Restore Files To: Drop-Down box is set to Original Location. Also notice we cannot change this selection. But does that mean the Mailbox database currently in production will be replaced by the one we restore from backup? No, this is not the case. First, we haven't dismounted the production Mailbox database, and second, we haven't enabled the *This Database Can Be Overwritten By A Restore* option on the Mailbox database property page. Because of this, the Mailbox database will be restored to the recovery storage group we just created.

Now specify the Exchange Server to which you want to restore the respective Mailbox database, and then enter a temporary location for the log and patch files. Lastly, check **Last Restore Set** (Log File Replay will start after this restore completes) since this is the last restore set. When you are done, click **OK** and wait for the restore job to complete. Then, click the **Close** button.

The respective files have now been restored to the RSG*xxxxxxxxx* folder, as you can see in Figure 10.20.

Figure 10.20 The Restored Mailbox Database in Windows Explorer

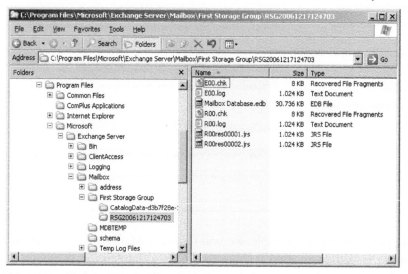

Since we didn't check the *Mount Database After Restore* option, the Mailbox database will now be in a dismounted state. With this in mind, let's switch back to the ExTRA Task Center. As shown in Figure 10.21, we now have several new recovery storage group–related tasks available. Since the Mailbox database needs to be mounted before we can extract data from it, we have to click **Mount or dismount databases in the recovery storage group**.

On the **Mount or Dismount Database** page, check the respective Mailbox database and click **Mount selected database** (Figure 10.22).

Figure 10.21 Selecting Mount or Dismount Databases in the Recovery Storage Group

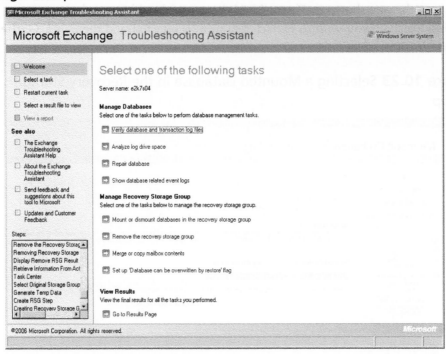

Figure 10.22 Mounting the Mailbox Database Using the ExTRA Tool

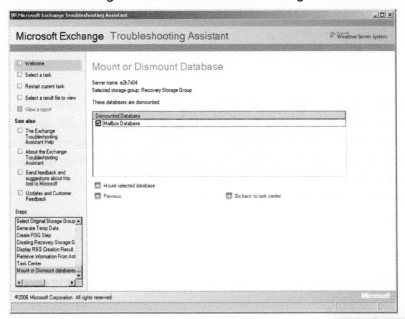

Once the Mailbox database has been mounted, click **Go back to task center**, and then select **Merge or copy mailbox content**. This will bring us to a screen similar to the one shown in Figure 10.23, here you should just make sure the Mailbox database you wish to extract data from is selected, and then click **Gather merge information**.

Figure 10.23 Selecting a Mounted Database in the Recovery Storage Group

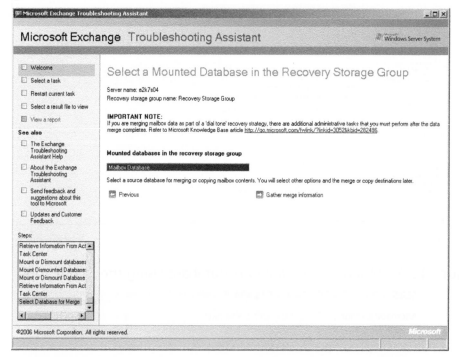

We now have the option of swapping the Mailbox database mounted to the RSG and the linked production Mailbox database (a recommended step if you're performing a dial-tone database restore) by checking Swap Database Configurations, as can be seen in Figure 10.24. Since this option will swap the two databases, both of them need to be dismounted, which will affect mail service to the end users whose mailboxes are stored in the respective database.

Figure 10.24 The Database Swap Option

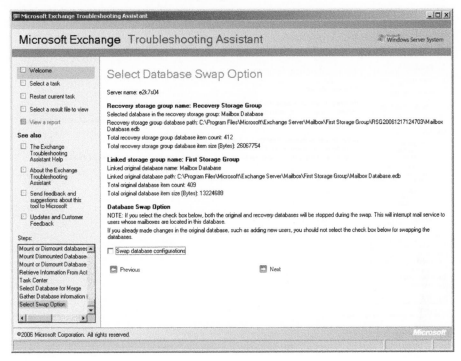

Since we aren't dealing with a dial-tone database restore in this example, just click **Next**.

On the **Select Merge Options** page, click **Perform pre-merge tasks** (Figure 10.25).

Figure 10.25 Specifying Merge Options

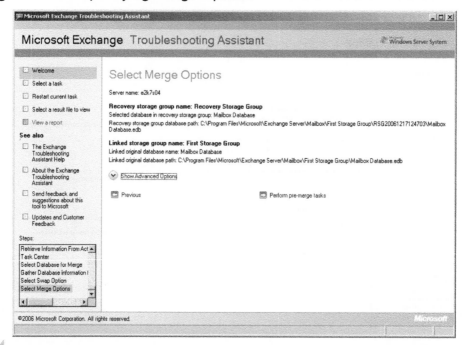

NOTE

Note that you have the option of clicking Show Advanced Options. Under the Advanced options, we can specify different match and filtering options, as well as the bad item limit. This is also the place where you specified whether all merge mailbox data should be merged to the respective mailboxes in the production Mailbox database, or whether they should be copied to a single target mailbox.

The final step is to select the mailboxes you want to merge. You do this by checking the box to the left of each user name in the list, as shown in Figure 10.26.

Figure 10.26 Selecting the Mailboxes to Merge

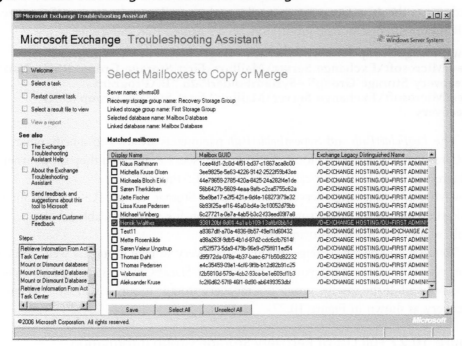

Now wait for the tool to merge the mailbox data from the Mailbox database in the recovery storage group for the selected mailbox. When the mailbox data merge has completed, you should be able to see the content deleted from the production Mailbox database. You don't even need to restart the Outlook or OWA client for the restored data to appear!

When you have merged or copied the required Mailbox data, you can use ExTRA to dismount and then remove the recovery storage group. Be sure you delete the files in the RSG*xxxxxxxxx* folder after you have removed it so the files don't take up valuable disk space.

Managing Recovery Storage Groups Using the Exchange Management Shell

As mentioned earlier in this chapter, you can also manage an RSG using the Exchange Management Shell (EMS). If you know your cmdlets, restoring mailbox data from a Mailbox database in a recovery storage group can be done a lot faster than when you're using ExTRA.

The first step is to create the RSG. In order to create an RSG via the EMS, you need to run the *New-StorageGroup* cmdlet with the *−Recovery* parameter. So, to create an RSG for the first storage group on a server named E2K7S04, type:

New-StorageGroup −Server E2K7S04 −LogFolderPath "E:\Program Files\Microsoft\Exchange Server\Mailbox\First Storage Group\RSG −Name "Recovery Storage Group" −SystemFolderPath "E:\Program Files\Microsoft\Exchange Server\Mailbox\First Storage Group\RSG" −Recovery

The *LogFolderPath* and *SystemFolderPath* parameters are used to specify where the RSG-related files should be located. As you can see, we specified they should them to be restored to a subfolder called RSG under E:\Program Files\Microsoft\Exchange Server\Mailbox\First Storage Group\RSG. If you intend to do the same, please make sure there's sufficient disk space available for the Mailbox database you're restoring from backup.

To see if a respective storage group is a recovery storage group (as well as many other types of information), you can use the *Get-StorageGroup <storage group name>* | *FL* command. If the storage group is a recovery storage group, it will say True under Recovery, as shown in Figure 10.27

Figure 10.27 Full List of Recovery Storage Group Information

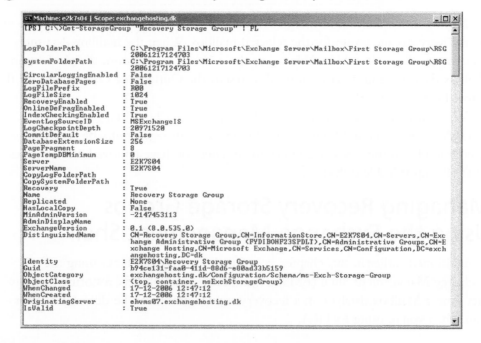

The next step is to add a recovery database (either moved, copied, or restored from backup) to the RSG, this is done by running the *New-MailboxDatabase* cmdlet with the *MailboxDatabaseToRecover* parameter. So, to add a recovery database to the recovery storage group on a server named E2KS04 with the edb file path pointing to E:\Program Files\Microsoft\Exchange Server\Mailbox\First Storage Group\RSG, type:

New-MailboxDatabase −MailboxDatabaseToRecover "Mailbox Database" −StorageGroup "E2K7S04\Recovery Storage Group" −EDBFilePath "E:\Program Files\Microsoft\Exchange Server\Mailbox\First Storage Group\RSG\Mailbox Database.edb"

With the Mailbox Database created in the recovery storage group, we now need to configure it to allow overwrites by running the *Set-MailboxDatabase* cmdlet with the *−AllowRestore* parameter. To allow file restores for the recovery database just created, type:

Set-MailboxDatabase -Identity "E2K7S04\Recovery Storage Group\Mailbox Database" -AllowFileR
estore $true

Now that we have created a recovery database in the recovery storage group and allowed it to be overwritten by a file restore, it's time to restore the mailbox database version from which you want to extract and copy or merge data to the mailbox database in production. To do so, launch the Windows 2003 Backup tool and restore the respective Mailbox database version using the same steps as we did when we used the ExTRA to recover Mailbox data.

We now need to mount the restore Mailbox database using the *Mount-Database* cmdlet. In order to do so, type:

Mount-Database −Identity "E2K7S04\Recovery Storage Group\Mailbox Database"

With the Mailbox database mounted, we can now extract Mailbox data from it. For example, if you want to merge the mailbox data of an existing user in the recovery database to the production Mailbox database, you need to type:

Restore-Mailbox −Identity <username> -RSGDatabase "servername\RSG name\database name"

In Figure 10.28, we recovered mailbox data for a user called Test User 1 on a server named E2K7S04.

Figure 10.28 Restoring Mailbox Data from a Mailbox in a Recovery Storage Group

```
Machine: e2k7s04 | Scope: exchangehosting.dk                                    _ □ ×
[PS] C:\>Restore-Mailbox -Identity "TestUser1" -RSGDatabase "e2k7s04\Recovery Storage Group\Mailbox
Database"

Confirm
Are you sure you want to perform this action?
Recovering mailbox content from the mailbox 'Test User 1' in the recovery database
'E2K7S04\Recovery Storage Group\Mailbox Database' into the mailbox for 'Test User 1
<Testuser1@exchangehosting.dk>'. The operation can take a long time.
[Y] Yes  [A] Yes to All  [N] No  [L] No to All  [S] Suspend  [?] Help (default is "Y"):
```

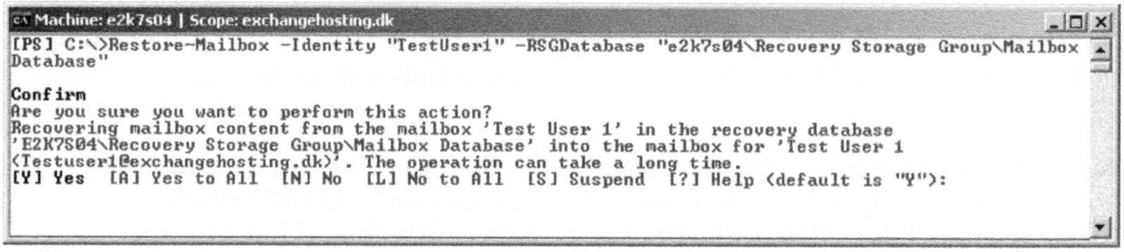

> **NOTE**
>
> Depending on the size of the mailbox to be recovered, this merging process can take a long time.

If you need to recover mailbox data for all users in the RSG, you would need to use the following command:

Get-MailboxStatistics -Database "Recovery Storage Group\Mailbox Database" | Restore-Mailbox

Let's suppose the mailbox in the recovery database that you want to recover data from has in the meantime been deleted from the production Mailbox database. In this case, you have the option of recovering the mailbox data to a target folder in another mailbox by using the following command:

Restore-Mailbox –RSGMailbox "Test User 1" -RSGDatabase "servername\RSG name\database name" –Identity "Test User 2" –TargetFolder "Test User 1 Recovered data"

Just as with recovering data using the ExTRA tool, when using the Exchange Management Shell you should remember to remove the RSG after the required data has been recovered. To do so, first run the command to remove the recovery database:

Remove-MailboxDatabase –Identity "E2K7S04\Recovery Storage Group\Mailbox Database"

Click **Yes** to the confirmation warning, and then type the following command in order to remove the RSG:

Remove-StorageGroup –Identity "E2K7S04\Recovery Storage Group"

Finally, delete the RSG folder manually using Windows Explorer.

Recovering an Exchange 2007 Server Using the RecoverServer Switch

What could be worse than facing one or more seriously corrupted Exchange 2007 mailbox databases? Yes, you guessed right: facing a completely dead Exchange 2007 Server. In this section, I'll shine some light on the steps necessary to restore an Exchange 2007 Server that has experienced a major hardware failure causing a complete loss of data. As is the case with Exchange 2000 and 2003, you can recover an Exchange 2007 Server in a fairly straightforward way. As you probably know, we could use the DisasterRecovery switch to recover a dead Exchange 2000 or 2003 Server on new hardware, but with Exchange 2007 this switch no longer exists. Instead, it has been replaced by the new RecoverServer switch, which is similar to the DisasterRecovery switch. The interesting thing about the RecoverServer switch is that it can be used to recover all types of Exchange 2007 Server roles, except the Edge Transport Server role, which uses ADAM and not the Active Directory to store configuration data.

> **NOTE**
>
> To recover a server with the Edge Transport Server role installed, you must use the cloned configuration tasks to export and import configuration information.

When you run Setup with the RecoverServer switch on a new Windows 2003 Server that is configured with the same name as the one that has crashed or is permanently down for some reason, Setup will read the configuration information for the respective Exchange 2007 server from the Active Directory. In addition to applying the roles and settings stored in Active Directory, Setup will, as is the case when installing an Exchange 2007 Server role without the RecoverServer switch, install the Exchange files and services required for the respective Exchange 2007 server role(s). This means that local customizations done on the server (such as Mailbox databases, Receive connectors, custom OWA settings, SSL certificates, and so on) need to be re-created or recovered manually afterwards.

In this section, we'll go through the steps necessary to recover an Exchange 2007 server with the Hub Transport, Mailbox Server, and Client Access Server roles installed.

Restoring and Configuring the Operating System

When you have received a replacement server or replacements for the failed hardware components, it's important you configure and partition the disk sets in the new server so they are identical to the way they were configured in the failed server. When the hardware is configured according to the documentation you wrote for the failed Exchange 2007 (which you did write, right?), we can begin installing the operating system from the Windows 2003 Server 64-bit media. When Windows 2003 Server has been installed, it's important you install the Windows Components required by the Exchange Server 2007 Server roles, as well as any service packs and Windows updates that were applied on the failed server.

In addition to that already mentioned, you should also make sure you name the new server with the same server name. Before doing so, however, it's important the failed Exchange 2007 server be turned off. In addition, you should add the server to the respective Active Directory domain, first resetting the computer account for the respective Exchange 2007 server. In order to reset the computer account, you must perform the following steps:

1. Log on to a domain controller or another server with the Adminpak installed in the Active Directory domain, and then open the **Active Directory Users and Computers (ADUC) MMC** snap-in.

2. In the ADUC MMC snap-in, navigate to the organizational unit (OU) containing your computer accounts (by default, the Computers OU), right-click the computer account that should be reset, and then select **Reset Account**, as shown in Figure 10.29.

Figure 10.29 Resetting the Computer Account in the ADUC MMC Snap-in

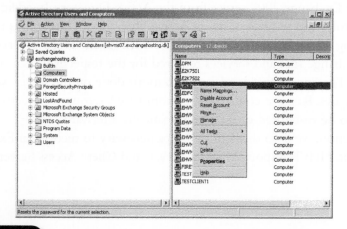

3. Click **Yes** to the warning in the dialog box that appears, and then click **OK**.

We can now join the new server to the domain without issues. Do so and perform the required reboot.

Installing Exchange 2007 Using the RecoverServer Switch

Now that Windows 2003 has been installed properly, we can move on and start installing Exchange 2007 by running Setup.exe with the RecoverServer switch. In order to do so, perform the following steps:

1. Click **Start | Run** and type **CMD**. Then, press **Enter**.

2. Change to the directory or media containing your Exchange 2007 Setup files, and then type **Setup.com /M:RecoverServer**. As can be seen in Figure 10.30, Exchange 2007 Setup will now prepare the Exchange 2007 setup, and then perform the mandatory prerequisite checks. Finally, it will begin to copy the Exchange files and then configure each Exchange 2007 Server role by reading the required configuration information from Active Directory.

Figure 10.30 Recovering an Exchange 2007 Server Using the RecoverServer Switch

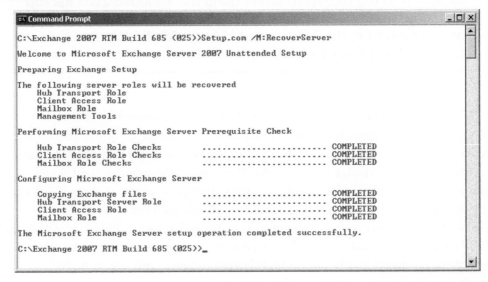

NOTE

If you're recovering an Exchange 2007 server with the Hub Transport Server role installed, and this is the only Exchange 2007 server with this role installed, its recommended you run Setup.com /M:RecoverServer with the /DoNotStartTransport syntax since there's a few post-recovery steps that should be completed before this role is made active.

When the Exchange setup has completed each phase successfully, we're close to calling the server recovery a success. However, there are a few post-recovery steps that need to be finished, depending on what Exchange 2007 Server roles are installed on the server. It's obvious a recovered server with the Mailbox Server role must have the respective Mailbox database and Public Folder database restored from backup, or copied back from the disks on the old server (if possible). If the Public Folders are replicated with other Exchange 2000/2003 or 2007 servers in the Exchange organization, you don't need to restore it since an empty Public Folder database will be backfilled from the other Public folder server(s).

NOTE

If you need to restore one or more Mailbox and/or Public Folder databases to the recovered server using the Windows 2003 Backup tool, note that you must catalog the respective backup (.BKF). This is done by selecting the **Restore and Manage Media** tab, and then clicking **Tools | Catalog** a backup file in the menu.

If the Hub Transport Server role is installed on the recovered Exchange 2007 server, you may also need to restore any saved message queue databases (which in Exchange 2007 are stored in an ESE database and not in the NTFS file system as was the case with Exchange 2000 and 2003) and place them in the right folder (should be done while the Microsoft Exchange Transport service is stopped, which is why it's a good idea to run the RecoverServer switch with the /DoNotStartTransport syntax if you're recovering an Exchange 2007 server with the Hub Transport Server role installed), as well as reconfigure any Receive connectors since these are stored locally on the Hub Transport Server and not in Active Directory, as is the case with Send Connectors.

In addition, you may need to restore the Client Access Server settings (custom OWA files and/or virtual directories). Custom virtual folder settings can be restored by using the script method mentioned earlier in this chapter.

NOTE

Although it should be the most comprehensive, as well as fastest, way to recover a server using the RecoverServer switch, it's worth mentioning that it's fully supported to restore an Exchange 2007 Server by restoring the System State as well as all the Exchange installation files. Bear in mind, however, that this method requires you restore Exchange 2007 on the same hardware.

Recovering an Exchange 2007 Cluster Using the RecoverCMS Switch

To finish off this chapter, we wanted to talk a little about how you can recover an Exchange 2007 clustered mailbox server (both CCR and SCC) by using the *ExSetup.exe* command with the RecoverCMS switch. Since we're talking about restoring a cluster, many of you may think the tasks involved are terribly complex. As a matter of fact, it's a relatively simple task. The biggest challenge is rebuilding the Windows 2003 cluster itself, which is a pretty harmless process. Once you have rebuilt the Windows 2003 cluster on new hardware, you need to install the Passive Clustered Mailbox Role on one of the Windows 2003 cluster nodes, navigate to the Exchange Bin folder (which, by default, is located under C:\Program Files\Microsoft\Exchange Server\), and then run the following command:

ExSetup.exe /RecoverCMS /CMSName:<name of the clustered mailbox server> /CMSIPAddress:<IP address of the clustered mailbox server>

When the clustered mailbox server has been recovered successfully (if the recovered clustered mailbox server is based on a CCR), you need to enable replication as replication, which, by default, will be in a suspended state after recovery using the RecoverCMS switch. In addition you must (both when recovering a CCR and SCC) start the Exchange System Attendant service manually since it will stop right after the clustered mailbox server has been recovered.

The next step is to restore the respective Mailbox and/or Public Folder databases that existed on the failed clustered mailbox server from backup, or move/copy them from their respective locations.

NOTE

If you're recovering a Single Copy Cluster (SCC) and stored the Mailbox and Public Folder databases on a storage area network (SAN), you won't need to restore the databases from backup as long as each node points to the same shared storage subsystem that the failed clustered mailbox server did.

When any required Mailbox and/or Public Folder databases have been restored, you should now install the Passive Clustered Mailbox Role on the second node (and if recovering an SCC, any additional nodes). If you recovered a clustered mailbox server that is based on SCC, we can now call the recovery of the clustered mailbox server a success, but if you use CCR, there's one final task to complete, and that is to reseed the replica and resume replication. To reseed the second copy of the database(s), you should run the following command in the Exchange Management Shell:

Update-StorageGroupCopy –Identity: <Servername\Name of StorageGroup>

When the storage group(s) have been reseeded, you can resume replication by running:

Resume-StorageGroupCopy –Identity:<Servername>\Name of Storage Group>

So, this was not as difficult as you had imagined it, right?

Restoring Mailbox Databases Using the Improved Database Portability Feature

As those of you with plenty of disaster recovery experience from Exchange 2003 might be aware, Mailbox database portability (that is mounting a Mailbox database to an alternative Exchange Server) was rather limited in this version of Exchange, actually the only options available were to mount the respective Mailbox database into a recovery storage group (RSG), into a storage group on a server with the same name as the failed server, or into the storage group on an Exchange Server in the same administrative group. Although mailbox databases were portable between Exchange 2003 servers (on the same service pack level) in the same administrative group, certain tasks were involved with this procedure. You had to rename the Mailbox databases appropriately, as well as re-link each mailbox in the database to an Active Directory user account before the mailbox could be accessible to an end user. In addition, several other issues might exist if the Mailbox database contained a System Attendant mailbox. Finally, depending on what type of third-party applications were running on the particular Exchange server, it was also best practice to reboot the server once the Mailbox database move was completed.

With Exchange 2007, the Mailbox database portability feature has been improved drastically. Now you can port and recover a Mailbox database to any server in the Exchange 2007 organization, and because of the new Autodiscover service, all Outlook 2007 clients will be redirected to the new server automatically the first time they try to connect after the Mailbox database has been mounted on another Exchange 2007 server.

NOTE

Since only Outlook 2007 clients can take advantage of the new Autodiscover service introduced in Exchange 2007, any legacy clients (Outlook 2003 and earlier) won't be redirected to the new server automatically.

Some of you might wonder if Exchange 2007 (unlike Exchange 2003) allows you to port or recover a Public Folder database to another server. The answer is no. Doing so is still not supported since it will break Public Folder replication. The proper method for moving a Public Folder database to another server is to add the respective server to the Public Folder replica list.

Okay, now that you have heard how cool the new Mailbox database portability improvements in Exchange 2007 are, let's take a look at the steps needed they entail:

First, it's important you make sure the Mailbox database you wish to port or recover to another server is in a clean shutdown state. If not, you must perform a soft recovery of the database, which is done by running Eseutil /R <ENN> against it. ENN is the prefix of the storage group to which you want to commit any existing transaction log files. One method you can use to find this prefix is to open the property page of the respective storage group containing the Mailbox database you wish to port or recover to another Exchange 2007 server (see Figure 10.31).

Figure 10.31 The Transaction Log Files Prefix

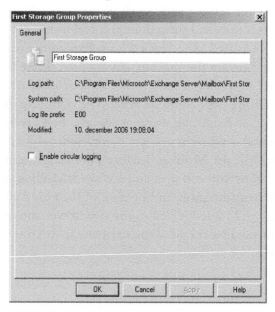

Once the Mailbox database is in a clean shutdown state, the next step is to move the Mailbox database (.EDB file, transaction log files, and Exchange Search catalog) to the system path folder of the respective storage group on the other server, and then create a new Mailbox database in the storage group using the following command:

New-MailboxDatabase –StorageGroup <Servername>\<Name of Storage Group> -Name <Name of Mailbox Database>

In this example, you will mount a database named Mailbox database to the Third Storage Group on an Exchange 2007 Server called EHVMS08. Therefore, the command we need to run is shown in Figure 10.32.

Figure 10.32 Creating a New Mailbox Database in the Third Storage Group

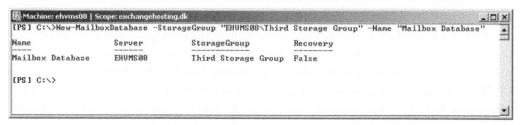

Because Exchange 2007 won't create an .EDB file for a newly created Mailbox database before it's mounted for the first time, using the *New-MailboxDatabe* cmdlet to create a new Mailbox database, while the Mailbox Database.edb file is placed in the folder of the Third Storage Group will not conflict in any way. Actually, you can just move ahead and mount the ported Mailbox database.

NOTE

> It's important that the name of the new Mailbox database you create using the *New-MailboxDatabase* cmdlet matches the name of the Mailbox database you ported or recovered from the old Exchange 2007 Server; otherwise, you won't be able to mount it.

To mount the Mailbox database, you can use the Mount-Database "Mailbox Database" or the Exchange Management Console. When the Mailbox database has been mounted appropriately, there's only one more task to complete, and that is to modify (re-link) the Active Directory user account objects associated with a mailbox in the Mailbox database that we ported to a new server, so they point to the correct server. This can be done by using the following command:

Get-Mailbox –Database "E2K7S04\Mailbox Database" | Move-Mailbox –TargetDatabase "EHVMS08\Mailbox Database" –ConfigurationOnly: $True

You then must confirm that you wish to perform this operation. Type **Y** for Yes, and press **Enter**.

NOTE

> If you receive an error when trying to run this command, check to make sure the Mailbox database is mounted on the old Exchange 2007 server.

Now would be a good time to access a few mailboxes (using Outlook 2007 or OWA 2007) stored in the Mailbox database we ported so you can verify the end users still have mailbox connectivity.

Summary

In this chapter, we took a look at how to properly back up the different server roles in Exchange 2007. We then went through how you restore an Exchange 2007 Server with one or more server roles installed, as well as how you can restore a corrupt Mailbox or Public Folder database using the Windows 2003 Backup tool, and if this isn't an option, how you can repair a corrupt database using Eseutil. We also had walked through how you can recover mailbox data using the improved Recovery Storage Group (RSG) feature. In addition, I showed you how it's possible to recover a failed Exchange 2007 server using the RecoverServer and RecoverCMS switches. Lastly, we talked about the improvements that have been made regarding database portability in Exchange 2007.

Solutions Fast Track

Backing Up Exchange 2007 Using Windows 2003 Backup

☑ Frequent backups of the Exchange 2007 servers in an organization are important operational tasks, which perhaps can be a bit trivial, but should be taken very seriously. I can only imagine one thing that's worse than a complete failure of an Exchange 2007 server, and that's a complete failure of an Exchange 2007 server without having any backups to restore from.

☑ One of the most important things to back up regarding Exchange 2007 Mailbox Servers are the databases that hold user mailboxes and public data.

☑ Since Exchange 2007 databases still use ESE, you can (just as with previous versions of Exchange) back them up using the Exchange-aware native Windows 2003 backup tool.

☑ Exchange 2007 supports two different backup methods. The first is a legacy streaming backup, which is a backup method based on the ESE application programming interface (API) that allows you to back up one or more storage groups at the same time. However, only one backup job can run against a specific storage group. Then we have the Volume Shadow Copy Service (VSS) backup method, which some of you may know from Exchange 2003, where it was first introduced. The interesting thing about VSS is that this method, in addition to what the legacy streaming backup method offers, can also take an online backup of the copy database when using either Local Continuous Replication or Cluster Continuous Replication in your setup.

Restoring Exchange 2007 Storage Groups and Databases Using Windows 2003 Backup

☑ It's important you understand that a restore of a Mailbox database will copy the database file (.EDB) into its original location on the disk, and thereby overwrite any existing .EDB file.

☑ Once a restore has completed, the log files will be replayed into the restored version of the database. In addition to the log files, a file called Restore.env will also be copied to the specified temporary folder, and this file is the one that keeps control of which storage group the log files belong to, as well as the database paths and range of log files that have been restored.

Repairing a Corrupt or Damaged Exchange 2007 Database Using Eseutil

☑ There may be situations where you either don't have a proper backup set to restore a particular database from, or perhaps you have found out that the database you just restored, in order to replace a corrupt or damaged database, is corrupt or damaged itself. In such situations, you have the option of repairing the database using Extensible Storage Engine Utilities for Microsoft Exchange Server (Eseutil).

☑ Eseutil hasn't changed much from Exchange 2003 since Exchange still uses ESE databases when speaking Exchange 2007. This means that pretty much all of the switches and parameters available in Eseutil are the same as in previous versions.

☑ As in previous versions, Eseutil is located in the Bin folder under your Exchange installation path, which in Exchange 2007, by default, is C:\Program Files\Microsoft\Exchange Server.

☑ When a database corruption occurs, 99.9 percent of the time it's caused by the underlying hard disk drive subsystem.

Restoring Mailbox Data Using the Recovery Storage Group Feature

☑ The Recovery Storage Group (RSG) feature, which was originally introduced back in Exchange 2003, gives you (the Exchange administrator) the option of mounting a second copy of a mailbox database (typically a mailbox database restored from backup). This way, you can extract data during work hours from one or more mailboxes in the respective database without affecting the production databases.

☑ With Exchange 2007, the RSG feature is accessed using the new Database Recovery Management tool, which is found under the Exchange Toolbox work center. You can also work with RSGs using the Exchange Management Shell (EMS).

☑ When you have merged or copied the required Mailbox data, you can use ExTRA to dismount and then remove the Recovery Storage Group. Be sure you delete the files in the RSG*xxxxxxxxx* folder again after you have removed it so the files don't take up valuable disk space.

Recovering an Exchange 2007 Server Using the RecoverServer Switch

☑ Just as with Exchange 2000 and 2003, you can recover an Exchange 2007 Server in a fairly straightforward way. As you perhaps know, we could use the DisasterRecovery switch to recover a dead Exchange 2000 or 2003 Server on new hardware, but with Exchange 2007 this switch no longer exists. Instead, it has been replaced by the new RecoverServer switch, which is similar to the DisasterRecovery switch.

☑ The RecoverServer switch can be used to recover all types of Exchange 2007 Server roles except for the Edge Transport Server role, which uses ADAM and not the Active Directory to store configuration data.

☑ If you're recovering an Exchange 2007 Server with the Hub Transport Server role installed, and this is the only Exchange 2007 Server with this role installed, it's recommended you run Setup.com /M:RecoverServer with the /DoNotStartTransport syntax since there's a few post-recovery steps that should be completed before this role is made active.

☑ When you run Setup with the RecoverServer switch on a new Windows 2003 Server that is configured with the same name as the one that has crashed or is permanently down for some reason, Setup will read the configuration information for the respective Exchange 2007 server from the Active Directory. In addition to applying the roles and settings stored in Active Directory, Setup will (just as when installing an Exchange 2007 Server role without the RecoverServer switch) install the Exchange files and services required for the respective Exchange 2007 server role(s).

Recovering an Exchange 2007 Cluster Using the RecoverCMS Switch

☑ You can recover an Exchange 2007 clustered mailbox server (both CCR and SCC) by using the *ExSetup.exe* command with the RecoverCMS switch.

☑ If you're recovering a Single Copy Cluster (SCC) and have stored the Mailbox and Public Folder databases on a storage area network (SAN), you won't need to restore the databases from backup as long as each node points to the same shared storage subsystem as the failed clustered mailbox server did.

Recovering Mailbox Databases Using the Improved Database Portability Feature

☑ With Exchange 2007, the Mailbox database portability feature has been improved drastically. Now you can port and recover a Mailbox database to any server in the Exchange 2007 organization, and because of the new Autodiscover service, all Outlook 2007 clients will be redirected to the new server automatically the first time they try to connect after the Mailbox database has been mounted on another Exchange 2007 server.

☑ It's important that the name of the new Mailbox database you create using the *New-MailboxDatabase* cmdlet matches the name of the Mailbox database you ported or recovered from the old Exchange 2007 Server. Otherwise, you won't be able to mount it.

Frequently Asked Questions

The following Frequently Asked Questions, answered by the authors of this book, are designed to both measure your understanding of the concepts presented in this chapter and to assist you with real-life implementation of these concepts. To have your questions about this chapter answered by the author, browse to **www.syngress.com/solutions** and click on the **"Ask the Author"** form.

Q: Now that we have Local Continuous Replication (LCR) and Cluster Continuous Replication (CCR), should you still take regular backups of the Exchange 2007 databases using a backup application?

A: It's important to understand that LCR and CCR aren't replacements for traditional regular backups. Instead, they are meant to serve as the primary fast recovery solution in case one or more of your production databases shuts down. But with LCR or CCR, you can change your backup schedule from daily to weekly backups.

Q: I heard you can take backups of the passive databases when using LCR or CCR, but I don't have the option of choosing the passive database in Windows 2003 Backup?

A: You're right in that LCR or CCR gives you the option of performing the backup of the passive database(s), but although the Windows 2003 Backup tool supports Volume Shadow Copy Service (VSS) backups, this is only the case when performing file-level–based backups of the databases. In order to perform a backup of the passive databases, you must use a third-party backup solution that supports VSS backups or Microsoft's Data Protection Manager version 2 (DPM v2), which at the time of this writing is still a beta product.

Q: How do you create and manage a Recovery Storage Group (RSG) in the Exchange 2007 Management Console?

A: You don't. With Exchange 2007, the RSG feature cannot be managed using the Exchange Management Console, as was the case in Exchange 2003. Instead, you must create and manage RSGs using the Database Recovery Management tool (which can be found beneath the Toolbox work center node) or the Exchange Management Shell.

Q: Is it possible to restore a Public Folder database to a Recovery Storage Group (RSG) in Exchange 2007?

A: No. Unfortunately, the RSG feature is still limited to Mailbox databases only.

Q: Can I recover all types of Exchange 2007 Server roles using the new RecoverServer switch?

A: Yes, almost. The only Exchange 2007 Server role that cannot be recovered using the RecoverServer switch is the Edge Transport server since this server doesn't belong to the Active Directory. To recover an Edge Transport server, you must instead use the cloned configuration method.

Microsoft Vista:
The International
Community

Microsoft vs. The World: What's the Issue?

Most Americans are probably aware of Microsoft's legal troubles in the United States with the federal government's antitrust division of the Justice Department and various states. However, the company's legal department has been busy handling the negative attentions of other countries around the world for more than a decade. As a result of various rulings by the European Union and countries in Asia, Microsoft made several changes to Vista. If it's not exceedingly careful, more changes may yet be required, causing the company even more legal, financial, and technical headaches.

Microsoft Vista: The EU Fixes

Microsoft has a long history of legal problems in Europe, almost as lengthy and involved as the company's run-ins with federal and state governments in the United States. In July 1994, after a four-year investigation by the U.S. Justice Department, Microsoft signed a consent decree governing the licensing of Windows. At the same time, the company made a similar agreement with the European Commission, which allowed the European Union to keep an eye on Microsoft's compliance for the next six years. Unfortunately for Microsoft, the European Union took its responsibilities very seriously.

The 2004 Ruling

A little more than three years later, Microsoft was in hot water with the European Commission again (as it was also with the Justice Department in the United States). On October 16, 1997, the European Union announced that it was opening another probe of the company to investigate whether it was illegally leveraging its operating system (OS) monopoly. In 1998, the European Commission expanded its inquiry after receiving complaints from Sun Microsystems that Microsoft would not reveal necessary application program interfaces (APIs) needed to interface with Windows NT.

These sorts of legal reviews can take quite a bit of time, so it's no surprise that it wasn't until August 2000 that the European Commission finally levied formal charges against Microsoft for withholding information from competitors that they needed in order to work with Microsoft's servers. One year later, in August 2001, a second charge was added to the complaint: that Microsoft's tying of Windows Media Player to the Windows OS illegally leveraged a monopoly product—in this case, the

OS—to promote another—the Media Player—to the detriment of competitors and consumers.

August 2003: A Preliminary Decision

By November 2002, Microsoft's antitrust suit in the United States was coming to an end, as U.S. District Judge Colleen Kollar-Kotelly approved most of the settlement between the company and the government. In its home country, Microsoft received the equivalent of a slap on the wrist and an admonishment to go and sin no more— pretty please?—but things were proceeding differently in Europe. On August 6, 2003, antitrust regulators in Europe announced that they had reached a preliminary decision against Microsoft that would require the corporation to resolve the issues around its server APIs and its media software. In the former instance, Microsoft would have to provide better, more complete technical information to competitors so that their software could more seamlessly interoperate with Windows; in the latter, Microsoft would have to somehow reduce the linkages between its OS and its media software. At this point, the decision was still not final, but Microsoft was encouraged to comment and involve itself productively in the process.

That Microsoft in fact was not interested in working constructively with the European Commission can been seen in an idea the company proffered to regulators in February 2004. Microsoft suggested that one way to reduce the ties between Windows Media Player and Windows would be to bundle a CD along with Windows that would contain media software by Real and other rivals. This scheme was rejected by EU antitrust head Mario Monti, who rightly understood that only a tiny minority of consumers would even look at such a CD, much less go to the trouble of installing any software on it. By March 18, 2004, only a month later, settlement talks between Monti and Microsoft's Steve Ballmer had inextricably broken down due to an inability to reach an agreement that both sides could accept. The only question now was exactly how bad the final ruling would be for Microsoft.

March 2004: The Ruling

On March 24, 2004, the Commission of the European Communities unanimously ruled against Microsoft in a 302-page ruling. The fact that Microsoft is an abusive monopoly—the basis for the rest of the Commission's findings—was clearly established:

```
(435) ... Microsoft, with its market shares of over 90%, occupies almost the
whole market - it therefore approaches a position of complete monopoly, and
can be said to hold an overwhelmingly dominant position.
(460) ... there is significant evidence that the protection granted by the
applications barrier to entry enables Microsoft to behave to a very large
```

```
extent independently of its competitors, its customers and ultimately of
consumers.
(464) ... for its client PC operating system product, Microsoft operated on
a profit margin of approximately 81%. This is high by any measure.
```

A monopoly in itself is not illegal; however, a company in a monopoly position has certain responsibilities that other companies do not possess, or, as the Commission puts it in paragraph 542, "an undertaking enjoying a dominant position is under a special responsibility not to engage in conduct that may distort competition." Microsoft, unfortunately, failed to restrain itself in two areas, as detailed by the European Union: the workgroup server market and streaming multimedia.

Workgroup Servers

In the case of servers, the ruling goes into great detail about the company's errant actions before finally making a strong conclusion about the effects of those failures to engage with competitors in a fair way:

```
(546) ... Microsoft is abusing its dominant position by refusing to supply
Sun and other undertakings with the specifications for the protocols used by
Windows work group servers in order to provide file, print and group and user
administration services to Windows work group networks, and allow these
undertakings to implement such specifications for the purpose of developing
and distributing interoperable work group server operating system products.
...
(589) ... Microsoft's refusal puts Microsoft's competitors at a strong
competitive disadvantage in the work group server operating system market,
to an extent where there is a risk of elimination of competition.
(692) It follows from the foregoing considerations that Microsoft's
behaviour risks eliminating competition in the work group server operating
system market, due to the indispensability of the input that it refuses to
supply to its competitors.
```

If you've never read a legal finding of fact, which is what Americans would call the European Commission's report, you might be surprised to find that the document actually displays a very thorough understanding of the technical issues involved in the case. For instance, the ruling does a good job summarizing the heart of the issue when it comes to workgroup interop:

```
(182) ... the proper functioning of a Windows work group network relies on
an architecture of client-to-server and server-to-server interconnections
and interactions, which ensures a transparent access to the core work group
server services (for Windows 2000 / Windows 2003, this "Windows domain
architecture" can be termed an "Active Directory domain architecture").
(183) When a non-Microsoft work group server is added to a Windows work
group network, the degree of interoperability with the Windows domain
```

architecture that such a work group server is able to achieve will have an
impact on the efficiency with which that work group server delivers its
services to the users of the network. ...

(184) This means that other work group server operating system vendors that
want to compete for customers having an existing investment in Windows need
access to information relating to interoperability with the Windows domain
architecture.

Those paragraphs do a pretty good job of boiling down a complex topic into
something easily understandable by techies, lawyers, and governments, which is a lot
harder than it might appear. Further in the document, the writers present specific
examples of the ways in which Microsoft hogties competitors; one in particular is
expressed succinctly in a way that completely undercuts Microsoft's claims of inno-
cence:

(243) Microsoft explains that "Active Directory supports versions 2 and 3 of
the Lightweight Directory Access Protocol ('LDAP'), which is the industry
standard directory access protocol".

(244) However, Microsoft has extended LDAP in a proprietary fashion and
failed to disclose the extensions that it has made.

Nice try, Microsoft, but the Commission saw through this attempt at chicanery.
Claiming to support standards while at the same time extending those standards in
secret, nondocumented ways is a perversion of the process, not a shining example of
the correct way to conduct business.

Windows Media Player

In its analysis of Windows Media Player, or WMP, the European Commission's findings astutely recognized the power of tying an app to an overwhelmingly popular
OS, a power that Microsoft not only recognizes, but also leverages to an extreme:

(844) Through tying WMP with Windows, Microsoft ensures that WMP is as
ubiquitous on PCs worldwide as Windows is. No other distribution mechanism
or combination of distribution mechanisms attains this universal
distribution. Microsoft obviously controls this mode of distribution and (no
longer) affords competing media player vendors access to it.

(845) Users who find WMP pre-installed on their client PCs are indeed in
general less likely to use alternative media players as they already have an
application which delivers media streaming and playback functionality. ...

(857) In conclusion, tying WMP creates disincentives for OEMs to ship third
party (streaming) media players pre-installed on their PCs.

Microsoft argued that users could always download another, competing media
app, such as Real Player, but the report not only saw the problems with that argument but also performed a neat bit of logical jujitsu by using Microsoft's own argu-

ment against it. If downloading is so easy and painless for end users, why doesn't Microsoft unbundle its software so that users have to download it, thus placing it on an equal footing with rivals?

(866) Yet another reason why downloading does not constitute as efficient a distribution channel as OEM pre-installation is that downloading is viewed as complicated by a not insignificant number of users, while using the pre-installed product is not. In this respect, it is also relevant that a significant number of download attempts are not successfully concluded. ...

(871) For the above reasons, downloading is not an adequate alternative to pre-installation, that is to say, it is not an alternative which would off-set the negative impact that tying WMP has on competition. Incidentally, if Microsoft seriously considers that downloading is an equivalent alternative to pre-installation, its insistence on maintaining its current privilege of automatic pre-installation appears inconsistent.

The result of Microsoft's illegal conjoining of its OS and its media player? A decrease in the competition necessary for a healthy market, which hurts other businesses and ultimately consumers:

(980) Microsoft thus interferes with the normal competitive process which would benefit users in terms of quicker cycles of innovation due to unfettered competition on the merits. Tying of WMP increases the content and applications barrier to entry which protects Windows and it will facilitate the erection of such a barrier for WMP. A position of market strength achieved in a market characterised by network effects - such as the media player market - is sustainable, as once the network effects work in favour of a company which has gained a decisive momentum, they will amount to entry barriers for potential competitors.

(981) This shields Microsoft from effective competition from potentially more efficient media player vendors which could challenge its position. Microsoft thus reduces the talent and capital invested in innovation of media players, not least its own and anti-competitively raises barriers to market entry. Microsoft's conduct affects a market which could be a hotbed for new and exciting products springing forth in a climate of undistorted competition.

(982) Moreover, tying of WMP allows Microsoft to anti-competitively expand its position in adjacent media-related software markets and weaken effective competition to the eventual detriment of consumers. ...

(984) There is therefore a reasonable likelihood that tying WMP with Windows will lead to a lessening of competition so that the maintenance of an effective competition structure will not be ensured in the foreseeable future. For these reasons, tying WMP with Windows violates the prohibition to abuse a dominant position ...

The Report's Conclusion

After an exhaustive detailing of the facts and issues involved in Microsoft's abuse of its monopoly position vis-à-vis workgroup servers and media software, the European Commission comes to a conclusion regarding the impact of those abuses on the overall markets for those products. In other words, Microsoft has definitely abused its monopoly position to leverage its own products and inhibit competition, but have the company's actions been *significant*? If abuses have occurred but aren't that far-reaching, the punishment will be vastly reduced in severity. Unfortunately for Microsoft, the report doesn't mince words at this point:

(1070) As regards the market for work group server operating systems, the abuse has already contributed to Microsoft achieving a dominant position in that market, and risks eliminating competition on that market.

(1071) As regard the market for streaming media players, the abuse has already contributed to Microsoft achieving a leading position in that market. Evidence described in this Decision suggests that the market may already be tipping in favour of WMP.

(1072) In conclusion, the Commission considers that the impact of Microsoft's abuses on the relevant markets has been significant.

March 2004: The Punishment

The only matter left was the punishment, which was to take two forms: remedies and fines. Although the meaning of a fine is obvious, a *remedy* is designed to change behavior by setting standards for Microsoft's behavior, a sort of dos and don'ts list for ongoing business.

The Remedies

In the case of workgroup servers, the solution is clear: "(999) Microsoft should be ordered to disclose complete and accurate specifications for the protocols used by Windows work group servers in order to provide file, print and group and user administration services to Windows work group networks." So that competitors can interoperate with Windows servers, Microsoft must make available—without "imposing unreasonable conditions" and on a "non-discriminatory basis"—the information those rivals need to work on a Windows network.

In the realm of media players, the decision goes even further by ordering Microsoft to "(1011) … offer a version of Windows for client PCs which does not include Windows Media Player. The remedy applies to Windows licensed directly to end users (home users via retail and corporate customers) and licensed to OEMs …". This is far-reaching, as it's not just a matter of a government telling a company to reveal information, but going beyond that to tell the business how to present and sell its products. However, in this case, the European Commission made it clear that Microsoft had over-reached and caused too much damage, and only a remedy this severe would suffice.

The Fine

As for the fine, here we enter the realm of very large numbers. Because the Commission found that Microsoft's behavior was "particularly anti-competitive" and had a "significant impact" on the "entire EEA [European Economic Area]," it was necessary to make the fine hurt … as much as it is possible to hurt a company with literally tens of billions of dollars in the bank. Following the reasoning in the report as the writers determine upon a good number is actually humorous, because the numbers are so large:

(1075) The initial amount of the fine to be imposed on Microsoft to reflect the gravity of the infringement should be … EUR 165,732,101.

(1076) When calculating the initial amount of the fine, account should be taken of the necessity of setting the fine at a level that ensures that it has a sufficient deterrent effect. … Given Microsoft's significant economic capacity, in order to ensure a sufficient deterrent effect on Microsoft, the initial amount should be adjusted upwards by a factor of 2 to EUR 331,464,203.

(1077) … For the purposes of the calculation of the fine, the overall duration of Microsoft's infringement is 5 years and 5 months, that is, an infringement of long duration.

(1078) Consequently, the amount of the fine to be imposed on the basis of the gravity of the infringement should therefore be increased by 50% to take account of its duration. On that basis, the basic amount of the fine is EUR 497,196,304.

A fine of more than €497 million translates into about $613 million, which is a big amount, even for Microsoft. In fact, it was so big that it set records.

The March 2004 Ruling in Practice

Of course, Microsoft appealed to the European Union Court of First Instance in June 2004. The wheels of justice grind slowly, so it took another six months for the Court of First Instance to reject Microsoft's appeal and order the company to start complying with the remedies detailed in the European Commission's ruling. At that point, Microsoft began preparing to license information about its protocols and creating a version of Windows for Europe that lacked Windows Media Player.

Windows Media Player

A sign of Microsoft's tendency to act like a recalcitrant child when ordered to perform an action it doesn't wish to do appeared when the company first announced the name it had settled on for the WMP-less version of its OS: "Windows XP Reduced Media Edition," which is so baldly awful that it is actually laughable. By late January, the European Commission had made its displeasure with that name known, and Microsoft withdrew it from consideration, finally announcing in June 2005—more than a year after the initial orders and six months after losing to an appeals court—the availability of Windows XP Home Edition N and Windows XP Professional Edition N. The *N*, of course, stood for "No Media Player."

Workgroup Servers

That remedy was taken care of, at least, but the documentation of protocols proved to be another story entirely. By December 2005—a *year* after being ordered to provide the necessary information by the Court of First Instance—Microsoft still had not produced the necessary paperwork. The European Commission, tired of the company's dilly-dallying, filed an objection with the European courts and threatened an additional fine of about $2.37 million per day until Microsoft completed its legal obligations.

Soon enough, Microsoft was back in court, appealing the Commission's new orders and offering to simply license the miles of spaghetti source code that make up Windows to rivals, because, as General Counsel Brad Smith helpfully contended, "The Windows source code is the ultimate documentation." The courts in Europe saw through this legal obfuscation and, even though Microsoft had provided 8,500 pages of technical documentation to the European Commission by July 2006, the continent's antitrust regulators went ahead and voted unanimously to impose a $357 million fine on Microsoft for failing to abide by the 2004 ruling, the first time a company was ever penalized for not living up to an antitrust order. In addition, the Commission went on to promise additional fines of $3.8 million each day after July 31 if the correct documents were not produced in a useful, and usable, fashion.

Microsoft said it was trying as hard as it could to comply with the order; in fact, it claimed to have 300 employees working full-time on the project. At the same time, the European Commission said that what Microsoft was handing over to them was "incomplete, inaccurate and unusable." The threats of further fines seemed to bring Microsoft back to its senses, and it worked harder to prepare the necessary documentation that it was required to produce, while at the same time, the European Union was even more explicit as to exactly what documentation was needed to comply with the order.

Again, time passed at a snail's pace, as it so often does in the world of justice. The latest word on the 2004 case came in November 2006. On November 16, the European Commission complained again that Microsoft had not given it all the documentation that was required—now more than two years after the initial order!—and threatened daily fines of $3.9 million if the problem wasn't rectified within one week. Neelie Kroes, the European competition commissioner, explained that Microsoft's actions simply had not been good enough: "I am not impressed if someone says 90 percent of the information is already there when we need 100 percent. It's a jigsaw and some parts are missing."

Lo and behold, by November 23, Microsoft had submitted even more technical specs to the European Union, enough so that the Commission was finally able to state "the dossier from Microsoft is worth testing." As of this writing, that testing is presumably occurring, but as to the ultimate success or failure of Microsoft's documentation, only time—and the antitrust regulators of the European Union—will tell.

Vista

During the trials and travails of Microsoft as it dealt with—or rather, tried to evade and then was forced to deal with—the 2004 orders issued by the European Commission, work in Redmond, Washington, continued on Vista. It's easy to forget that the entire time period of the EU ruling and its aftermath, from 2004 to late 2006, corresponds with the final years of Microsoft's work on Vista. So, as one arm of the company was reacting to Europe's antitrust investigation of Windows 2000 and Windows XP, another branch of the same corporation was writing the code that would become its next-generation OS. It would be difficult, if not impossible, to imagine that prior legal skirmishes would not impact the shape of Vista's development, and in fact, that's precisely what happened.

Problems Begin

It was not until 2006 that fault lines began to appear. In March, Competition Commissioner Neelie Kroes, the successor to Mario Monti, notified Microsoft via letter that the European Union was concerned that some parts of Vista might not conform to the 2004 orders. Specifically, the European Commission focused on two items: features that Microsoft was planning to include in its new OS (such as Net search, DRM and security, and XPS, a fixed document formatting technology designed to compete with PDF) that might prove to be cases of anticompetitive bundling, and whether the company would disclose technical details to other companies so that they could make their products work with, and compete with, Vista. In other words, the first issue was an extension of the problems found in 2004 with the bundling of Windows Media Player, and the second issue followed on the concerns about competition in the workgroup server market.

Steve Ballmer, CEO of Microsoft, replied to Kroes' March 2006 letter on April 11. In his missive, he specifically addressed concerns about XPS by offering four solutions, as delineated by *The New York Times*: "The options included adding P.D.F.-reading software in Vista, letting PC makers hide Microsoft's document format and related software, letting PC makers in Europe remove the document software and offering a higher-priced version of Vista in Europe that includes the software." The response of the European commissioners is not recorded, but it seems likely that they continued to follow a hands-off policy as much as possible during Microsoft's design and development of Vista, only warning the company to follow antitrust law in Europe.

In March, the Commission was simply tapping Microsoft on the shoulder and reminding it to keep the decision of two years earlier in mind. It was a reminder, and nothing more. On July 4, 2006, Kroes thought it expedient to follow up her earlier concerns with a letter to Microsoft containing 79 questions about Vista, with an August 31 deadline for a response. The exact contents of that letter remain confidential, but it must have impressed the normally bold executives at Microsoft, because only a week later, Chief Counsel Brad Smith revealed that the company offered again to create a version of Vista for Europe lacking the XPS capabilities, which evidently was not seen as necessary by the regulators in Brussels, and had also willingly incorporated a few of the tweaks suggested by European antitrust officials.

However, by August 2006, tensions were rising again, this time due to the PatchGuard kernel protection feature found on 64-bit versions of Vista. Symantec and a few other, smaller security companies began to complain that PatchGuard was going to hurt their ability to provide next-generation security solutions to Windows users. Even worse, Microsoft was up to its old tricks by failing to fully inform the companies that would be affected by PatchGuard and its changes to the Windows kernel. As John Pescatore, a Gartner analyst, put it, "This is a complex issue, but Microsoft has definitely been deficient in including the impacted software makers early on. That definitely does work to their advantage from a competitive viewpoint." Although no one disputed the fact that the Windows core is horribly insecure, and that the company obviously needed to tighten things up in an effort to lessen the nonstop security patches that have plagued those who rely on Windows over the past decade, it seemed that Microsoft was engaging in the same behavior that repeatedly landed it in court on both sides of the Atlantic.

Threats and a Response

Perhaps that possibility raised the ire of execs inside Microsoft, or perhaps the pressures of complying with the original 2004 ruling were starting to wear on key decision makers inside the corporation, or perhaps Ballmer and his associates saw it as a necessary bluff in a game of high-stakes poker. We may never know the reason behind the action Microsoft took in August 2006, but it doubtlessly did not endear the company to Neely and the rest of the officials in the European Union's antitrust arm. On August 25, Microsoft publicly complained in an SEC filing that the guidance it was receiving from the European Commission was so unclear that it might perhaps have to delay the introduction of Vista in Europe. Because Microsoft didn't know exactly how the European Union wanted it to design and develop its software, it would just have to wait before proceeding onward, thereby causing the rollout of Vista in Europe to be retarded, perhaps by several months or even longer.

This threat—more than likely hollow, and designed to make the European Commission look bad while allowing Microsoft to continue playing the innocent act—resulted in four members of the European Parliament penning a letter of protest to Competition Commissioner Neelie Kroes. That letter warned in no uncertain terms that the actions of Kroes and her associates were "endangering the ability of European business to compete globally" and should be tempered. How did this letter find its way to the international press? Through Microsoft releasing it to the public, an action undoubtedly performed solely in the interest of informing the citizens of Europe and America, we're sure.

The European Commission was not amused, and fired back. Jonathan Todd, a spokesman, explained that "'It is not up to us to tell Microsoft what it has to do to Vista. The onus is on Microsoft to design its product in conformity with European competition laws, which it is well aware of." In other words, Microsoft knows the law in Europe—it should, because it's been in court so many times—and it should make sure that Vista conforms to that law. If Microsoft oversteps the boundaries deliberately, the Commission will respond, but it will not oversee every decision by Microsoft as it develops its software.

Four Areas of Concern

A few days later, the Competition Commission went further, this time warning Microsoft specifically to ensure that competition could thrive even in the face of new security features in Vista. Although the regulators would not reveal to the public exactly what their concerns were, preferring to speak directly only to Microsoft, the company went ahead and revealed four areas of concern: PatchGuard, BitLocker, Windows Defender, and Windows Security Center.

The issues surrounding PatchGuard had been known for a few months. BitLocker—which allows users to encrypt hard drives—could potentially lock out other products that perform the same task; the same problem was found to exist with Windows Defender, because many other companies sell antispyware software. In addition, until Release Candidate 1 of Vista, third-party antispyware software could not automatically disable Windows Defender in order to prevent a confusing duplication of efforts; instead, users were required to turn off Defender themselves, an obviously scary or even intimidating task to many people. RC 1 fixed that problem, but the Commission was still worried that the free bundled Windows Defender might stifle competition. Finally, rivals were concerned that the Windows Security Center might lack a neutral point of view and somehow favor Microsoft's own products or downplay their own software instead.

The Competition Commission's spokesman, Jonathan Todd, used the biological metaphor of the monoculture—common in discussions of computer security and related issues—to explain the concerns of the Commission when it came to Microsoft's new security products (in a monoculture, there is the danger that a disease or virus will affect all similar organisms catastrophically, leading to mass death): "If business and home users are deprived of choice, a security 'monoculture' based on Microsoft products may lead to less innovation and could harm all computer users. Security risks could increase, and not decrease." In other words, if everyone is using Windows Defender as their antispyware tool, a hack that routes around or damages that program could potentially affect everyone using Windows, thus providing worse security than before, when there is a far wider variety of antispyware software in use.

The question now was, how would Steve Ballmer's company respond? A week earlier, Microsoft had used the stick—the threat of delays—but this time the company decided to use a carrot instead. On September 14, it proudly revealed the findings of a study that it had happened to sponsor ("The economic impact of Microsoft Windows Vista"), a study that found that within one year after its release, Vista would be installed on more than 30 million computers in the six EU countries studied.

The icing on the cake was the study's assertion that 1 million IT jobs in those six countries, including 100,000 new jobs, would be related in some way to Vista. Even better—the icing on the icing, as it were—was the study's promise that for every single euro Microsoft earned on Vista, other companies in Europe associated with the Vista ecosystem would see 14 euros; for Americans, that translates into Microsoft earning about $1.27, and everyone else earning $17.76, billions of times over. Microsoft is never afraid of being obvious, as the trumpeting of this study shows.

October 2006: Microsoft's Concessions

With the deadline of November fast approaching for Vista to be delivered for manufacturing and release to businesses, and the next deadline of January 2007 for the consumer release close behind, Microsoft had little room to spare. On October 13, 2006, Microsoft held a press conference to announce changes it was making to Vista in order to satisfy regulators in Europe (and South Korea, but more on that later). Brad Smith, General Counsel for the corporation, walked listeners through alterations in three areas: security, search, and XPS, and emphasized that Vista would not be delayed in Europe or Korea, but would instead see a simultaneous worldwide release.

Security

Microsoft elected to make three changes to Vista's security system, involving the Windows Security Center, PatchGuard, and the Windows Welcome Center. The Security Center is designed to inform a user about the status of her computer's firewall, antivirus and antispyware software, and automatic updates. Symantec, McAfee, and other security vendors were afraid that Microsoft would monopolize (pun only slightly intended) the Security Center and force third-party apps to secondary positions, thus denigrating those vendors and their programs and confusing customers.

To get around this issue, Microsoft agreed to provide an API for security companies to control where security alerts are sent. That way, the system won't send the same alert to both the Windows Security Center and a third-party console. For instance, if a user installs a product from Symantec that provides its own security center, the Symantec product will appear to be the source of security alerts. Smith explained that Microsoft was still going to monitor the status of the system's security, however, in a way that would protect the user:

[I]f the user uninstalls the second console, for example, or the second console decides that it is no longer going to send those alerts, Windows Security Center will re-start. That means that users will not receive duplicate alerts, but that the alternative console can send the alert instead. However, from our perspective, it also means that we know that users will receive at least one alert …

As long as Microsoft accurately detects what the other security center is doing—or not doing—and thereby avoids restarting erroneously, this move seems both smart and fair.

The objections to PatchGuard's behavior were a bit more difficult to fix, however. PatchGuard is an important feature for 64-bit versions of Vista that prevents malware authors—but also security software vendors and even Microsoft itself (supposedly)—from modifying the kernel. Vendors, however, complained that PatchGuard was going to prevent them from putting into place important security software. Microsoft was not about to remove PatchGuard, as it was simply too important to the company's hopes in securing Windows. Instead, the company would create APIs that would enable Symantec and similar companies to access the Windows kernel in a secure fashion. As Smith explained, such an approach would ensure that "PatchGuard will be retained, the security of the kernel will be protected, and yet security vendors will have an opportunity to meet their needs."

When a user first boots his PC, the Windows Welcome Center displays basic info about the computer, including links to various configuration choices and offers from Microsoft … including Windows Live OneCare security suite, Microsoft's antivirus software, and more. As a result of concerns that this would obviously provide extreme advantages to Microsoft's security products, the company added links to alternative security products as well. Smith also pointed out that, on top of that, Dell, HP, or any of the other thousands of Windows OEMs could change this link:

```
I would also note that the link that we have created to our offerings is an
optional link, and any PC manufacturer can delete it if they desire. In
fact, if Symantec or anyone else wants to negotiate an exclusive agreement
with an original equipment manufacturer (OEM) or PC manufacturer to replace
both of those links and install, in their place, a link only to their own
offering, they are free to do so.
```

This seems entirely reasonable and could definitely benefit both OEMs and security companies: security companies will undoubtedly want to make deals with the Dells of the world and expand their customer base, and the Dells will look favorably on the opportunities to make a bit more cash in the low-margin PC business.

Search

Google and Microsoft are locked in a battle over Internet search, with Google leading the way, so it's no surprise that Google was worried that Microsoft could arrange things in Internet Explorer 7 to highly favor, or even restrict, users to the MSN Live search engine. In actuality, however, things will not be that dangerous for Google and other search engines.

Users upgrading from Internet Explorer 6 to Internet Explorer 7, or from XP to Vista, will see a screen that lists their current default search site and ask them whether they'd like to continue using that choice or pick from another list of choices that includes everything from Google and Yahoo! to Ask and AOL. Of course, Microsoft's MSN search engine is a choice, but it's not even first in the list, so it's not more favored than any other option. If the user doesn't make a choice, nothing will be selected for her, but she'll continue to see it every time she launches Internet Explorer 7 until she finally makes up her mind.

There is an exception to this process, however: If someone buys a copy of Windows Vista at the store and installs it himself on a computer, then yes, MSN Live Search will be the default. That's a pretty rare occurrence, true, but Microsoft really should reuse the screen it displays for upgrades in this case as well, in order to avoid any suggestion of favoritism.

Finally, users can change the default at any time, and can add additional search engines to the drop-down list available in the instant search box. However, many if not most users will never be aware of these search engines, because few people investigate a program's options, so the default will be what those folks use to search the Web. Power users will enjoy the fact that they have variety in the instant search box, but the vast majority of users will never know that they have the option.

XPS

It's no secret that Microsoft's new XML Paper Specification (XPS) document technology is designed to go after Adobe's ubiquitous PDF format; Brad Smith himself recognized the fact when he admitted that XPS is "a new format that competes with Adobe's PDF format." In order to avoid the appearance of impropriety and anticompetitive positioning, Microsoft has promised to submit XPS to a standards body (although that hasn't happened at the time of this writing) and license it royalty-free so that anyone else can also implement it. Further, Microsoft is going to add an agreement not to sue for intellectual property infringement involving the use of XPS.

This is a great sign, but a lot will depend upon how easy it is to actually work with the XPS spec. If the documentation is clear and logical, we may see XPS appear in a wide variety of apps, just as PDF currently does; if the documentation is instead obtuse and heavily dependent upon proprietary technologies, this may just be empty promises on Microsoft's part. The former seems more likely for XPS, but it will take time for this process to play out entirely.

Immediate Results of the October Press Conference

Brad Smith was representing Microsoft during that press conference of October 13, and his words were extremely conciliatory toward Commissioner Kroes and her compatriots in Europe. It seems that Microsoft finally recognized that it could catch more flies with honey than with vinegar, and tempered its words accordingly:

We received guidance from the Commission on Windows Vista that was very clear and constructive. It provided us with the clarity that we needed in

```
order to move forward and make design decisions. Where there were questions
or areas of uncertainty, we were able to have the type of constructive
dialogue that eliminated that uncertainty, and that was extremely helpful. …
it is much easier to ensure that one obeys the speed limit when one knows
what the speed limit is …
```

Microsoft's announcement, however, did not mean that the European Commission had informed the company that it was now going to adopt a laissez faire policy toward Vista. In a statement delivered the same day as Smith's meeting with reporters, the regulators stated their point of view: "The commission has not given a green light to Microsoft to deliver Vista. Microsoft must shoulder its own responsibilities to ensure that Vista is fully compliant with competition rules and in particular with the principles laid down in the March 2004 commission antitrust decision concerning Microsoft." The European Union made it clear that it would continue to closely monitor Vista and the effects the OS had on the marketplace. If regulators received complaints, they would investigate. Microsoft—and Vista— weren't out of the woods yet, and undoubtedly would not be for quite some time.

A few days later, on October 16, Microsoft claimed that it had placed the necessary information that Symantec, McAfee, and other security vendors needed to interface with the Windows Security Center on a Web site for developers. Asked for comment the same day, a Symantec spokesperson simply replied, "We still don't know if we have everything we need or not." Regardless, because the OS was due to be delivered to businesses on October 25, Microsoft's actions were still going to make life difficult for software developers working at those other companies, who would now face long hours and tight deadlines.

And then things really blew up.

Putting Out Fire with Gasoline

Just two days later, on October 18, both McAfee and Symantec complained publicly about the quality of the information they had received from Microsoft. A McAfee corporate communications VP explained the situation in which the security company found itself:

```
We did receive a document from Microsoft yesterday that contained the SDK
for Windows Security Centre only. We continue to have questions pertaining
to this document and have asked Microsoft for meetings and/or additional
clarification … To date, we have not had any cooperation from MS and no
response on McAfee's repeated requests to review the information. … we have
not received anything at all from Microsoft concerning PatchGuard.
```

Symantec also released a statement claiming that it "has yet to actually see the final detailed information needed to address our concerns regarding Windows Security Centre or PatchGuard."

Microsoft CEO Steve Ballmer sometimes has a bad habit of trying to put out a fire with gasoline, and this tendency unfortunately immediately reared its head. Later on the same day as the publication of Symantec and McAfee's protests, Ballmer was quoted as saying, in response to a question about the complaints from security vendors, "We are through that ... We're prepared to release our product." This was not a response calculated to reduce tensions, but undoubtedly cooler heads inside the company prevailed, because Microsoft quickly announced that matters could be discussed at an online PowerPoint briefing for security companies that was scheduled to take place the following night.

Unfortunately, that meeting turned out to be more of a debacle than an educational experience. The online presentation, utilizing Microsoft's Live Meeting technology, had numerous problems, including incorrect invitations and crashes, resulting in a truncated presentation that members of McAfee and Symantec were unable to attend. In reports published later that day, a Microsoft spokesperson disputed problems reported with the meeting (although at least one attendee unaffiliated with Symantec or McAfee corroborated the foul-up on his blog), and went on to explain Microsoft's plans for resolving issues around PatchGuard.

It was Microsoft's plan, according to the spokesperson, to invite 150 security vendors to join with it to develop a security services API for Vista that would enable those companies to work with PatchGuard. Microsoft was not going to allow rivals—or even itself, the company claimed—to disable or work around PatchGuard; instead, security software would have to work alongside the new technology. Essentially, the 150 or so participants in the process would create a list of requirements that they all needed in order to implement their security software with PatchGuard, and then Microsoft would code the necessary APIs in Vista. Obviously such a process would take a great deal of time, which is why the spokesperson emphasized that the APIs would not be in place until Service Pack (SP) 1 of Vista was rolled out.

It seems highly likely that this plan will at least raise regulators' eyebrows in Brussels, although it has not so far. Microsoft is in essence asking 150 companies to reveal their plans and aims for their products to a company that is itself competing with them in many areas, and has made it clear that it intends to compete in more. Further, the timetable is far enough in the future that it gives Microsoft plenty of time to solidify its plans and thereby inhibit competition. Finally, the company has gotten into trouble with the European Union time and time again for extending deadlines in ways that inhibit competition, and its stated intentions for PatchGuard are similar enough to past behaviors as to cause consternation to Neelie Kroes and her associates. The fact that McAfee's attorneys in Brussels were issuing vociferous complaints only increases the likelihood that the European Commission will step in, although such actions have not taken place as of early January 2007.

Initial Release of the PatchGuard APIs

As 2006 drew to a close, Microsoft made one last big announcement relating to Vista's security and antitrust concerns: On December 19, it released the draft of the PatchGuard APIs it had created with, it turned out, input from 26 vendors. Four different API classes were created, according to Ben Fathi, VP for the Windows core OS:

```
The first set of APIs is around creating and opening processes and threads …
giving them the ability to set a policy in place that says when a thread is
created or when a process is created what kind of security precautions they
want to take. The second area is around protection of security software to
make sure the security software that gets installed on the system is not
itself being modified by viruses. The third one is around memory-based
controls. The fourth area is image loading operations … that allows security
software to block the loading of certain executables or DLLs [dynamic link
libraries] into memory.
```

The draft would be available for comment through January 31, 2007, with the final solidified APIs seeing the light of day with the release of Vista SP1, supposed to appear sometime in 2007. At least one bitter critic of Microsoft's action appeared to be mollified, as McAfee's Chief Scientist, George Heron, was quoted in the news as stating, in reference to the APIs, that "it appears [Microsoft] did a good job on those. Overall, McAfee is quite pleased with the path that Microsoft is taking."

And on that positive note, admittedly one of only a few uttered over the course of a contentious year as Vista wrapped up its development under the gaze of the European Union's Competition Commission, 2006 ended. Vista had changed as a result of the European Union, but whether those alterations would be enough to forestall further legal action by the continent's regulators remains to be seen. One thing is certain: It will be long, complicated, and hard-fought, but it will undoubtedly be fascinating to observe as well.

Microsoft and Japan

Japan's Fair Trade Commission (FTC) hasn't yet demanded changes in Vista, but it very well could. A long-standing dispute between the Japanese FTC and Microsoft is still not resolved, and shows no signs of wrapping up anytime soon.

The Raid in Tokyo

On February 26, 2004, the FTC raided Microsoft's Tokyo offices looking for information on a contract provision Microsoft had OEM PC manufacturers sign. The contracts specified that in return for a license to preinstall Windows on computers they sold, signees could not sue Microsoft for any violations of their patents. On behalf of Japanese companies such as Sony, NEC, and Hitachi, the FTC investigated.

That same day, in what the company claimed was a complete coincidence, Microsoft announced that it would remove the clause from future contracts: "Microsoft recently reviewed this provision again after receiving comments on it from some of its OEM customers. Microsoft has decided that, given its focus on improving customer satisfaction, it would delete the provision in its entirety from the next round of OEM contracts, which will take effect later this year." However, the corporation continued to deny that it had violated any law and went so far as to assert that the patent provision was lawful in Japan, the United States, and the European Union.

The JFTC's Recommendation and Microsoft's Response

The Japanese FTC was not convinced, however, and continued its investigations. On July 13, 2004, the FTC issued a "Recommendation to Microsoft Corporation" that found that Microsoft had violated Japan's Antimonopoly Act and ordered it to remove the offending clauses from past contracts as well as refrain from using them in the future. Specifically, Microsoft cannot contractually prevent Windows licensees "from suing, bringing, prosecuting, assisting or participating in any judicial, administrative or any other kinds of proceedings against Microsoft, its subsidiaries, or other licensees for infringement of the licensees' patents."

Microsoft did not back down. Instead, it issued a press release explaining that "we respectfully disagree with the conclusions reached by the JFTC at this stage of the process, and will avail ourselves of the mechanism set out in the Law and regulations to seek a review of this decision." In essence, Microsoft would not remove the provision from past contracts, and it would not admit that the clause had ever been illegal. However, neither would the JFTC remove its order.

And there it stands. Meetings between Microsoft lawyers and the JFTC occur regularly, but the entire process is nowhere near completion, and the case continues moving forward, albeit at a pace that would make glaciers impatient. So far, the JFTC has not publicly commented on Vista or asked for changes to the OS, but that could change at any time. Of course, by the time that conflict would be resolved,

Vista could be a legacy OS years out of date … which we're sure would suit Microsoft just fine.

Microsoft Vista: The Korean Fixes

In some ways, Microsoft's legal adventures in South Korea are remarkably similar to those it experienced in Japan: Both feature that country's FTC and a raid on corporate offices, and both have taken years to work their way through each country's legal system. In the case of South Korea, however, the FTC in that nation has achieved concrete results.

The Complaint

On September 5, 2001, Daum Communications, providers of an incredibly popular Web portal and related communications services in Korea, filed a complaint against Microsoft for including software providing instant messaging, telephony, and digital image handling in the upcoming Windows XP (XP appeared on store shelves in October 2001). In particular, the Windows Instant Messenger (IM) was a problem for Daum, which at that time had about 20 percent of the IM market in Korea.

Not much happened, but Daum's irritations at what it saw as Microsoft's anti-competitive software bundling continued, to the point where Daum finally brought suit in Korean courts in April 2004. That action, plus RealNetwork's complaints about Microsoft's inclusion of a media player with Windows, finally inspired the Korean FTC to act, so it raided Microsoft's Korean offices in June 2004.

The FTC finally focused its complaints in two areas: the bundling of Windows Media streaming services with Windows Server, and the inclusion of Windows Media Player with the Windows desktop OS (the latter being the same issue that got Microsoft into hot water with the European Competition Commission). It took more than a year, but Microsoft finally got so frustrated with the FTC's investigation that it threatened in October 2005 to withdraw Windows from Korea entirely if it was forced to remove software from Windows. This was a faint likelihood, however, given the amount of money the company makes in Korea, one of the most technically advanced countries in Asia.

In November, Microsoft settled for $30 million with Daum, so at least that lawsuit was no longer a problem. That didn't mean the probe by the KFTC was over, however. In an apparent about-face with the angry October 2005 statements, or, more likely, in a case of business sense winning out over emotion, Oliver Roll, a Microsoft spokesperson in Singapore, reiterated the company's commitment to South Korea as "one of the most vibrant markets in Asia."

The KFTC's Decision

December 7, 2005 saw the Korean FTC's decision: a $32 million fine and an order to unbundle both Windows Messenger and Windows Media Player from Windows. However, it was a bit more complicated than that. Microsoft was to offer two versions of Windows: one without Windows Media Player and Windows Messenger, and one containing the software but also including links to download competitors' IM and media player software. In addition, Microsoft would have to mail CDs to existing Windows users containing IM and media player software from rivals. Finally, Windows Server would have to remove Windows Media Service and make it available as a download, but not as an automatic part of the OS.

Microsoft understandably wasn't happy, and complained that the decision would lead to "chilling innovation" before making it clear that it would appeal; at the same time, the company reiterated that it was going to continue to sell Windows in Korea.

Two Versions of XP

Microsoft did in fact appeal in March 2006, and on July 4, the Korean High Court in Seoul rejected the company's request for a stay in following the orders of the KFTC. That meant Microsoft could continue in its appeal to overturn the ruling of the regulators, but it had to follow through on those orders immediately; if it later won its case in court, it could return to doing business as it had previously.

Accordingly, August 23 saw the introduction in Korea of two versions of Windows XP: one without IM and media software (known as the KN version), and one with the software but also with links to competitors (known as the K version).

Two Versions of Vista

Meanwhile, Microsoft continued to work on Vista, and in the October 2006 press conference conducted by Brad Smith, the General Counsel for Microsoft also revealed that after two months of talks with Korea, Vista would continue the FTC's rulings concerning XP into the new OS.

Just as there had been an XP K and an XP KN version of Windows, there were be K and KN variants of Vista as well. However, although K versions of all the various types of Vista will be released at the same time Vista is launched worldwide, the KN alternatives will see a more complicated schedule. KN versions of Home Basic and Business will be released in January 2007; however, KN versions of Premium and Ultimate won't go on sale until SP1 comes out, due to the inclusion of Media

Center features that depend on Windows Media Player. Microsoft is going to need the extra time in order to figure out how to work around that limitation.

Because Vista won't include an IM program anyway, that restriction by the KFTC won't be an issue; Microsoft will simply include a link to the Windows Live Messenger program as it was intending to do anyway.

Microsoft undoubtedly hopes that it can still reverse the KFTC's decision and ship the version of Vista that it wants to make available, with its software included and without links to competitors. It's unclear at this time whether Korean antitrust regulators will find other objections to Vista, but it's obvious that the Koreans are unafraid of challenging the world's largest software company when they think that it has broken the law.

Notes and Sources

Interested readers may want to follow up the events and statements recorded in this appendix by checking out the following sources.

Microsoft Vista: The EU Fixes

Details about Microsoft's 1994 consent decree can be found in *The Washington Post*'s "Microsoft Settles Case With Justice" (www.washingtonpost.com/wp-srv/ business/longterm/microsoft/stories/1994/settle071794.htm). The announcement of the European Union's 1997 probe is listed on an excellent resource for those interested in Microsoft's legal troubles: "U.S. v. Microsoft Timeline," from *The Washington Post*, which covers 1990–2002 (www.washingtonpost.com/wp-dyn/business/specials/microsofttrial/timeline). The announcement of formal charges in 2000 and 2001, as well as many other details in the European antitrust conflict, can be seen on two other timelines, both from *InformationWeek*: "The European Union Vs. Microsoft: A Timeline Of Events" (www.informationweek.com/story/ showArticle.jhtml?articleID=190302510), which covers the years between 1998 and 2006, and "Timeline: EU's Pursuit Of Microsoft" (www.informationweek.com/ story/showArticle.jhtml?articleID=18401563), which goes from 1994 to 2004.

The March 2004 Ruling

The initial PDF containing the text of the European Commission's ruling, titled "COMMISSION DECISION of 24.03.2004 relating to a proceeding under Article 82 of the EC Treaty (Case COMP/C-3/37.792 Microsoft)," can be found downloaded as a PDF from http://europa.eu.int/comm/competition/antitrust/cases/ decisions/37792/en.pdf. Information about the second huge fine that Microsoft received for failing to comply with the European Commission's 2004 antitrust ruling, and the threatened $3.8 million-per-day fine on top of that, can be found in many places, but *The New York Times'* "Regulators Penalize Microsoft In Europe" (http://select.nytimes.com/search/restricted/article?res=F10712FC35540C708DDD AE0894DE404482) contains a wealth of interesting information. The complaint by the European Union that Microsoft's initial cut at documentation was "incomplete, inaccurate and unusable" can be read in the same article.

The actions between Microsoft and the European Commission in November 2006 are detailed in *The New York Times'* "Europe Warns Microsoft Over Compliance" (http://select.nytimes.com/search/restricted/article?res= F40C17F73C5A0C758DDDA80994DE404482) and "Microsoft Gives Europe Antitrust Documents" (http://select.nytimes.com/search/restricted/article?res= F10D17FD385A0C778EDDA80994DE404482).

Vista

Neelie Kroes' letter to Microsoft in March 2006 about Vista is discussed in CNET's "EU voices concerns over Microsoft's Vista" (http://news.com.com/EU+voices+ concerns+over+Microsofts+Vista/2100-1016_3-6055501.html). Microsoft's response in April, as well as further details about the now-famous 79 questions, can be found in *The New York Times'* "Regulators Penalize Microsoft In Europe" of July 13, 2006 (http://select.nytimes.com/search/restricted/article?res=F10712FC35540C708DDD AE0894DE404482). More information about the jockeying back and forth in July is disclosed in *The Financial Times'* July 12 article titled "Microsoft closer to European truce" (http://search.ft.com/searchArticle?id=060712007839) and *Business Week*'s "A European Faceoff over Microsoft Vista" (http://yahoo.businessweek.com/globalbiz/ content/sep2006/gb20060913_243817.htm).

The quotation by Gartner's John Pescatore, as well as further information about the problems security vendors have with Vista's PatchGuard feature, is from CNET's "Windows defense handcuffs good guys" (http://news.com.com/2102-7355_3-6104379.html?tag=st.util.print), which was published August 11, 2006.

The SEC filing by Microsoft in August in which it warned of delays in Europe for Vista is covered in *The New York Times'* "Microsoft Warns Europeans New System Could Be Delayed" (http://select.nytimes.com/search/restricted/ article?res=F40F13F83C550C7B8CDDA00894DE404482) and the BBC's "Microsoft in EU Vista stand-off" (http://news.bbc.co.uk/2/hi/ business/5325690.stm), and the reply by the four European Parliament members is discussed in *InfoWorld*'s "EU criticized for action against Microsoft" (www.infoworld.com/article/06/09/07/HNeucriticized_1.html).

The Competition Commission's warnings to Microsoft about its bundling of security products with Vista are well covered in *The New York Times*' "Plan for Vista Draws Warning To Microsoft From Europe" (http://select.nytimes.com/search/restricted/article?res=FB0711F83E550C708DDDA00894DE404482) and CNET's "Vista's European battleground" (http://news.com.com/2102-7348_3-6116354.html?tag=st.util.print).

Microsoft's study describing the myriad benefits of Vista to the European economy is explored in *InfoWorld*'s "Microsoft tries to dazzle EU with Vista's benefits" (www.infoworld.com/article/06/09/14/HNmicrosoftdazzleeu_1.html). Glyn Moody dissects the flim-flammery of the study in his "Microsoft's Masterpiece of FUD," at *Linux Journal*'s Web site (www.linuxjournal.com/node/1000097).

The October Concessions

The October 13, 2006 press conference given by Microsoft's General Counsel, Brad Smith, is an excellent source of details on the changes the company made to Vista as a result of conversations with the European Union's Competition Commission. You can find "Brad Smith Press Conference Transcript: Announcement Regarding Release of Windows Vista in Europe and Korea" at www.microsoft.com/presspass/exec/bradsmith/10-13-06VistaRelease.mspx.

Microsoft's announcement was big news, and was reported in a number of places. Good sources include *eWeek*'s "Microsoft: Vista Set to Ship Without Regional Changes" (www.eweek.com/article2/0,1895,2029752,00.asp), *The New York Times*' "Microsoft Makes Changes in Windows Vista to Suit Foreign Regulators" (http://select.nytimes.com/search/restricted/article?res=F30615FA3A540C778DDDA90994DE404482), *The Seattle Post-Intelligencer*'s "Microsoft to change Vista" (http://seattlepi.nwsource.com/business/288671_msftvista14.html), and CNET's "Microsoft changes Vista over antitrust concerns" (http://news.com.com/Microsoft+changes+Vista+over+antitrust+concerns/2100-1016_3-6125560.html). Paul Thurrott gives the matter the most thorough coverage while keeping his usual pro-Microsoft spin in "Last Minute Changes to Windows Vista" (www.winsupersite.com/showcase/winvista_changes.asp).

The Commission's response to Microsoft's announcement is discussed in ITPro's "Microsoft makes changes to Vista in EU, S. Korea" (www.itpro.co.uk/servers/news/95628/microsoft-makes-changes-to-vista-in-eu-s-korea.html).

Squabbling over Security

The October squabbling between Microsoft and various security software vendors is covered in a series of articles. The initial delivery of Windows Security Center information, later rejected, can be followed in AP's "Microsoft: Working With Security Vendors" (http://biz.yahoo.com/ap/061016/eu_microsoft.html?.v=5), The Register's "McAfee dismisses Microsoft's security overtures" (www.theregister.co.uk/2006/10/18/vista_securityinfo_not_enough/), and Reuters' "Microsoft takes step to carry out EU bargain" (http://yahoo.reuters.com/news/articlehybrid.aspx?storyID=urn:newsml:reuters.com:20061018:MTFH39542_2006-10-18_22-34-31_L18922351&type=comktNews&rpc=44), which also includes Ballmer's dismissal of the security companies' concerns.

The meeting that turned into a fiasco is covered by CNET in "Security rivals shut out of Microsoft meeting" (http://news.com.com/Security+rivals+shut+out+of+Microsoft+meeting/2100-1009_3-6127559.html). BetaNews gives Microsoft's side of the story in "Vista SP1 to Include Common Security APIs for Partners" (www.betanews.com/article/Vista_SP1_to_Include_Common_Security_APIs_for_Partners/1161305514), but a blog entry by Alex Eckelberry, an employee of Sunbelt Software who was involved in the aborted attempt, disputes Microsoft's assurances of business as usual (although he is sympathetic to Microsoft about the problems it experienced); Eckelberry's description, titled "Much ado about nothing," can be found at http://sunbeltblog.blogspot.com/2006/10/much-ado-about-nothing.html.

Finally, further disputations between Microsoft and McAfee can be read in VNUnet's "McAfee blasts Microsoft's 'hollow security promises'" (www.vnunet.com/vnunet/news/2166897/mcafee-blasts-microsoft-hollow), Reuters' "Microsoft says McAfee 'inaccurate, inflammatory'" (http://yahoo.reuters.com/news/articlehybrid.aspx?storyID=urn:newsml:reuters.com:20061020:MTFH78676_2006-10-20_08-46-57_L20513055&type=comktNews&rpc=44), and BetaNews' "MS to McAfee: Stop Lying to the Public" (www.betanews.com/article/MS_to_McAfee_Stop_Lying_to_the_Public/1161357132).

The news of Microsoft's release of the initial draft of the PatchGuard APIs was carried by *Computerworld* in "Microsoft releases first draft of PatchGuard APIs" (www.computerworld.com/action/article.do?command=viewArticleBasic&articleId=9006251); an interview with Microsoft VP Ben Fathi that revealed further details was available as well at "Q&A: Fathi explains draft API release for PatchGuard" (www.computerworld.com/action/article.do?command=viewArticleBasic&articleId=9006269). McAfee's positive response can be found in *Forbes'* "Microsoft Opens Up" (www.forbes.com/2006/12/19/microsoft-vista-security-tech-security-cx_ll_1219microsoft.html).

Microsoft and Japan

News of the Tokyo office raids by the Japanese FTC were carried by *The Financial Times* in "Microsoft probed by Japan's anti-trust agency" (http://search.ft.com/searchArticle?id=040226005847). Microsoft's own PR firm put out "Statement by Microsoft Corporation on Reports of Japanese Fair Trade Commission Inquiry" (www.microsoft.com/presspass/press/2004/feb04/02-26jftcstatement.mspx) as well, which also explained that the company had already dropped the troublesome patent provisions on its own accord. The BBC also carried Microsoft's announcement that it was removing the offending patent suit clause in "Microsoft ends 'unfair' contract" (http://news.bbc.co.uk/2/hi/business/3488186.stm).

The order by the FTC to cease utilizing the patent clause can be read in a PDF published by the government agency itself, titled "The JFTC renders a Recommendation to Microsoft Corporation" and available at www.jftc.go.jp/e-page/pressreleases/2004/july/040713.pdf. Microsoft's refusal to abide by the order comes straight from the horse's mouth: "Statement by Microsoft Corporation on Japanese Fair Trade Commission Recommendation" (www.microsoft.com/presspass/press/2004/jul04/07-13jftcstatementpr.mspx). TechNewsWorld has more information in its story, "Microsoft Rebuffs Japanese Antitrust Inquiry" (www.technewsworld.com/story/35093.html).

Continuing meetings between the Fair Trade Commission and Microsoft are documented in *InfoWorld*'s December 21, 2004 "Japan's FTC, Microsoft meet again in licensing case" (www.infoworld.com/article/04/12/21/HNjapanmslicensing_1.html) and July 27, 2005 "Microsoft set for long battle with Japanese regulators" (www.infoworld.com/article/05/07/27/HNmslongbattle_1.html).

Microsoft Vista: The Korean Fixes

The news of Daum Communications' complaint against Microsoft in Korea was given by the BBC in "South Korean firm to sue Microsoft" (http://news.bbc.co.uk/2/hi/business/1526221.stm). The search of Microsoft's Korean offices by the Fair Trade Commission was reported in *NetworkWorld*'s "Microsoft Korea office searched in anti-trust probe" (www.networkworld.com/news/2004/0611microkorea.html).

Microsoft's angry threat to leave the Korean market if it didn't like the FTC's decision came from *The Financial Times*' "Microsoft threatens to pull Windows from Korea" (http://search.ft.com/searchArticle?id=051028004070).

The eventual settlement between Daum and Microsoft can be found in *The Financial Times*' "Microsoft settles with S Korea's Daum" (http://search.ft.com/searchArticle?id=051111001499) and *InfoWorld*'s "Microsoft settles with Daum for $30M" (www.infoworld.com/article/05/11/11/ HNmsdaumsettle_1.html), which also contains the quotation by spokesperson Oliver Roll affirming Microsoft's support for doing business in Korea.

Changes to XP

Although the KFTC's decision was covered worldwide in the news, the most in-depth article was probably *InfoWorld*'s "Update: Microsoft fined $32M by South Korea" (www.infoworld.com/article/05/12/07/HNmicrosoftfined_1.html). Of course, Microsoft also explained its side of the story in "Microsoft Statement on Korean Fair Trade Commission Decision" (www.microsoft.com/presspass/press/ 2005/dec05/12-06KFTCPR.mspx).

Microsoft announced its appeal of the decision in "Microsoft Appeals Korea Fair Trade Commission Decision" (www.microsoft.com/presspass/press/2006/mar06/03-26KFTCAppealPR.mspx); it announced the failure of its request for a stay in "Microsoft Statement Regarding the Korean Court's Decision" (www.microsoft. com/presspass/legal/07-04-06KoreaStatement.mspx). The news of a release of XP conforming to the demands of Korean regulators came in *The Financial Times*' "Microsoft to release new Windows in Korea" (http://search.ft.com/searchArticle?id=060823004080).

Vista

The record of the now famous press conference of October 13, titled "Brad Smith Press Conference Transcript: Announcement Regarding Release of Windows Vista in Europe and Korea," can be found on Microsoft's site at www.microsoft.com/press-pass/exec/bradsmith/10-13-06VistaRelease.mspx. News of those changes was reported in many places, including *InternetNews*' "Vista on Track: Microsoft Bends For E.U., Korea" (www.internetnews.com/ent-news/article.php/3637851).

The details about the delays in the Korean versions of Vista came from Paul Thurrott's "Last Minute Changes to Windows Vista" (www.winsupersite.com/show-case/winvista_changes.asp), with the details about the differing release schedules for the K and KN versions appearing in CNET's "Microsoft scrambles to ship Vista in Korea" (http://news.com.com/Microsoft+scrambles+to+ship+ Vista+in+Korea/2100-1016_3-6125751.html).

Summary

Microsoft's history with the antitrust divisions of governments in America, Europe, and Asia is nothing short of contentious. Part of the company's DNA is to resist any effort by regulators to rein in its excesses, no matter how egregious, which has resulted in years of legal maneuvers and millions of dollars in expense.

However, it must be said that the strategy has by and large paid off for Microsoft, as it has escaped relatively unscathed from its court battles. Vista did see a few changes, some of them significant, in the areas of search, XPS, media players, and especially security. Once Vista reaches wide distribution and users, businesses, and governments have time to really discover the full ramifications of the OS, we may see more antitrust challenges and more changes. Given Microsoft's legal history, it seems a certainty.

Microsoft Vista:
The EULA

This appendix was written by Scott Granneman, a monthly columnist for both SecurityFocus *and* Linux Magazine. *He comments on various problematic clauses in Vista's EULA that he first addressed in his column titled "Surprises Inside Microsoft Vista's EULA," which he wrote for* SecurityFocus *in October 2006. He also addresses the Vista EULA's restrictions on benchmark testing, virtualization, and Digital Rights Management (DRM).*

Introduction

Even though precious few users actually read it, Microsoft's End User License Agreement (EULA) has actually always been both incredibly important and problematic at the same time. Important because it governs what users may and may not do with the operating system (OS) that so many people around the world buy … uh, license, and problematic because many of the stipulations in the EULA are troublesome in the powers they grant Microsoft.

Anyone who's familiar with Microsoft's past EULAs knows about the controversial clauses present long before Vista, and Vista's EULAs contain them as well. The piece of the EULA promising that if you disagree with the license, just go ahead and return it to the retailer for a refund—a fruitless process that ends up leading the person seeking the refund on an endless round of phone calls between computer manufacturers and Microsoft, each insisting that it is the responsibility of the other party to pay up—is right in the beginning, just as in past EULAs. Mandatory activation, guaranteeing that at least some people will get stuck when their copy of Windows mysteriously "forgets" it's been activated already, is there. The statement that Microsoft is in no way liable for any failures of its OS, with damages limited to the actual cost of the software? Oh yeah. It's there.

That said, Microsoft—or the lawyers writing the EULA—should be given credit, because the EULAs for Vista are the clearest and easiest ever to come out of the company. Oh, there's still legalese to be found in there—"The laws of the state where you live govern all other claims, including claims under state consumer protection laws, unfair competition laws, and in tort"—but it's at a lower percentage when compared with any other EULA to come out of Redmond. That's good for consumers, and Microsoft is to be commended for that action.

Criticism and Change

When drafts of the Vista EULA first began circulating, there were several problematic clauses that raised quite a hue and cry. I wrote a column for *SecurityFocus* in October 2006 titled "Surprises Inside Microsoft Vista's EULA" that covered several of the more egregious legal claims upon which Microsoft was insisting. In particular, I called out clause 15 in the EULA—"REASSIGN TO ANOTHER DEVICE"—which originally read as follows:

```
Software Other than Windows Anytime Upgrade. The first user of the software
may reassign the license to another device one time. If you reassign the
license, that other device becomes the "licensed device."
```

This seemed to me egregious and unfair to exactly those users who support Microsoft by paying for licenses in the store instead of just acquiring them with new machines. As I wrote in my column:

```
As I read this, you go to the store and buy a copy of Vista, which you
install on a PC you had in your office. A year later, another PC becomes
available that's a bit more up-to-date, so you decide to transfer your Vista
license to that machine.
```

```
You're now finished with that Vista license. Done. Game over, man. Whether
you shelled out $199 for Home Basic or broke the bank with the $399 Ultimate
makes no difference. You've reassigned the license twice, and that's all
that Microsoft allows."
```

My column was reprinted in *The Register*, and picked up by both Slashdot and Digg, resulting in quite a lot of discussion and debate. Several other individuals, in both articles and blogs, were making the same points, and it seems that Microsoft actually listened. A few days after my column came out, links to the Vista EULA disappeared from Microsoft's Web site. When they returned, the wording that I had protested had changed:

```
Software Other than Windows Anytime Upgrade. You may uninstall the software
and install it on another device for your use. You may not do so to share
this license between devices.
```

This is much clearer, and it's also in accord with what most users understand and expect. It was good of Microsoft—both for itself and for users—to clarify this issue.

Unfortunately, two other clauses in the Vista EULA still contain troubling language, language that serves no purpose except to help Microsoft at the expense of customers and competitors. These two clauses cover benchmark testing and the use of Vista in virtualized environments, and anyone who signs on to the EULA should give them serious thought.

Benchmark Testing

Microsoft is releasing several different versions of Vista, which definitely complicates any discussion of the EULA, because the first question one must ask about a clause is "Which version of Vista has this condition in its license?" In the case of the benchmarking limitations, look in the software licenses for Windows Vista Home Basic, Windows Vista Home Premium, Windows Vista Business, and Windows Vista Ultimate. Together, those cover a huge percentage of Vista users, whose software will now be bound by the following restrictions:

```
MICROSOFT .NET BENCHMARK TESTING. The software includes one or more
components of the .NET Framework 3.0 (".NET Components"). You may conduct
internal benchmark testing of those components. You may disclose the results
```

```
of any benchmark test of those components, provided that you comply with the
conditions set forth at http://go.microsoft.com/fwlink/?LinkID=66406.
Notwithstanding any other agreement you may have with Microsoft, if you
disclose such benchmark test results, Microsoft shall have the right to
disclose the results of benchmark tests it conducts of your products that
compete with the applicable .NET Component, provided it complies with the
same conditions set forth at http://go.microsoft.com/fwlink/?LinkID=66406.
```

The problem with the preceding words is not that end users will have to go to a Microsoft Web site before conducting benchmarks; indeed, you'd be hard-pressed to find *any* end users who do perform benchmarking tests. Instead, this is a problem because those who do conduct benchmarking—reviewers in magazines and on Web sites, in particular—will be hamstrung.

To put this situation in terms of cars, it's as though Ford insisted that any tests of its automobiles had to be governed by rules that it set in place—rules that Ford could change at any time! Would that be bad for your average car buyer? Yes, but not because Joe Carbuyer would be out testing Fords, but rather because *Consumer Reports* and the myriad other organizations and publications that do examine cars—tests that Joe uses to know which cars are safe and which are deathtraps, for instance—would have to work under rigged and unreal conditions.

Rigging the Tests

It's bad enough that benchmark testers first have to stick to a Web page that Microsoft can change at any time—how'd you like to find out that the month of work you just went through has been invalidated thanks to a new change on that Web page?—but the actual language at http://go.microsoft.com/fwlink/?LinkID= 66406 should give one pause. At the time of this writing, the terms say this:

```
(3) your benchmark testing was performed using all performance tuning and
best practice guidance set forth in the product documentation and/or on
Microsoft's support Web sites, and uses the latest updates, patches, and
fixes available for the .NET Component and the relevant Microsoft operating
system.
```

This might seem fairly innocuous, but it's not. Microsoft is ensuring that if you run its products through a trial, you must first tweak those products exactly according to Microsoft's specifications ... which, coincidentally enough, will undoubtedly most favor Microsoft. Worse, there can sometimes be an enormous gap between the way Microsoft wants admins to configure systems and the actual configurations admins use. What would you rather read: the results of studies conducted in a spotlessly idealistic setup or those conducted in the real world? Which would give you more insight into how the product actually works?

And what about the demand that analysts must use the "latest updates, patches, and fixes"? How in the world are we going to know whether the latest version is actually better than the last one—or the one before that—if assessments are forbidden from comparing and contrasting the two versions without running afoul of the EULA?

The result of Microsoft's language in the EULA pertaining to benchmarking? Results that can be incorrect, unreal, or distorted. Is that what we want in the studies and reviews we read? Are limitations on benchmarking and the publishing of results ever a good idea? In this case, when we're working with the software that powers more than 90 percent of the world's desktops, it seems a disastrously unfortunate limitation, and one that should be abandoned as soon as possible.

Virtualization

The technology of virtualization has been around for more than 40 years in one form or another, but in the past five years or so, as desktops have become faster and more powerful, it's finally reached the point where even those machines can reap the advantages of virtualization. For those who don't know, the process of virtualization on a PC goes something like this (assuming you already have Windows installed and running):

1. Install virtualization software such as VMware (the market leader), Parallels (the market leader on Macs, with a fine product for computers running Windows as well), or Microsoft's own Virtual PC.

2. Open the virtualization software and create a new virtual machine (VM)—essentially, a large, multigigabyte (8? 10? bigger?) file that will contain the contents of the next step.

3. Within the new VM, install and configure the OS of your choice: Windows 2000, Windows XP, another copy of Windows Vista (with a different license than the machine containing your virtualized environment), Linux (I recommend Ubuntu), or pretty much any OS that you can install on Intel-compatible hardware.

4. Repeat steps 2 and 3 for any other OSes you want to install, and you're finished.

Let's say you installed a copy of Windows XP to use for testing in step 3. To use it, you'd open VMware (or whatever virtualization software you decided to use) and then select the VM you want to run—in this case, Windows XP. A few moments later, a window will open—a window like any other on your computer—showing

Windows XP booting really fast. Once the booting process completes, you will be staring at a Windows XP desktop running in a window surrounded by your Windows Vista desktop. This is really Windows XP, not a fake or gutted version of the OS. You may notice a 5 percent or so decrease in performance, but that's it, and many tasks will actually be far faster within the virtualized environment than they would be running on the bare metal of the machine (there is one exception: software, such as games, that requires 3D acceleration of the video card, but that's normally not an issue for most users of virtualization).

That's virtualization in a nutshell, and hopefully your mind is spinning with ideas now that you know how easy it is to set up and use. Is there a piece of software that refuses to run on Vista, but still works great on XP? Need to test Web sites with different versions of Internet Explorer? Want to verify that a new piece of software won't break on production machines? How about creating a virtual network on your machine so that you can examine network security software? Or would you like to run Internet Explorer and other potentially risky software on the Net without the risk of infecting your main OS? Switched to an Intel-based MacBook Pro running Mac OS X but still want to run Vista? In every case, virtualization to the rescue!

Sounds great, doesn't it? Then why is Microsoft hurting users of its OS who want to take advantage of this fantastic technology?

Virtualization Controls

To understand what I mean by that, let's take a quick look at the versions of Vista that Microsoft will be selling, along with the prices for each edition:

- Starter (OEM pricing only)
- Home Basic ($199, or $99 upgrade)
- Home Premium ($239, or $159 upgrade)
- Business ($299, or $199 upgrade)
- Enterprise (OEM pricing only)
- Ultimate ($399, or $259 upgrade)

Got that? Now, let's look at a particular clause tucked away in the Vista EULA for Home Basic and Home Premium:

```
USE WITH VIRTUALIZATION TECHNOLOGIES.  You may not use the software
installed on the licensed device within a virtual (or otherwise emulated)
hardware system.
```

What's that mean? Quite simply, you cannot create a virtualized environment on any computer and then install Home Basic or Home Premium within it. This proscription is not found in the EULAs for Business and Ultimate, however. For those editions, the EULA instead lacks one little word that carries with it a great meaning: "not."

```
USE WITH VIRTUALIZATION TECHNOLOGIES.  You may use the software installed on
the licensed device within a virtual (or otherwise emulated) hardware system
on the licensed device.
```

There is no technology in place actually preventing you from installing Home Basic or Home Premium inside VMware or any other virtualization software. Instead, Microsoft is using licensing and the withholding of support as its hammer. If you call Microsoft to request help with Home Premium, and the person on the other end of the phone finds out that you're running it inside Virtual PC, the support session is over.

This is a naked attempt to force people interested in taking advantage of virtualization to spend more money on Vista. If I'm a Web developer who just wants to test Internet Explorer 7 by installing Vista inside a virtual machine on my XP box, why can't I be allowed to simply pay for Home Basic and use that? From Microsoft's perspective, I shouldn't, when I can be forced to pay the company an additional $100 for Vista Business edition.

If you ask Microsoft, the company's spokespersons will give you some twaddle about how virtualization is "not yet mature enough for broad consumer adoption" and that "consumers don't understand the risks of running virtual machines." That's complete bunkum, as the technology most definitely is "mature," but logically, these are ridiculous statements: If virtualization was in fact not yet mature, forcing people to spend an additional 100 clams to try it out sure ain't gonna help it become mature! Even more ludicrous is the idea that a VM introduces risk; if anything, it actually reduces risk by allowing knowledgeable users to insulate their main OS from the dangers of the Internet. Microsoft is simply making feeble excuses for a business decision designed to rake in more cash from the public. Apparently, if something costs $299 instead of $199, Microsoft no longer cares about the "maturity" or "risks" of a technology, or maybe those problems just magically melt away.

It may be pointed out that if you're a subscriber to the Microsoft Developer Network (MSDN), then yes, you are allowed to use Home Basic or Home Premium in a VM. Again, notice that there is clearly nothing technical that prevents users from installing those OSes in Parallels or even Virtual PC; it's just Microsoft's whim. This might sound like a solution for some of the problems I posited earlier, but an

MSDN subscription isn't cheap, and will be onerous to small Web developers testing Internet Explorer and other folks who just want to make limited use of Vista.

DRM and Virtualization

Even in Business and Ultimate, however, Microsoft still put into place restrictions on use of those OSes. The full wording of the virtualization clause in those EULAs reads as follows:

```
USE WITH VIRTUALIZATION TECHNOLOGIES. You may use the software installed on
the licensed device within a virtual (or otherwise emulated) hardware system
on the licensed device. If you do so, you may not play or access content or
use applications protected by any Microsoft digital, information or
enterprise rights management technology or other Microsoft rights management
services or use BitLocker. We advise against playing or accessing content or
using applications protected by other digital, information or enterprise
rights management technology or other rights management services or using
full volume disk drive encryption.
```

So, you can use Business and Ultimate inside virtual environments, but you cannot use or view any content locked up using DRM. This ends up covering a lot of potential territory, as Microsoft's DRM is spreading, tentacle-like, into more and more applications and files, especially Windows Audio and Office documents. This is less onerous than simply prohibiting the use of an entire OS for virtualization, but this restriction still unfairly limits what users can do with the software they bought.

Let's say a Mac or Linux user decides to honor Microsoft's wishes about which OS to run inside a VM, and so goes ahead and ponies up for Vista Business or Ultimate. That user may decide to run Microsoft's Office 2007 inside his Vista VM, so he can read and create documents in the new Office 2007 XML formats. If that user should receive a document that is "protected" by Microsoft's DRM, too bad. The EULA says no—again, not for technical reasons, as Microsoft's DRM will work just as well in a virtual environment as it does on a version of Vista installed directly on a machine—and so the user ends up suffering because of Microsoft's business decisions. Now he's required to buy a new PC. This is both unfair and unreasonable.

We haven't really talked much about Vista Enterprise, which is unique in the Vista family when it comes to virtualization. Windows journalist Paul Thurrott explains how it works:

```
Windows Vista Enterprise is a special case. With that version of Vista,
which will be made available only to volume license customers, users will be
able to install a single licensed copy of Vista on one physical PC and up to
four VMs, simultaneously. Those four VMs, however, must all be installed on
the same Vista Enterprise-based PC, and they must be used by the same user.
```

Again we see Microsoft favoring one class of customer over another and putting dollars instead of technology first. Virtualization is one of the most exciting and useful tools available to computer users today, and it holds the potential to solve many important problems in the areas of security, testing, and reliability. Microsoft should be promoting its use instead of attempting to stifle and control its growth. The wording in the Vista EULA that shamelessly attempts to limit what users can do in virtualized environments with Vista is bad for users, bad for the technology industry, and bad for Microsoft. It should be removed.

Notes and Sources

Interested readers may want to follow up the events and statements recorded in this appendix by checking out the following sources.

EULA Overview

You can read the EULAs for Vista by going to the official "Find License Terms for Software Licensed from Microsoft" page at www.microsoft.com/about/legal/useterms and searching for Vista from the pull-down menu.

My *SecurityFocus* article, "Surprises Inside Microsoft Vista's EULA," can be found at www.securityfocus.com/columnists/420. The reprint at *The Register* is located at www.theregister.co.uk/2006/10/29/microsoft_vista_eula_analysis. The Slashdot discussion, which generated 382 comments, can be followed at http://yro.slashdot.org/article.pl?sid=06/11/02/1751222, and the Digg postings (904 of them) are on http://digg.com/tech_news/Surprises_Inside_Microsoft_Vista_s_EULA_2.

Benchmarking

Ed Foster, in his excellent Gripelog, wrote a piece titled "A Vista of Licensed Censorship" (www.gripe2ed.com/scoop/story/2006/10/24/0456/5625) that looks at several aspects of the Vista EULA. In particular, he covers the benchmarking problem with his usual brio and intelligence.

If you want to read Microsoft's ".NET Framework Benchmark Testing Terms," head to http://msdn2.microsoft.com/en-us/library/ms973265.aspx.

Virtualization

If you're interested in learning more about virtualization, check out Wikipedia's article on the subject at http://en.wikipedia.org/wiki/Virtual_machine, or read the explanation offered by VMware, one of the leading software companies in this arena, at www.vmware.com/virtualization. In the area of security, a column I wrote for *SecurityFocus*—"Virtualization for security" (www.securityfocus.com/columnists/397)—may interest you.

More about VMware is at www.vmware.com, and you can read about Parallels at www.parallels.com/en/products/workstation. Microsoft's Virtual PC can be found at www.microsoft.com/windows/virtualpc/default.mspx.

In my list of OSes you can install in a virtualized environment, I mentioned Ubuntu, an excellent version of Linux, which you can read about and acquire for free at www.ubuntu.com.

I wrote a column for *SecurityFocus* a few years ago that looks at the DRM Microsoft is injecting into its Office suite: "Learning to Love Big Brother" (www.securityfocus.com/columnists/165). Sadly, it's still relevant today.

Paul Thurrott's "Licensing Changes to Windows Vista" explains Microsoft's policies regarding Vista Enterprise and virtualization at www.winsupersite.com/showcase/winvista_licensing.asp.

Summary

In some ways—principally ease of reading and clarifying that users may uninstall a copy of Vista on one machine to reinstall the same copy on another computer—the EULA for Vista is a marked improvement over previous Windows EULAs. Unfortunately, Microsoft's EULA for Vista still contains within it two problematic clauses: one governing the ways in which benchmarking tests must be run, and one tightly constricting how users may install Vista inside virtualization environments. None of these restrictions benefits consumers, and it would be in Microsoft's best interests to change those limitations in future EULAs.

Index

Syngress: *The Definition of a Serious Security Library*

Syn·gress (sin-gres): *noun, sing.* Freedom from risk or danger; safety. See *security*.

Syngress IT Security Project Management Handbook

Susan Snedaker

The definitive work for IT professionals responsible for the management of the design, configuration, deployment and maintenance of enterprise-wide security projects. Provides specialized coverage of key project areas including Penetration Testing, Intrusion Detection and Prevention Systems, and Access Control Systems.

ISBN: 1-59749-076-8

Price: $59.95 US $77.95 CAN

Combating Spyware in the Enterprise

Paul Piccard

Combating Spyware in the Enterprise is the first book published on defending enterprise networks from increasingly sophisticated and malicious spyware. System administrators and security professionals responsible for administering and securing networks ranging in size from SOHO networks up to the largest enterprise networks will learn to use a combination of free and commercial anti-spyware software, firewalls, intrusion detection systems, intrusion prevention systems, and host integrity monitoring applications to prevent the installation of spyware, and to limit the damage caused by spyware that does in fact infiltrate their networks.

ISBN: 1-59749-064-4

Price: $49.95 US $64.95 CAN

Practical VoIP Security

Thomas Porter

After struggling for years, you finally think you've got your network secured from malicious hackers and obnoxious spammers. Just when you think it's safe to go back into the water, VoIP finally catches on. Now your newly converged network is vulnerable to DoS attacks, hacked gateways leading to unauthorized free calls, call eavesdropping, malicious call redirection, and spam over Internet Telephony (SPIT). This book details both VoIP attacks and defense techniques and tools.

ISBN: 1-59749-060-1

Price: $49.95 U.S. $69.95 CAN

Syngress: *The Definition of a Serious Security Library*

Syn·gress (sin–gres): *noun, sing.* Freedom from risk or danger; safety. See *security*.

Cyber Spying: Tracking Your Family's (Sometimes) Secret Online Lives

Dr. Eric Cole, Michael Nordfelt, Sandra Ring, and Ted Fair

Have you ever wondered about that friend your spouse e-mails, or who they spend hours chatting online with? Are you curious about what your children are doing online, whom they meet, and what they talk about? Do you worry about them finding drugs and other illegal items online, and wonder what they look at? This book shows you how to monitor and analyze your family's online behavior.

ISBN: 1-93183-641-8

Price: $39.95 US $57.95 CAN

Stealing the Network: How to Own an Identity

Timothy Mullen, Ryan Russell, Riley (Caezar) Eller, Jeff Moss, Jay Beale, Johnny Long, Chris Hurley, Tom Parker, Brian Hatch
The first two books in this series "Stealing the Network: How to Own the Box" and "Stealing the Network: How to Own a Continent" have become classics in the Hacker and Infosec communities because of their chillingly realistic depictions of criminal hacking techniques. In this third installment, the all-star cast of authors tackle one of the fastest-growing crimes in the world: Identity Theft. Now, the criminal hackers readers have grown to both love and hate try to cover their tracks and vanish into thin air...

ISBN: 1-59749-006-7

Price: $39.95 US $55.95 CAN

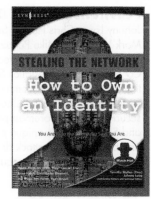

Software Piracy Exposed

Paul Craig, Ron Honick

For every $2 worth of software purchased legally, $1 worth of software is pirated illegally. For the first time ever, the dark underground of how software is stolen and traded over the Internet is revealed. The technical detail provided will open the eyes of software users and manufacturers worldwide! This book is a tell-it-like-it-is exposé of how tens of billions of dollars worth of software is stolen every year.

ISBN: 1-93226-698-4

Price: $39.95 U.S. $55.95 CAN

SYNGRESS®

Syngress: *The Definition of a Serious Security Library*

Syn·gress (sin–gres): *noun, sing.* Freedom from risk or danger; safety. See *security*.

Phishing Exposed

Lance James, Secure Science Corporation,
Joe Stewart (Foreword)

If you have ever received a phish, become a victim of a phish, or manage the security of a major e-commerce or financial site, then you need to read this book. The author of this book delivers the unconcealed techniques of phishers including their evolving patterns, and how to gain the upper hand against the ever-accelerating attacks they deploy. Filled with elaborate and unprecedented forensics, Phishing Exposed details techniques that system administrators, law enforcement, and fraud investigators can exercise and learn more about their attacker and their specific attack methods, enabling risk mitigation in many cases before the attack occurs.

ISBN: 1-59749-030-X

Price: $49.95 US $69.95 CAN

Penetration Tester's Open Source Toolkit

Johnny Long, Chris Hurley, SensePost,
Mark Wolfgang, Mike Petruzzi

This is the first fully integrated Penetration Testing book and bootable Linux CD containing the "Auditor Security Collection," which includes over 300 of the most effective and commonly used open source attack and penetration testing tools. This powerful tool kit and authoritative reference is written by the security industry's foremost penetration testers including HD Moore, Jay Beale, and SensePost. This unique package provides you with a completely portable and bootable Linux attack distribution and authoritative reference to the toolset included and the required methodology.

ISBN: 1-59749-021-0

Price: $59.95 US $83.95 CAN

Google Hacking for Penetration Testers

Johnny Long, Foreword by Ed Skoudis

Google has been a strong force in Internet culture since its 1998 upstart. Since then, the engine has evolved from a simple search instrument to an innovative authority of information. As the sophistication of Google grows, so do the hacking hazards that the engine entertains. Approaches to hacking are forever changing, and this book covers the risks and precautions that administrators need to be aware of during this explosive phase of Google Hacking.

ISBN: 1-93183-636-1

Price: $44.95 U.S. $65.95 CAN

Syngress: *The Definition of a Serious Security Library*

Syn·gress (sin–gres): *noun, sing.* Freedom from risk or danger; safety. See *security.*

Cisco PIX Firewalls:
Configure, Manage, & Troubleshoot

Charles Riley, Umer Khan, Michael Sweeney

Cisco PIX Firewall is the world's most used network firewall, protecting internal networks from unwanted intrusions and attacks. Virtual Private Networks (VPNs) are the means by which authorized users are allowed through PIX Firewalls. Network engineers and security specialists must constantly balance the need for air-tight security (Firewalls) with the need for on-demand access (VPNs). In this book, Umer Khan, author of the #1 best selling PIX Firewall book, provides a concise, to-the-point blueprint for fully integrating these two essential pieces of any enterprise network.

ISBN: 1-59749-004-0

Price: $49.95 US $69.95 CAN

Configuring Netscreen Firewalls

Rob Cameron

Configuring NetScreen Firewalls is the first book to deliver an in-depth look at the NetScreen firewall product line. It covers all of the aspects of the NetScreen product line from the SOHO devices to the Enterprise NetScreen firewalls. Advanced troubleshooting techniques and the NetScreen Security Manager are also covered..

ISBN: 1--93226-639-9

Price: $49.95 US $72.95 CAN

Configuring Check Point
NGX VPN-1/FireWall-1

Barry J. Stiefel, Simon Desmeules

Configuring Check Point NGX VPN-1/Firewall-1 is the perfect reference for anyone migrating from earlier versions of Check Point's flagship firewall/VPN product as well as those deploying VPN-1/Firewall-1 for the first time. NGX includes dramatic changes and new, enhanced features to secure the integrity of your network's data, communications, and applications from the plethora of blended threats that can breach your security through your network perimeter, Web access, and increasingly common internal threats.

ISBN: 1--59749-031-8

Price: $49.95 U.S. $69.95 CAN

SYNGRESS®

Syngress: *The Definition of a Serious Security Library*

Syn·gress (sin-gres): *noun, sing.* Freedom from risk or danger; safety. See *security.*

Syngress: *The Definition of a Serious Security Library*

Syn·gress (sin–gres): *noun, sing.* Freedom from risk or danger; safety. See *security.*

Syngress: *The Definition of a Serious Security Library*

Syn·gress (sin-gres): *noun, sing.* Freedom from risk or danger; safety. See *security*.

Configuring SonicWALL Firewalls

Chris Lathem, Ben Fortenberry, Lars Hansen
Configuring SonicWALL Firewalls is the first book to deliver an in-depth look at the SonicWALL firewall product line. It covers all of the aspects of the SonicWALL product line from the SOHO devices to the Enterprise SonicWALL firewalls. Advanced troubleshooting techniques and the SonicWALL Security Manager are also covered.

ISBN: 1-59749-250-7
Price: $49.95 US $69.95 CAN

Perfect Passwords:
Selection, Protection, Authentication

Mark Burnett

User passwords are the keys to the network kingdom, yet most users choose overly simplistic passwords (like password) that anyone could guess, while system administrators demand impossible to remember passwords littered with obscure characters and random numerals. Author Mark Burnett has accumulated and analyzed over 1,000,000 user passwords, and this highly entertaining and informative book filled with dozens of illustrations reveals his findings and balances the rigid needs of security professionals against the ease of use desired by users.

ISBN: 1-59749-041-5
Price: $24.95 US $34.95 CAN

Syngress: *The Definition of a Serious Security Library*

Syn·gress (sin-gres): *noun, sing.* Freedom from risk or danger; safety. See *security.*

How to Cheat at Managing Windows Server Update Services

Brian Barber

If you manage a Microsoft Windows network, you probably find yourself overwhelmed at times by the sheer volume of updates and patches released by Microsoft for its products. You know these updates are critical to keep your network running efficiently and securely, but staying current amidst all of your other responsibilities can be almost impossible. Microsoft's recently released Windows Server Update Services (WSUS) is designed to streamline this process. Learn how to take full advantage of WSUS using Syngress' proven "How to Cheat" methodology, which gives you everything you need and nothing you don't.

ISBN: 1-59749-027-X

Price: $39.95 US $55.95 CAN

How to Cheat at IT Project Management

Susan Snedaker

Most IT projects fail to deliver – on average, all IT projects run over schedule by 82%, run over cost by 43% and deliver only 52% of the desired functionality. Pretty dismal statistics. Using the proven methods in this book, you'll find that IT project you work on from here on out will have a much higher likelihood of being on time, on budget and higher quality. This book provides clear, concise, information and hands-on training to give you immediate results. And, the companion Web site provides dozens of templates for managing IT projects.

ISBN: 1-59749-037-7

Price: $44.95 U.S. $64.95 CAN

SYNGRESS®

Syngress: *The Definition of a Serious Security Library*

Syn·gress (sin-gres): *noun, sing.* Freedom from risk or danger; safety. See *security*.

Managing Cisco Network Security, Second Edition

Offers updated and revised information covering many of Cisco's security products that provide protection from threats, detection of network security incidents, measurement of vulnerability and policy compliance, and management of security policy across an extended organization. These are the tools that you have to mount defenses against threats. Chapters also cover the improved functionality and ease of the Cisco Secure Policy Manager software used by thousands of small-to-midsized businesses, and a special section on Cisco wireless solutions.

ISBN: 1-931836-56-6
Price: $69.95 USA $108.95 CAN

How to Cheat at Managing Microsoft Operations Manager 2005

Tony Piltzecker, Rogier Dittner, Rory McCaw, Gordon McKenna, Paul M. Summitt, David E. Williams

My e-mail takes forever. My application is stuck. Why can't I log on? System administrators have to address these types of complaints far too often. With MOM, system administrators will know when overloaded processors, depleted memory, or failed network connections are affecting their Windows servers long before these problems bother users. Readers of this book will learn why when it comes to monitoring Windows Server System infrastructure, MOM's the word.

ISBN: 1-59749-251-5
Price: $39.95 U.S. $55.95 CAN

SYNGRESS®

Syngress: *The Definition of a Serious Security Library*

Syn·gress (sin–gres): *noun, sing.* Freedom from risk or danger; safety. See *security*.

SYNGRESS®

Syngress: *The Definition of a Serious Security Library*

Syn·gress (sin-gres): *noun, sing.* Freedom from risk or danger; safety. See *security*.

Syngress: *The Definition of a Serious Security Library*

Syn·gress (sin–gres): *noun, sing.* Freedom from risk or danger; safety. See *security.*

"Thieme's ability to be open minded, conspiratorial, ethical, and subversive all at the same time is very inspiring."—*Jeff Moss, CEO, Black Hat, Inc.*

Richard Thieme's Islands in the Clickstream: Reflections on Life in a Virtual World

Richard Thieme is one of the most visible commentators on technology and society, appearing regularly on CNN radio, TechTV, and various other national media outlets. He is also in great demand as a public speaker, delivering his "Human Dimension of Technology" talk to over 50,000 live audience members each year. *Islands in the Clickstream* is a single volume "best of Richard Thieme."

ISBN: 1-931836-22-1

Price: $29.95 US $43.95 CAN

"Thieme's Islands in the Clickstream is deeply reflective, enlightening, and refreshing." —*Peter Neumann, Stanford Research Institute*

"Richard Thieme takes us to the edge of cliffs we know are there but rarely visit ... he wonderfully weaves life, mystery, and passion through digital and natural worlds with creativity and imagination. This is delightful and deeply thought provoking reading full of "aha!" insights." —*Clinton C. Brooks, Senior Advisor for Homeland Security and Asst. Deputy Director, NSA*

"WOW! You eloquently express thoughts and ideas that I feel. You have helped me, not so much tear down barriers to communication, as to leverage these barriers into another structure with elevators and escalators."
—*Chip Meadows, CISSP, CCSE, USAA e-Security Team*

"Richard Thieme navigates the complex world of people and computers with amazing ease and grace. His clarity of thinking is refreshing, and his insights are profound." —*Bruce Schneier, CEO, Counterpane*

"I believe that you are a practioner of wu wei, the effort to choose the elegant appropriate contribution to each and every issue that you address." —*Hal McConnell (fomer intelligence analyst, NSA)*

"Richard Thieme presents us with a rare gift. His words touch our heart while challenging our most cherished constructs. He is both a poet and pragmatist navigating a new world with clarity, curiosity and boundless amazement." —*Kelly Hansen, CEO, Neohapsis*

"Richard Thieme combines hi-tech, business savvy and social consciousness to create some of the most penetrating commentaries of our times. A column I am always eager to read."—*Peter Russell, author "From Science to God"*

"These reflections provide a veritable feast for the imagination, allowing us more fully to participate in Wonder. This book is an experience of loving Creation with our minds." —*Louie Crew, Member of Executive Council of The Episcopal Church*

"The particular connections Richard Thieme makes between mind, heart, technology, and truth, lend us timely and useful insight on what it means to live in a technological era. Richard fills a unique and important niche in hacker society!" —*Mick Bauer, Security Editor, Linux Journal*

SYNGRESS®

Syngress: *The Definition of a Serious Security Library*

Syn·gress (sin-gres): *noun, sing.* Freedom from risk or danger; safety. See *security*.

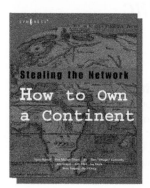

This License Agreement shall be construed and governed in accordance with the laws of the Commonwealth of Massachusetts. If any provision of this License Agreement is held to be contrary to law, that provision will be enforced to the maximum extent permissible and the remaining provisions will remain in full force and effect.

*If you do not agree, please return this product to the place of purchase for a refund.

Printed and bound by CPI Group (UK) Ltd, Croydon, CR0 4YY

03/10/2024

01040342-0007